Annie E. Hove

Winchester

Va

October 20th 1897

INTRODUCTION

TO

ENGLISH LITERATURE

INCLUDING

A NUMBER OF CLASSIC WORKS.

WITH NOTES.

BY

F. V. N. PAINTER, A.M.

PROFESSOR OF MODERN LANGUAGES AND LITERATURE IN ROANOKE COLLEGE.
AUTHOR OF A HISTORY OF EDUCATION, LUTHER ON EDUCATION,
HISTORY OF CHRISTIAN WORSHIP, ETC.

LEACH, SHEWELL, & SANBORN,

BOSTON.   NEW YORK.   CHICAGO.

ELECTROTYPING BY C. J. PETERS & SON.

PRESSWORK BY BERWICK & SMITH.

PREFACE.

THIS work is an attempt to solve the problem of teaching English literature. The ordinary manuals, it is believed, have ceased to give general satisfaction. This result was inevitable; for the principle upon which they are based is fundamentally at variance with educational science. While containing a great deal *about* English literature, these works do not teach English literature itself; and it is not unusual for a student to finish them without being acquainted with a single classic work, or having acquired the least fondness for sterling literature. It is the recognition of these facts that has caused many teachers to desire and seek something better.

The subject of English literature is of great extent; no other nationality has a richer intellectual heritage. Its history extends through twelve hundred years, and the list of authors and of their productions is almost endless. Some knowledge of this literature is an indispensable part of a liberal education. Simply as information, this knowledge is of far more importance to us than an acquaintance with any other literature, ancient or modern. And as an educating instrumentality, it possesses great value. Its critical study disciplines the attention, refines the taste, and cultivates the memory and judgment. But of more importance than any of these particulars, is its value in awakening mind. English literature is peculiarly adapted, in the hands of a competent teacher, to produce a genuine thirst for knowledge and culture — a thirst which once awakened rarely fails, in this age of books, to attain its end.

But the vast extent of English literature makes it a difficult subject to handle successfully in the class-room. Two leading mistakes, which have been embodied in numerous text-books, are easily made. On the one hand, a treatment too comprehensive in its scope necessitates a painful meagreness of details ; and the result is that the subject, with its bare biographical facts and its broad generalizations, remains confused and barren in the learner's mind. He is told many things *about* English literature, but he is not once permitted to see and examine for himself. On the other hand, brief illustrative extracts, with a short biographical notice of each writer, leaves the student unacquainted with English literature in its wonderful course of development. While learning many names and perhaps some choice bits of poetry and prose, he knows nothing of the writers in relation to one another, and to the times in which they lived.

Evidently some plan of selection and arrangement that might avoid these two erroneous methods is desirable. Greater fulness of treatment should be secured by the omission of unimportant writers; and in addition to this, the characteristics of each period, which are related alike to all the writers belonging to it, should be traced at some length. Fortunately English literature lends itself readily to this two-fold treatment. The long course of our literature is broken up into a number of periods marked by the presence of new and weighty influences; and in each period there are a few writers that stand, by reason of their ability and enduring works, in positions of recognized pre-eminence. These are our classic authors; and it is with their writings, in connection with the moulding influence of epoch and surroundings, that the formal study of English literature should begin. This plan, which it is hoped will be found embodied in the present work, not only gives the student what is rightly called a philosophy of our literature, but also leads him to a direct acquaintance with the literature itself.

A moment's examination will show the structure of the present work. The treatment of the representative writers of each period is sufficiently extended to allow considerable fulness of biographical and critical detail. This, it is hoped, will add to the interest of the work, and also be useful in developing a literary taste. The selections are representative pieces; and, studied with the help of the critical and explanatory notes, they will be found sufficient to give the student a clear idea of each author. To secure greater completeness of treatment, and also to encourage independent investigation, it is recommended that the less prominent authors, a list of which is prefixed to each period, be made from time to time the subject of essays and discussions in class. This will be found upon trial an interesting and profitable exercise.

The plan here adopted is the outgrowth of long experience; and it is believed that the faithful use of the book in the class-room can hardly fail to cultivate a taste for English literature, to give a clear conception of the general course of its development, to impart a considerable knowledge of our leading classic authors, and to stimulate further study in this interesting and valuable department of liberal culture.

F. V. N. PAINTER.

Salem, Virginia.
November, 1894.

CONTENTS.

PAGE

INTRODUCTION 1

I.

FORMATIVE PERIOD, 1066–1400 19

CHAUCER, PROLOGUE 24

II.

FIRST CREATIVE PERIOD, 1558–1625 75

SPENSER, FAERY QUEENE 84

BACON, ESSAYS 137

SHAKESPEARE, MERCHANT OF VENICE 172

III.

CIVIL WAR PERIOD, 1625–1660 273

MILTON, L'ALLEGRO AND IL PENSEROSO 280

IV.

THE RESTORATION, 1660–1700 311

DRYDEN, RELIGIO LAICI 316

V.

THE QUEEN ANNE PERIOD, 1700–1745 347

ADDISON, SIR ROGER DE COVERLEY 352

POPE, ESSAY ON CRITICISM 377

VI.

PAGE

AGE OF JOHNSON, 1745–1800 421

BURNS, THE COTTER'S SATURDAY NIGHT, ETC. 426

GOLDSMITH, THE DESERTED VILLAGE 454

JOHNSON, AKENSIDE 479

VII.

THE NINETEENTH CENTURY 499

SCOTT, THE TALISMAN 508

BYRON, THE PRISONER OF CHILLON 526

WORDSWORTH, TINTERN ABBEY AND INTIMATIONS OF IMMORTALITY 548

TENNYSON, ELAINE 575

ENGLISH LITERATURE.

INTRODUCTION.

HISTORY treats chiefly of the deeds of a people ; literature records their thoughts and feelings. It is thus intimately connected with the intellectual life of a nation,
of which it is the product and expression. No literature
is fully intelligible without an acquaintance with the conditions under which it originated. The three leading
factors that determine its character are *race*, *epoch*, and
surroundings. Each race has its fundamental traits, which
give it individuality in the world. The Teuton, with his
serious, reflective, persistent temper, is quite different from
the Celt, with his vivacity, wit, and ready enthusiasm.
These differences are naturally reflected in the literature
of the two races.

Again, every age has its peculiar interests, culture, and
tendencies. Literature cannot divorce itself from the
spirit of the time in which it is produced. For instance,
the dramas of Shakespeare, which reflect all the intellectual wealth and freedom of the age of Elizabeth, could not
have been written in the rude period of the Norman
Conquest.

The third great formative principle in literature is
environment, or physical and social conditions. The lit-

erature produced in the presence of a sterile soil and rigorous climate must necessarily be different in tone and coloring from that produced in the midst of fruitful fields and under sunny skies.   And, in like manner, its quantity and quality will be affected, to a greater or less degree, by a state of war or peace, intelligence or ignorance, wealth or poverty, freedom or persecution.

It is not enough to be acquainted with the isolated facts of a literature ; we should study them in connection with the various causes by which they were moulded and by which they are bound together in unity.   This study of causes and influences gives us a philosophy of literature, without which an acquaintance with separate authors will leave us superficial.   But it is a mistake to suppose that race, epoch, and surroundings will explain everything in literature ; there is a personal element of great importance.   From time to time men of great genius appear, and rising by native strength high above the level of their age, become centres of a new and weighty influence in literature.   This truth is exemplified by Luther in Germany, and Bacon in England, each of whom profoundly affected the subsequent literary development of his country.

English literature embodies the results of English thought and feeling.   It shares in the greatness of the English people.   It combines French vivacity with German depth.   If Germany excels in scholarship, and France in taste, England has produced a literature that in comprehensive scope and general excellence is second to none. No department of literature has been left uncultivated. Poets have sung in sweet and lofty strains ; novelists have artistically portrayed every phase of society ; orators have convinced the judgment and moved the heart ; scientists have revealed the laws of the physical world ; and philosophers have deeply pondered the mysteries of existence.

This literature is a heritage in which English-speaking people may feel a just pride, a subject to which they should give careful study. Only through literature can we obtain an adequate acquaintance with the best products of the English mind — a knowledge that is indispensable to liberal culture. (English literature begins with Bede in the seventh century, and extends through the long period of twelve hundred years to the present time. Its course has been an ever-widening stream.

The original inhabitants of the British Isles, within historic times, were Celts — a part of the first great Aryan wave that swept over Europe. They were partially conquered by the Romans, 55 B.C., and Britain continued under Roman dominion, as a province of the Empire, for nearly five hundred years. Then followed, in the fifth and sixth centuries of our era, the invasion by the Angles, Saxons, and Jutes — Teutonic tribes that inhabited Schleswig, Jutland, and adjacent territory on the continent. They supplanted the native Celts as completely as their descendants exterminated the American Indians. In the following centuries they laid the foundation of England — a word signifying the land of the Angles.

In the character of these Teutonic tribes are to be found the fundamental traits of the English people and of English literature. In their continental home they led a semi-barbarous and pagan life. The sterile soil and dreary climate fostered a serious disposition and developed great physical strength. Courage was esteemed a leading virtue, and cowardice was punished with drowning. No other men were ever braver. They welcomed the fierce excitement of danger; and in rude vessels they sailed from coast to coast on expeditions of piracy, war, and pillage. Laughing at storms and shipwrecks, these daring sea-kings sang: "The blast of the tempest aids our oars; the bellowing of heaven, the howling of the thunder, hurts us not; the hurricane is our servant, and drives us whither we wish to go."

With an unconquerable love of independence, they preferred death to slavery. Refined tastes and delicate instincts were crushed out by their inhospitable surroundings; and their pleasures, consisting chiefly of drinking, gambling, and athletic sports, were coarse and repulsive. Yet under their coarsest enjoyments we discover a sturdy, masculine strength. They felt the presence of the mysterious forces of nature, and deified them in a colossal mythology. Traces of their religion are seen in the names of the days of the week. Their sense of obligation and duty was strong; and having once pledged fidelity to a leader or cause, they remained loyal to death. They honored woman and revered virtue. In a word, the Anglo-Saxons possessed a native virtue and strength which, ennobled by Christianity, and refined by culture, raised their descendants to a pre-eminent position among the nations of the earth.

The Anglo-Saxon invasion swept away the British church which had been established under Christian Rome. A reign of paganism was once more introduced, and held sway for a hundred and fifty years. Then occurred an event that changed the character of English history. In 597 Gregory, who filled the papal chair at Rome, sent St.

Augustine with a band of missionaries to labor among the Anglo-Saxons. While yet an abbot, Gregory's interest had been awakened by the fair faces and flaxen hair of a group of Saxon youths exposed for sale in the slave-market at Rome. "Who are they?" he asked. "Angles," was the reply. "It suits them well," he said, "with faces so angel-like. From what country do they come?" "From Deiri," said the merchant. "*De ira!*"[1] exclaimed the pious monk, "then they must be delivered from the wrath of God. What is the name of their king?" "Aella," he was told. "Aella!" he replied, seizing on the word as of good omen, "then shall Alleluia be sung in his land."

Augustine proceeded to Kent, where he was kindly received by Ethelbert. The king had married Bertha, a Frankish princess of Christian training, through whose influence his pagan prejudices had been largely overcome. When, by means of interpreters, Augustine had set forth the nature of Christianity in a lengthy address, the king said: "Your words and promises are very fair; but as they are new to us, and of uncertain import, I cannot approve of them so far as to forsake that which I have so long followed with the whole English nation. But because you are come from far into my kingdom, and, as I conceive, are desirous to impart to us those things which you believe to be true and most beneficial, we will not molest you, but give you favorable entertainment, and take care to supply you with your necessary sustenance; nor do we forbid you to preach and gain as many as you can to your religion."[2]

---

[1] Latin, meaning "*from the wrath.*"
[2] Bede, Ecclesiastical History, B. I. ch. xxv.

The missionaries took up their residence at Canterbury. Christianity made rapid progress. Within a year from the landing of Augustine upon the shores of Kent, Ethelbert and thousands of his people became Christians. Missionary zeal carried the new religion to other parts of England. Edwin, the powerful king of Northumbria, was led to call a council for the purpose of considering its adoption. An aged ealderman arose and spoke as follows : " So seems life, O King, as a sparrow's flight through the hall where a man is sitting at meat in winter-tide with the warm fire lighted on the hearth, but the chill rain-storm without. The sparrow flies in at one door and tarries for a moment in the light and heat of the hearth-fire, and then flying forth from the other, vanishes into the wintry darkness whence it came. So tarries for a moment the life of man in our sight, but what is before it and what after it, we know not. If this new teaching tell us aught certainly of these, let us follow it."

The native seriousness of the Anglo-Saxon character offered a favorable soil for the growth of Christianity. The gospel was peculiarly adapted to the needs of this people. In restraining brutal pleasures, inculcating benevolent affections, and promoting intellectual culture, it supplied what was wanting in English character, and imparted an element essential to the highest development of the national life. England was once more brought in line with the highest European civilization ; and the culture, arts, and sciences, that had fled before the pagan conquerors, returned with Christianity.

The Anglo-Saxons were too much engaged in the active employments of life to have either inclination or leisure for literary culture. In spite of the education that followed in the wake of Christianity, the masses remained in ignorance, and even kings were sometimes unable to write their names. The monasteries, which grew out of the ascetic spirit then prevailing in the church, constituted the principal educational agency. The secular schools of pagan Rome had long since disappeared. The church regarded education as one of its exclusive functions, and under its direction nearly all instruction had a theological or ecclesiastical aim. Purely secular studies were pursued only in the interests of the church. The course of instruction in the convent or monastic schools embraced the so-called seven liberal arts — grammar, logic, rhetoric, arithmetic, geometry, astronomy, and music — to which seven years were devoted. Latin, the language of the church, was made the basis of education, to the general neglect of the mother-tongue. The works of the church fathers were chiefly read, though expurgated copies of the Latin classics were also used.

England produced its share of distinguished scholars, among whom were Alcuin, Bede, and Erigena. In the preface of one of his works Alcuin warmly commends study : "Oh, ye, who enjoy the youthful age, so fitted for your lessons, learn ! Be docile. Lose not the day in idle things. The passing hour, like the wave, never returns again. Let your early years flourish with the study of the virtues, that your age may shine with great honors. Use these happy days. Learn, while young, the art of eloquence, that you may be a safeguard and defender of those whom you value. Acquire the conduct and manners so beautiful in youth, and your name will become celebrated through the world. But as I wish you not to be sluggish, so neither be proud. I worship the recesses of the devout and humble breast." [1]

The first literature of a people is poetry. In national, as in individual life, the imagination is strong during the period of youth. An acquaintance with Anglo-Saxon life and character enables us to anticipate the spirit of their poetry. Not love, but war and religion, form its leading themes. The language is abrupt, elliptical, highly metaphorical, but often of overpowering energy. In form, Anglo-Saxon poetry consists of short, exclamatory, alliterative verses. Narrative poems, recited to the accompaniment of a musical instrument, often formed a part of their ale-drinking banquets.

The most important Anglo-Saxon poem that has descended to us is " Beowulf," an epic of six thousand short lines. It was probably composed in its present form in the eighth century, but the deeds it celebrates belong to a much earlier period. It possesses great value, not only for philology, but also for history, since it portrays the manners and customs of our Anglo-Saxon forefathers before they left their continental home. The hero of the poem is Beowulf, who, sailing to the land of the Danes, slew a monster of the fens called Grendel, whose nightly ravages brought dismay into the royal palace. After slaying the monster of the marshes, Beowulf returned to his native country, where he became king and ruled fifty years. But at last, in attacking a wrathful dragon " under the earth, nigh to the sea wave," he was mortally wounded. At his burial, " about the mound rode his hearth-sharers, who sang that he was of kings, of men, the mildest, kind-

[1] Turner, History of the Anglo-Saxons, Vol. II.

est, to his people sweetest, and the readiest in search of praise." Such, in a word, is the substance of the story, but it gives no idea of the interest of the details.

Cædmon, the earliest of English poets, lived in the latter part of the seventh century. He has with justice been called ("the Milton of our forefathers;") and his poems are strongly suggestive of "Paradise Lost." He seems to have been a laborer on the lands attached to the monastery of St. Hilda at Whitby, and was advanced in years before his poetical powers were developed. When at festive gatherings it was agreed that all present should sing in turn, Cædmon was accustomed, as the harp approached him, quietly to retire with a humiliating sense of his want of skill. Having left the banqueting hall on one occasion, he went to the stable, where it was his turn to care for the horses. In a vision an angel appeared to him and said, "Cædmon, sing a song to me." He answered, "I cannot sing; for that is the reason why I left the entertainment, and retired to this place." "Nevertheless," said the heavenly visitor, "thou shalt sing." "What shall I sing?" inquired the poet, as he felt the movement of an awakening power. "Sing the beginning of created things," said the angel.

His mission was thus assigned him. In the morning the good abbess Hilda, with a company of learned men, witnessed an exhibition of his newly awakened powers; and concluding that heavenly grace had been bestowed upon him, she bade him lay aside his secular habit and received him into the monastery as a monk. Here he led a humble, exemplary life in the exercise of his poetic gifts. "He sang the creation of the world, the origin of man, and all the history of Genesis; and made many verses on the departure of the children of Israel out of Egypt, and their entering into the Land of Promise, with many other histories from Holy Writ . . . by which he endeavored to turn away all men from the love of vice, and to excite in them the love of, and application to, good actions." [1]

The following description of the Creation illustrates Cædmon's manner of amplifying the simple Scripture narrative : —

> " There was not yet then here,
> Except gloom like a cavern,
> Any thing made.
> But the wide ground
> Stood deep and dim
> For a new lordship,
> Shapeless and unsuitable.
> On this with his eyes he glanced,
> The King stern in mind,
> And the joyless place beheld.
> He saw the dark clouds
> Perpetually press
> Black under the sky,
> Void and waste;
> Till that this world's creation
> Through the word was done
> Of the King of Glory."

Though rude in form, Cædmon's Paraphrase contains genuine poetry. It is the product of admirable genius, but genius fettered by unfavorable surroundings and lack of culture.

Bede may be justly regarded as the father of English prose. From an interesting autobiographical sketch at the close of his "Ecclesiastical History," we learn the leading events in his unpretentious life. He was born in

---

[1] Bede, Ecclesiastical History, B. IV. ch. xxiv.

673, near the monastery of Jarrow in northern England. As pupil, deacon, and priest, he passed his entire life in that monastic institution. The leisure that remained to him after the faithful performance of his various official duties, he assiduously devoted to learning ; for he always took delight, as he tells us, " in learning, teaching, and writing." He was an indefatigable worker, and wrote no less than forty-five separate treatises, including works on Scripture, history, hymnology, astronomy, grammar, and rhetoric, in which is embodied all the learning of his age.

His scholarship and aptness as a teacher gave celebrity to the monastic school at Jarrow, which was attended at one time by six hundred monks in addition to many secular students. His fame extended as far as Rome, whither he was invited by Pope Sergius, who wished the benefit of his counsel. He led an eminently simple, devout, and earnest life. He declined the dignity of abbot, lest the duties of the office might interfere with his studies. As a writer he was clear, succinct, and artless. His " Ecclesiastical History," which was composed in Latin, is our chief source of information in regard to the early Anglo-Saxon church. The credulity he exhibits in regard to ecclesiastical miracles was characteristic of his time.

His pupil Cuthbert has left us a pathetic account of his death. Industrious to the last, he was engaged on an Anglo-Saxon version of St. John. It was Wednesday morning, the 27th of May. One of his pupils, who was acting as scribe, said to him : " Dearest master, there is still one chapter wanting ; do you think it troublesome to be asked any more questions ? " He answered, " It is no trouble. Take your pen and write fast." In the afternoon he called his friends together, distributed a few sim-

ple gifts, and then amidst their tears bade them a solemn
farewell. At sunset his scribe said : " Dear master, there
is yet one sentence not written." He answered, " Write
quickly." " It is finished now," said the scribe at last.
" You have spoken truly," the aged scholar replied, " it is
finished. Receive my head into your hands, for it is a
great satisfaction to me to sit facing the holy place where
I was wont to pray." And thus on the pavement of his
little cell, in the year 735, he quietly passed away with
the last words of the solemn chant, " Glory be to the
Father, and to the Son, and to the Holy Ghost."

Thus closed the life of the first great English scholar.
Not inaptly did later ages style him the Venerable Bede.
" First among English scholars, first among English theologians, first among English historians, it is in the monk
of Jarrow that English literature strikes its roots. In the
six hundred scholars who gathered round him for instruction he is the father of our national education. In his
physical treatises he is the first figure to which our
science looks back." [1]

Not many sovereigns deserve a place in literature because of their own writings. But Alfred was as great
with the pen as with the sword. His history, around
which legendary stories have gathered, reads in its reality
like a piece of fiction. Known ages ago as the " darling
of the English," he grows in greatness with the passing
years. The unfavorable surroundings of his life serve as
a foil to set off his virtues.

He was born in 849. A part of his childhood was
spent in Rome, while much of its ancient splendor still
remained. At the residence of King Æthelwulf, his

---

[1] Green, History of the English People, Vol. I.

father, he learned not only the manly sports of the Anglo-Saxon youth, — running, leaping, wrestling, hunting, — but also the various occupations pertaining to the household, the workshop, and the tilling of the soil. He had a passion for the heroic songs of his people, and even before learning to read he had committed many of them to memory. Blessed with a healthful precocity of mind, he treasured up all this varied knowledge, and utilized it with rare wisdom in after years.

At the age of twenty-three he ascended the throne, and spent a considerable part of his subsequent life in conflict with the Danes, who in great numbers were making a descent upon the cultivated districts of England and France for the sake of pillage. At one time he was reduced to the extremity of fleeing with a few followers before the pagan invaders. But adversity, as with every vigorous nature, called forth a greater energy and determination. Gathering about him a body of strong and true men, he at length turned upon the foe, surprised and defeated them, and conquered a favorable peace. By the superior military organization of his people, by the founding of an English navy, and, above all, by his pre-eminent ability as a commander, he succeeded in repelling all subsequent attacks by the northern invaders, and saved England to the Anglo-Saxon race.

In the leisure that followed his treaties of peace, Alfred devoted himself assiduously to the elevation and welfare of his people. He rebuilt ruined towns, restored demolished monasteries, established a fixed code of laws, and encouraged every form of useful industry. The king himself set the example of diligent labor. By means of six wax candles which, lighted in succession, burned twenty-four hours, he introduced a rigid system into his work. He carried with him a little book in which he noted the valuable thoughts that occurred to him from time to time. When he came to the throne, the learning which a century before had furnished Europe with some of its most eminent scholars had fallen into decay. "To so low a depth has learning fallen among the English nation," he says, "that there have been very few on this side of the Humber who were able to understand the English of their service, or to turn an epistle out of Latin into English; and I know that there were not many beyond the Humber who could do it."

With admirable tact and wisdom he set about remedying the evil. He studied Latin himself that he might provide his people with useful books; he invited learned scholars from the continent to his court; and he established in the royal palace a school for the instruction of noble youth. His efforts were grandly successful; and in less than a generation England was again blessed with intelligence and prosperity. Among the books he translated into Anglo-Saxon were Bede's "Ecclesiastical History;" Orosius' "Universal History," the leading text-book on that subject in the monastic schools for several centuries; and Boethius' "Consolations of Philosophy," a popular book among thoughtful people during the Middle Ages. These translations were not always literal. Alfred rather performed the work of editor, paraphrasing, omitting, adding, as best served his purpose. In the work of Boethius he frequently departed from the text to introduce reflections of his own. To him belongs the honor of having furnished England with its first body of literature in the native tongue.

He died in 901. The governing purpose of his life he pointed out in a single sentence : "This I can now truly say, that so long as I have lived, I have striven to live worthily, and after my death to leave my memory to my descendants in good works." In him the Anglo-Saxon stock reached its highest development. His character was based on a profound belief in the abiding presence of God. But rising above the ascetic spirit of his time, he devoted himself to the duties of his royal station. To great vigor in action he added the force of patient and invincible endurance. While he watched with capacious intellect over the interests of his entire realm, he led with great simplicity a genial and affectionate life with his family and friends. After ages have made no mistake in calling him Alfred the Great.

FORMATIVE PERIOD.

REPRESENTATIVE WRITER.
GEOFFREY CHAUCER.

OTHER PROMINENT WRITERS.

Poets. — LAYAMON, ORMIN, LANGLAND, GOWER.
Prose Writer. — WYCLIFFE.

I.

THE FORMATIVE PERIOD.

(1066–1400.)

GENERAL SURVEY. — The designation "formative period" is applied to the centuries lying between the Norman Conquest and the death of Chaucer. It is a period of great importance for English history and English literature. England passed under a succession of alien rulers, and the state of society underwent a great change. For a long time violent antagonisms existed between Norman conqueror and Saxon subject. Their languages were kept distinct ; and a French and an Anglo-Saxon literature existed side by side, while Latin, as the language of the church and of scholars, added to the confusion.

But toward the close of the period, especially in the fourteenth century, the people of England became more homogeneous. The Normans coalesced with the Anglo-Saxons, and added new elements to the English character. At the same time the Anglo-Saxon language, which had hitherto maintained its highly inflected character, made a gradual transition into modern English. It gave up its complicated inflections, and received into its vocabulary a host of foreign elements, chiefly from the French. The new tongue, which gradually supplanted French and Latin, gained official recognition in 1362, when it became the language of the courts of law ; and the following year it was employed in the speech made at the opening of Parliament.

The name of Normans is given to the Scandinavians who, at the beginning of the tenth century, conquered a home in the northern part of France. They speedily adopted the language and customs of the subjugated country, and rapidly advanced in refinement and culture. By intermarriage with the native population, a vivacious Celtic element was introduced into the grave Teutonic disposition. Though of kindred blood with the Anglo-Saxons, the Normans, by their stay in France, developed a new, and in many respects admirable, type of character.

Along with their native Teutonic strength they acquired a versatile and imitative temper, which made them accessible to new ideas, and prepared them to be leaders in general progress. Losing their slow, phlegmatic temperament, they became impulsive and impatient of restraint. Their intellects acquired a nimble quality, quick in discernment, and instantaneous in decision. Delicacy of feeling produced aversion to coarse pleasures. They delighted in a gay social life, with hunting, hawking, showy equipage, and brilliant festivities. Diplomacy in a measure supplanted daring frankness. Brilliant superficiality took the place of grave thoughtfulness. Such were the people that were to rule in England, to introduce their language and customs, and, amalgamated at last, to impart a needed element to the English character.

In 1066 William, Duke of Normandy, landed on the English coast to enforce his claim to the English throne. In the battle of Hastings he gained a complete victory over the force under Harold, and won the title of Conqueror. He distributed England in the form of fiefs among his followers, and reduced the Anglo-Saxon population to a condition of serfdom. Feudal castles were erected in every part of England ; and the barons or lords, supported by the labors of a great body of dependants, lived in idleness and luxury. These baronial residences became centres of knightly culture. Here noble youths acquired courtly graces, and wandering minstrels entertained the assembled household with their songs. Brilliant tournaments from time to time brought together the beauty and chivalry of the whole realm. French became the social language of the ruling classes ; and the Anglo-Saxons, reduced to servitude, were despised. It required many generations to break down this harsh antagonism.

The social condition of England in the thirteenth and fourteenth centuries was most intimately related to the first great outburst of English literature. The Normans and the Saxons were drawn more closely together. When compelled to give up the hope of establishing a kingdom on the continent, the Norman fixed his thoughts upon his island home. The valor of the Saxons on many a field of France had conquered the respect of their haughty rulers. A restraint was set upon absolutism by the provisions of the Great Charter. The growth of cities and towns had been rapid, and there existed in all parts of England a wealthy and influential citizen class. The serfs of the time of the Conquest had risen to the rank of free peasants. Parliament was divided into two bodies, and the people acquired a growing influence in the affairs of government. The amalgamation of the two races that had lived side by side for centuries was gradually completed, and the great English nation, in its modern form, had its beginning — a nation that in its type of character is second to none in the history of the world.

But many evils still existed. The nobility lived in luxury and extravagance, while the peasants lived in squalor and want. The public taste was coarse, and the state of morals low. Highwaymen rendered travel unsafe. Through gross abuses of its power and the extensive corruption of its representatives, the church had in large measure lost its hold upon the people. Immense revenues, five times greater than that of the crown, were paid into the coffers at Rome. Half the soil of England was in the hands of the clergy. The immorality of the friars was notorious, and provoked vigorous denunciation and resistance. Yet there were faithful pastors and prelates, who, like Chaucer's poor parson, taught " Christes lore " and followed it themselves ; and magnificent cathedrals were built to stand as objects of admiration for succeeding ages.

The substantial element in all literature is knowledge. This was not lacking in the fourteenth century. Various agencies contributed to the general increase of knowledge. The Crusades had opened up the Orient and brought new ideas into vogue. The literature of France — the long narrative poems of the *trouvère* and the short love ballads of the *troubadour* — introduced a new taste and furnished improved models of style. The legends that had gathered about the names of Charlemagne, Alexander, and King Arthur, appealed strongly to the imagination of the age. The monasteries had multiplied in their *scriptoria* the writings of the ancients. Through Arabic influence and

the general awakening in Europe, learning was held in
greater esteem and prosecuted with more vigor. It was
no longer confined to the representatives of the church.
Ecclesiastical and secular schools were greatly multiplied
for the instruction of the young. Universities and colleges were founded in considerable numbers, some of the
most illustrious colleges at Oxford and Cambridge being
established at this time. Along with scholasticism, which
rigidly applied the logic of Aristotle to the development
of theology, the ancient classics of Greece and Rome were
beginning to receive attention. The nobility began to
take interest in letters. In Italy brilliant writers — Dante,
Petrarch, and Boccaccio — made permanent contributions
to the literature of the world. Thus a great store of
material was accumulated in the fourteenth century —
material that awaited the master-workman soon to appear.

GEOFFREY CHAUCER.

ABOVE all his contemporaries of the fourteenth century stands the figure of Geoffrey Chaucer. He is called by Tennyson —

> " . . . The first warbler, whose sweet breath
> Preluded those melodious bursts that fill
> The spacious times of great Elizabeth
> With sounds that echo still.''

He owes his pre-eminence to several facts. First of all, he was gifted by nature with extraordinary poetic genius, which embodied itself in a number of imperishable works. He is justly called by Dryden "the father of English poetry." Besides, he was peculiarly favored in the circumstances of his life. In the field, at the court, in his business relations, he acquired a wide range of knowledge, which lent support to his great natural abilities. His culture exhibited, for the age in which he lived, almost a cosmopolitan completeness. And lastly, beyond any other man of his time, he fixed the fluctuating language of the age in a permanent form, and laid a firm basis for the English of the present day. Like Homer in Greece, Chaucer stands pre-eminent in the early literature of England; and among the great English poets of subsequent ages, not more than three or four — Shakespeare, Milton, Spenser, and Tennyson — deserve to be placed in the same rank.

As with some other great authors, comparatively little is known of Chaucer's life. The most painstaking investigations have been comparatively fruitless. The time of his birth is a matter of dispute — the two dates given for that event being 1328 and 1340. His father, as well as his grandfather, was a

London wine-dealer. Nothing definite is known in regard to his education. The opinion formerly held that he studied at Cambridge or Oxford is without any satisfactory foundation. In the year 1357 an authentic record shows him attached to the household of Lady Elizabeth, wife of Prince Lionel, in the capacity of a page. In 1359 he accompanied Edward III. in an invasion of France; and having been captured by the French, he was ransomed by the English king for sixteen pounds. The time and circumstances of his marriage are involved in obscurity, though it is tolerably certain that his domestic life was not happy. He subsequently served on embassies to Genoa, Flanders, and France, and acquitted himself to the satisfaction of the Crown. He filled the office of comptroller of customs in the port of London; and like many others of strong literary bent, he appears to have felt the irksomeness of his routine duties: —

> " . . . When thy labor done all is,
> And hast y-made reckonings,
> Instead of rest and newe things
> Thou go'st home to thine house anon,
> And there as dumb as any stone
> Thou sittest at another book."

In 1386 Chaucer was elected a member of Parliament, where he did not distinguish himself. In 1387, as well as can be determined, he lost his wife. After some vicissitudes of fortune, in which he found it necessary at one time to address a " Complaint to his Purse," he died in circumstances of comfort and peace, Oct. 25, 1400. His body lies in Westminster Abbey, where his tomb is an object of tender interest in the famous Poets' Corner.

Chaucer was small and slender in stature, looked upon the ground as he walked, and seemed absent or distracted in manner. This much is brought out in the few graphic touches with which the host of the Tabard and leader of the Canterbury pilgrims draws the poet's portrait. After a most pathetic

tale related by the prioress, Harry Bailly, as was meet, was
the first to interrupt the silence : —

> " And then at first he looked upon me,
> And saide thus : 'What man art thou?' quoth he;
> 'Thou lookest as thou wouldest find a hare,
> For ever upon the ground I see thee stare.
> Approach more near, and looke merrily !
> Now 'ware you, sirs, and let this man have space.
> He in the waist is shaped as well as I;
> This were a puppet in an arm to embrace
> For any woman, small and fair of face.
> He seemeth elfish by his countenance,
> For unto no wight doth he dalliance.' "

While the outward circumstances of Chaucer's life are so
imperfectly known, we have abundant means to judge of his
character and attainments. He is revealed to us in his writings. He was familiar with the court life of his time, but we
cannot believe that he surrendered himself entirely to its vices
and empty formalities. While he was not indifferent to the
enjoyments of social life, he set his heart on higher things.
He recognized true worth wherever he found it, regardless of
the accident of birth or wealth. He seems in no small measure to have embodied the integrity and gentleness which he
fondly ascribes to the character of the gentleman : —

> " Look, who that is most virtuous alway
> Privy and open, and most intendeth aye
> To do the gentle deedes that he can,
> Take him for the greatest gentleman.
> Christ wills we claim of Him our gentleness,
> Not of our elders for their old riches."

Chaucer was a diligent student, with a passionate fondness
for books :

> " And as for me, though I have knowledge slight,
> In bookes for to read I me delight,
> And to them give I faith and full credence,
> And in my heart have them in reverence."

He was familiar with the scholastic learning of his time. He was acquainted with French, Latin, and Italian, and drew upon the literature of all these languages for the material of his writings. Unlike his contemporary Gower, he was not overborne by the weight of his learning. His native intellectual strength was exhibited in his extraordinary power of assimilation. In common with many other great poets, he was a prodigious borrower, using his lofty genius, not in the work of pure invention, but in glorifying materials already existing. He is a striking illustration of the personal element in literature. Gower and Langland worked in the presence of the abundant literary materials of the fourteenth century; but only Chaucer had the ability to lay hold of it and to mould it into imperishable forms.

Chaucer's love of nature was remarkable. It rivalled his passion for books. He tells us that there is nothing that can take him from his reading, —

> " Save, certainly, when that the month of May
> Is come, and that I hear the fowles sing,
> And see the flowers as they begin to spring,
> Farewell my book, and my devotion."

His poetic nature responded to the beauties of the morning landscape, the matin carols of the birds, and the glories of the rising sun. The May-time was his favorite season; and long before Burns and Wordsworth, he loved and sang of the daisy. The sight of this flower, as it opened to the sun, lightened his sorrow : —

> " And down on knees anon right I me set
> And as I could this freshe flower I grette,
> Kneeling always till it unclosed was
> Upon the small, and soft, and sweete grass."

But he was a sympathetic and keen observer of men. He has never been excelled in portraiture. No other literature possesses such a portrait gallery as is contained in the Prologue to the Canterbury Tales. The various pilgrims at the Tabard can be seen and painted. Observe, for example, the fine touches in the picture of the friar : —

> " Somewhat he lisped for his wantonness
> To make his English sweet upon his tongue ;
> And in his harping, when that he had sung,
> His eyen twinkled in his head aright,
> As do the starres in a frosty night."

Though Dryden and Goldsmith have imitated Chaucer in describing an ideal pastor, they have both fallen below their master. Yet with this keenness of observation, this power to detect the peculiarities and foibles of men, there is no admixture of cynicism. There is satire, but it is thornless. Chaucer's writings are pervaded by an atmosphere of genial humor, kindness, tolerance, humanity. He says of the lawyer, —

> " No where so busy a man as he there n'as,
> And yet he seemed busier than he was."

He does full justice to the doctor of physic's various attainments, and then adds,

> " His study was but litel on the Bible."

Chaucer's treatment of woman in his works is full of interest. He is fond of satirizing the foibles supposed to be peculiar to the sex. But he is not wholly lost to chivalrous sentiment, and nowhere else can we find higher and heartier praise of womanly patience, purity, and truth. He appears to have written the " Legend of Good Women " as a kind of amends for the injustice done the sex in the rest of his writings. After all, his real sentiments, let us hope, are found in the following lines : —

> " Alas, howe may we say on hem but well,
> Of whom we were yfostered and ybore,
> And ben all our socoure, and trewe as stele,
> And for our sake ful oft they suffre sore?
> Without women were al our joy ylore."

To many other admirable traits, Chaucer added that of courage in misfortune. His cheerful humor never deserted him. In his latter years he was sometimes without money; but instead of repining, he made a song to his empty purse : —

> " I am sorry now that ye be so light,
> For certes ye now make me heavy cheer."

There are passages in his works that are very offensive to modern taste ; but they are not to be charged so much to Chaucer's love of indecency, as to the grossness of his age and to his artistic sense of justice. This is his own apology; and in the prologue to one of the most objectionable tales, he begs his gentle readers —

> " For Goddes love, as deme not that I say
> Of evil intent, but that I mote reherse
> Hir tales alle, al be they bettre or werse,
> Or elles falsen some of my matere."

Then he adds the kindly warning : —

> " And therefore who so list it not to here,
> Turn over the leef, and chese another tale."

Upon the whole, the estimate of James Russell Lowell seems discriminating and just : " If character may be divined by works, he was a good man, genial, sincere, hearty, temperate of mind, more wise, perhaps, for this world than the next, but thoroughly human, and friendly with God and man."

Chaucer's literary career may be divided into three periods. The first period is characterized by the influence of French models. He began his literary life with the translation of the *Roman de la Rose* — a poem of more than 22,000 lines, composed in the preceding century by Guillaume de Lorris and Jean de Meung. In the original works that followed this translation — among which may be mentioned "The Court of Love" and "Chaucer's Dream" — the influence of French models is clearly apparent.

The second period is characterized by an Italian influence, which showed itself in a more refined taste and more elegant handling of material. Italy was the first modern nation to produce a notable literature. Before Chaucer was born, Dante had written the *Divina Commedia;* and when the English poet was but two years old, Boccaccio was crowned in the Capitol at Rome. When in 1372 Chaucer was sent on a mission to Italy, it is possible that he met Boccaccio and Petrarch. Be that as it may, there can be no doubt that his mission led to a greater interest in Italian literature, from which he borrowed some of his choicest stories. To the Italian period are to be ascribed "Troilus and Cressida," taken from Boccaccio, and "The House of Fame," in which the influence of Dante can be traced. Italy helped Chaucer to unfold his native powers.

The third period in his literary career is distinctly English. His powers reached their full maturity; and instead of depending upon foreign influence, the poet walked independent in his conscious strength. It was during this period, extending from about 1384 to the time of his death, that his greatest work, the "Canterbury Tales," was produced.

This work calls for special notice. The idea seems to have been suggested by Boccaccio's *Decameron.* During the prevalence of the plague in Florence in 1348, seven ladies and three gentlemen, all young, rich, and cultivated, retire to a beautiful villa a few miles from the city; and in order to pass the time more agreeably, they relate to one another a series of tales. Such is the plan of the *Decameron.* Chaucer adopted the idea of a succession of stories, but invented a happier occasion for their narration.

One evening in April a company of twenty-nine pilgrims, of various conditions in life, meet at the Tabard, a London inn, on their way to the shrine of St. Thomas à Becket at Canterbury. At supper the jolly, amiable host offers to accompany them as guide; and in order to relieve the tedium of the journey, he proposes that each one shall tell two tales on the way to the tomb and the same number on their return. The one narrating the best tale is to receive a supper at the expense of the others. The poet joins the party; and in the "Prologue" he gives us, with great artistic and dramatic power, a description of the pilgrims. The various classes of English society — a knight, a lawyer, a doctor, an Oxford student, a miller, a prioress, a monk, a farmer — are all placed before us with marvellous distinctness. Not a single peculiarity of feature, dress, manner, or character escapes the microscopic scrutiny of the poet. The tales that follow — the whole number contemplated was never completed — are adapted to the several narrators; and, taken altogether, they form the greatest literary work ever composed on the same plan.

THE PROLOGUE.

WHAN that Aprille with his schowres swoote
The drought of Marche hath perced to the roote,
And bathed every veyne in swich licour,
Of which vertue engendred is the flour ;
Whan Zephirus eek with his swete breethe   5
Enspired hath in every holte and heethe
The tendre croppes, and the yonge sonne
Hath in the Ram his halfe cours i-ronne,
And smale fowles maken melodie,
That slepen al the night with open eye,   10
So priketh hem nature in here corages : —
Thanne longen folk to gon on pilgrimages,
And palmers for to seeken straunge strondes,
To ferne halwes, kouthe in sondry londes :
And specially, from every schires ende   15
Of Engelond, to Caunterbury they wende,
The holy blisful martir for to seeke,
That hem hath holpen whan that they were seeke.
    Byfel that, in that sesoun on a day,
In Southwerk at the Tabard as I lay,   20
Redy to wenden on my pilgrimage
To Caunterbury with ful devout corage,
At night was come into that hostelrie
Wel nyne and twenty in a compainye,
Of sondry folk, by aventure i-falle   25
In felaweschipe, and pilgryms were thei alle,
That toward Caunterbury wolden ryde ;
The chambres and the stables weren wyde,
And wel we weren esed atte beste.
And schortly, whan the sonne was to reste,   30
So hadde I spoken with hem everychon,
That I was of here felaweschipe anon,
And made forward erly for to ryse,
To take our wey ther as I yow devyse.

But natheles, whil I have tyme and space,   35
Or that I forther in this tale pace,
Me thinketh it acordaunt to resoun,
To telle yow al the condicioun
Of eche of hem, so as it semede me,
And whiche they weren, and of what degre;   40
And eek in what array that they were inne:
And at a knight than wol I first bygynne.

     A KNIGHT ther was, and that a worthy man,
That from the tyme that he first bigan
To ryden out, he lovede chyvalrye,   45
Trouthe and honour, fredom and curteisie.
Ful worthi was he in his lordes werre,
And therto hadde he riden, noman ferre,
As wel in Cristendom as in hethenesse,
And evere honoured for his worthinesse.   50
At Alisaundre he was whan it was wonne,
Ful ofte tyme he hadde the bord bygonne
Aboven alle naciouns in Pruce.
In Lettowe hadde he reysed and in Ruce,
No cristen man so ofte of his degre.   55
In Gernade atte siege hadde he be
Of Algesir, and riden in Belmarie.
At Lieys was he, and at Satalie,
Whan they were wonne; and in the Greete see
At many a noble arive hadde he be.   60
At mortal batailles hadde he ben fiftene,
And foughten for oure feith at Tramassene
In lystes thries, and ay slayn his foo.
This ilke worthi knight hadde ben also
Somtyme with the lord of Palatye,   65
Ageyn another hethen in Turkye:
And everemore he hadde a sovereyn prys.
And though that he was worthy, he was wys,
And of his port as meke as is a mayde.
He nevere yit no vileinye ne sayde   70
In al his lyf, unto no maner wight.
He was a verray perfight gentil knight.

But for to tellen you of his array,
His hors was good, but he ne was nought gay.
Of fustyan he werede a gepoun   75
Al bysmotered with his habergeoun.
For he was late ycome from his viage,
And wente for to doon his pilgrimage.
    With him ther was his sone, a yong SQUYER,
A lovyere, and a lusty bacheler,   80
With lokkes crulle as they were leyd in presse.
Of twenty yeer of age he was I gesse.
Of his stature he was of evene lengthe,
And wonderly delyvere, and gret of strengthe.
And he hadde ben somtyme in chivachie,   85
In Flaundres, in Artoys, and Picardie,
And born him wel, as of so litel space,
In hope to stonden in his lady grace.
Embrowded was he, as it were a mede
Al ful of fresshe floures, white and reede.   90
Syngynge he was, or floytynge, al the day;
He was as fressh as is the moneth of May.
Schort was his goune, with sleeves longe and wyde.
Wel cowde he sitte on hors, and faire ryde.
He cowde songes make, and wel endite,   95
Juste and eek daunce, and wel purtreye and write.
So hote he lovede, that by nightertale
He sleep nomore than doth a nightyngale.
Curteys he was, lowely, and servysable,
And carf byforn his fader at the table.   100
    A YEMAN hadde he and servauntz nomoo
At that tyme, for him luste ryde soo;
And he was clad in coote and hood of grene.
A shef of pocok arwes brighte and kene
Under his belte he bar ful thriftily.   105
Wel cowde he dresse his takel yemanly;
His arwes drowpede nought with fetheres lowe.
And in his hond he bar a mighty bowe.
A not-heed hadde he with a broun visage.
Of woode-craft well cowde he al the usage.   110

Upon his arm he bar a gay bracer,
And by his side a swerd and bokeler,
And on that other side a gay daggere,
Harneysed wel, and scharp as poynt of spere ;
A Cristofre on his brest of silver schene. 115
An horn he bar, the bawdrik was of grene ;
A forster was he sothly, as I gesse.

 Ther was also a Nonne, a PRIORESSE,
That of hire smylyng was ful symple and coy ;
Hire gretteste ooth ne was but by seynt Loy ; 120
And sche was cleped madame Eglentyne.
Ful wel sche sang the servise divyne,
Entuned in hire nose ful semely ;
And Frensch sche spak ful faire and fetysly,
After the scole of Stratford atte Bowe, 125
For Frensch of Parys was to hire unknowe.
At mete wel i-taught was sche withalle ;
Sche leet no morsel from hire lippes falle,
Ne wette hire fyngres in hire sauce deepe.
Wel cowde sche carie a morsel, and wel keepe, 130
That no drope ne fille uppon hire breste.
In curteisie was set ful moche hire leste. *pleasure*
Hire overlippe wypede sche so clene,
That in hire cuppe was no ferthing sene
Of greece, whan sche dronken hadde hire draughte. 135
Ful semely after hire mete sche raughte,
And sikerly sche was of gret disport,
And ful plesaunt, and amyable of port,
And peynede hire to countrefete cheere
Of court, and ben estatlich of manere, 140
And to ben holden digne of reverence.
But for to speken of hire conscience,
Sche was so charitable and so pitous,
Sche wolde weepe if that sche sawe a mous
Caught in a trappe, if it were deed or bledde. 145
Of smale houndes hadde sche, that she fedde
With rosted flessh, or mylk and wastel breed.
But sore wepte sche if oon of hem were deed,

Or if men smot it with a yerde smerte:
And al was conscience and tendre herte.　　150
Ful semely hire wympel i-pynched was;
Hire nose tretys; hire eyen greye as glas;
Hire mouth ful smal, and therto softe and reed;
But sikerly sche hadde a fair forheed.
It was almost a spanne brood, I trowe;　　155
For hardily sche was not undergrowe.
Ful fetys was hire cloke, as I was waar.
Of smal coral aboute hire arm sche baar
A peire of bedes gauded al with grene;
And theron heng a broch of gold ful schene,　　160
On which was first i-write a crowned A,
And after *Amor vincit omnia.*
Another NONNE with hire hadde sche,
That was hire chapeleyne, and PRESTES thre.

　　A MONK ther was, a fair for the maistrie,　　165
An out-rydere, that lovede venerye;
A manly man, to ben an abbot able.
Ful many a deynté hors hadde he in stable:
And whan he rood, men mighte his bridel heere
Gynglen in a whistlyng wynd as cleere,　　170
And eek as lowde as doth the chapel belle.
Ther as this lord was kepere of the selle,
The reule of seynt Maure or of seint Beneyt,
Bycause that it was old and somdel streyt,
This ilke monk leet olde thinges pace,　　175
And held after the newe world the space.
He gaf not of that text a pulled hen,
That seith, that hunters been noon holy men;
Ne that a monk, whan he is reccheles
Is likned to a fissch that is waterles;　　180
This is to seyn, a monk out of his cloystre.
But thilke text held he not worth an oystre.
And I seide his opinioun was good.
What schulde he studie, and make himselven wood,
Uppon a book in cloystre alway to powre,　　185
Or swynke with his handes, and laboure,

As Austyn byt?   How schal the world be served?
Lat Austyn have his swynk to him reserved.
Therfore he was a pricasour aright;
Greyhoundes he hadde as swifte as fowel in flight;   190
Of prikyng and of huntyng for the hare
Was al his lust, for no cost wolde he spare.
I saugh his sleves purfiled atte honde
With grys, and that the fyneste of a londe.
And for to festne his hood under his chynne   195
He hadde of gold y-wrought a curious pynne:
A love-knotte in the grettere ende ther was.
His heed was balled, that schon as eny glas,
And eek his face as he hadde ben anoynt.
He was a lord ful fat and in good poynt;   200
His eyen steepe, and rollyng in his heede,
That stemede as a forneys of a leede;
His bootes souple, his hors in gret estate.
Now certeinly he was a fair prelate;
He was not pale as a for-pyned goost.   205
A fat swan lovede he best of eny roost.
His palfrey was as broun as is a berye.

A FRERE ther was, a wantown and a merye,
A lymytour, a ful solempne man.
In alle the ordres foure is noon that can   210
So moche of daliaunce and fair langage.
He hadde i-mad ful many a mariage
Of yonge wymmen, at his owne cost.
Unto his ordre he was a noble post.
Ful wel biloved and famulier was he   215
With frankeleyns over-al in his cuntre,
And eek with worthi wommen of the toun:
For he hadde power of confessioun,
As seyde himself, more than a curat,
For of his ordre he was licentiat.   220
Ful sweetely herde he confessioun,
And plesaunt was his absolucioun;
He was an esy man to geve penaunce
Ther as he wiste han a good pitaunce;

For unto a poure ordre for to give 225
Is signe that a man is wel i-schrive.
For if he gaf, he dorste make avaunt,
He wiste that a man was repentaunt.
For many a man so hard is of his herte,
He may not wepe although him sore smerte. 230
Therfore in stede of wepyng and preyeres,
Men moot give silver to the poure freres.
His typet was ay farsed ful of knyfes
And pynnes, for to give faire wyfes.
And certeynli he hadde a mery noote; 235
Wel couthe he synge and pleyen on a rote.
Of yeddynges he bar utterly the prys.
His nekke whit was as the flour-de-lys.
Therto he strong was as a champioun.
He knew the tavernes wel in every toun, 240
And everych hostiler and tappestere,
Bet then a lazer, or a beggestere,
For unto swich a worthi man as he
Acordede not, as by his faculté,
To han with sike lazars aqueyntaunce. 245
It is not honest, it may not avaunce,
For to delen with no swich a poraille,
But al with riche and sellers of vitaille.
And overal, ther as profyt schulde arise,
Curteys he was, and lowely of servyse. 250
Ther nas no man nowher so vertuous.
He was the beste beggere in his hous,
For though a widewe hadde noght oo schoo,
So plesaunt was his *in principio*,
Yet wolde he have a ferthing or he wente. 255
His purchas was wel bettre than his rente.
And rage he couthe as it were right a whelpe,
In love-dayes couthe he mochel helpe.
For ther he was not lik a cloysterer,
With thredbare cope as is a poure scoler, 260
But he was lik a maister or a pope.
Of double worstede was his semy-cope,

That rounded as a belle out of the presse.
Somwhat he lipsede, for his wantownesse,
To make his Englissch swete upon his tunge ; 265
And in his harpyng, whan that he hadde sunge,
His eyghen twynkled in his heed aright,
As don the sterres in the frosty night.
This worthi lymytour was cleped Huberd.

A MARCHAUNT was ther with a forked berd, 270
In motteleye, and high on horse he sat,
Uppon his heed a Flaundrisch bevere hat ;
His botes clapsed faire and fetysly.
His resons he spak ful solempnely,
Sownynge alway thencres of his wynnynge. 275
He wolde the see were kept for eny thinge
Betwixe Middelburgh and Orewelle.
Wel couthe he in eschaunge scheeldes selle.
This worthi man ful wel his wit bisette ;
Ther wiste no wight that he was in dette, 280
So estatly was he of governaunce,
With his bargayns, and with his chevysaunce.
For sothe he was a worthi man withalle,
But soth to sayn, I not how men him calle.

A CLERK ther was of Oxenford also, 285
That unto logik hadde longe i-go.
As lene was his hors as is a rake,
And he was not right fat, I undertake ;
But lokede holwe, and therto soberly.
Ful thredbare was his overeste courtepy, 290
For he hadde geten him yit no benefice,
Ne was so worldly for to have office.
For him was levere have at his beddes heede
Twenty bookes, i-clad in blak or reede,
Of Aristotle and his philosophie, 295
Then robes riche, or fithele, or gay sawtrie.
But al be that he was a philosophre,
Yet hadde he but litel gold in cofre ;
But al that he mighte of his frendes hente,
On bookes and on lernyng he it spente, 300

And busily gan for the soules preye
Of hem that gaf him wherwith to scoleye.
Of studie took he most cure and most heede.
Not oo word spak he more than was neede,
And that was seid in forme and reverence   305
And schort and quyk, and ful of heye sentence.
Sownynge in moral vertu was his speche,
And gladly wold he lerne, and gladly teche.

A Sergeant of the Lawe, war and wys,
That often hadde ben atte parvys,   310
Ther was also, ful riche of excellence.
Discret he was, and of gret reverence :
He semede such, his wordes weren so wise,
Justice he was ful often in assise,
By patente, and by pleyn commissioun ;   315
For his science, and for his heih renoun,
Of fees and robes hadde he many oon.
So gret a purchasour was nowher noon.
Al was fee symple to him in effecte,
His purchasyng mighte nought ben enfecte.   320
Nowher so besy a man as he ther nas,
And yit he seemede besier than he was.
In termes hadde he caas and domes alle,
That fro the tyme of Kyng William were falle.
Therto he couthe endite, and make a thing,   325
Ther couthe no wight pynche at his writyng ;
And every statute couthe he pleyn by roote.
He rood but hoomly in a medlé coote,
Gird with a seynt of silk, with barres smale ;
Of his array telle I no lenger tale.   330

A Frankeleyn was in his compaynye ;
Whit was his berde, as is the dayesye.
Of his complexioun he was sangwyn.
Wel lovede he by the morwe a sop in wyn.
To lyven in delite was al his wone,   335
For he was Epicurus owne sone,
That heeld opynyoun that pleyn delyt
Was verraily felicité perfyt.

An houshaldere, and that a gret, was he ;
Seynt Julian he was in his countré.   340
His breed, his ale, was alway after oon ;
A bettre envyned man was nowher noon.
Withoute bake mete was nevere his hous,
Of flessch and fissch, and that so plenteuous,
Hit snewede in his hous of mete and drynke,   345
Of alle deyntees that men cowde thynke.
After the sondry sesouns of the yeer,
So chaungede he his mete and his soper.
Ful many a fat partrich hadde he in mewe,
And many a brem and many a luce in stewe.   350
Woo was his cook, but-if his sauce were
Poynaunt and scharp, and redy al his gere.
His table dormant in his halle alway
Stood redy covered al the longe day.
At sessiouns ther was he lord and sire.   355
Ful ofte tyme he was knight of the schire.
An anlas and a gipser al of silk
Heng at his girdel, whit as morne mylk.
A schirreve hadde he ben, and a countour ;
Was nowher such a worthi vavasour.   360
    An HABERDASSHERE and a CARPENTER,
A WEBBE, a DEYERE, and a TAPICER,
And they were clothed alle in oo lyveré,
Of a solempne and a gret fraternité.
Ful fressh and newe here gere apiked was ;   365
Here knyfes were i-chaped nat with bras,
But al with silver wrought ful clene and wel,
Here gurdles and here pouches every del.
Wel semede ech of hem a fair burgeys,
To sitten in a geldehalle on a deys.   370
Everych for the wisdom that he can,
Was schaply for to ben an alderman.
For catel hadde they inough and rente,
And eek here wyfes wolde it wel assente ;
And elles certeyn were thei to blame.   375
It is ful fair to ben yclept *Madame,*

And to gon to vigilies al byfore,
And han a mantel riallyche i-bore.
　　A Cook thei hadde with hem for the nones,
To boylle chyknes with the mary bones, 380
And poudre-marchaunt tart, and galyngale.
Wel cowde he knowe a draughte of Londone ale.
He cowde roste, and sethe, and broille, and frie,
Maken mortreux, and wel bake a pye.
But gret harm was it, as it thoughte me, 385
That on his schyne a mormal hadde he,
For blankmanger that made he with the beste.
　　A Schipman was ther, wonyng fer by weste :
For ought I woot, he was of Dertemouthe.
He rood upon a rouncy, as he couthe, 390
In a gowne of faldyng to the kne.
A daggere hangyng on a laas hadde he
Aboute his nekke under his arm adoun.
The hoote somer hadde maad his hew al broun ;
And certeinly he was a good felawe. 395
Ful many a draughte of wyn hadde he ydrawe
From Burdeux-ward, whil that the chapman sleep.
Of nyce conscience took he no keep.
If that he faughte, and hadde the heigher hand,
By water he sente hem hoom to every land. 400
But of his craft to rekne wel his tydes,
His stremes and his daungers him bisides,
His herbergh and his mone, his lodemenage,
Ther was non such from Hulle to Cartage.
Hardy he was, and wys to undertake ; 405
With many a tempest hadde his berd ben schake.
He knew wel alle the havenes, as thei were,
From Gootlond to the cape of Fynystere,
And every cryke in Bretayne and in Spayne ;
His barge y-cleped was the Maudelayne. 410
　　With us ther was a Doctour of Phisik,
In al this world ne was ther non him lyk
To speke of phisik and of surgerye ;
For he was grounded in astronomye.

He kepte his pacient wonderly wel   415
In houres by his magik naturel.
Wel cowde he fortunen the ascendent
Of his ymages for his pacient.
He knew the cause of every maladye,
Were it of hoot or cold, or moyste, or drye,   420
And where engendred, and of what humour ;
He was a verrey parfight practisour.
The cause i-knowe, and of his harm the roote,
Anon he gaf the syke man his boote.
Ful redy hadde he his apotecaries,   425
To sende him dragges, and his letuaries,
For ech of hem made other for to wynne ;
Here frendschipe nas not newe to begynne.
Wel knew he the olde Esculapius,
And Deiscorides, and eek Rufus ;   430
Old Ypocras, Haly, and Galien ;
Serapyon, Razis, and Avycen ;
Averrois, Damascien, and Constantyn ;
Bernard, and Gatesden, and Gilbertyn.
Of his diete mesurable was he,   435
For it was of no superfluité,
But of gret norisching and digestible.
His studie was but litel on the Bible.
In sangwin and in pers he clad was al,
Lined with taffata and with sendal.   440
And yit he was but esy of dispence ;
He kepte that he wan in pestilence.
For gold in phisik is a cordial,
Therfore he lovede gold in special.

A good WIF was ther of byside BATHE,   445
But sche was somdel deef, and that was skathe.
Of cloth-makyng she hadde such an haunt,
Sche passede hem of Ypres and of Gaunt.
In al the parisshe wyf ne was ther noon
That to the offryng byforn hire schulde goon,   450
And if ther dide certeyn so wroth was sche,
That sche was out of alle charité.

Hire keverchefs ful fyne weren of grounde ;
I durste swere they weygheden ten pounde
That on a Sonday were upon hire heed.   455
Hire hosen weren of fyn scarlet reed,
Ful streyte y-teyd, and schoos ful moyste and newe.
Bold was hire face, and fair, and reed of hewe.
Sche was a worthy womman al hire lyfe,
Housbondes at chirche dore sche hadde fyfe,   460
Withouten other compainye in youthe ;
But therof needeth nought to speke as nouthe.
And thries hadde sche ben at Jerusalem ;
Sche hadde passed many a straunge streem ;
At Rome sche hadde ben, and at Boloyne,   465
In Galice at seynt Jame, and at Coloyne.
Sche cowde moche of wandryng by the weye.
Gat-tothed was sche, sothly for to seye.
Uppon an amblere esily sche sat,
Ywympled wel, and on hire heed an hat   470
As brood as is a bokeler or a targe ;
A foot-mantel aboute hire hipes large,
And on hire feet a paire of spores scharpe.
In felaweschipe wel cowde sche lawghe and carpe.
Of remedyes of love sche knew parchaunce,   475
For of that art sche couthe the olde daunce.

    A good man was ther of religioun,
And was a poure PERSOUN of a toun ;
But riche he was of holy thought and werk.
He was also a lerned man, a clerk   480
That Cristes gospel trewely wolde preche ;
His parischens devoutly wolde he teche.
Benigne he was, and wonder diligent,
And in adversité ful pacient ;
And such he was i-proved ofte sithes.   485
Ful loth were him to curse for his tythes,
But rather wolde he geven out of dowte,
Unto his poure parisschens aboute,
Of his offrynge, and eek of his substaunce.
He cowde in litel thing han suffisaunce.   490

Wyd was his parische, and houses fer asonder,
But he ne lafte not for reyne ne thonder,
In siknesse nor in meschief to visite
The ferreste in his parissche, moche and lite,
Uppon his feet, and in his hond a staf.　　495
This noble ensample to his scheep he gaf,
That first he wroughte, and afterward he taughte,
Out of the gospel he the wordes caughte,
And this figure he addede eek therto,
That if gold ruste, what schal yren doo?　　500
For if a prest be foul, on whom we truste,
No wonder is a lewed man to ruste;
And schame it is, if that a prest take kepe,
A [foule] schepherde and a clene schepe;
Wel oughte a prest ensample for to give,　　505
By his clennesse, how that his scheep schulde lyve.
He sette not his benefice to hyre,
And leet his scheep encombred in the myre,
And ran to Londone, unto seynte Poules,
To seeken him a chaunterie for soules,　　510
Or with a bretherhede to ben withholde;
But dwelte at hoom, and kepte wel his folde,
So that the wolf ne made it not myscarye;
He was a schepherde and no mercenarie.
And though he holy were, and vertuous,　　515
He was to sinful man nought despitous,
Ne of his speche daungerous ne digne,
But in his teching discret and benigne.
To drawe folk to heven by fairnesse,
By good ensample, this was his busynesse:　　520
But it were eny persone obstinat,
What so he were, of high or lowe estat,
Him wolde he snybbe scharply for the nones.
A bettre preest, I trowe, ther nowher non is.
He waytede after no pompe and reverence,　　525
Ne makede him a spiced conscience,
But Cristes lore, and his apostles twelve,
He taughte, but first he folwede it himselve.

With him ther was a PLOUGHMAN, was his brother,
That hadde i-lad of dong ful many a fother,   530
A trewe swynkere and a good was he,
Lyvynge in pees and perfight charitee.
God lovede he best with al his hoole herte
At alle tymes, though him gamede or smerte,
And thanne his neighebour right as himselve.   535
He wolde thresshe, and therto dyke and delve,
For Cristes sake, with every poure wight,
Withouten hyre, if it laye in his might.
His tythes payede he ful faire and wel,
Bothe of his owne swynk and his catel.   540
In a tabard he rood upon a mere.

    Ther was also a Reeve and a Mellere,
A Sompnour and a Pardoner also,
A Maunciple, and my self, ther were no mo.

    The MELLERE was a stout carl for the nones,   545
Ful big he was of braun, and eek of boones;
That prevede wel, for overal ther he cam,
At wrastlynge he wolde have alwey the ram.
He was schort schuldred, brood, a thikke knarre,
Ther nas no dore that he nolde heve of harre,   550
Or breke it at a rennyng with his heed.
His berd as ony sowe or fox was reed,
And therto brood, as though it were a spade.
Upon the cop right of his nose he hade
A werte, and theron stood a tuft of heres,   555
Reede as the berstles of a sowes eeres.
His nose-thurles blake were and wyde.
A swerd and bokeler baar he by his side,
His mouth as wyde was as a gret forneys.
He was a janglere and a golyardeys,   560
And that was most of synne and harlotries.
Wel cowde he stele corn, and tollen thries;
And yet he hadde a thombe of gold pardé.
A whit cote and a blew hood werede he.
A baggepipe wel cowde he blowe and sowne,   565
And therwithal he broughte us out of towne.

A gentil MAUNCIPLE was ther of a temple,
Of which achatours mighten take exemple
For to be wyse in beyying of vitaille.
For whether that he payde, or took by taille,   570
Algate he waytede so in his achate,
That he was ay biforn and in good state.
Now is not that of God a ful fair grace,
That such a lewed mannes wit schal pace
The wisdom of an heep of lernede men?   575
Of maystres hadde he moo than thries ten,
That were of lawe expert and curious;
Of which ther were a doseyne in that house,
Worthi to ben stiwardes of rente and lond
Of any lord that is in Engelond,   580
To make him lyve by his propre good,
In honour detteles, but-if he were wood,
Or lyve as scarsly as hym list desire;
And able for to helpen al a schire
In any caas that mighte falle or happe;   585
And yit this maunciple sette here aller cappe.
    The REEVE was a sklendre colerik man,
His berd was schave as neigh as evere he can.
His heer was by his eres ful round i-shorn.
His top was docked lyk a preest biforn.   590
Ful longe wern his legges, and ful lene,
Y-lik a staf, ther was no calf y-sene.
Wel cowde he kepe a gerner and a bynne:
Ther was non auditour cowde on him wynne.
Wel wiste he by the droughte, and by the reyn,   595
The yeeldyng of his seed, and of his greyn.
His lordes scheep, his neet, his dayerie,
His swyn, his hors, his stoor, and his pultrie,
Was holly in this reeves governynge,
And by his covenaunt gaf the rekenynge,   600
Syn that his lord was twenti yeer of age;
Ther couthe no man bringe him in arrerage.
Ther nas baillif, ne herde, ne other hyne,
That he ne knew his sleighte and his covyne;

They were adrad of him, as of the dethe.   605
His wonyng was ful fair upon an hethe,
With grene trees i-schadwed was his place.
He cowde bettre than his lord purchace.
Ful riche he was astored prively,
His lord wel couthe he plese subtilly,   610
To geve and lene him of his owne good,
And have a thank, and yet a cote, and hood.
In youthe he lerned hadde a good mester ;
He was a wel good wrighte, a carpenter.
This reeve sat upon a ful good stot, *stallion*   615
That was al pomely gray, and highte Scot.
A long surcote of pers uppon he hade,
And by his side he bar a rusty blade.
Of Northfolk was this reeve of which I telle,
Byside a toun men clepen Baldeswelle.   620
Tukked he was, as is a frere, aboute,
And evere he rood the hyndreste of the route. *company*

summoner   A Sompnour was ther with us in that place,
That hadde a fyr-reed cherubynes face,
For sawceflem he was, with eyghen narwe.   625
And [quyk] he was, and [chirped], as a sparwe,
With skalled browes blake, and piled berd ;
Of his visage children weren aferd.
Ther nas quyksilver, litarge, ne bremstoon,
Boras, ceruce, ne oille of tartre noon,   630
Ne oynement that wolde clense and byte,
That him mighte helpen of his whelkes white,
Ne of the knobbes sittyng on his cheekes.
Wel lovede he garleek, onyouns, and ek leekes,
And for to drinke strong wyn reed as blood. *mad*   635
Thanne wolde he speke, and crye as he were wood.
And whan that he wel dronken hadde the wyn,
Than wolde he speke no word but Latyn.
A fewe termes hadde he, tuo or thre,
That he hadde lerned out of som decree ;   640
No wonder is, he herde it al the day ;
And eek ye knowen wel, how that a jay

Can clepen Watte, as wel as can the pope.
But who so wolde in other thing him grope,
Thanne hadde he spent al his philosophie, 645
Ay, *Questio quid juris*, wolde he crye.
He was a gentil harlot and a kynde ;
A bettre felawe schulde men noght fynde.
He wolde suffre for a quart of wyn
A good felawe to have his concubyn 650
A twelf moneth, and excuse him atte fulle :
And prively a fynch eek cowde he pulle.
And if he fond owher a good felawe,
He wolde techen him to han non awe
In such caas of the archedeknes curs, 655
But-if a mannes soule were in his purs ;
For in his purs he scholde y-punyssched be.
" Purs is the erchedeknes helle," quod he.
But well I woot he lyede right in dede ;
Of cursyng oghte ech gulty man him drede ; 660
For curse wol slee right as assoillyng saveth ;
And also war him of a *significavit*.
In daunger hadde he at his owne gise
The yonge gurles of the diocise,
And knew here counseil, and was al here reed. 665
A garland hadde he set upon his heed,
As gret as it were for an ale-stake ;
A bokeler hadde he maad him of a cake.

  With him ther rood a gentil PARDONER
Of Rouncivale, his frend and his comper, 670
That streyt was comen from the court of Rome.
Ful lowde he sange, ' Com hider, love, to me.'
This sompnour bar to him a stif burdoun,
Was nevere trompe of half so gret a soun,
This pardoner hadde heer as yelwe as wex, 675
But smothe it heng, as doth a strike of flex ;
By unces hynge his lokkes that he hadde,
And therwith he his schuldres overspradde.
Ful thinne it lay, by culpons on and oon,
But hood, for jolitee, ne werede he noon, 680

For it was trussed up in his walet.
Him thoughte he rood al of the newe get,
Dischevele, sauf his cappe, he rood al bare.
Suche glaryng eyghen hadde he as an hare.
A vernicle hadde he sowed upon his cappe.   685
His walet lay byforn him in his lappe,
Bret-ful of pardoun come from Rome al hoot.
A voys he hadde as smal as eny goot.
No berd hadde he, ne nevere scholde have,
As smothe it was as it were late i-schave;   690
I trowe he were a geldyng or a mere.
But of his craft, fro Berwyk into Ware,
Ne was ther such another pardoner.
For in his male he hadde a pilwebeer,
Which that, he seide, was oure lady veyl: 695
He seide, he hadde a gobet of the seyl
That seynt Peter hadde, whan that he wente
Uppon the see, til Jhesu Crist him hente.
He hadde a croys of latoun ful of stones,
And in a glas he hadde pigges bones.   700
But with these reliques, whan that he fond
A poure persoun dwellyng uppon lond,
Upon a day he gat him more moneye
Than that the persoun gat in monthes tweye.
And thus with feyned flaterie and japes,   705
He made the persoun and the people his apes.
But trewely to tellen atte laste,
He was in churche a noble ecclesiaste.
Wel cowde he rede a lessoun or a storye,
But altherbest he sang an offertorie;   710
For wel he wyste, whan that song was songe,
He moste preche, and wel affyle his tonge,
To wynne silver, as he right wel cowde;
Therefore he sang ful meriely and lowde.

     Now have I told you schortly in a clause   715
Thestat, tharray, the nombre, and eek the cause
Why that assembled was this compainye
In Southwerk at this gentil hostelrie,

That highte the Tabard, faste by the Belle.
But now is tyme to yow for to telle   720
How that we bare us in that ilke night,
Whan we were in that hostelrie alight;
And after wol I telle of oure viage,
And al the remenaunt of oure pilgrimage.
But first I pray you of your curteisie,   725
That ye ne rette it nat my vileinye,
Though that I pleynly speke in this matere,
To telle you here wordes and (here cheere;)
Ne though I speke here wordes proprely.
For this ye knowen also wel as I,   730
Whoso schal telle a tale after a man,
He moot reherce, as neigh as evere he can,
Everych word, if it be in his charge,
Al speke he nevere so rudelyche and large;
Or elles he moot telle his tale untrewe,   735
Or feyne thing, or fynde wordes newe.
He may not spare, although he were his brother;
He moot as wel seyn oo word as another.
Crist spak himself ful broode in holy writ,
And wel ye woote no vileinye is it.   740
Eek Plato seith, whoso that can him rede,
The wordes mote be cosyn to the dede.
Also I praye you to forgeve it me,
Al have I nat set folk in here degre
Here in this tale, as that thei schulde stonde: 745
My wit is schort, ye may wel understonde.

    Greet cheere made oure host us everchon,
And to the souper sette he us anon;
And servede us with vitaille atte beste.
Strong was the wyn, and (wel to drynke us leste.   750
A semely man oure hoost he was withalle
For to han been a marschal in an halle;
A large man he was with eyghen stepe,
A fairer burgeys was ther noon in Chepe:
Bold of his speche, and wys and wel i-taught,   755
And of manhede him lakkede right naught.

Eek therto he was right a mery man,
And after soper playen he bygan,
And spak of myrthe amonges othre thinges,
Whan that we hadde maad our rekenynges;   760
And sayde thus : " Lo, lordynges, trewely
Ye ben to me right welcome hertely :
For by my trouthe, if that I schal not lye,
I saugh nought this yeer so mery a companye
At oones in this herbergh as is now.   765
Fayn wolde I (don yow mirthe,) wiste I how.
And of a mirthe I am right now bythought,
To doon you eese, and it schal coste nought.
Ye goon to Caunterbury; God you speede,
The blisful martir (quyte you youre meede !)   770
And wel I woot, as ye gon by the weye,
Ye (schapen yow to talen) and to pleye ;
For trewely confort ne mirthe is noon
To ryde by the weye domb as a stoon ;
And therfore wol I maken you disport,   775
As I seyde erst, and don you som confort.
And if yow liketh alle by oon assent
Now for to standen at my juggement,
And for to werken as I schal you seye,
To morwe, whan ye riden by the weye,   780
Now by my fader soule that is deed,
But ye be merye, I wol geve myn heed.
Hold up youre hond withoute more speche."
Oure counseil was not longe for to seche ;
Us thoughte it nas nat worth to make it wys,   785
And grauntede him withoute more avys,
And bad him seie his verdite, as him leste.
" Lordynges," quoth he, " now herkneth for the beste ;
But taketh it not, I praye you, in desdeyn ;
This is the poynt, to speken schort and pleyn,   790
That ech of yow to schorte with oure weie,
In this viage, schal telle tales tweye,
To Caunterburi-ward, I mene it so,
And hom-ward he schal tellen othere tuo,

Of aventures that whilom han bifalle.   795
And which of yow that bereth him best of alle,
That is to seyn, that telleth in this caas
Tales of best sentence and most solas,
Schal han a soper at oure alther cost
Here in this place sittynge by this post,   800
Whan that we come ageyn from Caunterbury.
And for to maken you the more mery,
I wol myselven gladly with you ryde,
Right at myn owen cost, and be youre gyde.
And whoso wole my juggement withseie   805
Schal paye al that we spenden by the weye.
And if ye vouchesauf that it be so,
Telle me anoon, withouten wordes moo,
And I wole erely schape me therfore."
This thing was graunted, and oure othes swore   810
With ful glad herte, and prayden him also
That he wold vouchesauf for to doon so,
And that he wolde ben oure governour,
And of oure tales jugge and reportour,
And sette a souper at a certeyn prys;   815
And we wolde rewled ben at his devys,
In heygh and lowe; and thus by oon assent
We been acorded to his juggement.
And thereupon the wyn was fet anoon;
We dronken, and to reste wente echoon,   820
Withouten eny lenger taryinge.
A morwe whan the day bigan to sprynge,
Up roos oure host, and was oure alther cok,
And gadrede us togidre alle in a flok,
And forth we riden a litel more than pass,   825
Unto the waterynge of seint Thomas.
And there oure host bigan his hors areste,
And seyde; " Lordes, herkneth if yow leste.
Ye woote youre forward, and I it you recorde.
If even-song and morwe-song accorde,   830
Lat se now who schal telle first a tale.
As evere moot I drinke wyn or ale,

Whoso be rebel to my juggement
Schal paye for al that by the weye is spent.
Now draweth cut, er that we ferrer twynne;   835
He which that hath the schorteste schal bygynne."
" Sire knight," quoth he, " my maister and my lord,
Now draweth cut, for that is myn acord.
Cometh ner," quoth he, " my lady prioresse;
And ye, sir clerk, lat be youre schamefastnesse,   840
Ne studieth nat; ley hand to, every man."
      Anon to drawen every wight bigan,
And schortly for to tellen as it was,
Were it by aventure, or sort, or cas,
The soth is this, the cut fil to the knight,   845
Of which ful blithe and glad was every wight;
And telle he moste his tale as was resoun,
By forward and by composicioun,
As ye han herd; what needeth wordes moo?
And whan this goode man seigh that it was so,   850
As he that wys was and obedient
To kepe his forward by his fre assent,
He seyde: " Syn I schal bygynne the game,
What, welcome be thou cut, a Goddes name:
Now lat us ryde and herkneth what I seye."   855
      And with that word we riden forth oure weye;
And he bigan with right a merie chere
His tale anon, and seide in this manere.

NOTES TO CHAUCER'S PROLOGUE.

(The numbers refer to lines.)

THE language of Chaucer exhibits the fusion of Teutonic and French elements. Dropping most of the Anglo-Saxon inflections, it passes from a synthetic to an analytic condition, in which the relations of words are expressed, not by different terminations, but by separate words. It is essentially modern, but the following peculiarities are to be noted. The plural of nouns is usually formed by the ending *es,* which is pronounced as a distinct syllable; but in words of more than one syllable, the ending is *s.* Instead of *es,* we sometimes meet with *is* and *us.* Some nouns which originally ended in *an* have *en* or *n ;* as, *asschen,* ashes; *been,* bees; *eyen,* eyes. The possessive or genitive case, singular and plural, is usually formed by adding *es ;* as, his *lordes* werre (wars); *foxes* tales. But *en* is sometimes used in the plural; as, his *eyen* sight. The dative case singular ends in *e ;* as, *holte, bedde.* The adjective is inflected. After demonstrative and possessive adjectives and the definite article, the adjective takes the ending *e ;* as, the *yonge* sonne; his *halfe* cours. But in adjectives of more than one syllable, this *e* is usually dropped. The plural of adjectives is formed by adding *e ;* as, *smale* fowles. But adjectives of more than one syllable, and all adjectives in the predicate, omit the *e.* The comparative is formed by the addition of *er,* though the Anglo-Saxon form *re* is found in a few words; as, *derre,* dearer; *ferre,* farther. The personal pronouns are as follows : —

	SINGULAR.	PLURAL.
Nom.	I, Ich, Ik,	we,
Poss.	min (myn), mi (my),	our, oure,
Obj.	me.	us.
Nom.	thou (thow, tow),	ye,
Poss.	thin (thyn), thi (thy),	your, youre,
Obj.	the, thee.	yow, you.

	Masc.	*Fem.*	*Neut.*	*All Genders.*
Nom.	he,	she, sche,	hit, it, yt,	thei, they,
Poss.	his,	hire, hir,	his,	here, her, hir,
Obj.	him.	hire, hir, here.	hit, it, yt.	hem.

The present indicative plural of verbs ends in *en* or *e;* as, we *loven* or *love*. The infinitive ends in *en* or *e;* as, *speken, speke,* to speak. The present participle usually ends in *yng* or *ynge*. The past participle of strong verbs ends in *en* or *e,* and (as well as the past participle of weak verbs) is often preceded by the prefix *y* or *i,* answering to the Anglo-Saxon and modern German *ge;* as, *ironne, yclept*. The following negative forms deserve attention: *nam,* am not; *nys,* is not; *nas,* was not; *nere,* were not; *nath,* hath not; *nadde,* had not; *nylle,* will not; *nolde,* would not; *nat, not, noot,* knows not. Adverbs are formed from adjectives by adding *e;* as, *brighte,* brightly; *deepe,* deeply. Other peculiarities will be explained in the notes.

VERSIFICATION. — The prevailing metre in the Canterbury Tales is iambic pentameter in rhyming couplets. Occasionally there are eleven syllables in a line, and sometimes only nine. Short, unemphatic syllables are often slurred over; as,

" Sche gad | *ereth* flour | es par | ty white | and rede."

Words from the French usually retain their native pronunciation; that is, are accented on the last syllable. Final *e* is usually sounded as a distinct syllable except before *h,* a following vowel, in the personal pronouns *oure, youre, hire, here,* and in many polysyllables. The *ed* of the past indicative and past participle, and the *es* of the plural and of the genitive, form separate syllables.

In exemplification of the foregoing rules, the opening lines of the Prologue are here divided into their component iambics:—

" Whan that | April | le, with | his schow | res swoote
The drought | of Marche | hath per | ced to | the roote,
And ba | thed eve | ry veyne | in swich | licour,
Of which | vertue | engen | dred is | the flour;
Whan Ze | phirus | eek with | his swe | te breethe
Enspi | red hath | in eve | ry holte | and heethe
The ten | dre crop | pes, and | the yon | ge sonne
Hath in | the Ram | his hal | fe cours | i-ronne,
And sma | le fow | les ma | ken me | lodie,
That sle | pen al | the night | with o | pen eye,
So pri | keth hem | nature | in here | corages: —
Thanne lon | gen folk | to gon | on pil | grimages,
And pal | mers for | to see | ken straun | ge strondes,
To fer | ne hal | wes, couthe | in son | dry londes;
And spe | cially | from eve | ry schi | res ende
Of En | gelond | to Caunt | terbury | they wende,
The ho | ly blis | ful mar | tir for | to seeke,
That hem | hath holp | en whan | that they | were seeke."

1. *Whan that* = when. A frequent phrase in Chaucer. — *Swoote* = sweet. The final *e* is the sign of the plural.

2. *Marche.* Final *e* is silent before words beginning with *h* or a vowel. *Roote.* The *e* denotes the dative.

3. *Swich* = such. A. S. *swilc*, such; from *swa*, so, and *lic*, like.

4. *Vertue* = power. Retains French accent on the last syllable.

5. *Eek* = also. — *Swete.* The final *e* denotes the definite declension with the possessive *his*. — *Breethe.* Final *e* for the dative. So with *holte* and *heethe* in the following line. *Holt* = wood, grove.

7. *Yonge sonne.* The final *e* of *yonge* for the definite declension with *the*. The sun is called young, because it has not long entered upon its annual course.

8. *Ram.* The first constellation of the Zodiac, corresponding to the latter part of March and the first half of April. It is the part in April that the sun has run. — *I-ronne*, p. p. of *ronne*, to run. The prefixes *i* and *y* usually denote the past participle, and correspond to the A. S. *ge*. Cf. modern German.

9. *Smale.* Final *e* denoting the plural. — *Maken* is a plural form, as also *slepen* in the following line.

11. *Priketh* = inciteth, prompteth. — *Hem, here.* See list of pronouns under Chaucer's "Diction." — *Corages* = hearts, spirits. French *courage*, from Lat. *cor*, heart.

12. *To gon* = to go.

13. *Palmers* = persons bearing palm-branches in token of having been to the Holy Land. — *Straunge strondes* = strange strands or foreign shores.

14. *Ferne halwes, kouthe* = old, or distant saints known, etc. *Kouthe*, from the A. S. *cunnan*, to know. Cf. uncouth.

16. *Wende* = go. The past tense is *wente*, English *went*.

17. *The holy blisful martir*, Thomas à Becket. Read a sketch of his life.

18. *Holpen*, p. p. *helpen*, to help.

19. *Byfel* = it befell or chanced; an impers. verb.

20. *Tabard* = a sleeveless jacket or coat, formerly worn by nobles in war. It was the sign of a well-known inn in Southwark, London.

25. *By aventure i-falle* = by adventure, or chance fallen, etc.

29. *Esed atte beste* = accommodated in the best manner. *Atte*, contraction for the A. S. *at tham* = at the.

31. *Everychon* = every one.

34. *Ther as I yow devyse* = where I describe to you. *Ther as* = where.

35. *Natheless* = nevertheless. A. S. *na the laes* = not the less.

36. *Or that* = ere that. *Or*, from A. S. *aer*, before, soon. *Pace* = pass.

37. *Me thinketh* = it seems to me. *Me* is the dative after the impers. verb *it thinketh*. From the A. S. *thyncan*, to seem; quite distinct from *thencan*, to think.

45. *Chyvalrye* = chivalry. Old French *chevalerie*, from *cheval*, a horse; Latin, *caballus*.

47. *Werre* = wars.

48. *Noman ferre* = no man farther. *Ferre*, comp. of *fer*, far.

49. *Hethenesse* = heathendom. Like many other knights of his age, he had served as a volunteer under foreign princes.

51. *Alisaundre* = Alexandria. It was taken in 1365 by Pierre de Lusignan, King of Cyprus.

52. *He hadde the bord bygonne.* An obscure expression. Perhaps he had been placed at the head of the table (bord) by way of distinction; or *bord* may be the Low Ger. *boort* = joust, tournament.

53. *Aboven alle naciouns.* He took precedence over the representatives of all other nations at the Prussian court. *Pruce* = Prussia. It was not unusual for English knights to serve in Prussia, with the Knights of the Teutonic order, who were constantly warring with their heathen neighbors in *Lettowe* (Lithuania) and in *Ruce* (Russia).

54. *Reysed* = made an expedition. A. S. *raesan*, to rush, attack. Cf. Ger. *reisen*, to travel.

56. *Gernade* = Granada. The city of Algezir was taken from the Moorish king of Granada in 1344.

57. *Belmarie* and *Tramassene* (line 62) were Moorish kingdoms in Africa.

58. *Lieys*, in Armenia, was taken from the Turks by Pierre de Lusignan about 1367, and *Satalie* (Attalia) by the same prince about 1352.

59. *Greete sea.* Great sea is a name applied to that part of the Mediterranean lying between the Greek islands and the coast of Syria. See Numbers xxxiv. 6.

60. *Arive* = arrival or disembarkation of troops; here a hostile landing probably. — *Be* = been. In the next line the form is *ben*.

63. *Lystes* = lists, the ground enclosed for a tournament.

64. *Ilke* = same. A. S. *ylc*, same. Cf. " of that ilk."

65. *Palatye* = Palathia, in Anatolia or Asia Minor.

67. *Sovereyn prys* = highest praise.

68. *Worthy* = brave, bold.

70. *Vileinye* = villany, foul language.

71. *No maner wight* = no manner of wight or person.

72. *Perfight* = perfect.

74. *Ne . . . nought.* A double negative form. Cf. French *ne . . . pas.* *Nought* = A. S. *na*, no, not, and *wiht*, whit, thing. The adv. *not* is a further contraction. — *Gay* = lively, fast; or perhaps decked out in various trappings.

75. *Gepoun* = a short cassock or cloak.

76. *Bysmotered* = besmutted or soiled. — *Habergeoun* = habergeon, a coat of mail, composed of little iron rings, extending from the neck to the waist, or lower.

77. *Viage* = voyage, journey, travels. He made the pilgrimage in the dress worn on his knightly expeditions.

79. *Squyer* = squire, an attendant upon a knight. Old French, *escuyer*, Low Lat., *scutarius*, shield-bearer, Latin, *scutum*, a shield.

81. *Lokkes crulle* = locks curled.

83. *Evene lengthe* = moderate or usual height.

84. *Delyvere* = active, quick.

85. *Chivachie* = military expedition or service. Fr. *chevauchée* (from *cheval*), a raid or expedition of cavalry.

88. *Lady grace* = lady's grace. *Lady* for *ladye*, genitive singular; the ending was in A. S. *an*.

89. *Embrowded* = embroidered, in his dress.

91. *Floytynge* = fluting, playing the flute.

95. *Endite* = relate.

96. *Purtreye* = draw, sketch.

97. *Nightertale* = night-time.

99. *Servysable* = willing to be of service.

100. *Carf* = carved, past of *kerven*, to carve; A. S. *ceorfan.*

101. *Yemen* = yeoman. — *No moo* = no more.

102. *Him luste* = it pleased him. — *Ryde* is inf. = to ride.

104. *Pocok arwes* = arrows winged with peacock feathers.

109. *Not-heed* = cropped head; sometimes explained as *nut-head*, or head like a nut.

111. *Bracer* = a covering for the arm to protect it from the bow-string.

112. *Bokeler* = buckler, shield.

115. *Cristofre* = a brooch with the image of St. Christopher, who was regarded with special reverence by the middle and lower classes. — *Schene* = bright, beautiful; A. S. *scyne*, fair. Cf. Eng., *sheen*; Ger. schön.

116. *Bawdrik* = baldric, girdle, belt.

117. *Forster* = forester. Ger. *förster.* — *Sothly* = truly, soothly.

120. *Seynt Loy* = St. Louis; according to others, St. Eligius.

124. *Fetysly* = prettily, cleverly.

126. *Frensch of Parys.* The French of Paris, then as now, was the

standard. The French in England was not pure. — *Unknowe* = unknown. The *n* of the past part. is frequently dropped.

129. *Sauce* = saucer. Forks and spoons had not yet come into use.

131. *No drope ne fille* = no drop fall. Double negative, as in French and Anglo-Saxon.

132. *Leste* = pleasure, delight.

134. *Ferthing* = small quantity. Literally, a fourth part. A. S. *feorth*, fourth, and diminutive suffix *ing*.

136. *Raughte* = reached. Preterit of *reche*.

137. *Sikerly* = surely. Cf. Ger. *sicherlich*. — *Disport* = sport, diversion. She was fond of gayety.

139. *Peynede hire* = she took pains. — *Countrefete cheere* = imitate the manner. Formerly no bad association belonged to the word *counterfeit*.

140. *Estatlich* = stately, high-bred.

141. *Digne* = worthy. French *digne*, Lat. *dignus*.

147. *Wastel breed* = cake bread, or bread made of the finest flour. Dogs were usually fed on coarse bread baked for the purpose.

149. *Men* = indef. pronoun *one;* sometimes written *me*. It has unfortunately become obsolete. German *man*, French *on*. — *Smerte* = smartly.

151. *Wympel* = a linen covering for the neck and shoulders. — *I-pynched* = plaited, or gathered into folds.

152. *Tretys* = slender, well-proportioned.

156. *Hardily* = assuredly, certainly.

157. *Fetys* = neat, pretty. See l. 124.

159. *Gauded al with grene* = having large green gauds or beads. The reference is to a rosary. See Webster.

162. *Amor vincit omnia* = love conquers all things.

164. *Chapeleyne* = chaplain or assistant. — *Prestes thre*. Priests were connected with nunneries for the purpose of saying mass.

165. *A fair for the maistrie* = a fair one for obtaining the mastery.

166. *Out-rydere* = one who rides after hounds in hunting.

170. *Gynglen* = jingling. Fashionable riders were accustomed to hang small bells on their bridles and harness.

172. *Ther as* = where. — *Selle* = cell. Originally applied to the small chamber occupied by each monk, but afterwards also to a religious house or inferior monastery.

173. *Seynt Maur — seint Beneyt* = St. Maur, St. Benedict. The latter founded the order of Benedictines at the beginning of the sixth century. St. Maur was a disciple of St. Benedict. The Bendictine mode of life was originally severely ascetic.

174. *Somdel streyt* = somewhat strict.

175. *This ilke* = this same.   A. S. *ylc*, same.

176. *Space* = path, steps.   Other readings are *trace* and *pace*.

177. *A pulled hen* = a moulting or worthless hen, neither laying eggs nor fit for food.

179. *Reccheles* = reckless, careless.   A. S. *reccan*, to think.

182. *Thilke* = that, the like.   A. S. *thylc*, that, the like.

183. *Seide* = should say.   Pret. of Subjunctive.

184. *What* = why, wherefore. — *Wood* = mad, foolish.   Cf. Ger. *Wuth*, rage.

186. *Swynke* = to toil, labor.

187. *As Austyn byt* = As Augustine bids.   St. Augustine of Canterbury urged a faithful adherence to the monastic vows upon his clergy.

188. Let Augustine, or Austin, have his toil kept for himself.

189. *Pricasour* = hard rider, one who spurs his horse. — *Aright* = on right, indeed.

191. *Prikyng* = riding.   Cf. Spenser's —

> " A gentle knight was pricking on the plaine."

192. *Lust* = pleasure.   Other forms are *leste*, *list*.

193. *Purfiled atte honde* = embroidered at the hand or cuff.   Fr. *pour-filer*, to embroider.   *Atte*, see l. 29.

194. *Grys* = fur of the Siberian squirrel.   French *gris*, gray.

200. *In good poynt* = French *en bon point*, rotundity of figure.

201. *Steepe* = bright.

202. *Stemede as a forneys of a leed* = shone as a furnace of a caldron (*leed*).

203. *Bootes souple.*   High boots of soft leather were worn, fitting closely to the leg.

205. *For-pyned* = wasted away.   *For* is intensive.   Cf. Eng. *pine*.

208. *Frere* = friar. — *Wantoun* = playful, sportive; literally, untrained, uneducated.

209. *Lymytour* = a begging friar to whom a certain district or *limit* was assigned.

210. *The ordres foure* = the four orders of mendicant friars.   These were the Dominicans or Black friars, the Franciscans or Gray friars, the Carmelites or White friars, and the Austin friars. — *Can* = knows.   Present tense of A. S. *cunnan*, to know.

211. *Daliaunce and fair langage* = gossip and flattery.

214. *Post* = pillar or support.

220. *Licentiat* = one who has license from the Pope to grant absolution in all cases.   Curates were required to refer certain cases to the bishop.

224. *Ther as he wiste han* = where he knew he would have. *Han*, inf. contracted from *haven.* — *Pitaunce* = meal of victuals, or small allowance of anything.

226. *I-schrive* = confessed. The *n* of the past part. is dropped.

233. *His typet was ay farsed* = His hood was always stuffed. Says an old writer: "When the order degenerated, the friar combined with the spiritual functions the occupation of pedler, huckster, mountebank, and quack doctor."

236. *Rote* = a kind of harp.

237. *Yeddynges* = ballads or romantic tales.

237. *Bar utterly the prys* = took unquestionably the prize.

238. *Flour-de-lys* = lily. Now written *fleur-de-lis.*

241. *Tappestere* = bar-maid. The corresponding masculine was *tapper*. *Ster* was originally the feminine suffix of agency. Cf. *spinster.*

242. *Bet* = better. — *Lazer* = leper, from Lazarus in the parable.

243. *Swich* = such. See note l. 3.

245. *Sike* = sick.

247. *Poraille* = poor people, rabble.

253. *Nogt oo schoo* = not one shoe.

254. *In principio.* At each house the *lymytour* began his speech, " *In principio erat verbum* " = in the beginning was the Word.

255. *Ferthing.* See note l. 134.

256. *Purchas* = proceeds of his begging. — *Rente* = regular income.

258. *Love-dayes* = days fixed to settle difficulties by arbitration.

259. *For ther* = further.

260. *Cope* = cloak or vestment of a priest. Cf. Eng. *cape.* *Semy-cope* (l. 262) = a short cape or cloak.

263. *Belle out of the press* = bell from the mould.

264. *Lipsede* = lisped.

270. *Forked berd.* This was the fashion among franklins and burghers.

273. *Clapsed* = clasped.

275. *Sownynge — thencres* = sounding the increase.

276. *For eny thinge* = at all hazards.

277. *Middelburgh and Orewelle.* Middleburgh is still a port of the island of Walcheren in the Netherlands. *Orewelle* is now the port of Harwich.

278. *Scheeldes* = French crowns (*écus*) from the figure of a shield on one side.

279. *His wit bisette* = employed his wit or knowledge.

281. *Governaunce* = management.

282. *Chevysaunce* = agreement for borrowing money.

284. *Not* = Know not. *Ne* and *wot*.

285. *Clerk* = an ecclesiastic or man of learning; here a university student. — *Oxenford* = Oxford; not derived from the A. S. *oxna*, oxen, but from a Celtic word meaning *water*.

289. *Holwe* = hollow.

290. *Overeste courtépy* = uppermost short cloak.

292. *Office* = secular calling, in contrast with *benefice*, an ecclesiastical living.

293. *Levere* = preferable. *Him* is dat. after *levere*. Cf. Ger. *lieber*.

295. Aristotle was a celebrated Greek philosopher. He was the founder of the Peripatetic school of philosophy, and the tutor of Alexander the Great. Born 384 B.C.

296. *Fithele* = fiddle. — *Sawtrie* = psaltery, a kind of harp.

299. *Hente* = get, take.

302. *Scoleye* = to attend school, to study. Poor students were accustomed to beg for their support at the universities.

303. *Cure* = care.

306. *Heye sentence* = high meaning or lofty sentiment.

309. *Sergeant of the lawe* = a lawyer of the highest rank. The Lat. phrase is *serviens ad legem*. — *War* = wary.

310. *Atte parvys* = at the porch, of St. Paul's, where lawyers were accustomed to meet for consultation.

312. *Of gret reverence* = worthy of great respect or reverence.

318. *Purchasour* = prosecutor. French *pourchasser*, to hunt after.

319. *Al was fee simple to him.* This seems to mean that all cases were clear to him. See etymology of *fee* in Webster.

320. His prosecution might not be tainted (*enfecte*) or contaminated with any illegality.

323. *Caas and domes* = cases and dooms, or precedents and decisions.

325. *Make a thing* = make or draw up a contract.

326. *Pynche at* = find fault with.

328. *Medlé coote* = coat of mixed stuff or color.

329. *Seynt of silk* = girdle of silk. Cf. Eng. cincture.

332. *Dayesye* = daisy; literally, *day's eye*. Chaucer's favorite flower.

334. *By the morwe* = early in the morning. — *Sop in wyn* = bread dipped in wine; according to Bacon, more intoxicating than wine itself.

335. *Wone* = pleasure, desire. Cf. Ger. *Wonne*, bliss.

336. Epicurus, a famous Greek philosopher, who assumed pleasure to be the highest good.

337. *Pleyn delyt* = full delight or perfect physical enjoyment.

340. *Seynt Julian* = The patron saint of travellers and hospitality.

341. *Alway after oon* = always the same.

342. *Envyned* = provided with wine.

345. *Hit snewede* = it snowed or abounded.

348. *Mete and soper* = food and drink. See etymology of *supper* in Webster.

349. *Mewe* = cage or coop.

350. *Brem* = bream. — *Luce* = pike. — *Stewe* = fish-pond.

351. *Woo was his cook* = woe was it to his cook. — *But-if* = unless, if not.

353. *Table dormant.* Previous to the fourteenth century the tables were rough boards laid on trestles; tables *dormant*, or with fixed legs, were then introduced, and standing in the hall were looked upon as evidences of hospitality.

355. *Sessiouns* = The county courts.

336. *Knight of the schire* = representative in Parliament.

357. *Anlas* = knife or dagger. — *Gipser* = pouch.

359. *Schirreve* = shire reeve, sheriff. Reeve, A. S. *gerefa*, = officer, governor. — *Countour* = auditor of accounts, or county treasurer. Cf. Fr. *compter*, to count.

360. *Vavasour* = one next in dignity to a baron; landholder of the middle class.

361. *Haberdasshere* = dealer in " notions " — ribbons, pins, etc.

362. *Webbe* = weaver. Cf. Ger. *Weber*. — *Tapicer* = worker in tapestry.

363. *Lyveré* = livery; here the uniform of the trade guild to which they belonged.

365. *Apiked* = cleaned, kept neat.

366. *I-chaped* = having plates of metal at the point of the sheath or scabbard.

368. *Del* = part, portion. A. S. *dael*, a portion. Cf. Eng. *dole* and Ger. *Theil*.

369. *Burgeys* = burgess; here a person of the middle class.

370. *Geldehalle* = guild-hall. — *Deys* = dais; here the raised platform at the upper end of the hall, on which were seats for persons of distinction.

371. *That he can* = that he knows.

372. *Schaply* = fit. From *to shape*, hence *adapted*.

373. *Catel* = property. Cf. Eng. *chattels* and *cattle*. — *Rente* = rent, revenue, income. Cf. Eng. *render*.

377. *Vigilies* = vigils, or eves of festival days, when the people were accustomed to meet at the church for merrymaking. They wore their best clothes, and the wealthier women had their mantles, which were brought for show as well as protection, carried by servants.

378. *Riallyche* = royally.

379. *For the nones* = for the nonce. The older spelling is *for then ones* = for the once, for the occasion. The *n*, which is the sign of the dat. (A. S. *tham*, *than*), is carried over to the following word.

380. *Mary bones* = marrow bones.

381. *Poudre-marchaunt tart* = a tart or acid flavoring powder. — *Galyn-gale* = the root of an aromatic species of sedge found in the south of England.

382. *London ale* was held in high esteem at that time.

384. *Mortreux* = a kind of soup, of which the principal ingredients were fowl, fresh pork, bread-crumbs, eggs, and saffron; so called from being brayed in a *mortar*.

386. *Mormal* = cancer. French *mort-mal*.

387. *Blank manger* = blanc-mange, white food, composed of minced chicken, eggs, flour, sugar, and milk. This dish he could make with the best of his fellow-cooks.

388. *Wonyng fer by weste* = dwelling far in the west. Cf. Ger. *wohnen*, to dwell.

389. *Dertemouth* = Dartmouth, on the south-west coast of England.

390. *Rouncy* = a common hack-horse. — *As he couthe* = as well as he could. As a seaman, he was not accustomed to riding.

391. *Gowne of faldyng* = gown or robe of coarse cloth.

392. *Laas* = belt, strap. Cf. Eng. *lace*.

397. *Burdeux* = Bordeaux, a city of south-west France. — *Chapman* = merchant or supercargo. A. S. *ceap*, trade, and *mann*, man.

401. *Craft* = calling.

403. *Herbergh* = harbor, place of shelter. Cf. Eng. *harbor*. — *Mone* = moon, as influencing the tides. — *Lodemenage* = pilotage. Cf. Eng. *lode*, *lodestar*, *lodestone*.

404. *Hulle* = Hull, a seaport on the north-east coast of England. — *Cartage* = Cartagena, a city on the south-east coast of Spain.

408. *Gootland* = Gothland, an island in the Baltic belonging to Sweden. — *Fynystere* = Finisterre, a cape on the north-west coast of Spain.

409. *Cryk* = creek, harbor.

414. *Astronomye* = astrology, the art of judging of the influence of the stars on the human body, etc. The medical science of the Middle Ages paid attention to astrological and superstitious observances.

415. *Kepte* = watched.

416. *Houres* = astrological hours. "He carefully watched for a favorable star in the ascendant."

417. *Fortunen* = to make fortunate. The practice here referred to is spoken of more fully in Chaucer's *House of Fame*, ll. 169–180: —

" Ther saugh I pleyen jugelours
      .   .   .

        And clerkes cek, which conne wel
        Alle this magike naturel,
        That craftely doon her ententes
        To maken in certeyn ascendentes
        Ymages, lo! thrugh which magike
        To make a man ben hool or syke."

420. The four humors of the body, to which all diseases were referred.

424. *Boote* = remedy.

426. *Dragges and his letuaries* = drugs and his electuaries.

429. Esculapius was the god of medicine among the Greeks.

430–434. The writers here mentioned were the leading medical authorities of the Middle Ages. *Deyscorides*, or *Dioscorides*, a physician in Cilicia of the first century. *Rufus*, a Greek physician of Ephesus of the time of Trajan. *Ypocras*, or *Hippocrates*, a Greek physician of the fourth century, called the father of medicine. *Haly*, an Arabian physician of the eleventh century. *Galen*, scarcely second in rank to Hippocrates, a Greek physician of the second century. *Serapyon*, an Arabian physician of the eleventh century. *Rhasis* was a Spanish Arab of the ninth century. *Avycen*, an Arabian physician of the eleventh century. *Averrois*, or *Averroes*, an Arabian scholar of the twelfth century. *Damascien*, or *Damascenus*, an Arabian physician of the ninth century. *Constantyn*, or *Constantius Afer*, a physician of Carthage, and one of the founders of the University of Salerno. *Bernard*, a professor of medicine at Montpellier in France, and contemporary of Chaucer. *Gatesden*, or *John of Gaddesden*, physician to Edward III., the first Englishman to hold the position of royal physician. *Gilbertyn*, supposed to be the celebrated Gilbertus Anglicus.

439. *Sangwin and in pers* = a cloth of blood-red and sky-blue (*pers*).

440. *Taffata* = thin silk. — *Sendal* = a rich, thin silk, highly esteemed for lining.

441. *Esy of dispense* = moderate in his expenditures.

442. *Wan in pestilence* = won in pestilence; a reference to the great pestilence of 1348 and 1349.

445. *Of byside Bathe* = from near Bath.

446. *Somdel* = somewhat. — *Skathe* = misfortune, loss.   A. S. *sceathan*, to harm, injure.   Cf. Eng., *scathe*, and Ger. *schaden*.

447. *Haunt* = skill, practice.

448. *Ypres* and *Ghent* (Gaunt) were the greatest cloth-markets on the continent.

450. *To the offryng.*   An allusion to Relic Sunday, when the people went to the altar to kiss the relics.

453. *Keverchefs* = kerchief, a square piece of cloth used to cover the head. French *couvre-chef*, the latter coming from Lat. *caput*.

457. *Moyste* = soft, supple.

460. Marriages were celebrated at the door of the church.

462. *As nouthe* = at present. *Nouthe* = *now + the* = *now + then*, just now, at present.

465. *Boloyne* = Bologna, where was preserved an image of the Virgin Mary.

466. In Galicia at the shrine of St. James. It was believed that the body of the apostle had been conveyed thither. — *Coloyne* = Cologne, where the bones of the three wise men or kings of the East, who came to see the infant Jesus, are said to be preserved.

467. *Cowde* = knew.

468. *Gat-tothed.* This word is variously explained. Equivalent, perhaps, to *gap-toothed*, having the teeth some distance apart.

470. *Y-wympled* = having a wimple or covering for the neck. See note on l. 151.

472. *Foot-mantel* = a riding-skirt probably.

473. *Spores* = spurs.

474. *Carpe* = to jest, chaff. It now means *to find fault with*.

476. *The olde daunce* = the old game, or customs.

478. *Persoun of a toun* = a parish priest or parson. Lat. *persona*. Blackstone says: "A *parson, persona ecclesiæ*, is one that hath full possession of all the rights of a parochial church. He is called *parson, persona*, because by his person the church, which is an invisible body, is represented." Skeat justly observes that "this reason may well be doubted, but without affecting the etymology."

482. *Parischens* = parishioners.

485. *Sithes* = times. A. S. *sith*, time. Cf. Ger., *Zeit*.

486. *Loth* = odious, hateful. It was odious to him to excommunicate those who failed to pay tithes due him.

489. *Offrynge* = voluntary contributions of his parishioners. — *Substance* = income of his benefice or the property he had acquired.

492. *Ne lafte not* = did not cease.

493. *Meschief* = misfortune.

494. *Moche and lite* = great and small.

502. *Lewed* = unlearned, ignorant.

503. *Kepe* = heed.

507. *To hyre* = He did not let out his parish to a strange curate, while he ran to London to seek a chantry at St. Paul's — a more congenial and lucrative employment. The chantries were endowments for singing masses for souls.

511. *To ben withholde* = to be maintained.

516. *Nought despitous* = not pitiless, cruel.

517. *Daungerous ne digne* = domineering nor haughty.

523. *Snybbe* = snub, reprove. — *For the nones.* See note l. 379.

525. *Waytede after* = sought or looked for.

526. *Spiced* = over-scrupulous.

530. *I-lad* = drawn out, carried. — *Fother* = load, cart-load.

531. *Swynkere* = laborer.

534. *Though him gamede or smerte* = though it pleased or pained him.

536. *Dyke and delve* = to ditch and dig.

541. *Tabard.* See note l. 20. — *Mere* = mare. People of quality would not ride upon a mare.

542. *Reeve* = steward, bailiff, officer. — *Mellere* = miller.

543. *Sompnour* = summoner, in ecclesiastical courts. — *Pardoner* = seller of pardons or indulgences.

544. *Maunciple* = an officer who purchased provisions for a college, etc. Lat. *manceps*, purchaser, contractor.

545. *Carl* = churl, hardy fellow. A.S. *ceorl*, country-man, churl.

547. That proved he well, for everywhere he came. — *Overal ther* = everywhere, wherever. Cf. Ger. *überall*, everywhere.

548. *Ram.* A ram was the usual prize at wrestling matches.

549. *Knarre* = knot. He was a thick-set, muscular fellow.

550. *Nolde = ne + wolde* = would not. — *Heve of harre* = heave, or lift, off its hinges.

551. *Rennyng* = running.

554. *Upon the cop right* = right upon the top. Cf. Eng. *coping*.

556. *Berstles* = bristles. A. S. *byrst*, a bristle, by a common transposition of the consonants. Cf. Ger. *bürste*, brush.

557. *Nose-thurles* = nostrils. A. S. *thyrel*, a hole.

560. *Janglere* = great talker, babbler. — *Golyardeys* = buffoon at rich men's tables; a teller of ribald stories.

563. *Thombe of gold* refers to the miller's skill in testing the quality of meal or flour by rubbing it between his thumb and forefinger. — *Pardé* = par Dieu, a common oath.

568. *Achatours* = purchasers, caterers. Fr. *acheter*, to buy.

570. *By taille* = by tally; i.e., on credit. Fr. *tailler*, to cut, referring to the score cut on wood.

571. *Algate* = always. — *Waytede so in his achate* = watched so in his purchase.

572. *Ay biforn* = always before or ahead of others.

574. *Pace* = pass, surpass.

581. *Propre good* = own property.

582. *But-if he were wood* = unless he were mad.

583. *As hym list desire* = as it pleases him to desire.

586. *Sette here aller cappe* = set all their caps — an expression meaning to outwit, overreach.

590. His head was *docked*, or closely cut in front like a priest.

594. *Auditour* = accountant.

597. *Neet* = cattle. Cf. *neat*, cattle.

598. *Stoor* = stock, store.

603. *Herde* = herdsman. — *Hyne* = hind, servant, farm-laborer.

604. *Covyne* = deceit.

605. *Adrad* = afraid. — *The dethe* = the pestilence or plague.

606. *Wonyng* = dwelling. Cf. Ger. *Wohnung*, dwelling.

613. *Mester* = trade. French *métier*.

615. *Stot* = stallion.

616. *Pomely gray* = dappled gray.

617. *Of pers.* See note on l. 439.

621. *Tukked* = clothed in the long dress of a friar.

622. *Hyndreste of the route* = hindmost of the company.

623. *Sompnour.* See note l. 543.

625. *Sawceflem* = having a red, pimpled face. — *Narwe* = narrow.

627. *Skalled* = having the *scall* or scab. — *Piled berd* = thin beard, or bare in patches.

629. *Litarge* = litharge.

630. *Boras* = borax. — *Ceruce* = white lead.

632. *Whelkes* = blotches, pimples.

636. *Wood.* See note l. 184.

643. *Can clepen Watte* = can call Wat, or Walter.

644. *Grope* = try, test; literally, to feel with the hands.

646. *Questio quid juris* = The question is, what is the law in the case.

652. *Pulle a fynch* was a common expression for cheating a novice.

653. *Owher* = anywhere.

656. *But-if.* See note ll. 351 and 582.

660. Each guilty man ought to be afraid of excommunication (*cursyng*).

661. *Assoillyng* = absolution. O. Fr. *assoiller*, Lat. *absolvere*.

662. *War him* = warn him. — *Significavit* = a writ of excommunication, which usually began, "Significavit nobis venerabilis frater," etc.

663. *In daunger* = in his power or jurisdiction. — *At his owne gise* = after his own fashion (*gise*).

664. *Gurles* = young people of both sexes.

665. *Al here reed* = wholly their adviser.

667. *Ale-stake* = sign-post in front of an ale-house. It was usual to attach an ivy bush to an *ale-stake*.

673. *Burdoun* = bass.

676. *Strike of flex* = hank of flax.

677. *Unces* = small, separate portions.

679. *By culpons on and oon* = by shreds or strands one by one.

681. *Trussed* = packed up.

682. *Him thought* = it seemed to him. See note l. 37. — *The newe get* = the new fashion.

683. *Sauf his cappe* = except his cap.

685. *Vernicle* = a miniature copy of the picture of Christ, which is said to have been miraculously imprinted on a handkerchief preserved in St. Peter's at Rome.

691. *Geldyng* = eunuch.

694. *Male* = bag, valise. — *Pilwebeer* = pillow-case.

695. *Oure lady veyl* = our lady's veil. See note l. 88.

696. *Gobet* = piece.

698. *Hente* = took, seized.

699. *Latoun* = a kind of brass or tinned iron.

700. *Pigges bones*, which he pretended were the bones of some saint.

702. *Poure persoun* = poor parson.

705. *Japes* = tricks, impostures.

712. *Affyle* = file, polish.

726. That you do not ascribe (*rette*) it to my ill-breeding (*vileinye*).

728. *Here cheere* = their appearance.

741. Plato, a famous Greek philosopher, born about 420 B.C.

742. *Cosyn* = kindred or in keeping with. The language should be in keeping with the thing described.

744. *Al* = although. Cf. Eng. *albeit.*

750. *Wel to drynke us leste* = it pleased us well to drink.

753. *Eygen stepe.* See note l. 201.

754. *Chepe* = Cheapside, a leading street in London, on which the wealthiest burgesses or citizens lived.

758. *Playen* = to make sport.

761. *Lordynges* = sirs, gentlemen. Dim. of *lord.*

765. *Herbergh* = inn. See note l. 403.

766. *Don yow mirthe* = cause you mirth. Cf. Eng. " *I do you to wit*" = I cause you to know.

770. *Quyte you youre meede* = grant you your reward.

772. *Schapen yow to talen* = prepare yourselves, or get ready, to tell tales (*talen*).

782. *But ye be merye* = if ye be not merry.

784. *Seche* = seek.   Cf. Ger. *suchen.*

785. *To make it wys* = to make it a matter of serious deliberation.

786. *Avys* = advice, consideration.   Cf. Fr. *avis.*

787. *Verdite* = verdict, judgment.

791. *To schorte* = to shorten.

798. *Of best sentence and most solas* = the most instructive and the most amusing.

799. *At oure alther cost* = at the cost of us all.

810. *Oure othes swore* = we swore our oaths.

816. *Devys* = decision, direction.

819. *Fet* = fetched.   A. S. *fetian*, to fetch.

822. *A morwe* = on the morrow, the 18th of April.

823. *Our alther cok* = cock or leader for us all.

825. *A litel more than paas* = a little faster than a pace or walk.

826. The watering of St. Thomas was at the second mile-stone on the old road to Canterbury.

827. *Bigan — areste* = halted.   *Bigan* is sometimes used as an auxiliary = did.

829. *Forward* = promise, covenant.   A. S. *foreword*, covenant, agreement.

831. *Lat se* = let us see.

835. *Ferrer twynne* = farther depart or travel.

838. *Acord* = decision.

840. *Lat be youre schamfastnesse* = let be your modesty.   See etymology of *shamefaced* in Webster or Skeat.

844. *Aventure, or sort, or cas* = by chance, or luck, or accident.

845. *Soth* = truth.   Cf. Eng. *in sooth.*

847. *As was resoun* = as was reasonable.

848. *Forward* = see note l. 829.   *Composicioun* = agreement.

850. *Seigh* = saw.

854. *A Goddes name* = in God's name.

857. *Right a merie chere* = a right merry countenance.

FIRST CREATIVE PERIOD.

REPRESENTATIVE WRITERS.

SPENSER, BACON, SHAKESPEARE.

OTHER PROMINENT WRITERS.

Poets. — DANIEL, DRAYTON, DONNE.

Prose Writers. — ASCHAM, LYLY, SIDNEY, HOOKER, RALEIGH.

Dramatists. — MARLOWE, GREEN, JONSON, BEAUMONT, FLETCHER.

II.

FIRST CREATIVE PERIOD.

1558-1625.

GENERAL SURVEY. — This period, which includes the reigns of Elizabeth and James I., is one of great interest. In the long course of English literature there is no other period that deserves more careful attention. It was the natural outcome of forces that had been accumulating for a hundred years. It is sometimes called the Elizabethan era, because the successful reign of that queen supplied the opportunity for a splendid manifestation of literary genius. Peace, prosperity, and general intelligence are the necessary conditions for the creation of a great national literature — a truth that finds abundant exemplification in the age of Pericles in Athens, of Augustus in Rome, and of Louis XIV. in France. While these conditions do not explain genius, which must be referred to the immediate agency of the Creator, they make it possible for genius to realize its best capabilities. The reign of Elizabeth, with its increase of intelligence and national power, furnished the occasion and the stimulus under which Spenser, Shakespeare, and Bacon produced their immortal works. At one great bound English literature reached an excellence that for variety of interest and weight of thought has scarcely been surpassed.

The century and a half lying between the death of

Chaucer and the accession of Elizabeth may be considered as a retrogressive era. The potential forces that called the father of English poetry into being seemed to subside; and not a single writer in either prose or poetry attained to the first or even the second rank. English literature, as a whole, did not reach respectable mediocrity. The only names that need to be mentioned here are Caxton, who introduced printing into England, and Sir Thomas More, a brilliant courtier under Henry VIII., whose "Utopia" — the land of Nowhere — has the rare distinction of having contributed a new word to our language. The cause of this barrenness is to be found partly in the repression of free inquiry by the church and Parliament, partly in the social disorder connected with the Wars of the Roses, and partly in the varied and important interests that engaged general attention.

The century preceding the accession of Elizabeth was an era of awakened mind and intellectual acquisition. The revival of learning was an event of vast importance, not only in the intellectual life of England, but also of all Europe. It had its central point in the capture of Constantinople by the Turks in 1453, which caused many Greek scholars to seek refuge in Italy. As ancient learning had already begun to receive attention there, these scholarly fugitives were warmly welcomed. Noble and wealthy patronage was not wanting; and soon the classic literature of Greece and Rome was studied with almost incredible enthusiasm. The Popes received the new learning under their protection; libraries were founded, manuscripts collected, and academies established.

Eager scholars from England, France, and Germany sat at the feet of Italian masters, in order afterward to bear beyond the Alps the precious seed of the new culture. Its beneficent effects soon became apparent. Greek was introduced into the great universities of England. Erasmus, the most brilliant scholar of his time, taught at Oxford. It became the fashion to study the ancient classics ; and Elizabeth, Jane Grey, and other noble ladies are said to have been conversant with Plato, Xenophon, and Cicero in the original. The taste, the eloquence, the refined literary culture, of Athens and pagan Rome were restored to the world ; and "gradually, by an insensible change, men were raised to the level of the great and healthy minds which had freely handled ideas of all kinds fifteen centuries before."[1]

The remarkable inventions and discoveries of the fifteenth century contributed, in a noteworthy degree, to awaken intellect, and lift men to a higher plane of knowledge. The printing-press was invented about the middle of the century, and in less than a decade it was brought to such perfection that the whole Bible appeared in type in 1456. It became a powerful aid in the revival of learning. It at once supplanted the tedious and costly process of copying books by hand, and brought the repositories of learning within reach of the common people. Gunpowder, which had been invented the previous century, came into common use, and wrought a salutary change in the organization of society. It destroyed the military prestige of the knightly order, brought the lower classes into greater prominence, and contributed to the abolition of serfdom. The mariner's compass greatly furthered navigation. Instead of creeping along the shores of the Mediterranean or the Atlantic, seamen boldly ventured upon

[1] Taine, English Literature, Vol. I.

unknown waters.   In 1492 Columbus discovered America ;
and six years later Vasca da Gama, rounding the Cape of
Good Hope, sailed across the Indian Ocean to Calcutta.
Voyages of discovery followed in rapid succession, new
continents were added to the map, and the general store
of knowledge was greatly increased.

The greatest event in history since the advent of
Christ is the Reformation of the sixteenth century.   It
was essentially a religious movement which sought to correct the errors in doctrine and practice that had crept into
the church and long given rise to deep dissatisfaction.   In
connection with the co-operating influences spoken of in
the preceding paragraphs, the Reformation began a new
stage in human progress, marking the close of the Middle
Ages and the dawn of the modern era.   There is scarcely
an important interest that it did not touch.   It secured
greater purity and spirituality in religion, contributed
much to the elevation of the laity and the advancement of
woman, confirmed the separation of the secular and the
ecclesiastical power, established the right of liberty of
conscience, gave an extraordinary impulse to literature and
science, and, in a word, promoted all that distinguishes
and ennobles our modern civilization.

When the reformatory movement, which began with
Martin Luther in Germany in 1517, extended to England,
it found a receptive soil.   Traditions of Wycliffe still survived ; the new learning was friendly to reform ; and men
of high civil and ecclesiastical rank had inveighed against
existing abuses.   Though Henry VIII. at first remained
faithful to the Roman Catholic Church, and even wrote
a book against the German reformer, he afterwards, for
personal and selfish reasons, withdrew his support, and

encouraged the reformatory work of his ministers and of Parliament. In 1534 the Act of Supremacy was passed, by which the king was made the supreme head of the Church of England, and empowered to "repress and amend all such errors and heresies as, by any manner of spiritual jurisdiction, might and ought to be lawfully reformed."

Without attempting to trace the general effects of the Reformation in England — a factor that enters with a moulding influence into all the subsequent history of the country — some of its immediate results upon English literature are briefly indicated. In 1526 Tyndale published his translation of the New Testament, which was followed soon afterwards by other portions of the Bible. Nearly every year, for half a century, saw a new edition issue from the press. Tyndale's translation was made with great ability, and served as the basis of subsequent versions until, in 1611, King James's version, embodying all the excellences of previous efforts, gained general acceptance.

The Scriptures in English were seized upon with great avidity by the common people. The results were far-reaching and salutary. The study of the Bible stimulated mental activity ;. its precepts ennobled character and governed conduct ; its language improved the common speech ; and its treasures of history and poetry added to the popular intelligence. It gave an impulse to general education ; and it became at once, what it has since remained, the occasion of high scholarship and of a considerable body of literature. Latimer, whose vigorous sermons advanced the cause of the Reformation in different parts of England, is a type of the unbroken line of able preachers whose influence since upon the social, moral, and intellectual life of the English people cannot be estimated. Religious services were conducted in English; and in 1549 the "Book of Common Prayer," which has been absorbed into the life of succeeding generations, was published, and its use, to the exclusion of all other forms, prescribed by law.

When Elizabeth ascended the throne in 1558, the fortunes of England were at a low ebb. The people were exasperated by Mary's misgovernment and persecution, and the bitter animosity between Protestants and Catholics was apparently beyond reconciliation. Humiliated by defeat in France, the country was threatened with invasion. There was neither army nor navy. "If God start not forth to the helm," wrote the Council in an appeal to the country, "we be at the point of greatest misery that can happen to any people, which is to become thrall to a foreign nation." By the marriage of Mary, Queen of Scots, to the dauphin of France, Scotland became a new menace. These were some of the difficulties Elizabeth encountered on assuming the sovereignty. In dealing with them she showed extraordinary courage and wisdom; and in a long reign of forty-five years, she raised England to the front rank among European nations, and awakened in the English people an aggressive and dauntless spirit.

As a woman, the character of Elizabeth is far from admirable. She was vain, coarse, haughty, vindictive, profane, mendacious. But as a queen, she in large measure justified the esteem in which she has been generally held. She was earnest, prudent, far-seeing, wise, and, above all, unselfishly devoted to the interests of her realm. She surrounded herself with able counsellors; and, as a rule, her administration was characterized by a spirit of moderation. She extinguished the fires of persecution that had been lighted under Mary; and, though exacting outward conformity to the established religion, she made no inquisition into the private opinions of her people.

England gradually became Protestant in spirit, and the head of the Protestant movement in Europe. The successive dangers arising from fanatical conspiracies were happily averted. The papal bull of excommunication, which absolved the English people from their allegiance to the queen, came to nothing; the Jesuit emissaries failed in their attempt to incite a revolt; and finally the combined efforts of the Papacy and of Spain to subdue England and re-establish Catholicism by force were frustrated by the destruction of the Armada. With these triumphs over foes at home and abroad, England acquired a new self-respect and confidence, and entered upon her career of maritime and commercial pre-eminence.

In spite of the difficulties and dangers belonging to the earlier years of Elizabeth's reign, the interests of the people were wisely cared for. When coming into conflict with Parliament, the queen gracefully surrendered her despotic tendencies. She abolished monopolies, which had abused their privileges and become oppressive. Salutary laws were passed for the employment of the mendicant classes, which the cruel policy of preceding reigns had left as a residuum of discontent and menace to the country.

The condition of the middle class was greatly improved. Better methods of tilling the soil gave a new impetus to agriculture. The growth of manufactures was rapid. Instead of sending her fleeces to Holland,

England developed every department of woollen manufacture. The mineral products of the country — iron,
coal, tin — were increased. With the wars in the Netherlands, which destroyed for a time the trade of Antwerp
and Bruges, London became the commercial centre of
Europe. At her wharves were found the gold and sugar
of the New World, the cotton of India, and the silk of the
East. English vessels made their way everywhere —
catching cod at Newfoundland, seeking new trade centres
in the Baltic, and extending commerce in the Mediterranean.

This activity in agriculture, manufacture, and commerce brought wealth and comfort. The dwellings were
improved. Carpets took the place of rushes; the introduction of chimneys brought the pleasures of the fireside;
gloomy castles, built for military strength, gave place to
elegant palaces, surrounded by Italian gardens. Grammar
schools and colleges were established; and the printing-
press, freely used for the promulgation and defence of
facts and opinions, advanced the general intelligence. A
learned woman herself, Elizabeth lent her influence and
that of her court to the cause of letters. While the
dungeon and the stake were crushing out intellectual
freedom in Italy and Spain; while France was distracted
by internal religious dissension; while foreign oppression
was destroying the trade of the Netherlands, — England,
under the prosperous reign of Elizabeth, was constantly
gaining in wealth, intelligence, and power.

These outward conditions could not fail to have an
influence upon the thought and feeling of the English nation, and to manifest themselves in the literary productions
of the time. The proud success achieved by England in

the face of great odds naturally aroused a vigorous and dauntless spirit. The Englishman of that day became aggressive, persisted in the face of obstacles, drew back before no dangers, despaired of no success. With the growing prominence of his country, his views became comprehensive and penetrating. He was forced to think with a large horizon. Called upon to deal with large interests, his intellect expanded and his character became weighty; engaged in conducting large enterprises, he developed large executive powers.

Life became intense and rich in all its relations. No interest, whether social, political, commercial, or religious, escaped attention. The energies of the English people were strung to the highest pitch, and wrought the best results of which the English mind is capable. To say nothing of minor writers, Hooker's " Ecclesiastical Polity " is a master-piece in the field of theology. Spenser's " Faery Queene," with its unexampled richness of imagination, is a fountain from which the poets of succeeding generations have drawn inspiration. And Shakespeare, with his many-sided and inexhaustible intellect, stands easily at the head of the world's great dramatists. With its great achievements, we may well call this the *first creative period* in our literature.

EDMUND SPENSER.   150

For more than one hundred and fifty years no poet worthy
to bear the mantle of Chaucer had appeared in England.   But
mighty movements had been going on in Europe — the revival
of letters, great inventions and discoveries, and the widespread
religious movement known as the Reformation.   It was an age
of great thoughts and aspirations, and of marvellous achievement.   The time had at length come, under the prosperous and
illustrious reign of Elizabeth, for English greatness to mirror
itself in literature.   A group of great writers arose.   To Edmund Spenser belongs the honor of having been the first
genius to reflect the greatness of his age and country in an
imperishable poem, and to add new lustre to a splendid period
in English history.

As with Chaucer, we have to lament the meagreness of
detail connected with the life of Spenser.   The year 1552,
which is determined by an incidental and not wholly conclu-
sive reference in one of his sonnets, is commonly accepted as
the year of his birth.   The place of his birth, not otherwise
known, is likewise determined by a passage in his " Prothala-
mion," a poem written near the close of his life : —

> " At length they all to merry London came,
>   To merry London, my most kindly nurse,
>   That to me gave this life's first native source,
>   Though from another place I take my name,
>   An house of ancient fame."

Nothing is known of his parents ; but, as he was a charity
student, it is to be inferred that they were in humble circumstances.   He received his preparatory training at the Merchant

Taylor School, and at the age of seventeen entered Pembroke Hall, Cambridge, where he earned his board by acting as sizar or waiter. He took the degree of Bachelor of Arts in 1572, and that of Master of Arts four years later. The particulars of his life at Cambridge are, for the most part, matters of mere conjecture. We may safely infer from his broad scholarship that he was a diligent student. His writings show an intimate acquaintance, not only with classical antiquity, but also with the great writers — Chaucer, Dante, Tasso, Ariosto, Marot — of the dawning modern era.

A friendship with Gabriel Harvey, a fellow of Pembroke Hall, and an enthusiastic writer and educator, was not without influence upon his poetical career. Harvey encouraged Spenser in his early literary efforts; but it is fortunate that his advice failed to turn the poet's genius to the drama. After leaving the university, Spenser spent a year or two in the north of England (it is impossible to be more definite), where he wrote his first important work, ("The Shepherd's Calendar.") It was inspired by a deep but unfortunate affection for a country lass, who appears in the poem under the anagrammatic name of Rosalinde. Her identity, a puzzle to critics, remained for a long time undetermined; but an American writer, with great ingenuity, has shown almost beyond question that the young lady was Rose Daniel, sister to the poet of that name.[1]

The poem consists of twelve eclogues, named after the months of the year. It contains a variety of measures, all of which are distinguished for their harmony. Nothing so admirable in metre and phrase had appeared since Chaucer. Many archaic words were introduced under the impression, as we are told in a prefatory epistle addressed to Harvey, "that they bring great grace, and, as one would say, authority to the verse." Though less finished than some subsequent poems, "The Shepherd's Calendar" showed a master's touch, and announced the presence of a great poet in England.

[1] See *Atlantic Monthly*, November, 1858.

Upon the advice of Harvey, Spenser went to London. He met Sir Philip Sidney, by whom he was introduced at court, and put in the way of preferment. He fell in readily with court life, wore a pointed beard and fashionable moustache, and acquired a light tone in speaking of women — a levity that soon gave place to a truly chivalrous regard. In 1580 he was appointed secretary to Lord Grey, deputy to Ireland, and accompanied that official through the bloody scenes connected with the suppression of Desmond's rebellion. The duties assigned him were ably performed ; and, in recognition of his services, he received in 1586, as a grant, Kilcolman Castle and three thousand acres of land in the county of Cork. Here he afterwards made his home, occasionally visiting London to seek preferment or to publish some new work. Though his home was not without the attraction of beautiful surroundings, he looked upon his life there as a sort of banishment. In one of his poems he speaks of —

> " My luckless lot,
> That banisht had myself, like wight forlore,
> Into that waste, where I was quite forgot."

But however disagreeable to the feelings of Spenser, who continued to feel a longing for the " sweet civilities " of London, it can hardly be doubted that his experience in Ireland was favorable to the development of his poetic gifts, and found a favorable reflection in his greatest poem. It gave a vivid realism to his descriptions that in all probability would otherwise have been wanting.

In 1589 he was visited by Sir Walter Raleigh, to whom he read the first three books of the " Faery Queene." Seated in the midst of an attractive landscape, the poet and the hero make a pleasing picture as they discuss the merits of a work that is to begin a new era in English literature. Raleigh was so delighted with the poem that he urged the author to take it to London — advice that was eagerly followed. The poet was granted an audience by Elizabeth, and favored with the patronage of several noble ladies; but further than a pension of fifty pounds, which does not appear to have been regularly paid, he received no substantial recognition.

This result was a disappointment to Spenser, who had hoped that his literary fame would lead to higher political preferment. In "Colin Clout's Come Home Again," a poem in which the incidents of this visit are embodied, he speaks of the court in a tone of disappointment and bitterness. In a prefatory letter addressed to Raleigh, who figures in the poem under the title of "Shepherd of the Ocean," Spenser says that the work agrees "with the truth in circumstance and matter;" and from this declaration it may be inferred that his portrayal of court-life was drawn, not from imagination, but from experience.

> For, sooth to say, it is no sort of life
> For shepherd fit to lead in that same place,
> Where each one seeks with malice, and with strife,
> To thrust down other in foul disgrace,
> Himself to raise: and he doth soonest rise
> That best can handle his deceitful wit
> In subtle shifts. . . . . .
> To which him needs a guileful, hollow heart
> Masked with fair dissembling courtesy,
> A filed tongue furnisht with terms of art,
> No art of school, but courtiers' schoolery.
> For arts of school have there small countenance,
> Counted but toys to busy idle brains,
> And there professors find small maintenance,
> But to be instruments of others' gains,
> Nor is there place for any gentle wit
> Unless to please it can itself apply."

In "Mother Hubbard's Tale," which exhibits Spenser's genius in satire, and is the most interesting of his minor pieces, he has spoken of the court in some vigorous lines. This poem was published in 1591; and though composed, as the author tells us, "in the raw conceit of youth," it shows the touch of his mature years. No doubt it expresses his own bitter experience : —

> "Full little knowest thou that hast not tried
> What hell it is in suing long to abide;
> To lose good days that might be better spent;
> To waste long nights in pensive discontent;
> To speed to-day, to be put back to-morrow;
> To feed on hope, to pine with fear and sorrow;
> To have thy prince's grace, yet want her peers';
> To have thy asking, yet wait many years;
> To fret thy soul with crosses and with cares;
> To eat thy heart through comfortless despairs;
> To fawn, to crouch, to wait, to ride, to run,
> To spend, to give, to want, to be undone.
> Unhappy wight, born to disastrous end,
> That doth his life in so long tendance spend!"

The first three books of the "Faery Queene" were published in 1590, and were received with an outburst of applause. Spenser took rank as the first of living poets. "The admiration of this great poem," says Hallam, "was unanimous and enthusiastic. No academy had been trained to carp at his genius with minute cavilling; no recent popularity, no traditional fame (for Chaucer was rather venerated than much in the hands of the reader) interfered with the immediate recognition of his supremacy. The 'Faery Queene' became at once the delight of every accomplished gentleman, the model of every poet, and the solace of every scholar." Spenser remained in London about a year in the enjoyment of his newly-won reputation, and in the pursuit of preferment. But in the latter he was disappointed, and returned to Ireland, as we have seen, with a feeling of resentment toward the manners and morals of the court.

In 1594 he married a lady by the name of Elizabeth — her family name remaining uncertain. In his " Amoretti, or Sonnets," he describes the beginning and progress of his affection.

These sonnets are interesting, not only for their purity and delicacy of feeling, but also for the light they throw on the poet's life. Whatever may have been the real character of the Irish maiden he celebrates, in the poems she is idealized into great beauty. It was only after a protracted suit that the poet met with encouragement and was able to say, —

> "After long storms' and tempests' sad assay,
> Which hardly I endured heretofore,
> In dread of death, and dangerous dismay,
> With which my silly bark was tossed sore;
> I do at length descry the happy shore,
> In which I hope ere long for to arrive:
> Fair soil it seems from far, and fraught with store
> Of all that dear and dainty is alive.
> Most happy he! that can at last atchyve
> The joyous safety of so sweet a rest;
> Whose least delight sufficeth to deprive
> Remembrance of all pains which him opprest.
>   All pains are nothing in respect of this;
>   All sorrows short that gain eternal bliss."

The marriage, which took place in 1594, was celebrated in an "Epithalamion," which ranks as the noblest bridal song ever written.

In 1596 Spenser wrote his "View of the State of Ireland," which shows, not the poet's hand, but that of a man of affairs. It is rigorous in policy and inexorable in spirit. He sees but one side of the subject. After an elaborate review of the history, character, and institutions of the Irish, which are pronounced full of "evil usages," he lays down his plan of pacification. Garrison Ireland with an adequate force of infantry and cavalry; give the Irish twenty days to submit; and after that time, hunt down the rebels like wild beasts. "If they be well followed one winter, ye shall have little work to do with them the next summer." Famine would complete the work of the sword; and in less than two years, Spenser thought, the country would be peaceful and open to English colonists. Submission or extermination — this was the simple solution of the Irish problem he proposed. "Bloody and cruel" he recognized it to be; but holding the utter subjugation of Ireland necessary to the preservation of English power and the Protestant religion, he would not draw back "for the sight of any such rueful object as must thereupon follow."

In 1598 Spenser was appointed sheriff of Cork: and Tyrone's rebellion breaking out soon afterward, Kilcolman Castle was sacked and burned. The poet and his wife escaped with difficulty, and it is probable that their youngest child, who was left behind, perished in the flames. In 1599 Spenser, overcome by misfortunes, died in a common London inn, and was buried in Westminster Abbey, near the tomb of his master, Chaucer. His life was full of disappointment. He never obtained the preferment to which he aspired, and he felt his failure with all the keenness of sensitive genius. And yet, under different and happier circumstances, his great natural gifts would probably not have borne such rich fruitage.

All that we know of Spenser is of good report. He had the esteem and friendship of the best people of his time; he was faithful in his attachments, and irreproachable in his outward life. In his comparative seclusion he was able to forget the hard realities of his lot, and to dwell much of the time in an ideal world; and the poetic creations, which he elaborated in the quietude of Kilcolman Castle, had the good fortune to gain immediate and hearty recognition. He has been aptly styled "the poet's poet;" and it is certain that his writings, especially the "Faery Queene," have been a perennial source of inspiration and power to his successors. Pope read him in his old age with the same zest as in his youth. Dryden looked up to him as master; and Milton called him "our sage and serious poet, whom I dare be known to think a better teacher than Scotus or Aquinas."

As already stated, the first three books of the "Faery Queene" were published in 1590. Three more books appeared in 1596 — an interval that indicates the conscientious labor

Spenser bestowed upon his productions. The plan of the work contemplated no fewer than twelve books; but in its present incomplete state it is one of the longest poems in the language. There is a tradition that three unpublished books were burned in the destruction of Kilcolman Castle, but it is probably without foundation. The "Faery Queene" is Spenser's master-piece. Keenly sympathizing with all the great interests and movements of his time, he embodied in this work his noblest thoughts and feelings. Here his genius had full play, and attained the highest results of which it was capable. In this poem the Elizabethan age is reflected in all its splendor.

The stanza of the poem was the poet's own invention, and properly bears his name. It is singularly melodious and effective, and has since been made the medium of some of the finest poetry in our language. Though somewhat difficult in its structure, Spenser handled it with masterly ease and skill, and poured forth his treasures of description, narrative, reflection, feeling, and fancy, without embarrassment.

The poem is itself an allegory, a form that the poet took some pains to justify. In a prefatory letter addressed to Raleigh, the author fully explains his plan, and makes clear what would otherwise have remained obscure. " The generall end, therefore, of all the booke," he says, " is to fashion a gentleman or noble person in vertuous and gentle discipline. Which for that I conceived shoulde be most plausible and pleasing, beeing coloured with an historicall fiction, the which the most part of men delight to read, rather for varietie of matter than for profit of the ensample : I chose the historie of King Arthure, as most fit for the excellencie of his person, beeing made famous by many men's former works, and also furthest from the danger of envie, and suspicion of present time." Prince Arthur is the central figure of the poem, in whose person, Spenser says, "I sette forth magnificence in particular, which vertue, for that (according to Aristotle and the rest) is the perfection of all the rest and containeth in it them all, therefore in the whole course I mention the deeds of Arthure appliable to that vertue, which I write of in that booke."

By *magnificence* Spenser meant *magnanimity*, which, according to Aristotle, contains all the moral virtues. Twelve other knights are made the representatives or patrons of so many separate virtues. The Knight of the Red Cross represents *holiness ;* Sir Guyon, *temperance ;* Britomartis, a lady knight, *chastity ;* and so on. But the allegory is double. In addition to the abstract moral virtues, the leading characters represent contemporary persons. The Faery Queene stands for the glory of God in general, and for Queen Elizabeth in particular ; Arthur for *magnanimity*, and also for the Earl of Leicester ; the Red Cross Knight for *holiness*, and also for the model Englishman ; Una for *truth*, and also for the Protestant Church ; Duessa for *falsehood*, and also for the Roman Church, etc. But in this second part of the allegory a close resemblance is not to be expected, as flattery often guides the poet's pen or warps his judgment. While an acquaintance with the allegory is necessary for a complete understanding of the poem, it adds perhaps but little to the interest of perusal. The poem possesses an intrinsic interest as a narrative of adventure ; and our sympathy with the actual personages moving before us causes us to lose sight of their typical character.

The " Faery Queene," it must be confessed, is defective in construction. Spenser intended to follow the maxim of Horace and the example of Homer and Virgil by plunging into the midst of his story ; but he failed in his purpose, and a prose introduction, in the shape of a letter to Raleigh, became necessary to understand the poem. " The methode of a poet historicall is not such as of an historiographer. For an historiographer discourseth of affaires orderly as they were done, accounting as well the times as the actions ; but a poet thrusteth into the middest, even where it most concerneth him, and there recoursing to the things forepast, and divining of things to come, maketh a pleasing analysis of all. The beginning, therefore, of my historie, if it were to be told by an historiographer, should be the twelfth booke, which is the last; where I devise that the Faery Queene kept her annuall feast twelve daies; upon which twelve severall dayes, the occasions of the twelve severall adventures hapned, which being undertaken by xii. severall knights, are in these twelve books severally handled and discoursed."

The first book, of which two cantos are hereafter given, is the most interesting of all. In the letter already quoted it is explained as follows : " In the beginning of the feast there presented him selfe a tall clownish younge man, who falling before the Queene of Faeries desired a boone (as the manner then was) which during that feast she might not refuse ; which was that hee might have the atchievement of any adventure, which during that feast should happen ; that being granted, he rested him selfe on the floore, unfit through his rusticitie for a better place. Soone after entred a faire ladie in mourning weedes, riding on a white asse, with a dwarfe behind her leading a warlike steed, that bore the armes of a knight, and his speare in the dwarfe's hand. She falling before the Queene of Faeries complayned that her father and mother, an ancient king and queene, had bene by an huge dragon many yeers shut up in a brazen castle, who thence suffered them not to issew : and therefore besought the Faery Queene to assigne her some one of her knights to take on him that exployt. Presently that clownish person upstarting, desired that adventure ; whereat the Queene much wondering, and the lady much gain-saying, yet he earnestly importuned his desire. In the end the lady told him, that unlesse that armour which she brought would serve him (that is the armour of a Christian man specified by Saint Paul, v. Ephes.) that he could not succeed in that enterprise, which being forth-with put upon him with due furnitures thereunto, he seemed the goodliest man in al that company, and was well liked of the lady. And eftesoones taking on him knighthood, and mounting on that strange courser, he went forth with her on that adventure : where beginneth the first booke, viz., —

' A gentle knight was pricking on the plaine,' etc."

The allegory of the "Faery Queene" is nowhere more worthy of study than in the first book. Like Bunyan's pilgrim, the Red Cross Knight shows the conflicts of the human soul in its effort to attain to holiness. This is the sublimest of all conflicts. The knight, clad in Christian armor, sets forth to make war upon the dragon, the Old Serpent. After a time the light of heaven is shut out by clouds, and the warrior loses his way in the "wandering wood," the haunt of Error.

> " For light she hated as the deadly bale,
>   Ay wont in desert darkness to remaine,
> Where plain none might her see, nor she see any plain."

Only after a long and bitter struggle, typifying the conflicts of the earnest soul in search of truth, does the knight succeed in vanquishing this dangerous foe. This danger passed, another follows. The hero, with his fair companion, at length encounters —

> " An aged sire, in long blacke weedes yclad,
>   His feet all bare, his beard all hoarie gray,
>   And by his belt his booke he hanging had;
>   Sober he seemde, and very sagely sad,
>   And to the ground his eyes were lowly bent,
>   Simple in shew, and voide of malice bad,
>   And all the way he prayed, as he went,
> And often knockt his breast, as one that did repent."

This was Archimago or Hypocrisy, who deceives the Knight with his magic art. Truth is made to seem falsehood, and falsehood truth. This deception is the cause of all his subsequent trouble — his struggle with Sans Foy or Infidelity, his companionship with Duessa or Falsehood, his sojourn and trials at the palace of Pride, and his capture and imprisonment by the giant Orgoglio or Antichrist. He is finally delivered by Arthur, and conducted by Una to the house of Holiness, where he is taught repentance. Spiritual discipline frees him from all his stains, and sends him forth once more protected with his celestial armor. He meets the grim Dragon, and after a prolonged conflict gloriously triumphs. The book naturally ends with his betrothal to Una or Truth, emblematic of eternal union. Through trials and suffering to final victory and truth — this is the history of every earnest soul ; and never before was it portrayed with such magnificent imagery and in such melodious language.

As will be readily comprehended, a striking feature of the poem is its unlikeness to actual life. In no small degree it appears artificial and unreal. The personages are somewhat shadowy. A large part of the incident and sentiment belongs to an ideal age of chivalry. All this is apt to affect the realistic or prosaic reader unpleasantly. But the poem should be approached in the spirit with which it was written. Instead of stopping to criticise the ideas, fashions, and superstitions of the Middle Ages, we should surrender ourselves into the magician's hands, and follow him submissively and sympathetically through the ideal realms into which he leads us. The poem then becomes, in the words of Lowell, " the land of pure heart's ease, where no ache or sorrow of spirit can come."

Spenser was surpassingly rich in imagination — that faculty without which no great poem is possible. He possessed an extraordinary power for appreciating and portraying beauty. His mind was extremely capacious ; and, gathering all the literary treasures of the past, whether mediæval, classic, or Christian, he gave them new and fadeless forms. His invention was almost inexhaustible. His facility in description sometimes betrayed him into tedious excess. In his fondness for details, he occasionally wrote passages that are simply nauseating. His style lacks the classic qualities of brevity, force, and self-restraint. But we shall nowhere else find a more flowing and melodious verse, an atmosphere of finer sentiment, and a larger movement or richer coloring. He may be fairly styled the Rubens of English poetry. Every canto of the " Faery Queene " presents passages in which thought, diction, and melody are combined in exquisite harmony.

THE FIRST BOOKE OF THE FAERY QUEENE,

CONTAYNING THE LEGEND OF THE KNIGHT OF THE RED CROSSE, OR OF HOLINESSE.

I.

Lo ! I, the man whose Muse whylome did maske,
As time her taught, in lowly Shepheards weeds,
Am now enforst, a farre unfitter taske,
For trumpets sterne to chaunge mine oaten reeds,
And sing of knights and ladies gentle deeds ;
Whose praises having slept in silence long,
Me, all to meane, the sacred Muse areeds
To blazon broade emongst her learned throng :
Fierce warres and faithful loves shall moralize my song.

II.

Helpe then, O holy virgin, chiefe of nyne,
Thy weaker Novice to performe thy will ;
Lay forth out of thine everlasting scryne
The antique rolles, which there lye hidden still,
Of Faery knights, and fayrest Tanaquill,
Whom that most noble Briton Prince so long
Sought through the world, and suffered so much ill,
That I must rue his undeserved wrong :
O, helpe thou my weake wit, and sharpen my dull tong !

III.

And thou, most dreaded impe of highest Jove,
Faire Venus sonne, that with thy cruell dart
At that good knight so cunningly didst rove,
That glorious fire it kindled in his hart ;
Lay now thy deadly heben bowe apart,
And with thy mother mylde come to mine ayde ;
Come, both ; and with you bring triumphant Mart,
In loves and gentle jollities arraid,
After his murdrous spoyles and bloudie rage allayd.

IV.

And with them eke, O Goddesse heavenly bright,
Mirrour of grace and majestie divine,
Great ladie of the greatest isle, whose light
Like Phœbus lampe throughout the world doth shine,
Shed thy faire beames into my feeble eyne,
And raise my thoughtes, too humble and too vile,
To thinke of that true glorious type of thine,
The argument of mine afflicted stile:
The which to heare vouchsafe, O dearest dread. a while.

CANTO I.

The patron of true Holinesse,
Foule Errour doth defeate;
Hypocrisie, him to entrappe,
Doth to his home entreate.

I.

A GENTLE Knight was pricking on the plaine,
Ycladd in mightie armes and silver shielde,
Wherein old dints of deepe woundes did remaine,
The cruell markes of many a bloody fielde;
Yet armes till that time did he never wield:
His angry steede did chide his foming bitt,
As much disdayning to the curbe to yield:
Full jolly knight he seemd, and faire did sitt,
As one for knightly giusts and fierce encounters fitt.

II.

And on his brest a bloodie crosse he bore,
The deare remembrance of his dying Lord,
For whose sweete sake that glorious badge he wore,
And dead, as living ever, him ador'd:
Upon his shield the like was also scor'd,
For soveraine hope which in his helpe he had.
Right, faithfull, true he was in deede and word;
But of his cheere did seeme too solemne sad;
Yet nothing did he dread, but ever was ydrad.

III.

Upon a great adventure he was bond,
That greatest Gloriana to him gave,
(That greatest glorious queene of Faery lond,)
To winne him worshippe, and her grace to have,
Which of all earthly things he most did crave:
And ever as he rode his hart did earne
To prove his puissance in battell brave
Upon his foe, and his new force to learne;
Upon his foe, a dragon horrible and stearne.

IV.

A lovely ladie rode him faire beside,
Upon a lowly asse more white then snow,
Yet she much whiter; but the same did hide
Under a vele, that wimpled was full low;
And over all a blacke stole shee did throw:
As one that inly mournd, so was she sad,
And heavie sate upon her palfrey slow;
Seemed in heart some hidden care she had;
And by her in a line a milkewhite lambe she lad.

V.

So pure and innocent, as that same lambe,
She was in life and every vertuous lore;
And by descent from royall lynage came,
Of ancient kinges and queenes, that had of yore
Their scepters stretcht from east to westerne shore,
And all the world in their subjection held;
Till that infernall feend with foule uprore
Forwasted all their land, and them expeld;
Whom to avenge she had this knight from far compeld.

VI.

Behind her farre away a dwarfe did lag,
That lasie seemd, in being ever last,
Or wearied with bearing of her bag
Of needments at his backe.   Thus as they past,

The day with cloudes was suddeine overcast,
And angry Jove an hideous storme of raine
Did poure into his lemans lap so fast,
That everie wight to shrowd it did constrain;
And this faire couple eke to shroud themselves were fain.

VII.

Enforst to seeke some covert nigh at hand,
A shadie grove not farr away they spide,
That promist ayde the tempest to withstand;
Whose loftie trees, yclad with sommers pride,
Did spred so broad, that heavens light did hide,
Not perceable with power of any starr:
And all within were pathes and alleies wide, *alleys*
With footing worne, and leading inward farr:
Faire harbour that them seems; so in they entred ar.

VIII.

And foorth they passe, with pleasure forward led,
Joying to heare the birds sweete harmony,
Which, therein shrouded from the tempest dred,
Seemd in their song to scorne the cruell sky.
Much can they praise the trees so straight and hy,
The sayling pine; the cedar proud and tall;
The vine-propp elme; the poplar never dry;
The builder oake, sole king of forrests all;
The aspine good for staves; the cypresse funerall;

IX.

The laurell, meed of mightie conquerours
And poets sage; the firre that weepeth still;
The willow, worne of forlorne paramours;
The eugh, obedient to the benders will;
The birch for shaftes; the sallow for the mill;
The mirrhe sweete-bleeding in the bitter wound;
The warlike beech; the ash for nothing ill;
The fruitfull olive; and the platane round;
The carver holme; the maple seeldom inward sound.

X.

Led with delight, they thus beguile the way,
Untill the blustring storme is overblowne;
When, weening to returne whence they did stray,
They cannot finde that path, which first was showne,
But wander too and fro in waies unknowne,
Furthest from end then, when they neerest weene,
That makes them doubt their wits be not their owne :
So many pathes, so many turnings seene,
That which of them to take in diverse doubt they been.

XI.

At last resolving forward still to fare,
Till that some end they finde, or in or out,
That path they take, that beaten seemd most bare,
And like to lead the labyrinth about;
Which when by tract they hunted had throughout,
At length it brought them to a hollowe cave
Amid the thickest woods.   The champion stout
Eftsoones dismounted from his courser brave,
And to the dwarfe a while his needless spere he gave.

XII.

" Be well aware," quoth then that ladie milde,
" Least suddaine mischiefe ye too rash provoke :
The danger hid, the place unknowne and wilde,
Breedes dreadfull doubts : oft fire is without smoke,
And perill without show : therefore your stroke,
Sir knight, with-hold, till further tryall made."
" Ah ladie," sayd he, " shame were to revoke
The forward footing for an hidden shade :
Vertue gives her selfe light through darknesse for to wade."

XIII.

" Yea but," quoth she, " the perill of this place
I better wot than you : though nowe too late
To wish you backe returne with foule disgrace,
Yet wisedome warnes, whilest foot is in the gate,

To stay the steppe, ere forced to retrate.
This is the wandring wood, this *Errours den*,
A monster vile, whom God and man does hate,
Therefore I read beware." " Fly, fly," quoth then
The feareful dwarfe, " This is no place for living men."

XIV.

But, full of fire and greedy hardiment,
The youthfull knight could not for ought be staide ;
But forth unto the darksom hole he went,
And looked in : his glistring armor made
A little glooming light, much like a shade
By which he saw the ugly monster plaine,
Halfe like a serpent horribly displaide,
But th'other halfe did womans shape retaine,
Most lothsom, filthie, foule, and full of vile disdaine.

XV.

And, as she lay upon the durtie ground,
Her huge long taile her den all overspred,
Yet was in knots and many boughtes upwound,
Pointed with mortall sting.   Of her there bred
A thousand yong ones, which she dayly fed,
Sucking upon her poisnous dugs ; each one
Of sundrie shapes, yet all ill-favored :
Soone as that uncouth light upon them shone,
Into her mouth they crept, and suddain all were gone.

XVI.

Their dam upstart out of her den effraide,
And rushed forth, hurling her hideous taile
About her cursed head ; whose folds displaid
Were stretcht now forth at length without entraile.
She lookt about, and seeing one in mayle,
Armed to point, sought backe to turne againe ;
For light she hated as the deadly bale,
Ay wont in desert darknes to remaine,
Where plain none might her see, nor she see any plaine.

XVII.

Which when the valiant elfe perceiv'd, he lept
As lyon fierce upon the flying pray,
And with his trenchand blade her boldly kept
From turning backe, and forced her to stay:
Therewith enrag'd she loudly gan to bray,
And turning fierce her speckled taile advaunst,
Threatning her angrie sting, him to dismay;
Who, nought aghast, his mightie hand enhaunst:
The stroke down from her head unto her shoulder glaunst.

XVIII.

Much daunted with that dint her sence was dazd;
Yet kindling rage her selfe she gathered round,
And all attonce her beastly bodie raizd
With double forces high above the ground:
Tho, wrapping up her wrethed sterne arownd,
Lept fierce upon his shield, and her huge traine
All suddenly about his body wound,
That hand or foot to stirr he strove in vaine.
God helpe the man so wrapt in Errours endlesse traine!

XIX.

His lady, sad to see his sore constraint,
Cride out, "Now, now, Sir knight, shew what ye bee;
Add faith unto your force, and be not faint;
Strangle her, or els she sure will strangle thee."
That when he heard, in great perplexitie,
His gall did grate for griefe and high disdaine;
And, knitting all his force, got one hand free,
Wherewith he grypt her gorge with so great paine,
That soone to loose her wicked bands did her constraine.

XX.

Therewith she spewd out of her filthie maw
A floud of poyson horrible and blacke,
Full of great lumps of flesh and gobbets raw,
Which stunck so vildly, that it forst him slacke

His grasping hold, and frome her turne him backe :
Her vomit full of bookes and papers was,
With loathly frogs and toades, which eyes did lacke,
And creeping sought way in the weedy gras :
Her filthie parbreake all the place defiled has.

XXI.

As when old Father Nilus gins to swell
With timely pride above the Ægyptian vale,
His fattie waves doe fertile slime outwell, .
And overflow each plaine and lowly dale :
But, when his later spring gins to avale,
Huge heapes of mudd he leaves, wherein there breed
Ten thousand kindes of creatures, partly male
And partly femall, of his fruitful seed ;
Such ugly monstrous shapes elswher may no man reed.

XXII.

The same so sore annoyed has the knight,
That, welnigh choked with the deadly stinke,
His forces faile, ne can no lenger fight :
Whose corage when the feend perceivd to shrinke,
She poured forth out of her hellish sinke
Her fruitfull cursed spawne of serpents small,
(Deformed monsters, fowle, and blacke as inke,)
Which swarming all about his legs did crall,
And him encombred sore, but could not hurt at all.

XXIII.

As gentle shepheard in sweete eventide,
When ruddy Phœbus gins to welke in west,
High on an hill, his flocke to vewen wide,
Markes which doe byte their hasty supper best ;
A cloud of cumbrous gnattes doth him molest,
All striving to infixe their feeble stinges,
That from their noyance he no where can rest ;
But with his clownish hands their tender wings
He brusheth oft, and oft doth mar their murmurings.

XXIV.

Thus ill bestedd, and fearefull more of shame
Then of the certeine perill he stood in,
Halfe furious unto his foe he came,
Resolvd in minde all suddenly to win,
Or soone to lose, before he once would lin;
And stroke at her with more then manly force,
That from her body, ful of filthie sin,
He raft her hatefull heade without remorse :
A streame of cole-black blood forth gushed from her corse.

XXV.

Her scattered brood, soone as their parent deare
They saw so rudely falling to the ground,
Groning full deadly all with troublous feare
Gathred themselves about her body round,
Weening their wonted entrance to have found
At her wide mouth ; but, being there withstood,
They flocked all about her bleeding wound,
And sucked up ther dying mothers bloud ;
Making her death their life, and eke her hurt their good.

XXVI.

That detestable sight him much amazde,
To see th' unkindly impes, of heaven accurst,
Devoure their dam ; on whom while so he gazd,
Having all satisfide their bloudy thurst,
Their bellies swolne he saw with fulnesse burst
And bowels gushing forth : well worthy end
Of such, as drunke her life, the which them nurst
Now needeth him no lenger labour spend,
His foes have slaine themselves, with whom he should contend.

XXVII.

His lady seeing all that chaunst from farre,
Approcht in hast to greet his victorie ;
And saide, " Faire knight, borne under happie starre,
Who see your vanquisht foes before you lye,
Well worthie be you of that armory,

Wherein ye have great glory wonne this day,
And prov'd your strength on a strong enimie,
Your first adventure: many such I pray,
And henceforth ever wish that like succeed it may!"

XXVIII.

Then mounted he upon his steede againe,
And with the lady backward sought to wend:
That path he kept, which beaten was most plaine,
Ne ever would to any byway bend;
But still did follow one unto the end,
The which at last out of the wood them brought.
So forward on his way (with God to frend)
He passed forth, and new adventure sought:
Long way he traveiled, before he heard of ought.

XXIX.

At length they chaunst to meet upon the way
An aged sire, in long blacke weedes yclad,
His feete all bare, his beard all hoarie gray,
And by his belt his booke he hanging had;
Sober he seemde, and very sagely sad;
And to the ground his eyes were lowly bent,
Simple in shew, and voide of malice bad;
And all the way he prayed as he went,
And often knockt his brest, as one that did repent.

XXX.

He faire the knight saluted, louting low,
Who faire him quited, as that courteous was;
And after asked him, if he did know
Of straunge adventures, which abroad did pas.
"Ah! my dear sonne," quoth he, "how should, alas!
Silly old man, that lives in hidden cell,
Bidding his beades all day for his trespas,
Tydings of warre and worldly trouble tell?
With holy father sits not with such thinges to mell.

XXXI.

"But if of daunger, which hereby doth dwell,
And homebredd evil ye desire to heare,

Of a straunge man I can you tidings tell,
That wasteth all this countrie, farre and neare."
" Of suche," saide he, " I chiefly doe inquere ;
And shall thee well rewarde to shew the place,
In which that wicked wight his dayes doth weare :
For to all knighthood it is foule disgrace,
That such a cursed creature lives so long a space."

XXXII.

" Far hence," quoth he, " in wastfull wildernesse
His dwelling is, by which no living wight
May ever passe, but thorough great distresse."
" Now," saide the ladie, " draweth tow'rd night ;
And well I wote, that of your later fight
Ye all forwearied be ; for what so strong,
But, wanting rest, will also want of might ?
The sunne, that measures heaven all day long,
At night doth baite his steedes the ocean waves emong.

XXXIII.

" Then with the sunne take, Sir, your timely rest,
And with new day new worke at once begin :
Untroubled night, they say, gives counsell best."
" Right well, Sir knight, ye have advised bin,"
Quoth then that aged man : " the way to win
Is wisely to advise ; now day is spent ;
Therefore with me ye may take up your in
For this same night." The knight was well content ;
So with that godly father to his home they went.

XXXIV.

A litle lowly hermitage it was,
Downe in a dale, hard by a forest's side,
Far from resort of people that did pas
In traveill to and froe : a little wyde
There was an holy chappell edifyde,
Wherein the hermite dewly wont to say
His holy thinges each morne and eventyde :
Thereby a christall streame did gently play,
Which from a sacred fountaine welled forth alway.

XXXV.

Arrived there, the litle house they fill,
Ne looke for entertainement, where none was ;
Rest is their feast, and all thinges at their will :
The noblest mind the best contentment has.
With faire discourse the evening so they pas ;
For that olde man of pleasing wordes had store,
And well could file his tongue as smooth as glas :
He told of saintes and popes, and evermore
He strowd an *Ave-Mary* after and before.

XXXVI.

The drouping night thus creepeth on them fast ;
And the sad humor loading their eyeliddes,
As messenger of Morpheus, on them cast
Sweet slombring deaw, the which to sleep them biddes ;
Unto their lodgings then his guestes he riddes :
Where when all drownd in deadly sleepe he findes,
He to his studie goes ; and there amiddes
His magick bookes, and artes of sundrie kindes,
He seekes out mighty charmes to trouble sleepy minds.

XXXVII.

Then choosing out few words most horrible,
(Let none them read) thereof did verses frame ;
With which, and other spelles like terrible,
He bad awake blacke Plutoes griesly Dame ;
And cursed heven ; and spake reprochful shame
Of highest God, the Lord of life and light.
A bold bad man, that dar'd to call by name
Great Gorgon, prince of darkness and dead night ;
At which Cocytus quakes, and Styx is put to flight.

XXXVIII.

And forth he cald out of deepe darknes dredd
Legions of Sprights, the which, like litle flyes
Fluttring about his ever-damned hedd,
Awaite whereto their service he applyes,
To aide his friendes, or fray his enimies :

Of those he chose out two, the falsest twoo,
And fittest for to forge true-seeming lyes ;
The one of them he gave a message to,
The other by him selfe staide other worke to doo.

XXXIX.

He, making speedy way through spersed ayre,
And through the world of waters wide and deepe,
To Morpheus house doth hastily repaire.
Amid the bowels of the earth full steepe,
And low, where dawning day doth never peepe,
His dwelling is ; there Tethys his wet bed
Doth ever wash, and Cynthia still doth steepe
In silver deaw his ever-drouping hed,
Whiles sad Night over him her mantle black doth spred.

XL.

Whose double gates he findeth locked fast ;
The one faire fram'd of burnisht yvory,
The other all with silver overcast ;
And wakeful dogges before them farre doe lye,
Watching to banish Care their enimy,
Who oft is wont to trouble gentle Sleepe.
By them the sprite doth passe in quietly,
And unto Morpheus comes, whom drowned deepe
In drowsie fit he findes ; of nothing he takes keepe.

XLI.

And, more to lulle him in his slumber soft,
A trickling streame from high rock tumbling downe,
And ever-drizling raine upon the loft,
Mixt with a murmuring winde, much like the sowne
Of swarming bees, did cast him in a swowne.
No other noyse, nor peoples troublous cryes,
As still are wont t' annoy the walled towne,
Might there be heard ; but carelesse Quiet lyes
Wrapt in eternall silence farre from enimyes.

XLII.

The messenger approching to him spake ;
But his waste wordes retournd to him in vaine :

So sound he slept, that nought mought him awake.
Then rudely he him thrust, and pusht with paine,
Whereat he gan to stretch : but he againe
Shooke him so hard, that forced him to speake.
As one then in a dreame, whose dryer braine
Is tost with troubled sights and fancies weake,
He mumbled soft, but would not all his silence breake.

XLIII.

The sprite then gan more boldly him to wake,
And threatned unto him the dreaded name
Of Hecaté : whereat he gan to quake,
And, lifting up his lompish head, with blame
Halfe angrie asked him, for what he came.
" Hether," quoth he, " me Archimago sent,
He that the stubborne sprites can wisely tame,
He bids thee to him send for his intent
A fit false dreame, that can delude the sleepers sent."

XLIV.

The god obayde ; and, calling forth straight way
A diverse dreame out of his prison darke,
Delivered it to him, and downe did lay
His heavie head, devoide of careful carke ;
Whose sences all were straight benumbd and starke.
He, backe returning by the yvorie dore,
Remounted up as light as chearefull larke ;
And on his litle winges the dreame he bore
In hast unto his lord, where he him left afore.

XLV.

Who all this while, with charmes and hidden artes,
Had made a lady of that other spright,
And fram'd of liquid ayre her tender partes,
So lively, and so like in all mens sight,
That weaker sence it could have ravisht quight :
The maker selfe, for all his wondrous witt,
Was nigh beguiled with so goodly sight.
Her all in white he clad, and over it
Cast a black stole, most like to seeme for Una fit.

XLVI.

Now, when that ydle dreame was to him brought,
Unto that elfin knight he bad him fly,
Where he slept soundly void of evil thought,
And with false shewes abuse his fantasy,
In sort as he him schooled privily.
And that new creature, borne without her dew,
Full of the makers guyle, with usage sly
He taught to imitate that lady trew,
Whose semblance she did carrie under feigned hew.

XLVII.

Thus, well instructed, to their worke they haste;
And, comming where the knight in slomber lay,
The one upon his hardie head him plaste,
And made him dreame of loves and lustfull play,
That nigh his manly hart did melt away.

.   .   .   .

XLIX.

In this great passion of unwonted lust,
Or wonted feare of doing ought amis,
He starteth up, as seeming to mistrust
Some secret ill, or hidden foe of his.
Lo! there before his face his ladie is,
Under blacke stole hyding her bayted hooke;
And as halfe blushing offred him to kis,
With gentle blandishment and lovely looke,
Most like that virgin true, which for her knight him took.

L.

All cleane dismayd to see so uncouth sight,
And half enraged at her shamelesse guise,
He thought have slaine her in his fierce despight;
But, hastie heat tempring with sufferance wise,
He stayde his hand; and gan himselfe advise
To prove his sense, and tempt her faigned truth.
Wringing her hands, in wemens pitteous wise,
Tho can she weepe, to stirre up gentle ruth
Both for her noble blood, and for her tender youth.

LI.

And sayd, " Ah Sir, my liege lord, and my love,
Shall I accuse the hidden cruell fate,
And mightie causes wrought in heaven above,
Or the blind god, that doth me thus amate,
For hoped love to winne me certaine hate?
Yet thus perforce he bids me do, or die.
Die is my dew ; yet rew my wretched state,
You, whom my hard avenging destinie
Hath made judge of my life or death indifferently.

LII.

" Your owne deare sake forst me at first to leave
My fathers kingdom " — There she stopt with teares ;
Her swollen hart her speech seemd to bereave ;
And then againe begun : " My weaker yeares,
Captiv'd to fortune and frayle worldly feares,
Fly to your fayth for succour and sure ayde :
Let me not die in languor and long teares."
" Why, dame," quoth he, " what hath ye thus dismayd?
What frayes ye, that were wont to comfort me affrayd ? "

LIII.

" Love of your selfe," she saide, " and deare constraint,
Lets me not sleepe, but waste the wearie night
In secret anguish and unpittied plaint,
Whiles you in carelesse sleepe are drowned quight."
Her doubtfull words made that redoubted knight
Suspect her truth ; yet since no untruth he knew,
Her fawning love with foule disdainefull spight
He would not shend ; but said, " Deare dame, I rew,
That for my sake unknowne such griefe unto you grew :

LIV.

" Assure your selfe, it fell not all to ground ;
For all so deare as life is to my hart,
I deeme your love, and hold me to you bound :
Ne let vaine feares procure your needlesse smart,
Where cause is none ; but to your rest depart."

Not all content, yet seemd she to appease
Her mournefull plaintes, beguiled of her art,
And fed with words that could not chose but please ;
So, slyding softly forth she turnd as to her ease.

LV.

Long after lay he musing at her mood,
Much griev'd to thinke that gentle dame so light,
For whose defence he was to shed his blood.
At last, dull wearines of former fight
Having yrockt asleepe his irkesome spright,
That troublous dreame gan freshly tosse his braine
With bowres, and beds, and ladies deare delight :
But, when he saw his labour all was vaine,
With that misformed spright he backe returnd againe.

CANTO II.

The guilefull great Enchaunter parts
The Redcrosse Knight from Truth :
Into whose stead faire Falshood steps,
And workes him woefull ruth.

I.

By this the northerne wagoner had set
His sevenfold teme behind the stedfast starre
That was in ocean waves yet never wet,
But firme is fixt, and sendeth light from farre
To al that in the wide deepe wandring arre ;
And chearefull chaunticlere with his note shrill
Had warned once, that Phœbus fiery carre
In hast was climbing up the easterne hill,
Full envious that night so long his roome did fill :

II.

When those accursed messengers of hell,
That feigning dreame, and that faire-forged spright,
Came to their wicked maister, and gan tel
Their bootelesse paines, and ill succeeding night :

Who, all in rage to see his skilfull might
Deluded so, gan threaten hellish paine,
And sad Prosérpines wrath, them to affright.
But, when he saw his threatning was but vaine,
He cast about, and searcht his baleful bokes againe.

VI.

Retourning to his bed in torment great,
And bitter anguish of his guilty sight,
He could not rest; but did his stout heart eat,
And wast his inward gall with deepe despight,
Yrkesome of life, and too long lingring night.
At last faire Hesperus in highest skie
Had spent his lampe, and brought forth dawning light;
Then up he rose, and clad him hastily:
The dwarfe him brought his steed; so both away do fly.

VII.

Now when the rosy-fingred Morning faire,
Weary of aged Tithones saffron bed,
Had spred her purple robe through deawy aire,
And the high hils Titan discovered,
The royall virgin shooke off drousyhed;
And, rising forth out of her baser bowre,
Lookt for her knight, who far away was fled,
And for her dwarfe, that wont to wait each howre:
Then gan she wail and weepe to see that woeful stowre.

VIII.

And after him she rode, with so much speede
As her slowe beast could make; but all in vaine;
For him so far had borne his light-foot steede,
Pricked with wrath and fiery fierce disdaine,
That him to follow was but fruitlesse paine:
Yet she her weary limbes would never rest;
But every hil and dale, each wood and plaine,
Did search, sore grieved in her gentle brest,
He so ungently left her, whome she loved best.

IX.

But subtill Archimago, when his guests
He saw divided into double parts,
And Una wandring in woods and forrésts,
(Th' end of his drift,) he praisd his divelish arts,
That had such might over true meaning harts:
Yet rests not so, but other meanes doth make,
How he may worke unto her further smarts;
For her he hated as the hissing snake,
And in her many troubles did most pleasure take.

X.

He then devisde himselfe how to disguise;
For by his mighty science he could take
As many formes and shapes in seeming wise,
As ever Proteus to himselfe could make:
Sometime a fowle, sometime a fish in lake,
Now like a foxe, now like a dragon fell;
That of himselfe he ofte for feare would quake,
And oft would flie away. O who can tell
The hidden powre of herbes, and might of magick spel!

XI.

But now seemde best the person to put on
Of that good knight, his late beguiled guest:
In mighty armes he was yclad anon,
And silver shield; upon his coward brest
A bloody crosse, and on his craven crest
A bounch of heares discolourd diversly.
Full jolly knight he seemde, and wel addrest;
And, when he sate upon his courser free,
Saint George himselfe ye would have deemed him to be.

XII.

But he, the knight, whose semblaunt he did beare,
The true Saint George, was wandered far away,
Still flying from his thoughts and gealous feare:
Will was his guide, and griefe led him astray.

At last him chaunst to meete upon the way
A faithlesse Sarazin, all armde to point,
In whose great shield was writ with letters gay
Sans foy ; full large of limbe and every joint
He was, and cared not for God or man a point.

XIII.

Hee had a faire companion of his way,
A goodly lady clad in scarlot red,
Purfled with gold and pearle of rich assay ;
And like a Persian mitre on her hed
Shee wore, with crowns and owches garnished,
The which her lavish lovers to her gave :
Her wanton palfrey all was overspred
With tinsell trappings, woven like a wave,
Whose bridle rung with golden bels and bosses brave.

XIV.

With faire disport, and courting dalliaunce,
She intertainde her lover all the way :
But, when she saw the knight his speare advaunce,
She soone left off her mirth and wanton play,
And bad her knight addresse him to the fray,
His foe was nigh at hand.   He, prickte with pride,
And hope to winne his ladies hearte that day,
Forth spurred fast ; adowne his coursers side
The red bloud trickling staind the way, as he did ride.

XV.

The Knight of the Redcrosse, when him he spide
Spurring so hote with rage dispiteous,
Gan fairely couch his speare, and towards ride :
Soone meete they both, both fell and furious,
That, daunted with theyr forces hideous,
Their steeds doe stagger, and amazed stand ;
And eke themselves, too rudely rigorous,
Astonied with the stroke of their owne hand,
Doe backe rebutte, and ech to other yealdeth land.

XVI.

As when two rams, stird with ambitious pride,
　Fight for the rule of the rich fleeced flocke,
　Their horned fronts so fierce on either side
　Doe meete, that, with the terror of the shocke,
　Astonied, both stand sencelesse as a blocke,
　Forgetfull of the hanging victory :
　So stood these twaine, unmoved as a rocke,
　　Both staring fierce, and holding idely
The broken reliques of their former cruelty.

XVII.

The Sarazin, sore daunted with the buffe,
　Snatcheth his sword, and fiercely to him flies ;
　Who well it wards, and quyteth cuff with cuff :
　Each others equall puissaunce envies,
　And through their iron sides with cruell spies
　Does seeke to perce ; repining courage yields
　No foote to foe : the flashing fier flies,
　　As from a forge, out of their burning shields ;
And streams of purple bloud new die the verdant fields.

XVIII.

" Curse on that Cross," quoth then the Sarazin,
" That keepes thy body from the bitter fitt ;
　Dead long ygoe, I wote, thou haddest bin,
　Had not that charme from thee forwarned itt :
　But yet I warne thee now assured sitt,
　And hide thy head." Therewith upon his crest
　With rigor so outrageous he smitt,
　　That a large share it hewd out of the rest,
And glauncing downe his shield from blame him fairly blest.

XIX.

Who, thereat wondrous wroth, the sleeping spark
　Of native virtue gan eftsoones revive ;
　And at his haughty helmet making mark,
　So hugely stroke, that it the steele did rive,
　And cleft his head : he, tumbling downe alive,

With bloudy mouth his mother earth did kis,
Greeting his grave : his grudging ghost did strive
With the fraile flesh ; at last it flitted is,
Whither the soules do fly of men that live amis.

XX.

　The lady, when she saw her champion fall,
Like the old ruines of a broken towre,
Staid not to waile his woefull funerall ;
But from him fled away with all her powre :
Who after her as hastily gan scowre,
Bidding the dwarfe with him to bring away
The Sarazins shield, signe of the conqueroure :
Her soone he overtooke, and bade to stay ;
For present cause was none of dread her to dismay.

XXI.

　Shee turning backe, with ruefull countenance
Cride, " Mercy, mercy, Sir, vouchsafe to show
On silly dame, subject to hard mischaunce,
And to your mighty wil ! "　Her humblesse low
In so ritch weedes, and seeming glorious show,
Did much emmove his stout heroicke heart ;
And said, " Deare dame, your suddein overthrow
Much rueth me ; but now put feare apart,
And tel, both who ye be, and who that tooke your part."

XXII.

　Melting in teares, then gan shee thus lament ;
" The wretched woman, whom unhappy howre
Hath now made thrall to your commandement,
Before that angry heavens list to lowre,
And fortune false betraide me to thy powre,
Was (O what now availeth that I was !)
Borne the sole daughter of an Emperour ;
He that the wide West under his rule has,
And high hath set his throne where Tiberis doth pas.

XXIII.

"He, in the first flowre of my freshest age,
Betrothed me unto the onely haire
Of a most mighty king, most rich and sage;
Was never prince so faithfull and so faire,
Was never prince so meeke and debonaire;
But, ere my hoped day of spousall shone,
My dearest lord fell from high honors staire
Into the hands of hys accursed fone,
And cruelly was slaine; that shall I ever mone.

XXIV.

"His blessed body, spoild of lively breath,
Was afterward, I know not how, convaid,
And fro me hid: of whose most innocent death
When tidings came to mee, unhappy maid,
O, how great sorrow my sad soule assaid!
Then forth I went his woefull corse to find,
And many yeares throughout the world I straid,
A virgin widow; whose deepe wounded mind
With love long time did languish, as the striken hind.

XXV.

"At last it chaunced this proud Sarazin
To meete me wandring; who perforce me led
With him away; but yet could never win;
There lies he now with foule dishonor dead,
Who, whiles he livde, was called proud Sans foy,
The eldest of three brethren; all three bred
Of one bad sire, whose youngest is Sans joy;
And twixt them both was born the bloudy bold Sans loy.

XXVI.

"In this sad plight, friendlesse, unfortunate,
Now miserable I Fidessa, dwell,
Craving of you, in pitty of my state,
To doe none ill, if please ye not doe well."

He in great passion al this while did dwell,
More busying his quicke eies her face to view,
Then his dull eares to heare what shee did tell;
And said, " Faire lady, hart of flint would rew
The undeserved woes and sorrowes, which ye shew,

XXVII.

" Henceforth in safe assuraunce may ye rest,
Having both found a new friend you to aid,
And lost an old foe that did you molest;
Better new friend then an old foe is said."
With chaunge of chear the seeming simple maid
Let fall her eien, as shamefast, to the earth,
And yeelding soft, in that she nought gainsaid,
So forth they rode, he feining seemely merth,
And shee coy lookes : so dainty, they say, maketh derth.

XXVIII.

Long time they thus together traveiled ;
Til, weary of their way, they came at last
Where grew two goodly trees, that faire did spred
Their armes abroad, with gray mosse overcast ;
And their greene leaves, trembling with every blast,
Made a calme shadowe far in compasse round :
The fearefull shepheard, often there aghast,
Under them never sat, ne wont there sound
His mery oaten pipe ; but shund th' unlucky ground.

XXIX.

But this good knight, soone as he them can spie,
For the coole shade him thither hastly got :
For golden Phœbus, now ymounted hie,
From fiery wheeles of his faire chariot
Hurled his beame so scorching cruell hot,
That living creature mote it not abide ;
And his new lady it endured not.
There they alight, in hope themselves to hide
From the fierce heat, and rest their weary limbs a tide.

XXX.

Faire seemely pleasaunce each to other makes,
With goodly purposes, there as they sit;
And in his falsed fancy he her takes
To be the fairest wight that lived yit;
Which to expresse, he bends his gentle wit;
And, thinking of those braunches greene to frame
A girlond for her dainty forehead fit
He pluckt a bough; out of whose rifte there came
Smal drops of gory bloud, that trickled down the same.

XXXI.

Therewith a piteous yelling voice was heard,
Crying, " O spare with guilty hands to teare
My tender sides in this rough rynd embard;
But fly, ah! fly far hence away, for feare
Least to you hap that happened to me heare,
And to this wretched lady, my deare love;
O too deare love, love bought with death too deare!"
Astond he stood, and up his heare did hove;
And with that suddein horror could no member move.

XXXII.

At last whenas the dreadfull passion
Was overpast, and manhood well awake;
Yet musing at the straunge occasion,
And doubting much his sence, he thus bespake:
" What voice of damned ghost from Limbo lake,
Or guilefull spright wandring in empty aire,
Both which fraile men doe oftentimes mistake,
Sends to my doubtful eares these speaches rare,
And ruefull plaints, me bidding guiltlesse blood to spare?"

XXXIII.

Then, groning deep; " Nor damned ghost," quoth he,
" Nor guileful sprite to thee these words doth speake;
But once a man Fradubio, now a tree;
Wretched man, wretched tree! whose nature weake

A cruell witch, her cursed will to wreake,
Hath thus transformed, and plast in open plaines,
Where Boreas doth blow full bitter bleake,
And scorching sunne does dry my secret vaines ;
For though a tree I seme, yet cold and heat me paines."

XXXIV.

" Say on, Fradubio, then, or man or tree,"
Quoth then the knight ; " by whose mischievous arts
Art thou misshaped thus, as now I see ?
He oft finds med'cine who his griefe imparts ;
But double griefs afflict concealing harts ;
As raging flames who striveth to suppresse."
" The author then," said he, " of all my smarts,
Is one Duessa, a false sorceresse,
That many errant knights hath broght to wretchednesse.

XXXV.

" In prime of youthly yeares, when corage hott
The fire of love, and joy of chevalree
First kindled in my brest, it was my lott
To love this gentle lady, whome ye see
Now not a lady, but a seeming tree ;
With whome, as once I rode accompanyde,
Me chaunced of a knight encountred bee,
That had a like faire lady by his syde ;
Lyke a faire lady, but did fowle Duessa hyde.

XXXVI.

" Whose forged beauty he did take in hand
All other dames to have exceeded farre ;
I in defence of mine did likewise stand,
Mine, that did then shine as the morning starre.
So both to batteill fierce arraunged arre ;
In which his harder fortune was to fall
Under my speare ; such is the dye of warre.
His lady, left as a prise martiall,
Did yield her comely person to be at my call.

XXXVII.

" So doubly lov'd of ladies, unlike faire,
Th' one seeming such, the other such indeede,
One day in doubt I cast for to compare
Whether in beauties glorie did exceede ;
A rosy girlend was the victors meede,
Both seemde to win, and both seemde won to bee ;
So hard the discord was to be agreede.
Frælissa was as faire as faire mote bee,
And ever false Duessa seemde as faire as shee.

XXXVIII.

" The wicked witch, now seeing all this while
The doubtfull ballaunce equally to sway,
What not by right, she cast to win by guile ;
And, by her hellish science raisd streight way
A foggy mist that overcast the day,
And a dull blast that breathing on her face
Dimmed her former beauties shining ray,
And with foule ugly forme did her disgrace :
Then was she fayre alone, when none was faire in place.

XXXIX.

" Then cride she out, ' Fye, fye, deformed wight,
Whose borrowed beautie now appeareth plaine
To have before bewitched all mens sight :
O ! leave her soone, or let her soone be slaine.'
Her loathly visage viewing with disdaine,
Eftsoones I thought her such as she me told,
And would have kild her ; but with faigned paine
The false witch did my wrathfull hand withhold :
So left her, where she now is turned to treën mould.

XL.

" Thensforth I tooke Duessa for my dame,
And in the witch unweeting joyd long time ;
Ne ever wist but that she was the same ;
Till on a day (that day is everie prime,

When witches wont do penance for their crime,)
I chaunst to see her in her proper hew,
Bathing her selfe in origane and thyme :
A filthy foule old woman I did vew,
That ever to have toucht her I did deadly rew.

XLI.

" Her neather partes misshapen, monstruous,
Were hidd in water ; that I could not see ;
But they did seeme more foule and hideous,
Then womans shape man would beleeve to bee.
Thensforth from her most beastly companie
I gan refraine, in minde to slipp away,
Soone as appeard safe opportunitie :
For danger great, if not assurd decay,
I saw before mine eyes, if I were knowne to stray.

XLII.

" The divelish hag by chaunges of my cheare
Perceiv'd my thought ; and, drownd in sleepie night,
With wicked herbes and oyntments did besmeare
My body all, through charmes and magicke might,
That all my senses were bereaved quight :
Then brought she me into this desert waste,
And by my wretched lovers side me pight ;
Where now enclosd in wooden wal full faste,
Banisht from living wights, our wearie daies we waste."

XLIII.

" But how long time," said then the Elfin knight,
" Are you in this misformed hous to dwell ? "
" We may not chaunge," quoth he, " this evill plight,
Till we be bathed in a living well :
That is the terme prescribed by the spell."
" O how," sayd he, " mote I that well out find,
That may restore you to your wonted well ? "
" Time and suffised fates to former kynd
Shall us restore ; none else from hence may us unbynd."

XLIV.

The false Duessa, now Fidessa hight,
Heard how in vaine Fradubio did lament,
And knew well all was true.   But the good knight,
Full of sad feare and ghastly dreriment,
When all this speech the living tree had spent,
The bleeding bough did thrust into the ground,
That from the blood he might be innocent,
And with fresh clay did close the wooden wound:
Then, turning to his lady, dead with feare her fownd.

XLV.

Her seeming dead he found with feigned feare,
As all unweeting of that well she knew;
And paynd himselfe with busie care to reare
Her out of carelesse swowne.   Her eyelids blew,
And dimmed sight with pale and deadly hew,
At last she up gan lift; with trembling cheare
Her up he tooke, (too simple and too trew,)
And oft her kist.   At length, all passed feare,
He set her on her steede, and forward forth did beare.

NOTES TO THE FAERY QUEENE.

(The numbers refer to lines.)

I. 1. *Lo ! I, the man.* — An imitation of the lines prefixed to Virgil's Æneid. — *Whylome* = formerly, in time past. A. S. *hwilum*, dat. pl. of *hwil*, time, and so meaning *at times*.

2. *Lowly Shepheards weeds.* — A reference to "The Shepherd's Calendar," published in 1579. See sketch of Spenser. — *Weeds* = garments. A. S. *waed*, garment. Now used chiefly in the phrase, "a widow's weeds."

4. *Oaten reeds.* — The musical instrument, made of the hollow joint of oat straw, which the poet employed as "lowly shepherd."

7. *Areeds* = advises, commands. A. S. *araedan*, to tell, speak.

8. *To blazon broade* = to proclaim abroad.

II. 1. *O holy Virgin, chiefe of nyne.* — Clio, first of the nine Muses. She presided over history and epic poetry.

2. *Thy weaker novice* = thy too weak novice. A Latinism not infrequent in Spenser.

3. *Scryne* = a case or chest for keeping books. A. S. *scrin*, Lat. *scrinium*, a chest. Mod. Eng. *shrine*, a place in which sacred things are deposited.

5. *Tanaquill*, an ancient British princess, here intended to represent Queen Elizabeth.

6. *Briton Prince* = King Arthur.

III. 1. *Dreaded impe of highest Jove* = Cupid or Love; in mythology sometimes represented as the son of Jupiter and Venus. *Impe* = scion or offspring; formerly used in a good sense.

3. *Rove* = to shoot an arrow, not point blank, but with an elevation.

5. *Heben* = of ebony wood, ebon; from the Hebrew *hobnim*, ebony wood, through Gr., Lat., and Fr. From Heb. *eben*, a stone.

7. *Mart* = Mars, the god of war.

IV. 3. *Great ladie* = Queen Elizabeth. Two years after the defeat of the Armada, she deserved this title; but as much can hardly be said of the appellation "goddesse heavenly bright," as the Queen was in her fifty-seventh year. But such was the abject flattery of the age.

5. *Eyne* = eyes. Written also *eyen;* both are old plu. forms. A. S. *eage*, plu. *eagan.*

7. *Type of thine* = Una, or Truth.

8. *Argument* = subject-matter; *afflicted* = lowly, humble; *stile* = pen. The whole line may be rendered, *The subject-matter of my lowly pen.*

9. *Dread* = object of reverence.

Canto I.

I.   1. *A gentle Knight* = the Knight of the Red Cross, representing Holiness, and also the model Englishman.   See remarks on the "Faery Queene." — *Pricking* = to ride or spur on quickly.

2. *Ycladd* = past par. of clad.   *Y* stands for the A. S. prefix *ge*, affixed to any part of the verb, but especially to the past par.   Cf. Ger. *ge*, prefix of the past par.   Of very frequent occurrence in Spenser. — *Mightie armes* = the Christian armor described in the last chapter of Ephesians.   See introductory remarks.

5. *Yet armes*, etc. — See introductory remarks.   The knight had hitherto been "a tall clownish young man."

8. *Jolly* = handsome; Fr. *joli*, gay, pretty.

9. *Giusts* = jousts, tilts, or encounters on horseback at tournaments. O. Fr. *joster*, Lat. *juxtare*, to approach.   From *juxta*, near.

II.   1. *Bloodie* = red.

4. *And dead, as living ever*, etc. — A reference to Rev. i. 18.   "I am he that liveth, and was dead; and, behold, I am alive for evermore."

8. *Cheere* = face, countenance.   O. Fr. *chiere*, Lat. *cara*, face, Gr. *kara*, the head.

9. *Ydrad* = past par. of dread.   See *Ycladd*, stanza i., line 2.

III.   2. *Gloriana* = The Faery Queene, who "stands for the *glory of God* in general, and for Queen Elizabeth in particular."   See introductory remarks.

6. *Earne* = yearn.   A. S. *gyrnan*, to yearn; from *georn*, desirous.

9. *His foe, a dragon* = Satan, or the powers of evil, in general, and the Papacy in particular.

IV.   1. *Lovely ladie* = Una, or Truth, in general, and the Protestant Church in particular.   See introduction. — *Faire* = fairly, the *e* being an adverbial termination.

3. *Yet she much whiter.* — Hallam criticises this as absurd, (Lit. of Europe, Vol. I. p. 354) referring it to Una's outward appearance, and not, as Spenser intended, to her inward purity.

4. *Wimpled* = plaited or folded like the white cloth worn by nuns around the neck.

5. *Stole* = a long robe. A. S. *stole* = Lat. *stola* = Gr. *stolē*, a robe.

8. *Seemed* = it seemed. Spenser often omits the subject with impersonal verbs.

9. *Lad* = led. A. S. *laedan*.

V. 3. *From royall lynage.* — Una, Truth, or the Protestant Church, traces her lineage, not from the Papacy, but from the Church Universal.

8. *Forwasted* = utterly wasted. *For* (Ger. *ver*) is an A. S. prefix, generally with the sense of *loss* or *destruction*, but frequently also, as here, *intensive*.

VI. 1. *A dwarfe.* — The significance of the dwarf is doubtful; but probably he is intended to represent *prudence*, as he bears the " bag of needments at his backe."

5. *Suddeine* = suddenly. See note stanza iv., line 1.

7. *Leman* = a sweetheart, or one loved, of either sex. A. S. *leof*, dear, and *mann*, a person.

8. *To shrowd* = to take shelter.

VII. 2. *A shadie grove* = the wood of Error, at first enchanting, but at last leading astray.

VIII. 6. *Sayling pine.* — A reference to its use for masts of sailing ships.

7. *The vine-propp elm.* — In Italy the elm was anciently used to prop or support the vine.

9. *The cypresse funerall.* — The cypress was anciently used to adorn tombs, and hence came to be an emblem of mourning.

IX. 2. *The firre that weepeth* = that distilleth resin.

3. *The willow* = the badge of deserted lovers.

4. *The eugh, obedient*, etc. — A reference to the fact that bows were made of the yew.

5. *The sallow* = a kind of willow.

6. *The mirrhe sweete-bleeding*, etc. — The myrrh, which has a bitter taste, exudes a sweet-smelling gum.

7. *The warlike beech.* — So called because suitable for warlike arms, or because used by the ancients for war-chariots.

9. *The carver holme* = evergreen oak, good for carving. " Every one knows," says Hallam, "that a natural forest never contains such a variety of species; nor, indeed, could such a medley as Spenser, treading in the steps of Ovid, has brought from all soils and climates, have existed long if planted by the hands of man."

X. 3. *Weening* = thinking. A. S. *wenan*, to imagine, hope; from *wen*, expectation, hope.

7. *Doubt* = fear. This was the common meaning in Middle English. Fr. *douter*, Lat. *dubitare*, to doubt.

XI. 4. *And like to lead the labyrinth about* = and likely to lead out of the labyrinth. — *About* = A. S. *abutan*, for *onbutan* = *on* + *be* + *utan*, on by the outside.

5. *Tract* = track, path.

8. *Eftsoones* = soon after, immediately.   A. S. *eftsone*.

XII.   7. *Shame were to revoke* = it were shame to recall.

XIII.   4. *In the gate* = in the way.

7. *Does*. — A singular for a plural verb; a not infrequent solecism in Spenser's time.

8. *Read* = advise.   A.S. *raedan*, to advise.   Cf. stanza i. line 7.

XIV.   1. *Greedy hardiment* = hardihood, or intrepidity, eager for adventure.

7. *Displaide* = unfolded.   O. Fr. *despleier* = Lat. *dis*, apart, and *plicare*, to fold.

9. *Full of vile disdaine* = full of vileness exciting disdain.

XV.   3. *Boughtes* = bends, folds.

8. *Uncouth* = unknown, strange.   A. S. *un*, not, and *cuth*, known, past par. of *cunnan*.

XVI.   1. *Upstart* = upstarted.

4. *Without entraile* = without fold or entanglement.

6. *Armed to point* = armed at every point, completely.

7. *Bale* = evil, destruction.   A. S. *bealu*, disaster, destruction.

XVII.   1. *Elfe* = the knight, so called because coming from fairyland.

3. *Trenchand* = trenchant, cutting.   Fr. *trencher*, to cut.   The *and* is an old participial form.

7. *Threatning* = brandishing.

8. *Enhaunst* = raised, lifted up.

XVIII.   1. *Dint* = blow.   A. S. *dynt*, blow.

5. *Tho* = then.   A. S. *tha*.

6. *Traine* = tail.   Fr. *train*, a tail.

9. *Traine* = snare.   Fr. *traine*.   From Lat. *trahere*, to draw.

XIX.   6. *His gall did grate* = his anger stirred.   The gall was anciently supposed to be the seat of anger.

8. *Gorge* = throat.   Fr. *gorge*, throat.

XX.   3. *Gobbets* = mouthfuls, little lumps.   O. Fr. *gobet*, a morsel of food; from *gob*, a gulp, with diminutive suffix *et*.

6. *Full of bookes and papers*. — A reference no doubt to the numerous scurrilous attacks by Roman Catholic writers upon Queen Elizabeth and Protestantism.

9. *Parbreake* = vomit.   This stanza is to be contemplated only with averted face !

XXI.   5. *To avale* = to fall, sink.   O. Fr. *avaler*, from Lat. *ad vallem*, to the valley, downward.   Cf. *avalanche*.

7. *Ten thousand kindes of creatures.* This was commonly believed by the writers of Spenser's day.

9. *Reed* = perceive, discover. See stanza xiii., line 8.

XXII. 3. *Ne* = nor.

5. *Sinke* = a receptable for filth.

XXIII. 2. *Phœbus* = the sun. — *To welke* = to fade, to grow dim.

7. *Noyance* = annoyance. O. Fr. *anoi* = Lat. *in odio*, in hatred.

XXIV. 1. *Ill bestedd* = badly situated.

5. *Lin* = cease. A. S. *linnan*, to cease.

8. *Raft* = reft; preterit of *reave*. A. S. *reofan*, to deprive.

XXVI. 2. *Impes.* See stanza iii., line 1.

7. *Her life the which them nurst. The which* refers to *her.* In Spenser's day *which* was often used for *who;* as "Our Father *which* art in heaven."

9. *Should contend* = was to contend, or should have contended.

XXVII. 1. *Chaunst* = happened.

3. *Borne under happie starre.* A reference to astrology, or the belief in the influence of the stars upon the destiny of man.

5. *Armory* = armor. See introduction.

9. *That like succeed it may* = that like victories may succeed or follow it.

XXVIII. 2. *To wend* = to go. A. S. *wendan*, to go. Of special interest as supplying the preterit of *to go*.

4. *Ne* = nor.

7. *With God to frend* = With God for friend.

XXIX. 2. *An aged sire* = Archimago, or Hypocrisy.

XXX. 1. *Louting* = bowing. A. S. *lutan*, to stoop.

2. *Quite* = to requite, to satisfy a claim.

6. *Silly* = simple, harmless. "The word has much changed its meaning," says Skeat. "It meant *timely;* then *lucky, happy, blessed, innocent, simple, foolish.*" A. S. *saelig*, happy, prosperous. Cf. Ger. *selig.*

7. *Bidding his beades* = saying, or praying his prayers. *Beade* = prayer; A. S. *bed*, a prayer, from A. S. *biddan*, to pray. Cf. Ger. *Gebet.*

9. *Sits not* = it sits not, is not becoming. Cf. Fr. *il sied*, it is becoming. — *To mell* = to meddle, interfere with. O. Fr. *meller, mesler*, from Lat. *misculare*, to mix.

XXXII. 3. *Thorough* = through. A. S. *thurh*. Cf. Ger. *durch.*

5. *Wote* = know. A. S. *witan*, to know.

6. *Forwearied* = thoroughly weary. See stanza v., line 8.

9. *Doth baite* = doth feed. Literally *bait* = to make to bite. To *bait* a bear is to make the dogs bite him; to *bait* a horse is to make him eat.

XXXIII. 7. *In* = inn. A. S. *inn*, a lodging.

XXXIV. 4. *A little wyde* = a little apart.

5. *Edifyde* = built. O. Fr. *edifier*, Lat. *ædificare*, to build, = *ædes*, a building, and *facere*, to make.

6. *Wont* = was wont. *Wont* is properly a past par. of *won*, to dwell, to be used to.

XXXV. 9. *Ave-Mary* = Ave Maria, an invocation to the Virgin Mary.

XXXVI. 2. *And the sad humor*, etc. = the sweet "slombring deaw," cast on them by Morpheus, the god of sleep and dreams.

5. *Riddes* = conducts, removes. A. S. *hredan*, to deliver.

XXXVII. 4. *Blacke Plutoes griesly Dame*. Pluto is the god of the infernal regions, or realms of darkness; hence the epithet *black*. His wife is Proserpine, whom Pluto carried off as she was gathering flowers in Sicily. As the inflicter of men's curses on the dead, she is called *grisly*, hideous.

8. *Great Gorgon* = Not Medusa, a sight of whom turned the beholder to stone, but Demo-gorgon, an evil divinity that ruled the spirits of the lower world.

9. *Cocytus* = A river of the infernal region, a branch of the Styx. The former is known as the river of lamentation, the latter as the river of hate. The other two rivers of Hades are Acheron, the river of grief, and Phlegethon, the river of burning. So Milton speaks

> " Of four infernal rivers, that disgorge
> Into the burning lake their baleful streams :
> Abhorred Styx, the flood of deadly hate ;
> Sad Acheron, of sorrow black and deep ;
> Cocytus, named of lamentation loud,
> Heard on the rueful stream ; fierce Phlegethon,
> Whose waves of torrent fire inflame with rage."
>
> *Paradise Lost*, ii. 577.

XXXVIII. 2. *Sprights* = spirits. *Sprite* is the more correct spelling. From Fr. *esprit*, spirit.

5. *Fray* = frighten, terrify. A short form for *affray*. O. Fr. *effraier*, to frighten, = Low. Lat. *exfrigidare*.

XXXIX. 1. *Spersed* = dispersed. Lat. *dis*, apart, and *spargere*, to scatter.

6. *Tethys* = the wife of Oceanus, and daughter of Uranus and Terra.

7. *Cynthia* = the goddess of the moon; called also Diana and Artemis.

XL. 4. *Dogges before them farre doe lye* = dogs lie at a distance in front of them.

9. *Takes keepe* = takes heed or care.

XLII. 3. *Mought* = might. A. S. *mugan*, to be able.

6. *That forced* = that he forced.

7. *Dryer braine*. — Spenser seems to consider a " dry brain " the source of troubled dreams.

XLIII. 3. *Hecaté* = an infernal divinity, who at night sends from the lower world all kinds of demons and phantoms.

9. *Sleepers sent* = sleeper's sensation.

XLIV. 2. *Diverse dreame* = a diverting or distracting dream. Lat. *dis*, apart, and *vertere*, to turn.

4. *Carke* = anxiety, care. A. S. *carc*, care.

5. *Starke* = stiff, rigid. A. S. *stearc*, strong, stiff.

9. *Afore* = before. A. S. *onforan*, in front, before.

XLV. 9. *Stole* = a long robe. See stanza iv., line 5.

XLVI. 5. *In sort as* = in the manner that.

6. *Borne without her dew* = born unnaturally; or, perhaps, without the due qualities of a real woman.

7. *Usage sly* = sly or artful conduct.

XLVII. 3. *Hardie* = strong, brave. Fr. *hardi*, stout, bold.

L. 1. *Uncouth* = unknown, strange. See stanza xv., line 8.

4. *Sufferance* = moderation.

6. *To prove his sense, and tempt her faigned truth* = to test the evidence of his senses, and try her professed sincerity.

8. *Tho* = then. See stanza xviii., line 5. — *Can* = began. — *Ruth* = pity, compassion.

LI. 4. *The blind god* = Cupid, the god of love. — *Amate* = subdue, daunt. O. Fr. *amatir*, from *mat*, weak, dull.

7. *Die* = to die. — *Rew* = rue, lament.

LII. 1. *Your own dear sake*, etc. —This is false. See introduction for an account of Una's coming to the court of the Faery Queene.

3. *To bereave* = to take away, to deprive her of. A. S. *be*, and *reafian*, to rob.

9. *Frayes* = frightens. See stanza xxxviii., line 5.

LIII. 5. *Doubtfull* = exciting doubt, suspicions.

8. *Shend* = reproach, spurn. A. S. *scendan*, to reproach. — *Rew* = rue, lament.

LIV. 1. *It fell not all to ground* = it was not all lost or thrown away.

7. *Beguiled of her art* = craftily deluded out of an opportunity to exercise her art.

LV. 5. *Irksome spright* = wearied spirit.

8. *When he saw*, etc., = when the dream saw. The dream is personified.

9. *That misformed spright* = the feigned Una.

CANTO II.

I.   1. *The northern wagoner* = Boötes, the son of Ceres and Iasion, who, being plundered of all his possessions by his brother Pluto, invented the plough, to which he yoked two oxen, and cultivated the soil to procure subsistence for himself.   As a reward for this discovery, he was translated to heaven by his mother, with the plough and yoke of oxen, where he constitutes a constellation in the northern heavens.   The name Boötes means ox-driver, and he is here represented as the driver of Charles's Wain or Wagon, one of the names of the cluster of seven stars, commonly called the *Dipper*, in the constellation of *Ursa Major* or the Great Bear.

2. *His sevenfold teme* = Charles's Wain or Wagon.   *Wain*, A. S. *waegn*, which passed into the form *waen* by the loss of *g*, just as the A. S. *regn* (Ger. *regen*) became *ren* = rain. — *Stedfast starre* = the Pole star, which, not setting in our latitude, " was in ocean waves yet never wet."

7. *Phœbus fiery carre* = the sun, which in mythology was regarded as the chariot driven daily by the sun-god Phœbus across the sky.

III, IV, V.   These stanzas relate a vile imposture practised by Archimago on the Red Cross Knight, whereby the latter was led to believe in the wanton unfaithfulness of Una.

VI.   4. *Gall* = the seat of anger, as was anciently supposed.

6. *Hesperus* = the evening star usually; but here evidently the morning star.   In both cases the planet Venus is meant.

VII.   1. *Rosy-fingered Morning*.   This is a frequent Homeric phrase.

> " Soon as the rosy-finger'd queen appeared,
> Aurora, lovely daughter of the dawn,
> Towards the camp of Greece they took their way,
> And friendly Phœbus gave propitious gales."
>
> *Iliad*, Book I., l. 619.

2. *Aged Tithones* = the spouse of Eos, or Morning.   According to the myth, Eos, in asking immortality for her beloved Tithonus, forgot to ask at the same time eternal youth; and hence, in his old age, he became decrepit.

4. *Titan* = the sun; so called as the offspring of Hyperion, one of the Titans.

5. *Drousyhed* = drowsyhood or drowsiness.   The suffix *head* and *hood*, as in *godhead*, *manhood*, is derived from the A. S. *had*, state, condition.

6. *Bowre* = chamber; often a lady's apartment.   A. S. *bur*, a chamber, from *buan*, to build.

9. *Stowre* = peril, disturbance, battle.   O. Fr. *estur, estor ;* Old Norse, *styrr*, stir, tumult, battle.

VIII. 4. *Pricked* = stung; agreeing with *him* in the preceding line.

IX. 4. *Drift* = purpose or object aimed at.

6. *Doth make* = doth devise or machinate. With the latter *make* is etymologically related.

X. 4. *Proteus* = the " old man of the sea," who tended the seal-flocks of Poseidon or Neptune. He had the gift of prophecy, and of endless transformation. Proteus was very unwilling to prophesy, and tried to escape by adopting all manner of shapes and disguises; but if he found his endeavors useless, he at length resumed his proper form and spoke unerringly of the future.

6. *Fell* = fierce, cruel. A. S. *fel*, fierce, dire.

9. *Might of magick spell.* When Spenser wrote, the belief in magic was still strong, and the arts of Archimago were not regarded as impossible.

XI. 1. *But now seemde best* = but now it seemed best to him.

6. *Discolourd diversly* = variously or diversely colored.

7. *Jolly* = handsome. Fr. *joli*, pretty. *Addrest* = prepared, dressed. Fr. *adresser*.

9. *Saint George himselfe* = the patron of chivalry and the tutelary saint of England. His origin is obscure, though he was no doubt a real personage. At the council of Oxford in 1222, his feast was ordered to be kept as a national festival.

XII. 1. *Semblaunt* = semblance. Fr. *sembler*, to seem; from Lat. *simulare*, to assume the appearance of.

2. *The true Saint George* = the Red Cross Knight. See introduction.

4. *Will* = wilfulness; that is, he was governed by the will alone, and not, as when Una was with him, by truth.

8. *Sans foy* = without faith, or faithless.

XIII. 2. *A goodly lady* = Duessa, representing Falsehood in general, and the Church of Rome in particular; for which reason she is described as " clad in scarlet red," referring to Rev. xvii. 4 — a passage applied to the Papacy by many Protestant commentators.

3. *Purfled* = embroidered on the edge. O. Fr. *pourfiler*, to trim a tinsel; from *pour* (Lat. *pro*) and *filer*, to twist threads; from *fil*, a thread.

4. *Persian mitre* = a lofty mitre or cap.

5. *Owches* = ouches or ornaments; also sockets, in which precious stones are set. See Ex. xxviii. 11.

9. *Bosses brave* = fair ornaments. *Boss* = a protuberant ornament on any work.

XIV. 5. *Addresse* = prepare. See stanza xi., line 7.

XV. 2. *Dispiteous* = pitiless, cruel.

3. *Towards ride* = ride towards him.

8. *Astonied* = astonished, astounded, stunned. *Astonish* and *astound*,

are corruptions of the older form *astony*, which is derived by Skeat from A. S. *astunian*, to stun or amaze completely, intimately confused with the O. Fr. *estonner*, to amaze.

9. *Rebutte* = recoil.   Fr. *re*, back, and *bouter*, to thrust.

XVI. 6. *Hanging* = doubtful, undecided.

9. *Broken reliques* = Shattered spears.

XVII. 1. *Buffe* = blow. O. Fr. *bufe*, a blow.

3. *Quyteth* = requiteth.

4. *Each others equall*, etc. = each envies the equal valor of the other, and seeks with cruel glances to pierce his side armed with iron. For this use of " *their*," compare Matt. xviii. 25: " If ye from your hearts forgive not every one his brother *their* trespasses."

XVIII. 2. *The bitter fitt* = the bitter throes of death.

3. *Wote* = know. A. S. *wat*, present tense of *witan*, to know.

5. *Assured sitt* = keep a firm seat in your saddle.

8. *It* = the Saracen's sword.

9. *Blest* = preserved.

XIX. 1. *Who* = the Red Cross Knight.

3. *Making mark* = taking aim.

7. *Grudging ghost did strive* = his spirit, unwilling to depart, strove with " the fraile flesh."

XX. 5. *Who* = the Red Cross Knight. — *Scowre* = ride rapidly. O. Fr. *escurer*, to scour; from Lat. *ex*, used here as intensive prefix, and *curare*, to take care.

XXI. 3. *Silly dame* = simple, harmless dame. See Canto I., stanza xxx., line 6.

4. *Her humblesse* = her humility.

7. *And said* = and he said.

8. *Rueth* = grieveth, afflicteth.

XXII. 4. *Before that angry heavens list to lowre* = before it pleased the angry heavens to lower. *List* is here impersonal with the dative. A. S. *lystan*, to please.

8. *Daughter of an Emperour*. — Duessa, representing the Papacy, here traces her descent from the Roman empire. " The Popes at Rome looked on themselves (partially at least) as inheritors of the Imperial position."

XXIII. 2. *Onely haire* = only heir.

5. *Debonaire* = courteous, gracious. O. Fr. *de bon aire*, of good mien or appearance.

8. *Fone* = foes. *Fone* is an old plural. A. S. *fan*, plu. of *fah*, foe.

XXIV. 5. *Assaid* = affected. O. Fr. *essaier*, to judge of a thing.

XXV. 7. *Sans joy* = without joy, joyless.

8. *Sans loy* = without loy, lawless.

XXVI. 2. *Fidessa*. — Duessa assumes this name, which implies truth, in order to deceive the Red Cross Knight.

4. *If please* = if it please.

XXVII. 4. *Is said* = it is said.

5. *Chear* = face, countenance. See Canto I., stanza ii., line 8.

6. *Eien* = eyes. Written also *eyne* and *eyen ;* both are old plural forms. A. S. *eage*, plu. *eagen*. — *Shamefast* = shamefaced; an absurd modern spelling, as *face* has nothing to do with it. A. S. *scamfaest ;* from *scamu*, shame, and *faest*, fast, firm.

9. *Dainty maketh derth* = coyness creates desire. *Derth* is literally dearness; from A. S. *deore*, dear, with the suffix *th*, as in *heal-th, leng-th*.

XXVIII. 8. *Ne wont there sound* = nor was wont there to sound.

XXIX. 1. *Can spie* = gan or began to see.

3. *Phœbus* = the sun. See stanza ii., line 7.

6. *Mote* = might. A. S. *ic mot*, I am able.

9. *Tide* = time, season. A. S. *tid*, time.

XXX. 1. *Faire seemely pleasaunce* = pleasing and proper courtesy.

2. *Goodly purposes* = agreeable conversation. *Purposes*, from O. Fr. *purpos*, mod. Fr. *propos*, talk, discourse.

XXXI. 8. *Astond* = astonished. See stanza xv., line 8. — *His heare did hove* = his hair did rise. *Hove* = heave.

XXXII. 1. *Whenas* = when.

4. *Bespake* = spoke.

5. *Limbo* = the borders of hell. Written also *limbus*. See Webster.

8. *Speaches rare* = thin-sounding discourse. Lat. *rarus*, thin, rare.

XXXIII. 3. *Fradubio* = doubtful. Spenser indicates the fate of those who waver between truth and falsehood.

6. *Plast* = placed.

7. *Boreas* = the north wind.

XXXV. 9. *Lyke a faire lady, but did*, etc. = like a fair lady, but she did hide or cover the foul Duessa.

XXXVI. 1. *Forged beauty* = false or counterfeit beauty. — *Did take in hand* = did undertake to maintain by the sword.

7. *Dye of war* = die or chance of war.

XXXVII. 3. *I cast* = I resolved or planned.

4. *Whether* = which of the two. A. S. *hwather*, which of two. Cf. Matt. xxvii. 21.

8. *Frælissa* = fragile, frail.

XXXVIII. 5. *A foggy mist.* — The effect of slander in blasting a fair reputation is here depicted. The Jesuits slandered Queen Elizabeth for the purpose of injuring her influence with the English people.

9. *In place* = in the place or on the spot.

XXXIX.　1.　*Wight* = person, creature.　A. S. *wiht*, creature, person. Formerly both masculine and feminine; here it refers to Fraelissa.

9.　*Treën mould* = form of a tree.　*Treën* is an adj. with the suffix *n* or *en*, as in *leathern, wooden.*

XL.　2.　*Unweeting* = unknowing, unwitting.　A. S. *witan*, to know.

3.　*Wist* = knew.　A. S. *wiste*, past tense of witan, to know.

4.　*Everie prime* = every spring.　It was commonly believed that witches had to do penance once a year in some unsightly form.

7.　*Origane* = an herb used in baths for cutaneous diseases.

XLII.　1.　*Cheare* = face, countenance; as usual in Spenser.

7.　*Pight* = fixed, placed.　Cf., *pitch.*

XLIII.　7.　*Wonted well* = wonted or accustomed weal.

8.　*Suffised fates*, etc. = the fates satisfied shall restore us to our former shape and condition.

XLIV.　1.　*Hight* = called.　A. S. *hatan*, to be called.　"A most singular word, presenting the sole instance in English of a *passive* verb."　Skeat.

4.　*Dreriment* = sorrow, dreariness.　A. S. *dreorig*, sad.

XLV.　2.　*Unweeting* = unknowing.　See stanza xl., line 2.

6.　*She up gan lift* = she began to uplift.

FRANCIS BACON.

IN this era of great writers, the name of Francis Bacon, after those of Shakespeare and Spenser, stands easily first. He was great as a lawyer, as a statesman, as a philosopher, as an author — great in everything, alas! but character. Though his position in philosophy is still a matter of dispute, there can be little doubt that he deserves to rank with Plato and Aristotle, who for two thousand years ruled the philosophic world.

It is claimed by some critics that Bacon's method of philosophizing is wanting in either novelty or value, and that no investigator follows his rules. There is much truth in this claim, and yet Bacon's influence in modern science is pre-eminent. That which has counted for most in his philosophical writings is his spirit. In proud recognition of modern ability and modern advantages, he threw off the tyranny of the ancients. "It would indeed be dishonorable," he says, "to mankind if the regions of the material globe, the earth, the sea, the stars, should be so prodigiously developed and illustrated in our age, and yet the boundaries of the intellectual globe should be confined to the narrow discoveries of the ancients."

He looked upon knowledge, not as an end in itself, to be enjoyed as a luxury, but as a means of usefulness in the service of men. The mission of philosophy is to ameliorate man's condition — to increase his power, to multiply his enjoyments, and to alleviate his sufferings. He discarded the speculative philosophy which seeks to build up a system from the inner resources of the mind. However admirable in logical acuteness and consistency, such systems are apt to be without truth or utility. "The wit and mind of man," says Bacon, "if it work upon matter, which is the contemplation of the creatures of

God, worketh according to the stuff, and is limited thereby; but if it work upon itself, as the spider worketh his web, then it is endless, and brings forth indeed cobwebs of learning, admirable for the fineness of thread and work, but of no substance or profit."

He constantly urged an investigation of nature, whereby philosophy might be planted on a solid foundation, and receive continual accretions of truth. *Investigation, experiment, verification* — these are characteristic features of the Baconian philosophy, and the powerful instruments with which modern science has achieved its marvellous results.

Francis Bacon was born in London, Jan. 22, 1561. His father, Sir Nicholas Bacon, was a man full of wit and wisdom, comprehensive in intellect, retentive to a remarkable degree in memory, and so dignified in appearance and bearing that Queen Elizabeth was accustomed to say, "My Lord Keeper's soul is well lodged." His mother was no less remarkable as a woman. She was the daughter of Sir Anthony Cooke, tutor to King Edward VI., from whom she received a careful education. She was distinguished not only for her womanly and conjugal virtues, but also for her learning, having translated a work from Italian, and another from Latin.

Thus Bacon was fortunate in his parents, whose intellectual superiority he inherited, and also in the time of his birth, "when," as he says, "learning had made her third circuit; when the art of printing gave books with a liberal hand to men of all fortunes; when the nation had emerged from the dark superstitions of popery; when peace throughout all Europe permitted the enjoyment of foreign travel and free ingress to foreign scholars; and, above all, when a sovereign of the highest intellectual attainments, at the same time that she encouraged learning and learned men, gave an impulse to the arts, and a chivalric and refined tone to the manners of the people."

He was delicate in constitution, but extraordinary in intellectual power. Son of a Lord Keeper, and nephew of a Secretary of State, he was brought up in surroundings that were highly favorable to intellectual culture and elegant manners. His youthful precocity attracted attention. Queen Elizabeth, delighted with his childish wisdom and gravity, playfully called him her "Young Lord Keeper." When she asked him one day how old he was, with a delicate courtesy beyond his years, he replied: "Two years younger than your majesty's happy reign." His disposition was reflective and serious; and it is related of him that he stole away from his playmates to indulge his spirit of investigation.

At the early age of thirteen he matriculated in Trinity College, Cambridge, and, with rare penetration, soon discovered the leading defects in the higher education of the time. The principle of authority prevailed in instruction to the suppression of free inquiry. The university was engaged, not in broadening the field of knowledge by discovery of new truth, but in disseminating simply the wisdom of the ancients. Aristotle was dictator, from whose utterances there was no appeal. "In the universities," he says, "all things are found opposite to the advancement of the sciences; for the readings and exercises are here so managed that it cannot easily come into any one's mind to think of things out of the common road; or if, here and there, one should venture to use a liberty of judging, he can only impose the task upon himself without obtaining assistance from his fellows; and, if he could dispense with this, he will still find his industry and resolution a great hindrance to his fortune. For the studies of men in such places are confined, and pinned down to the writings of certain authors; from which, if any man happens to differ, he is presently reprehended as a disturber and innovator."

Though meeting with little sympathy in his spirit of free investigation, Bacon still followed the bent of his genius. While yet a student, he planned the immortal work which was to influence the subsequent course of philosophy. His opinions of the defects existing in the universities were only confirmed by age. Some years after leaving Cambridge he advocated the establishment of a college which should be devoted to the discovery of new truths — "a living spring to mix with the stagnant waters." He complained that there was no school for the training of statesmen — a fact that seemed to him prejudicial, not only to science, but also to the state — and that the weighty affairs of the kingdom were entrusted to men whose only qualifications were a "knowledge of Latin and Greek, and verbal criticisms upon the dead languages."

After a residence of three years at the university, he went to Paris under the care of the English ambassador at the French Court. He was sent on a secret mission to Elizabeth, and discharged its duties with such ability as to win the queen's approbation. He afterwards travelled in the French provinces, and met many distinguished men — statesmen, philosophers, authors — who were impressed by his extraordinary gifts and attainments. The death of his father recalled him to England in 1579; and finding himself without adequate means to lead a life of philosophic investigation, it became necessary for him, as he expresses it, "to think how to live, instead of living only to think."

The two roads open to him were law and politics; and with his antecedents he naturally inclined to the latter. He applied to his uncle, Lord Burleigh, for a position; but the prime minister, fearing, it is said, the abilities of his nephew, used his influence to prevent the young applicant from obtaining a place of importance and emolument. Thus disappointed in his hopes, Bacon was reluctantly obliged to betake himself to the law. He gave himself with industry to his calling, and in a few years attained distinction for legal knowledge and skill. As might naturally be supposed from the philosophic cast of his mind, his studies were not confined to precedents and authorities, but extended to the universal principles of justice and the whole circle of knowledge. In 1590 he was made counsel-extraordinary to the queen — a position, it seems, of more honor than profit.

With this appointment began his political career. He

sought worldly honors and wealth, but chiefly, as there is reason to believe, in order that he might at last enjoy a competency, which would allow him to retire from official cares and pursue his philosophical studies without distraction. In 1592 he was elected a member of Parliament from Middlesex. He advocated comprehensive improvements in the law. On one occasion he incurred the queen's displeasure by opposing the early payment of certain subsidies to which the House had consented. When her displeasure was formally communicated to him, he calmly replied that "he spoke in discharge of his conscience and duty to God, to the queen, and to his country."

His connection with Parliament was characterized by activity, and his integrity at this time kept him from sacrificing the interests of England at the foot of the throne. As an orator he became affluent, weighty, and eloquent. "No man," says Ben Jonson, "ever spake more neatly, more pressly, more weightily, or suffered less emptiness, less idleness in what he uttered: no member of his speech but consisted of its own graces. His hearers could not cough or look aside from him without loss; he commanded when he spoke, and had his judges angry and pleased at his devotion. No man had their affections more in his power; the fear of every man that heard him was lest he should make an end."

In 1594 the office of solicitor-general became vacant, and Bacon set to work to obtain it. Every influence within his reach was brought to bear upon the queen. Lord Essex, the favorite of Elizabeth, interested himself especially in his behalf. But every effort proved unavailing. Bacon, like Spenser, felt the bitterness of seeking preferment at court, and complained that he was like a child following a bird which, when almost within reach, continually flew farther. "I am weary of it," he said, "as also of wearying my friends."

To assuage his keen disappointment, Essex bestowed upon him an estate, valued at eighteen hundred pounds, in the beautiful village of Twickenham. The earl continued to befriend him through a long period. When Bacon wished to marry Lady Hatton, a woman of large fortune, Essex supported his suit with a strong letter to her parents. But in spite of Bacon's merit and his noble patron's warmth, the heart of the lady remained untouched; and fortunately for Bacon, as a biographer suggestively remarks, she afterwards became the wife of his great rival, Sir Edward Coke.

When, a few years later, Essex, through his imprudence, incurred the queen's disfavor, and by his treason forfeited his life, Bacon appeared against him. For this act he has been severely censured. Macaulay especially, in his famous essay, displays the zeal of an advocate in making him appear in a bad light, affirming that "he exerted his professional talents to shed the earl's blood, and his literary talents to blacken the earl's memory." Though it cannot be maintained that Bacon acted the part of a high-minded, generous friend, or that his course was in any way justifiable, an impartial survey of the facts does not justify Macaulay's severity.

In 1597 Bacon published a collection of ten essays, which were afterwards increased to fifty-eight. If he had written nothing else, these alone would have entitled him to an honorable place in English literature. Though brief in form, they are weighty in thought. The style is clear; and the language, as in the essay on "Adversity," often rises into great beauty. They were composed, as he tells us, as a recreation from severer studies, but contain, nevertheless, the richest results of his thinking and experience. They were popular from the time of their publication; they were at once translated into French, Italian, and Latin, and no fewer than six editions appeared during the author's life.

Though it is through his other writings — the *Novum Organum* and "The Advancement of Learning" — that he has exerted the greatest influence, it is the "Essays" that have been most widely read, coming home, as he says, "to men's business and bosoms." Archbishop Whately said : "I am old-fashioned enough to admire Bacon, whose remarks are taken in and assented to by persons of ordinary capacity, and seem nothing very profound; but when a man comes to reflect and observe, and his faculties enlarge, he then sees more in them than he did at first, and more still as he advances further; his admiration of Bacon's profundity increasing as he himself grows intellectually. Bacon's wisdom is like the seven-league boots, which would fit the giant or the dwarf, except only that the dwarf cannot take the same stride in them."

The distinguished Scotch philosopher, Dugald Stewart, bears similar testimony, which indeed is confirmed by the judgment of every competent reader: "The small volume to which he has given the title of ' Essays,' the best known and the most popular of all his works, is one of those where the superiority of his genius appears to the greatest advantage; the novelty and depth of his reflections often receiving a strong relief from the triteness of the subject. It may be read from beginning to end in a few hours, and yet after the twentieth perusal one seldom fails to remark in it something overlooked before. This, indeed, is a characteristic of all Bacon's writings, and is only to be accounted for by the inexhaustible aliment they furnish to our own thoughts, and the sympathetic activity they impart to our torpid faculties."

After the accession of James I. in 1603, whose favor he made great efforts to placate, Bacon rose rapidly in position and honor. That year he was elevated to the order of knighthood, and the following year appointed salaried counsel to the king — a mark of favor almost without precedent. In 1613 he was advanced to the office of attorney-general. In 1617 he was created Lord Keeper of the Great Seal of England — a dignity of which he was proud; and the following year he was made Lord High Chancellor, the summit of his ambition and political elevation.

Fond of elegant surroundings, he lived in great state, with liveried servants, beautiful mansions, and magnificent gardens. He was inconsiderate and lavish in his expenditures; and while laboring with conscientious fidelity to improve the laws of the kingdom and to facilitate the administration of justice, his personal character, it must be acknowledged, did not remain above suspicion and reproach. He was unduly subservient to the king; and to maintain his outward splendor, he accepted presents, if not bribes, from persons interested in his judicial decisions. Being tried by Parliament, he made confession to twenty-eight charges of corruption, whereupon he was condemned to pay a fine of forty thousand pounds, to be imprisoned in the Tower during the king's pleasure, and to be debarred from any office in the state. Thus, in 1621, Bacon fell from his high position, ruined in fortune and broken in spirit. Though released from the Tower after an imprisonment of two days, and relieved also of the payment of the fine, he never recovered from his disgrace.

It is difficult now to determine the extent of his guilt. It is certain that he was not, what Pope pronounced him, "the meanest of mankind." The truth probably is that he was morally weak rather then basely corrupt. Though he received presents or bribes, it can hardly be shown that he purposely perverted justice. It was not unusual for judges at that day to receive presents. There is no sufficient reason to doubt his sincerity and justice when he wrote : "For the briberies and gifts wherewith I am charged, when the book of hearts shall be opened, I hope I shall not be found to have the troubled fountain of the corrupt heart, in a depraved habit of taking rewards to pervert justice; howsoever I may be frail, and partake of the abuses of the time." He was, in some measure, a victim of secret enmity and parliamentary clamor ; and in his will he did wisely to appeal from the prejudice about him to the impartial judgment of posterity. "For my name and memory," he pathetically writes, "I leave it to men's charitable speeches, to foreign nations, and the next ages."

The colossal cast of Bacon's mind is seen in his great philosophical scheme entitled the "*Instauratio Magna*, or the Great Institution of True Philosophy," which embodies his principal writings. It was to consist of six parts, the completion of which was necessarily beyond the power of one man or even of one age.

I. *Divisions of the Sciences.* "This part exhibits a summary, or universal description, of such science and learning as mankind is, up to this time, in possession of."

II. *Novum Organum; or, Precepts for the Interpretation of Nature.* "The object of the second part is the doctrine touching a better and more perfect use of reasoning in the investigation of things, and the true helps of the understanding ; that it may by this means be raised, as far as our human and mortal nature will admit, and be enlarged in its powers so as to master the arduous and obscure secrets of nature."

III. *Phenomena of the Universe; or, Natural and Experimental History on which to found Philosophy.* "The third part of our work embraces the phenomena of the universe ; that is to say, experience of every kind, and such a natural history as can form the foundation of an edifice of philosophy."

IV. *Scale of the Understanding.* "The fourth part . . . is in fact nothing more than a particular and fully developed application of the second part."

V. *Precursors or Anticipations of the Second Philosophy.* "We compose this fifth part of the work of those matters which we have either discovered, tried, or added."

VI. *Sound Philosophy, or Active Science.* "Lastly, the sixth part of our work (to which the rest are subservient and auxiliary) discloses and propounds that philosophy which is reared and formed by the legitimate, pure, and strict method of investigation previously taught and prepared. But it is both beyond our power and expectation to perfect and conclude this last part."

In the first part of this vast scheme Bacon embodied, in a revised form, the " Advancement of Learning," his earliest philosophical work, published in 1605. It made a complete survey of the field of learning, for the purpose of indicating what departments of knowledge had received due attention, and what subjects yet needed cultivation. It is a rich mine of wisdom and learning. But the most celebrated part of the *Instauratio Magna* is the *Novum Organum*, in which Bacon's philosophical method is unfolded. It is written in the form of aphorisms, several of which, including the first, are here given as indicating the character of the whole work : —

" I. Man, as the minister and interpreter of nature, does and understands as much as his observations on the order of nature, either with regard to things or the mind, permit him, and neither knows nor is capable of more.

" IX. The sole cause and root of almost every defect in the sciences is this ; that whilst we falsely admire and extol the powers of the human mind, we do not search for its real helps.

" XIX. There are and can exist but two ways of investigating and discovering truth. The one hurries on rapidly from the senses and particulars to the most general axioms ; and from them as principles and their supposed indisputable truth derives and discovers the intermediate axioms. This is the way now in use. The other constructs its axioms from the senses and particulars, by ascending continually and gradually, till it finally arrives at the most general axioms, which is the true but unattempted way."

A well-known and valuable portion of the *Novum Organum* is the discussion of the influences which warp the human mind in the pursuit of truth. These warping influences Bacon calls *idols ;* and his exposition of the subject, which cannot be fully inserted here, has never been surpassed in analytical scope and power.

"XXXIX. Four species of idols beset the human mind ; to which, for distinction's sake, we have assigned names, calling the first, idols of the tribe ; the second, idols of the den ; the third, idols of the market ; the fourth, idols of the theatre.

" XLI. The idols of the tribe are inherent in human nature, and the very tribe or race of man. For man's sense is falsely asserted to be the standard of things. On the contrary, all the perceptions, both of the senses and the mind, bear reference to man, and not to the universe, and the human mind resembles those uneven mirrors, which impart their own properties to different objects, from which rays are emitted, and distort and disfigure them.

"XLII. The idols of the den are those of each individual. For everybody (in addition to the errors common to the race of man) has his own individual den or cavern, which intercepts and corrupts the light of nature ; either from his own peculiar and singular disposition, or from his education and intercourse with others, or from his reading, and the authority acquired by those whom he reverences and admires, or from the different impressions produced on the mind, as it happens to be pre-occupied and predisposed, or equable and tranquil, and the like ; so that the spirit of man (according to its several dispositions) is variable, confused, and, as it were, actuated by chance ; and Heraclitus said well that men search for knowledge in lesser worlds, and not in the greater or common world.

"XLIII. There are also idols formed by the reciprocal intercourse and society of man with man, which we call idols of the market, from the commerce and association of man with each other. For men converse by means of language ; but words are formed at the will of the generality ; and there arises from a bad and unapt formation of words a wonderful obstruction to the mind. Nor can the definitions and explanations, with which learned men are wont to guard and protect themselves in some instances afford a complete remedy ; words still manifestly force the understanding, throw everything into confusion, and lead mankind into vain and innumerable controversies and fallacies.

"XLIV. Lastly, there are idols which have crept into men's minds from the various dogmas of peculiar systems of philosophy, and also from the perverted rules of demonstration, and these we denominate idols of the theatre. For we regard all the systems of philosophy hitherto received or imagined, as so many plays brought out and performed, creating fictitious and theatrical worlds. Nor do we speak only of the present systems, or of the philosophy and sects of the ancients, since numerous other plays of a similar nature can be still composed and made to agree with each other, the causes of the most opposite errors being generally the same. Nor, again, do we allude merely to general systems, but also to many elements and axioms of sciences, which have become inveterate by tradition, implicit credence, and neglect. We must, however, discuss each species of idols more fully and distinctly, in order to guard the human understanding against them."

However much men may differ in their estimate of Bacon's method and position in philosophy, all agree in recognizing his intellectual greatness. It would be easy to fill pages with the glowing tributes that have been paid him, not only by English, but also by French and German writers. Hallam, who is not given to inconsiderate panegyric, says: "If we compare what may be found in the sixth, seventh, and eighth books *De Augmentis;* in the Essays, the History of Henry VII., and the various short treatises contained in his works on moral and political wisdom, and on human nature, from experience of which all such wisdom is drawn, with the Rhetoric, Ethics, and Politics of Aristotle, or with the historians most celebrated for their deep insight into civil society and human character; with Thucidides, Tacitus, Philip de Comines, Machiavel, Davila, Hume, we shall, I think, find that one man may almost be compared with all of these together."

An able German scholar assigns Bacon a high rank as a philosopher and educator because he was "the first to say to the learned men who lived and toiled in the languages and writings of antiquity, and who were mostly only echoes of the old Greeks and Romans, yea, who knew nothing better than to be such: 'There is also a present, only open your eyes to recognize its splendor. Turn away from the shallow springs of traditional natural science, and draw from the unfathomable and ever-freshly flowing fountain of creation. Live in nature with active senses; ponder it in your thoughts, and learn to comprehend it, for thus you will be able to control it. Power increases with knowledge.' " [1]

Bacon had unswerving faith in the power of truth, and he confidently looked forward to a time when the value of his teachings would be recognized. The fulfilment of the following prediction establishes the character and mission of the prophet: "I have held up a light in the obscurity of philosophy," he says, "which will be seen centuries after I am dead. It will be seen amid the erection of temples, tombs, palaces, theatres, bridges, making noble roads, cutting canals, granting multitudes of charters and liberties for comfort of decayed companies and corporations; the foundation of colleges and lectures for learning and the education of youth; foundations and institutions of orders and fraternities for nobility, enterprise, and obedience; but, above all, the establishing good laws for the regulation of the kingdom, and as an example to the world."

[1] Raumer, Geschichte der Pädagogik.

BACON'S ESSAYS.

OF TRUTH.

"WHAT is truth?"[1] said jesting[2] Pilate, and would not stay for an answer. Certainly there be that[3] delight in giddiness,[4] and count it a bondage to fix a belief; affecting[5] free-will in thinking, as well as in acting. And though the sects of philosophers[6] of that kind be gone, yet there remain certain discoursing[7] wits, which are of the same veins, though there be not so much blood in them as was in those of the ancients. But it is not only the difficulty and labour which men take in finding out of truth, nor, again, that, when it is found, it imposeth[8] upon men's thoughts, that doth bring lies in favour; but a natural though corrupt love of the lie itself. One of the later schools of the Grecians examineth the matter, and is at a stand[9] to think what should be in it, that men should love lies, where neither they make for pleasure, as with poets,[10] nor for advantage, as with the merchant, but for the lie's sake. But I cannot tell: this same truth is a naked and open daylight, that doth not show the masques and mummeries and triumphs of the world half so stately and daintily[11] as candle-lights. Truth may perhaps come to the price of a pearl, that showeth best by day, but it will not rise to the price[12] of a diamond or carbuncle,[13] that showeth best in varied lights. A mixture of a lie doth ever add pleasure. Doth any man doubt that, if there were taken out of men's minds vain opinions, flattering hopes, false valuations, imaginations as one would, and the like, it would leave the minds of a number of men poor shrunken things, full of melancholy and indisposition, and unpleasing to themselves? One of the fathers,[14] in great severity, called poesy *vinum dæmonum*,[15] because it filleth the imagination, and yet it is but with the shadow of a lie. But it is not the lie that passeth through the mind, but the lie that sinketh in, and settleth in it, that doth the hurt, such as we spake of before. But howsoever[16] these things are thus in men's depraved judgments and affections, yet truth, which only doth judge itself, teacheth, that the inquiry of truth, which is the love-making or wooing of it, the knowledge of truth, which is the presence of it, and the belief of truth, which is the enjoying of it, is the sovereign good of human nature. The first creature[17] of God, in the works of the days, was the light of the sense; the last was the light of reason; and His sabbath work ever since is the illumination of His Spirit. First, He breathed light upon the face of the matter, or chaos; [18] then He breathed light into the face of man; and still He breatheth and inspireth light into the face of His chosen. The poet that beautified the sect,[19] that was otherwise inferior to the rest, saith yet excellently well: "It is a pleasure to stand upon the shore, and to see ships tossed upon the sea; a pleasure to stand in the window of a castle, and to see a battle, and the adventures [20] thereof below: but no pleasure is comparable to the standing upon the vantage ground of truth," (a hill not to be commanded,[21] and where the air is always clear and serene,) "and to see the errors and wanderings, and mists and tempests, in the vale below:" so [22] always that this prospect [23] be with pity, and not with swelling or pride. Certainly it is Heaven upon Earth to have a man's mind move in charity, rest in Providence, and turn upon the poles of truth.

To pass from theological and philosophical truth to the truth of civil business: It will be acknowledged, even by those that practise it not, that clear and round [24] dealing is the honour of man's nature, and that mixture of falsehood is like alloy [25] in coin of gold and silver, which may make the metal work the better, but it embaseth [26] it. For these winding and crooked courses are the goings of the serpent; which goeth basely upon the belly, and not upon the feet. There is no vice that doth so cover a man with shame as to be found false and perfidious: and therefore Montaigne [27] saith prettily, when he inquired the reason why the word of the lie should be such a disgrace and such an odious charge: saith he, "If it be well weighed, to say that a man lieth, is as much as to say that he is brave towards God, and a coward towards men. For a lie faces God, and shrinks from man." Surely the wickedness of falsehood and breach of faith cannot possibly be so highly expressed, as in that it shall be the last peal to call the judgments of God upon the generations of men; it being foretold that, when "Christ cometh," He shall not "find faith upon the Earth."

OF REVENGE.

REVENGE is a kind of wild justice, which the more Man's nature runs to, the more ought law to weed it out: for, as for the first wrong, it doth but offend the law, but the revenge of that wrong putteth the law out of office. Certainly, in taking revenge, a man is but even with his enemy, but in passing it over he is superior; for it is a prince's part to pardon: and Solomon, I am sure, saith, "It is the glory of a man to pass by an offence."[1] That which is past is gone and irrevocable,[2] and wise men have enough to do with things present and to come; therefore they do but trifle with themselves that labour in past matters. There is no man doth a wrong for the wrong's sake, but thereby to purchase himself profit, or pleasure, or honour, or the like; therefore why should I be angry with a man for loving himself better than me? And if any man should do wrong merely out of ill-nature, why, yet it is but like the thorn or briar, which prick and scratch because they can do no other. The most tolerable sort of revenge is for those wrongs which there is no law to remedy; but then let a man take heed the revenge be such as there is no law to punish, else a man's enemy is still beforehand, and it is two for one. Some, when they take revenge, are desirous the party should know whence it cometh: this is the more generous; for the delight seemeth to be not so much in doing the hurt as in making the party repent: but base and crafty cowards are like the arrow that flieth in the dark. Cosmus, Duke of Florence,[3] had a desperate[4] saying against perfidious or neglecting[5] friends, as if those wrongs were unpardonable. "You shall read," saith he, "that we are commanded to forgive our enemies; but you never read that we are commanded to forgive our friends." But yet the spirit of Job was in a better tune: "Shall we," saith he, "take good at God's hands, and not be content to take evil also?"[6] and so of friends in a proportion. This is certain, that a man that studieth revenge keeps his own wounds green, which otherwise would heal and do well. Public revenges[7] are for the most part fortunate; as that for the death of Cæsar;[8] for the death of Pertinax;[9] for the death of Henry the Third of France;[10] and many more. But in private revenges it is not so; nay, rather vindictive persons live the life of witches; who, as they are mischievous, so end they unfortunate.[11]

OF ADVERSITY.

IT was a high speech of Seneca, (after the manner of the Stoics,[1]) that "the good things which belong to prosperity are to be wished, but the good things that belong to adversity are to be admired," — *Bona rerum secundarum optabilia, adversarum mirabilia.* Certainly, if miracles be the command over Nature, they appear most in adversity. It is yet a higher speech of his than the other, (much too high for a heathen,) " It is true greatness to have in one the frailty of a man, and the security of a god," — *Vere magnum habere fragilitatem hominis, securitatem dei.* This would have done better in poesy, where transcendencies [2] are more allowed ; and the poets indeed have been busy with it ; for it is in effect the thing which is figured in that strange fiction of the ancient poets, which seemeth not to be without mystery ; [3] nay, and to have some approach to the state of a Christian ; " that Hercules,[4] when he went to unbind Prometheus, (by whom human nature is represented,) sailed the length of the great ocean in an earthen pot or pitcher," lively describing Christian resolution, that saileth in the frail bark of the flesh through the waves of the world. But, to speak in a mean,[5] the virtue of prosperity is temperance, the virtue of adversity is fortitude, which in morals is the more heroical virtue. Prosperity is the blessing of the Old Testament, adversity is the blessing of the New, which carrieth the greater benediction, and the clearer revelation of God's favour. Yet, even in the Old Testament, if you listen to David's harp, you shall hear as many hearse-like airs [6] as carols ; and the pencil of the Holy Ghost hath laboured more in describing the afflictions of Job than the felicities of Solomon. Prosperity is not without many fears and distastes ; and adversity is not without comforts and hopes. We see in needleworks and embroideries, it is more pleasing to have a lively work upon a sad and solemn ground, than to have a dark and melancholy work upon a lightsome ground : judge, therefore, of the pleasure of the heart by the pleasure of the eye. Certainly virtue is like precious odours, most fragrant when they are incensed,[7] or crushed : for prosperity doth best discover vice, but adversity doth best discover virtue.

OF MARRIAGE AND SINGLE LIFE

He that hath wife and children hath given hostages to fortune ; for they are impediments [1] to great enterprises, either of virtue or mischief. Certainly the best works, and of greatest merit for the public, have proceeded from the unmarried or childless men, which [2] both in affection and means have married and endowed the public. Yet it were great reason that those that have children should have greatest care of future times, unto which they know they must transmit their dearest pledges. Some there are who, though they lead a single life, yet their thoughts do end with themselves, and account future times impertinences ; [3] nay, there are some other that account wife and children but as bills of charges;[4] nay, more, there are some foolish rich covetous men that take a pride in having no children, because[5] they may be thought so much the richer; for perhaps they have heard some talk, "Such an one is a great rich man," and another except to it, "Yea, but he hath a great charge[6] of children;" as if it were an abatement to his riches.   But the most ordinary cause of a single life is liberty, especially in certain self-pleasing and humorous[7] minds, which are so sensible of every restraint, as they will go near to think their girdles and garters to be bonds and shackles.   Unmarried men are best friends, best masters, best servants; but not always best subjects, for they are light to run away, and almost all fugitives are of that condition.   A single life doth well with churchmen,[8] for charity will hardly water the ground where it must first fill a pool.[9]   It is indifferent for judges and magistrates; for if they be facile and corrupt, you shall have a servant five times worse than a wife.   For soldiers, I find the generals commonly, in their hortative,[10] put men in mind of their wives and children; and I think the despising of marriage amongst the Turks maketh the vulgar soldier more base.   Certainly wife and children are a kind of discipline of humanity; and single men, though they be many times more charitable, because their means are less exhaust,[11] yet, on the other side, they are more cruel and hard-hearted, (good to make severe inquisitors,) because their tenderness is not so oft called upon.   Grave natures, led by custom, and therefore constant, are commonly loving husbands, as was said of Ulysses, *Vetulam suam prætulit immortalitati*.[12]   Chaste women are often proud and froward, as presuming upon the merit of their chastity.   It is one of the best bonds, both of chastity and obedience, in the wife, if she think her husband wise, which she will never do if she find him jealous.   Wives are young men's mistresses, companions for middle age, and old men's nurses; so as[13] a man may have a quarrel[14] to marry when he will: but yet he was reputed one of the wise men that made answer to the question when a man should marry, "A young man not yet, an elder man not at all."   It is often seen that bad husbands have very good wives; whether it be that it raiseth the price of their husbands' kindness when it comes, or that the wives take a pride in their patience; but this never fails, if the bad husbands were of their own choosing, against their friends' consent; for then they will be sure to make good their own folly.

OF GREAT PLACE.

MEN in great place are thrice servants, — servants of the sovereign or State, servants of fame, and servants of business ; so as [1] they have no freedom, neither in their persons, nor in their actions, nor in their times. It is a strange desire to seek power and to lose liberty ; or to seek power over others, and to lose power over a man's self. The rising unto place is laborious, and by pains men come to greater pains ; and it is sometimes base, and by indignities [2] men come to dignities. The standing is slippery, and regress is either a downfall, or at least an eclipse, which is a melancholy thing : *Cum non sis qui fueris, non esse cur velis vivere.*[3] Nay, retire men cannot when they would, neither will they when it were reason,[4] but are impatient of privateness even in age and sickness, which require the shadow ; [5] like old townsmen, that will be sitting at their street-door, though thereby they offer age to scorn. Certainly great persons had need to borrow other men's opinions to think themselves happy ; for if they judge by their own feeling, they cannot find it : but if they think with themselves what other men think of them, and that other men would fain be as they are, then they are happy as it were by report, when, perhaps, they find the contrary within ; for they are the first that find their own griefs, though they be the last that find their own faults. Certainly men in great fortunes are strangers to themselves, and while they are in the puzzle [6] of business they have no time to tend their health either of body or mind. *Illi mors gravis incubat, qui notus nimis omnibus, ignotus moritur sibi.*[7] In place there is license to do good or evil, whereof the latter is a curse ; for in evil the best condition is not to will,[8] the second not to can.[9] But power to do good is the true and lawful end of aspiring ; for good thoughts, though God accept them, yet towards men are little better than good dreams, except they be put in act ; and that cannot be without power and place, as the vantage and commanding ground. Merit and good works is the end of man's motion, and conscience [10] of the same is the accomplishment of man's rest ; for if a man can be partaker of God's theatre,[11] he shall likewise be partaker of God's rest : *Et conversus Deus ut aspiceret opera, quæ fecerunt manus suæ, vidit quod omnia essent bona nimis ;* [12] and then the Sabbath.

In the discharge of thy place set before thee the best examples, for imitation is a globe [13] of precepts ; and after a time set before thee thine own example, and examine thyself strictly whether thou didst not best at first. Neglect not, also, the examples of those that have carried themselves ill in the same place; not to set off thyself by taxing their memory, but to direct thyself what to avoid. Reform, therefore, without bravery [14] or scandal of former times and persons; but yet set it down to thyself, as well to create good precedents as to follow them. Reduce things to the first institution, and observe wherein and how they have degenerated; but yet ask counsel of both times, — of the ancient time what is best, and of the later time what is fittest. Seek to make thy course regular, that men may know beforehand what they may expect; but be not too positive and peremptory; and express thyself well when thou digressest from thy rule. Preserve the right of thy place, but stir not questions of jurisdiction; and rather assume thy right in silence, and *de facto*,[15] than voice [16] it with claims and challenges. Preserve likewise the rights of inferior places; and think it more honour to direct in chief than to be busy in all. Embrace and invite helps and advices touching the execution of thy place; and do not drive away such as bring thee information as meddlers, but accept of them in good part.

The vices of authority are chiefly four, — delays, corruption, roughness, and facility.[17] For delays, give easy access; keep times appointed; go through with that which is in hand, and interlace not business but of necessity. For corruption, do not only bind thine own hands or thy servants' hands from taking, but bind the hands of suitors also from offering; for integrity used doth the one, but integrity professed, and with a manifest detestation of bribery, doth the other; and avoid not only the fault, but the suspicion. Whosoever is found variable, and changeth manifestly without manifest cause, giveth suspicion of corruption: therefore always, when thou changest thine opinion or course, profess it plainly, and declare it, together with the reasons that move thee to change, and do not think to steal it.[18] A servant or a favourite, if he be inward,[19] and no other apparent cause of esteem, is commonly thought but a by-way to close [20] corruption. For roughness, it is a needless cause of discontent: severity breedeth fear, but roughness breedeth hate. Even reproofs from authority ought to be grave, and not taunting. As for facility, it is worse than bribery; for bribes come but now and then; but if importunity or idle respects [21] lead a man, he shall never be without; as Solomon saith, "To respect persons is not good; for such a man will transgress for a piece of bread."

It is most true that was anciently spoken, — "A place showeth the man;" and it showeth some to the better and some to the worse. *Omnium consensu capax imperii, nisi imperasset*,[22] saith Tacitus of Galba; but of Vespasian he saith, *Solus imperantium, Vespasianus mutatus in melius;*[23] though the one was meant of sufficiency, the other of manners and affection. It is an assured sign of a worthy and generous spirit, whom honour amends; for honour is, or should be, the place of virtue; and as in Nature things move violently to their place, and calmly in their place, so virtue in ambition is violent, in authority settled and calm. All rising to great place is by a winding stair; and if there be factions, it is good to side [24] a man's self whilst he is in the rising, and to balance himself when he is placed. Use the memory of thy predecessor fairly and tenderly; for, if thou dost not, it is a debt will sure be paid when thou art gone. If thou have colleagues, respect them; and rather call them when they look not for it, than exclude them when they have reason to look to be called. Be not too sensible or too remembering of thy place in conversation and private answers to suitors; but let it rather be said "When he sits in place, he is another man."

OF SEEMING WISE.

IT hath been an opinion, that the French are wiser than they seem, and the Spaniards seem wiser than they are; but, howsoever it be between nations, certainly it is so between man and man; for, as the apostle saith of godliness, "Having a show of godliness, but denying the power thereof;"[1] so certainly there are, in points of wisdom and sufficiency,[2] that do nothing or little very solemnly; *magno conatu nugas.*[3] It is a ridiculous thing, and fit for a satire, to persons of judgment, to see what shifts these formalists have, and what prospectives[4] to make superficies to seem body, that hath depth and bulk. Some are so close and reserved, as [5] they will not show their wares but by a dark light, and seem always to keep back somewhat; and when they know within themselves they speak of that they do not well know, would nevertheless seem to others to know of that which they may not well speak. Some help themselves with countenance and gesture, and are wise by signs; as Cicero saith of Piso, that when he answered him he fetched one of his brows up to his forehead, and bent the other down to his chin; *Respondes, altero ad frontem sublato, altero ad mentum depresso supercilio, crudelitatem tibi non placere.*[6] Some think to bear[7] it by speaking a great word, and being peremptory; and go on, and take by admittance that which they cannot make good. Some, whatsoever is beyond their reach, will seem to despise, or make light of it, as impertinent or curious;[8] and so would have their ignorance seem judgment. Some are never without a difference,[9] and commonly, by amusing men with a subtilty, blanch [10] the matter; of whom A. Gellius saith, *Hominem delirum, qui verborum minutiis rerum frangit pondera.*[11] Of which kind also Plato, in his *Protagoras*, bringeth in Prodicus in scorn, and maketh him make a speech that consisteth of distinctions from the beginning to the end. Generally, such men, in all deliberations, find ease to be of the negative side, and affect a credit to object and foretell difficulties; for, when propositions are denied, there is an end of them; but if they be allowed, it requireth a new work; which false point of wisdom is the bane of business. To conclude, there is no decaying merchant, or inward beggar,[12] hath so many tricks to uphold the credit of their wealth as these empty persons have to maintain the credit of their sufficiency. Seeming wise men may make shift to get opinion; but let no man choose them for employment; for, certainly, you were better take for business a man somewhat absurd than over-formal.

OF DISCOURSE.

SOME in their discourse desire rather commendation of wit, in being able to hold all arguments, than of judgment, in discerning what is true; as if it were a praise to know what might be said, and not what should be thought. Some have certain commonplaces and themes wherein they are good, and want variety; which kind of poverty is for the most part tedious, and, when it is once perceived, ridiculous. The honourablest part of talk is to give the occasion; and again to moderate and pass to somewhat else; for then a man leads the dance. It is good in discourse, and speech of conversation, to vary, and intermingle speech of the present occasion with arguments, tales with reasons, asking of questions with telling of opinions, and jest with earnest; for it is a dull thing to tire, and, as we say now, to jade any thing too far. As for jest, there be certain things which ought to be privileged from it, namely, religion, matters of State, great persons, any man's present business of importance, and any case that deserveth pity; yet there be some that think their wits have been asleep, except they dart out somewhat that is piquant, and to the quick. That is a vein which would be bridled: *Parce, puer, stimulis, et fortius utere loris.*[1] And, generally, men ought to find the difference between saltness and bitterness. Certainly, he that hath a satirical vein, as he maketh others afraid of his wit, so he had need be afraid of others' memory. He that questioneth much shall learn much, and content much, but especially if he apply his questions to the skill of the persons whom he asketh ; for he shall give them occasion to please themselves in speaking, and himself shall continually gather knowledge : but let his questions not be troublesome, for that is fit for a poser ;[2] and let him be sure to leave other men their turns to speak : nay, if there be any that would reign and take up all the time, let him find means to take them off, and to bring others on, as musicians use to do with those that dance too long galliards.[3] If you dissemble sometimes your knowledge of that[4] you are thought to know, you shall be thought, another time, to know that you know not. Speech of a man's self ought to be seldom, and well chosen. I knew one was wont to say in scorn, " He must needs be a wise man, he speaks so much of himself : " and there is but one case wherein a man may commend himself with good grace, and that is in commending virtue in another, especially if it be such a virtue whereunto himself pretendeth. Speech of touch[5] toward others should be sparingly used ; for discourse ought to be as a field, without coming home to any man. I knew two noblemen, of the west part of England, whereof the one was given to scoff, but kept ever royal cheer in his house ; the other would ask of those that had been at the other's table, " Tell truly, was there never a flout or dry blow[6] given ? " To which the guest would answer, " Such and such a thing passed." The lord would say, " I thought he would mar a good dinner." Discretion of speech is more than eloquence ; and to speak agreeably[7] to him with whom we deal, is more than to speak in good words, or in good order. A good continued speech, without a good speech of interlocution, shows slowness ; and a good reply, or second speech, without a good settled speech, showeth shallowness and weakness. As we see in beasts, that those that are weakest in the course, are yet nimblest in the turn ; as it is betwixt the greyhound and the hare. To use too many circumstances,[8] ere one come to the matter, is wearisome ; to use none at all, is blunt.

OF RICHES.

I CANNOT call riches better than the baggage of virtue : the Roman word is better, *impedimenta ;* [1] for as the baggage is to an army, so is riches [2] to virtue ; it cannot be spared nor left behind, but it hindereth the march ; yea, and the care of it sometimes loseth or disturbeth [3] the victory.   Of great riches there is no real use, except it be in the distribution ; the rest is but conceit : [4] so saith Solomon, " Where much is, there are many to consume it ; and what hath the owner but the sight of it with his eyes ? " [5]   The personal fruition [6] in any man cannot reach [7] to feel great riches : there is a custody of them, or a power of dole [8] and donative [9] of them, or a fame of them, but no solid use to the owner.   Do you not see what feigned [10] prices are set upon little stones and rarities? and what works of ostentation are undertaken, because [11] there might seem to be some use of great riches?   But then you will say, they may be of use to buy men out of dangers or troubles ; as Solomon saith, " Riches are as a stronghold in the imagination of the rich man : " [12] but this is excellently expressed, that it is in imagination, and not always in fact ; for, certainly, great riches have sold more men than they have bought out.   Seek not proud [13] riches, but such as thou mayest get justly, use soberly, distribute cheerfully, and leave contentedly : yet have no abstract [14] nor friarly [15] contempt of them ; but distinguish, as Cicero [16] saith well of Rabirius Posthumus, [17] *In studio rei amplificandæ apparebat, non avaritiæ prædam, sed instrumentum bonitati quæri.* [18]   Hearken also to Solomon, and beware of hasty gathering of riches : *Qui festinat ad divitias, non erit insons.* [19]   The poets feign, that when Plutus [20] (which is riches) is sent from Jupiter, [21] he limps, and goes slowly ; but when he is sent from Pluto, [22] he runs, and is swift of foot ; meaning, that riches gotten by good means and just labour pace slowly ; but when they come by the death of others, (as by the course of inheritance, testaments, and the like,) they come tumbling upon a man : but it might be applied likewise to Pluto, taking him for the Devil ; for when riches come from the Devil, (as by fraud and oppression, and unjust means,) they come upon speed. [23]   The ways to enrich are many, and most of them foul : parsimony is one of the best, and yet is not innocent ; for it withholdeth men from works of liberality and charity.   The improvement of the ground is the most natural obtaining of riches, for it is our great mother's blessing, the Earth ; but it is slow ; and yet, where men of great wealth do stoop to husbandry, it multiplieth riches exceedingly.   I knew a nobleman in England that had the greatest audits [24] of any man in my time, — a great grazier, a great sheep-master, a great timberman, a great collier, a great corn-man, a great lead-man, and so of iron, and a number of the like points of husbandry; so as the earth seemed a sea to him in respect of the perpetual importation. It was truly observed by one, that himself [25] "came very hardly to a little riches, and very easily to great riches;" for when a man's stock is come to that, that he can expect the prime of markets,[26] and overcome [27] those bargains which for their greatness are few men's money, and be partner in the industries of younger men, he cannot but increase mainly.[28] The gains of ordinary trades and vocations are honest, and furthered by two things, chiefly, — by diligence, and by a good name for good and fair dealing; but the gains of bargains are of a more doubtful nature, when men shall wait upon others' necessity; broke [29] by servants and instruments to draw them [30] on; put off others cunningly that would be better chapmen,[31] and the like practices, which are crafty and naught: [32] as for the chopping [33] of bargains, when a man buys not to hold, but to sell over again, that commonly grindeth double, both upon the seller and upon the buyer. Sharings [34] do greatly enrich, if the hands be well chosen that are trusted. Usury [35] is the certainest means of gain, though one of the worst; as that whereby a man doth eat his bread, *in sudore vultùs alieni;* [36] and, besides, doth plough upon Sundays: but yet, certain though it be, it hath flaws; for that the scriveners [37] and brokers do value [38] unsound men to serve their own turn.[39] The fortune in being the first in an invention, or in a privilege, doth cause sometimes a wonderful overgrowth in riches, as it was with the first sugar-man [40] in the Canaries: [41] therefore, if a man can play the true logician, to have as well judgment as invention, he may do great matters, especially if the times be fit. He that resteth upon gains certain shall hardly grow to great riches: and he that puts all upon adventures doth oftentimes break and come to poverty: it is good, therefore, to guard adventures with certainties that may uphold losses. Monopolies, and coemption [42] of wares for re-sale, where they are not restrained, are great means to enrich; especially if the party have intelligence what things are like to come into request, and so store himself beforehand. Riches gotten by service, though it be of the best rise,[43] yet when they are gotten by flattery, feeding humours,[44] and other servile conditions, they may be placed amongst the worst. As for fishing for testaments and executorships, (as Tacitus saith of Seneca, *Testamenta et orbos tanquam indagine capi,*[45]) it is yet worse, by how much men submit themselves to meaner persons than in service.

Believe not much them that seem to despise riches, for they despise them that despair of them; and none worse [46] when they come to them. Be not penny-wise: [47] riches have wings, and sometimes they fly away of themselves, sometimes they must be set flying to bring in more. Men leave their riches either to their kindred or to the public; and moderate portions prosper best in both. A great state left to an heir is as a lure to all the birds of prey round about to seize on him, if he be not the better stablished in years and judgment: likewise, glorious [48] gifts and foundations are like sacrifices without salt; and but the painted sepulchres of alms, which soon will putrefy and corrupt inwardly. Therefore measure not thine advancements [49] by quantity, but frame them by measure: and defer not charities till death; for, certainly, if a man weigh it rightly, he that doth so is rather liberal of another man's than of his own.

OF STUDIES.

STUDIES serve for delight, for ornament, and for ability.[1] Their chief use for delight is in privateness and retiring;[2] for ornament, is in discourse; and for ability, is in the judgment and disposition[3] of business: for expert men can execute, and perhaps judge of particulars, one by one; but the general counsels, and the plots and marshalling[4] of affairs come best from those that are learned. To spend too much time in studies, is sloth; to use them too much for ornament, is affectation; to make judgment[5] wholly by their rules, is the humour[6] of a scholar: they perfect nature, and are perfected by experience: for natural abilities are like natural plants, that need pruning by study; and studies themselves do give forth directions too much at large, except they be bounded in by experience. Crafty[7] men contemn studies, simple men admire them, and wise men use them; for they teach not their own use; but that is a wisdom without them and above them, won by observation. Read not to contradict and confute, nor to believe and take for granted, nor to find talk and discourse, but to weigh and consider. Some books are to be tasted, others to be swallowed, and some few to be chewed and digested; that is, some books are to be read only in parts; others to be read, but not curiously;[8] and some few to be read wholly, and with diligence and attention. Some books also may be read by deputy, and extracts made of them by others; but that would be only in the less important arguments, and the meaner sort of books; else distilled books are, like common distilled waters, flashy[9] things. Reading maketh a full man, conference[10] a ready man, and writing an exact man; and therefore, if a man write little, he had need have a great memory; if he confer little, he had need have a present wit; and if he read little, he had need have much cunning, to seem to know that he doth not. Histories make men wise; poets witty;[11] the mathematics subtile; natural philosophy deep; moral, grave; logic and rhetoric, able to contend: *Abeunt studia in mores:*[12] nay, there is no stond[13] or impediment in the wit, but may be wrought out by fit studies: like as diseases of the body may have appropriate exercises,— bowling[14] is good for the stone and reins,[15] shooting[16] for the lungs and breast, gentle walking for the stomach, riding for the head and the like; — so, if a man's wit be wandering,[17] let him study the mathematics, for in demonstrations, if his wit be called away never so little, he must begin again; if his wit be not apt to distinguish or find differences, let him study the schoolmen,[18] for they are *Cymini sectores;*[19] if he be not apt to beat over[20] matters, and to call up one thing to prove and illustrate another, let him study the lawyers' cases: so every defect of the mind may have a special receipt.

NOTES TO BACON'S ESSAYS.

OF TRUTH.

1. See John xviii. 38. "Pilate saith unto him, What is truth?"

2. This was hardly the attitude of the Roman governor. "Any one of Bacon's acuteness, or a quarter of it," says Whately, "might easily have perceived, had he at all attended to the context of the narrative, that never was any one less in a *jesting* mood than Pilate on this occasion."

3. *That.* — The antecedent is omitted; insert *persons* or *people* after "be."

4. *Giddiness* = unsteadiness; want of certainty or of fixed beliefs.

5. *Affecting* = aiming at; from Lat. *ad*, to, and *facere*, to do, act.

6. *Philosophers of that kind.* — A reference probably to Pyrrho and Carneades. Pyrrho, a Greek philosopher of the third century B.C., maintained that certainty could not be attained in anything; hence he is known as the founder of scepticism. Carneades, a philosopher at Cyrene in Africa the second century B.C., held that all the knowledge the human mind is capable of attaining is not science but opinion.

7. *Discoursing* = discursive, rambling; from Lat. *dis*, apart, and *currere*, to run.

8. *Imposeth* = layeth restraints upon; from Lat. *in*, on, upon, and *ponere*, to place.

9. *At a stand* = perplexed.

10. Bacon does not make a distinction between *fiction* and *falsehood*. Poetry is opposed, not to truth, but to fact.

11. *Daintily* = elegantly.

12. *Price* = value. O. Fr. *pris*, Lat. *pretium*, price.

13. *Carbuncle* = a gem of a deep red color. Lat. *carbo*, a live coal.

14. *Fathers.* — This name is applied to the leading ecclesiastical writers of the first five or six centuries after Christ.

15. *Vinum dæmonum* = the wine of demons. This quotation is from Augustine, the greatest of the Latin fathers, who was born in Numidia in 354.

16. *Howsoever* = although.

17. *Creature* = created thing.

18. *Chaos* = the original unorganized condition of matter, out of which it was believed the universe was created.

19. *Sect* = the followers of Epicurus, a Greek philosopher of the fourth century B.C., who held that pleasure is the highest good. Though his life was blameless, his followers made his philosophy a cloak for luxury and licentiousness. The poet referred to is Lucretius, a Latin author of the first century B.C., whose poem *De Rerum Natura* is largely devoted to an exposition of the Epicurean philosophy.

20. *Adventures* = fortunes, chances.

21. *Commanded* = overlooked from some higher hill.

22. *So* = provided.

23. *Prospect* = view, survey. Lat. *pro*, before, and *specere*, to look.

24. *Round* = fair, candid, plain.

25. *Alloy* = a baser metal mixed with a finer. O. Fr. *à loi*, according to law, used with reference to the mixing of metals in coinage.

26. *Embaseth* = debaseth.

27. *Montaigne*, a celebrated French essayist of the sixteenth century. He died in 1592.

OF REVENGE.

1. Prov. xix. 11. "The discretion of a man deferreth his anger; and it is his glory to pass over a transgression."

2. *Irrevocable* = cannot be recalled. Lat. *ir* (for *in*), not, *re*, back, and *vocare*, to call.

3. Cosmo de Medici, born 1519, was chief of the Florentine republic. He "possessed the astuteness of character, the love of elegance, and taste for literature, but not the frank and generous spirit, that had distinguished his great ancestors."

4. *Desperate* = exceedingly severe.

5. *Neglecting* = negligent, neglectful.

6. Job ii. 10. The Authorized Version is slightly different.

7. *Public revenges* = punishments inflicted upon persons guilty of some crime against the state.

8. Julius Cæsar, the leading general, statesman, and orator (excepting Cicero) of his time, was assassinated in the year 44 B.C. Not one of his assassins, it is said, died a natural death.

9. Pertinax, born 126 A.D., was made emperor of Rome by the assassins of his predecessor, Commodus. After a reign of eighty-six days he was put to death by the soldiers, who objected to the reforms he proposed to introduce in the army.

10. Henry III. of France was assassinated in 1589 by Jacques Clement,

a fanatical Dominican friar, who was himself slain on the spot by the royal guard.

11. Witches were supposed to be women who had entered into a compact with the devil, by whose aid they were enabled to perform extraordinary feats, but into whose power they passed entirely at death. "So end they unfortunate."

OF ADVERSITY.

1. *Stoics* = followers of Zeno, who taught that men should be free from passion, unmoved by joy or grief, and submit without complaint to the unavoidable necessity by which all things seem to be governed.

2. *Transcendencies* = exaggerations.

3. *Mystery* = secret meaning.

4. Hercules, the most celebrated of the Grecian heroes, was the ideal of human perfection as conceived in the heroic age. With high qualities of mind he possessed extraordinary physical strength, which was shown in his "twelve labors." Among his other wonderful achievements he released Prometheus, who, for having stolen fire from heaven for mortals, had been chained by Jupiter's command to the rocks of Mount Caucasus.

5. *In a mean* = with moderation.

6. *Hearse-like airs* = funereal tunes.

7. *Incensed* = set on fire. Lat. *in*, in, upon, and *candere*, to burn, to glow.

OF MARRIAGE AND SINGLE LIFE.

1. *Impediments* = hindrances. Lat. *in*, and *pes*, *pedis*, foot. Frequently used, in the original, to denote *baggage*, especially of armies.

2. *Which* = who. *Which* was formerly used for persons as well as for things. "Our Father *which* art in heaven." Matt. vi. 9.

3. *Impertinences* = things irrelevant. This is the original sense. Lat. *in*, not, and *pertinere*, to pertain to.

4. *Charges* = cost, expense.

5. *Because* = in order that, on this account that. Cf. Matt. xx. 31. "And the multitude rebuked them, *because* they should hold their peace."

6. *Charge* = load or burden. Fr. *charge*, load, burden; Lat. *carrus*, car, wagon. Cf. *cargo* and *caricature*.

7. *Humorous* = governed by humor or caprice.

8. *Churchman* = an ecclesiastic or clergyman.

9. *Fill a pool* = bear the expenses of a family.

10. *Hortatives* = exhortations. Lat. *hortari*, to excite, exhort.

11. *Exhaust* = drained, exhausted. Lat. *ex*, out of, and *haurire*, to draw, the past part. being *exhaustum*.

12. "He preferred his aged wife to immortality." Ulysses was shipwrecked on the coast of Ogygia, the island home of the goddess Calypso. She detained him eight years, and proposed to confer immortality upon him. But with beautiful fidelity the Grecian hero preferred to return to his native Ithaca and his wife Penelope.

13. *So as =* so that. In Bacon *as* is frequently used in the sense of *that*.

14. *Quarrel =* cause, reason, excuse. Formerly a not infrequent meaning. O. Fr. *querele;* Lat. *querela*, a complaint, from *queri*, to complain.

OF GREAT PLACE.

1. *So as =* so that. See note 13 of the preceding Essay.

2. *Indignities =* basenesses, meannessess. Lat. *in*, not, and *dignus*, worthy.

3. "Since thou art no longer what thou wast, there is no reason why thou shouldst wish to live."

4. *Reason =* right, reasonable. O. Fr. *raison*, from Lat. *rationem*, reason.

5. *Shadow =* retirement.

6. *Puzzle =* perplexity.

7. "Death presses heavily upon him who, too well known to all others, dies unknown to himself."

8. *To will =* to be willing, to desire. Cf. John vii. 17. "If any man *will* do his will, he shall know of the doctrine, whether it be of God."

9. *To can =* to be able.

10. *Conscience =* consciousness. This is an old meaning. Lat. *con*, together with, and *scire*, to know.

11. *Theatre =* sphere or scheme of operation. An unusual and obsolete meaning.

12. "And God turned to behold the works which his hands had made, and he saw that everything was very good." Gen. i. 31.

13. *Globe =* body, circle.

14. *Bravery =* bravado. Used in this sense also by Milton and Shakespeare.

15. *De facto =* in fact.

16. *Voice =* announce, declare.

17. *Facility =* readiness of compliance, pliability.

18. *Steal it =* do it secretly. So in Shakespeare: "'Twere good, methinks, to *steal* our marriage."

19. *Inward =* intimate. So Job xix. 19. "All my *inward* friends abhorred me."

20. *Close =* hidden or secret.

21. *Respects* = considerations, motives

22. "One whom all would have considered fit for rule, if he had not ruled."

23. "Alone of all the emperors, Vespasian was changed for the better."

24. *To side* = to lean to one side.

OF SEEMING WISE.

1. 2 Tim. iii. 5.

2. *Sufficiency* = ability, full power. So 2 Cor. iii. 5. "Our sufficiency is of God."

3. "Trifles with great effort."

4. *Prospectives* = perspective glasses. They make things appear different from what they are.

5. *As* = that, as often in Bacon.

6. "With one brow raised to your forehead, the other bent downward to your chin, you answer that cruelty does not please you."

7. *To bear* = to gain or win.

8. *Impertinent* = irrelevant. — *Curious* = over-nice.

9. *Difference* = subtle distinction.

10. *Blanch* = avoid, evade.

11. "A foolish man who fritters away matters by trifling with words."

12. *Inward beggar* = a man secretly insolvent.

OF DISCOURSE.

1. "Boy, spare the spur, and hold the reins more lightly." Ovid.

2. *Poser* = a close examiner. Fr. *poser*, to put a question.

3. *Galliards* = a gay, lively dance, much in fashion in Bacon's time.

4. *That* = what, that which. Frequently so used. Cf. John iii. 11. "We speak *that* we do know."

5. *Speech of touch* = speech of particular application, personal hits.

6. *Dry blow* = sarcastic remark.

7. *Agreeably* = in a manner suited to.

8. *Circumstances* = unimportant particulars. Lat. *circum*, around, and *stare*, to stand.

OF RICHES.

1. *Impedimenta* = baggage, especially of an army. See notes on "Of Marriage and Single Life."

2. *Riches*. — This noun is really singular, though commonly used in the plural. Fr. *richesse*.

3. *Disturbeth* = interferes with. Lat. *dis*, apart, and *turbare*, to trouble; from *turba*, disorder, tumult.

4. *Conceit* = imagination, fancy.   O. Fr. *conceit*, pastpart. of *concevoir;* Lat. *conceptus*, from *con*, together, and *capere*, to take, hold.

5. Eccles. v. 11.   The language of the Authorized Version is somewhat different.

6. *Fruition* = enjoyment.   Coined as if from *fruitio*.   Lat. *frui*, to enjoy.

7. *Reach* = extend.

8. *Dole* = distribution.   A. S. *dael*, division; it is a doublet of deal. Cf. Ger. *theil*, part.

9. *Donative* = gift.   Lat. *donare*, to give.

10. *Feigned* = fictitious.

11. *Because* = in order that.   See note 5 on "Of Marriage and Single Life."

12. Prov. xviii. 11.   In the Authorized Version, "The rich man's wealth is his strong city."   Also Prov. x. 15.

13. *Proud* = giving reason or occasion for pride.

14. *Abstract* = withdrawn from the concrete; not considering the uses that may be made of wealth.   Lat. *abs*, from, and *trahere*, to draw.

15. *Friarly* = like a friar, one of whose vows was poverty.

16. *Cicero*, the greatest of Roman orators, was born 106 B.C., and murdered 43 B.C.

17. *Rabirius Posthumus*, a Roman knight, was accused by the Senate of having lent large sums of money to the king of Egypt for unlawful purposes. He was defended by Cicero and acquitted.

18. "In his desire to increase his wealth it was evident that he sought, not the gratification of avarice, but the means of doing good."

19. Prov. xxviii. 20: "He that maketh haste to be rich shall not be innocent."

20. *Plutus* = the god of riches.

21. *Jupiter* = the supreme deity of Roman mythology.

22. *Pluto* = the god of shades, or of the infernal regions, brother of Neptune and Jupiter.

23. *Upon speed* = in or with speed.

24. *Audits* = rent-roll or account of income.   Lat. *audire*, to hear.

25. *Himself* = he himself.

26. *Expect the prime of market* = wait for the best markets.   So in Heb. x. 13.   "*Expecting* till his enemies be made his footstool."

27. *Overcome* = come upon, take advantage of.

28. *Mainly* = greatly.

29. *Broke* = to transact business through a *broker* or middle man.   Here in the fut. tense with "shall" from the preceding clause understood.

30. *Them* = those pressed by necessity.

31. *Chapmen* = traders, merchants.   A. S. *ceap*, trade, and *mann*, man. Cf. Eng. *cheap*.

32. *Naught* = naughty, bad.

33. *Chopping* = bartering, exchanging.   *Chopping of bargains* means *speculating*.

34. *Sharings* = partnerships.

35. *Usury* = interest; now illegal or exorbitant interest, charged for the use of money.   Lat. *usura*, from *uti*, to use.

36. " In the sweat of another's brow."

37. *Scriveners* = scribes, persons who draw up contracts, especially in money matters.

38. *Value* = represented as financially sound.

39. *Turn* = convenience, purpose.

40. *Sugar-man* = planter of the sugar-cane.

41. *Canaries* = Canary Islands, off the north-west coast of Africa, noted in the early part of the sixteenth century for the production of sugar.

42. *Coemption* = the purchase of the whole quantity of any commodity. Lat. *co*, for *con*, together, and *emere*, to buy.

43. *Of the best rise* = of the best kind or most lucrative sort.

44. *Feeding humours* = indulging caprices or flattering whims.

45. " Wills and childless parents taken as with a net."

46. *None worse* = none are worse.

47. *Penny-wise* = niggardly when important interests are at stake.

48. *Glorious* = ostentatious.

49. *Advancements* = gifts of money or property.

OF STUDIES.

1. *Ability* = power to accomplish things.

2. *Privateness and retiring* = privacy and retirement.

3. *Disposition* = arrangement.   Lat. *dis*, apart, and *ponere*, to place.

4. *Plots and marshalling* = complicated plans and arranging in due order.

5. *To make judgment* = to judge.

6. *Humour* = practice or habit.

7. *Crafty* = expert, skilful, practical.

8. *Curiously* = carefully, attentively.   Lat. *cura*, care.

9. *Flashy* = transitorily bright; showy, but useless.

10. *Conference* = conversation, discussion.

11. *Witty* = inventive, brilliant.

12. " Studies pass into manners."

13. *Stond* = stop, hesitation.   An old form of *stand*.

14. *Bowling* = playing at bowls, a game corresponding to ten-pins.

15. *Stone and reins* = gravel and kidneys. The *gravel* is a disease produced by small calculous concretions in the kidneys and bladder.

16. *Shooting*, that is, with bow and arrow.

17. *Wandering* = hard to concentrate on a subject.

18. *Schoolmen* = the scholars of the Middle Ages, who applied the logic of Aristotle to theology.

19. *Cymini sectores* = splitters of cummin.

20. *To beat over* = to examine thoroughly.

WILLIAM SHAKESPEARE.

If Shakespeare had left an autobiography, we should esteem it one of our greatest literary treasures. If some Boswell had dogged his footsteps, noted carefully the incidents of his every-day life, and recorded the sentiments and thoughts that dropped spontaneously from his lips, how eagerly we should read the book to gain a clearer insight into the great master's soul. As it is, we are shut up to very meagre records, to names and dates found in business accounts or legal documents; and the greatest genius of all literature is concealed behind his works almost in the haze of a myth. We are dependent, not upon history, but upon fancy, to fill up the measure of what must have been an interesting, varied, and bountiful life.

William Shakespeare was born in Stratford-on-Avon, April 23, 1564. On his father's side, he was of Saxon lineage; on his mother's side, he was of Norman descent; and in his character the qualities of these two races — Saxon sturdiness and Norman versatility — were exquisitely harmonized. His father, John Shakespeare, was a glover, wool-dealer, and yeoman, who attained prominence in Stratford as an alderman and bailiff. He was a man of substantial qualities, and for many years lived in easy circumstances; but afterwards, when his son was passing into early manhood, he suffered a sad decline in fortune. William's mother, Mary Arden, was brought up on a landed estate; and besides inheriting from her the finer qualities of his mind, the future poet probably learned under her influence to appreciate the exceeding beauty of gentle and tender womanhood.

His education was received in the free school of Stratford,

and included, besides the elementary branches of English, the rudiments of classical learning — the "small Latin and less Greek" which Ben Jonson attributed to him. His acquisitive powers were extraordinary; and, as is evident from his works, this elementary training, which appears so inadequate, was afterwards increased by rich stores of learning and wisdom. He exhibits not only a wide general knowledge, but also a technical acquaintance with several callings, including law, medicine, and divinity.

In 1582, at the youthful age of eighteen, he married Ann Hathaway, who was eight years his senior. Whether the marriage was a matter of choice or, as some believe, a necessity forced upon him, does not clearly appear. His wife, the daughter of a substantial yeoman, was not unworthy of him; and the marriage was probably a love-match, which proudly disdained the disparity in years. It is assumed by many critics that the union was necessarily an unhappy one; but an examination of the evidence leads to a different conclusion. In his sonnets there are several loving passages that seem to refer to his wife; and as soon as he had acquired wealth in his theatrical career in the metropolis, he returned to Stratford to spend his last years in the bosom of his family.

Several years after his marriage, at the age of twenty-two, he went to London. There is a tradition that his departure from Stratford was the result of a deer-stealing escapade, for which he was sharply prosecuted by an irate landlord.. Though the poaching is probably not a myth, his departure may be satisfactorily explained on other grounds. Conscious no doubt of his native genius, it was but natural for him to seek his fortune amidst the opportunities afforded in a large city.

His poetic gifts and his acquaintance with the drama, as learned through visiting troupes in his native village, naturally drew him to the theatre. He held at first a subordinate position, and worked upwards by degrees. He recast plays and performed as an actor, for which his handsome and shapely form peculiarly fitted him. "The top of his performance," says an old historian, "was the Ghost in his own Hamlet." His progress was rapid, and at the end of six years he had achieved no small reputation. His success aroused the envy of some of his fellow playwrights; and Greene, in a scurrilous pamphlet, accused him of plagiarism, calling him "an upstart crow beautified with our feathers."

His ability attracted the attention of the court and the nobility. To the young Earl of Southampton he dedicated in 1593 his "Venus and Adonis," which the poet, in a short and manly dedicatory letter, styles "the first heir of my invention;" and in return he is said to have received from that nobleman the princely gift of a thousand pounds. In Spenser's "Colin Clout's Come Home Again," we find this reference to Shakespeare:—

> " And there, though last not least, is Aetion;
> A gentler shepherd may nowhere be found;
> Whose muse, full of high thought's invention,
> Doth, like himself, heroically sound."

His plays delighted Elizabeth, who was a steady patron of the drama; and there is a tradition that the queen was so pleased with Falstaff in "King Henry the Fourth," that she requested the poet to continue the character in another play and to portray him in love. The result was "The Merry Wives of Windsor."

Unlike many of his fellow dramatists, Shakespeare avoided a life of extravagance and dissipation. He showed that high literary genius is not inconsistent with business sagacity. Not content with being actor and author, he became a large shareholder in the Blackfriars and the Globe, the two leading theatres of his day. Wealth accumulated; and with an affectionate remembrance of his native town, he purchased in 1597 a handsome residence in Stratford. He continued to make judicious investments; and a careful estimate places his income in 1608 at about four hundred pounds a year — equivalent to $12,000 at the present time.

We have several pleasing glimpses of his social life in London. He had a reputation for civility and honesty; he frequented the Mermaid, where he met Ben Jonson and the other leading wits of his day. Beaumont probably had him in mind when he wrote: —

> " What things have we seen
> Done at the Mermaid! Heard words that have been
> So nimble, and so full of subtile flame,
> As if that every one from whence they came
> Had meant to put his whole wit in a jest,
> And had resolved to live a fool the rest
> Of his dull life."

The following testimony of the rough, upright Ben Jonson is of special value: " I loved the man, and do honor his memory, on this side idolatry, as much as any. He was indeed honest, and of an open and free nature ; had an excellent phantasy, brave notions, and gentle expressions."

With wealth and genius, it was not unnatural for the poet to desire a higher social rank. Accordingly, we find that in 1599, no doubt through his influence, a coat-of-arms was granted to his father. He grew tired of the actor's profession, chafing under its low social standing and its enslaving exactions upon his time and person. In one of his sonnets he writes, —

> " Alas ! 'tis true I have gone here and there,
> And made myself a motley to the view;
> Gor'd mine own thoughts, sold cheap what is most dear,
> Made old offences of affections new;
> Most time it is that I have looked on truth
> Askance and strangely."

It is probable that Shakespeare ceased to be an actor in 1604, though he continued to write for the stage, and produced all his greatest master-pieces after that date. About 1611 he retired to his native town to live in quiet domestic enjoyment. How great the contrast with the excitements, labors, and vanities of his career in London ! The last five years of his life were spent in domestic comforts, local interests, the entertainment of friends, the composition of one or two great dramas, with an occasional visit to the scene of his former struggles and triumphs. He died April 23, 1616, on the anniversary of his birth, and was buried in the parish church of Stratford. If we may credit tradition, he rose from a sick bed to entertain Jonson and Drayton, and the convivial excesses of the occasion brought on a fatal relapse. His tomb bears the following inscription, —

> " Good friend, for Jesus' sake forbear,
> To dig the dust enclosed here :
> Blest be the man that spares these stones,
> And curst be he that moves my bones."

Such are the principal but meagre facts in the outward life of this great man. Were this all we know of him, how incomplete and unsatisfactory our knowledge ! But there is another life besides the outward and visible one — a life of the soul. It is by the aims, thoughts, and feelings of this interior life that the character and greatness of a man are to be judged. Outward circumstances are, in a large measure, fortuitous ; at most they but aid or hinder the operations of the spirit within — plume or clip its wings. It is when we turn to this interior life of Shakespeare, and measure its creations and experiences, that we learn his unapproachable greatness. Many other authors have surpassed him in the variety and splendor of outward circumstances ; many warriors and statesmen and princes have been occupied with larger national interests ; but where is the man that can compare with him in the richness and extent of this life of the soul ?

There is no class of society, from kings to beggars, from queens to hags, with which he has not entered into the closest sympathy, thinking their thoughts and speaking their words. By his overpowering intuition, he comprehended, in all their extent, the various hopes, fears, desires, and passions of the human heart ; and, as occasion arose, he gave them the most perfect utterance they have ever found. Every age and country — early England, mediæval Italy, ancient Greece and Rome — were all seized in their essential features.

There were no thoughts too high for his strong intellect to grasp ; and the great world of nature, with its mysteries, its abounding beauty, its subtle harmonies, its deep moral teachings, he irradiated with the light of his genius. If, as a poet has said, "we live in thoughts, not years, in feelings, not in figures on the dial," how infinitely rich the quarter of a century Shakespeare spent in London ! In comparison with his all-embracing experience, the career of an Alexander, or Cæsar, or Napoleon, with its far-extending ambition and manifold interests, loses its towering greatness ; for the English poet lived more than they all.

It is a mistake to suppose that Shakespeare owed everything to nature, and that in his productions he was guided alone by instinct. This view was maintained by his earliest biographer, Rowe, who says, "Art had so little, and nature so large a share in what Shakespeare did, that for aught I know the performances of his youth were the best." An examination of his works in their chronological order shows that his genius underwent a process of development, and was perfected by study, knowledge, and experience. His earliest dramas, such as "Henry VI.," "Love's Labor's Lost," "Comedy of Errors," and "The Two Gentlemen of Verona," all of which were composed prior to 1591, are lacking in the freedom and perfection of his later works. They show the influence of the contemporary stage, and declamation often takes the place of genuine passion.

But after this apprentice work, the poet passed into the full possession of his powers, and produced, during what may be regarded the middle period of his literary career, an uninterrupted succession of master-pieces, among which may be mentioned "The Merchant of Venice," "A Midsummer Night's Dream," "Romeo and Juliet," "As You Like It," "Hamlet," and most of his English historical plays. All these appeared before 1600. With increasing age and experience, the poet passed on to profounder themes. It was during this final stage of his development that he gave "King Lear," "Macbeth," and "Othello" to the world, the two former in 1605, and the latter in 1609.

But in one particular his earlier and his later dramas are alike. The personality of the poet is concealed in them all. He enters into sympathy with all his creations, but he can be identified with none. He is greater than any one of them, or than all of them combined; for it is in him that they all originated and find their unity. Thus to create and project into the world a large number of independent beings is an evidence of the highest genius. Byron could not do it; for through all his works, whatever may be the names of his characters, we recognize the lawless, passionate, misanthropic poet himself. The same is true of Goethe and Victor Hugo, who embody in their works their didactic principles or their idealized experience. Among the world's great writers, Shakespeare and Homer almost alone are hidden behind their works like a mysterious presence.

Shakespeare possessed a profound knowledge of his art. This is obvious both from Hamlet's famous instruction to the players, and from the structure of his dramas. He has been criticised for discarding classic rules; but the censure is most unjust. Genius has an inalienable right to prescribe its own creative forms. He laid aside the hampering models of antiquity in order to give the world a new and richer dramatic form. The simple action of the ancient drama could not be adjusted to his great and complex themes. His works possess the one great essential characteristic—that of organic unity. After Shakespeare had completed his apprenticeship, his dramas embody an almost faultless structure; they are not pieces of elaborate and elegant patchwork, but of consistent and regular growth. We can but wonder at the range and power of that intellect which grasped a multitude of characters, brought them into contact, carried them through a great variety of incidents, portrayed with justice and splendor the profoundest feelings and thoughts, traced their reciprocal influence, and symmetrically conducted the whole to a striking and pre-determined conclusion.

It scarcely detracts from his greatness that, instead of inventing his themes and characters, he borrowed them from history and literature. His borrowing was not slavish and weak. Whatever materials he appropriated from others, he reshaped and glorified; and he is no more to be censured than is the sculptor who takes from the stone-cutter the rough marble that he afterwards transforms into a Venus de Medici or a Greek Slave. His works constitute a world in themselves; and with its inhabitants — with Hamlet, Othello, Macbeth, Portia, Shylock, and many others — we are as well acquainted as with the personages of history.

The poet exhibits an almost perfect acquaintance with human nature. His creations are not personified moral qualities or individualized passions, but real persons. They are beings of flesh and blood; but by their relations and reciprocal influence they are lifted above the dull and commonplace. Shakespeare removes the veil that hides from common vision the awful significance of human influence, and reveals it in its subtle workings and mighty results. He enables us to see, beneath a placid or rippling surface, the deep currents that move society.

As his mode of expression was always suited to his changing characters, he exemplified every quality of style in turn. His faculties and taste were so exquisitely adjusted, that his manner was always in keeping with his matter. He drew with equal facility on the Saxon and the Latin elements of our language, and attained with both the same incomparable results. He had a prodigious faculty for language, surpassing in copiousness every other English writer. The only term that adequately describes his manner of writing is *Shakespearian* — a term that comprehends a great deal. It includes vividness of imagination, depth of thought, delicacy of feeling, carefulness of observation, discernment of hidden relations, and whatever else may be necessary to clothe thought in expressions of supreme fitness and beauty.

Far above every other writer of ancient or modern times Shakespeare voices, in its manifold life, the human soul. This fact makes his works a storehouse of riches, to which we constantly turn. Are we oppressed at times with a morbid feeling of the emptiness of life? How perfectly Shakespeare voices our sentiment: —

> " Life's but a walking shadow, a poor player
> That struts and frets his hour upon the stage,
> And then is heard no more: it is a tale
> Told by an idiot, full of sound and fury,
> Signifying nothing."

Or again: —

> " We are such stuff
> As dreams are made of, and our little life
> Is rounded with a sleep."

If we recognize the fact that somehow there is a mysterious power controlling our lives, we are told

> " There's a divinity that shapes our ends,
> Rough-hew them how we will."

But, as our consciousness tells us, we are not wholly at the mercy of this overruling agency: —

> " Our remedies oft in ourselves do lie,
> Which we ascribe to heaven; the fated sky
> Gives us free scope, only doth backward push
> Our slow designs when we ourselves are dull."

What beautiful expression he gives to the trite observation that contentment is better than riches!

> " 'Tis better to be lowly born,
> And range with humble livers in content,
> Than to be perk'd up in glistering grief,
> And wear a golden sorrow."

What clear expression he gives to the indistinct feeling of beauty that sometimes comes to us in the presence of some object in nature! He surprises its secret, and embodies it in an imperishable word: —

" How sweet the moonlight *sleeps* upon this bank ! "

But why multiply illustrations, when they are found on almost every page of his works?

And what shall be said of Shakespeare's influence? He so entirely eclipsed his contemporary dramatists that their works are scarcely read. There are passages in his works that we could wish omitted — panderings to the corrupt taste of the time. But they are exceptional, and at heart the poet's sympathy, as in the case of every truly great man, is on the side of virtue. His writings, as a whole, carry with them the uplifting power of high thought, noble feeling, and worthy deeds.

Many of his thoughts and characters pass into the intellectual life of each succeeding generation. "Hamlet," "The Merchant of Venice," and "Romeo and Juliet," are read by nearly every young student ; and to have read any one of Shakespeare's master-pieces intelligently marks an epoch in the intellectual life of youth. But his dramas give pleasure not alone to the young. With minds enriched by experience and study, we turn, in the midst of active life, to his works for recreation and instruction. He but appears greater with our enlarged capacity to appreciate him. If he gathered about him a circle of cultivated friends and admirers in his life, he has shown himself still stronger in death. The circle has widened until it comprehends many lands.

He has exerted a noteworthy influence upon foreign literature, especially in Germany and France. Translated into the languages of these countries, his works have been extensively studied, admired, and imitated. He is lectured on in German universities, and some of his ablest critics have been German and French. He has stimulated a prodigious amount of intellectual activity; and his biographers, editors, translators, critics, and commentators are numbered by the hundred. No other English author has gathered about him such an array of scholarship and literary ability.

There is no abatement of interest in his works. Societies are organized for their systematic study, and periodicals are devoted to their illustration. There is no likelihood that he will ever be superseded; as he wrote in the proud presentiment of genius, —

> " Not marble, nor the gilded monuments
>   Of princes, shall outlive this powerful rhyme."

Future ages will turn to his works as a mirror of nature, and find in them the most perfect expression of their deepest and most precious experience. It is safe to say that his productions are as imperishable as the English language or the English race.

THE MERCHANT OF VENICE.

DRAMATIS PERSONÆ.

THE DUKE OF VENICE.
THE PRINCE OF MOROCCO, ⎫ suitors to
THE PRINCE OF ARRAGON, ⎭ Portia.
ANTONIO, a merchant of Venice.
BASSANIO, his kinsman, suitor likewise to
    Portia.
SALARINO, ⎫
SALANIO,   ⎬ friends to Antonio and
GRATIANO, ⎪   Bassanio.
SALERIO,   ⎭
LORENZO, in love with Jessica.
SHYLOCK, a rich Jew.
TUBAL, a Jew, his friend.
LAUNCELOT GOBBO, the clown, servant to
    Shylock.

OLD GOBBO, father to Launcelot.
LEONARDO, servant to Bassanio.
BALTHASAR, ⎫ servants to Portia.
STEPHANO, ⎭

PORTIA, a rich heiress.
NERISSA, her waiting-maid.
JESSICA, daughter to Shylock.

  Magnificoes of Venice, Officers of the Court
    of Justice, Gaoler, Servants to Portia,
    and other Attendants.

SCENE: *Partly at Venice, and partly at
    Belmont, the seat of Portia, on the
    Continent.*

ACT I.

SCENE I. *Venice. A street.*

Enter ANTONIO, SALARINO, *and* SALANIO.

ANTONIO. In sooth,[1] I know not why I am so sad :
It wearies me ; you say it wearies you ;
But how I caught it, found it, or came by it,
What stuff 'tis made of, whereof it is born,
I am to learn ;
And such a want-wit[2] sadness makes of me
That I have much ado[3] to know myself.

    SALARINO. Your mind is tossing on the ocean ;
There, where your argosies[4] with portly sail,
Like signiors[5] and rich burghers on the flood,
Or, as it were, the pageants[6] of the sea,
Do overpeer[7] the petty traffickers,
That curtsy to them, do them reverence,
As they fly by them with their woven wings.

    SALANIO. Believe me, sir, had I such venture[8] forth,
The better part of my affections would
Be with my hopes abroad. I should be still[9]
Plucking the grass, to know where sits the wind,

Peering in maps for ports and piers and roads; [10]
And every object that might make me fear
Misfortune to my ventures out of doubt
Would make me sad.

    SALARINO.   My wind cooling my broth
Would blow me to an ague, when I thought
What harm a wind too great at sea might do.
I should not see the sandy hour-glass run,
But I should think of shallows and of flats,
And see my wealthy Andrew dock'd in sand, [11]
Vailing [12] her high-top lower than her ribs
To kiss her burial.   Should I go to church
And see the holy edifice of stone,
And not bethink me straight [13] of dangerous rocks,
Which touching but my gentle vessel's side,
Would scatter all her spices on the stream,
Enrobe the roaring waters with my silks,
And, in a word, but even now worth this, [14]
And now worth nothing?   Shall I have the thought
To think on this, and shall I lack the thought
That such a thing bechanc'd would make me sad?
But tell not me; I know, Antonio
Is sad to think upon his merchandise.

    ANTONIO.   Believe me, no: I thank my fortune for it,
My ventures are not in one bottom [15] trusted,
Nor to one place; nor is my whole estate
Upon the fortune of this present year:
Therefore my merchandise makes me not sad.

    SALARINO.   Why, then you are in love.

    ANTONIO.   Fie, fie!

    SALARINO.   Not in love neither?   Then let us say you are sad,
Because you are not merry: and 'twere as easy
For you to laugh and leap and say you are merry,
Because you are not sad.   Now, by two-headed Janus, [16]
Nature hath framed strange fellows in her time:
Some that will evermore peep through their eyes [17]
And laugh like parrots at a bag-piper,
And other [18] of such vinegar aspect
That they'll not show their teeth in way of smile,
Though Nestor [19] swear the jest be laughable.

Enter BASSANIO, LORENZO, *and* GRATIANO.

SALANIO.   Here comes Bassanio, your most noble kinsman,
Gratiano and Lorenzo.   Fare ye well:
We leave you now with better company.

SALARINO.   I would have stay'd till I had made you merry,
If worthier friends had not prevented [20] me.

ANTONIO.   Your worth is very dear in my regard.
I take it, your own business calls on you
And you embrace the occasion to depart.

SALARINO.   Good morrow, my good lords.

BASSANIO.   Good signiors both, when shall we laugh? say, when?
You grow exceeding strange: [21] must it be so?

SALARINO.   We'll make our leisures to attend on yours.

                              [*Exeunt* SALARINO *and* SALANIO.

LORENZO.   My Lord Bassanio, since you have found Antonio,
We two will leave you: but at dinner-time,
I pray you, have in mind where we must meet.

BASSANIO.   I will not fail you.

GRATIANO.   You look not well, Signior Antonio;
You have too much respect upon [22] the world:
They lose it that do buy it with much care:
Believe me, you are marvellously changed.

ANTONIO.   I hold the world but as the world, Gratiano:
A stage where every man must play a part,
And mine a sad one.

GRATIANO.   Let me play the fool: [23]
With mirth and laughter let old wrinkles come,
And let my liver rather heat with wine
Than my heart cool with mortifying groans.
Why should a man, whose blood is warm within,
Sit like his grandsire cut in alabaster?
Sleep when he wakes and creep into the jaundice
By being peevish?   I tell thee what, Antonio —
I love thee, and it is my love that speaks —
There are a sort of men whose visages
Do cream and mantle [24] like a standing pond,
And do [25] a wilful stillness entertain,
With purpose to be dress'd in an opinion [26]
Of wisdom, gravity, profound conceit, [27]

As who should say [28] " I am Sir Oracle,
And when I ope my lips let no dog bark !"
O my Antonio, I do know of these
That therefore only are reputed wise
For saying nothing, who, I am very sure,
If they should speak, would almost damn those ears
Which, hearing them, would call their brothers fools.[29]
I'll tell thee more of this another time :
But fish not, with this melancholy bait,
For this fool gudgeon,[30] this opinion.
Come, good Lorenzo.   Fare ye well awhile :
I'll end my exhortation after dinner.

LORENZO.   Well, we will leave you then till dinner-time :
I must be one of these same dumb wise men,
For Gratiano never lets me speak.

GRATIANO.   Well, keep me company but two years moe,[31]
Thou shalt not know the sound of thine own tongue.

ANTONIO.   Farewell : I'll grow a talker for this gear.[32]

GRATIANO.   Thanks, i' faith, for silence is only commendable
In a neat's tongue dried.   [*Exeunt* GRATIANO *and* LORENZO.

ANTONIO.   Is that any thing now?

BASSANIO.   Gratiano speaks an infinite deal of nothing, more
than any man in all Venice.   His reasons are as two grains of
wheat hid in two bushels of chaff : you shall seek all day ere you
find them, and when you have them, they are not worth the
search.

ANTONIO.   Well, tell me now what lady is the same
To whom you swore a secret pilgrimage,
That you to-day promised to tell me of?

BASSANIO.   'Tis not unknown to you, Antonio,
How much I have disabled mine estate,
By something [33] showing a more swelling port [34]
Than my faint means would grant continuance :
Nor do I now make moan to be abridged
From such a noble rate ; [35] but my chief care
Is to come fairly off from the great debts
Wherein my time something too prodigal
Hath left me gag'd.[36]   To you, Antonio,
I owe the most, in money and in love,
And from your love I have a warranty

To unburden all my plots and purposes
How to get clear of all the debts I owe.

    ANTONIO.   I pray you, good Bassanio, let me know it;
And if it stand, as you yourself still [37] do,
Within the eye of honour,[38] be assured,
My purse, my person, my extremest means,
Lie all unlock'd to your occasions.

    BASSANIO.   In my school-days, when I had lost one shaft
I shot his fellow of the self-same flight [39]
The self-same way, with more advised [40] watch,
To find the other forth,[41] and by adventuring both
I oft found both: I urge this childhood proof,[42]
Because what follows is pure innocence.
I owe you much, and like a wilful [43] youth,
That which I owe is lost; but if you please
To shoot another arrow that self way [44]
Which you did shoot the first, I do not doubt,
As I will watch the aim, or to find both
Or bring your latter hazard back again
And thankfully rest debtor for the first.

    ANTONIO.   You know me well, and herein spend but time
To wind about my love with circumstance; [45]
And out of doubt you do me now more wrong
In making question of my uttermost [46]
Than if you had made waste of all I have:
Then do but say to me what I should do
That in your knowledge may by me be done,
And I am prest [47] unto it: therefore speak.

    BASSANIO.   In Belmont is a lady richly left; [48]
And she is fair and, fairer than that word,
Of wondrous virtues: sometimes [49] from her eyes
I did receive fair speechless messages:
Her name is Portia, nothing undervalued [50]
To Cato's daughter, Brutus' Portia: [51]
Nor is the wide world ignorant of her worth,
For the four winds blow in from every coast
Renowned suitors, and her sunny locks
Hang on her temples like a golden fleece;
Which makes her seat of Belmont Colchos' strand,[52]
And many Jasons come in quest of her.

O my Antonio, had I but the means
To hold a rival place with one of them,[53]
I have a mind presages me such thrift,[54]
That I should questionless be fortunate !

ANTONIO. Thou know'st that all my fortunes are at sea ;
Neither have I money nor commodity [55]
To raise a present sum : therefore go forth ;
Try what my credit can in Venice do ;
That shall be rack'd, even to the uttermost,
To furnish thee to Belmont, to fair Portia.
Go, presently [56] inquire, and so will I,
Where money is, and I no question make
To have it of my trust or for my sake.[57]   [*Exeunt.*

SCENE II. *Belmont. A room in* PORTIA'S *house.*

Enter PORTIA *and* NERISSA.

PORTIA. By my troth,[1] Nerissa, my little body is aweary of this great world.

NERISSA. You would be, sweet madam, if your miseries were in the same abundance as your good fortunes are : and yet, for aught I see, they are as sick that surfeit with too much as they that starve with nothing. It is no mean happiness therefore, to be seated in the mean : superfluity comes sooner by white hairs, but competency lives longer.

PORTIA. Good sentences and well pronounced.

NERISSA. They would be better, if well followed.

PORTIA. If to do were as easy as to know what were good to do, chapels had been churches and poor men's cottages princes' palaces. It is a good divine that follows his own instructions : I can easier teach twenty what were good to be done, than be one of the twenty to follow mine own teaching. The brain may devise laws for the blood, but a hot temper leaps o'er a cold decree : such a hare is madness the youth, to skip o'er the meshes of good counsel the cripple. But this reasoning is not in the fashion to choose me a husband. O me, the word " choose !" I may neither choose whom I would nor refuse whom I dislike ; so is the will of a living daughter curbed by the will of a dead father. Is it not hard, Nerissa, that I cannot choose one nor refuse none ?[2]

NERISSA. Your father was ever virtuous : and holy men at their death have good inspirations: therefore the lottery, that he hath devised in these three chests of gold, silver and lead, whereof who chooses his meaning chooses you, will, no doubt, never be chosen by any rightly but one who shall rightly love. But what warmth is there in your affection towards any of these princely suitors that are already come?

PORTIA. I pray thee, over-name them; and as thou namest them, I will describe them; and, according to my description, level at [3] my affection.

NERISSA. First, there is the Neapolitan prince.

PORTIA. Ay, that's a colt [4] indeed, for he doth nothing but talk of his horse; and he makes it a great appropriation [5] to his own good parts, that he can shoe him himself.

NERISSA. Then there is the County Palatine. [6]

PORTIA. He doth nothing but frown, as who should say " If you will not have me, choose:" he hears merry tales and smiles not: I fear he will prove the weeping philosopher [7] when he grows old, being so full of unmannerly sadness in his youth. I had rather be married to a death's head with a bone in his mouth than to either of these. God defend me from these two!

NERISSA. How say you by [8] the French lord, Monsieur Le Bon?

PORTIA. God made him, and therefore let him pass for a man. In truth, I know it is a sin to be a mocker: but, he! why, he hath a horse better than the Neapolitan's, a better bad habit of frowning than the Count Palatine; he is every man in no man; if a throstle sing, he falls straight a capering; he will fence with his own shadow: if I should marry him, I should marry twenty husbands. If he would despise me, I would forgive him, for if he love me to madness, I shall never requite him.

NERISSA. What say you then to Falconbridge, the young baron of England?

PORTIA. You know I say nothing to [9] him, for he understands not me, nor I him: he hath neither Latin, French, nor Italian, and you will come into the court and swear that I have a poor pennyworth in the English. He is a proper [10] man's picture, but, alas, who can converse with a dumbshow? How oddly he is suited! [11] I think he bought his doublet [12] in Italy, his round hose [13] in France, his bonnet [14] in Germany, and his behaviour everywhere.

NERISSA. What think you of the Scottish lord, his neighbour?

PORTIA. That he hath a neighbourly charity in him, for he borrowed a box of the ear of the Englishman, and swore he would pay him again when he was able : I think the Frenchman became his surety and sealed under [15] for another.

NERISSA.   How like you the young German, the Duke of Saxony's nephew?

PORTIA.   Very vilely in the morning, when he is sober, and most vilely in the afternoon, when he is drunk : when he is best he is a little worse than a man, and when he is worst, he is little better than a beast : an [16] the worst fall that ever fell, I hope I shall make shift to go without him.

NERISSA.   If he should offer to choose, and choose the right casket, you should [17] refuse to perform your father's will, if you should refuse to accept him.

PORTIA.   Therefore, for fear of the worst, I pray thee, set a deep glass of Rhenish wine on the contrary [18] casket, for if the devil be within and that temptation without, I know he will choose it.   I will do any thing, Nerissa, ere I'll be married to a sponge.

NERISSA.   You need not fear, lady, the having any of these lords : they have acquainted me with their determinations ; which is indeed to return to their home and to trouble you with no more suit, unless you may be won by some other sort [19] than your father's imposition [20] depending on the caskets.

PORTIA.   If I live to be as old as Sibylla, [21] I will die as chaste as Diana, unless I be obtained by the manner of my father's will.   I am glad this parcel of wooers are so reasonable, for there is not one among them but I dote on his very absence, and I pray God grant them a fair departure.

NERISSA.   Do you not remember, lady, in your father's time, a Venetian, a scholar and a soldier, that came hither in company of the Marquis of Montferrat?

PORTIA.   Yes, yes, it was Bassanio ; as I think, he was so called.

NERISSA.   True, madam : he, of all the men that ever my foolish eyes looked upon, was the best deserving a fair lady.

PORTIA.   I remember him well, and I remember him worthy of thy praise.

Enter a Serving-man.

How now ! what news?

SERVANT.   The four [22] strangers seek for you, madam, to take their leave : and there is a forerunner come from a fifth, the Prince of Morocco, who brings word the prince his master will be here to-night.

PORTIA. If I could bid the fifth welcome with so good a heart as I can bid the other four farewell, I should be glad of his approach : if he have the condition [23] of a saint and the complexion of a devil, I had rather he should shrive [24] me than wive me.

Come, Nerissa. Sirrah, go before.

Whiles we shut the gates upon one wooer, another knocks at the door.

[*Exeunt.*

SCENE III. *Venice. A public place.*

Enter BASSANIO *and* SHYLOCK.

SHYLOCK. Three thousand ducats ; [1] well.

BASSANIO. Ay, sir, for three months.

SHYLOCK. For three months ; well.

BASSANIO. For the which, as I told you, Antonio shall be bound.

SHYLOCK. Antonio shall become bound ; well.

BASSANIO. May you stead [2] me? will you pleasure me? shall I know your answer?

SHYLOCK. Three thousand ducats, for three months, and Antonio bound.

BASSANIO. Your answer to that.

SHYLOCK. Antonio is a good man. [3]

BASSANIO. Have you heard any imputation to the contrary?

SHYLOCK. Oh, no, no, no, no : my meaning in saying he is a good man is to have you understand me that he is sufficient. Yet his means are in supposition : [4] he hath an argosy bound to Tripolis, another to the Indies ; I understand, moreover, upon the Rialto, [5] he hath a third at Mexico, a fourth for England, and other ventures he hath, squandered [6] abroad. But ships are but boards, sailors but men : there be land-rats and water-rats, water-thieves and land-thieves, I mean pirates, and then there is the peril of waters, winds and rocks. The man is, notwithstanding, sufficient. Three thousand ducats ; I think I may take his bond.

BASSANIO. Be assured you may.

SHYLOCK. I will be assured I may ; and, that I may be assured, I will bethink me. May I speak with Antonio?

BASSANIO. If it please you to dine with us.

SHYLOCK. Yes, to smell pork ; to eat of the habitation which your prophet the Nazarite conjured the devil into. [7] I will buy with you, sell with you, talk with you, walk with you, and so following, but I

will not eat with you, drink with you, nor pray with you.   What news
on the Rialto ?   Who is he comes here ?

Enter ANTONIO.

BASSANIO.   This is Signior Antonio.

SHYLOCK.   [*Aside*] How like a fawning publican he looks !
I hate him for he is a Christian,
But more for that in low simplicity
He lends out money gratis and brings down
The rate of usance [8] here with us in Venice.
If I can catch him once upon the hip,[9]
I will feed fat the ancient grudge I bear him.
He hates our sacred nation, and he rails,
Even there where merchants most do congregate,
On me, my bargains and my well-won thrift,
Which he calls interest.[10]   Cursed be my tribe,
If I forgive him.

BASSANIO.   Shylock, do you hear ?

SHYLOCK.   I am debating of my present store,
And, by the near guess of my memory,
I cannot instantly raise up the gross
Of full three thousand ducats.   What of that ?
Tubal, a wealthy Hebrew of my tribe,
Will furnish me.   But soft ! how many months
Do you desire ?   [*To* ANTONIO.]   Rest you fair,[11] good signior ;
Your worship was the last man in our mouths.

ANTONIO.   Shylock, although I neither lend nor borrow
By taking nor by giving of excess,[12]
Yet to supply the ripe wants [13] of my friend,
I'll break a custom.   Is he yet possess'd [14]
How much ye would?

SHYLOCK.   Ay, ay, three thousand ducats.

ANTONIO.   And for three months.

SHYLOCK.   I had forgot ; three months ; you told me so.
Well then, your bond ; and let me see ; but hear you ;
Methought [15] you said you neither lend nor borrow
Upon advantage.

ANTONIO.   I do never use it.

SHYLOCK.   When Jacob grazed his uncle Laban's sheep —
This Jacob from our holy Abram was,

As his wise mother wrought in his behalf,
The third possessor; ay, he was the third [16] —

    ANTONIO.   And what of him? did he take interest?

    SHYLOCK.   No, not take interest, not, as you would say,
Directly interest: mark what Jacob did
When Laban and himself were compromised [17]
That all the eanlings [18] which were streak'd and pied
Should fall as Jacob's hire. [19]
This was a way to thrive, and he was blest:
And thrift is blessing, if men steal it not.

    ANTONIO.   This was a venture, sir, that Jacob served for;
A thing not in his power to bring to pass,
But sway'd and fashion'd by the hand of heaven.
Was this inserted [20] to make interest good?
Or is your gold and silver ewes and rams?

    SHYLOCK,   I cannot tell; I make it breed as fast:
But note me, signior.

    ANTONIO.   Mark you this, Bassanio, [21]
The devil can cite Scripture for his purpose.
An evil soul producing holy witness
Is like a villain with a smiling cheek,
A goodly apple rotten at the heart;
O, what a goodly outside falsehood hath!

    SHYLOCK.   Three thousand ducats; 'tis a good round sum.
Three months from twelve; then, let me see; the rate —

    ANTONIO.   Well, Shylock, shall we be beholding [22] to you?

    SHYLOCK.   Signior Antonio, many a time and oft
In the Rialto you have rated me
About my moneys and my usances:
Still have I borne it with a patient shrug,
For sufferance is the badge of all our tribe.
You call me misbeliever, cut-throat dog,
And spit upon my Jewish gaberdine, [23]
And all for use of that which is mine own.
Well then, it now appears you need my help:
Go to, [24] then; you come to me, and you say,
" Shylock, we would have moneys: " you say so;
You, that did void your rheum upon my beard
And foot me as you spurn a stranger cur
Over your threshold: moneys is your suit.

What should I say to you?   Should I not say
" Hath a dog money? is it possible
A cur can lend three thousand ducats?"   Or
Shall I bend low and in a bondman's key,
With bated breath and whispering humbleness,
Say this ;
" Fair sir, you spit on me on Wednesday last ;
You spurn'd me such a day ; another time
You call'd me dog ; and for these courtesies
I'll lend you thus much moneys?"

ANTONIO.   I am as like to call thee so again,
To spit on thee again, to spurn thee too.
If thou wilt lend this money, lend it not
As to thy friends ; for when did friendship take
A breed [25] for barren metal of his friend?
But lend it rather to thine enemy,
Who [26] if he break, thou mayst with better face
Exact the penalty.

SHYLOCK.   Why, look you, how you storm!
I would be friends with you and have your love,
Forget the shames that you have stain'd me with,
Supply your present wants and take no doit [27]
Of usance for my moneys, and you'll not hear me :
This is kind I offer.

BASSANIO.   This were kindness.

SHYLOCK.   This kindness will I show.
Go with me to a notary, seal me there
Your single bond ; and, in a merry sport,
If you repay me not on such a day,
In such a place, such sum or sums as are
Express'd in the condition, [28] let the forfeit
Be nominated for an equal [29] pound
Of your fair flesh, to be cut off and taken
In what part of your body pleaseth me.

ANTONIO.   Content, i' faith : I'll seal to such a bond
And say there is much kindness in the Jew.

BASSANIO.   You shall not seal to such a bond for me :
I'll rather dwell [30] in my necessity.

ANTONIO.   Why, fear not, man ; I will not forfeit it :
Within these two months, that's a month before

This bond expires, I do expect return
Of thrice three times the value of this bond.

    SHYLOCK.   O father Abram, what these Christians are,
Whose own hard dealings teaches [31] them suspect
The thoughts of others! Pray you, tell me this;
If he should break his day, [32] what should I gain
By the exaction of the forfeiture?
A pound of man's flesh taken from a man
Is not so estimable, profitable neither,
As flesh of muttons, beefs, or goats. I say,
To buy his favour, I extend this friendship:
If he will take it, so; if not, adieu;
And, for my love, I pray you wrong me not.

    ANTONIO.   Yes, Shylock, I will seal unto this bond.

    SHYLOCK.   Then meet me forthwith at the notary's;
Give him direction for this merry bond,
And I will go and purse the ducats straight,
See to my house, left in the fearful guard [33]
Of an unthrifty knave, and presently
I will be with you.

    ANTONIO.   Hie [34] thee, gentle Jew.   [*Exit* SHYLOCK.
The Hebrew will turn Christian: he grows kind.

    BASSANIO.   I like not fair terms and a villain's mind.

    ANTONIO.   Come on: in this there can be no dismay;
My ships come home a month before the day.   [*Exeunt.*

ACT II.

SCENE I. *Belmont. A room in* PORTIA'S *house.*

Flourish of Cornets. Enter the PRINCE OF MOROCCO *and his train*;
    PORTIA, NERISSA, *and others attending.*

    MOROCCO.   Mislike [1] me not for my complexion,
The shadow'd livery of the burnish'd sun,
To whom I am a neighbour and near bred.
Bring me the fairest creature northward born,
Where Phœbus' fire scarce thaws the icicles,
And let us make incision for your love,
To prove whose blood is reddest, [2] his or mine.

I tell thee, lady, this aspect of mine
Hath fear'd [3] the valiant: by my love, I swear
The best-regarded [4] virgins of our clime
Have loved it too: I would not change this hue,
Except to steal your thoughts, my gentle queen.

    PORTIA.   In terms of choice I am not solely led
By nice [5] direction of a maiden's eyes;
Besides, the lottery of my destiny
Bars me the right of voluntary choosing:
But if my father had not scanted [6] me,
And hedged me by his wit, [7] to yield myself
His wife who wins me by that means I told you,
Yourself, renowned prince, then stood [8] as fair
As any comer I have look'd on yet
For my affection.

    MOROCCO.   Even for that I thank you:
Therefore, I pray you, lead me to the caskets
To try my fortune. By this scimitar,
That slew the Sophy [9] and a Persian prince
That won three fields of Sultan Solyman,[10]
I would outstare the sternest eyes that look,
Outbrave the heart most daring on the earth,
Pluck the young sucking cubs from the she-bear,
Yea, mock the lion when he roars for prey,
To win thee, lady. But, alas the while!
If Hercules and Lichas [11] play at dice
Which is the better man, the greater throw
May turn by fortune from the weaker hand:
So is Alcides [12] beaten by his page;
And so may I, blind fortune leading me,
Miss that which one unworthier may attain,
And die with grieving.

    PORTIA.   You must take your chance,
And either not attempt to choose at all
Or swear, before you choose, if you choose wrong
Never to speak to lady afterward
In way of marriage: therefore be advised.[13]

    MOROCCO.   Nor will not. Come, bring me unto my chance.

    PORTIA.   First, forward to the temple: [14] after dinner
Your hazard shall be made.

MOROCCO.   Good fortune then !
To make me blest or cursed'st among men.   [*Cornets, and exeunt.*

SCENE II.   *Venice.   A street.*

Enter LAUNCELOT.

LAUNCELOT.   Certainly my conscience will serve me to run from this Jew my master.   The fiend is at mine elbow and tempts me, saying to me " Gobbo, Launcelot Gobbo, good Launcelot," or " good Gobbo," or " good Launcelot Gobbo, use your legs, take the start, run away."   My conscience says " No ; take heed, honest Launcelot ; take heed, honest Gobbo," or, as aforesaid, " honest Launcelot Gobbo ; do not run ; scorn running with thy heels."   Well, the most courageous fiend bids me pack : " Via ! " [1] says the fiend ; " away ! " says the fiend ; " for the heavens, [2] rouse up a brave mind," says the fiend, " and run."   Well, my conscience, hanging about the neck of my heart, says very wisely to me, " My honest friend Launcelot, being an honest man's son," or rather an honest woman's son ; for indeed my father did something smack, something grow to, [3] he had a kind of taste ; well, my conscience says, " Launcelot, budge not."   " Budge," says the fiend.   " Budge not," says my conscience.   " Conscience," say I, " you counsel well ; "   " Fiend," say I, " you counsel well : " to be ruled by my conscience, I should stay with the Jew my master, who, God bless the mark, [4] is a kind of devil ; and, to run away from the Jew, I should be ruled by the fiend, who, saving your reverence, is the devil himself.   Certainly the Jew is the very devil incarnal ; [5] and, in my conscience, my conscience is but a kind of hard conscience, to offer to counsel me to stay with the Jew.   The fiend gives the more friendly counsel : I will run, fiend ; my heels are at your command ; I will run.

Enter OLD GOBBO, *with a basket.*

GOBBO.   Master young man, you, I pray you, which is the way to master Jew's ?

LAUNCELOT. [*Aside*]   O heavens, this is my true-begotten father ! who, being more than sand-blind, [6] high-gravel-blind, knows me not : I will try confusions [7] with him.

GOBBO.   Master young gentleman, I pray you, which is the way to master Jew's ?

LAUNCELOT.   Turn up on your right hand at the next turning, but, at the next turning of all, on your left ; marry, [8] at the very next turning, turn of no hand, but turn down indirectly to the Jew's house.

GOBBO.   By God's sonties,[9] 'twill be a hard way to hit.   Can you tell me whether one Launcelot, that dwells with him, dwell with him or no?

LAUNCELOT.   Talk you of young Master Launcelot?   [*Aside*] Mark me now; now will I raise the waters.[10] — Talk you of young Master Launcelot?

GOBBO.   No master,[11] sir, but a poor man's son: his father, though I say it, is an honest exceeding poor man and, God be thanked, well to live.

LAUNCELOT.   Well, let his father be what a' will,[12] we talk of young Master Launcelot.

GOBBO.   Your worship's friend and Launcelot, sir.

LAUNCELOT.   But I pray you, ergo,[13] old man, ergo, I beseech you, talk you of young Master Launcelot?

GOBBO.   Of Launcelot, an't [14] please your mastership.

LAUNCELOT.   Ergo, Master Launcelot.   Talk not of Master Launcelot, father;[15] for the young gentleman, according to Fates and Destinies and such odd sayings, the Sisters Three and such branches of learning, is indeed deceased, or, as you would say in plain terms, gone to heaven.

GOBBO.   Marry, God forbid ! the boy was the very staff of my age, my very prop.

LAUNCELOT.   Do I look like a cudgel or a hovel-post,[16] a staff or a prop?   Do you know me, father ?

GOBBO.   Alack the day, I know you not, young gentleman: but, I pray you, tell me, is my boy, God rest his soul, alive or dead ?

LAUNCELOT.   Do you not know me, father ?

GOBBO.   Alack, sir, I am sand-blind; I know you not.

LAUNCELOT.   Nay, indeed, if you had your eyes, you might fail of the knowing me: it is a wise father that knows his own child.   Well, old man, I will tell you news of your son: give me your blessing: truth will come to light; murder cannot be hid long; a man's son may, but at the length truth will out.

GOBBO.   Pray you, sir, stand up:[17] I am sure you are not Launcelot, my boy.

LAUNCELOT.   Pray you, let's have no more fooling about it, but give me your blessing: I am Launcelot, your boy that was, your son that is, your child that shall be.

GOBBO.   I cannot think you are my son.

LAUNCELOT.   I know not what I shall think of that: but I am Launcelot, the Jew's man, and I am sure Margery your wife is my mother.

GOBBO.   Her name is Margery, indeed: I'll be sworn, if thou be Launcelot, thou art mine own flesh and blood.   Lord worshipped might he be!   what a beard hast thou got!   thou hast more hair on thy chin than Dobbin my fill-horse [18] has on his tail.

LAUNCELOT.   It should seem then that Dobbin's tail grows backward: I am sure he had more hair of his tail than I have of my face when I last saw him.

GOBBO.   Lord, how art thou changed!   How dost thou and thy master agree?   I have brought him a present.   How 'gree you now?

LAUNCELOT.   Well, well: but, for mine own part, as I have set up my rest [19] to run away, so I will not rest till I have run some ground.   My master's a very Jew: give him a present! give him a halter: I am famished in his service; you may tell every finger I have with my ribs.   Father, I am glad you are come: give me [20] your present to one Master Bassanio, who indeed gives rare new liveries: if I serve not him, I will run as far as God has any ground.   O rare fortune! here comes the man: to him, father; for I am a Jew, if I serve the Jew any longer.

Enter BASSANIO, *with* LEONARDO *and other followers.*

BASSANIO.   You may do so; but let it be so hasted that supper be ready at the farthest by five of the clock.   See these letters delivered; put the liveries to making, and desire Gratiano to come anon to my lodging.   [*Exit a Servant.*

LAUNCELOT.   To him, father.

GOBBO.   God bless your worship!

BASSANIO.   Gramercy! [21] wouldst thou aught with me?

GOBBO.   Here's my son, sir, a poor boy, —

LAUNCELOT.   Not a poor boy, sir, but the rich Jew's man; that would, sir, as my father shall specify —

GOBBO.   He hath a great infection, [22] sir, as one would say, to serve —

LAUNCELOT.   Indeed, the short and the long is, I serve the Jew, and have a desire, as my father shall specify, —

GOBBO.   His master and he, saving your worship's reverence, are scarce cater-cousins [23] —

LAUNCELOT.   To be brief, the very truth is that the Jew, having done me wrong, doth cause me, as my father, being, I hope, an old man, shall frutify [24] unto you, —

GOBBO.   I have here a dish of doves that I would bestow upon your worship, and my suit is —

LAUNCELOT,   In very brief, the suit is impertinent [25] to myself, as your worship shall know by this honest old man ; and, though I say it, though old man, yet poor man, my father.

BASSANIO.   One speak for both.   What would you?

LAUNCELOT.   Serve you, sir.

GOBBO.   That is the very defect [26] of the matter, sir.

BASSANIO.   I know thee well ; thou hast obtain'd thy suit :
Shylock thy master spoke with me this day,
And hath preferr'd [27] thee, if it be preferment
To leave a rich Jew's service, to become
The follower of so poor a gentleman.

LAUNCELOT.   The old proverb [28] is very well parted between my master Shylock and you, sir : you have the grace of God, sir, and he hath enough.

BASSANIO.   Thou speak'st it well.   Go, father, with thy son.
Take leave of thy old master and inquire
My lodging out.   Give him a livery
More guarded [29] than his fellows' : see it done.

LAUNCELOT.   Father, in.   I cannot get a service, no ; I have ne'er a tongue in my head.   Well, if any man in Italy have a fairer table [30] which doth offer to swear upon a book, I shall have good fortune.   Go to, here's a simple line of life, [31] here's a small trifle of wives : alas, fifteen wives is nothing ! eleven widows and nine maids is a simple coming-in for one man : and then to scape drowning thrice, and to be in peril of my life with the edge of a feather-bed ; [32] here are simple scapes.   Well, if Fortune be a woman, she's a good wench for this gear.   Father, come ; I'll take my leave of the Jew in the twinkling of an eye.   [*Exeunt* LAUNCELOT *and* OLD GOBBO.

BASSANIO.   I pray thee, good Leonardo, think on this :
These things being bought and orderly bestow'd
Return in haste, for I do feast to-night
My best-esteemed acquaintance : hie thee, go.

LEONARDO.   My best endeavours shall be done herein.

Enter GRATIANO.

GRATIANO. Where is your master?

LEONARDO. Yonder, sir, he walks. [*Exit.*

GRATIANO. Signior Bassanio!

BASSANIO. Gratiano!

GRATIANO. I have a suit to you.

BASSANIO. You have obtain'd it.

GRATIANO. You must not deny me: I must go with you to Belmont.

BASSANIO. Why then you must. But hear thee, Gratiano;
Thou art too wild, too rude and bold of voice;
Parts that become thee happily enough
And in such eyes as ours appear not faults;
But where thou art not known, why, there they show
Something too liberal.[33] Pray thee, take pain
To allay with some cold drops of modesty
Thy skipping [34] spirit, lest through thy wild behaviour
I be misconstrued in the place I go to
And lose my hopes.

GRATIANO. Signior Bassanio, hear me:
If I do not put on a sober habit,
Talk with respect and swear but now and then,
Wear prayer-books in my pocket, look demurely,
Nay more, while grace is saying, hood mine eyes
Thus with my hat,[35] and sigh and say "amen,"
Use all the observance of civility,[36]
Like one well studied in a sad ostent [37]
To please his grandam, never trust me more.

BASSANIO. Well, we shall see your bearing.

GRATIANO. Nay, but I bar to-night: you shall not gauge me
By what we do to-night.

BASSANIO. No, that were pity:
I would entreat you rather to put on
Your boldest suit of mirth, for we have friends
That purpose merriment. But fare you well:
I have some business.

GRATIANO. And I must to Lorenzo and the rest:
But we will visit you at supper-time. [*Exeunt.*

SCENE III. *The same. A room in Shylock's house.*

Enter JESSICA *and* LAUNCELOT.

JESSICA.   I am sorry thou wilt leave my father so :
Our house is hell, and thou, a merry devil,
Didst rob it of some taste of tediousness.
But fare thee well, there is a ducat for thee :
And, Launcelot, soon at supper shalt thou see
Lorenzo, who is thy new master's guest :
Give him this letter ; do it secretly ;
And so farewell : I would not have my father
See me in talk with thee.

LAUNCELOT.   Adieu ! tears exhibit [1] my tongue. Most beautiful
pagan, most sweet Jew, adieu : these foolish drops do something
drown my manly spirit : adieu.

JESSICA.   Farewell, good Launcelot.   [*Exit* LAUNCELOT.
Alack, what heinous sin is it in me
To be ashamed to be my father's child !
But though I am a daughter to his blood,
I am not to his manners.   O Lorenzo,
If thou keep promise, I shall end this strife,
Become a Christian and thy loving wife.   [*Exit.*

SCENE IV. *The same. A street.*

Enter GRATIANO, LORENZO, SALARINO, *and* SALANIO.

LORENZO.   Nay, we will slink away in supper-time,
Disguise us at my lodging and return,
All in an hour.

GRATIANO.   We have not made good preparation.

SALARINO.   We have not spoke us yet of torch-bearers. [1]

SALANIO.   'Tis vile, unless it may be quaintly order'd,
And better in my mind not undertook.

LORENZO.   'Tis now but four o'clock : we have two hours.
To furnish us.

Enter LAUNCELOT, *with a letter.*

Friend Launcelot, what's the news ?

LAUNCELOT.   An [2] it shall please you to break up [3] this, it shall
seem to signify.

LORENZO. I know the hand: in faith, 'tis a fair hand,
And whiter than the paper it writ on
Is the fair hand that writ.

GRATIANO.   Love-news, in faith.

LAUNCELOT. By your leave, sir.

LORENZO. Whither goest thou ?

LAUNCELOT. Marry, sir, to bid my old master the Jew to sup
to-night with my new master the Christian.

LORENZO. Hold here, take this : tell gentle Jessica
I will not fail her ; speak it privately.   [*Exit* LAUNCELOT.
Go, gentlemen,
Will you prepare you for this masque to-night ?
I am provided of [4] a torch-bearer.

SALARINO. Ay, marry, I'll be gone about it straight.

SALANIO. And so will I.

LORENZO.   Meet me and Gratiano
At Gratiano's lodging some hour hence.

SALARINO. 'Tis good we do so.

                              [*Exeunt* SALARINO *and* SALANIO.

GRATIANO. Was not that letter from fair Jessica ?

LORENZO. I must needs tell thee all. She hath directed
How I shall take her from her father's house,
What gold and jewels she is furnish'd with,
What page's suit she hath in readiness.
If e'er the Jew her father come to heaven,
It will be for his gentle daughter's sake :
And never dare misfortune cross her foot,
Unless she do it under this excuse,
That she is issue to a faithless Jew.
Come, go with me ; peruse this as thou goest :
Fair Jessica shall be my torch-bearer.   -   [*Exeunt.*

SCENE V. *The same. Before* SHYLOCK'S *house.*

Enter SHYLOCK *and* LAUNCELOT.

SHYLOCK. Well, thou shalt see, thy eyes shall be thy judge,
The difference of old Shylock and Bassanio : —
What, Jessica ! — thou shalt not gormandize,
As thou hast done with me : — What, Jessica ! —

And sleep and snore, and rend apparel out : —
Why, Jessica, I say !

    LAUNCELOT.   Why, Jessica !

    SHYLOCK. Who bids thee call ? I do not bid thee call.

    LAUNCELOT. Your worship was wont to tell me that I could do nothing without bidding.

Enter JESSICA.

    JESSICA. Call you ? what is your will ?

    SHYLOCK. I am bid forth [1] to supper, Jessica :
There are my keys. But wherefore should I go ?
I am not bid for love ; they flatter me :
But yet I'll go in hate, to feed upon
The prodigal Christian. Jessica, my girl,
Look to my house. I am right loath to go :
There is some ill a-brewing towards my rest,
For I did dream of money-bags to-night.

    LAUNCELOT. I beseech you, sir, go : my young master doth expect your reproach.[2]

    SHYLOCK. So do I his.

    LAUNCELOT. An they have conspired together, I will not say you shall see a masque ; but if you do, then it was not for nothing that my nose fell a-bleeding on Black-Monday [3] last at six o'clock i' the morning falling out that year on Ash-Wednesday was four year, in the afternoon.

    SHYLOCK. What, are there masques? Hear you me, Jessica :
Lock up my doors ; and when you hear the drum
And the vile squealing of the wry-neck'd fife,[4]
Clamber not you up to the casements then,
Nor thrust your head into the public street
To gaze on Christian fools with varnish'd faces,
But stop my house's ears, I mean my casements :
Let not the sound of shallow foppery enter
My sober house. By Jacob's staff,[5] I swear,
I have no mind of feasting [6] forth to-night :
But I will go. Go you before me, sirrah ;
Say I will come.

    LAUNCELOT. I will go before sir. Mistress, look out at window, for all this ;

                 There will come a Christian by,
                 Will be worth a Jewess' eye.   *[Exit.*

SHYLOCK. What says that fool of Hagar's offspring,[7] ha?
JESSICA. His words were "farewell mistress;" nothing else.
SHYLOCK. The patch[8] is kind enough, but a huge feeder;
Snail-slow in profit, and he sleeps by day
More than the wild-cat: drones hive not with me:
Therefore I part with him, and part with him
To one that I would have him help to waste
His borrow'd purse. Well, Jessica, go in:
Perhaps I will return immediately:
Do as I bid you; shut doors after you:
Fast bind, fast find;
A proverb never stale in thifty mind.   [*Exit.*

JESSICA. Farewell; and if my fortune be not crost,
I have a father, you a daughter, lost.   [*Exit.*

SCENE VI. *The same.*

Enter GRATIANO *and* SALARINO, *masqued.*

GRATIANO. This is the pent-house under which Lorenzo
Desired us to make stand.
SALARINO.   His hour is almost past.
GRATIANO. And it is marvel he out-dwells[1] his hour,
For lovers ever run before the clock.
SALARINO. O, ten times faster Venus' pigeons[2] fly
To seal love's bonds new-made, than they are wont
To keep obliged[3] faith unforfeited!
GRATIANO. That ever holds: who riseth from a feast
With that keen appetite that he sits down?
Where is the horse that doth untread again
His tedious measures with the unbated fire
That he did pace them first? All things that are
Are with more spirit chased than enjoy'd.
How like a younker or a prodigal
The scarfed[4] bark puts from her native bay,
Hugg'd and embraced by the strumpet wind!
How like the prodigal doth she return,
With over-weather'd[5] ribs and ragged sails,
Lean, rent and beggar'd by the strumpet wind!
SALARINO. Here comes Lorenzo: more of this hereafter.

Enter LORENZO.

LORENZO. Sweet friends, your patience for my long abode; [6]
Not I, but my affairs, have made you wait:
When you shall please to play the thieves for wives,
I'll watch as long for you then. Approach;
Here dwells my father Jew. Ho! who's within?

Enter JESSICA, *above, in boy's clothes.*

JESSICA. Who are you? Tell me, for more certainty,
Albeit I'll swear that I do know your tongue.

LORENZO. Lorenzo, and thy love.

JESSICA. Lorenzo, certain, and my love indeed,
For who [7] love I so much? And now who knows
But you, Lorenzo, whether I am yours?

LORENZO. Heaven and thy thoughts are witness that thou art.

JESSICA. Here, catch this casket; it is worth the pains.
I am glad 'tis night, you do not look on me,
For I am much ashamed of my exchange: [8]
But love is blind and lovers cannot see
The pretty follies that themselves commit;
For if they could, Cupid himself would blush
To see me thus transformed to a boy.

LORENZO. Descend, for you must be my torch-bearer.

JESSICA. What, must I hold a candle to my shames?
They in themselves, good sooth, [9] are too too light.
Why, 'tis an office of discovery, love;
And I should be obscured.

LORENZO. So are you, sweet,
Even in the lovely garnish of a boy.
But come at once;
For the close [10] night doth play the runaway,
And we are stay'd for at Bassanio's feast.

JESSICA. I will make fast the doors, and gild myself
With some more ducats, and be with you straight. [*Exit above.*

GRATIANO. Now, by my hood, a Gentile and no Jew.

LORENZO. Beshrew me [11] but I love her heartily;
For she is wise, if I can judge of her,
And fair she is, if that mine eyes be true,
And true she is, as she hath proved herself,

And therefore, like herself, wise, fair and true,
Shall she be placed in my constant soul.

Enter JESSICA, *below.*

What, art thou come?   On, gentlemen ; away !
Our masquing mates by this time for us stay.

[*Exit with* JESSICA *and* SALARINO.

Enter ANTONIO.

ANTONIO.   Who's there?
GRATIANO.   Signior Antonio !
ANTONIO.   Fie, fie, Gratiano ! where are all the rest?
'Tis nine o'clock : our friends all stay for you.
No masque to-night : the wind is come about ;
Bassanio presently will go aboard :
I have sent twenty out to seek for you.
GRATIANO.   I am glad on't ;[12] I desire no more delight
Than to be under sail and gone to-night.   [*Exeunt.*

SCENE VII.   *Belmont.   A room in* PORTIA'S *house.*

Flourish of Cornets.   Enter PORTIA *with the* PRINCE OF MOROCCO,
and their trains.

PORTIA.   Go draw aside the curtains and discover
The several caskets to this noble prince.
Now make your choice.
MOROCCO.   The first, of gold, who[1] this inscription bears,
" Who chooseth me shall gain what many men desire ; "
The second, silver, which this promise carries,
" Who chooseth me shall get as much as he deserves ; "
This third, dull lead, with warning all as blunt,[2]
" Who chooseth me must give and hazard all he hath."
How shall I know if I do choose the right?
PORTIA.   The one of them contains my picture, prince :
If you choose that, then I am yours withal.
MOROCCO.   Some God direct my judgment !   Let me see ;
I will survey the inscriptions back again.
What says this leaden casket?
" Who chooseth me must give and hazard all he hath."

Must give! for what? for lead? hazard for lead?
This casket threatens.   Men that hazard all
Do it in hope of fair advantages :
A golden mind stoops not to shows of dross ;
I'll then nor give nor hazard aught for lead.
What says the silver with her virgin hue?
" Who chooseth me shall get as much as he deserves."
As much as he deserves !   Pause there, Morocco,
And weigh thy value with an even hand :
If thou be'st rated by thy estimation,[3]
Thou dost deserve enough ; and yet enough
May not extend so far as to the lady :
And yet to be afeard of my deserving
Were but a weak disabling[4] of myself.
As much as I deserve !   Why, that's the lady :
I do in birth deserve her, and in fortunes,
In graces and in qualities of breeding ;
But more than these, in love I do deserve.
What if I stray'd no further, but chose here ?
Let's see once more this saying graved in gold ;
" Who chooseth me shall gain what many men desire."
Why, that's the lady ; all the world desires her ;
From the four corners of the earth they come,
To kiss this shrine,[5] this mortal breathing saint :
The Hyrcanian deserts[6] and the vasty wilds
Of wide Arabia are as throughfares now
For princes to come view fair Portia :
The watery kingdom, whose ambitious head
Spits in the face of heaven, is no bar
To stop the foreign spirits, but they come,
As o'er a brook, to see fair Portia.
One of these three contains her heavenly picture.
Is't like that lead contains her?   'Twere damnation
To think so base a thought : it were too gross
To rib her cerecloth in the obscure grave.
Or shall I think in silver she's immured,
Being ten times undervalued[7] to tried gold ?
O sinful thought !   Never so rich a gem
Was set in worse than gold.   They have in England
A coin that bears the figure of an angel

Stamped in gold, but that's insculp'd upon;[8]
But here an angel in a golden bed
Lies all within.   Deliver me the key:
Here do I choose, and thrive I as I may!

PORTIA.   There, take it, prince; and if my form lies there,
Then I am yours.   [*He unlocks the golden casket.*

MOROCCO.   O hell! what have we here?
A carrion Death,[9] within whose empty eye
There is a written scroll!   I'll read the writing.

[*Reads*]   All that glisters is not gold;
           Often have you heard that told:
           Many a man his life hath sold
           But my outside to behold:
           Gilded tombs do worms infold.
           Had you been as wise as bold,
           Young in limbs, in judgment old,
           Your answer had not been inscroll'd:
           Fare you well; your suit is cold.

      Cold, indeed; and labour lost:
        Then, farewell, heat, and welcome, frost!
Portia, adieu.   I have too grieved a heart
To take a tedious leave: thus losers part.[10]

                [*Exit with his train.   Flourish of Cornets.*

PORTIA.   A gentle riddance.   Draw the curtains, go.
Let all of his complexion choose me so.   [*Exeunt.*

                SCENE VIII.   *Venice.   A street.*

                Enter SALARINO *and* SALANIO.

SALARINO.   Why, man, I saw Bassanio under sail:
With him is Gratiano gone along;
And in their ship I'm sure Lorenzo is not.

SALANIO.   The villain Jew with outcries raised the duke,
Who went with him to search Bassanio's ship.

SALARINO.   He came too late, the ship was under sail:
But there the duke was given to understand
That in a gondola were seen together
Lorenzo and his amorous Jessica:
Besides, Antonio certified the duke
They were not with Bassanio in his ship.

SALANIO.   I never heard a passion [1] so confused,
So strange, outrageous, and so variable,
As the dog Jew did utter in the streets:
"My daughter!   O my ducats!   O my daughter!
Fled with a Christian!   O my Christian ducats!
Justice! the law! my ducats, and my daughter!
A sealed bag, two sealed bags of ducats,
Of double ducats, stolen from me by my daughter!
And jewels, two stones, two rich and precious stones,
Stolen by my daughter!   Justice! find the girl;
She hath the stones upon her, and the ducats."

SALARINO.   Why, all the boys in Venice follow him,
Crying, his stones, his daughter, and his ducats.

SALANIO.   Let good Antonio look he keep his day,[2]
Or he shall pay for this.

SALARINO.   Marry, well remember'd.
I reason'd [3] with a Frenchman yesterday,
Who told me, in the narrow seas that part
The French and English, there miscarried
A vessel of our country richly fraught:
I thought upon Antonio when he told me,
And wish'd in silence that it were not his.

SALANIO.   You were best [4] to tell Antonio what you hear;
Yet do not suddenly, for it may grieve him.

SALARINO.   A kinder gentleman treads not the earth.
I saw Bassanio and Antonio part:
Bassanio told him he would make some speed
Of his return: he answer'd, "Do not so;
Slubber [5] not business for my sake, Bassanio,
But stay the very riping [6] of the time;
And for the Jew's bond which he hath of me,
Let it not enter in your mind of love: [7]
Be merry, and employ your chiefest thoughts
To courtship and such fair ostents [8] of love
As shall conveniently [9] become you there:"
And even there, his eye being big with tears,
Turning his face, he put his hand behind him,
And with affection wondrous sensible [10]
He wrung Bassanio's hand; and so they parted.

SALANIO.   I think he only loves the world for him.

I pray thee, let us go and find him out
And quicken his embraced heaviness [11]
With some delight or other.
    SALARINO.   Do we so.[12]   *[Exeunt.*

    SCENE IX.   *Belmont.   A room in* PORTIA'S *house.*

Enter NERISSA *with a Servitor.*

    NERISSA.   Quick, quick, I pray thee; draw the curtain straight:[1]
The Prince of Arragon hath ta'en his oath,
And comes to his election[2] presently.

Flourish of Cornets.   Enter the PRINCE OF ARRAGON, PORTIA,
and their trains.

    PORTIA.   Behold, there stand the caskets, noble prince:
If you choose that wherein I am contain'd,
Straight shall our nuptial rites be solemnized:
But if you fail, without more speech, my lord,
You must be gone from hence immediately.
    ARRAGON.   I am enjoin'd by oath to observe three things:
First, never to unfold to any one
Which casket 'twas I chose; next, if I fail
Of the right casket, never in my life
To woo a maid in way of marriage:
Lastly,
If I do fail in fortune of my choice,
Immediately to leave you and be gone.
    PORTIA.   To these injunctions every one doth swear
That comes to hazard for my worthless self.
    ARRAGON.   And so have I address'd me.[3]   Fortune now
To my heart's hope![4]   Gold; silver; and base lead.
"Who chooseth me must give and hazard all he hath."
You shall look fairer, ere I give or hazard.
What says the golden chest? ha! let me see
"Who chooseth me shall gain what many men desire.'
What many men desire! that "many" may be meant
By [5] the fool multitude, that choose by show,
Not learning more than the fond eye doth teach;
Which pries not to the interior, but, like the martlet,[6]

Builds in the weather on the outward wall,
Even in the force and road of casuality.
I will not choose what many men desire,
Because I will not jump with [7] common spirits
And rank me with the barbarous multitudes.
Why, then to thee, thou silver treasure-house;
Tell me once more what title thou dost bear:
" Who chooseth me shall get as much as he deserves: "
And well said too; for who shall go about
To cozen fortune and be honourable
Without the stamp of merit ?   Let none presume
To wear an undeserved dignity.
O, that estates, degrees and offices
Were not derived corruptly, and that clear honour
Were purchased by the merit of the wearer!
How many then should cover that stand bare!
How many be commanded that command!
How much low peasantry would then be glean'd
From the true seed of honour! and how much honour
Pick'd from the chaff and ruin [8] of the times
To be new-varnish'd!   Well, but to my choice:
" Who chooseth me shall get as much as he deserves."
I will assume desert.   Give me a key for this,
And instantly unlock my fortunes here.

> *[He opens the silver casket.*

PORTIA.   Too long a pause for that which you find there.
ARRAGON.   What's here? the portrait of a blinking idiot,
Presenting me a schedule!   I will read it.
How much unlike art thou to Portia!
How much unlike my hopes and my deservings!
" Who chooseth me shall have as much as he deserves."
Did I deserve no more than a fool's head?
Is that my prize? are my deserts no better?
PORTIA.   To offend, and judge,[9] are distinct offices
And of opposed natures.
ARRAGON.   What is here ?
[*Reads*] The fire seven times tried this:
        Seven times tried that judgment is,
        That did never choose amiss.
        Some there be that shadows kiss;

Such have but a shadow's bliss :
There be fools alive, I wis,[10]
Silver'd o'er; and so was this.
Take what wife you will to bed,
I will ever be your head :
So be gone : you are sped.[11]

Still more fool I shall appear
By the time[12] I linger here :
With one fool's head I came to woo,
But I go away with two.
Sweet, adieu.   I'll keep my oath,
Patiently to bear my wroth.[13]

Exeunt ARRAGON *and train.*

PORTIA.   Thus hath the candle singed the moth.
O, these deliberate fools ! when they do choose,
They have the wisdom by their wit to lose.
NERISSA.   The ancient saying is no heresy,
Hanging and wiving goes by destiny.
PORTIA.   Come, draw the curtain, Nerissa.

Enter a Servant.

SERVANT.   Where is my lady?
PORTIA.   Here : what would my lord?[14]
SERVANT.   Madam, there is alighted at your gate
A young Venetian, one that comes before
To signify the approaching of his lord ;
From whom he bringeth sensible regreets,[15]
To wit, besides commends[16] and courteous breath,
Gifts of rich value.   Yet[17] I have not seen
So likely an ambassador of love :
A day in April never came so sweet,
To show how costly summer was at hand,
As this fore-spurrer comes before his lord.
PORTIA.   No more, I pray thee : I am half afeard
Thou wilt say anon he is some kin to thee,
Thou spend'st such high-day wit in praising him.
Come, come, Nerissa ; for I long to see
Quick Cupid's post[18] that comes so mannerly.
NERISSA.   Bassanio, lord Love,[19] if thy will it be !   [*Exeunt.*

ACT III.

SCENE I.   *Venice.   A street.*

Enter SALANIO *and* SALARINO.

SALANIO.   Now, what news on the Rialto?

SALARINO.   Why, yet it lives there unchecked that Antonio hath
a ship of rich lading wrecked on the narrow seas; the Goodwins,[1]
I think they call the place; a very dangerous flat and fatal, where the
carcases of many a tall ship lie buried, as they say, if my gossip Report be an honest woman of her word.

SALANIO.   I would she were as lying a gossip in that as ever
knapped ginger[2] or made her neighbours believe she wept for the
death of a third husband.   But it is true, without any slips of pro-
lixity or crossing the plain highway of talk, that the good Antonio, the
honest Antonio, — O that I had a title good enough to keep his name
company! —

SALARINO.   Come, the full stop.

SALANIO.   Ha! what sayest thou?   Why, the end is, he hath
lost a ship.

SALARINO.   I would it might prove the end of his losses.

SALANIO.   Let me say "amen" betimes, lest the devil cross my
prayer, for here he comes in the likeness of a Jew.

Enter SHYLOCK.

How now, Shylock! what news among the merchants?

SHYLOCK.   You knew, none so well, none so well as you, of my
daughter's flight.

SALARINO.   That's certain: I, for my part, knew the tailor that
made the wings she flew withal.[3]

SALANIO.   And Shylock, for his own part, knew the bird was
fledged; and then it is the complexion[4] of them all to leave the dam.

SHYLOCK.   My own flesh and blood to rebel!

SALARINO.   There is more difference between thy flesh and hers
than between jet and ivory; more between your bloods than there is
between red wine and Rhenish.   But tell us, do you hear whether
Antonio have had any loss at sea or no?

SHYLOCK.   There I have another bad match:[5] a bankrupt, a
prodigal, who dare scarce show his head on the Rialto; a beggar,
that was used to come so smug[6] upon the mart; let him look to his

bond: he was wont to call me usurer; let him look to his bond: he was wont to lend money for a Christian courtesy; let him look to his bond.

SALARINO. Why, I am sure, if he forfeit, thou wilt not take his flesh: what's that good for?

SHYLOCK. To bait fish withal: if it will feed nothing else, it will feed my revenge. He hath disgraced me, and hindered me half a million; [7] laughed at my losses, mocked at my gains, scorned my nation, thwarted my bargains, cooled my friends, heated mine enemies; and what's his reason? I am a Jew. Hath not a Jew eyes? hath not a Jew hands, organs, dimensions, senses, affections, passions? fed with the same food, hurt with the same weapons, subject to the same diseases, healed by the same means, warmed and cooled by the same winter and summer, as a Christian is? If you prick us, do we not bleed? if you tickle us, do we not laugh? if you poison us, do we not die? and if you wrong us, shall we not revenge? If we are like you in the rest, we will resemble you in that. If a Jew wrong a Christian, what is his humility? Revenge. If a Christian wrong a Jew, what should his sufferance be by Christian example? Why, revenge. The villany you teach me, I will execute, and it shall go hard but I will better the instruction.

Enter a Servant.

SERVANT. Gentlemen, my master Antonio is at his house and desires to speak with you both.

SALARINO. We have been up and down to seek him.

Enter TUBAL.

SALANIO. Here comes another of the tribe: a third cannot be matched, unless the devil himself turn Jew.

[*Exeunt* SALANIO, SALARINO, *and Servant.*

SHYLOCK. How now, Tubal! what news from Genoa? hast thou found my daughter?

TUBAL. I often came where I did hear of her, but cannot find her.

SHYLOCK. Why, there, there, there, there! a diamond gone, cost me two thousand ducats in Frankfort! [8] The curse never fell upon our nation till now; I never felt it till now; two thousand ducats in that; [9] and other precious, precious jewels. I would my daughter were dead at my foot, and the jewels in her ear! would she were hearsed at my foot, and the ducats in her coffin! No news of them?

Why, so: and I know not what's spent in the search: why, thou loss upon loss! the thief gone with so much, and so much to find the thief; and no satisfaction, no revenge: nor no ill luck stirring but what lights on my shoulders; no sighs but of my breathing; no tears but of my shedding.

TUBAL. Yes, other men have ill luck too: Antonio, as I heard in Genoa, —

SHYLOCK. What, what, what? ill luck, ill luck?

TUBAL. Hath an argosy cast away, coming from Tripolis.

SHYLOCK. I thank God, I thank God. Is't true, is't true?

TUBAL. I spoke with some of the sailors that escaped the wreck.

SHYLOCK. I thank thee, good Tubal: good news, good news! ha, ha! where? in Genoa?

TUBAL. Your daughter spent in Genoa, as I heard, in one night fourscore ducats.

SHYLOCK. Thou stickest a dagger in me: I shall never see my gold again: fourscore ducats at a sitting! fourscore ducats!

TUBAL. There came divers of Antonio's creditors in my company to Venice, that swear he cannot choose but break.

SHYLOCK. I am very glad of it: I'll plague him; I'll torture him: I am glad of it.

TUBAL. One of them showed me a ring that he had of your daughter for a monkey.

SHYLOCK. Out upon her! Thou torturest me, Tubal: it was my turquoise; [10] I had it of Leah when I was a bachelor: I would not have given it for a wilderness of monkeys.

TUBAL. But Antonio is certainly undone.

SHYLOCK. Nay, that's true, that's very true. Go, Tubal, fee me an officer; bespeak him a fortnight before. I will have the heart of him, if he forfeit; for, were he out of Venice, I can make what merchandise I will. Go, go, Tubal, and meet me at our synagogue; go, good Tubal; at our synagogue, Tubal.   [*Exeunt.*

SCENE II. *Belmont. A room in* PORTIA'S *house.*

Enter BASSANIO, PORTIA, GRATIANO, NERISSA, *and Attendants.*

PORTIA. I pray you, tarry: pause a day or two
Before you hazard; for, in choosing wrong,
I lose your company: therefore forbear awhile.

There's something tells me, but it is not love,
I would not lose you; and you know yourself,
Hate counsels not in such a quality.
But lest you should not understand me well, —
And yet a maiden hath no tongue but thought, —
I would detain you here some month or two
Before you venture for me.   I could teach you
How to choose right, but I am then forsworn;[1]
So will I never be: so may you miss me;
But if you do, you'll make me wish a sin,
That I had been forsworn.   Beshrew[2] your eyes,
They have o'erlook'd me[3] and divided me;
One half of me is yours, the other half yours,
Mine own, I would say; but if mine, then yours,
And so all yours.   O, these naughty times
Put bars between the owners and their rights!
And so, though yours, not yours.   Prove it so,[4]
Let fortune go to hell for it, not I.
I speak too long; but 'tis to peize[5] the time,
So eke it and to draw it out in length,
To stay you from election.

    BASSANIO.   Let me choose;
For as I am, I live upon the rack.

    PORTIA.   Upon the rack, Bassanio! then confess
What treason there is mingled with your love.

    BASSANIO.   None but that ugly treason of mistrust,
Which makes me fear[6] the enjoying of my love:
There may as well be amity and life
'Tween snow and fire, as treason and my love.

    PORTIA.   Ay, but I fear you speak upon the rack,
Where men enforced do speak anything.

    BASSANIO.   Promise me life, and I'll confess the truth.

    PORTIA.   Well then, confess and live.

    BASSANIO.   " Confess " and " love "
Had been the very sum of my confession:
O happy torment, when my torturer
Doth teach me answers for deliverance!
But let me to my fortune and the caskets.

    PORTIA.   Away, then! I am lock'd in one of them:
If you do love me, you will find me out.

Nerissa and the rest, stand all aloof.
Let music sound while he doth make his choice;
Then, if he lose, he makes a swan-like end,[7]
Fading in music: that the comparison
May stand more proper, my eye shall be the stream
And watery death-bed for him.   He may win;
And what is music then?   Then music is
Even as the flourish[8] when true subjects bow
To a new-crowned monarch: such it is
As are those dulcet sounds in break of day
That creep into the dreaming bridegroom's ear
And summon him to marriage.   Now he goes,
With no less presence, but with much more love,
Than young Alcides,[9] when he did redeem
The virgin tribute paid by howling Troy
To the sea-monster: I stand for sacrifice;
The rest aloof are the Dardanian wives,[10]
With bleared visages, come forth to view
The issue of the exploit.   Go, Hercules!
Live thou, I live: with much, much more dismay
I view the fight than thou that makest the fray.

Music, *whilst* BASSANIO *comments on the caskets to himself.*

SONG.

Tell me where is fancy bred,
Or in the heart or in the head?
How begot, how nourished?
        Reply, reply.
It is engender'd in the eyes,
With gazing fed; and fancy dies
In the cradle where it lies.
        Let us all ring fancy's knell:
        I'll begin it, — Ding, dong, bell.

ALL.   Ding, dong, bell.
BASSANIO.   So may the outward shows be least themselves:
The world is still deceiv'd with ornament.
In law, what plea so tainted and corrupt
But, being season'd with a gracious voice,
Obscures the show of evil?   In religion,
What damned error, but some sober brow

Will bless it and approve [11] it with a text,
Hiding the grossness with fair ornament?
There is no vice so simple but assumes
Some mark of virtue on his [12] outward parts:
How many cowards, whose hearts are all as false
As stairs of sand, wear yet upon their chins
The beards of Hercules and frowning Mars,
Who, inward search'd, have livers white as milk; [13]
And these assume but valour's excrement [14]
To render them redoubted!   Look on beauty,
And you shall see 'tis purchas'd by the weight;
Which therein works a miracle in nature,
Making them lightest that wear most of it:
So are those crisped snaky golden locks
Which make such wanton gambols with the wind,
Upon supposed fairness, [15] often known
To be the dowry of a second head,
The skull that bred them in the sepulchre.
Thus ornament is but the guiled [16] shore
To a most dangerous sea; the beauteous scarf
Veiling an Indian beauty; [17] in a word,
The seeming truth which cunning times put on
To entrap the wisest.   Therefore, thou gaudy gold,
Hard food for Midas, [18] I will none of thee;
Nor none of thee, thou pale and common drudge
'Tween man and man: but thou, thou meagre lead,
Which rather threatenest than dost promise aught,
Thy plainness moves me more than eloquence;
And here choose I: joy be the consequence!

    PORTIA [*Aside*].   How all the other passions fleet to air,
As doubtful thoughts, and rash-embraced despair,
And shuddering fear, and green-eyed jealousy!
O love, be moderate; allay thy ecstasy;
In measure rain thy joy; scant this excess.
I feel too much thy blessing: make it less,
For fear I surfeit.

    BASSANIO.   What find I here?   [*Opening the leaden casket.*
Fair Portia's counterfeit! [19]   What demi-god
Hath come so near creation?   Move these eyes?
Or whether, riding on the balls of mine,

Seem they in motion?   Here are sever'd lips,
Parted with sugar breath : so sweet a bar
Should sunder such sweet friends.   Here in her hairs
The painter plays the spider and hath woven
A golden mesh to entrap the hearts of men
Faster than gnats in cobwebs : but her eyes, —
How could he see to do them? having made one,
Methinks it should have power to steal both his
And leave itself unfurnish'd.[20]   Yet look, how far
The substance of my praise doth wrong this shadow
In underprizing it, so far this shadow
Doth limp behind the substance.   Here's the scroll,
The continent [21] and summary of my fortune,

[*Reads*] You that choose not by the view,
          Chance as fair and choose as true !
          Since this fortune falls to you,
          Be content and seek no new.
          If you be well pleas'd with this
          And hold your fortune for your bliss,
          Turn you where your lady is
          And claim her with a loving kiss.

A gentle scroll.   Fair lady, by your leave ;
I come by note,[22] to give and to receive.
Like one of two contending in a prize,[23]
That thinks he hath done well in people's eyes,
Hearing applause and universal shout,
Giddy in spirit, still gazing in a doubt
Whether those peals of praise be his or no,
So, thrice-fair lady, stand I, even so ;
As doubtful whether what I see be true,
Until confirm'd, sign'd, ratified by you.
      PORTIA.   You see me, Lord Bassanio, where I stand,
Such as I am : though for myself alone
I would not be ambitious in my wish,
To wish myself much better ; yet, for you
I would be trebled twenty times myself ;
A thousand times more fair, ten thousand times
More rich ;
That only to stand high in your account,

I might in virtues, beauties, lïvings,[24] friends,
Exceed account; but the full sum of me
Is sum of — something, which, to term in gross,
Is an unlesson'd girl, unschool'd, unpractised;
Happy in this, she is not yet so old
But she may learn; happier than this,
She is not bred so dull but she can learn;
Happiest of all in that her gentle spirit
Commits itself to yours to be directed,
As from her lord, her governor, her king.
Myself and what is mine to you and yours
Is now converted: but now I was the lord
Of this fair mansion, master of my servants,
Queen o'er myself; and even now, but now,
This house, these servants and this same myself
Are yours, my lord: I give them with this ring;
Which when you part from, lose, or give away,
Let it presage the ruin of your love
And be my vantage to exclaim on you.[25]

    BASSANIO.   Madam, you have bereft me of all words,
Only my blood speaks to you in my veins;
And there is such confusion in my powers
As, after some oration fairly spoke
By a beloved prince, there doth appear
Among the buzzing pleased multitude;
Where every something, being blent together,
Turns to a wild of nothing, save of joy,
Express'd and not express'd.   But when this ring
Parts from this finger, then parts life from hence:
Oh, then be bold to say Bassanio's dead!

    NERISSA.   My lord and lady, it is now our time,
That have stood by and seen our wishes prosper,
To cry, good joy: good joy, my lord and lady!

    GRATIANO.   My lord Bassanio and my gentle lady,
I wish you all the joy that you can wish;
For I am sure you can wish none from me:[26]
And when your honours mean to solemnize
The bargain of your faith, I do beseech you,
Even at that time I may be married too.

    BASSANIO.   With all my heart, so[27] thou canst get a wife.

GRATIANO.   I thank your lordship, you have got me one.
My eyes, my lord, can look as swift as yours :
You saw the mistress, I beheld the maid ;
You lov'd, I lov'd, for intermission [28]
No more pertains to me, my lord, than you.
Your fortune stood upon the casket there,
And so did mine too, as the matter falls ;
For wooing here until I sweat again,
And swearing till my very roof was dry
With oaths of love, at last, if promise last,[29]
I got a promise of this fair one here
To have her love, provided that your fortune
Achiev'd her mistress.

    PORTIA.   Is this true, Nerissa?

    NERISSA.   Madam, it is, so you stand pleas'd withal.

    BASSANIO.   And do you, Gratiano, mean good faith?

    GRATIANO.   Yes, faith, my lord.

    BASSANIO.   Our feast shall be much honour'd in your marriage.

    GRATIANO.   But who comes here?   Lorenzo and his infidel?
What, and my old Venetian friend Salerio?

    Enter LORENZO, JESSICA, *and* SALERIO, *a messenger from*
Venice.

    BASSANIO.   Lorenzo and Salerio, welcome hither ;
If that the youth of my new interest here
Have power to bid you welcome.   By your leave,
I bid my very [30] friends and countrymen,
Sweet Portia, welcome.

    PORTIA.   So do I, my lord :
They are entirely welcome.

    LORENZO.   I thank your honour.   For my part, my lord,
My purpose was not to have seen you here ;
But meeting with Salerio by the way,
He did entreat me, past all saying nay,
To come with him along.

    SALERIO.   I did, my lord ;
And I have reason for it.   Signor Antonio
Commends him [31] to you.   *[Gives* BASSANIO *a letter.*

    BASSANIO.   Ere I ope his letter,
I pray you, tell me how my good friend doth.

SALERIO.   Not sick, my lord, unless it be in mind;
Nor well, unless in mind: his letter there
Will show you his estate.[32]

GRATIANO.   Nerissa, cheer yon stranger; bid her welcome.
Your hand, Salerio: what's the news from Venice?
How doth that royal merchant, good Antonio?
I know he will be glad of our success;
We are the Jasons, we have won the fleece.

SALERIO.   I would you had won the fleece that he hath lost.

PORTIA.   There are some shrewd [33] contents in yon same paper,
That steals the colour from Bassanio's cheek:
Some dear friend dead; else nothing in the world
Could turn so much the constitution
Of any constant [34] man.   What, worse and worse!
With leave, Bassanio; I am half yourself,
And I must freely have the half of anything
That this same paper brings you.

BASSANIO.   O sweet Portia,
Here are a few of the unpleasant'st words
That ever blotted paper!   Gentle lady,
When I did first impart my love to you,
I freely told you, all the wealth I had
Ran in my veins, I was a gentleman;
And then I told you true; and yet, dear lady,
Rating myself at nothing, you shall see
How much I was a braggart.   When I told you
My state was nothing, I should then have told you
That I was worse than nothing; for indeed
I have engag'd myself to a dear friend,
Engag'd my friend to his mere [35] enemy,
To feed my means.   Here is a letter, lady;
The paper as the body of my friend,
And every word in it a gaping wound,
Issuing life-blood.   But is it true, Salerio?
Have all his ventures failed?   What, not one hit?
From Tripolis, from Mexico and England,
From Lisbon, Barbary and India?
And not one vessel scape the dreadful touch
Of merchant-marring rocks?

SALERIO.   Not one, my lord.

Besides, it should appear,[36] that if he had
The present money to discharge the Jew,
He would not take it.   Never did I know
A creature, that did bear the shape of man,
So keen and greedy to confound [37] a man:
He plies the duke at morning and at night,
And doth impeach the freedom of the state,[38]
If they deny him justice: twenty merchants,
The duke himself, and the magnificoes [39]
Of greatest port, have all persuaded with him;
But none can drive him from the envious plea [40]
Of forfeiture, of justice and his bond.

    JESSICA.   When I was with him I have heard him swear
To Tubal and to Chus, his countrymen,
That he would rather have Antonio's flesh
Than twenty times the value of the sum
That he did owe him: and I know, my lord,
If law, authority, and power deny not,
It will go hard with poor Antonio.

    PORTIA.   Is it your dear friend that is thus in trouble?

    BASSANIO.   The dearest friend to me, the kindest man,
The best-condition'd [41] and unwearied spirit
In doing courtesies, and one in whom
The ancient Roman honour more appears
Than any that draws breath in Italy.

    PORTIA.   What sum owes he the Jew?

    BASSANIO.   For me three thousand ducats.

    PORTIA.   What, no more?
Pay him six thousand, and deface the bond;
Double six thousand, and then treble that,
Before a friend of this description
Shall lose a hair through my Bassanio's fault.
First go with me to church and call me wife,
And then away to Venice to your friend;
For never shall you lie by Portia's side
With an unquiet soul.   You shall have gold
To pay the petty debt twenty times over:
When it is paid, bring your true friend along.
My maid Nerissa and myself meantime
Will live as maids and widows.   Come, away!

For you shall hence upon your wedding day:
Bid your friends welcome, show a merry cheer: [42]
Since you are dear bought, I will love you dear.
But let me hear the letter of your friend.

BASSANIO. [*Reads*] " Sweet Bassanio, my ships have all miscarried,
my creditors grow cruel, my estate is very low, my bond to the Jew is
forfeit; and since in paying it, it is impossible I should live, all debts
are cleared between you and I,[43] if I might but see you at my death.
Notwithstanding, use your pleasure: if your love do not persuade you
to come, let not my letter."

PORTIA.   O love, dispatch all business, and be gone !
BASSANIO.   Since I have your good leave to go away,
   I will make haste: but, till I come again,
No bed shall e'er be guilty of my stay,
   No rest be interposer 'twixt us twain.   [*Exeunt.*

SCENE III.   *Venice.   A street.*

Enter SHYLOCK, SALARINO, ANTONIO, *and Gaoler.*

SHYLOCK.   Gaoler, look to him: tell not me of mercy;
This is the fool that lent out money gratis:
Gaoler, look to him.
ANTONIO.   Hear me yet, good Shylock.
SHYLOCK.   I'll have my bond; speak not against my bond:
I have sworn an oath that I will have my bond.
Thou call'dst me dog before thou hadst a cause;
But, since I am a dog, beware my fangs:
The duke shall grant me justice.   I do wonder,
Thou naughty gaoler, that thou art so fond [1]
To come [2] abroad with him at his request.
ANTONIO.   I pray thee, hear me speak.
SHYLOCK.   I'll have my bond; I will not hear thee speak:
I'll have my bond; and therefore speak no more.
I'll not be made a soft and dull-eyed [3] fool,
To shake the head, relent, and sigh, and yield
To Christian intercessors.   Follow not;
I'll have no speaking; I will have my bond.   [*Exit.*
SALARINO.   It is the most impenetrable cur
That ever kept [4] with men.

ANTONIO.   Let him alone:
I'll follow him no more with bootless prayers.
He seeks my life; his reason well I know:
I oft deliver'd from his forfeitures
Many that have at times made moan to me;
Therefore he hates me.

SALARINO.   I am sure the duke
Will never grant this forfeiture to hold.

ANTONIO.   The duke cannot deny the course of law: [5]
For the commodity [6] that strangers have
With us in Venice, if it be denied,
Will much impeach the justice of his state;
Since that the trade and profit of the city
Consisteth of all nations.   Therefore go:
These griefs and losses have so bated [7] me,
That I shall hardly spare a pound of flesh
To-morrow to my bloody creditor.
Well, gaoler, on.   Pray God, Bassanio come
To see me pay his debt, and then I care not!   [*Exeunt.*

SCENE IV.   *Belmont.   A room in* PORTIA'S *house.*

Enter PORTIA, NERISSA, LORENZO, JESSICA, *and* BALTHASAR.

LORENZO.   Madam, although I speak it in your presence,
You have a noble and a true conceit [1]
Of god-like amity; which appears most strongly
In bearing thus the absence of your lord.
But if you knew to whom you show this honour,
How true a gentleman you send relief,
How dear a lover [2] of my lord your husband,
I know you would be prouder of the work
Than customary bounty can enforce you. [3]

PORTIA.   I never did repent for doing good,
Nor shall not now: for in companions
That do converse and waste the time together,
Whose souls do bear an equal yoke of love,
There must be needs a like proportion
Of lineaments, of manners and of spirit;
Which makes me think that this Antonio,
Being the bosom lover of my lord,

Must needs be like my lord.   If it be so,
How little is the cost I have bestow'd
In purchasing the semblance of my soul
From out the state of hellish misery!
This comes too near the praising of myself:
Therefore no more of it : hear other things.
Lorenzo, I commit into your hands
The husbandry and manage[4] of my house
Until my lord's return : for mine own part,
I have toward heaven breath'd a secret vow
To live in prayer and contemplation,
Only attended by Nerissa here,
Until her husband and my lord's return :
There is a monastery two miles off;
And there will we abide.   I do desire you
Not to deny this imposition,[5]
The which my love and some necessity
Now lays upon you.

    LORENZO.   Madam, with all my heart :
I shall obey you in all fair commands.

    PORTIA.   My people do already know my mind,
And will acknowledge you and Jessica
In place of Lord Bassanio and myself.
And so farewell, till we shall meet again.

    LORENZO.   Fair thoughts and happy hours attend on you!

    JESSICA.   I wish your ladyship all heart's content.

    PORTIA.   I thank you for your wish, and am well pleased
To wish it back on you : fare you well, Jessica.

                    [Exeunt JESSICA *and* LORENZO.

Now, Balthasar,
As I have ever found thee honest-true,
So let me find thee still.   Take this same letter,
And use thou all the endeavour of a man
In speed to Padua :[6] see thou render this
Into my cousin's hand, Doctor Bellario ;
And, look, what notes and garments he doth give thee,
Bring them, I pray thee, with imagined speed[7]
Unto the tranect,[8] to the common ferry
Which trades to Venice.   Waste no time in words,
But get thee gone : I shall be there before thee.

BALTHASAR.   Madam, I go with all convenient [9] speed.   [*Exit.*

PORTIA.   Come on, Nerissa; I have work in hand
That you yet know not of: we'll see our husbands
Before they think of us.

NERISSA.   Shall they see us?

PORTIA.   They shall, Nerissa; but in such a habit,
That they shall think we are accomplished
With that we lack.   I'll hold thee any wager,
When we are both accoutred like young men,
I'll prove the prettier fellow of the two,
And wear my dagger with the braver grace,
And speak between the change of man and boy
With a reed voice,[10] and turn two mincing steps
Into a manly stride, and speak of frays
Like a fine bragging youth, and tell quaint [11] lies,
How honourable ladies sought my love,
Which I denying, they fell sick and died;
I could not do withal; [12] then I'll repent,
And wish, for all that, that I had not kill'd them;
And twenty of these puny lies I'll tell,
That men shall swear I have discontinu'd school
Above a twelvemonth.   I have within my mind
A thousand raw [13] tricks of these bragging Jacks,[14]
Which I will practise.
But come, I'll tell thee all my whole device [15]
When I am in my coach, which stays for us
At the park gate; and therefore haste away,
For we must measure twenty miles to-day.   [*Exeunt.*

SCENE V.   *The same.   A garden.*

Enter LAUNCELOT *and* JESSICA.

LAUNCELOT.   Yes, truly; for, look you, the sins of the fathers are
to be laid upon the children: therefore, I promise ye, I fear you.[1]   I
was always plain with you, and so now I speak my agitation[2] of the
matter: therefore be of good cheer, for truly I think you are damned.
There is but one hope in it that can do you any good; and that is but
a kind of base hope neither.

JESSICA.   And what hope is that, I pray thee?

LAUNCELOT.   Marry, you may partly hope that you are not the Jew's daughter.

JESSICA.   That were a kind of base hope, indeed: so the sins of my mother should be visited upon me.

LAUNCELOT.   Truly then I fear you are damned both by father and mother: thus when I shun Scylla, your father, I fall into Charybdis,[3] your mother: well, you are gone both ways.

JESSICA.   I shall be saved by my husband;[4] he hath made me a Christian.

LAUNCELOT.   Truly, the more to blame he: we were Christians enow[5] before; e'en as many as could well live, one by another.   This making of Christians will raise the price of hogs: if we grow all to be pork-eaters, we shall not shortly have a rasher[6] on the coals for money.

Enter LORENZO.

JESSICA.   I'll tell my husband, Launcelot, what you say: here he comes.

LORENZO.   I shall grow jealous of you shortly, Launcelot.

JESSICA.   Nay, you need not fear us, Lorenzo: Launcelot and I are out.[7]   He tells me flatly, there is no mercy for me in heaven, because I am a Jew's daughter: and he says, you are no good member of the commonwealth, for in converting Jews to Christians, you raise the price of pork.

LORENZO.   I think the best grace of wit will shortly turn into silence, and discourse grow commendable in none only but parrots.   Go in, sirrah; bid them prepare for dinner.

LAUNCELOT.   That is done, sir: they have all stomachs.

LORENZO.   Goodly Lord, what a wit-snapper are you! then bid them prepare dinner.

LAUNCELOT.   That is done too, sir; only " cover " is the word.

LORENZO.   Will you cover then, sir?

LAUNCELOT.   Not so, sir, neither; I know my duty.[8]

LORENZO.   Yet more quarrelling with occasion[9] !   Wilt thou show the whole wealth of thy wit in an instant?   I pray thee, understand a plain man in his plain meaning: go to thy fellows; bid them cover the table, serve in the meat, and we will come in to dinner.

LAUNCELOT.   For the table, sir, it shall be served in; for the meat, sir, it shall be covered; for your coming in to dinner, sir, why, let it be as humours and conceits shall govern.   [*Exit.*

LORENZO.   O dear discretion,[10] how his words are suited!

The fool hath planted in his memory
An army of good words ; and I do know
A many [11] fools, that stand in better place,
Garnish'd [12] like him, that for a tricksy word
Defy the matter. [13]   How cheer'st thou, [14] Jessica?
And now, good sweet, say thy opinion,
How dost thou like the Lord Bassanio's wife ?

  JESSICA.   Past all expressing.   It is very meet
The Lord Bassanio live an upright life ;
For, having such a blessing in his lady,
He finds the joys of heaven here on earth ;
And if on earth he do not merit it, then
In reason he should never come to heaven.
Why, if two gods should play some heavenly match
And on the wager lay two earthly women,
And Portia one, there must be something else
Pawn'd with the other, for the poor rude world
Hath not her fellow.

  LORENZO.   Even such a husband
Hast thou of me as she is for a wife.

  JESSICA.   Nay, but ask my opinion too of that.

  LORENZO.   I will anon : first, let us go to dinner.

  JESSICA.   Nay, let me praise you while I have a stomach

  LORENZO.   No, pray thee, let it serve for table-talk ;
Then, howsoe'er thou speak'st, 'mong other things
I shall digest it.

  JESSICA. Well, I'll set you forth. [15]   [*Exeunt.*

ACT IV.

  SCENE I.   *Venice.   A court of justice.*

  Enter the DUKE, *the Magnificoes,* ANTONIO, BASSANIO,
GRATIANO, SALERIO, *and others.*

  DUKE.   What, is Antonio here?

  ANTONIO.   Ready, so please your grace.

  DUKE.   I am sorry for thee : thou art come to answer
A stony adversary, an inhuman wretch
Uncapable [1] of pity, void and empty
From any dram of mercy.

ANTONIO.   I have heard
Your grace hath ta'en great pains to qualify[2]
His rigorous course; but since he stands obdurate
And that[3] no lawful means can carry me
Out of his envy's reach,[4] I do oppose
My patience to his fury, and am arm'd
To suffer, with a quietness of spirit,
The very tyranny and rage of his.
        DUKE.   Go one, and call the Jew into court.
        SALERIO.   He is ready at the door: he comes, my lord.

Enter SHYLOCK.

        DUKE.   Make room, and let him stand before our face.
Shylock, the world thinks, and I think so too,
That thou but lead'st this fashion of thy malice
To the last hour of act; and then 'tis thought
Thou'lt show thy mercy and remorse[5] more strange
Than is thy strange apparent cruelty;
And where[6] thou now exact'st the penalty,
Which is a pound of this poor merchant's flesh,
Thou wilt not only loose[7] the forfeiture,
But, touch'd with human gentleness and love,
Forgive a moiety[8] of the principal;
Glancing an eye of pity on his losses,
That have of late so huddled on his back,
Enow to press a royal merchant down
And pluck commiseration of his state
From brassy bosoms and rough hearts of flint,
From stubborn Turks and Tartars, never train'd
To offices of tender courtesy.
We all expect a gentle answer, Jew.
        SHYLOCK.   I have possess'd your grace of what I purpose,
And by our holy Sabbath have I sworn
To have the due and forfeit of my bond:
If you deny it, let the danger light
Upon your charter[9] and your city's freedom.
You'll ask me, why I rather choose to have
A weight of carrion flesh than to receive
Three thousand ducats: I'll not answer that:
But, say, it is my humour: is it answer'd?

What if my house be troubled with a rat,
Am I be pleased to give ten thousand ducats
To have it baned ?   What, are you answer'd yet?
Some men there are love not a gaping pig ; [10]
Some, that are mad if they behold a cat ;
Some, when they hear the bagpipe : for affection,
Mistress of passion,[11] sways it to the mood
Of what it likes or loathes.   Now, for your answer :
As there is no firm reason to be render'd,
Why he cannot abide a gaping pig ;
Why he, a harmless necessary cat ;
Why he, a woollen bagpipe ; but of force
Must yield to such inevitable shame
As to offend, himself being offended ;
So can I give no reason, nor I will not,
More than a lodg'd [12] hate and a certain loathing
I bear Antonio, that I follow thus
A losing suit against him.   Are you answer'd ?

BASSANIO.   This is no answer, thou unfeeling man,
To excuse the current [13] of thy cruelty.

SHYLOCK.   I am not bound to please thee with my answers.

BASSANIO.   Do all men kill the things they do not love?

SHYLOCK.   Hates any man the thing he would not kill?

BASSANIO.   Every offence is not a hate at first.

SHYLOCK.   What, wouldst thou have a serpent sting thee twice?

ANTONIO.   I pray you, think you question [14] with the Jew :
You may as well go stand upon the beach
And bid the main flood [15] bate his usual height ;
You may as well use question with the wolf
Why he hath made the ewe bleat for the lamb ;
You may as well forbid the mountain pines
To wag their high tops and to make no noise,
When they are fretten [16] with the gusts of heaven ;
You may as well do anything most hard,
As seek to soften that — than which what's harder?—
His Jewish heart : therefore, I do beseech you,
Make no more offers, use no farther means,
But with all brief and plain conveniency [17]
Let me have judgment [18] and the Jew his will.

BASSANIO.   For thy three thousand ducats here is six.

SHYLOCK.   If every ducat in six thousand ducats
Were in six parts and every part a ducat,
I would not draw them ; I would have my bond.
    DUKE.   How shalt thou hope for mercy, rendering none ?
    SHYLOCK.   What judgment shall I dread, doing no wrong?
You have among you many a purchas'd slave,
Which, like your asses and your dogs and mules,
You use in abject and in slavish parts,[19]
Because you bought them : shall I say to you,
Let them be free, marry them to your heirs ?
Why sweat they under burthens ? let their beds
Be made as soft as yours and let their palates
Be season'd with such viands ?   You will answer
" The slaves are ours : " so do I answer you :
The pound of flesh, which I demand of him,
Is dearly bought ; 'tis mine and I will have it.
If you deny me, fie upon your law !
There is no force in the decrees of Venice.
I stand for judgment : answer ; shall I have it ?
    DUKE.   Upon my power [20] I may dismiss this court,
Unless Bellario, a learned doctor,
Whom I have sent for to determine [21] this,
Come here to-day.
    SALERIO.   My lord, here stays without
A messenger with letters from the doctor,
New come from Padua.
    DUKE.   Bring us the letters ; call the messenger.
    BASSANIO.   Good cheer, Antonio! What, man, courage yet!
The Jew shall have my flesh, blood, bones, and all,
Ere thou shalt lose for me one drop of blood.
    ANTONIO.   I am a tainted wether of the flock,
Meetest for death : the weakest kind of fruit
Drops earliest to the ground ; and so let me :
You cannot better be employ'd, Bassanio,
Than to live still and write mine epitaph.

       Enter NERISSA, *dressed like a lawyer's clerk.*
    DUKE.   Came you from Padua, from Bellario?
    NERISSA.   From both, my lord.   Bellario greets your grace.
                    [Presenting a letter.

BASSANIO.   Why dost thou whet thy knife so earnestly?

SHYLOCK.   To cut forfeiture from that bankrupt there.

GRATIANO.   Not on thy sole, but on thy soul, harsh Jew,
Thou makest thy knife keen; but no metal can,
No, not the hangman's [22] axe, bear half the keenness
Of thy sharp envy.[23]   Can no prayers pierce thee?

SHYLOCK.   No, none that thou hast wit [24] enough to make.

GRATIANO.   O, be thou damn'd, inexecrable [25] dog!
And for thy life let justice be accused.[26]
Thou almost makest me waver in my faith
To hold opinion with Pythagoras,[27]
That souls of animals infuse themselves
Into the trunks of men: thy currish spirit
Govern'd a wolf, who, hang'd [28] for human slaughter,
Even from the gallows did his fell [29] soul fleet,[30]
And, whilst thou lay'st in thy unhallow'd dam,
Infused itself in thee; for thy desires
Are wolvish, bloody, starved and ravenous.

SHYLOCK.   Till thou canst rail the seal from off my bond,
Thou but offend'st [31] thy lungs to speak so loud:
Repair thy wit, good youth, or it will fall
To cureless ruin.   I stand here for law.

DUKE.   This letter from Bellario doth commend
A young and learned doctor to our court.
Where is he?

NERISSA.   He attendeth here hard by,
To know your answer, whether you'll admit him.

DUKE.   With all my heart.   Some three or four of you
Go give him courteous conduct to this place.
Meantime the court shall hear Bellario's letter.

CLERK.   [*Reads*] " Your Grace shall understand that at the receipt of your letter I am very sick: but in the instant that your messenger came, in loving visitation was with me a young doctor of
Rome; his name is Balthasar.   I acquainted him with the cause in
controversy between the Jew and Antonio the merchant: we turned
o'er many books together: he is furnished with my opinion; which,
bettered with his own learning, the greatness whereof I cannot enough
commend, comes with him, at my importunity, to fill up [32] your grace's
request in my stead.   I beseech you, let his lack of years be no impediment to let him lack [33] a reverend estimation; for I never knew

so young a body with so old a head. I leave him to your gracious
acceptance, whose trial shall better publish his commendation."

DUKE. You hear the learn'd Bellario, what he writes:
And here, I take it, is the doctor come.

Enter PORTIA, *dressed like a doctor of laws.*

Give me your hand. Came you from old Bellario?
    PORTIA. I did, my lord.
    DUKE.   You are welcome: take your place.[34]
Are you acquainted with the difference
That holds this present question [35] in the court?
    PORTIA. I am informed throughly of the cause.
Which is the merchant here, and which the Jew?
    DUKE. Antonio and old Shylock, both stand forth.
    PORTIA. Is your name Shylock?
    SHYLOCK.   Shylock is my name.
    PORTIA. Of a strange nature is the suit you follow;
Yet in such rule [36] that the Venetian law
Cannot impugn [37] you as you do proceed.
You stand within his danger, [38] do you not?
    ANTONIO. Ay, so he says.
    PORTIA.   Do you confess the bond?
    ANTONIO. I do.
    PORTIA.   Then must the Jew be merciful.
    SHYLOCK. On what compulsion must I? tell me that.
    PORTIA. The quality of mercy is not strain'd,[39]
It droppeth as the gentle rain from heaven
Upon the place beneath; it is twice blest;
It blesseth him that gives and him that takes:
'Tis mightiest in the mightiest: it becomes
The throned monarch better than his crown;
His sceptre shows the force of temporal power,
The attribute to awe and majesty,
Wherein doth sit the dread and fear of kings;
But mercy is above this sceptred sway;
It is enthroned in the hearts of kings,
It is an attribute to God himself;
And earthly power doth then show likest God's
When mercy seasons justice. Therefore, Jew,
Though justice be thy plea, consider this,

That, in the course of justice, none of us
Should see salvation : we do pray for mercy ;
And that same prayer doth teach us all to render
The deeds of mercy.　I have spoke thus much
To mitigate the justice of thy plea ;
Which if thou follow, this strict court of Venice
Must needs give sentence 'gainst the merchant there.

　　SHYLOCK.　My deeds upon my head !　I crave the law,
The penalty and forfeit of my bond.

　　PORTIA.　Is he not able to discharge the money?

　　BASSANIO.　Yes, here I tender it for him in the court
Yea, twice the sum : if that will not suffice,
I will be bound to pay it ten times o'er,
On forfeit of my hands, my head, my heart :
If this will not suffice, it must appear
That malice bears down truth.[40]　And I beseech you,
Wrest once the law to your authority :
To do a great right, do a little wrong,
And curb this cruel devil of his will.

　　PORTIA.　It must not be ; there is no power in Venice
Can alter a decree established :
'Twill be recorded for a precedent,
And many an error by the same example
Will rush into the state : it cannot be.

　　SHYLOCK.　A Daniel [41] come to judgment !　yea, a Daniel !
O wise young judge, how I do honour thee !

　　PORTIA.　I pray you, let me look upon the bond.

　　SHYLOCK.　Here 'tis, most reverend doctor, here it is.

　　PORTIA.　Shylock, there's thrice thy money offer'd thee.

　　SHYLOCK.　An oath, an oath, I have an oath in heaven :
Shall I lay perjury upon my soul?
No, not for Venice.

　　PORTIA.　　　　Why, this bond is forfeit ;
And lawfully by this the Jew may claim
A pound of flesh, to be by him cut off
Nearest the merchant's heart.　Be merciful :
Take thrice thy money ; bid me tear the bond.

　　SHYLOCK.　When it is paid according to the tenour.
It doth appear you are a worthy judge ;
You know the law, your exposition

Hath been most sound : I charge you by the law,
Whereof you are a well-deserving pillar,
Proceed to judgment : by my soul I swear
There is no power in the tongue of man
To alter me : I stay here on my bond.

    ANTONIO.   Most heartily I do beseech the court
To give the judgment.

    PORTIA.   Why then, thus it is :
You must prepare your bosom for his knife.

    SHYLOCK.   O noble judge ! O excellent young man !

    PORTIA.   For the intent and purpose of the law
Hath full relation [42] to the penalty
Which here appeareth due upon the bond.

    SHYLOCK.   'Tis very true : O wise and upright judge !
How much more elder [43] art thou than thy looks !

    PORTIA.   Therefore lay bare your bosom.

    SHYLOCK.   Ay, his breast :
So says the bond : doth it not, noble judge ?
" Nearest his heart : " those are the very words.

    PORTIA.   It is so.   Are there balance [44] here to weigh
The flesh ?

    SHYLOCK.   I have them ready.

    PORTIA.   Have by some surgeon, Shylock, on your charge, [45]
To stop his wounds, lest he do bleed to death.

    SHYLOCK.   Is it so nominated in the bond ?

    PORTIA.   It is not so express'd : but what of that ?
'Twere good you do so much for charity.

    SHYLOCK.   I cannot find it ; 'tis not in the bond.

    PORTIA.   You, merchant, have you any thing to say ?

    ANTONIO.   But little : I am arm'd and well prepar'd.
Give me your hand, Bassanio : fare you well !
Grieve not that I am fall'n to this for you ;
For herein Fortune shows herself more kind
Than is her custom : it is still her use [46]
To let the wretched man outlive his wealth,
To view with hollow eye and wrinkled brow
An age of poverty ; from which lingering penance
Of such misery doth she cut me off.
Commend me to your honourable wife :
Tell her the process of Antonio's end ;

Say how I loved you, speak me fair in death; [47]
And, when the tale is told, bid her be judge
Whether Bassanio had not once a love.
Repent but you that you shall lose your friend,
And he repents not that he pays your debt;
For if the Jew do cut but deep enough,
I'll pay it presently with all my heart.[48]

BASSANIO.   Antonio, I am married to a wife
Which is as dear to me as life itself;
But life itself, my wife, and all the world,
Are not with me esteem'd above thy life:
I would lose all, ay, sacrifice them all
Here to this devil, to deliver you.

PORTIA.   Your wife would give you little thanks for that,
If she were by, to hear you make the offer.

GRATIANO.   I have a wife, whom, I protest, I love:
I would she were in heaven, so she could
Entreat some power to change this currish Jew.

NERISSA.   'Tis well you offer it behind her back;
The wish would make else an unquiet house.

SHYLOCK.   [*Aside*] These be the Christian husbands.   I have a
         daughter;
Would any of the stock of Barrabas
Had been her husband rather than a Christian
[*Aloud*] We trifle time: I pray thee, pursue sentence.

PORTIA.   A pound of that same merchant's flesh is thine:
The court awards it, and the law doth give it.

SHYLOCK.   Most rightful judge!

PORTIA.   And you must cut this flesh from off his breast:
The law allows it, and the court awards it.

SHYLOCK.   Most learned judge!   A sentence!   Come, prepare!

PORTIA.   Tarry a little; there is something else.
This bond doth give thee here no jot of blood;
The words expressly are "a pound of flesh:"
Take then thy bond, take thou thy pound of flesh;
But, in the cutting it, if thou dost shed
One drop of Christian blood, thy lands and goods
Are, by the laws of Venice, confiscate
Unto the state of Venice.

GRATIANO.   O upright judge!   Mark, Jew: O learned judge!

SHYLOCK.   Is that the law?

PORTIA.   Thyself shalt see the act:
For, as thou urgest justice, be assured
Thou shalt have justice, more than thou desirest.

GRATIANO.   O learned judge! Mark, Jew: a learned judge!

SHYLOCK.   I take this offer, then; pay the bond thrice
And let the Christian go.

BASSANIO.   Here is the money.

PORTIA.   Soft!
The Jew shall have all justice; soft! no haste:
He shall have nothing but the penalty.

GRATIANO.   O Jew! an upright judge, a learned judge!

PORTIA.   Therefore prepare thee to cut off the flesh.
Shed thou no blood, nor cut thou less nor more
But just a pound of flesh: if thou cut'st more
Or less than a just [49] pound, be it but so much
As makes it light or heavy in the substance, [50]
Or the division of the twentieth part
Of one poor scruple, nay, if the scale do turn
But in the estimation of a hair,
Thou diest and all thy goods are confiscate.

GRATIANO.   A second Daniel, a Daniel, Jew!
Now, infidel, I have you on the hip.

PORTIA.   Why doth the Jew pause? take thy forfeiture.

SHYLOCK.   Give me my principal, and let me go.

BASSANIO.   I have it ready for thee; here it is.

PORTIA.   He hath refused it in the open court:
He shall have merely justice and his bond.

GRATIANO.   A Daniel, still say I, a second Daniel!
I thank thee, Jew, for teaching me that word.

SHYLOCK.   Shall I not have barely my principal?

PORTIA.   Thou shalt have nothing but the forfeiture,
To be so taken at thy peril, Jew.

SHYLOCK.   Why, then the devil give him good of it!
I'll stay no longer question.

PORTIA.   Tarry, Jew:
The law hath yet another hold on you.
It is enacted in the laws of Venice,
If it be proved against an alien
That by direct or indirect attempts

He seek the life of any citizen,
The party 'gainst the which he doth contrive [51]
Shall seize one half his goods; the other half
Comes to the privy coffer of the state;
And the offender's life lies in the mercy
Of the duke only, 'gainst all other voice.
In which predicament, I say, thou stand'st;
For it appears, by manifest proceeding,
That indirectly and directly too
Thou hast contrived against the very life
Of the defendant; and thou hast incurr'd
The danger formerly [52] by me rehears'd.
Down therefore and beg mercy of the duke.

GRATIANO.   Beg that thou mayst have leave to hang thyself:
And yet, thy wealth being forfeit to the state,
Thou hast not left the value of a cord;
Therefore thou must be hang'd at the state's charge.

DUKE.   That thou shalt see the difference of our spirits,
I pardon thee thy life before thou ask it:
For half thy wealth, it is Antonio's;
The other half comes to the general state,
Which humbleness may drive unto a fine.[53]

PORTIA.   Ay, for the state, not for Antonio.

SHYLOCK.   Nay, take my life and all; pardon not that:
You take my house when you do take the prop
That doth sustain my house; you take my life
When you do take the means whereby I live.

PORTIA.   What mercy can you render him, Antonio?

GRATIANO.   A halter gratis; nothing else, for God's sake.

ANTONIO.   So please my lord the duke and all the court
To quit the fine for one half of his goods,
I am content; so he will let me have
The other half in use,[54] to render it,
Upon his death, unto the gentleman
That lately stole his daughter:
Two things provided more, that, for this favour,
He presently become a Christian;
The other, that he do record a gift,
Here in the court, of all he dies possess'd,
Unto his son Lorenzo and his daughter.

DUKE. He shall do this, or else I do recant
The pardon that I late pronounced here.
PORTIA. Art thou contented, Jew? what dost thou say?
SHYLOCK. I am content.
PORTIA.   Clerk, draw a deed of gift.
SHYLOCK. I pray you, give me leave to go from hence;
I am not well: send the deed after me,
And I will sign it.
DUKE.   Get thee gone, but do it.
GRATIANO. In christening shalt thou have two godfathers;
Had I been judge, thou shouldst have had ten more,[55]
To bring thee to the gallows, not the font.   [*Exit* SHYLOCK.
DUKE. Sir, I entreat you home with me to dinner.
PORTIA. I humbly do desire your grace of pardon:
I must away this night toward Padua,
And it is meet I presently set forth.
DUKE. I am sorry that your leisure serves you not.[56]
Antonio, gratify [57] this gentleman,
For, in my mind, you are much bound to him.

                         [*Exeunt* DUKE *and his train.*

BASSANIO. Most worthy gentleman, I and my friend
Have by your wisdom been this day acquitted
Of grievous penalties; in lieu whereof,
Three thousand ducats, due unto the Jew,
We freely cope [58] your courteous pains withal.[59]
ANTONIO. And stand indebted, over and above,
In love and service to you evermore.
PORTIA. He is well paid that is well satisfied;
And I, delivering you, am satisfied
And therein do account myself well paid:
My mind was never yet more mercenary.[60]
I pray you, know me when we meet again:
I wish you well, and so I take my leave.
BASSANIO. Dear sir, of force [61] I must attempt [62] you further:
Take some remembrance of us, as a tribute
Not as a fee: grant me two things, I pray you,
Not to deny me, and to pardon me.
PORTIA. You press me far, and therefore I will yield.
[*To* ANTONIO] Give me your gloves, I'll wear them for your sake;
[*To* BASSANIO] And, for your love, I'll take this ring from you:

Do not draw back your hand ; I'll take no more ;
And you in love shall not deny me this.

BASSANIO.   This ring, good sir, alas, it is a trifle !
I will not shame myself to give you this.

PORTIA.   I will have nothing else but only this ;
And now methinks I have a mind to it.

BASSANIO.   There's more depends on this than on the value.
The dearest ring in Venice will I give you,
And find it out by proclamation :
Only for this, I pray you, pardon me.

PORTIA.   I see, sir, you are liberal in offers :
You taught me first to beg ; and now methinks
You teach me how a beggar should be answer'd.

BASSANIO.   Good sir, this ring was given me by my wife ;
And when she put it on, she made me vow
That I should neither sell nor give nor lose it.

PORTIA.   That 'scuse [63] serves many men to save their gifts.
An if [64] your wife be not a mad-woman,
And know how well I have deserved the ring,
She would not hold out enemy for ever,
For giving it to me.   Well, peace be with you !

[Exeunt PORTIA *and* NERISSA.

ANTONIO.   My Lord Bassanio, let him have the ring :
Let his deservings and my love withal
Be valued 'gainst your wife's commandment.

BASSANIO.   Go, Gratiano, run and overtake him ;
Give him the ring, and bring him, if thou canst,
Unto Antonio's house : away ! make haste.   *[Exit* GRATIANO.
Come, you and I will thither presently ;
And in the morning early will we both
Fly toward Belmont : come, Antonio.   *[Exeunt.*

SCENE II.   *The same.   A street.*

Enter PORTIA *and* NERISSA.

PORTIA.   Inquire the Jew's house out, give him this deed
And let him sign it : we'll away to-night
And be a day before our husbands home :
This deed will be well welcome to Lorenzo.

Enter GRATIANO.

GRATIANO.   Fair sir, you are well o'erta'en :
My Lord Bassanio upon more advice [1]
Hath sent you here this ring, and doth entreat
Your company at dinner.
    PORTIA.   That cannot be :
His ring I do accept most thankfully :
And so, I pray you, tell him : furthermore,
I pray you, show my youth old Shylock's house.
    GRATIANO.   That will I do.
    NERISSA.   Sir, I would speak with you.
[*Aside to* PORTIA] I'll see if I can get my husband's ring,
Which I did make him swear to keep for ever.
    PORTIA.   [*Aside to* NERISSA] Thou may'st, I warrant.   We shall
        have old swearing [2]
That they did give the rings away to men ;
But we'll outface them, and outswear them too.
[*Aloud*] Away ! make haste : thou know'st where I will tarry.
    NERISSA.   Come, good sir, will you shew me to this house?
                                      [*Exeunt.*

ACT V.

SCENE I.   *Belmont.*   *Avenue to* PORTIA'S *house.*

Enter LORENZO *and* JESSICA.

LORENZO.   The moon shines bright : in such a night as this,
When the sweet wind did gently kiss the trees
And they did make no noise, in such a night
Troilus [1] methinks mounted the Troyan walls
And sigh'd his soul toward the Grecian tents,
Where Cressid lay that night.
    JESSICA.   In such a night
Did Thisbe [2] fearfully o'ertrip the dew
And saw the lion's shadow ere himself
And ran dismay'd away.
    LORENZO.   In such a night
Stood Dido [3] with a willow in her hand
Upon the wild sea banks and wav'd her love
To come again to Carthage.

JESSICA.   In such a night
Medea[4] gather'd the enchanted herbs
That did renew old Æson.

LORENZO.   In such a night
Did Jessica steal from the wealthy Jew
And with an unthrift love did run from Venice
As far as Belmont.

JESSICA.   In such a night
Did young Lorenzo swear he loved her well,
Stealing her soul with many vows of faith
And ne'er a true one.

LORENZO.   In such a night
Did pretty Jessica, like a little shrew,
Slander her love, and he forgave it her.

JESSICA. I would out-night[5] you, did no body come;
But, hark, I hear the footing of a man.

Enter STEPHANO.

LORENZO. Who comes so fast in silence of the night?
STEPHANO. A friend.
LORENZO. A friend! what friend? your name, I pray you, friend?
STEPHANO. Stephano is my name; and I bring word
My mistress will before the break of day
Be here at Belmont: she doth stray about
By holy crosses,[6] where she kneels and prays
For happy wedlock hours.

LORENZO.   Who comes with her?
STEPHANO. None but a holy hermit and her maid.
I pray you, is my master yet return'd?

LORENZO. He is not, nor we have not heard from him.
But go we in, I pray thee, Jessica,
And ceremoniously let us prepare
Some welcome for the mistress of the house.

Enter LAUNCELOT.

LAUNCELOT. Sola, sola! wo ha, ho! sola, sola!
LORENZO. Who calls?
LAUNCELOT. Sola! did you see Master Lorenzo? Master Lo-
renzo, sola, sola!
LORENZO. Leave hollaing, man: here.

LAUNCELOT.   Sola! where? where?

LORENZO.   Here.

LAUNCELOT.   Tell him there's a post come from my master, with his horn full of good news: my master will be here ere morning.

[*Exit.*

LORENZO.   Sweet soul, let's in, and there expect [7] their coming.
And yet no matter: why should we go in?
My friend Stephano, signify, I pray you,
Within the house, your mistress is at hand;
And bring your music forth into the air.   [*Exit* STEPHANO.
How sweet the moonlight sleeps upon this bank!
Here will we sit and let the sounds of music
Creep in our ears: soft stillness and the night
Become the touches of sweet harmony.
Sit, Jessica.   Look how the floor of heaven
Is thick inlaid with patines [8] of bright gold:
There's not the smallest orb which thou behold'st
But in his motion like an angel sings, [9]
Still quiring [10] to the young-eyed cherubins;
Such harmony is in immortal souls;
But whilst this muddy vesture of decay
Doth grossly close it in, we cannot hear it.

Enter Musicians.

Come, ho! and wake Diana [11] with a hymn:
With sweetest touches pierce your mistress' ear
And draw her home with music.   [*Music.*

JESSICA.   I am never merry when I hear sweet music.

LORENZO.   The reason is, your spirits are attentive:
For do but note a wild and wanton herd,
Or race of youthful and unhandled colts,
Fetching mad bounds, bellowing and neighing loud,
Which is the hot condition of their blood;
If they but hear perchance a trumpet sound,
Or any air of music touch their ears,
You shall perceive them make a mutual [12] stand,
Their savage eyes turn'd to a modest gaze
By the sweet power of music: therefore the poet
Did feign that Orpheus [13] drew trees, stones and floods;
Since nought so stockish, [14] hard and full of rage,

But music for the time doth change his nature.
The man that hath no music in himself,
Nor is not moved with concord of sweet sounds,
Is fit for treasons, stratagems and spoils; [15]
The motions of his spirit are dull as night
And his affections dark as Erebus: [16]
Let no such man be trusted.   Mark the music.

Enter PORTIA *and* NERISSA.

PORTIA.   That light we see is burning in my hall.
How far that little candle throws its beams!
So shines a good deed in a naughty world.
    NERISSA.   When the moon shone, we did not see the candle.
    PORTIA.   So doth the greater glory dim the less:
A substitute shines brightly as a king
Until a king be by, and then his state
Empties itself, as doth an inland brook
Into the main of waters.   Music! hark!
    NERISSA.   It is your music, madam, of the house.
    PORTIA.   Nothing is good, I see, without respect: [17]
Methinks it sounds much sweeter than by day.
    NERISSA.   Silence bestows that virtue on it, madam.
    PORTIA.   The crow doth sing as sweetly as the lark
When neither is attended, [18] and I think
The nightingale, if she should sing by day,
When every goose is cackling, would be thought
No better a musician than the wren.
How many things by season season'd are [19]
To their right praise and true perfection!
Peace, ho! the moon sleeps with Endymion [20]
And would not be awaked.   [*Music ceases.*
    LORENZO.   That is the voice,
Or I am much deceived, of Portia.
    PORTIA.   He knows me as the blind man knows the cuckoo,
By the bad voice.
    LORENZO.   Dear lady, welcome home.
    PORTIA.   We have been praying for our husbands' healths,
Which speed, we hope, the better for our words.
Are they return'd?
    LORENZO.   Madam, they are not yet;

But there is come a messenger before,
To signify their coming.

    PORTIA.   Go in, Nerissa;
Give order to my servants that they take
No note at all of our being absent hence;
Nor you, Lorenzo; Jessica, nor you.   [*A tucket* [21] *sounds.*

    LORENZO. Your husband is at hand; I hear his trumpet:
We are no tell-tales, madam; fear you not.

    PORTIA. This night methinks is but the daylight sick;
It looks a little paler: 'tis a day,
Such as the day is when the sun is hid.

   Enter BASSANIO, ANTONIO, GRATIANO, *and their followers.*

    BASSANIO. We should hold day with the Antipodes,
If you would walk in absence of the sun. [22]

    PORTIA. Let me give light, but let me not be light;
For a light wife doth make a heavy husband,
And never be Bassanio so for me:
But God sort all! [23] You are welcome home, my lord.

    BASSANIO. I thank you, madam. Give welcome to my friend.
This is the man, this is Antonio,
To whom I am so infinitely bound.

    PORTIA. You should in all sense [24] be much bound to him,
For, as I hear, he was much bound for you.

    ANTONIO. No more than I am well acquitted of.

    PORTIA. Sir, you are very welcome to our house:
It must appear in other ways than words,
Therefore I scant this breathing courtesy. [25]

    GRATIANO. [*To* NERISSA] [26] By yonder moon I swear you do
           me wrong;
In faith, I gave it to the judge's clerk:
Would he were dead that had it, for my part,
Since you do take it, love, so much to heart.

    PORTIA. A quarrel, ho, already! what's the matter?

    GRATIANO. About a hoop of gold, a paltry ring
That she did give me, whose posy [27] was
For all the world like cutler's poetry
Upon a knife, "Love me, and leave me not."

    NERISSA. What talk you of the posy or the value?
You swore to me, when I did give it you,

That you would wear it till your hour of death
And that it should lie with you in your grave :
Though not for me, yet for your vehement oaths,
You should have been respective [28] and have kept it.
Gave it a judge's clerk ! no, God's my judge,
The clerk will ne'er wear hair on's face that had it.

    GRATIANO.   He will, an if he live to be a man.

    NERISSA.   Ay, if a woman live to be a man.

    GRATIANO.   Now, by this hand, I gave it to a youth,
A kind of boy, a little scrubbed boy,
No higher than thyself, the judge's clerk,
A prating boy, that begg'd it as a fee :
I could not for my heart deny it him.

    PORTIA.   You were to blame, I must be plain with you,
To part so slightly with your wife's first gift ;
A thing stuck on with oaths upon your finger
And so riveted with faith unto your flesh.
I gave my love a ring and made him swear
Never to part with it ; and here he stands ;
I dare be sworn for him he would not leave it
Nor pluck it from his finger, for the wealth
That the world masters.   Now, in faith, Gratiano,
You give your wife too unkind a cause of grief :
An 'twere to me, I should be mad at it.

    BASSANIO. [*Aside*] Why, I were best to cut my left hand off
And swear I lost the ring defending it.

    GRATIANO.   My Lord Bassanio gave his ring away
Unto the judge that begg'd it and indeed
Deserved it too : and then the boy, his clerk,
That took some pains in writing, he begg'd mine ;
And neither man nor master would take aught
But the two rings.

    PORTIA.   What ring gave you, my lord?
Not that, I hope, which you received of me.

    BASSANIO.   If I could add a lie unto a fault,
I would deny it ; but you see my finger
Hath not the ring upon it ; it is gone.

    PORTIA.   Even so void is your false heart of truth.
By heaven, I will never be your wife
Until I see the ring.

NERISSA.   No, nor I yours
Till I again see mine.

BASSANIO.   Sweet Portia,
If you did know to whom I gave the ring,
If you did know for whom I gave the ring,
And would conceive for what I gave the ring,
And how unwillingly I left the ring,
When nought would be accepted but the ring,
You would abate the strength of your displeasure.

PORTIA.   If you had known the virtue of the ring, [29]
Or half her worthiness that gave the ring,
Or your own honour to contain [30] the ring,
You would not then have parted with the ring.
What man is there so much unreasonable,
If you had pleased to have defended it
With any terms of zeal, wanted [31] the modesty
To urge the thing held as a ceremony? [32]
Nerissa teaches me what to believe:
I'll die for't but some woman had the ring.

BASSANIO.   No, by my honour, madam, by my soul,
No woman had it, but a civil doctor, [33]
Which did refuse three thousand ducats of me
And begg'd the ring; the which I did deny him
And suffer'd him to go displeas'd away;
Even he that did uphold the very life
Of my dear friend.   What should I say, sweet lady?
I was enforc'd to send it after him;
I was beset with shame and courtesy; [34]
My honour would not let ingratitude
So much besmear it.   Pardon me, good lady;
For, by these blessed candles of the night,
Had you been there, I think you would have begg'd
The ring of me to give the worthy doctor.

PORTIA.   Let not that doctor e'er come near my house:
Since he hath got the jewel that I loved,
And that which you did swear to keep for me,
I will become as liberal as you;
I'll not deny him any thing I have.

ANTONIO.   I am the unhappy subject of these quarrels.

PORTIA.   Sir, grieve not you; you are welcome notwithstanding.

BASSANIO. Portia, forgive me this enforced wrong;
And, in the hearing of these many friends,
I swear to thee, even by thine own fair eyes,
Wherein I see myself —

PORTIA. Mark you but that!
In both my eyes he doubly sees himself;
In each eye, one: swear by your double self,
And there's an oath of credit.

BASSANIO. Nay, but hear me:
Pardon this fault, and by my soul I swear
I never more will break an oath with thee.

ANTONIO. I once did lend my body for his wealth; [35]
Which, but for him that had your husband's ring,
Had quite miscarried: I dare be bound again,
My soul upon the forfeit, that your lord
Will never more break faith advisedly. [36]

PORTIA. Then you shall be his surety. Give him this,
And bid him keep it better than the other.

ANTONIO. Here, Lord Bassanio; swear to keep this ring.

BASSANIO. By heaven, it is the same I gave the doctor!

PORTIA. You are all amazed:
Here is a letter: read it at your leisure;
It comes from Padua, from Bellario:
There you shall find that Portia was the doctor,
Nerissa there her clerk: Lorenzo here
Shall witness I set forth as soon as you
And even but now return'd: I have not yet
Enter'd my house. Antonio, you are welcome;
And I have better news in store for you
Than you expect: unseal this letter soon;
There you shall find three of your argosies
Are richly [37] come to harbour suddenly: [38]
You shall not know by what strange accident
I chanced on this letter.

ANTONIO. I am dumb.

BASSANIO. Were you the doctor and I knew you not?

GRATIANO. Were you the clerk and yet I knew you not?

ANTONIO. Sweet lady, you have given me life and living; [39]
For here I read for certain that my ships
Are safely come to road.

PORTIA. How now, Lorenzo!
My clerk hath some good comforts too for you.

NERISSA. Ay, and I'll give them him without a fee.
There do I give to you and Jessica,
From the rich Jew, a special deed of gift,
After his death, of all he dies possess'd of.

LORENZO. Fair ladies, you drop manna in the way
Of starved people.

PORTIA. It is almost morning,
And yet I am sure you are not satisfied
Of these events at full. [40] Let us go in ;
And charge us there upon inter'gatories,
And we will answer all things faithfully. [41]

GRATIANO. Well, while I live I'll fear no other thing
So sore as keeping safe Nerissa's ring. [*Exeunt.*

NOTES TO THE MERCHANT OF VENICE.

THE essential thing in the drama is action. It is thus distinguished from the epic, which narrates heroic deeds, and from the lyric, which expresses intense emotion. The drama presents a series of grave or humorous incidents that terminate in a striking result. Its ultimate basis is found in our natural love of imitation; and hence it is not restricted to any race or age or country. India and China, Greece and Rome, no less than modern nations, delighted in dramatic exhibitions, and produced a notable dramatic literature. Obviously the drama is not inherently evil; and if it has often been condemned by pagan sage and Christian teacher, the condemnation has been evoked by the degeneracy and dissoluteness of the stage.

The principal species of the drama are tragedy and comedy. Tragedy represents an important and serious action, which usually has a fatal termination; it appeals to the earnest side of our nature, and moves our deepest feelings. Comedy consists in a representation of light and amusing incidents; it exhibits the foibles of individuals, the manners of society, and the humorous accidents of life. The laws of the drama are substantially the same for both tragedy and comedy. There must be unity in the dramatic action. This requires that the separate incidents contribute in some way to the development of the plot and to the final result or *dénouement*. A collection of disconnected scenes, no matter how interesting in themselves, would not make a drama.

The action of the drama should exhibit movement or progress, in which several stages may be clearly marked. The introduction acquaints us, more or less fully, with the subject to be treated. It usually brings before us some of the leading characters, and shows us the circumstances in which they are placed. In the "Merchant of Venice," for example, the First Scene reveals Antonio's ventures at sea, and Bassanio's desire to woo the fair Portia, which facts furnish the basis of the subsequent action. After the introduction follows the growth or development of the action toward the climax. From the days of Aristotle, this part of the drama has been called the tying of the knot, and it needs to be managed with great care. If the development is too slow, the interest lags; if too rapid, the climax appears tame. The interest of a drama depends in large measure upon the successful arrangement of the climax. In our best dramas it usually occurs near the middle of the piece.

In the " Merchant of Venice " it is reached in the Third Scene of the Third Act, where Antonio is in prison and Shylock will not hear of mercy. From this point the action proceeds to the close or *dénouement*. The knot is untied; the complications in which the leading characters have become involved are either happily removed, or lead to an inevitable catastrophe. Avoiding every digression, the action should go forward rapidly, in order not to weary the patience and dissipate the interest of the spectator. The *dénouement* should not be dependent upon some foreign element introduced at the last moment; but should spring naturally from the antecedent action.

In the " Merchant of Venice," the knot is untied at the end of the Fourth Act, where the over-reaching malice of Shylock meets its punishment, and the noble Antonio is triumphantly vindicated. But as Schlegel remarks, " the poet was unwilling to dismiss his audience with the gloomy impressions which Antonio's acquittal — effected with so much difficulty — and the condemnation of Shylock were calculated to leave behind them; he therefore added a Fifth Act by way of a musical afterlude to the piece itself."

In addition to unity of action, which is obviously the indispensable law of the drama, two other unities have been prescribed from a very early day. The one is unity of time, which requires that the action fall within the limits of a single day; the other is unity of place, which requires that the action occur in the same locality. While evidently artificial and dispensable, these latter unities conduce to clear and concise treatment. Among the Greeks and Romans the three unities, as they are called, were strictly observed; they have been followed also by the French drama; but the English stage, breaking away in the days of Elizabeth from every artificial restriction, recognizes unity of action alone. The " Merchant of Venice " includes a period of three months.

Act I. — Scene I.

1. *In sooth* = in truth. A. S. *soth*, truth. Cf. *forsooth, soothsayer*.

2. *Want-wit* = foolish, idiotic. This unaccountable sadness of Antonio has been called the keynote of the play. It forbodes coming disaster.

3. *Ado* = trouble. Contraction of Mid. Eng. *at do*.

4. *Argosies* = merchant vessels. From *Argo*, the name of the ship which carried Jason to Colchis in search of the Golden Fleece.

5. *Signiors* = lords. From Lat. *senior*, elder, through the Italian.

6. *Pageants* = shows, spectacles. Originally the movable scaffolds used in the miracle plays.

7. *Overpeer* = tower above, look over.

8. *Venture* = hazard, risk; especially, something sent to sea in trade. Etymologically, a headless form of *adventure*.

9. *Still* = constantly.

10. *Roads* = places where ships *ride* at anchor. A. S. *rad*, road.

11. *Wealthy Andrew dock'd in sand* = richly freighted ship stranded. The name is probably taken from Andrea Doria, a famous Genoese admiral.

12. *Vailing* = lowering. A headless form of the Fr. *avaler*, from Lat. *ad vallem*, to the valley.

13. *Straight* = at once, immediately. A. S. *streccan*, to stretch.

14. *Worth this* refers to some expressive gesture.

15. *Bottom* = merchant vessel.

16. *Janus* = a Latin deity represented with two faces looking in opposite directions. *January* is named after him. See Webster.

17. *Peep through their eyes*, because half shut with laughter.

18. *Other* = others; frequently used as a plural in Shakespeare.

19. *Nestor* = the gravest and oldest of the Grecian heroes at the siege of Troy.

20. *Prevented* = anticipated. This is the old sense; from Fr. *prevenir*, Lat. *prae*, before, and *venire*, to come.

21. *Exceeding strange* = exceedingly strange-like, quite strangers. *Exceeding* is often used as an adverb by Shakespeare.

22. *Respect upon* = regard, consideration for.

23. *Play the fool* = act the part of the fool, as seen in old comedies. His function was to show the comic side of things.

24. *Mantle* = become covered, as with a mantle.

25. *Do* has *who* understood as its subject. The whole line may be rendered thus: And who do maintain an obstinate silence.

26. *Opinion of wisdom* = reputation for wisdom.

27. *Conceit* = thought. In Shakespeare this word is used for *thought, conception, imagination*, but never in the sense of *vanity*.

28. *As who should say* = as if one should say; who being indefinite.

29. A reference to Matt. v. 22. "Whosoever shall say, Thou fool, shall be in danger of hell fire." If these silent persons should speak, they would provoke their hearers to say "thou fool," and thus bring them into danger of condemnation.

30. *Gudgeon* = a small fish that is easily caught. See Webster.

31. *Moe* = more.

32. *Gear* = matter, business, purpose. In Act II, Scene 2, we find: "Well, if Fortune be a woman, she's a good wench for this *gear*."

33. *Something* = somewhat. This use is common in Shakespeare.

34. *Swelling port* = great state, ostentatious manner of living.

35. *Rate* = manner, style.

36. *Gag'd* = engaged, pledged.

37. *Still* = constantly. See note 9.

38. *Within the eye of honour* = within the range of what is honorable.

39. *Self-same flight* = made for the same range, having the same length, weight, and feathering.

40. *Advised* = careful, considerate.

41. *To find the other forth* = to find the other out.

42. *Childhood proof* = test or experiment of childhood.

43. *Wilful* = obstinate in extravagance. Owing to the obscurity, " witless " and " wasteful " have been suggested for *wilful.*

44. *That self way* = that same way. This use of *self* is frequent in Shakespeare.

45. *Circumstance* = circumlocution.

46. *In making question,* etc. = in questioning my readiness to do my utmost for you.

47. *Prest* = ready. O. Fr. *prest,* now *prêt,* ready.

48. *Richly left* = with a large inheritance.

49. *Sometimes* = formerly. *Sometimes* and *sometime* were used indifferently by Shakespeare in this sense.

50. *Nothing undervalued* = not at all inferior.

51. *Brutus' Portia.* See Shakespeare's *Julius Cæsar,* in which Portia is a prominent character.

52. *Colchos' strand.* Colchis was situated at the eastern extremity of the Black Sea. Thither, according to Grecian mythology, Jason was sent in quest of the golden fleece, which, though it was guarded by a sleepless dragon, he succeeded in obtaining. The Argonautic expedition is referred to again in Act III. Scene 2: " We are the Jasons, we have won the fleece."

53. *With one of them* = as one of them.

54. *Thrift* = success.

55. *Commodity* = property, merchandise.

56. *Presently* = instantly, immediately.

57. *Of my trust,* etc. = on my credit as a merchant or as a personal favor.

SCENE II.

1. *Troth* = truth, of which it is an old form.

2. *Nor refuse none.* — We should now say, Nor refuse any. But the double negative had not yet disappeared from English in Shakespeare's day.

3. *Level at* = guess, aim at.

4. *Colt* = wild, rough youth.

5. *Appropriation* = credit.

6. *County Palatine* = Count Palatine.

7. *Weeping philosopher* = Heraclitus; so called because he wept over the follies of mankind. Democritus, who laughed at them, was called "The laughing philosopher."

8. *By* = of, about, concerning — a not unfrequent use of the word.

9. *Say to* is here playfully used in a different sense from that which Nerissa meant.

10. *Proper* = handsome.

11. *Suited* = dressed.

12. *Doublet* = a close-fitting coat, with skirts reaching a little below the girdle.

13. *Round hose* = coverings for the legs. *Doublet and hose* is equivalent to *coat and breeches*.

14. *Bonnet* = hat or head-dress. Since Shakespeare's day *bonnet* and *hat* have changed places.

15. *Sealed under*, that is, as surety he placed his name *under* that of the principal. There seems to be a sly hit at the constant assistance which the French promised the Scotch in their quarrels with the English.

16. *An* = if.

17. *Should* = would. These words were not fully differentiated by Shakespeare.

18. *Contrary* = wrong. So in "King John," IV. 2: "Standing on slippers which his nimble haste had falsely thrust upon contrary feet."

19. *Sort* = manner; or, possibly, lot, as in "Troilus and Cressida," I. 3: "Let blockish Ajax draw the sort to fight with Hector."

20. *Imposition* = imposed condition.

21. *Sibylla* is erroneously used as a proper noun. A sibyl was a woman supposed to be endowed with a spirit of prophecy. The reference here is to one to whom Apollo promised as many years of life as there were grains of sand in her hand.

22. *Four* is probably an oversight, as there were six of the strangers.

23. *Condition* = disposition, temper. This is a common meaning of the word in Shakespeare.

24. *Shrive* = to administer confession and absolution.

Scene III.

1. *Ducats* = coins first issued in the duchy of Apulia. From O. Fr. *ducat* = Ital. *ducato* = Low Lat. *ducatus*, duchy. So called because when first coined, about A.D. 1140, they bore the legend, "Sit tibi, Christe, datus, quem tu regis, iste *ducatus*." — Skeat. The Venetian silver ducat was worth about one dollar.

2. *May you stead me* = can you help me. *May* originally expressed *ability*.

3. *A good man* = a solvent man, one able to meet his obligations.

4. *In supposition* = in doubtful form, being risked at sea.

5. *Rialto* = the Exchange of Venice. From *rivo alto*, higher shore. The name was originally applied to the chief island in Venice.

6. *Squandered* = scattered, dispersed; this was the original sense of the word.

7. Referring to the permission given the devils to enter into the herd of swine. Matt. viii. 32.

8. *Usance* = interest.

9. *Catch upon the hip* = to get into one's power; a phrase used by wrestlers.

10. *Interest* was a term of reproach in Shakespeare's day, as *usury* is now. It was held disreputable to take compensation for the use of money, inasmuch, as it was said, "it is against nature for money to beget money."

11. *Rest you fair* = may you have fair fortune.

12. *Excess* = that which is paid in excess of the sum lent.

13. *Ripe wants* = wants that require immediate attention.

14. *Possess'd* = informed.

15. *Methought* = it seemed to me. From A. S. *thincan* = to seem. *To think* comes from A. S. *thencan*.

16. *The third*, counting Abraham as the first. Gen. xxvii.

17. *Compromis'd* = agreed.

18. *Eanling* = lamb just brought forth. *Yeanling* is another form of the word. From A. S. *eanian*, to bring forth.

19. See Gen. xxx. 31–43.

20. *Inserted*, that is, in the Scriptures.

21. These lines are spoken aside, while Shylock is occupied with his calculations.

22. *Beholding* = beholden, indebted. Shakespeare always uses the form in *ing*, *beholden* occurring not a single time in his writings.

23. *Gaberdine* = a coarse smock-frock or upper garment.

24. *Go to* = come; a phrase of exhortation.

25. *Breed* = interest, money *bred* from the principal.

26. *Who* is here without a verb. This use of the relative with a supplementary pronoun was not uncommon. "Which though it be not true, yet I forbear to note any deficiencies." — BACON.

27. *Doit* = a small Dutch coin, worth about a quarter of a cent.

28. *Condition* = agreement.

29. *Equal* = exact, equally balanced.

30. *Dwell* = continue, abide.

31. *Teaches* is usually regarded as a mistake, having the plural subject *dealings*. But Abbott regards it as an old Northern plural, which ended in *es*.

32. *Break his day* = fail to fulfil his engagement.

33. *Fearful guard* = protection to be feared.

34. *Hie* = haste.

ACT II. — Scene I.

1. *Mislike* = dislike, which Shakespeare commonly uses. *Mislike* is found only three times.

2. *Whose blood is reddest.* — Red blood was regarded as a sign of courage. Macbeth calls one of his frightened soldiers a "*lily-livered* boy."

3. *Fear'd* = terrified. *Fear* was often used transitively in this sense.

4. *Best-regarded* = most esteemed.

5. *Nice* = fastidious, fanciful. She intimates that judgment has something to do with her choice.

6. *Scanted* = limited, restricted.

7. *Wit* = wisdom. A. S. *witan*, to know. "*Will*" has been suggested as an emendation.

8. *Stood* = would stand.

9. *Sophy* = a common name for the emperor of Persia.

10. *Sultan Solyman.* — Probably Solyman the Magnificent, who reigned from 1520 to 1566.

11. *Lichas* was the servant of Hercules.

12. *Alcides* = another name for Hercules. So called because a descendant of Alceus.

13. *Advised* = deliberate, careful.

14. *Temple* = church, in which the prince was to take the oath just spoken of.

Scene II.

1. *Via* = away! Italian, from Lat. *via*, a way.

2. *For the heavens* = for Heaven's sake.

3. *Grow to* = "a household phrase applied to milk when burnt to the bottom of the saucepan, and thence acquiring an unpleasant taste." — Clark and Wright.

4. *God bless the mark* = a parenthetic apology for some coarse or profane remark.

5. *Incarnal* = incarnate; intended as a ludicrous blunder. A number of others occur in this scene.

6. *Sand-blind* = having a defect of sight, causing the appearance of small particles flying before the eyes. "High-gravel-blind" is an effort at wit.

7. *Confusions* = conclusions; another Gobboism. "To try conclusions" means to make experiments.

8. *Marry* = a corruption of Mary; originally a mode of swearing by the Virgin, but here a mere expletive.

9. *Sonties* = saints, of which it is probably a corruption.

10. *Raise the waters* = raise a storm or commotion.

11. *Master* was a title of respect that meant something in Shakespeare's day; hence Gobbo scruples to bestow it upon his son.

12. *What a' will* = what he will.

13. *Ergo* = therefore.

14. *An't* = An it; that is, if it.

15. *Father.* — As young people often used this term of address in speaking to old men, Gobbo did not recognize his son.

16. *Hovel-post* = a post to support a hovel or shed.

17. *Stand up.* — Launcelot had been kneeling, and, according to an old tradition, with his back to his father, who mistook the hair of his head for a beard.

18. *Fill-horse* = thill-horse, the horse that goes between the thills or shafts.

19. *Set up my rest* = made up my mind. "A metaphor taken from a game, where the highest stake the parties were disposed to venture was called the *rest*."

20. *Give me.* — The *me* is a dative of indirect personal reference, called in Latin the *dativus ethicus*.

21. *Gramercy* = great thanks. A corruption of the French *grand merci*.

22. *Infection* = affection or inclination; another Gobboism.

23. *Cater-cousins* = an expression of difficult explanation. Commonly regarded as a corruption of the French *quatre-cousins*, fourth cousins.

24. *Frutify* = certify, the word aimed at.

25. *Impertinent* = pertinent, as he means.

26. *Defect* = effect.

27. *Preferr'd* = recommended for promotion.

28. *The old proverb* = "The grace of God is gear enough."

29. *Guarded* = braided, trimmed.

30. *Table* = palm of the hand, on which Launcelot is gazing. As Hudson explains, this "*table* doth *not only* promise, *but* offer to swear upon a book, *that* I shall have good fortune."

31. *Line of life* = the line passing around the base of the thumb.

32. *Edge of a feather-bed* = an absurd variation of "edge of the sword."

33. *Liberal* = free, reckless.

34. *Skipping* = frolicsome.

35. *With my hat.* — Hats were worn at meals; but while grace was saying, they were taken off and held over the eyes.

36. *Civility* = refinement.

37. *Sad ostent* = grave demeanor.

SCENE III.

1. *Exhibit* = inhibit, as he means.

SCENE IV.

1. *Spoke as yet*, etc. = bespoken torch-bearers for us.

2. *An* = if.

3. *Break up* = break open.

4. *Provideth of* = provided with. The prepositions *of*, *with*, and *by* were often used interchangeably.

SCENE V.

1. *Bid forth* = invited out.

2. *Reproach* = approach — a Gobboism.

3. *Black-Monday.* "In the 34th of Edward III., the 13th of April, and the morrow after Easter-day, King Edward, with his host, lay before the city of Paris; which day was full of dark mist and hail, and so bitter cold, that many men died on their horses' backs with the cold. Wherefore unto this day it hath been called *Black-Monday.*" — STOWE, as quoted by Hudson.

4. *Fife* = fifer, probably. A writer in 1618 says: "A fifer is a wry-neckt musician."

5. *Jacob's staff.* — "By faith Jacob, when he was a dying, blessed both the sons of Joseph; and worshipped, leaning upon the top of his staff." Heb. xi. 21.

6. *Of feasting* = for feasting.

7. *Hagar's offspring* = Gentiles.

8. *Patch* = professional jester or fool; so called from his motley or patched dress.

SCENE VI.

1. *Out-dwells* = out-stays.

2. *Venus' pigeons.* — The chariot of Venus was drawn by doves.

3. *Obliged* = pledged, bound by contract.

4. *Scarfed* = decked with flags.
5. *Over-weather'd* = weather-beaten.
6. *Abode* = tarrying.
7. *Who* = whom. Shakespeare often omits the inflection.
8. *Exchange*, that is, of apparel.
9. *Good sooth* = in good truth.
10. *Close* = secret.
11. *Beshrew me* = curse me, used as a mild imprecation.
12. *On't* = of it.

SCENE VII.

1. *Who* = which. In the Elizabethan age, *who* and *which* were not fully differentiated. *Which* was often used of persons, as *who* of things. "Our Father *which* art in heaven." Matt. vi. 9.
2. *As blunt*, that is, as the "dull lead."
3. *Rated by thy estimation* = valued by thy reputation.
4. *Disabling* = disparaging.
5. *This shrine.* — Portia is compared to a saint's shrine, which pilgrims often made long journeys to kiss.
6. *Hyrcanian deserts* = an extended wilderness region lying south of the Caspian Sea.
7. *Ten times undervalued.* — This refers to silver, which in 1600 stood to gold in the proportion of ten to one in value.
8. *Insculp'd upon* = graven on the outside. The angel was in relief, and represented St. Michael piercing the dragon. The value of the coin was about ten shillings.
9. *Carrion Death* = a skull from which the flesh has disappeared.
10. *Part* = depart.

SCENE VIII.

1. *Passion* = passionate outcry.
2. *Keep his day*, that is, the day fixed for the payment of the borrowed money.
3. *Reason'd* = talked, conversed.
4. *You were best* = it were best for you.
5. *Slubber* = do carelessly, slur over.
6. *Riping* = ripeness.
7. *Mind of love* = loving mind.
8. *Ostents* = manifestations.
9. *Conveniently* = fitly, suitably.
10. *Sensible* = sensitive, deeply moved.

11. *Quicken his embraced heaviness* = enliven the sadness which he has embraced or given up to.

12. *Do we so* = let us do so. This is an imperative, 1st person, plural.

SCENE IX.

1. *Straight* = straightway, at once.

2. *Election* = choice.

3. *Address'd me* = prepared myself, made ready.

4. *Fortune now*, etc. = Success now to my heart's hope !

5. *By* = of. These two prepositions were not yet fully differentiated.

6. *Martlet* = the house-martin.

7. *Jump with* = agree with.

8. *Ruin* = refuse, rubbish.

9. *To offend, and judge*, etc. That is, the offender cannot sit in judgment on his own case.

10. *I wis* = I know. This is a blunder form for *ywis*, *iwis*, meaning certainly. "It is particularly to be noted," says Skeat, "that the commonest form in MSS. is *iwis*, in which the prefix (like most other prefixes) is frequently written *apart* from the rest of the word, and not unfrequently the *i* is represented by a capital letter so that it appears as *I wis*. Hence, by an extraordinary error, the *I* has often been mistaken for the 1st per. pron., and the verb *wis*, to know, has been thus created, and is given in many dictionaries ! "

11. *You are sped* = you are undone.

12. *By the time* = in proportion to the time.

13. *Wroth* = suffering, misery.

14. *My lord* is in jesting response to the servant's inquiry, "Where is *my lady ?* "

15. *Sensible regreets* = tangible or substantial greetings.

16. *Commends* = compliments.

17. *Yet* = up to this time.

18. *Post* = postman, courier.

19. *Lord Love* = Cupid.

ACT III. — SCENE I.

1. *The Goodwins* = the Goodwin Sands, off the eastern coast of Kent.

2. *Knapped ginger* = snapped or broke-up ginger — a favorite condiment with old people.

3. *Wings she flew withal* = the clothes in which she eloped.

4. *Complexion* = natural disposition.

5. *Match* = bargain.

6. *Smug* = spruce, trim, studiously neat.

7. *Hindered me*, etc. = kept me from gaining half a million ducats.

8. *Frankfort* = Frankfort-on-the-Maine, noted for its fairs.

9. *In that* = in that one diamond.

10. *Turquoise* = a mineral, brought from Persia, of a peculiar bluish-green color, susceptible of a high polish, and much esteemed as a gem. It was formerly supposed to fade or brighten with the wearer's health, and to change with the decay of a lover's affection.

Scene II.

1. *Forsworn* = perjured.

2. *Beshrew* = curse upon — used as a harmless imprecation.

3. *O'erlook'd me* = bewitched, fascinated me.

4. *Prove it so* = if it prove so.

5. *Peize* = retard, delay. From Fr. *peser*, to weigh.

6. *Fear* = doubt; that is, whether I shall ever enjoy.

7. *Swan-like end.* — An allusion to the belief that swans sing just before they die.

8. *Flourish.* — The coronation of English sovereigns is announced by a flourish of trumpets.

9. *Alcides* = Hercules. He rescued Hesione, daughter of Làomedon, when she was exposed as a sacrifice to appease the wrath of Neptune; and this he did, not from love, but for the reward of two horses promised by her father.

10. *Dardanian wives* = Trojan women.

11. *Approve* = prove, justify.

12. *His* = its.

13. *Livers white as milk* = an expression indicative of cowardice. Falstaff speaks of " the liver white and pale, which is the badge of pussillanimity and cowardice."

14. *Excrement* = the beard. From Lat. *excrescere*, to grow out.

15. *Supposed fairness* = fictitious beauty.

16. *Guiled* = beguiling.

17. *Indian beauty.* — This has been regarded a troublesome expression. "Dowdy," "gypsy," "favor," "visage," "feature," have been suggested in place of *beauty*. The difficulty seems to be removed by placing the emphasis on *Indian*, and regarding it as used in a derogatory sense. An *Indian* beauty, after all, is not apt to be a very desirable person.

18. *Food for Midas.* Midas prayed that everything he touched might turn to gold. His prayer being granted, he found himself without food, and prayed Bacchus to revoke the favor.

19. *Counterfeit* = portrait.

20. *Leave itself unfurnish'd*, that is, with a companion.

21. *Continent* = that which contains, container.

22. *I come by note* = I come by written warrant.

23. *In a prize* = for a prize.

24. *Livings* = estates, possessions.

25. *Vantage to exclaim on you* = warrant to cry out against you.

26. *None from me* = none away from me.

27. *So* = if, provided that.

28. *Intermission* = pause, delay.

29. *If promise last* = if promise hold; a play on words, often weak, so common in Shakespeare.

30. *Very* = true. O. Fr. *verai*, from Lat. *verax*, true.

31. *Him* = himself.

32. *Estate* = condition, state.

33. *Shrewd* = evil.

34. *Constant* = firm, steadfast.

35. *Mere* = absolute, thorough. Lat. *merus*, pure, unmixed.

36. *Should appear* = would appear.

37. *Confound* = ruin, destroy.

38. *Impeach the freedom*, etc. = denies that strangers have equal rights in the city.

39. *Magnificoes of greatest port* = grandees of highest rank.

40. *Envious plea* = malicious plea.

41. *Best-condition'd* = best disposed. The superlative here is carried over also to *unwearied*.

42. *Cheer* = countenance.

43. *You and I.* This mistake is not uncommon in Shakespeare and other writers of the time.

SCENE III.

1. *Fond* = foolish. This is the original sense of the word.

2. *To come* = as to come.

3. *Dull-eyed* = stupid, wanting in perception.

4. *Kept* = dwelt.

5. *Deny the course of law* = refuse to let the law take its course.

6. *Commodity* = traffic, commercial relations.

7. *Bated* = lowered, reduced.

Scene IV.

1. *Conceit* = idea, conception.

2. *Lover* = friend. A common signification.

3. *Customary bounty can enforce you* = ordinary benevolence can make you feel.

4. *Husbandry and manage* = stewardship and management.

5. *Imposition* = task or duty imposed.

6. *Padua* was famous for the learned jurists of its university.

7. *Imagined speed* = speed of thought or imagination.

8. *Tranect* = the name of the place where "the common ferry" or ferry-boat set out for Venice.

9. *Convenient* = proper, suitable.

10. *Reed voice* = shrill, piping voice.

11. *Quaint* = ingenious, elaborate.

12. *I could not do withal* = I could not help it.

13. *Raw* = crude, unskilful.

14. *Jacks* = a common term of contempt.

15. *All my whole device.* — A pleonasm not infrequent in Shakespeare.

Scene V.

1. *Fear you* = fear for you.

2. *Agitation* = cogitation — another blunder of Launcelot's.

3. *Scylla* = a rocky cape on the west coast of southern Italy. *Charybdis* is a celebrated whirlpool on the opposite coast of Sicily. Hence the frequent saying, "He falls into Scylla who seeks to avoid Charybdis."

4. *I shall be saved*, etc. — A reference, probably, to 1 Cor. vii. 14: "The unbelieving wife is sanctified by the husband."

5. *Enow* = enough.

6. *Rasher* = a thin slice of bacon.

7. *Are out* = have fallen out, quarrelled.

8. *I know my duty.* — Launcelot plays on the double meaning of "cover," namely, to lay the table, and to put on one's hat.

9. *Quarrelling with occasion* = using every opportunity to make perverse replies.

10. *Discretion* = discrimination.

11. *A many.* — This phrase is still used, though rarely, by poets. It is found in Tennyson's "Miller's Daughter," and Rolfe quotes from Gerald Massey: —

> "We've known a many sorrows, Sweet;
> We've wept a many tears."

12. *Garnish'd* = furnished, equipped.

13. *Defy the matter* = set the meaning at defiance.

14. *How cheer'st thou* = what spirits are you in?

15. *Set you forth* = describe you fully.

ACT IV. — SCENE I.

1. *Uncapable.* — Shakespeare uses also *incapable.* With a considerable number of words, the English prefix *un* and the Latin prefix *in* were used indifferently; as, uncertain, incertain; ungrateful, ingrateful.

2. *Qualify* = modify, moderate.

3. *And that* = and since. It is not unusual for the Elizabethan writers to use *that* in place of repeating a preceding conjunction. " *Though* my soul be guilty and *that* I think," etc. — BEN JONSON.

4. *Envy's reach* = reach of hatred or malice. *Envy* frequently had this meaning in Shakespeare's time. In Mark xv. 10 we read: " For he knew that the chief priests had delivered him for *envy.*"

5. *Remorse* = pity, relenting — a common meaning in the age of Elizabeth.

6. *Where* = whereas.

7. *Loose* = release, give up.

8. *Moiety* = portion, share, as often in Shakespeare. According to its etymology, it strictly means *a half.* From Fr. *moitié,* half.

9. *Charter.* — Shakespeare seems to have supposed that Venice held a charter from the German Emperor, which might be revoked for any flagrant act of injustice.

10. *A gaping pig* = a pig's head as roasted for the table.

11. *Passion* = feeling.

12. *Lodg'd* = fixed, abiding.

13. *Current* = course.

14. *Think you question* = consider that you are arguing.

15. *Main flood* = ocean tide.

16. *Fretten* = fretted.

17. *With all brief and plain conveniency* = " with such brevity and directness as befits the administration of justice." — WRIGHT.

18. *Have judgment* = receive sentence.

19. *Parts* = offices, employments.

20. *Upon my power* = by virtue of my prerogative. We still say, " on my authority."

21. *Determine* = decide.

22. *Hangman* = executioner.

23. *Envy* = malice. See note 4.

24. *Wit* = sense.

25. *Inexecrable* = that cannot be execrated enough. Another reading is " inexorable."

26. *And for thy life,* etc. = let justice be impeached for allowing thee to live.

27. *Pythagoras.* — A philosopher of the sixth century B.C., who taught the transmigration of souls.

28. *Who, hang'd,* etc. Another instance of the suspended nominative.

29. *Fell* = fierce, cruel. A. S. *fel,* cruel.

30. *Fleet* = flit, take flight.

31. *Offend'st* = hurtest, annoyest.

32. *To fill up* = to fulfil.

33. *No impediment to let him lack* = no hindrance to his receiving.

34. *Take your place,* probably beside the duke.

35. *Question* = trial.

36. *Such rule* = such regular form.

37. *Impugn* = oppose, controvert.

38. *Within his danger* = within his power.

39. *Strain'd* = constrained, forced.

40. *Truth* = honesty.

41. *A Daniel.* — See the " History of Susanna " in the Apocrypha, where " the Lord raised up the holy spirit of a young youth, whose name was Daniel," to confound the two wicked judges.

42. *Hath full relation* = is fully applicable.

43. *More elder.* — Double comparatives were frequently used by the Elizabethan writers.

44. *Balance.* — Though singular in form, it is used as a plural, as having two scales.

45. *On your charge* = at your expense.

46. *Still her use* = constantly her custom.

47. *Speak me fair in death* = speak well of me when I am dead.

48. *With all my heart.* — There is pathos in this jest.

49. *A just pound* = an exact pound.

50. *In the substance* = in amount, in the gross weight.

51. *Contrive* = plot.

52. *Formerly* = as aforesaid.

53. *Which humbleness,* etc. = which humble supplication on your part may induce me to commute into a fine.

54. *In use* = in trust.

55. *Ten more,* that is, to make up twelve jurymen, who were jestingly called " godfathers-in-law."

56. *Serves you not* = is not at your disposal.

57. *Gratify* = recompense.

58. *Cope* = requite, repay.

59. *Withal* = with; here used as a preposition governing *ducats.*

60. *More mercenary* = desirous for more pay than the satisfaction of doing good.

61. *Of force* = of necessity.

62. *Attempt* = tempt.

63. *'Scuse* = excuse. This shortened form occurs in only one other passage in Shakespeare.

64. *An if* = if; a pleonasm.

Scene II.

1. *Upon more advice* = upon further consideration.

2. *Old swearing.* — "Old" was an intensive epithet in common use.

ACT V. — Scene I.

1. *Troilus* was a son of Priam, king of Troy. He loved Cressida, daughter of the Grecian soothsayer, Calchas.

2. *Thisbe* was a beautiful Babylonian lady, with whom Pyramus was in love. They agreed to meet at the tomb of Ninus; but, on arriving there, Thisbe was frightened at the sight of a lioness that had just killed an ox. She fled, leaving her cloak behind. Pyramus, finding the cloak stained with blood, believed that a wild beast had killed her, and took his own life — an example which was followed by Thisbe.

3. *Dido* was Queen of Carthage. She loved Æneas, by whom she was deserted. The "willow in her hand" was the symbol of unhappy love.

4. *Medea* was the daughter of Æetes, king of Colchis. She assisted Jason in obtaining the Golden Fleece, and afterwards became his wife. She possessed magical powers, and in order to renew the youth of Aeson, the father of Jason, she boiled him in a caldron, into which she had cast "enchanted herbs."

5. *Out-night you* = beat you in this game of "In such a night."

6. *Holy crosses.* — These were numerous in Italy, being found not only in churches, but along the roads.

7. *Expect* = await.

8. *Patines* = the plate used for the sacramental bread. It was sometimes made of gold.

9. *Like an angel sings.* — A reference to " the music of the spheres."

10. *Quiring* = singing in concert.

11. *Diana* = the goddess of the moon.

12. *Mutual* = common.

13. *Orpheus* = a Thracian poet who accompanied the Argonauts, and had the power of moving inanimate objects by the music of his lyre.

14. *Stockish* = stupid, insensible.

15. *Spoils* = robbery, acts of plundering.

16. *Erebus* = the underworld, or region of the dead.

17. *Without respect* = absolutely, independent of circumstances.

18. *Attended* = attended to, heard attentively.

19. *Season'd are* = are made fit.

20. *Endymion.* — In Greek mythology Silene, or the moon, is represented as charmed with the beauty of Endymion, whom she put to sleep on Mount Latmos, that she might nightly kiss him unobserved.

21. *Tucket* = a flourish on a trumpet to announce an arrival.

22. *We should hold day*, etc. = we should have day at the same time with the Antipodes, if you, Portia, would walk abroad at night in the absence of the sun.

23. *God sort all* = God dispose or arrange all things.

24. *In all sense* = in all reason.

25. *Breathing courtesy* = courtesy consisting of mere breath or talk.

26. Gratiano and Nerissa have been talking apart in dumb show.

27. *Posy* = sentiment or motto inscribed on rings. A contraction of *poesy*. It was the custom to inscribe sentiments, usually in distichs, upon knives by means of *aqua fortis*.

28. *Respective* = mindful or regardful of your oath.

29. *The virtue of the ring* = the power of the ring. It gave its possessor a right to Portia and all she had.

30. *Contain* = retain.

31. *Wanted* = as to have wanted; dependent on " so much unreasonable."

32. *Ceremony* = a sacred thing.

33. *Civil doctor* = doctor of civil law.

34. *Shame and courtesy* = shame at being thought ungrateful, and a sense of what courtesy required.

35. *Wealth* = weal, prosperity.

36. *Advisedly* = deliberately.

37. *Richly* = richly laden.

38. *Suddenly* = unexpectedly.

39. *Living* = means of living, livelihood.

40. *Satisfied of these events at full* = fully satisfied concerning these events.

41. *Charge us upon inter'gatories*, etc. "In the Court of Queen's Bench, when a complaint is made against a person for a 'contempt,' the practice is that before sentence is finally pronounced he is sent into the Crown Office, and being there 'charged upon interrogatories,' he is made to swear that he will 'answer all things faithfully.'"

CIVIL WAR PERIOD.

REPRESENTATIVE WRITER.
JOHN MILTON.

OTHER PROMINENT WRITERS.

Poets. — WALLER, COWLEY, QUARLES, HERRICK, SUCKLING, CAREW.

Historian. — LORD CLARENDON.

Religious Writers. — TAYLOR, BAXTER, BUNYAN.

III.

CIVIL WAR PERIOD.

1625-1660.

GENERAL SURVEY. — Though short, this period is
worthy of careful study. It is characterized by a great
conflict that absorbed every other important interest.
The antagonistic elements in England were at last brought
into an armed contest for supremacy. Charles I. ascended the throne in 1625, and moulded his policy according to high notions of the divine right of kings. He
sought to establish an absolute monarchy. He assumed
a haughty tone in addressing the Commons, telling them
to "remember that parliaments were altogether in his
power for their calling, sitting, or dissolution, and that,
therefore, as he should find the fruits of them good or
evil, they were to be, or not to be."

Two Parliaments were convened in rapid succession,
but showed themselves unyielding to the royal will.
When the king demanded supplies, the Commons clam-
ored for redress of grievances. In each case the king
dissolved Parliament, and proceeded to levy taxes in
defiance of law. Resistance to the royal demands led to
immediate imprisonment ; and in order to exercise his
tyranny the better, he billeted soldiers among the people,
and in some places established martial law.

A third Parliament was called in 1629. Finding it still

more determined in resisting his arbitrary and tyrannical rule, the king resolved upon a change of tactics. After many attempted evasions, he was at last brought to ratify the Petition of Right, the second great charter of English liberty, which bound him not to levy taxes without the consent of Parliament, not to imprison any person except by due course of law, and not to govern by martial law.

The rejoicing of the Commons over this victory was of short duration. The king was by nature insincere and false, and, on principle, did not feel himself bound to keep faith with the people. After collecting the supplies that had been granted him, he violated the solemn pledge of the Petition of Right, and dissolved Parliament with every mark of royal displeasure. For the following eleven years no Parliament was called together, and the king ruled as a despot.

Throughout the whole course of his usurpation, the king was surrounded by bad advisers. Among them was the Duke of Buckingham, whom the Commons considered "the grievance of grievances;" Laud, Archbishop of Canterbury, who hated the Puritans more than he hated the Catholics; and Thomas Wentworth, Earl Strafford, who had been won from the side of Parliament by bribes and honors, and to whom Mr. Pym suggestively remarked, "You have left us, but we will never leave you while your head is upon your shoulders." In natural sympathy with the king were the nobility of the realm and the prelates of the Established Church. With the supremacy of the crown, the position of the nobility would be guaranteed against republican tendencies. Since Charles I. was a zealous Episcopalian, the bishops had every thing to gain from his absolutism. They warmly defended the divine right of kings. Here, then, we find two influential classes which were bound to the king by common sympathies and common interests. They were called Royalists.

The opposition, as we have seen, centred in the House of Commons, who represented the great middle class of England. They stood for constitutional government. For the most part they were Independents in religion, and looked upon the usages and episcopal organization of the Anglican Church as savoring of Romanism. They made the individual congregation the source of authority, and, rejecting all human traditions, appealed to the Scriptures alone as the standard of faith and practice. Their form of worship was simple.

In emancipating men from the arbitrary rule of an external authority in religion, their principles were favorable to human dignity and freedom. Though persecuted to a greater or less degree during the reigns of Elizabeth and James I., the Independents had increased. Their trials had made them an earnest and determined body. In contrast with what they regarded the formalism and worldliness of the Established Church, many of them had gone to the opposite extreme of ascetic rigor. They denounced every kind of amusement, excluded music and art from the churches, acquired a stern solemnity of countenance, and affected a Scriptural style of speech.

To escape the annoyances and persecutions to which they were exposed in England, thousands had voluntarily exiled themselves in Holland, or braved the trials and dangers of the New World. It will be readily understood that men of this character — men of deep conviction, of high conceptions of individual liberty, and of fearless courage — could not be friendly to royal despotism.

When placed in power in the House of Commons, they were stubborn and unyielding in their defence of constitutional liberty. They could not be deceived by promises nor terrified by threats. Thus constitutional government in the Commons was arrayed against despotism in the king.

At last the resources of peace were exhausted, and in 1642 an appeal was made to arms. It is not necessary to follow the course of the Civil War. The gay Cavaliers about the king were no match for the serious Puritans. " I raised such men as had the fear of God before them," said Cromwell, " and made some conscience of what they did, and from that day forward, I must say to you, they were never beaten, and wherever they engaged against the enemy they beat continually."

In 1649 Charles I. was brought to the block. England became a commonwealth, and with Cromwell as Lord Protector occupied a commanding position among European nations. The Protector was everywhere feared. He subjugated Ireland ; from Spain he demanded the right of free trade with the West Indies ; he suppressed the Barbary pirates of the Mediterranean ; he forced the Pope and Catholic rulers to cease their persecutions of Protestants. In treating with foreign sovereigns, he insisted on receiving the formal honors paid to the proudest monarchs of Europe. He returned two letters to Louis XIV. of France because they were not, as he thought, properly addressed. " What," exclaimed the French king to Cardinal Mazarin, " must I call this base fellow ' Our dear Brother Oliver ? ' " " Aye," replied the crafty minister, " or your father, if it will gain your ends ; or you will have him at the gates of Paris ! "

This was not a period favorable to literature. The genius of the nation was occupied with practical questions of the highest importance. The people were divided in sympathy between the king and Parliament. Much ability was absorbed in controversial writings of only temporary value. Anglicans, Catholics, Presbyterians, Independents, and Puritans were constantly in conflict. The Royalist poets, writing in the atmosphere of the court, could not easily be more than graceful versifiers. There was no leisure nor inspiration for great works.

On the other hand, Puritan poets were not more favorably situated. In the austere atmosphere of Puritanic piety, there is little encouragement for the grace and delicacy of poetry. The æsthetic sentiment is suppressed by ascetic views of life. The literary impulse finds expression only in devotional manuals, unadorned history, or severely logical theology. "The idea of the beautiful is wanting," says Taine, "and what is literature without it? The natural expression of the heart's emotions is proscribed, and what is a literature without it? They abolished as impious the free stage and the rich poesy which the Renaissance had brought them. They rejected as profane the ornate style and the ample eloquence which had been established around them by the imitation of antiquity and of Italy."

We find, however, one great exception. It is John Milton. Though a Puritan at heart, and a participator in the religious controversies and political movements of the period, he was able to rise above the narrowness of party spirit, and stands out as the one great literary figure of his age.

With the exception of Milton the poetic writers of this

period show a literary decadence. The large, creative spirit of the preceding era, which reflected the grandeur and power of the English people, was succeeded by a narrow, artificial spirit, which devoted its energies to the turning of small compliments and the tracing of remote resemblances. Since the time of Dr. Johnson, it has been customary to designate these writers, among whom we may mention Waller, Cowley, Quarles, Herrick, Suckling, and Carew, as *metaphysical poets.*

The term *artificial* or *fantastic* would perhaps be more accurately descriptive of their character. They were men of learning, but took too much pains to show it. They wrote not from the emotions of the heart, but from the deliberate choice of the will; and hence they succeeded not in giving voice to nature, but only in pleasing a false and artificial taste. They abound in far-fetched and violent figures; and though we may be surprised at their ingenuity in discovering remote resemblances, we smile at the incongruous result. Thus Carew sings: —

> " Ask me no more, whither do stray
> The golden atoms of the day;
> For in pure love, heaven did prepare
> Those powders to enrich your hair.
>
> Ask me no more, whither doth haste
> The nightingale, when May is past;
> For in your sweet dividing throat
> She winters, and keeps warm her note.
>
> Ask me no more, where those stars light,
> That downwards fall in dead of night;
> For in your eyes they sit, and there
> Fixed become, as in their sphere."

It is not in such laborious conceits that nature finds a voice. Speaking of these poets, Dr. Johnson says: "Their attempts were always analytic; they broke every image into fragments; and could no more represent, by their slender conceits and labored particularities, the prospects of nature, or the scenes of life, than he who dissects the sunbeam with a prism can exhibit the wide effulgence of a summer noon. What they wanted, however, of the sublime, they endeavored to supply by hyperbole; their amplification had no limits; they left not only reason but fancy behind them; and produced combinations of confused magnificence that not only could not be credited, but could not be imagined."

Yet a happy trifle was now and then hit upon. At rare intervals nature seems to have broken through the casing of artificiality. Francis Quarles gives forcible poetic expansion to Job's prayer, "Oh that thou wouldest hide me in the grave, that thou wouldest keep me secret, until thy wrath be past."

> " Ah, whither shall I fly? What path untrod
> Shall I seek out to escape the flaming rod
> Of my offended, of my angry God? "

There is a light, careless spontaneity about the little song of Herrick's beginning, —

> " Gather the rose-buds while ye may,
> Old Time is still a flying;
> And this same flower that smiles to-day
> To-morrow will be dying."

JOHN MILTON.

In the period under consideration, Milton stands out in solitary grandeur. Intimately associated with the political and religious movements of his time, and identified in principle and in life with the Puritan party, he still rises grandly above the narrowness of his age. In one work at least he rivals the great achievements of the age of Elizabeth. He deserves to be recognized as the sublimest poet of all times. The far-fetched conceit of Dryden, whose genuine appreciation of Milton at a time when the Puritan poet was not in fashion is much to his credit, hardly surpasses the truth : —

> " Three poets, in three distant ages born,
> Greece, Italy, and England did adorn.
> The first in loftiness of thought surpassed;
> The next in majesty; in both the last.
> The force of nature could no further go:
> To make a third, she joined the other two."

John Milton was born in London, Dec. 9, 1608. His father, a man of the highest integrity, had been disinherited for espousing the Protestant cause; but, taking up the profession of a scrivener, he acquired the means of giving his son a liberal education. His mother, a woman of most virtuous character, was especially distinguished for her neighborhood charities. The private tutor of Milton was Thomas Young, a Puritan minister, who was afterwards forced to leave the kingdom on account of his religious opinions. Milton showed extraordinary aptness in learning ; and when in 1624 he was sent to Cambridge, he was master of several languages, and had read extensively in philosophy and literature. He remained at the university seven years, and took the usual degrees.

The education of his time did not, however, meet with his approval, and in several of his works he has criticised the subjects and methods of study with astonishing independence and wisdom. His educational writings deservedly rank him as one of the notable educational reformers of modern times. "And for the usual method of teaching arts," he says, "I deem it to be an old error of universities, not yet well recovered from the scholastic grossness of barbarous ages, that, instead of beginning with arts most easy (and those be such as are most obvious to the senses), they present their young, unmatriculated novices at first coming with the most intellective abstractions of logic and metaphysics; so that they, having but newly left those grammatic flats and shallows, where they stuck unreasonably long to learn a few words with lamentable construction, and now on the sudden transported under another climate, to be tossed and turmoiled with their unballasted wits in fathomless and unquiet depths of controversy, do for the most part grow into hatred and contempt of learning, mocked and deluded all this while with ragged notions and babblements, while they expected delightful and worthy knowledge."

Milton was designed by his parents for the church. But as he approached maturity, he perceived that his religious convictions and ecclesiastical independence would not allow him to enter the Established Church. We here see, perhaps, the effects of his Puritan training. Speaking of this matter he says : "Coming to some maturity of years, and perceiving what tyranny had invaded the church, that he who would take orders must subscribe slave, and take an oath withal, which unless he took with a conscience that he would relish, he must either perjure or split his faith, I thought better to prefer a blameless silence before the sacred office of speaking, bought and begun with servitude and forswearing."

In 1632 he left the university amidst the regrets of the fellows of his college, and retired to his father's house at Horton in Buckinghamshire. Here he spent five years in laborious study, in the course of which he perused all the Greek and Latin writers of the classic period. He also studied Italian, and was accustomed, as he tells us, "to feast with avidity and delight on Dante and Petrarch." To use his own expression, he was letting his wings grow. In a letter to a friend, he gives us some interesting particulars in regard to his studies and habits of life. "You well know," he says, "that I am naturally slow in writing, and averse to write. It is also in my favor that your method of study is such as to admit of frequent interruptions, in which you visit your friends, write letters, or go abroad ; but it is my way to suffer no impediment, no love of ease, no avocation whatever, to chill the ardor, to break the continuity, or divert the completion of my literary pursuits."

It was during this period of studious retirement that he produced several of his choicest poems, among which are "Comus," "L'Allegro," and "Il Penseroso." "Comus" is the most perfect mask in any language. But "in none of the works of Milton," says Macaulay, "is his peculiar manner more happily displayed than in 'Allegro' and the 'Penseroso.' It is impossible to conceive that the mechanism of language can be brought to a more exquisite degree of perfection. These poems differ from others, as attar of roses differs from ordinary rose water, the close-packed essence from the thin diluted mixture. They are indeed not so much poems as collections of hints, from each of which the reader is to make a poem for himself. Every epithet is a text for a stanza."

At the time these two poems were written, they stood as the highwater mark of English poetry. In their sphere they have never been excelled. In spite of little inaccuracies of description (for Milton was too much in love with books to be a close observer of nature), we find nowhere else such an exquisite delineation of country life and country scenes. These idylls are the more remarkable, because their light, joyous spirit stands in strong contrast with the elevation, dignity, and austerity of his other poems.

At length Milton began to tire of his country life, and to long for the pleasures and benefits of travel. In 1638 he left England for a tour on the Continent. At Paris he met Grotius, one of the most learned men of his age, who resided at the French capital as ambassador from the Queen of Sweden. After a few days he went to Italy, and visited all the principal cities. He was everywhere cordially received by men of learning, who were not slow to recognize his genius. In his travels he preserved an admirable and courageous independence. Even under the shadow of St. Peter's he made no effort to conceal his religious opinions. "It was a rule," he says, "which I laid down to myself in those places, never to be the first to begin any conversation on religion ; but if any question were put to me concerning my faith, to declare it without any reserve or fear. . . . For about the space of two months, I again openly defended, as I had done before, the reformed religion in the very metropolis of Popery."

The Italians, who were frugal in their praise of men from beyond the Alps, received some of Milton's productions with marks of high appreciation. This had the effect to confirm his opinion of his own power, and to stimulate his hope of achieving something worthy of remembrance. "I began thus to assent both to them, and divers of my friends at home," he tells us in an interesting passage, "and not less to an inward prompting, which now grew daily upon me, that, by labor and intense study (which I take to be my portion in this life), I might perhaps leave something so written to after-times as they should not willingly let die." He was about to extend his travels into Sicily and Greece when the news of the civil commotions in England caused him to change his purpose ; "for I thought it base," he says, "to be travelling for amusement abroad, while my fellow-citizens were fighting for liberty at home."

Not being called to serve the state in any official capacity on his arrival in London, he rented a spacious house in which he conducted a private school. He sought to exemplify, in some measure at least, his educational theories.   He held that languages should be studied for the sake of the literary treasures they contain.   He accordingly laid but little stress on minute verbal drill, and sought to acquaint his pupils with what was best in classic literature.   A long list of Latin and Greek authors was read.   Besides, he attached much importance to religious instruction ; and on Sunday he dictated to his pupils an outline of Protestant theology.

But this school has called forth some unfavorable criticism upon its founder.   Dr. Johnson, who delights in severe reflections, calls attention to the contrast between the lofty sentiment and small performance of the poet, who, " when he reaches the scene of action, vapors away his patriotism in a private boarding-school."   The animadversion is unjust.   Though modestly laboring as a teacher, Milton's talents and learning were sincerely devoted to the service of his country.   He has himself given us what ought to be a satisfactory explanation.   " Avoiding the labors of the camp," he says, "in which any robust soldier would have surpassed me, I betook myself to those weapons which I could wield with most effect; and I conceived that I was acting wisely when I thus brought my better and more valuable faculties, those which constituted my principal strength and consequence, to the assistance of my country and her honorable cause."

In 1641 he published his first work in prose, " Of Reformation in England, and the Causes that hitherto have Hindered It."   It is an attack upon the bishops and the Established Church.   The same year appeared two other controversial works, " Of Prelatical Episcopacy," which he maintains is without warrant from apostolic times, and "The Reason of Church Government," which is an argument against prelacy. With these works Milton threw himself into the bitter controversies of the age.   It was a matter, not of choice, but of duty.   He felt called to add the weight of his learning and eloquence to the side of the Puritans, who were perhaps inferior to their prelatical opponents in scholarship.   He tells us himself that he " was not disposed to this manner of writing, wherein knowing myself inferior to myself, led by the genial power of nature to another task, I have the use, as I may account it, but of my left hand."

In 1643, in his thirty-fifth year, Milton married Mary Powell, daughter of a justice of the peace in Oxfordshire. She was of Royalist family, and had been brought up in the leisure and gayety of affluence. It is not strange, therefore, that she found the meagre fare and studious habits of her husband's house distasteful. After a month in this scholastic abode, she made a visit to her father's home, from which she refused to return. Her husband's letters were left unanswered, and his messenger was dismissed with contempt. Milton felt this breach of duty on her part very keenly, and resolved at once to repudiate his wife on the ground of disobedience and desertion.

In support of his course, he published in 1644 a treatise entitled, " The Doctrine and Discipline of Divorce," and the year following his " Tetrachordon," or expositions on the four chief places of Scripture which treat of marriage. He maintains " that indisposition, unfitness, or contrariety of mind, arising from a cause in nature unchangeable, hindering, and likely to hinder, the main benefits of conjugal society, which are solace and peace," is a justifiable ground of divorce. As might be expected, he argued with great skill ; but he was smarting at the time under a sense of personal humiliation and wrong, and it may be doubted whether he himself afterwards approved of his extreme position. His views were bitterly assailed.

At last a reconciliation between him and his wife was effected. When one day she suddenly appeared before him, and on her knees begged his forgiveness, his generous impulses were deeply moved. He received her into his home again, and ever afterwards treated her with affection ; and when her family, because of their Royalist sympathies fell into distress, he generously extended his protection to her father and brothers. The incidents of this reconciliation are supposed to have given rise to a beautiful passage in "Paradise Lost," where Eve is described as humbly falling in tears and disordered tresses at the feet of Adam, and suing for pardon and peace. And then —

> "She ended, weeping; and her lowly plight,
> Immovable till peace obtain'd from fault
> Acknowledged and deplored, in Adam wrought
> Commiseration; soon his heart relented
> Towards her, his life so late, and sole delight,
> Now at his feet submissive in distress;
> Creature so fair his reconcilement seeking,
> His counsel, whom she had displeased, his aid."

This same year, 1644, saw the publication of two other treatises that will long survive. The one is the "Areopagitica, or Speech for the Liberty of Unlicensed Printing," the other is his "Tractate on Education." In the latter he has set forth in brief compass his educational views, and made many suggestions for the improvement of the current system. It has been pronounced Utopian in character; but it is to be noted that many educational reforms of recent years have been in the line indicated by Milton.

His definition of education, which has been often quoted, presents a beautiful ideal. "I call a complete and generous education," he says, "that which fits a man to perform justly, skilfully, and magnanimously all the offices, both private and public, of peace and war." But he does not contemplate practical efficiency in the secular duties of life as the sole end of education. Its highest aim is character. "The end of learning is," he says, "to repair the ruins of our first parents by regaining to know God aright, and out of that knowledge to love him, to imitate him, to be like him, as we may the nearest by possessing our souls of true virtue, which being united to the heavenly grace of faith, makes up the highest perfection."

Languages are to be studied in order to learn the useful things embodied in the literatures of those peoples that have made the highest attainments in wisdom. "And though a linguist should pride himself to have all the tongues that Babel cleft the world into, yet if he have not studied the solid things in them, as well as the words and lexicons, he were nothing so much to be esteemed a learned man as any yeoman or tradesman competently wise in his mother dialect only."

He held that the subjects studied and the tasks imposed should be wisely adapted to the learner's age and progress; and he strongly denounces the "preposterous exaction" which forces "the empty wits of children to compose themes, verses, and orations, which are the acts of ripest judgment and the final work of a head filled by long reading and observing with elegant maxims and copious invention." The outline of studies he proposes includes nearly the whole circuit of learning — a curriculum of heroic mould. Milton himself seems to have been conscious of the vastness of his plan; and he concludes the "Tractate" with the remark, "that this is not a bow for every man to shoot in that counts himself a teacher, but will require sinews almost equal to those which Homer gave Ulysses."

Milton continued to live in private, giving his life to instructing his pupils, and to discussing questions relating to the public weal. In 1649, two weeks after the execution of Charles I., he published his "Tenure of Kings and Magistrates," in which he undertook to prove that it is lawful, and has been held so in all ages, for any who have the power, to call to account a tyrant or wicked king, and, after due conviction, to depose and put him to death. This treatise marked a turning-point in his career. The Council of State of the new Commonwealth, pleased with his courage and republicanism, called him to the secretaryship for foreign tongues. It became his duty to prepare the Latin letters which were addressed by the Council to foreign princes. Later he served as Cromwell's Latin Secretary — an office he held throughout the Protectorate.

His literary and controversial activity, however, did not cease in his official life. His "Eikonoklastes," or Image-breaker, was written in 1649 to counteract the influence of the "Eikon Basilike," or Royal Image, a book that had an immense circulation, and tended to create a reaction in public sentiment in favor of the monarchy. A still more important work was his Latin "Pro Populo Anglicano Defensio," which was written in reply to a treatise by Salmasius, a scholar of Leyden, in which an effort was made to vindicate the memory of Charles I., and to bring reproach upon the Commonwealth. In spite of failing vision and the warning of his physicians, Milton threw himself with great ardor into his task, and in 1651 published his "Defensio," one of the most masterly controversial works ever written. He practically annihilated his opponent. The Commonwealth, it was said, owed its standing in Europe to Cromwell's battles and Milton's books.

During the Protectorate, Milton's life was uneventful. He bore his blindness, which had now become total, with heroic fortitude, upheld by the faith that —

> "They also serve who only stand and wait."

At the Restoration, though specially named for punishment, he somehow escaped the scaffold. His life, however, was for some years one of solitude and dejection. His own feelings are put into the mouth of his Samson : —

> "Now blind, disheartened, shamed, dishonored, quelled,
>   To what can I be useful? wherein serve
>   My nation, and the work from heaven imposed?
>   But to sit idle on the household hearth,
>   A burdensome drone, to visitants a gaze,
>   Or pitied object."

To add to his distress, his three daughters, whose rearing had been somewhat neglected, failed to prove a comfort to their father in his sore afflictions. They treated him with disrespect, sold his books by stealth, and rebelled against the drudgery of reading to him. Under these circumstances, it is hardly to be wondered at that he allowed himself to be persuaded into contracting a third marriage — a union that greatly added to the comfort and happiness of his last years.

But in all this period of trial, Milton had the solace of a noble task. He was slowly elaborating his "Paradise Lost," in which he realized the dream of his youth. Its main theme is indicated in the opening lines : —

> "Of man's first disobedience, and the fruit
> Of that forbidden tree, whose mortal taste
> Brought death into the world, and all our woe,
> With loss of Eden, till one greater Man
> Restore us, and regain the blissful seat,
> Sing, heavenly Muse, that on the secret top
> Of Oreb, or of Sinai, didst inspire
> That shepherd, who first taught the chosen seed,
> In the beginning, how the heavens and earth
> Rose out of chaos."

But the poem must be read before its grandeur can be appreciated. It is one of the world's great epics; and in majesty of plan and sublimity of treatment, it surpasses them all. The Eternal Spirit, which he invokes, seems to have touched his lips with hallowed fire. The splendors of heaven, the horrors of hell, and the beauties of Paradise are depicted with matchless power. The beings of the unseen world, angels and demons, exercise before us their mighty agency; and in the council chambers of heaven we hear the words of the Almighty. The poem comprehends the universe, sets forth the truth of divine government, and exhibits life in its eternal significance — a poem that rises above the petty incidents of earth with monumental splendor. It met with appreciation from the start. With a clear recognition of its worth, Dryden said, "This man cuts us all out, and the ancients too." Milton's modest house became a pilgrim's shrine, and men from every rank, not only from his native land, but also from abroad, came to pay him homage.

Milton's literary activity continued to the last, and enriched our literature with two other noble productions, "Paradise Re-

gained," and " Samson Agonistes." The former may be regarded as a sequel to " Paradise Lost ; " the latter is the most
powerful drama in our language after the Greek model. The
poet, unconsciously perhaps, identified himself with his Samson, and gave utterance to the profoundest emotions which had
been awakened by the mighty conflicts and sorrows of his own
life.

He died Nov. 8, 1674. He was a man of heroic mould.
In his solitary grandeur only one man of his age deserves to
be placed beside him — the great Protector, Oliver Cromwell.
His greatness was austere. In his life he had no intimate and
tender companionships ; and now our feeling toward him is admiration rather than love. His character was without blemish,
his aspirations pure and lofty, his courage undaunted, his intellectual vigor and power almost without parallel. But he was
conscious of his greatness, and, finding ample resources within
himself, he did not seek human sympathy. Wordsworth has
spoken truly, —

> "Thy soul was like a star, and dwelt apart."

Like his own " Paradise Lost," he appears, with his Titanic
proportions and independent loneliness, as the most impressive
figure in English literature.

L'ALLEGRO.

HENCE, loathèd Melancholy,
Of Cerberus and blackest Midnight born,
In Stygian cave forlorn,
　　'Mongst horrid shapes, and shrieks, and sights unholy!
Find out some uncouth cell,
　　Where brooding Darkness spreads his jealous wings,
　　And the night-raven sings:
There, under ebon shades, and low-brow'd rocks,
As ragged as thy locks,
　　In dark Cimmerian desert ever dwell.   10
　　But come, thou goddess fair and free,
In Heaven yclep'd Euphrosyne,
And by men, heart-easing Mirth;
Whom lovely Venus, at a birth,
With two sister Graces more,
To ivy-crownèd Bacchus bore:
Or whether, as some sager sing,
The frolick wind, that breathes the spring,
Zephyr, with Aurora playing,
As he met her once a-Maying;   20
There on beds of violets blue,
And fresh-blown roses wash'd in dew,
Fill'd her with thee a daughter fair,
So buxom, blithe, and debonair.
　　Haste thee, nymph, and bring with thee
Jest, and youthful jollity,
Quips, and cranks, and wanton wiles,
Nods, and becks, and wreathèd smiles,
Such as hang on Hebe's cheek,
And love to live in dimple sleek;   30
Sport that wrinkled Care derides,
And Laughter holding both his sides.
Come, and trip it, as you go,
On the light fantastick toe;
And in thy right hand lead with thee
The mountain-nymph, sweet Liberty;

And, if I give thee honour due,
Mirth, admit me of thy crew,
To live with her, and live with thee,
In unreprovèd pleasures free ;   40
To hear the lark begin his flight,
And singing, startle the dull night,
From his watch-tower in the skies,
Till the dappled dawn doth rise ;
Then to come, in spite of sorrow,
And at my window bid good morrow,
Through the sweet-briar, or the vine,
Or the twisted eglantine :
While the cock, with lively din,
Scatters the rear of darkness thin ;   50
And to the stack, or the barn-door,
Stoutly struts his dames before :
Oft list'ning how the hounds and horn
Cheerly rouse the slumb'ring morn,
From the side of some hoar hill,
Through the high wood echoing shrill :
Some time walking, not unseen,
By hedge-row elms, on hillocks green,
Right against the eastern gate,
Where the great sun begins his state   60
Robed in flames, and amber light,
The clouds in thousand liveries dight ;
While the plowman, near at hand,
Whistles o'er the furrow'd land,
And the milkmaid singeth blithe,
And the mower whets his sithe,
And every shepherd tells his tale
Under the hawthorn in the dale.
    Straight mine eye hath caught new pleasures,
Whilst the landskip round it measures ;   70
Russet lawns, and fallows gray,
Where the nibbling flocks do stray ;
Mountains, on whose barren breast
The lab'ring clouds do often rest ;
Meadows trim with daisies pide,
Shallow brooks, and rivers wide :

Towers and battlements it sees
Bosom'd high in tufted trees,
Where perhaps some beauty lies,
The Cynosure of neighbouring eyes.   80
Hard by, a cottage chimney smokes
From betwixt two aged oaks,
Where Corydon and Thyrsis, met,
Are at their savoury dinner set
Of herbs, and other country messes,
Which the neat-handed Phillis dresses;
And then in haste her bower she leaves,
With Thestylis to bind the sheaves;
Or, if the earlier season lead,
To the tann'd haycock in the mead.   90
Sometimes with secure delight
The upland hamlets will invite,
When the merry bells ring round,
And the jocund rebecks sound
To many a youth, and many a maid,
Dancing in the chequer'd shade;
And young and old come forth to play
On a sunshine holyday,
Till the livelong daylight fail:
Then to the spicy nut-brown ale,   100
With stories told of many a feat,
How faery Mab the junkets ate:
She was pinch'd and pull'd, she sed;
And he, by frier's lantern led,
Tells how the drudging goblin swet,
To earn his cream-bowl duly set,
When in one night, ere glimpse of morn,
His shadowy flale hath thresh'd the corn,
That ten day-labourers could not end:
Then lies him down the lubbar fiend,   110
And, stretch'd out all the chimney's length,
Basks at the fire his hairy strength;
And crop-full out of doors he flings,
Ere the first cock his matin rings.
Thus done the tales, to bed they creep,
By whispering winds soon lull'd asleep.

Tower'd cities please us then,
And the busy hum of men,
Where throngs of knights and barons bold,
In weeds of peace, high triumphs hold,   120
With store of ladies, whose bright eyes
Rain influence, and judge the prize
Of wit or arms, while both contend
To win her grace, whom all commend.
There let Hymen oft appear
In saffron robe, with taper clear,
And pomp, and feast, and revelry,
With mask, and antique pageantry;
Such sights as youthful poets dream
On summer eves by haunted stream.   130
Then to the well-trod stage anon,
If Jonson's learnèd sock be on;
Or sweetest Shakspeare, Fancy's child,
Warble his native wood-notes wild.
    And ever, against eating cares,
Lap me in soft Lydian airs,
Married to immortal verse;
Such as the meeting soul may pierce,
In notes, with many a winding bout
Of linkèd sweetness long drawn out,   140
With wanton heed and giddy cunning;
The melting voice through mazes running,
Untwisting all the chains that tie
The hidden soul of harmony;
That Orpheus' self may heave his head
From golden slumber on a bed
Of heap'd Elysian flowers, and hear
Such strains, as would have won the ear
Of Pluto, to have quite set free
His half-regained Eurydice.   150
    These delights if thou canst give,
Mirth, with thee I mean to live.

IL PENSEROSO.

HENCE, vain deluding Joys,
 The brood of Folly without father bred!
 How little you bested,
Or fill the fixèd mind with all your toys!
Dwell in some idle brain,
 And fancies fond with gaudy shapes possess,
 As thick and numberless
 As the gay motes that people the sun-beams;
 Or likest hovering dreams,
The fickle pensioners of Morpheus' train. 10
But hail, thou goddess, sage and holy,
Hail, divinest Melancholy!
Whose saintly visage is too bright
To hit the sense of human sight,
And therefore to our weaker view
O'erlaid with black, staid wisdom's hue;
Black, but such as in esteem
Prince Memnon's sister might beseem,
Or that starr'd Ethiop queen that strove
To set her beauty's praise above 20
The sea-nymphs', and their powers offended:
Yet thou art higher far descended:
Thee bright-hair'd Vesta, long of yore,
To solitary Saturn bore;
His daughter she; in Saturn's reign
Such mixture was not held a stain:
Oft in glimmering bowers and glades
He met her, and in secret shades
Of woody Ida's inmost grove,
Whilst yet there was no fear of Jove. 30
  Come, pensive Nun, devout and pure,
Sober, stedfast, and demure,
All in a robe of darkest grain,
Flowing with majestick train,
And sable stole of Cypress lawn,
Over thy decent shoulders drawn.

Come, but keep thy wonted state,
With even step, and musing gait;
And looks commércing with the skies,
Thy rapt soul sitting in thine eyes: 40
There, held in holy passion still,
Forget thyself to marble, till
With a sad leaden downward cast
Thou fix them on the earth as fast:
And join with thee calm Peace, and Quiet,
Spare Fast, that oft with gods doth diet,
And hears the Muses in a ring
Aye round about Jove's altar sing.
And add to these retirèd Leisure,
That in trim gardens takes his pleasure: 50
But first and chiefest with thee bring,
Him that yon soars on golden wing
Guiding the fiery-wheelèd throne,
The cherub Contemplation;
And the mute Silence hist along,
'Less Philomel will deign a song,
In her sweetest, saddest plight,
Smoothing the rugged brow of night,
While Cynthia checks her dragon yoke,
Gently o'er the accustom'd oak: 60
Sweet bird, that shunn'st the noise of folly,
Most musical, most melancholy!
Thee, chauntress, oft, the woods among,
I woo, to hear thy even-song;
And, missing thee, I walk unseen
On the dry smooth-shaven green,
To behold the wandering moon
Riding near her highest noon,
Like one that had been led astray
Through the heaven's wide pathless way;   70
And oft, as if her head she bow'd,
Stooping through a fleecy cloud.
Oft, on a plat of rising ground,
I hear the far-off curfeu sound,
Over some wide-water'd shore,
Swinging slow with sullen roar:

Or, if the air will not permit,
Some still removèd place will fit,
Where glowing embers through the room
Teach light to counterfeit a gloom;   80
Far from all resort of mirth,
Save the cricket on the hearth,
Or the bellman's drowsy charm,
To bless the doors from nightly harm.
Or let my lamp at midnight hour,
Be seen in some high lonely tower,
Where I may oft outwatch the Bear,
With thrice-great Hermes, or unsphere
The spirit of Plato, to unfold
What worlds or what vast regions hold   90
The mortal mind, that hath forsook
Her mansion in this fleshly nook:
And of those demons that are found
In fire, air, flood, or under ground,
Whose power hath a true consent
With planet, or with element.
Sometimes let gorgeous Tragedy
In sceptred pall come sweeping by,
Presenting Thebes, or Pelops' line,
Or the tale of Troy divine;   100
Or what, though rare, of later age
Ennobled hath the buskin'd stage.

    But, O sad Virgin, that thy power
Might raise Musæus from his bower!
Or bid the soul of Orpheus sing
Such notes, as, warbled to the string,
Drew iron tears down Pluto's cheek,
And made Hell grant what love did seek!
Or call up him that left half-told
The story of Cambuscan bold,   110
Of Camball and of Algarsife,
And who had Canace to wife,
That own'd the virtuous ring and glass;
And of the wondrous horse of brass,
On which the Tartar king did ride:
And if aught else great bards beside

In sage and solemn tunes have sung,
Of turneys, and of trophies hung;
Of forests and enchantments drear,
Where more is meant than meets the ear.   120
     Thus, Night, oft see me in thy pale career,
Till civil-suited Morn appear,
Not trick'd and frounced as she was wont
With the Attic boy to hunt,
But kercheft in a comely cloud,
While rocking winds are piping loud,
Or usher'd with a shower still,
When the gust hath blown his fill,
Ending on the rustling leaves,
With minute drops from off the eaves.   130
And, when the sun begins to fling
His flaring beams, me, Goddess, bring
To archèd walks of twilight groves,
And shadows brown, that Sylvan loves,
Of pine, or monumental oak,
Where the rude axe, with heavèd stroke,
Was never heard the nymphs to daunt,
Or fright them from their hallow'd haunt.
There in close covert by some brook,
Where no profaner eye may look,   140
Hide me from day's garish eye,
While the bee with honied thigh,
That at her flowery work doth sing,
And the waters murmuring,
With such consort as they keep,
Entice the dewy-feather'd sleep;
And let some strange mysterious Dream
Wave at his wings in aery stream
Of lively portraiture display'd,
Softly on my eyelids laid: 150
And, as I wake, sweet music breathe
Above, about, or underneath,
Sent by some Spirit to mortals good,
Or the unseen Genius of the wood.
     But let my due feet never fail
To walk the studious cloysters pale,

And love the high-embowèd roof,
With antick pillars massy proof,
And storied windows richly dight,
Casting a dim religious light: 160
There let the pealing organ blow,
To the full-voiced quire below,
In service high, and anthems clear,
As may with sweetness, through mine ear,
Dissolve me into ecstasies,
And bring all heaven before mine eyes.
    And may at last my weary age
Find out the peaceful hermitage,
The hairy gown and mossy cell,
Where I may sit and rightly spell   170
Of every star that heaven doth shew,
And every herb that sips the dew;
Till old experience do attain
To something like prophetic strain.
    These pleasures, Melancholy, give,
And I with thee will choose to live.

NOTES TO MILTON.

L'ALLEGRO.

(The numbers refer to lines.)

THE title *L'Allegro* is from the Italian, and signifies "the cheerful man."

1. *Melancholy* = a gloomy state of mind.   From Gr. *melan*, stem of *melas*, black, and *chole*, bile.   *Black bile* was thought to cause a gloomy state of mind.

2. *Cerberus* = the three-headed monster in the shape of a serpent-tailed dog, which, according to mythology, guarded the entrance to the infernal regions.   The genealogy here given is Milton's own invention.

3. *Stygian* = pertaining to the Styx, fabled by the ancients to be a river of hell, over which Charon rowed the souls of the dead; hence, hellish, infernal. — *Forlorn* = deserted; from A. S. *forloren*.   Cf. Ger. *verloren*, lost.

5. *Uncouth* = hideous; from A. S. *cunnan*, to know, and the prefix *un*. Literally, unknown.

7. *Night-raven* = a bird of ill-omen that cries in the night.

8. *Ebon* = dark or black.   This word has a long pedigree, running back through Fr., Lat., Gr., to the Hebrew *eben*, a stone.   It was applied to a kind of dense, hard wood, and afterwards came to denote simply a dark color. — *Low-brow'd* = beetle-browed, overhanging.

9. *Ragged* = rugged, to which it is related.   Skeat, in opposition to Webster, says there is no reason for connecting it with the A. S. *hracod*, torn, and that its resemblance to the Gr. '*rakos*, a shred of cloth, is accidental.

10. *Cimmerian* = pertaining to the Cimmerii, a people fabled in ancient times to dwell in profound and perpetual darkness.   A Cimmerian desert is one covered with deep and continual obscurity.

12. *Yclep'd* = called; from A. S. *clypian*, to call, the p.p. of which is *geclypod*.   The prefix *y* = A. S. *ge*. — *Euphrosyne* = Joy, one of the three Graces, her sisters being Aglaia, Beauty, and Thalia, Health.

14. *Venus* = the goddess of love and beauty.

16. *Bacchus* = the god of wine.

17. *Some sager sing* = an allusion, according to some, to Ben Jonson, and according to others, to Milton himself.

18. *Frolic* = joyous, sportive; from Dutch *vro*, glad, and suffix *lijk* = Eng. like. "It seems," says Skeat, "to be one of the rather numerous words imported from Dutch in the reign of Elizabeth."

19. *Zephyr* and *Aurora* are personifications of the *west wind* and *the dawn*.

22. *Fresh-blown*. *Blow*, meaning to bloom, is from A. S. *blowan*, and should not be confounded with *blow*, to puff, which is from A. S. *blawan*.

24. *Buxom* = possessing health and beauty combined with liveliness of manner. From A. S. *bugan*, to bend; the original meaning was pliable, obedient. Cf. Ger. *biegsam*, pliant. — *Debonair* = courteous; from Fr. *de bon air*, of good mien.

25. *Nymph* = in mythology a goddess of the mountains, forests, meadows, or waters; otherwise, a lovely maiden.

26. *Jollity* = merriment, gayety; from O. Fr. *joli*, joyful; derived from Scandinavian *jol*, festive. Cf. Eng. *Yule*.

27. *Quips* = playful taunts. It is of Celtic origin. — *Cranks* = puns or twisting of words. From an original root KRANK, to bend, twist. — *Wanton* = playful, sportive. The true sense is *unrestrained, uneducated;* from A. S. *wan*, lacking, and p.p. *togen*, educated, brought up. Webster gives a different etymology.

28. *Becks* = significant movements or signs with the head or hands; from A. S. *beacen*, a sign.

29. *Hebe* = the goddess of youth, and cupbearer of the gods.

34. *Fantastick* = capricious, indulging the vagaries of the imagination. From the Gr. *phantazein*, *f* taking the place of *ph*.

38. *Crew* = a company of people. It is of Scandinavian origin = old Icelandic *kru*. Webster derives it from Fr. *cru*, p.p. of *croitre*, to grow. The shade of contempt now adhering to the word did not formerly belong to it.

40. *Unreproved* = blameless, irreproachable, in which sense it is now obsolete.

44. *Dappled* = marked with spots of different colors; from Icel. *depill*, a spot. It has no connection with *apple*, as sometimes suggested.

48. *Eglantine* = honeysuckle or woodbine; usually sweet-brier, from which, however, Milton here distinguishes it. From Fr. *eglantine* = Low Lat. *aculentus*, prickly.

60. *State* = pomp, splendor.

61. *Amber* = a yellowish fossil rosin.

62. *Liveries* = the uniforms of servants or attendants; from Fr. *livrer*, to deliver, literally meaning a thing delivered, and applied to the clothes which a master gives his servant. — *Dight* = adorned; from A. S. *dihtan*, to set in order, arrange. The full form is *dighted*, p.p. of *dight*.

66. *Sithe* is the correct spelling of this word, which comes from the A. S. *sithe.* The *c* in our present spelling is a blunder.

67. *Tale* = reckoning by count, enumeration; from A. S. *tal*, a number. Cf. Ger. *Zahl.*

70. *Landskip* = landscape. The word was borrowed from the Dutch painters. Du. *landscap.*

71. *Fallows* = fields that have lain for some time unseeded or uncultivated. From A. S. *fealu*, yellowish, applied to ploughed land because of its yellowish color.

74. *Lab'ring* = in travail with rains and storms.

75. *Pide* = spotted; now spelled *pied.*

77. *Battlements* = notched or indented parapets, originally used only on fortifications, but afterwards employed on ecclesiastical and other buildings. See Webster.

78. *Bosom'd* = nestling and partly hidden.

79. *Lies* = stays or dwells, as very often in old English.

80. *Cynosure* = centre of attraction. From Lat. *cynosura*, the stars composing the constellation of the Lesser Bear, the last of which is the pole-star, or centre of attraction to the magnet. From Gr. *kuon*, dog, and *oura*, tale, meaning literally a dog's tail.

83. Corydon, Thyrsis, and Thestylis were shepherds, and Phillis, a maiden, in Virgil; here used as typical pastoral names.

85. *Messes* = dishes of food, without any tinge of contempt. From O. Fr. *mes*, dish = Low Lat. *missum*, that which is set or placed. "Not to be derived from A. S. *myse*, a table, nor from Lat. *mensa*, nor from O. H. Ger. *maz*, meat; all of which have been absurdly suggested." — SKEAT. The etymologies condemned are found in Webster.

87. *Bower* = a chamber, or lady's apartment; from A. S. *bur*, chamber, from *buan*, to dwell.

91. *Secure* = free from care or anxiety; from Lat. *se*, away, free from, and *cura*, care. The derivation from *sine cura*, though common, seems to be a mistake. The prefix *se* occurs in *secede, seduce*, etc.

94. *Rebecks* = a kind of fiddle, with two, three, or four strings. It comes from the Persian *rubab*, an instrument struck with a bow, through the Italian and French.

96. *Chequered* = marked with light and shade, like a checker-board. From O. Fr. *eschec* = Persian *Shah*, a king. *Checkmate* = *shah mat*, the king is dead.

98. *Holyday* = a day of amusement, joy, and gayety. In this sense the spelling *holiday* is preferable.

99. *Livelong* = long in passing.

100. *Spicy nut-brown ale* = ale seasoned with nutmeg, sugar, toast, and roasted apples. Shakespeare refers to it as the "gossips' bowl."

101. *Feat* = a striking act of strength, daring, or skill. From Fr. *fait*, p.p. of *faire*, to do, from Lat. *facere*.

102. *Mab* = the queen of the fairies. — *Junkets* = sweetmeats, dainties. The original meaning was *cream cheese* served up on rushes, whence its name. From Ital. *giunco*, a rush = Lat. *juncum*.

103. *She* and *he* = two of the party telling their tales over the spicy ale.

104. *Frier's lantern* = the *ignis fatuus*, or will-o'-the-wisp.

105. *Goblin* = a mischievous sprite or fairy. From O. Fr. *gobelin* = Low Lat. *gobelinus*, an extension of *cobalus* = Gr. *kobalos*, an impudent rogue, sprite.

110. *Lubbar* = a heavy, clumsy fellow; now spelled *lubber*. — *Fiend* = evil spirit; literally, enemy or hater. From A. S. *feond*, pres. p. of *feon*, to hate. Cf. Ger. *Feind*, enemy.

113. *Cropful* = having a full crop or belly. — *Flings* = rushes; literally, throws himself, the reflexive pronoun being omitted.

114. *Ere the first cock*, etc. This was the signal for ghosts and evil spirits to vanish. — *Matin* = morning. In the plural, morning prayers. From Fr. *matin* = Lat. matutinus, from Matuta, the goddess of morning.

120. *Weeds* = garments; from A. S. *waed*, garment. Commonly used now only in the phrase "widow's weeds," a widow's mourning dress.

121. *Store* = a great number.

122. *Rain influence*, upon the contending champions, as in the days of astrology the planets were supposed to do upon the lives of men.

124. *Her* = the lady of the tournament, by whom the prize was bestowed upon the successful knight. — *Grace* = favor; from Fr. *grace* = Lat. *gratia*, favor.

125. *Hymen* = the god of marriage; represented in the masks of the time as clad in yellow silk, and bearing a torch in his hand.

128. *Mask* = a dramatic entertainment in which masks were worn.

128. *Antique* = ancient. In present usage these words are discriminated: *ancient* is opposed to *modern;* as *ancient* landmarks, ancient institutions. *Antique* is used to designate what has come down from the ancients, or what is made in imitation of them; as, an *antique* cameo, an *antique* temple. *Antic* is a doublet of *antique*. — *Pageantry* = pompous exhibition or display. *Pageant* originally meant the sçaffold or platform on which the miracle plays were represented, and afterwards the play itself. From Lat. *pagina*, scaffold or stage. Webster's probable etymology is wrong.

131. *Anon* = immediately, at once; from A. S. *on an*, in one (moment). Cf. Eng. *at once*.

132. *Jonson* = Ben Jonson, who was still living when this compliment was paid him. — *Sock* = comedy; literally, the light-heeled shoe or sock worn by comic actors, whence a symbol for comedy. *Buskin*, a high-heeled boot or legging worn by tragic actors, has come to stand for tragedy.

136. *Lydian* = soft and voluptuous. From Lydia, a country in Asia Minor, whose people were notorious for luxurious effeminacy.

138. *Meeting* = sympathetic.

139. *Bout* = turn, bending; also spelled *bought*.

141. *Giddy* = mirthful; from A. S. *giddian*, to sing, to be merry. In present usage it means *unsteady, heedless*.

142. *Mazes* = intricacies.

145. *Orpheus* = a character in Greek mythology, who had power to move men and beasts, and even inanimate objects, by the music of his lyre. — *Heave* = raise; from A. S. *hebban*, to raise. Cf. Ger. *heben*, to lift. The connection of *heaven* with *heave* has not, according to Skeat, been clearly made out.

147. *Elysian* = pertaining to Elysium, the abode of the blessed in the other world. It was represented as a region of perpetual spring, clothed with continual verdure, enamelled with flowers, shaded by groves, and refreshed by never-failing fountains.

149. *Pluto* = the god of the infernal regions; son of Saturn, and brother of Jupiter and Neptune.

150. *Eurydice* = the wife of Orpheus. After her death, caused by the bite of a serpent, Orpheus descended into Hades, and so moved Pluto by his music that the god consented to her restoration to life, but only on the condition that the minstrel would not look back until the regions of day were reached. Fearing that his wife might not be following, the anxious husband cast a glance behind, and thereby lost her forever.

IL PENSEROSO.

Il Penseroso = the thoughtful man.

1. *Vain* = empty, worthless; from Fr. *vain* = Lat. *vanus*, empty.

3. *Bested* = assist.

4. *Fixed* = earnest, steady; from O. Fr. *fixe* = Lat. *fixus*, p.p. of *figere*, to fix.

6. *Fond* = foolish.

8. *Gay motes*, because of their lively motion in the sunbeam.

10. *Pensioners* = dependants. Through the Fr. from Lat. *pensus*, p.p. of *pendere*, to weigh out, to pay. Literally, those to whom money is weighed out or paid. — *Morpheus* = the god of dreams.

14. *To hit the sense* = to suit or be adapted to the sense.

18. *Memnon's sister* = some beautiful Ethiopian princess. Memnon, who was killed by Achilles in the Trojan war, was noted for his beauty. — *Beseem* = suit or become.

19. *Starr'd Ethiop Queen* = Cassiope, wife of Cepheus, king of Ethiopia. Having offended the Nereids by her presumption in setting herself above them in beauty, Neptune, sympathizing with the anger of the sea-maidens, laid waste the realms of Cepheus by an inundation and sea-monster. After her death Cassiope was changed into a constellation; whence the epithet *starred*.

23. *Vesta* = goddess of the fireside or domestic hearth. — *Of yore* = of old. From A. S. *geara*, formerly; originally genitive plu. of *gear*, year.

24. *Solitary Saturn* = the father of Jupiter, Neptune, and Pluto, who were concealed by their mother. He was accustomed to devour his offspring, whence he is called *solitary*.

29. *Ida* = woody mountains near Troy.

30. *No fear of Jove*, that is, before he was banished from the throne by Jupiter.

32. *Demure* = of modest look; from O. Fr. *de murs*, i.e., *de bons murs*, of good manners.

33. *Darkest grain* = Tyrian purple.

35. *Stole* = a long, loose garment reaching to the feet, the characteristic robe of the Roman matron; but here denoting probably a *hood* or *veil*, in which sense the word is used by Spenser. — *Cyprus lawn*. A dark kind of lawn was made in Cyprus. From Lat. *linum*, flax, through the French.

36. *Decent* = modest, because covered. From Fr. *decent* = pres. p. of *decere*, to become, to befit.

37. *Wonted state* = usual dignified bearing.

39. *Commercing* = communicating.

40. *Rapt* = enraptured; from Lat. *raptus*, p.p. of *rapere*, to transport.

41. *Passion* = devotion; from Fr. *passion* = Lat. *passionem*, from *pati*, to suffer.

42. *Forget thyself to marble* = become as insensible to surrounding objects as a statue.

43. *Leaden* = heavy.

44. *Fast* = firm, fixed.

52. *Yon* = yonder.

55. *Hist along* = bring along silently.

56. *'Less* = unless. — *Philomel* = the nightingale; literally, lover of song.

59. *Cynthia* = the moon. A surname of Diana, from Mt. Cynthus, in the island of Delos, where she was born. Her chariot, however, was not, according to classic mythology, drawn by dragons. Ovid speaks of the moon's "snow-white horses."

60. *Accustomed oak* = the particular oak in which the nightingale was accustomed to sing.

61. *Noise of folly* = the sounds of revelry.

68. *Highest noon* = highest point of ascension

73. *Plat* = a portion of flat, even ground; a variation of *plot*.

74. *Curfeu* = the ringing of a bell at nightfall as a signal to extinguish fires and lights. The custom was introduced into England by William the Conqueror.

78. *Removed* = remote. — *Will fit* = will be suitable.

80. *Counterfeit* = imitate; from Fr. *contre*, against, and *faire*, to make; Lat. *contra* and *facere*.

83. *Bellman's drowsy charm* = the watchman, who with a bell patrolled the streets at night before the establishment of the present police system, and called out the hours. *Charm* = song, incantation; from Fr. *charme* = Lat. *carmen*, song. The bellman frequently made use of rhyme; as, —

> " Mercie secure ye all and keep
> The goblin from ye, while ye sleep,
> Past one o'clock, and almost two,
> My masters all, good-day to you."

84. *Nightly harm* = harm at night.

87. *Outwatch the Bear.* — The "Bear" refers to the constellation of that name, which in England never sets. The poet means that he will remain awake all night.

88. *Thrice-great Hermes* = a personification of the Egyptian priesthood; to him was ascribed the invention of language and writing, geometry, arithmetic, astronomy, medicine, music, religion, etc.

89. *Plato* = a celebrated Greek philosopher born 429 B.C. To *unsphere* his spirit means to call it back from Elysium.

95. *Consent* = harmony, agreement. From Fr. *consentir* = Lat. *con*, for *cum*, together, and *sentire*, to feel.

98. *Sceptred pall* = royal robe. *Pall* = A. S. *paell*, from Lat. *palla*, a mantle.

99. Oedipus of Thebes, Pelops, and the heroes of the Trojan war, were the favorite subjects of Attic tragedy.

102. *Buskin'd.* — See note on *L'Allegro*, 132. Milton was probably thinking of *Hamlet*, *Othello*, and *King Lear*.

104. *Musæus* = an early Greek bard.

105. *Orpheus.* — See note on *L'Allegro*, 145, 150.

109. *Him* = Chaucer. The reference is to the " Squire's Tale," which was left unfinished. Cambuscan was a Tartar king, who had two sons, Camball and Algarsife, and a daughter Canace.

116. *Great bards beside* = probably Tasso, Ariosto, and Spenser, who were great favorites with Milton.

120. *Where more is meant*, etc. — A reference no doubt to Spenser's " Faery Queene," in which the poet had a high moral purpose.

122. *Civil-suited* = dressed in the garb of a plain citizen.

123. *Trick'd* = tricked out, showily dressed. — *Frounced* = frizzled and curled.

124. *Attic boy* = Cephalus, whom she carried off.

125. *Kercheft* = having the head covered. A more correct spelling would be *curchief;* from Fr. *couvre*, cover, and *chef*, head. Cf. *curfeu.*

134. *Sylvan* = Sylvanus, god of the woods. From Lat. *sylva*, woods.

136. *Heaved* = uplifted. See note on *L'Allegro*, 145.

140. *Profaner* = unsympathetic. From Lat. *pro*, before, and *fanum*, temple; hence, outside the temple, not sacred, secular.

142. *Honied thigh.* — This is a mistake, for the bee collects the honey in its crop. What we see on the " thigh " is pollen.

145. *Consort* = harmony of sounds.

156. *Studious cloysters pale* = an enclosure or place of retirement devoted to study and religion. He is probably thinking of St. Paul's, where he went to school.

157. *High-embowed* = with lofty arches.

158. *Antick.* — See note on *L'Allegro*, 128.

159. *Dight.* — See note on *L'Allegro*, 62.

170. *Spell* = read.

174. *Strain* = rank, character; in which sense it is now obsolete.

THE RESTORATION.

REPRESENTATIVE WRITER.

JOHN DRYDEN.

OTHER PROMINENT WRITERS.

Poet. — SAMUEL BUTLER.

Dramatists. — WYCHERLY, CONGREVE, FARQUHAR.

Diarists. — PEPYS, EVELYN.

Preachers. — BARROW, SOUTH, TILLOTSON.

Philosophers. — HOBBES, NEWTON, CUDWORTH, LOCKE.

Miscellaneous. — WALTON, TEMPLE.

IV.

THE RESTORATION.

1660-1700.

GENERAL SURVEY. — Every extreme tends to beget a reaction. Nowhere is the truth of this principle more strikingly exemplified than in England at the time of the Restoration. With all its moral earnestness and love of freedom, Puritanism had degenerated into a false and forbidding asceticism. It condemned many innocent pleasures. It clothed morality and religion in a garb of cant. The claims of the physical and intellectual parts of man were, under the influence of a terrific theology, sacrificed to his spiritual interests. All spontaneous joy and gayety were banished from life. The Puritan's steps were slow ; his face was elongated ; his tone had a nasal quality. He gave his children names drawn from the Scriptures ; and shutting his eyes to the beauties of the world about him, and forgetting the infinite love of God, he lived perpetually in the shadow of divine wrath. His religion, at war with nature and the gospel, degenerated into fanaticism, and weighed heavily upon the life of the English nation.

With the Restoration, Puritanism was overthrown. The Royalist party, with its sharp contrasts to Puritan principles, again came into power. The result in its moral effects was dreadful. The stream of license, which had been held in check for years, burst forth with fearful momentum. The reign of the flesh set in. Virtue was held to savor of Puritanism; duty was thought to smack of fanaticism; and integrity, patriotism, and honor were regarded as mere devices for self-aggrandizement. Under the lead of Charles II., himself a notorious libertine, the court became a scene of shameless and almost incredible debauchery. The effect upon literature can be easily imagined. It debased the moral tone of poetry and the drama to a shocking degree. As Dryden tells us in one of his epilogues, —

> " The poets who must live by courts, or starve,
> Were proud so good a government to serve;
> And, mixing with buffoons and pimps profane,
> Tainted the stage, for some small snip of gain."

But there are other respects in which the Restoration affected literature. Charles II. returned to England with French companions and French tastes. It was but natural, therefore, that English literature should be influenced by French models. It was the Augustan age of literature in France. Louis XIV., the most powerful monarch in Europe, had gathered about him the best literary talent of the age. Corneille, Molière, and Racine gave great splendor to dramatic poetry, and Boileau developed the art of criticism. But the French drama, besides following classical models in regard to the unities, imposed the burden of rhymed couplets upon dramatic composition. It was in obedience to the wish of Charles that rhyme was first introduced into the English drama. Through French influence the course of the drama, as it had been developed by the great Elizabethans, was seriously interrupted.

But in respect to literary criticism, the influence of France was more salutary. Boileau had displayed great critical acumen in estimating French authors, and had laid down correct principles by which to judge literary composition. The art of criticism took root in England. Dryden, whom Johnson calls the father of English criticism, sat at the feet of his great French contemporary, and in his numerous prefaces exhibited admirable judgment in weighing the productions both of ancient and modern times.

The Restoration gave a new impulse to natural science. Charles II. was himself something of a chemist, and even the profligate Buckingham varied his debaucheries with experiments in his laboratory. In 1662 the Royal Society was founded, and for half a century inventions and discoveries in science followed one another in rapid succession. The national observatory at Greenwich was established. The spirit of investigation showed great vigor. Halley studied the tides, comets, and terrestrial magnetism. Boyle improved the air-pump, and founded experimental chemistry. Mineralogy, zoölogy, and botany either had their beginning or made noteworthy progress at this time. It was the age of Sir Isaac Newton.

But this period was one of ferment and transition. Old faiths in politics, philosophy, and religion were being cast aside. Tradition and custom were summoned before the bar of reason. " From the moment of the Restoration," says Green, " we find ourselves all at once among the great currents of thought and activity which have gone on widening and deepening from that time to this. The England around us becomes our England, an England whose chief forces are industry and science, the love of popular freedom and of law, an England which presses steadily forward to a larger social justice and equality, and which tends more and more to bring every custom and tradition, religious, intellectual, and political, to the test of pure reason." The belief in the divine right of kings became a thing of the past. With the Revolution of 1688, which placed William of Orange on the throne, the prolonged conflict between the people and the king came to an end. The executive supremacy was transferred from the crown to the House of Commons.

The asperities of theological parties began to give way. Within the Church of England there arose a class of divines who, because of their tolerant views, were stigmatized as "latitudinarians." Avoiding the scholasticism of the preceding age, they studied Scripture with a genial spirit. The evils of strife, as well as a sense of danger from infidelity, made them desire Christian unity, which they recognized as the normal condition of the church. Among the most distinguished of these broad churchmen were Ralph Cudworth, Henry More, and John Tillotson.

A still more important movement in theology was the rise of Deism, which owed its prevalence to several co-operative causes. As we have seen, there was a general tendency to break away from the restraints of authority in every department of thought. The divisions and animosities of the church tended to unsettle the faith of many in the teachings of Christianity. And above all, perhaps, the license of the age sought to emancipate itself from the restraints of divine law.

In its progress Deism showed a rapid declension. It began with Lord Herbert of Cherbury, who reduced religion to five points : 1, that there is a God ; 2, that he is to be worshipped; 3, that piety and virtue are the principal parts of this worship; 4, that men should repent and forsake sin; and 5, that good will be rewarded and sin punished. This scheme of doctrine represents Deism at its best. The writings of the deists, among whom may be mentioned Hobbes, Blount, and Lord Bolingbroke, naturally called forth many replies. The controversy, which was protracted into the eighteenth century, was conducted with great ability on both sides. Among the defenders of Christianity, with whom ultimately remained the victory, were Cudworth, John Locke the philosopher, and Joseph Butler, the author of the famous " Analogy."

JOHN DRYDEN.

THE greatest name in the literature of this period is John Dryden. He does not deserve, indeed, to stand by the side of Chaucer, Spenser, Shakespeare, or Milton ; but after these great names he comes at the head of the second rank. It was the fault of his age that he was not greater. No man can wholly detach himself from the influences by which he is surrounded ; and Dryden came on the stage when a false taste prevailed, and when licentiousness gave moral tone to poetry. Living in the midst of burning religious and political questions, he was drawn into the vortex of controversy. He was always a partisan in some religious or political issue of the day. While this fact has given us some of the best satirical and didactic poems in our language, it did not contribute, perhaps, to the largest development of his poetical powers.

His aims were not high enough. "I confess," he said, "my chief endeavors are to delight the age in which I live. If the humor of this be for low comedy, small accidents, and raillery, I will force my genius to obey it." This was a voluntary degrading of his genius, and an intentional renouncing of the artistic spirit. Guided by such motives, it was impossible for him to attain the highest results. If, like Milton, he had concentrated all the energies of his strong nature on an epic poem, as he once con- templated, or on poetry as an art, his work would no doubt have been less faulty. But, taking him as he was, we cannot help admiring his genius, which created for him a distinct place in English literature.

Dryden was born of good family in Northamptonshire, in 1631. Both on his father's and his mother's side his ancestry was Puritan and republican. He was educated at Westminster school, under the famous Dr. Busby. A school-boy poem on the death of Lord Hastings had the distinction, and we may add the misfortune, of being published in connection with several other elegies called forth by the same event. Some of its conceits are exceedingly ridiculous. The young nobleman had died of the small-pox, and Dryden exclaims : —

> " Was there no milder way than the small-pox,
> The very filthiness of Pandora's box? "

Of the pustules he says : —

> " Each little pimple had a tear in it,
> To wail the fault its rising did commit."

And as the climax of this absurdity : —

> " No comet need foretell his change drew on,
> Whose corpse might seem a constellation."

Dryden's genius was slow in maturing, and much of his early work failed to give promise of his future eminence.

He entered Trinity College, Cambridge, in 1650, and took his degree of Bachelor of Arts in 1654. No details of his college life have come down to us, except his punishment on one occasion for " disobedience to the vice-master, and contumacy in taking his punishment, inflicted by him." In 1654, by the death of his father, he came into the possession of a small estate worth about sixty pounds a year. After leaving Cambridge, for which he entertained no great affection, he went to London, and served for a time as secretary to his cousin, Sir Gilbert Pickering, a favorite of Cromwell.

In 1658 he composed " Heroic Stanzas " on the death of Oliver Cromwell, which caused him to be spoken of as a rising poet. Though disfigured here and there by conceits, it is, upon the whole, a strong, manly poem, showing a just appreciation of the great Protector's life. His next effort does not reflect credit on his character.   It was the " Astræa Redux," written "on the happy restoration and return of his sacred Majesty, Charles II."   After his eulogy of Cromwell two years before, we are hardly prepared for such lines as these : —

> " For his long absence Church and State did groan;
>   Madness the pulpit, faction seized the throne :
>   Experienced age in deep despair was lost,
>   To see the rebel thrive, the loyal cross'd."

In 1663 he began to write for the stage.   Instead of seeking to elevate public morals, or to attain perfection in art, it is to the lasting discredit of Dryden that he pandered to the vicious taste of the time.   His first play, " The Wild Gallant," was not successful; and Pepys, in his " Diary," pronounced it " so poor a thing as ever I saw in my life."   Without following him through the vicissitudes of his dramatic career, it is enough to say that he wrote in all twenty-eight comedies and tragedies, and at length established his position as the first dramatist of his time.   For a long time he followed French models, but at last came to recognize and professedly to imitate the " divine Shakespeare."   In his comedies, as he tells us, he copied " the gallantries of the court."   When in later years Jeremy Collier severely attacked the immoralities of the stage, Dryden, unlike several of his fellow dramatists who attempted a reply, pleaded guilty, and retracted all thoughts and expressions that could be fairly charged with " obscenity, profaneness, or immorality."

In his tragedies he imitated the heroic style of Corneille. They contain much splendid declamation, which too often degenerates into bombast.   But frequently he reaches the height of genuine poetry.   Only a poet could have written these lines : —

> " Something like
>   That voice, methinks, I should have somewhere heard;
>   But floods of woe have hurried it far off
>   Beyond my ken of soul."

Or these : —

> " I feel death rising higher still and higher
> Within my bosom; every breath I fetch
> Shuts up my life within a shorter compass,
> And, like the vanishing sound of bells, grows less
> And less each pulse, till it be lost in air."

When he moralizes he is often admirable : —

> " The gods are just,
> But how can finite measure infinite?
> Reason ! alas, it does not know itself !
> Yet man, vain man, would with his short-lined plummet
> Fathom the vast abyss of heavenly justice.
> Whatever is, is in its causes just,
> Since all things are by fate.   But purblind man
> Sees but a part o' th' chain, the nearest links,
> His eyes not carrying to that equal beam
> That poises all above."

But the drama was not Dryden's sphere.   In his mind the
judgment had the ascendency over the imagination.   He was
strongest in analyzing, arguing, criticising.   He was a master
of satire — not indeed of that species which slovenly butchers
a man, to use his own comparison, but rather of that species
which has " the fineness of stroke to separate the head from
the body, and leave it standing in its place."   We shall say
nothing of his " Annus Mirabilis," a long poem on the Dutch
war and the London fire, except that it contains some of his
manliest lines.   It is not easy to surpass, —

> " Silent in smoke of cannon they come on; "

> " And his loud guns speak thick, like angry men; "

> " The vigorous seaman every port-hole plies,
> And adds his heart to every gun he fires."

In 1681 appeared the famous satire, " Absalom and Achitophel," the object of which was to bring discredit on the Earl

of Shaftesbury and his adherents, who were seeking to secure the succession to the throne for the Duke of Monmouth, Charles's eldest son. It has been called the best political satire ever written. There is no effort at playful and delicate art; the poem was composed in earnest, and it abounds in hard, sweeping, stunning blows. It was eagerly seized upon by the public, and in a year no fewer than nine editions were called for. The Earl of Shaftesbury figures as Achitophel : —

> " A name to all succeeding ages cursed:
> For close designs, and crooked counsels fit;
> Sagacious, bold, and turbulent of wit;
> Restless, unfix'd in principles and place;
> In power unpleased, impatient of disgrace:
> A fiery soul, which, working out its way,
> Fretted the pigmy-body to decay,
> And o'er-inform'd the tenement of clay;
> A daring pilot in extremity;
> Pleased with the danger, when the waves went high,
> He sought the storms; but, for a calm unfit,
> Would steer too nigh the sands to boast his wit."

The Duke of Buckingham is Zimri, whose character is outlined with astonishing power : —

> " A man so various, that he seemed to be
> Not one, but all mankind's epitome:
> Stiff in opinions, always in the wrong;
> Was every thing by starts, and nothing long:
> But in the course of one revolving moon,
> Was chymist, fiddler, statesman, and buffoon:
> Then all for women, painting, rhyming, drinking,
> Besides ten thousand freaks that died in thinking.
> Bless'd madman, who could every hour employ,
> With something new to wish, or to enjoy!
> Railing and praising were his usual themes;
> And both, to show his judgment, in extremes."

In 1682 appeared the "Religio Laici," which is appended for special study. As an exposition of a layman's faith, it was probably an honest presentation of Dryden's beliefs at the time. Whether intended to serve a political purpose or not, is a matter of dispute; but it attacks the Papists, and at the same time declares the "Fanatics," by whom are meant the Non-conformists, still more dangerous — a declaration that accorded well with Charles's policy of persecution. It is entirely didactic in character, and deservedly ranks as one of the very best poems of its class in English. Though it is closely argumentative throughout, it still contains passages of much beauty. The opening lines are justly admired : —

> "Dim as the borrowed beams of moon and stars
>   To lonely, weary, wandering travellers
>   Is Reason to the soul: and as on high
>   Those rolling fires discover but the sky,
>   Not light us here, so Reason's glimmering ray
>   Was lent, not to assure our doubtful way,
>   But guide us upward to a better day.
>   And as those nightly tapers disappear
>   When day's bright lord ascends our hemisphere,
>   So pale grows Reason at Religion's sight,
>   So dies, and so dissolves in supernatural light."

In the preface to the poem, Dryden has given us the ideal of style at which he aimed and which he largely realized : "If any one be so lamentable a critic as to require the smoothness, the numbers, and the turn of heroic poetry in this poem, I must tell him, that, if he has not read Horace, I have studied him, and hope the style of his Epistles is not ill imitated here. The expressions of a poem designed purely for instruction ought to be plain and natural, and yet majestic : for here the poet is presumed to be a kind of lawgiver, and those three qualities which I have named are proper to the legislative style. The florid, elevated, and figurative way is for the passions; for love and hatred, fear and anger, are begotten in the soul by showing their objects out of their true proportion, either greater than the life or less; but instruction is to be given by showing them what they naturally are. A man is to be cheated into passion, but to be reasoned into truth."

On the accession of James in 1685, Dryden became a Roman Catholic. This conversion has given rise to considerable discussion. Did it result from conviction or from self-interest? It is impossible to determine. But, in the moderate language of Johnson, " That conversion will always be suspected that apparently concurs with interest. He that never finds his error till it hinders his progress towards wealth or honor, will not be thought to love truth only for herself. Yet it may easily happen that information may come at a commodious time, and as truth and interest are not by any fatal necessity at variance, that one may by accident introduce the other. When opinions are struggling into popularity, the arguments by which they are opposed or defended become more known, and he that changes his profession would perhaps have changed it before, with the like opportunities of instruction. This was then the state of popery; every artifice was used to show it in its fairest form; and it must be owned to be a religion of external appearance sufficiently attractive."

As a result of this conversion we have the " Hind and Panther," a poem of twenty-five hundred lines, which is devoted to the defence of the Roman Church. This church is represented by the " milk-white hind," and the Church of England by the panther, a beautiful but spotted animal. Published at a time of heated religious controversy, it had a wide circulation. It was regarded by Pope as the most correct specimen of Dryden's versification ; and there can be no doubt that the author, knowing it would be criticised with the most unfriendly rigor, elaborated it with unusual care. The opening lines are beautiful : —

> ' A milk-white Hind, immortal and unchanged,
>   Fed on the lawns, and in the forest ranged;
>   Without unspotted, innocent within,
>   She feared no danger, for she knew no sin.

> Yet hath she oft been chased with horns and hounds
> And Scythian shafts, and many winged wounds
> Aimed at her heart; was often forced to fly,
> And doomed to death, though fated not to die.''

At the Revolution, Dryden did not abjure his faith, and, as a consequence, lost his office as poet laureate. In addition to the loss of his pension, which he could ill afford to suffer, he had the chagrin of seeing his rival, Shadwell, elevated to his place. Against him he wrote at this time one of his keenest satires, entitled, " Mac Flecknoe." Flecknoe, who had governed long, and —

> " In prose and verse was owned, without dispute,
> Through all the realms of Nonsense, absolute,''

at length decides to settle the succession of the state, —

> " And, pondering, which of all his sons was fit
> To reign, and wage immortal war with wit,
> Cried, ' 'Tis resolved; for nature pleads, that he
> Should only rule, who most resembles me.
> Shadwell alone my perfect image bears,
> Mature in dullness from his tender years:
> Shadwell alone, of all my sons, is he,
> Who stands confirm'd in full stupidity.
> The rest to some faint meaning make pretence,
> But Shadwell never deviates into sense.' ''

Once more thrown upon his pen for support, Dryden turned to the stage, but chiefly to translation. In 1693 he published a volume of miscellanies, which contained translations from Homer and Ovid; and a little later appeared the satires of Juvenal and Persius. His theory of translation, as set forth in his prefaces, is better than his practice. He takes liberties with his author; and, as was the case with him in all his writings, he is far from painstaking. Besides, instead of mitigating, he magnified their obscenity. But, upon the whole, the translations are of high excellence. The most important of his translations was that of Virgil's "Æneid," on which he labored three years. The public expectation was great, and it was not disappointed. Pope pronounced it "the most noble and spirited translation that I know in any language."

Among his songs and odes, the best known is "Alexander's Feast." He wrote it at a single sitting, and afterwards spent a fortnight in polishing it. It is justly considered one of the finest odes in our language. Dryden himself declared that it would never be surpassed. It was, perhaps, the last effort of his poetic genius, composed amid the pressing infirmities of age. It was fitting, to use the beautiful words of one of his heroes, that, —

> " A setting sun
> Should leave a track of glory in the skies."

He died May 1, 1700, and was buried with imposing pomp in Westminster Abbey.

Dryden's prose is scarcely less excellent than his verse. He wrote much on criticism in the form of prefaces to his various works. He avoided, as a rule, the common mistakes in the prose of his time — inordinately long sentences and tedious parenthetic clauses. He says he formed his prose style on Tillotson; but Tillotson never had the ease, point, and brilliancy of Dryden. He was a clear, strong thinker, with a great deal to say; and often compressing his thought into a few well-chosen words, he sent them forth like shots from a rifle. He delighted in argument; and on either side of a question, he could marshal his points with almost matchless skill. Whether attacking or defending the Roman Church, he showed equal power.

Dryden did not attain to the highest regions of poetry. He could not portray what is deepest and finest in human experience. His strong, masculine hands were too clumsy. He has no charm of pathos; he does not touch that part of our nature where "thoughts do often lie too deep for tears." But he was a virile thinker, and a master of the English tongue.

He had the gift of using the right word ; and in the words of Lowell, he " sometimes carried common-sense to a height where it catches the light of a diviner air, and warmed reason till it had well-nigh the illuminating property of intuition."

He made literature a trade. He wrote rapidly ; and having once finished a piece, he did not, year after year, patiently retouch it into perfection. Perhaps he wrote too much. Voltaire said that he " would have a glory without a blemish, if he had only written the tenth part of his works." Yet, in spite of his faults, we recognize and admire his extraordinary intellectual force, and the indisputable greatness of his literary work. At Will's coffee-house, where his chair had in winter a prescriptive place by the fire, and in summer a choice spot on the balcony, he was fitted, beyond all others of his time, to reign as literary dictator.

For the rest, we shall let Congreve speak — the poet whom Dryden implored " to be kind to his remains," and who was not untouched by the appeal. " Mr. Dryden," says his friend, " had personal qualities to challenge both love and esteem from all who were truly acquainted with him. He was of a nature exceedingly humane and compassionate, easily forgiving injuries, and capable of a prompt and sincere reconciliation with those who had offended him. Such a temperament is the only solid foundation of all moral virtues and sociable endowments. His friendship, when he professed it, went much beyond his professions, though his hereditary income was little more than a bare competency. As his reading had been extensive, so was he very happy in a memory tenacious of everything he read. He was not more possessed of knowledge than communicative of it, but then his communication of it was by no means pedantic, or imposed upon the conversation : but just such, and went so far, as by the natural turn of the discourse in which he was engaged, it was necessarily promoted or required. He was extremely ready and gentle in his correction of the errors of any writer who thought fit to consult him, and felt as ready and patient to admit of the reprehension of others in respect of his own oversight or mistakes. He was of very easy, I may say, of very pleasing access, but somewhat slow, and, as it were, diffident in his advances to others. He had something in his nature that abhorred intrusion into any society whatever : indeed, it is to be regretted that he was rather blamable in the other extreme ; for by that means he was personally less known, and consequently his character will become liable to misapprehension and misrepresentation. To the best of my knowledge and observation, he was, of all men that ever I knew, one of the most modest and the most easily to be discountenanced in his approaches either to his superiors or his equals."

RELIGIO LAICI;

OR A LAYMAN'S FAITH.

DIM as the borrowed beams of moon and stars
To lonely, weary, wandering travellers,
Is Reason to the soul: and as on high
Those rolling fires discover but the sky,
Not light us here, so Reason's glimmering ray
Was lent, not to assure our doubtful way,
But guide us upward to a better day.
And as those nightly tapers disappear
When day's bright lord ascends our hemisphere,
So pale grows Reason at Religion's sight,   10
So dies, and so dissolves in supernatural light.
Some few, whose lamp shone brighter, have been led
From cause to cause to Nature's secret head,
And found that one first principle must be;
But what or who that UNIVERSAL HE;
Whether some soul encompassing this ball,
Unmade, unmoved, yet making, moving all,
Or various atoms' interfering dance
Leapt into form (the noble work of chance,)
Or this great All was from eternity,   20
Not even the Stagirite himself could see,
And Epicurus guessed as well as he.
As blindly groped they for a future state,
As rashly judged of Providence and Fate.
But least of all could their endeavours find
What most concerned the good of human kind;
For Happiness was never to be found,
But vanished from them like enchanted ground.
One thought Content the good to be enjoyed;
This every little accident destroyed.   30
The wiser madmen did for Virtue toil,
A thorny, or at best a barren soil;

In Pleasure some their glutton souls would steep,
But found their line too short, the well too deep,
And leaky vessels which no bliss could keep.
Thus anxious thoughts in endless circles roll,
Without a centre where to fix the soul.
In this wild maze their vain endeavours end:
How can the less the greater comprehend?
Or finite Reason reach Infinity?   40
For what could fathom GOD were more than He.
 The Deist thinks he stands on firmer ground,
Cries *eureka*, the mighty secret's found:
God is that spring of good, supreme and best,
We made to serve, and in that service blest;
If so, some rules of worship must be given,
Distributed alike to all by Heaven;
Else God were partial, and to some denied
The means His justice should for all provide.
This general worship is to PRAISE and PRAY;   50
One part to borrow blessings, one to pay;
And when frail nature slides into offence,
The sacrifice for crime is penitence.
Yet since the effects of Providence, we find,
Are variously dispensed to human kind;
That vice triumphs and virtue suffers here,
(A brand that sovereign justice cannot bear:)
Our Reason prompts us to a future state,
The last appeal from Fortune and from Fate,
Where God's all-righteous ways will be declared,   60
The bad meet punishment, the good reward.
 Thus man by his own strength to Heaven would soar
And would not be obliged to God for more.
Vain, wretched creature, how art thou misled
To think thy wit these god-like notions bred!
These truths are not the product of thy mind,
But dropped from Heaven, and of a nobler kind.
Revealed Religion first informed thy sight,
And Reason saw not till Faith sprung the light.
Hence all thy natural worship takes its source: 70
'Tis Revelation what thou thinkst Discourse.

Else how com'st thou to see these truths so clear,
Which so obscure to heathens did appear ?
Not Plato these, nor Aristotle found,
Nor he whose wisdom oracles renowned.
Hast thou a wit so deep or so sublime,
Or canst thou lower dive or higher climb ?
Canst thou by reason more of Godhead know
Than Plutarch, Seneca, or Cicero ?
Those giant wits, in happier ages born,   80
When arms and arts did Greece and Rome adorn,
Knew no such system ; no such piles could raise
Of natural worship, built on prayer and praise
To one sole GOD :
Nor did remorse to expiate sin prescribe,
But slew their fellow creatures for a bribe :
The guiltless victim groaned for their offence,
And cruelty and blood was penitence.
If sheep and oxen could atone for men,
Ah ! at how cheap a rate the rich might sin !   90
And great oppressors might Heaven's wrath beguile
By offering his own creatures for a spoil !
        Darest thou, poor worm, offend Infinity ?
And must the terms of peace be given by thee ?
Then thou art Justice in the last appeal ;
Thy easy God instructs thee to rebel,
And, like a king remote and weak, must take
What satisfaction thou art pleased to make.
        But if there be a power too just and strong
To wink at crimes and bear unpunished wrong,   100
Look humbly upward, see his will disclose
The forfeit first, and then the fine impose :
A mulct thy poverty could never pay,
Had not eternal Wisdom found the way,
And with celestial wealth supplied thy store ;
His justice makes the fine, His mercy quits the score.
See God descending in thy human frame ;
The offended suffering in the offender's name :
All thy misdeeds to Him imputed see,
And all His righteousness devolved on thee.   110

For granting we have sinned, and that the offence
Of man is made against Omnipotence,
Some price that bears proportion must be paid,
And infinite with infinite be weighed.
See then the Deist lost : remorse for vice
Not paid, or paid inadequate in price :
What further means can Reason now direct,
Or what relief from human wit expect ?
That shows us sick ; and sadly are we sure
Still to be sick, till Heaven reveal the cure :   120
If then Heaven's will must needs be understood,
Which must, if we want cure and Heaven be good,
Let all records of will revealed be shown,
With Scripture all in equal balance thrown,
And our one Sacred Book will be that one.

    Proof needs not here ; for whether we compare
That impious, idle, superstitious ware
Of rites, lustrations, offerings, which before,
In various ages, various countries bore,
With Christian Faith and Virtues, we shall find   130
None answering the great ends of human kind,
But this one rule of life ; that shows us best
How God may be appeased and mortals blest.
Whether from length of time its worth we draw,
The world is scarce more ancient than the law :
Heaven's early care prescribed for every age,
First, in the soul, and after, in the page.
Or whether more abstractedly we look
Or on the writers or the written book,
Whence but from Heaven could men, unskilled in arts,   140
In several ages born, in several parts,
Weave such agreeing truths ? or how or why
Should all conspire to cheat us with a lie ?
Unasked their pains, ungrateful their advice,
Starving their gain and martyrdom their price.

    If on the Book itself we cast our view,
Concurrent heathens prove the story true :
The doctrine, miracles ; which must convince,
For Heaven in them appeals to human sense ;

And though they prove not, they confirm the cause, 150
When what is taught agrees with Nature's laws.
 Then for the style, majestic and divine,
It speaks no less than God in every line;
Commanding words, whose force is still the same
As the first fiat that produced our frame.
All faiths beside or did by arms ascend,
Or sense indulged has made mankind their friend;
This only doctrine does our lusts oppose,
Unfed by nature's soil, in which it grows,
Cross to our interests, curbing sense and sin; 160
Oppressed without and undermined within,
It thrives through pain; its own tormenters tires,
And with a stubborn patience still aspires.
To what can Reason such effects assign,
Transcending Nature, but to laws divine?
Which in that sacred volume are contained;
Sufficient, clear, and for that use ordained.
 But stay; the Deist here will urge anew,
No supernatural worship can be true;
Because a general law is that alone 170
Which must to all and everywhere be known:
A style so large as not this Book can claim,
Nor aught that bears Revealed Religion's name.
'Tis said the sound of a Messiah's birth
Is gone through all the habitable earth;
But still that text must be confined alone
To what was then inhabited, and known:
And what provision could from thence accrue
To Indian souls and worlds discovered new?
In other parts it helps, that, ages past, 180
The Scriptures there were known, and were embraced,
Till Sin spread once again the shades of night:
What's that to these who never saw the light?
 Of all objections this indeed is chief
To startle reason, stagger frail belief:
We grant, 'tis true, that Heaven from human sense
Has hid the secret paths of Providence;
But boundless wisdom, boundless mercy may

Find even for those bewildered souls a way;
If from His nature foes may pity claim,   190
Much more may strangers who ne'er heard His name.
And though no name be for salvation known,
But that of His Eternal Son's alone;
Who knows how far transcending goodness can
Extend the merits of that Son to man?
Who knows what reasons may His mercy lead,
Or ignorance invincible may plead?
Not only charity bids hope the best,
But more the great Apostle has exprest:
That if the Gentiles, whom no law inspired,   200
By nature did what was by law required,
They who the written rule had never known
Were to themselves both rule and law alone,
To Nature's plain indictment they shall plead
And by their conscience be condemned or freed.
Most righteous doom! because a rule revealed
Is none to those from whom it was concealed.
Then those who followed Reason's dictates right,
Lived up, and lifted high their natural light,
With Socrates may see their Maker's face,   210
While thousand rubric-martyrs want a place.
    Nor does it baulk my charity to find
The Egyptian Bishop of another mind;
For, though his Creed eternal truth contains,
'Tis hard for man to doom to endless pains
All who believed not all his zeal required,
Unless he first could prove he was inspired.
Then let us either think he meant to say
This faith, where published, was the only way;
Or else conclude that, Arius to confute,   220
The good old man, too eager in dispute,
Flew high; and, as his Christian fury rose,
Damned all for heretics who durst oppose.
    Thus far my charity this path hath tried,
(A much unskilful, but well meaning guide;)
Yet what they are, even these crude thoughts were bred
By reading that which better thou hast read,

Thy matchless author's work, which thou, my friend,
By well translating better dost commend.
Those youthful hours, which of thy equals most   230
In toys have squandered or in vice have lost,
Those hours hast thou to nobler use employed,
And the severe delights of truth enjoyed.
Witness this weighty book, in which appears
The crabbed toil of many thoughtful years,
Spent by thy author in the sifting care
Of Rabbins' old sophisticated ware
From gold divine, which he who well can sort
May afterwards make Algebra a sport;
A treasure which, if country curates buy,   240
They Junius and Tremellius may defy,
Save pains in various readings and translations,
And without Hebrew make most learned quotations;
A work so full with various learning fraught,
So nicely pondered, yet so strongly wrought
As Nature's height and Art's last hand required:
As much as man could compass, uninspired.
Where we may see what errors have been made
Both in the copier's and translator's trade:
How Jewish, Popish interests have prevailed,   250
And where Infallibility has failed.
   For some, who have his secret meaning guessed,
Have found our author not too much a priest;
For fashion-sake he seems to have recourse
To Pope and Councils and Tradition's force:
But he that old traditions could subdue
Could not but find the weakness of the new:
If Scripture, though derived from heavenly birth,
Has been but carelessly preserved on earth;
If God's own people, who of God before   260
Knew what we know, and had been promised more
In fuller terms of Heaven's assisting care,
And who did neither time nor study spare
To keep this Book untainted, unperplext,
Let in gross errors to corrupt the text,
Omitted paragraphs, embroiled the sense,

With vain traditions stopped the gaping fence,
Which every common hand pulled up with ease,
What safety from such brushwood-helps as these?
If written words from time are not secured,　　　270
How can we think have oral sounds endured?
Which thus transmitted, if one mouth has failed,
Immortal lies on ages are entailed;
And that some such have been, is proved too plain;
If we consider Interest, Church, and Gain.
　　Oh, but, says one, Tradition set aside,
Where can we hope for an unerring guide?
For since the original Scripture has been lost
All copies disagreeing, maimed the most,
Or Christian faith can have no certain ground　　　280
Or truth in Church tradition must be found.
　　Such an omniscient Church we wish indeed;
'Twere worth both Testaments, and cast in the Creed;
But if this mother be a guide so sure
As can all doubts resolve, all truth secure,
Then her infallibility as well
Where copies are corrupt or lame can tell;
Restore lost canon with as little pains,
As truly explicate what still remains;
Which yet no Council dare pretend to do,　　　290
Unless, like Esdras, they could write it new;
Strange confidence, still to interpret true,
Yet not be sure that all they have explained
Is in the blest original contained.
More safe and much more modest 'tis to say,
God would not leave mankind without a way:
And that the Scriptures, though not everywhere
Free from corruption, or entire, or clear,
Are uncorrupt, sufficient, clear, entire,
In all things which our needful faith require.　　　300
If others in the same glass better see,
'Tis for themselves they look, but not for me;
For MY salvation must its doom receive,
Not from what OTHERS, but what I, believe.
　　Must all tradition then be set aside?

This to affirm were ignorance or pride.
Are there not many points, some needful sure
To saving faith, that Scripture leaves obscure,
Which every sect will wrest a several way?
For what one sect interprets, all sects may.   310
We hold, and say we prove from Scripture plain,
That Christ is GOD; the bold Socinian
From the Scripture urges he's but MAN.
Now what appeal can end the important suit?
Both parts talk loudly, but the rule is mute.
    Shall I speak plain, and in a nation free
Assume an honest layman's liberty?
I think, according to my little skill,
To my own mother Church submitting still,
That many have been saved, and many may,   320
Who never heard this question brought in play.
The unlettered Christian, who believes in gross,
Plods on to Heaven and ne'er is at a loss;
For the strait gate would be made straiter yet,
Were none admitted there but men of wit.
The few by Nature formed, with learning fraught,
Born to instruct, as others to be taught,
Must study well the sacred page; and see
Which doctrine, this or that, does best agree
With the whole tenour of the work divine,   330
And plainliest points to Heaven's revealed design;
Which exposition flows from genuine sense,
And which is forced by wit and eloquence.
Not that Tradition's parts are useless here,
When general, old, disinteressed, and clear:
That ancient fathers thus expound the page
Gives truth the reverend majesty of age,
Confirms its force by biding every test,
For best authorities, next rules, are best;
And still the nearer to the spring we go,   340
More limpid, more unsoiled, the waters flow.
Thus, first traditions were a proof alone,
Could we be certain such they were, so known:
But since some flaws in long descent may be,

They make not truth but probability.
Even Arius and Pelagius durst provoke
To what the centuries preceding spoke.
Such difference is there in an oft-told tale,
But truth by its own sinews will prevail.
Tradition written, therefore, more commends   350
Authority than what from voice descends :
And this, as perfect as its kind can be,
Rolls down to us the sacred history :
Which, from the Universal Church received,
Is tried, and after for its self believed.

    The partial Papists would infer from hence,
Their Church in last resort should judge the sense.
But first they would assume with wondrous art
Themselves to be the whole, who are but part
Of that vast frame, the Church ; yet grant they were   360
The handers down, can they from thence infer
A right to interpret? or would they alone
Who brought the present claim it for their own?
The Book's a common largess to mankind,
Not more for them than every man designed ;
The welcome news is in the letter found ;
The carrier's not commissioned to expound.
It speaks its self, and what it does contain
In all things needful to be known is plain.

    In times o'ergrown with rust and ignorance   370
A gainful trade their clergy did advance ;
When want of learning kept the laymen low
And none but priests were authorized to know ;
When what small knowledge was in them did dwell
And he a God who could but read or spell ;
Then Mother Church did mightily prevail ;
She parcelled out the Bible by retail,
But still expounded what she sold or gave,
To keep it in her power to damn and save.
Scripture was scarce, and as the market went,   380
Poor laymen took salvation on content,
As needy men take money, good or bad ;
God's word they had not, but the priest's they had.

Yet, whate'er false conveyances they made,
The lawyer still was certain to be paid.
In those dark times they learned their knack so well,
That by long use they grew infallible.
At last, a knowing age began to inquire
If they the Book or that did them inspire;
And making narrower search they found, though late,   390
That what they thought the priest's was their estate,
Taught by the will produced, the written word,
How long they had been cheated on record.
Then every man, who saw the title fair,
Claimed a child's part and put in for a share,
Consulted soberly his private good,
And saved himself as cheap as e'er he could.

    'Tis true, my friend (and far be flattery hence),
This good had full as bad a consequence;
The Book thus put in every vulgar hand,   400
Which each presumed he best could understand,
The common rule was made the common prey,
And at the mercy of the rabble lay.
The tender page with horny fists was galled,
And he was gifted most that loudest bawled;
The spirit gave the doctoral degree,
And every member of a Company
Was of his trade and of the Bible free.
Plain truths enough for needful use they found,
But men would still be itching to expound;   410
Each was ambitious of the obscurest place,
No measure ta'en from Knowledge, all from GRACE.
Study and pains were now no more their care,
Texts were explained by fasting and by prayer:
This was the fruit the private spirit brought,
Occasioned by great zeal and little thought.
While crowds unlearned, with rude devotion warm,
About the sacred viands buzz and swarm;
The fly-blown text creates a crawling brood
And turns to maggots what was meant for food.   420
A thousand daily sects rise up and die,
A thousand more the perished race supply:

So all we make of Heaven's discovered will
Is not to have it or to use it ill.
The danger's much the same, on several shelves
If others wreck us or we wreck ourselves.

    What then remains but, waving each extreme,
The tides of ignorance and pride to stem?
Neither so rich a treasure to forego
Nor proudly seek beyond our power to know?   430
Faith is not built on disquisitions vain;
The things we must believe are few and plain:
But since men will believe more than they need
And every man will make himself a creed,
In doubtful questions 'tis the safest way
To learn what unsuspected ancients say;
For 'tis not likely we should higher soar
In search of Heaven than all the Church before;
Nor can we be deceived, unless we see
The Scripture and the Fathers disagree.   440
If after all they stand suspected still,
(For no man's faith depends upon his will,)
'Tis some relief, that points not clearly known
Without much hazard may be let alone;
And after hearing what our Church can say,
If still our reason runs another way,
That private reason 'tis more just to curb
Than by disputes the public peace disturb.
For points obscure are of small use to learn:
But common quiet is mankind's concern.   450

    Thus have I made my own opinions clear,
Yet neither praise expect nor censure fear;
And this unpolished rugged verse I chose
As fittest for discourse and nearest prose;
For while from sacred truth I do not swerve,
Tom Sternhold's or Tom Shadwell's rhymes will serve.

NOTES TO RELIGIO LAICI.

In the preface Dryden makes an elaborate apology. " A poem with so bold a title," he says, " and a name prefixed from which the handling of so serious a subject would not be expected, may reasonably oblige the author to say somewhat in defence both of himself and of his undertaking. In the first place, if it be objected to me that, being a layman, I ought not to have concerned myself with speculations which belong to the profession of divinity, I could answer that perhaps laymen, with equal advantages of parts and knowledge, are not the most incompetent judges of sacred things; but in the due sense of my own weakness and want of learning, I plead not this; I pretend not to make myself a judge of faith in others, but only to make a confession of my own. I lay no unhallowed hand upon the Ark, but wait on it with the reverence that becomes me at a distance. In the next place, I will ingenuously confess that the helps I have used in this small treatise were many of them taken from the works of our own reverend divines of the Church of England; so that the weapons with which I combat irreligion are already consecrated, though I suppose they may be taken down as lawfully as the sword of Goliath was by David, when they are to be employed for the common cause against the enemies of piety. I intend not by this to entitle them to any of my errors, which yet I hope are only those of charity to mankind; and such as my own charity has caused me to commit, that of others may more easily excuse."

LINES 1-11. In the preface Dryden says, among other things, of human reason: " That there is something above us, some principle of motion, our Reason can apprehend, though it cannot discover what it is by its own virtue. And, indeed, 'tis very improbable that we, who by the strength of our faculties cannot enter into the knowledge of any being, not so much as of our own, should be able to find out by them that supreme nature, which we cannot otherwise define than by saying it is infinite; as if infinite were definable, or infinity a subject for our narrow understanding. They who would prove religion by reason do but weaken the cause which they endeavor to support: 'tis to take away the pillars from our faith, and to prop it only with a twig; 'tis to design a tower like that of Babel, which, if it were possible (as it is not) to reach heaven, would come to nothing by the confusion of the workmen. For every man is building a several way; impotently conceited of his own model and his own materials: reason is always striving, and always at a loss; and of necessity it must so come to pass, while 'tis exercised about that which is not its proper object. Let us be content at last to know God by his own methods; at least, so much of him as he is pleased to reveal to us in the sacred Scriptures: to apprehend them to be the word of God is all our reason has to do; for all beyond it is the work of faith, which is the seal of Heaven impressed upon our human understanding.''

12–24. These refer to the speculations of several Greek philosophers. In lines 16, 17, we have the theory of Anaxagoras, who was born about 500 B.C. He advanced ''the idea of a world-forming intelligence (*nous*), absolutely separated from all matter and working with design.'' — 18–19. The theory of Democritus, who was born about 470 B.C. He taught that atoms are the ultimate material of all things. These atoms are in motion, and by their contact and various combinations they form what we call nature or the world. — 20 refers to the theory of Parmenides, who was born about 520 B.C. His fundamental position is this: ''*All is, non-entity is not.*'' Of this universal being he says:—

> '' Whole and self-generate, unchangeable, illimitable,
>   Never was nor yet shall be its birth. All is already
>   One from eternity.''

21. The Stagirite is Aristotle, one of the greatest of Greek philosophers, and tutor of Alexander the Great. He was born 384 B.C., at Stagira, a town in Macedonia; whence the name applied to him in the text.

22. Epicurus was a Greek philosopher, who was born in the island of Tamos, 341 B.C. He was a materialist, believing in the existence of matter only. He founded the school of philosophy called the Epicurean.

25–41. These lines contain the theories of various philosophers concerning *the highest good*. — 29. This refers to Aristippus, who was born in Cyrène, Africa, about 424 B.C. He is the founder of the Cyrenaic School of Philosophy. ''His maxim seems to have been,'' says Haven in his '' History of Philosophy,'' '' ' Be content with such things as you have, and by no means fret thyself on any account.' '' — 31. This refers to Antisthenes and his pupil Diogenes, the chief representatives of the cynic school of philosophy. With Antisthenes virtue is the supreme good. What is this virtue? Stern, determined resistance to all indulgence and pleasure — in a contempt of riches, honors, and even learning. — 33. Epicurus taught that pleasure is the highest good. His own life was temperate, simple, and pure. But his followers perverted his ethical principle, and made it an excuse for every sort of sensual indulgence.

42–61. These lines contain the system of Deism at its best. Consult the "General Survey" at the beginning of the chapter. In reference to the principles of Deism, Dryden maintains that they are not the result of unaided human reason, as is commonly believed; but that they have been derived through tradition from the revealed religion of Noah. He says: "I have assumed in my poem . . . that Deism, or the principles of natural worship, are only the faint remnants or dying flames of revealed religion in the posterity of Noah: and that our modern philosophers, nay, and some of our philosophizing divines, have too much exalted the faculties of our souls when they have maintained that by their force mankind has been able to find out that there is one supreme agent or intellectual being which we call God; that praise and prayer are his due worship; and the rest of those deducements, which I am confident are the remote effects of revelation, and unnattainable by our discourse, I mean as simply considered, and without the benefit of divine illumination. So that we have not lifted up ourselves to God by the weak pinions of our reason, but he has been pleased to descend to us; and what Socrates said of him, what Plato writ, and the rest of the heathen philosophers of several nations, is all no more than the twilight of revelation, after the sun of it was set in the race of Noah." — 43. *Eureka* was accented by Dryden, according to the Greek accentuation, on the first syllable. — 56. *Triumphs* was accented by Dryden on the last syllable.

62. Here begins the reply to the Deist. Dryden maintains that the Deistic principles just enumerated sprang in reality, not from reason, but from revelation, lines 62–71. This must be true, he argues, because these principles are so far superior to those of the wisest of ancient philosophers, lines 72–92. — 75 refers to Socrates, the celebrated Greek philosopher, who was born at Athens in the year 469 B.C. — 77. Plutarch, a Bœotian by birth, lived in the first century of our era. He is one of the most felicitous biographers that ever lived. His "Lives" are well known, but he wrote extensively also on moral subjects. — Seneca was a celebrated Roman writer on moral subjects. He was condemned to death by Nero in 65 A.D. — Cicero, the greatest orator of Rome, was born 106 B.C. He was slain by the soldiers of Antony, against whom he had delivered a series of celebrated philippics, in 43 B.C.

93–98. Dryden objects, further, that the Deist's system is guilty of the monstrous presumption of dictating the terms of peace with God. But, he argues in lines 99–110, if there be a God who takes cognizance of our sins, we should accept his terms of reconciliation.

111–125. Penitence, the Deist's remedy, is obviously not a sufficient atonement for sin. We have sinned against Omnipotence; and, —

"Some price that bears proportion must be paid."

Having thus shown the weakness of the Deistic system, and the necessity of a revelation, the poet finds it in the Scriptures.

126–145. Proofs of the divine origin of the Scriptures follow: it answers the great ends of life; it possesses high antiquity; its authors, though of different ages and countries, agree in doctrine. — 146–151. Its historical narratives are proved by heathen testimony, and its doctrine is confirmed by miracles. — 152–167. Its style and its opposition to our inclinations show it to be of God.

168–183 contain the Deist's objections to revealed religion. A religion that is restricted in extent and efficacy, he says, cannot come from a just God.

184–211 contain the poet's reply. He asserts, first (lines 186–197), that the boundless wisdom of God may have made some provisions for those who have not received the gospel; and, second, that according to the teaching of Paul, Rom. ii. 14, 15, the Gentiles or heathen are a law unto themselves, and shall be judged according to the light they have. — 193. *Son's* should be *Son*, according to present usage, though in Dryden's day it was correct as written. — 211. *Rubric-martyrs* = devotees of ecclesiastical forms.

212–223. This animadversion on the Egyptian bishop Athanasius (born at Alexandria 296 A.D.), Dryden was advised, as he tells us, by "a judicious and learned friend," to omit. For its retention he makes a long apology, which throws light on the passage. The introduction to the Creed of Athanasius is as follows: "Whosoever will be saved, before all things it is necessary that he hold the Catholic faith. Which faith except every one do keep whole and undefiled, without doubt he shall perish everlastingly." Dryden says: "And now for what concerns the holy bishop Athanasius, the Preface of whose Creed seems inconsistent with my opinion, which is, that heathens may possibly be saved: in the first place, I desire it may be considered that it is the Preface only, not the Creed itself, which, till I am better informed, is of too hard a digestion for my charity. It is not that I am ignorant how many several texts of Scripture seemingly support that cause; but neither am I ignorant how all those texts may receive a kinder and more mollified interpretation. Every man who is read in church history knows that Belief was drawn up after a long contestation with Arius, concerning the divinity of our blessed Saviour and his being one substance with the Father; and that, thus compiled, it was sent abroad among the Christian churches, as a kind of test, which whosoever took was looked on as an orthodox believer. It is manifest from hence, that the heathen part of the empire was not concerned in it; for its business was not to distinguish betwixt Pagans and Christians, but betwixt heretics and true believers. This, well considered, takes off the heavy weight of censure, which I would willingly avoid from so venerable a man ; for if this proposition, 'whosoever will be saved,' be restrained only to those to whom it was intended, and for whom it was composed, I mean the Christians, then the anathema reaches not the heathens, who had never heard of Christ and were nothing interested in that dispute. After all, I am far from blaming even that prefatory addition to the Creed, and as far from cavilling at the continuation of it in the Liturgy of the Church, where on the days appointed 'tis publicly read : for I suppose there is the same reason for it now in opposition to the Socinians as there was then against the Arians ; the one being a heresy, which seems to have been refined out of the other ; and with how much more plausibility of reason it combats our religion, with so much more caution to be avoided : and therefore the prudence of our Church is to be commended, which has interposed her authority for the recommendation of this Creed." — 220. Arius, the founder of Arianism, was born in Libya about the middle of the third century. He taught, among other things, that the Son of God was a created being, that he was not eternal, and that he was not of the same substance as the Father. His doctrines were condemned at the Council of Nice in the year 325, when the Nicene Creed was prepared.

224–251. Personal remarks addressed Mr. Henry Dickinson, of whom nothing is known farther than that he translated "The Critical History of the Old Testament" by Richard Simon, a priest of the Oratory in Paris, and a good Oriental scholar. Dryden says in the "Preface:" "It remains that I acquaint the reader, that the verses were written for an ingenious young gentleman, my friend, upon his translation of 'The Critical History of the Old Testament,' composed by the learned Father Simon : the verses therefore are addressed to the translator of that work, and the style of them is, what it ought to be, epistolary." — 241. Junius and Tremellius were two Calvinistic divines, whose translation of the Scriptures Simon criticised.

252–275. This is an argument against tradition as a source of religious doctrine. Dryden holds the Protestant doctrine that the Scripture is the only rule of faith and practice in religion. The Roman Catholic says that "not the Bible alone, but the Bible and Tradition, *both* infallibly interpreted by the Church, are the right Rule of Faith. (Deharbe's "Catechism of the Catholic Religion.") If the written Scriptures, the poet argues, have not escaped "gross errors," "how can we think oral sounds have endured?"

276–281. The Romanist argues for the necessity of an interpreting Church, without which "Christian faith can have no certain ground."

282–304. The poet replies that the claim of an infallibly interpreting Church is absurd, because, while it undertakes to interpret, it is impotent to determine the genuineness of the text. He affirms the Protestant doctrine that, in the language of the Thirty-nine Articles, "Holy Scripture containeth all things necessary to salvation." In reference to this whole subject, Dryden says: " By asserting the Scripture to be the canon of our faith, I have unavoidably created to myself two sorts of enemies: the Papists, indeed, more directly, because they have kept the Scripture from us what they could, and have reserved to themselves a right of interpreting what they have delivered under the pretence of infallibility: and the Fanatics more collaterally, because they have assumed what amounts to an infallibility in the private spirit, and have detorted those texts of Scripture which are not necessary to salvation to the damnable uses of sedition, disturbance, and destruction of the civil government."

305–315. To this doctrine of the sufficiency of the Scripture, it is objected that certainly tradition should not be utterly set aside; for in that case, each sect will interpret for itself; and thus, as in the case of the Socinian, error will be disseminated. — 312. *Socinian.* See Webster.

316–355. In reply, the poet says that a complete system of doctrinal theology is not necessary to salvation; that single texts are to be explained in the light of the whole Word of God; and that tradition, while not a source of doctrine, is helpful in determining the true sense of the Scriptures. — 346. *Pelagius* was a monk who lived in Britain in the fourth century, and denied the received doctrines in respect to original sin, free will, grace, and the merit of good works.

356, 357. A second objection of the Papist, namely, that his Church, having been the medium of transmitting both Scripture and ancient tradition, "should in the last resort judge the sense."

358–397. The poet replies that, apart from assuming "to be the whole, who are but part," "the carrier's not commissioned to expound;" and that, as a matter of fact, the Bible is a gift to mankind. In lines 370–397 he further reminds the Papist of the trade the priests made of the Word of God, when they, on account of their learning and the ignorance of the laity, were the recognized interpreters of Holy Writ.

398–426. The poet points out what he conceives to be abuses to which the Scriptures were subject in the hands of the Puritans.

427–450. Some wise rules to be observed in dealing with the Scriptures.

451–456. Conclusion. Sternhold and Shadwell were contemporary with Dryden. They are satirized again in "Absalom and Achitophel," and Dryden's "Mac Flecknoe" is a severe satire exclusively devoted to Shadwell.

THE QUEEN ANNE PERIOD.

REPRESENTATIVE WRITERS.

ADDISON AND POPE.

OTHER PROMINENT WRITERS.

Poets. — THOMSON, YOUNG, GAY.

Novelists. — DEFOE, RICHARDSON, FIELDING.

Essayists and Satirists. — STEELE, SWIFT.

V.

THE QUEEN ANNE PERIOD.

(1700–1745.)

GENERAL SURVEY. — It is not easy to characterize this period. Various names have been applied to it. In view of the elegant form and wide influence of literature, it has been called the *Augustan age.* It has been thought to resemble the flourishing period of Roman literature under Augustus, when Ovid, Horace, Cicero, and Virgil produced their immortal works.

If we consider the attention given to literary expression and the perfection of style exhibited by writers of this time, we may properly designate it as the *first critical period* of our literature. Prior to the beginning of the eighteenth century, our literature was creative rather than critical. The chief aim of Pope, the most representative writer of this age, was to attain correctness of form and style, which he believed had not been sufficiently regarded by previous writers.

Instead of adopting, however, either of the names indicated, it has seemed better to connect literature with the social, political, and religious conditions by which it was largely moulded, and to name the period under consideration after its representative sovereign, Queen Anne. She ascended the throne in 1702, and reigned till 1714; but

347

inasmuch as the same general influences continued opera-
tive for a longer time, the period is extended to the death
of Swift in 1745. It thus includes the reign of George I.,
and a part of the reign of George II.

In this period the political principles of the Revolution
became predominant. Absolutism gave place to constitutional government. The Tories and the Whigs became
well-marked parties, and in turn succeeded to the government. Corrupt political methods were frequently resorted
to in order to gain party ascendency. Walpole boasted
that every man had his price. An unselfish patriotism
was too often looked on as youthful enthusiasm, which the
coolness of age would cure. Leading statesmen led impure
and dissipated lives.

Yet in spite of these conditions, England attained to
great influence in Continental affairs. Victory attended
her arms on the Continent under the leadership of Marlborough. The battles of Blenheim, Ramillies, Oudenarde,
and Malplaquet brought the power of Louis XIV. to the
verge of destruction. The balance of power was restored
to Europe. The union of England and Scotland was
effected in 1707, and English sovereigns henceforth
reigned over the kingdom of *Great Britain.* The power
of English thought, as well as of English arms, was felt
abroad. Buffon found inspiration in its science; Montesquieu studied the institutions of England with great care;
and Rousseau borrowed many of his thoughts from Locke.
The English people once more became conscious of their
strength, and felt the uplifting power of great hopes and
splendid purposes.

In several particulars the state of society does not
present a pleasing picture. Education was confined to a

comparatively limited circle. Addison complained that there were families in which not a single person could spell, "unless it be by chance the butler or one of the footmen." Cock-fighting was the favorite sport of school-boys, and bull-baiting twice a week delighted the populace of London. The theatres were not yet fully redeemed from the licentiousness of the preceding period. Gambling was a common vice ; and, what appears strange to us, the women of the time showed a strong passion for this excitement. Speaking of Will's Coffee-house, the *Tatler* says : " This place is very much altered since Mr. Dryden frequented it. Where you used to see songs, epigrams, and satires in the hands of every one you met, you have now only a pack of cards." Fashionable hours became later ; and a considerable part of the night was frequently given to dissipation. Drunkenness increased with the introduction of gin. The police was not able to control the lawless classes, and in the cities mobs not infrequently vented their rage in conflagration and pillage. When Sir Roger de Coverley, as portrayed by Addison, went to the theatre, he armed his servants with cudgels for protection.

Woman had not yet found her true sphere ; and, in wealthy or fashionable circles, her time was devoted chiefly to dress, frivolity, and scandal. In the " Rape of the Lock," Pope gives us a glimpse of conversation in court circles : —

> " In various talk th' instructive hours they pass'd,
> Who gave the ball, or paid the visit last;
> One speaks the glory of the British queen,
> And one describes a charming Indian screen;
> A third interprets motions, looks, and eyes;
> At every word a reputation dies;
> Snuff, or the fan, supplies each pause of chat,
> With singing, laughing, ogling, and all that."

Belief in witchcraft had not entirely passed away. In 1712 a witch was condemned to death; and her prosecution was conducted, not by ignorant rustics, but by a learned author and an educated clergyman. It is in keeping with the belief of the time to find Sir Roger de Coverley puzzled over the character of Moll White, and piously advising her "to avoid all communication with the devil, and never to hurt any of her neighbor's cattle." Superstition was common, and people of every class had faith in omens. Religion was at a low ebb. Scepticism was extensively prevalent, especially among the higher classes, and many of the clergy thought more of the pleasures of the chase than of the care of souls. "Every one laughs," said Montesquieu, "if one talks of religion."

But there is also a more favorable side to the social condition of England during this period — some influences that contain the promise of a brighter day. In spite of the low state of Christianity, earnest men, like Doddridge, Watts, and William Law, were not wanting to inculcate a a genuine piety. The rise of Methodism under John Wesley and George Whitefield exerted a salutary influence upon the religious life of England. These great preachers, impressed by the realities of sin, redemption, and eternal life, urged these truths with surpassing eloquence upon the multitudes that flocked to hear them. Before the death of John Wesley, his followers numbered a hundred thousand, and the Established Church was awakened to a new zeal.

The great middle class of England came into greater prominence, and gradually formed a reading public. Literature became independent of patronage. It did not pretend to deal with the great problems of human thought, but as a rule confined itself to criticism, satire, wit, the minor morals, and the small proprieties of life. But through French and classic influences, these subjects were treated with a lightness of touch and elegance of form that have never been surpassed.

The clubs became an important feature of social life in London. Coffee-houses multiplied, till in 1708 they reached the number of three thousand. They became centres for the diffusion of intelligence. Here the leading political, literary, and social questions of the day were discussed.

Periodical publications became an important factor in the intellectual life of England. In 1714 no fewer than fourteen papers were published in London. The principal periodicals were the *Tatler, Spectator,* and *Guardian,* which were conducted in a manner not only to refine the taste, but also to improve the morals. Made up of brief, entertaining, and often elegant essays, and treating of every subject from epic poems to female toilets, they came to be welcomed at the club-house and breakfast-table, and exerted a wide and salutary influence upon the thought and life of the country.

JOSEPH ADDISON.

THERE is no other writer in English literature of whom we think more kindly than of Joseph Addison. Macaulay has given very strong expression to the same sentiment. "After full inquiry and impartial reflection," he says, "we have long been convinced, that he deserved as much love and esteem as can be justly claimed by any of our infirm and erring race."

We read his writings with a refined and soothing pleasure. They possess a genial humor and unvarying cheerfulness that are contagious and delightful. There is no other writer who has greater power to dispel gloominess. As seen through his pages, the world appears wrapped in a mellow light. We learn to think more kindly of men, to smile at human foibles, to entertain ennobling sentiments, to trust in an over-ruling providence.

He does not indeed usually treat of the deeper interests of human life; he is never profound; he does not try to exhaust a subject — to write it to the dregs. His sphere is rather that of minor morals, social foibles, and small philosophy. But if he is not deep, he is not trifling; and if he is not exhaustive, he is always interesting. He uses satire, but it is never cruel. It does not, like that of Swift, scatter desolation in its path. On the contrary, it is tempered with a large humanity, and like a gentle rain, dispenses blessings in its course. It leads, not to cynicism, but to tenderness.

He enlisted wit on the side of virtue; and by his inimitable humor, good sense, genial satire, and simple piety, he wrought a great social reform. "So effectually, indeed," says Macaulay, "did he retort on vice the mockery which had recently been directed against virtue, that, since his time, the open violation of decency has always been considered amongst us the sure mark of a fool."

Joseph Addison was born in Wiltshire in 1672, his father, a man of some eminence, being dean of Lichfield. Though there is a tradition that he once took a leading part in barring out his teacher, and on another occasion played truant, his youthful scholarship proves him to have been a diligent student.

From the school at Lichfield he passed to Charter House. Here he made the friendship of Steele, which, as we shall see, was not without influence upon his subsequent career and fame.

At the age of fifteen he entered Oxford with a scholarship far in advance of his years, attracted attention by his superior Latin verses, and was elected a scholar of Magdalen College, where he took his degree of Master of Arts in 1693. He was held in high regard for his ability and learning. His portrait now hangs in the college hall, and his favorite walk on the banks of the Cherwell is still pointed out.

After writing a number of Latin poems, which secured the praise of the great French critic Boileau, he made his first attempt in English verse in some lines addressed to Dryden, at that time pre-eminent among men of letters. This maiden effort had the good fortune to please the great author, and led to an interchange of civilities.

At this time Addison's mind seemed inclined to poetry; and he published some lines to King William, a translation of Virgil's fourth Georgic, and "An Account of the Greatest English Poets," all of which have but little to commend them except correct versification. The last poem is remarkable for having a discriminating criticism of Spenser, whose works the author at that time had not read. "So little sometimes," comments Dr. Johnson, "is criticism the effect of judgment."

Addison was a moderate Whig in politics, and by his poems had conciliated the favor of Somers and Montague, afterwards Earl of Halifax. In conformity with the wishes of his father and his own inclinations, he contemplated taking orders in the

Anglican Church; but through the influence of Montague, who was unwilling to spare him to the church, he was led to prepare himself for the public service.

He was granted a pension of three hundred pounds, and spent the next several years in travel on the Continent, visiting France, Italy, Switzerland, Germany, and Holland. He improved his opportunities in perfecting his knowledge of the French language, in visiting localities of historic interest, and in making the acquaintance of illustrious scholars and statesmen. His observations on the French people, as given in a letter to Montague, are worth reading: "Truly, by what I have yet seen, they are the happiest nation in the world. 'Tis not in the power of want or slavery to make them miserable. There is nothing to be met with in the country but mirth and poverty. Every one sings, laughs, and starves. Their conversation is generally agreeable; for if they have any wit or sense they are sure to show it. They never mend upon a second meeting, but use all the freedom and familiarity at first sight that a long intimacy or abundance of wine can scarce draw from an Englishman. Their women are perfect mistresses in this art of showing themselves to the best advantage. They are always gay and sprightly, and set off the worst faces in Europe with the best airs." In general his remarks upon the French character are not complimentary.

The immediate literary fruits of his travels were a poetical epistle to Lord Halifax, which ranks among his best verses, and " Remarks on Italy," in which his observations are made to illustrate the Roman poets. In his "Letter to Lord Halifax," he gives expression to his delight and enthusiasm in finding himself in the midst of scenes associated with his favorite authors : —

> " Poetic fields encompass me around,
>   And still I seem to tread on classic ground;
>   For here the Muse so oft her harp has strung,
>   That not a mountain rears its head unsung;
>   Renowned in verse each shady thicket grows,
>   And every stream in heavenly numbers flows."

Here should be mentioned also one of his best hymns. While sailing along the Italian coast, he encountered a fierce storm. The captain of the ship lost all hope, and confessed his sins to a Capuchin friar who happened to be on board. But the young English traveller solaced himself with the reflections embodied in the famous hymn : —

> " When all thy mercies, O my God,
> My rising soul surveys,
> Transported with the view I'm lost
> In wonder, love, and praise."

Towards the close of 1703 Addison returned to England, and was cordially received by his friends. He was enrolled at the Kit-Kat Club, and thus brought into contact with the chief lights of the Whig party. The way was soon opened to a public office.

The battle of Blenheim was fought in 1704 ; and Godolphin, the Lord Treasurer, wished to have the great victory worthily celebrated in verse. He was referred by Halifax to Addison. The result was " The Campaign," which was received with extraordinary applause both by the minister and the public. Its chief merit is the rejection of extravagant fiction, according to which heroes are represented as mowing down whole squadrons with their single arm, and a recognition of those qualities — energy, sagacity, and coolness in the hour of danger — which made Marlborough really a great commander. One passage in the poem has become famous : —

> " 'Twas then great Marlbro's mighty soul was proved
> That, in the shock of charging hosts unmoved,
> Amidst confusion, horror, and despair,
> Examined all the dreadful scenes of war;
> In peaceful thought the field of death surveyed,
> To fainting squadrons sent the timely aid,
> Inspired repulsed battalions to engage,
> And taught the doubtful battle where to rage.

> So when an angel by divine command
> With rising tempests shakes a guilty land,
> Such as of late o'er pale Britannia past,
> Calm and serene he drives the furious blast;
> And, pleased the Almighty's orders to perform,
> Rides in the whirlwind, and directs the storm."

This simile of the angel the *Tatler* pronounced " one of the noblest thoughts that ever entered into the heart of man."

From this time on the career of Addison was a brilliant one. In 1704, in grateful recognition of his poem, he received the Excise Commissionership, made vacant by the death of the celebrated John Locke. In 1706 he became one of the Under-Secretaries of State ; and two years later he entered Parliament, where, however, his natural timidity kept him from participating in the debates. In 1709 he was appointed Chief Secretary for Ireland ; and, while residing in that country, he entered upon that department of literature upon which his fame chiefly rests, and in which he stands without a rival.

This was in connection with the *Tatler*, a periodical begun by Steele in 1709. Sir Richard Steele, who was born in Dublin in 1671, had led a somewhat wayward life. He left Oxford without taking his degree, and enlisted in the Horse Guards — an imprudence that cost him an inheritance. He rose to the rank of captain, but was gay, reckless, and dissipated. His naturally tender heart was constantly overcome by his imperious appetites, and his life presents a series of alternate repentance and dissipation.

In 1701 he wrote the " Christian Hero " for the purpose of impressing the principles of virtue upon his own heart. It is filled with lofty sentiment, but remained without serious effect upon the author's irregular life. Then followed in annual succession several moderate comedies.

The literary ability evinced in his writings secured him the appointment of Gazetteer. This position gave him a monopoly of official news, and no doubt suggested the scheme of publishing a periodical. Accordingly he began the *Tatler*. Addison had not been consulted about the scheme, but promptly gave it his support.

In a few weeks after its first issue he began a series of contributions. The result may be best expressed in Steele's own words. " I fared," he said, " like a distressed prince who calls in a powerful neighbor to his aid. I was undone by my auxiliary. When I had once called him in, I could not subsist without dependence on him." Steele's own contributions, however, were of a high order, inferior only to those of his illustrious co-adjutor. The *Tatler* was published three times a week, and, after reaching two hundred and seventy-one numbers, was discontinued Jan. 2, 1711.

It was succeeded by the *Spectator*, which appeared six times a week. The first number was issued March 1, 1711,—two months after the discontinuance of the *Tatler*. It was considered at the time a bold undertaking; but the result more than justified the confidence of Steele and Addison, its promoters.

It is made up of an incomparable series of short essays, which have all the interest of fiction and the value of philosophy. They are represented as the productions of an imaginary spectator of the world, a description of whom in the first paper we recognize as a caricature of Addison himself. " Thus I live in the world," it is said, " rather as a spectator of mankind, than as one of the species, by which means I have made myself a speculative statesman, soldier, merchant, and artisan, without ever meddling with any practical part in life. I am very well versed in the theory of a husband or a father, and can discern the errors in the economy, business, and diversions of others, better than those who are engaged in them ; as standers-by discover blots, which are apt to escape those who are in the game. I never espoused any party with violence, and am resolved to observe an exact neutrality between the Whigs and Tories, unless I shall be forced to declare myself by the hostilities of either side. In short, I have acted in all the parts of my life as a looker-on, which is the character I intend to preserve in this paper."

The plan, it must be perceived, is excellent. Addison wrote about three-sevenths of the six hundred and thirty-five numbers. He poured into them all the wealth of his learning, observation, and genius. The variety is almost endless, but the purpose is always moral. He is a great teacher without being pedantic. His wholesome lessons are so seasoned with playful humor, gentle satire, and honest amiability, that they encounter no resistance. Vice becomes ridiculous, and virtue admirable. And his style is so easy, graceful, perspicuous, elegant, that it must remain a model for all time. "Give days and nights, sir," said the blunt Dr. Johnson, "to the study of Addison, if you mean to be a good writer, or what is more worth, an honest man."

The *Spectator* created a large constituency, and every number was eagerly waited for. It found a welcome in the coffee-houses and at many a breakfast-table. Its daily circulation was more than three thousand; and when the essays were published in book form, ten thousand copies of each volume were immediately called for, and successive editions were necessary to supply the popular demand.

In 1713 appeared Addison's tragedy of "Cato," the first four acts of which had been written years before in Italy. It was only at the urgent solicitation of his friends that he consented to its representation on the stage. Its success was astonishing. For a month it was played before crowded houses. Whigs and Tories vied with each other in its praise, applying its incidents and sentiments to current politics. "The Whigs applauded every line in which liberty was mentioned, as a satire on the Tories; and the Tories echoed every clap, to show that the satire was unfelt." It was translated into Italian and acted at Florence.

On its publication, however, its popularity began to abate. It was savagely attacked by Dennis. Addison was too amiable to write a reply. Pope, however, assailed the furious critic, but left the objections to the play in full force. It is probable that he was more desirous of scourging Dennis than of vindicating

Addison. At all events, Addison did not approve of the bitterness of Pope's reply, disclaimed all responsibility for it, and caused Dennis to be informed that whenever he thought fit to answer, he would do it in the manner of a gentleman. Of course Pope was mortified; and it is to this transaction that his dislike of Addison is probably to be traced.

"Cato" conforms to the classic writers, and abounds in noble sentiment. But it is lacking in high poetic or dramatic interest. A scene in the fifth act, which represents Cato alone, sitting in a thoughtful posture with Plato's "Immortality of the Soul" in his hand, and a drawn sword on the table by him, is well known.

> "It must be so — Plato, thou reason'st well! —
> Else whence this pleasing hope, this fond desire,
> This longing after immortality?
> Or whence this secret dread, and inward horror,
> Of falling into nought? why shrinks the soul
> Back on herself, and startles at destruction?
> 'Tis the divinity that stirs within us;
> 'Tis heaven itself, that points out an hereafter,
> And intimates eternity to man.
> Eternity! thou pleasing, dreadful thought!
> Through what variety of untried being,
> Through what new scenes and changes must we pass?
> The wide, th' unbounded prospect lies before me;
> But shadows, clouds, and darkness rest upon it.
> Here will I hold. If there's a power above us,
> (And that there is all nature cries aloud
> Through all her works,) he must delight in virtue;
> And that which he delights in, must be happy.
> But when! or where! — This world was made for Cæsar.
> I'm weary of conjectures. — This must end them.
>   [*Laying his hand on his sword.*]
>   Thus am I doubly armed; my death and life,
> My bane and antidote are both before me:
> This in a moment brings me to an end;
> But this informs me I shall never die.
> The soul, secured in her existence, smiles
> At the drawn dagger, and defies its point.

> The stars shall fade away, the sun himself
> Grow dim with age, and nature sink in years;
> But thou shalt flourish in immortal youth,
> Unhurt amidst the wars of elements,
> The wrecks of matter, and the crush of worlds."

In 1716, after a long courtship, Addison married Lady War-wick. She was a woman of much beauty, but also of proud and imperious temper. The marriage, it seems, did not add to his happiness. According to Dr. Johnson, the lady married him "on terms much like those on which a Turkish princess is espoused, to whom the Sultan is reported to pronounce, 'Daughter, I give thee this man for thy slave.'" His domestic infelicity caused him to seek more frequently the pleasures of the coffee-house. His fondness for wine likewise increased.

The year after his marriage he reached the summit of his political career as Secretary of State. But his health soon failed; and after holding office for eleven months, he resigned on a pension of fifteen hundred pounds. His complaint ended in dropsy. A shadow was cast over the last years of his life by a quarrel with Steele arising from a difference of political views. He died June 17, 1719. His last moments were per-fectly serene. To his stepson he said, "See how a Christian can die." His piety was sincere and deep. All nature spoke to him of God; and the Psalmist's declaration that "the heavens declare the glory of God," he wrought into a magnificent hymn : —

> " The spacious firmament on high,
> With all the blue ethereal sky,
> And spangled heavens, a shining frame,
> Their great Original proclaim."

Speaking of this hymn, Thackeray says : " It seems to me those verses shine like the stars. They shine out of a great deep calm. When he turns to Heaven, a Sabbath comes over that man's mind; and his face lights up from it with a glory of thanks and prayer. His sense of religion stirs through his whole being. In the fields, in the town ; looking at the birds in the trees ; at the children in the streets ; in the morning or in the moonlight ; over his books in his own room ; in a happy party at a country merry-making or a town assembly : good-will and peace to God's creatures, and love and awe of Him who made them, fill his pure heart and shine from his kind face. If Swift's life was the most wretched, I think Addison's was one of the most enviable. A life prosperous and beautiful — a calm death — an immense fame and affection afterwards for his happy and spotless name."

SIR ROGER DE COVERLEY.

I. SIR ROGER'S COUNTRY RESIDENCE.

HAVING often received an invitation from my friend Sir Roger de Coverley to pass away a month with him in the country, I last week accompanied him thither, and am settled with him for some time at his country-house, where I intend to form several of my ensuing speculations. Sir Roger, who is very well acquainted with my humor,[1] lets me rise and go to bed when I please, dine at his own table or in my chamber as I think fit, sit still and say nothing without bidding me be merry. When the gentlemen of the county come to see him, he only shows me at a distance. As I have been walking in his fields, I have observed them stealing a sight of me over an hedge,[2] and have heard the knight desiring them not to let me see them, for that I hated to be stared at.

I am the more at ease in Sir Roger's family, because it consists of sober and staid persons: for as the knight[3] is the best master in the world, he seldom changes his servants; and as he is beloved by all about him, his servants never care for leaving him : by this means his domestics are all in years, and grown old with their master. You would take his *valet-de-chambre*[4] for his brother, his butler is gray-headed, his groom is one of the gravest men that I have ever seen, and his coachman has the looks of a privy-councillor.[5] You see the goodness of the master even in the old house-dog, and in a gray pad[6] that is kept in the stable with great care and tenderness out of regard to his past services, though he has been useless for several years.

I could not but observe with a great deal of pleasure the joy that appeared in the countenances of these ancient domestics, upon my friend's arrival at his county-seat. Some of them could not refrain from tears at the sight of their old master; every one of them pressed forward to do something for him, and seemed discouraged if they were not employed. At the same time, the good old knight, with a mixture of the father and master of the family, tempered [7] the inquiries after his own affairs with several kind questions relating to themselves. This humanity [8] and good nature engages everybody to him, so that when he is pleasant upon any of them, all his family are in good humor, and none so much as the person whom he diverts himself with; on the contrary, if he coughs, or betrays any infirmity of old age, it is easy for a stander-by to observe a secret concern in the looks of all his servants.

My worthy friend has put me under the particular care of his butler, who is a very prudent man, and, as well as the rest of his fellow-servants, wonderfully desirous of pleasing me, because they have often heard their master talk of me as of his particular friend.

My chief companion, when Sir Roger is diverting himself in the woods or the fields, is a very venerable man, who is ever with Sir Roger, and has lived at his house in the nature [9] of a chaplain above thirty years. This gentleman is a person of good sense and some learning, of a very regular life and obliging conversation. He heartily loves Sir Roger, and knows that he is very much in the old knight's esteem, so that he lives in the family rather as a relation than a dependant.

I have observed in several of my papers, that my friend Sir Roger, amidst all his good qualities, is something of an humorist; and that his virtues, as well as imperfections, are, as it were, tinged [10] by a certain extravagance, which makes them particularly his, and distinguishes them from those of other men. This cast of mind, as it is generally very innocent in itself, so it renders his conversation highly agreeable and more delightful than the same degree of sense and virtue would appear in their common and ordinary colors. As I was walking with him last night, he asked me how I liked the good man whom I have just now mentioned; and without staying for my answer, told me that he was afraid of being insulted [11] with Latin and Greek at his own table; for which reason he desired a particular friend of his at the university to find him out a clergyman rather of plain sense than much learning, of a good aspect, a clear voice, a sociable temper, and, if possible, a man that understood a little of backgammon. [12] "My friend," says Sir Roger, "found me out this gentleman, who, besides the endowments required of him, is, they tell me, a good scholar, though he does not show it. I have given him the parsonage [13] of the parish; and because I know his value, have settled upon him a good annuity for life. If he outlives me, he shall find that he was higher in my esteem than perhaps he thinks he is. He has now been with me thirty years; and though he does not know I have taken notice of it, has never in all that time asked anything of me for himself, though he is every day soliciting me for something in behalf of one or other of my tenants his parishioners. There has not been a lawsuit in the parish since he has lived among them; if any dispute arises, they apply themselves to him for the decision; if they do not acquiesce in his judgment, which I think never happened above once or twice at most, they appeal to me. At his first settling with me, I made him a present of all the good sermons which have been printed in English, and only begged of him that every Sunday he would pronounce one of them in the pulpit. Accordingly, he has digested [14] them into such a series that they follow one another naturally, and make a continued system of practical divinity." [15]

As Sir Roger was going on with his story, the gentleman we were talking of came up to us; and upon the knight's asking him who preached to-morrow (for it was Saturday night), told us, the Bishop of St. Asaph in the morning, and Dr. South in the afternoon. He then showed us his list of preachers for the whole year, where I saw with a great deal of pleasure Archbishop Tillotson, Bishop Saunderson, Dr. Barrow, Dr. Calamy,[16] with several living authors, who have published discourses of practical divinity. I no sooner saw this venerable man in the pulpit, but I very much approved of my friend's insisting upon the qualifications of a good aspect and a clear voice; for I was so charmed with the gracefulness of his figure and delivery, as well as with the discourses he pronounced, that I think I never passed any time more to my satisfaction. A sermon repeated after this manner is like the composition of a poet in the mouth of a graceful actor.

I could heartily wish that more of our country clergy would follow this example, and instead of wasting their spirits in laborious compositions of their own, would endeavor after a handsome elocution, and all those other talents that are proper to enforce what has been penned by greater masters. This would not only be more easy to themselves, but more edifying to the people.

II. A SUNDAY AT SIR ROGER DE COVERLEY'S.

I AM always very well pleased with a country Sunday, and think, if keeping holy the seventh day were only a human institution, it would be the best method that could have been thought of for the polishing and civilizing of mankind. It is certain the country people would soon degenerate into a kind of savages and barbarians, were there not such frequent returns at a stated time, in which the whole village meet together with their best faces, and in their cleanliest habits,[1] to converse with one another upon different subjects, hear their duties explained to them, and join together in adoration of the Supreme Being. Sunday clears away the rust of the whole week, not only as it refreshes in their minds the notions of religion, but as it puts both the sexes upon appearing in their most agreeable forms, and exerting all such qualities as are apt to give them a figure in the eye of the village. A country fellow distinguishes himself as much in the churchyard as a citizen does upon the 'Change,[2] the whole parish politics being generally discussed in that place either after sermon or before the bell rings.

My friend Sir Roger being a good churchman,[3] has beautified the inside of his church with several texts of his own choosing. He has likewise given a handsome pulpit-cloth, and railed in the communion table at his own expense. He has often told me, that at his coming to his estate he found his parishioners very irregular; and that in order to make them kneel and join in the responses, he gave every one of them a hassock [4] and a Common Prayer-Book, and at the same time employed an itinerant singing-master, who goes about the country for that purpose, to instruct them rightly in the tunes of the psalms; upon which they now very much value themselves, and, indeed, outdo most of the country churches that I have ever heard.

As Sir Roger is landlord to the whole congregation, he keeps them in very good order, and will suffer nobody to sleep in it besides himself; for if by chance he has been surprised into a short nap at sermon, upon recovering out of it he stands up and looks about him, and if he sees anybody else nodding, either wakes them himself, or sends his servant to them. Several other of the old knight's particularities [5] break out upon these occasions. Sometimes he will be lengthening out a verse in the singing psalms, half a minute after the rest of the congregation have done with it; sometimes, when he is pleased with the matter of his devotion, he pronounces Amen three or four times to the same prayer, and sometimes stands up when everybody else is upon their knees, to count the congregation, or see if any of his tenants are missing.

I was yesterday very much surprised to hear my old friend, in the midst of the service, calling out to one John Matthews to mind what he was about, and not disturb the congregation. This John Matthews, it seems, is remarkable for being an idle fellow, and at that time was kicking his heels for his diversion. The authority of the knight, though exerted in that odd manner which accompanies him in all circumstances of life, has a very good effect upon the parish, who are not polite [6] enough to see anything ridiculous in his behavior; besides that the general good sense and worthiness of his character make his friends observe these little singularities as foils,[7] that rather set off than blemish his good qualities.

As soon as the sermon is finished, nobody presumes to stir till Sir Roger is gone out of the church. The knight walks down from his seat in the chancel [8] between a double row of his tenants, that stand bowing to him on each side ; and every now and then inquires how such an one's wife, or mother, or son, or father, does, whom he does not see at church ; which is understood as a secret reprimand to the person that is absent.

The chaplain has often told me that upon a catechizing day, when Sir Roger has been pleased with a boy that answers well, he has ordered a Bible to be given him next day for his encouragement; and sometimes accompanies it with a flitch [9] of bacon to his mother. Sir Roger has likewise added five pounds a year to the clerk's [10] place ; and that he may encourage the young fellows to make themselves perfect in the church-service, has promised, upon the death of the present incumbent, who is very old, to bestow it according to merit.

The fair understanding between Sir Roger and his chaplain, and their mutual concurrence in doing good, is the more remarkable, because the very next village is famous for the differences and contentions that rise between the parson [11] and the squire, who live in a perpetual state of war. The parson is always preaching at the squire; and the squire, to be revenged on the parson, never comes to church. The squire has made all his tenants atheists and tithe-stealers; [12] while the parson instructs them every Sunday in the dignity of his order, and insinuates to them in almost every sermon that he is a better man than his patron. In short, matters are come to such an extremity, that the squire has not said his prayers either in public or private this half-year; and that the parson threatens him, if he does not mend his manners, to pray for him in the face of the whole congregation.

Feuds of this nature, though too frequent in the country, are very fatal to the ordinary people, who are so used to be dazzled with riches that they pay as much deference to the understanding of a man of an estate as of a man of learning; and are very hardly [13] brought to regard any truth, how important soever it may be, that is preached to them, when they know there are several men of five hundred a year who do not believe it.

III. SIR ROGER'S VISIT TO WESTMINSTER ABBEY.

MY friend Sir Roger de Coverley told me the other night that he had been reading my paper upon Westminster [1] Abbey, " in which," says he, " there are a great many ingenious fancies." He told me, at the same time, that he observed I had promised another paper upon the tombs, and that he should be glad to go and see them with me, not having visited them since he had read history. I could not at first imagine how this came into the knight's head, till I recollected that he had been very busy all last summer upon Baker's *Chronicle*,[2] which he has quoted several times in his disputes with Sir Andrew Freeport [3] since his last coming to town. Accordingly, I promised to call upon him the next morning, that we might go together to the Abbey.

I found the knight under the butler's hands, who always shaves him. He was no sooner dressed, than he called for a glass of the Widow Trueby's water,[4] which he told me he always drank before he went abroad. He recommended to me a dram of it at the same time, with so much heartiness that I could not forbear drinking it.

As soon as I had got it down, I found it very unpalatable; upon which the knight, observing that I had made several wry faces, told me that he knew I should not like it at first, but that it was the best thing in the world against the stone or gravel.

I could have wished, indeed, that he had acquainted me with the virtues of it sooner; but it was too late to complain, and I knew what he had done was out of good-will. Sir Roger told me further, that he looked upon it to be very good for a man while he staid in town, to keep off infection, and that he got together a quantity of it upon the first news of the sickness [5] being at Dantzic: when of a sudden, turning short to one of his servants, who stood behind him, he bid him call a hackney-coach, [6] and take care it was an elderly man that drove it.

He then resumed his discourse upon Mrs. Trueby's water, telling me that the Widow Trueby was one who did more good than all the doctors and apothecaries in the country: that she distilled every poppy that grew within five miles of her; that she distributed her medicine *gratis* among all sorts of people; to which the knight added, that she had a very good jointure,[7] and that the whole country would fain have it a match between him and her; "and truly," says Sir Roger, "if I had not been engaged, perhaps I could not have done better."

His discourse was broken off by his man's telling him he had called a coach. Upon our going to it, after having cast his eye upon the wheels, he asked the coachman if his axle-tree was good. Upon the fellow's telling him he would warrant it, the knight turned to me, told me he looked like an honest man, and went in without further ceremony.

We had not gone far, when Sir Roger, popping out his head, called the coachman down from his box, and upon presenting himself at the window, asked him if he smoked. As I was considering what this would end in, he bid him stop by the way at any good tobacconist's, and take in a roll of their best Virginia.[8] Nothing material happened in the remaining part of our journey, till we were set down at the west end of the Abbey.

As we went up the body of the church, the knight pointed at the trophies [9] upon one of the new monuments, and cried out: "A brave man, I warrant him!" Passing afterward by Sir Cloudesley

Shovel,[10] he flung his hand that way, and cried : " Sir Cloudesley Shovel ! a very gallant man ! " As we stood before Busby's [11] tomb, the knight uttered himself again after the same manner : " Dr Busby ! a great man ! he whipped my grandfather ; a very great man ! I should have gone to him myself, if I had not been a blockhead ; a very great man ! "

We were immediately conducted into the little chapel [12] on the right hand. Sir Roger, planting himself at our historian's [13] elbow, was very attentive to everything he said, particularly to the account he gave us of the lord who had cut off the king of Morocco's head. Among several other figures, he was very well pleased to see the statesman Cecil [14] upon his knees ; and concluding them all to be great men, was conducted to the figure which represents that martyr [15] to good housewifery, who died by the prick of a needle. Upon our interpreter's telling us that she was a maid of honor to Queen Elizabeth, the knight was very inquisitive into her name and family ; and after having regarded her finger for some time, " I wonder," says he, "that Sir Richard Baker has said nothing of her in his *Chronicle*."

We were then conveyed to the two coronation chairs,[16] where my old friend, after having heard that the stone underneath the most ancient of them, which was brought from Scotland, was called Jacob's pillar, sat himself down in the chair ; and looking like the figure of an old Gothic king, asked our interpreter : " What authority they had to say that Jacob had ever been in Scotland ? " The fellow, instead of returning him an answer, told him " that he hoped his honor would pay his forfeit." [17] I could observe Sir Roger a little ruffled upon being thus trepanned ; [18] but our guide not insisting upon his demand, the knight soon recovered his good humor, and whispered in my ear, that if Will Wimble [19] were with us, and saw those two chairs, it would go hard but he would get a tobacco-stopper out of one or t'other of them.

Sir Roger, in the next place, laid his hand upon Edward III.'s [20] sword, and leaning upon the pommel of it, gave us the whole history of the Black Prince ; concluding, that in Sir Richard Baker's opinion, Edward III. was one of the greatest princes that ever sat upon the English throne.

We were then shown Edward the Confessor's [21] tomb ; upon which Sir Roger acquainted us, that he was the first that touched for the evil: [22] and afterward Henry IV.'s, [23] upon which he shook his head, and told us there was fine reading of the casualties of that reign.

Our conductor then pointed to that monument where there is the figure of one of our English kings without an head; [24] and upon giving us to know that the head, which was of beaten silver, had been stole away several years since : " Some Whig, I'll warrant you," says Sir Roger; " you ought to lock up your kings better; they will carry off the body too, if you do not take care."

The glorious names of Henry V. and Queen Elizabeth gave the knight great opportunities of shining, and of doing justice to Sir Richard Baker, " who," as our knight observed with some surprise, " had a great many kings in him, whose monuments he had not seen in the Abbey."

For my own part, I could not but be pleased to see the knight show such an honest passion for the glory of his country, and such a respectful gratitude to the memory of its princes.

I must not omit that the benevolence of my good old friend, which flows out toward every one he converses with, made him very kind to our interpreter, whom he looked upon as an extraordinary man, for which reason he shook him by the hand at parting, telling him that he should be very glad to see him at his lodgings in Norfolk Buildings, and talk over these matters with him more at leisure.

IV. DEATH OF SIR ROGER.

WE last night received a piece of ill news at our club, which very sensibly afflicted every one of us. I question not but my readers themselves will be troubled at the hearing of it. To keep them no longer in suspense, Sir Roger de Coverley is dead. He departed this life at his house in the country, after a few weeks' sickness. Sir Andrew Freeport has a letter from one of his correspondents in those parts, that informs him the old man caught a cold at the countysessions, as he was very warmly promoting an address of his own penning, in which he succeeded according to his wishes. But this particular comes from a Whig justice of peace, who was always Sir Roger's enemy and antagonist. I have letters both from the chaplain and Captain Sentry,[1] which mention nothing of it, but are filled with many particulars to the honor of the good old man. I have likewise a letter from the butler, who took so much care of me last summer when I was at the knight's house. As my friend, the butler, mentions, in the simplicity of his heart, several circumstances the others have passed over in silence, I shall give my reader a copy of his letter, without any alteration or diminution.

"HONORED SIR — Knowing that you was my old master's good friend, I could not forbear sending you the melancholy news of his death, which has afflicted the whole country as well as his poor servants, who loved him, I may say, better than we did our lives. I am afraid he caught his death at the last county-sessions, where he would go to see justice done to a poor widow woman and her fatherless children, that had been wronged by a neighboring gentleman; for you know, my good master was always the poor man's friend. Upon his coming home, the first complaint he made was, that he had lost his roast-beef stomach, not being able to touch a sirloin which was served up according to custom; and you know he used to take great delight in it. From that time forward he grew worse and worse, but still kept a good heart to the last. Indeed, we were once in great hope of his recovery, upon a kind message that was sent him from the widow lady [2] whom he had made love to the forty last years of his life; but this only proved a lightning before his death. He has bequeathed to this lady, as a token of his love, a great pearl necklace, and a couple of silver bracelets set with jewels, which belonged to my good lady his mother. He has bequeathed the fine white gelding that he used to ride a-hunting upon to his chaplain, because he thought he would be kind to him; and has left you all his books. He has moreover bequeathed to the chaplain a very pretty tenement, with good lands about it. It being a very cold day when he made his will, he left for mourning, to every man in the parish, a great frieze [3] coat, and to every woman a black riding-hood. It was a moving sight to see him take leave of his poor servants, commending us all for our fidelity, while we were not able to speak a word for weeping. As we most of us are grown gray-headed in our dear master's service, he has left us pensions and legacies, which we may live very comfortably upon the remaining part of our days. He has bequeathed a great deal more in charity, which is not yet come to my knowledge; and it is peremptorily said in the parish that he has left money to build a steeple to the church; for he was heard to say some time ago, that if he lived two years longer Coverley church should have a steeple to it. The chaplain tells everybody he made a very good end, and never speaks of him without tears. He was buried, according to his own directions, among the family of the Coverleys, on the left hand of his father Sir Arthur. The coffin was carried by six of his tenants, and the pall held up by six of the quorum.[4]   The whole parish followed the corpse with heavy hearts, and in their mourning suits; the men in frieze, and the women in riding-hoods.   Captain Sentry, my master's nephew, has taken possession of the Hall-house and the whole estate.   When my old master saw him a little before his death, he shook him by the hand, and wished him joy of the estate which was falling to him, desiring him only to make a good use of it, and to pay the several legacies and the gifts of charity, which he told him he had left as quit-rents [5] upon the estate.   The captain truly seems a courteous man, though he says but little.   He makes much of those whom my master loved, and shows great kindness to the old house-dog that you know my poor master was so fond of.   It would have gone to your heart to have heard the moans the dumb creature made on the day of my master's death.   He has never joyed himself since; no more has any of us.   It was the melancholiest day for the poor people that ever happened in Worcestershire.   This is all from, honored sir, your most sorrowful servant,

EDWARD BISCUIT.

P. S. — My master desired, some weeks before he died, that a book, which comes up to you by the carrier, should be given to Sir Andrew Freeport in his name."

This letter, notwithstanding the poor butler's manner of writing it, gave us such an idea of our good old friend, that upon the reading of it there was not a dry eye in the club.   Sir Andrew opening the book, found it to be a collection of acts of parliament.   There was in particular the Act of Uniformity, with some passages in it marked by Sir Roger's own hand.   Sir Andrew found that they related to two or three points which he had disputed with Sir Roger the last time he appeared at the club.   Sir Andrew, who would have been merry at such an incident on another occasion, at the sight of the old man's writing burst into tears, and put the book in his pocket. Captain Sentry informs me that the knight has left rings and mourning for every one in the club.

NOTES TO SIR ROGER DE COVERLEY.

THE Sir Roger de Coverley papers are taken from the *Spectator*, and well exhibit the elegant style and delicate humor of Addison.

I.

1. *Humor* = disposition. Fr. *humeur* = Lat. *humorem*, from *humere*, to be moist. Cf. *humid*.

2. *An hedge.* — Addison frequently uses *an* before a sounded *h*.

3. *Knight* = Sir Roger. A. S. *cniht*, a boy, servant. Cf. Ger. *Knecht*.

4. *Valet-de-chambre* = a body servant or personal attendant. Pronounced *văl-ā dĕ shăm-br*.

5. *Privy-councillor* = a member of the privy council; one of the distinguished persons selected by a sovereign to advise in the administration of the government. Equivalent to our *cabinet officer*.

6. *Pad* = an easy-paced horse.

7. *Tempered* = softened.

8. *Humanity* = kindness, benevolence.

9. *Nature* = character.

10. *Tinged* = slightly colored. Lat. *tingere*, to dye.

11. *Insulted*, etc. — Sir Roger, in common with the country gentlemen of the time, made but little pretension to learning.

12. *Backgammon.* — The common etymology derives it from the Welsh *bach*, little, and *cammon*, a battle. But this Skeat pronounces "a worthless guess."

13. *Parsonage* = the benefice or church living of the parish; not the house used as a residence by pastors.

14. *Digested* = distributed or arranged methodically.

15. *Divinity* = theology, or the science which treats of God, his laws, and moral government.

16. These were distinguished divines, three of whom, Tillotson, South, and Barrow, still deserve to be studied.

II.

1. *Habits* = attire, dress.

2. *'Change* = Exchange; that is, the place where the merchants, brokers, and bankers of a city meet at certain hours to transact business.

3. *Churchman* = an Episcopalian as distinguished from a Presbyterian or Congregationalist.

4. *Hassock* = a thick mat for kneeling in church.

5. *Particularities* = peculiarities, individual characteristics.

6. *Polite* = polished, refined.

7. *Foils* = anything that serves to set off another thing to advantage. See Webster.

8. *Chancel* = the part of a church between the communion table and the railing that encloses it. O. F. *chancel*, an enclosure, from Lat. *cancellus*, a grating.

9. *Flitch* = the side of a hog salted and cured.

10. *Clerk* = a parish officer, being a layman who leads in reading the responses of the Episcopal Church service.

11. *Parson* = a clergyman. *Parson* and *person* are the same word, from Lat. *persona*. Blackstone says: "A *parson*, *persona ecclesiæ*, is one that hath full possession of all the rights of a parochial church. He is called *parson*, *persona*, because by his person the church, which is an invisible body, is represented." — "This reason may well be doubted," says Skeat, "but without affecting the etymology."

12. *Tithe-stealers.* — A *tithe* is the tenth part of the increase arising from the profits of land and stock, allotted to the clergy for their support.

13. *Very hardly* = with great difficulty.

III.

In a previous number of the *Spectator* Addison tells us of Sir Roger's visit to London.

1. *Westminster Abbey* = a famous cathedral in London, in which the British sovereigns are crowned, and in which many of them are buried. Addison made it the subject of the twenty-sixth paper in the *Spectator*.

2. *Baker's Chronicle.* — Sir Richard Baker was born in 1568; and his book, the full title of which is "Chronicle of the Kings of England," was popular in the last century.

3. *Sir Andrew Freeport* was a member of the imaginary club, to which the Spectator and Sir Roger belonged.

4. *Widow Trueby's water* = a strong drink said to have been much used by the ladies as an exhilarant. From what we know of Addison's bibulous habits, we may conclude that his dislike is only assumed for effect.

5. *Sickness* = the plague, which prevailed at Dantzic in 1709.

6. *Hackney-coach* = a coach kept for hire.

7. *Jointure* = an estate settled on a wife, and which she is to enjoy after her husband's decease.

8. *Virginia* = a common name for tobacco in Addison's time.

9. *Trophies* = representations in marble of a pile of arms taken from a vanquished enemy.

10. *Sir Cloudesley Shovel.* — The visitors passed by his monument. A distinguished British admiral, commander-in-chief of the British fleets. Returning to England in 1707, his ship struck on the rocks near Scilly and sank with all on board. The body of Sir Cloudesley Shovel was found next day, and buried in Westminster Abbey.

11. Richard Busby was for fifty-five years, from 1640 to 1695, headmaster of Westminster School. It has been said that he " bred up the greatest number of learned scholars that ever adorned any age or nation.'' He was equally noted for his learning, assiduity, and application of the birch.

12. *Little chapel*, etc. = the chapel of St. Edmund. In cathedrals, *chapels* are usually annexed in the recesses on the sides of the aisles.

13. *Historian* = the guide who shows visitors through the Abbey.

14. *Robert Cecil*, Earl of Salisbury, was born in 1550 and died in 1612. In 1608 he was made Lord High Treasurer. A man of immense energy and far-reaching sagacity — the best minister of his time, but cold, selfish, and unscrupulous.

15. *Martyr*, etc. — This is described as " an elaborate statue of Elizabeth Russell of the Bedford family — foolishly shown for many years as the lady who died by the prick of a needle.'' Goldsmith characterizes the story as one of a hundred lies that the guide tells without blushing.

16. *Coronation chairs* = two chairs in the Chapel of Edward the Confessor used at the coronation of the sovereigns of Great Britain. The more ancient of the two contains the famous " Stone of Scone,'' on which the kings of Scotland were crowned. The stone was brought to England by Edward I. in 1304. The other coronation chair was placed in the Abbey in the reign of William and Mary.

17. *Forfeit*, that is, for sitting in the chair.

18. *Trepanned* = ensnared, caught. Another form of the verb is *trapan*. From Fr. *trappe*, a trap.

19. *Will Wimble* is described in one of the Coverley papers as " younger brother to a baronet. . . . He is now between forty and fifty, but being bred to no business, and born to no estate, he generally lives with his elder brother as superintendent of his game. He hunts a pack of dogs better than any man in the country, and is very famous for finding out a hare,'' etc. He was a neighbor and friend of Sir Roger.

20. *Edward III.* was born in 1312 and died in 1376. He gained many victories, including that of Crecy. During his reign many salutary laws were enacted, and art and literature flourished. The Black Prince was his son.

21. *Edward the Confessor*, king of the Anglo-Saxons, was born in 1004 and died in 1066, the year of the Conquest.

22. *The evil* = a scrofulous disease known as "king's evil." It was formerly believed that the touch of a king would cure it.

23. *Henry IV.* was born in 1366 and died in 1413, after a troubled reign of fourteen years.

24. The monument in question was that of Henry V., the hero of Agincourt. He was born in 1388 and died in 1422. The head of the effigy, which was of silver, was stolen at the time of the Protestant Reformation.

IV.

1. *Captain Sentry* was Sir Roger's nephew and heir.

2. *The widow lady* captivated Sir Roger in his early manhood. A full account of the circumstances will be found in the *Spectator* No. 113. Elsewhere Sir Roger says: "When I reflect upon this woman, I do not know whether in the main I am the worse for having loved her; whenever she is recalled to my imagination, my youth returns, and I feel a forgotten warmth in my veins. This affliction in my life has streaked all my conduct with a softness, of which I should otherwise have been incapable."

3. *Frieze* = a coarse woollen cloth with a nap on one side.

4. *Quorum* = justice-court.

5. *Quit-rent* = a rent reserved in grants of land, by the payment of which the tenant is quieted or quit from all other service.

ALEXANDER POPE.

THE greatest literary character of this period is Alexander Pope. In his life we find much to admire and much to condemn; but we cannot deny him the tribute of greatness. With his spiteful temper and habitual artifice we can have no sympathy; but we recognize in him the power of an indomitable will supported by genius and directed to a single object.

He triumphed over the most adverse circumstances. A lowly birth cut him off from social position; his Roman Catholic faith brought political ostracism; and a dwarfed, sickly, deformed body excluded him from the vocations in which wealth and fame are usually acquired. Yet, in spite of this combination of hostile circumstances, he achieved the highest literary distinction, attracted to him the most eminent men of his day, and associated on terms of equality with the proudest nobility.

Alexander Pope was born in London in 1688, the memorable year of the Revolution. His father, a Roman Catholic, was a linen merchant; and shortly after the poet's birth, he retired with a competent fortune to a small estate at Binfield in Windsor Forest.

Though delicate and deformed, the future poet is represented as having been a sweet-tempered child; and his voice was so agreeable that he was playfully called the "little nightingale." Excluded from the public schools on account of his father's faith, he passed successively under the tuition of three or four Roman priests, from whom he learned the rudiments of Latin and Greek. In after years he thought it no disadvantage that his education had been irregular; for, as he observed, he read the classic authors, not for the *words*, but for the *sense*.

At the age of twelve he formed a plan of study for himself, and plunged into the delights of miscellaneous reading with such ardor that he came near putting an end to his life. While dipping into philosophy, theology, and history, he delighted most in poetry and criticism; and either in the original or in translations (for he read what was easiest), he familiarized himself with the leading poets and critics of ancient and modern times. But in the strict sense of the term he never became a scholar. Seeing all other avenues of life closed to him, he early resolved to devote himself to poetry, to which no doubt he felt the intuitive impulse of genius. He showed remarkable precocity in rhyme. In his own language, —

> " As yet a child, nor yet a fool to fame,
> I lisp'd in numbers, for the numbers came."

He was encouraged in his early attempts by his father, who assigned him subjects, required frequent revisions, and ended with the encouragement, "These are good rhymes." Before venturing before the public as an author, he served a long and remarkable apprenticeship to poetry. Whenever a passage in any foreign author pleased him, he turned it into English verse. Before the age of fifteen he composed an epic of four thousand lines, in which he endeavored, in different passages, to imitate the beauties of Milton, Cowley, Spenser, Statius, Homer, Virgil, Ovid, and Claudian. " My first taking to imitating," he says, " was not out of vanity, but humility. I saw how defective my own things were, and endeavored to mend my manner by copying good strokes from others."

Among English authors he fixed upon Dryden as his model, for whom he felt so great a veneration that he persuaded some friends to take him to the coffee-house frequented by that distinguished poet. " Who does not wish," asks Johnson, " that Dryden could have known the value of the homage that was paid him, and foreseen the greatness of his young admirer ? "

His earliest patron, if such he may be called, was Sir William Trumbull, who, after serving as ambassador at Constantinoble under James II., and as secretary of state under William III., had withdrawn from public service and fixed his residence in the neighborhood of Binfield. The extraordinary precocity of the youthful poet delighted the aged statesman, who was accustomed to ride and discuss the classics with him. It was from him that Pope received the first suggestion to translate the "Iliad."

Another acquaintance belonging to this youthful period was William Walsh, a Worcestershire gentleman of fortune, who had some reputation at the time as a poet and critic. From him the ambitious youth received a bit of advice which has become famous: "We have had several great poets," he said, "but we have never had one great poet who was correct; and I advise you to make that your study and aim." This advice Pope evidently laid to heart.

At this time he made also the acquaintance of Wycherly, whose store of literary anecdote about a past generation greatly entertained him. Unfortunately, however, his assistance was asked in revising some of Wycherly's verses; and this task he performed with so much conscientiousness and ability — cutting out here and adding there — that the aged author was mortified and offended.

At the age of sixteen Pope circulated some "Pastorals," which were pronounced equal to anything Virgil had produced at the same age. Before he had passed his teens he was recognized as the most promising writer of his time, and was courted by the leading wits and people of fashion.

The first great work that Pope produced was the "Essay on Criticism," which was published in 1711. It was written two years previously, when the author was but twenty-one years of age. As was his custom with all his writings, he kept it by him for this period in order to revise and polish it. It shows a critical power and soundness of judgment that usually belong only to age and experience. It is true that the critical principles he lays down are not original or novel. At this time Pope had his head full of critical literature. Horace's

Ars Poetica and Boileau's *L'Art Poétique* were perfectly familiar to him, to say nothing of Quintilian and Aristotle. He embodied in his poem the principles he found in his authorities. But he did this with such felicity of expression and aptness of illustration as to win the admiration, not only of his contemporaries, but also of succeeding generations.

"One would scarcely ask," says Leslie Stephen, "for originality in such a case, any more than one would desire a writer on ethics to invent new laws of morality. We require neither Pope nor Aristotle to tell us that critics should not be pert nor prejudiced; that fancy should be regulated by judgment; that apparent facility comes by long training; that the sound should have some conformity to the meaning; that genius is often envied; and that dulness is frequently beyond the reach of reproof. We might even guess, without the authority of Pope, backed by Bacon, that there are some beauties which cannot be taught by method, but must be reached 'by a kind of felicity.'" Yet these commonplaces of criticism Pope has presented in inimitable form, exemplifying one of his own couplets : —

> "True wit is nature to advantage dressed;
> What oft was thought, but ne'er so well expressed."

The "Essay" is full of felicitous statements that instantly command the assent of the judgment, and fix themselves in the memory. Some of the lines are in daily use. Who has not heard that —

> "To err is human; to forgive, divine."

And also —

> "For fools rush in where angels fear to tread."

By the poet's striking presentation we are sometimes tempted to accept error for truth, as when he tell us, —

> "A little learning is a dangerous thing!
> Drink deep, or taste not the Pierian spring."

His own lines often furnish a happy exemplification of his maxims. He tells us, for instance, —

> " 'Tis not enough no harshness gives offence,
> The sound must seem an echo to the sense."

Then, by way of illustration, he continues, —

> "Soft is the strain when Zephyr gently blows,
> And the smooth stream in smoother numbers flows;
> But when loud surges lash the sounding shore,
> The hoarse, rough verse should like the torrent roar.
> When Ajax strives some rock's vast weight to throw,
> The line, too, labors, and the words move slow;
> Not so when swift Camilla scours the plain,
> Flies o'er th' unbending corn, and skims along the main."

But the poem is not without its faults. It would be too much to expect that; for, as he says, —

> " Whoever thinks a faultless piece to see,
> Thinks what ne'er was, nor is, nor e'er shall be."

Its extreme conciseness renders it obscure in places; words are sometimes used in a vague and variable sense; and there is a noticeable poverty of rhymes, "wit" and "sense" and "fools" being badly overworked. Yet, if he had written nothing else, this production alone would have given him a high rank as critic and poet.

The publication of the "Essay" was the beginning of a ceaseless strife with contemporary writers. In the following lines the youthful poet had the temerity to attack Dennis, whose acquaintance we made in the sketch of Addison : —

> "But Appius reddens at each word you speak,
> And stares tremendous with a threatening eye,
> Like some fierce tyrant in old tapestry."

This graphic picture inflamed the belligerent Dennis; and he made a bitter personal attack upon Pope, of whom, among other savage things, he says : " He may extol the ancients, but he has reason to thank the gods that he was born a modern ; for had he been born of Grecian parents, and his father consequently had by law had the absolute disposal of him, his life had been no longer than that of one of his poems — the life of half a day."

Though Pope affected to despise these attacks, yet his sensitive nature was deeply wounded by them. To some friends he remarked, when one of Cibber's pamphlets came into his hand, "These things are my diversion." But they noticed that his features, as he read, writhed with anguish; and when alone one of them expressed the hope that he might be preserved from such diversion as had been that day the lot of Pope. But, as we shall see, his revenge was terrific.

The next important production of Pope was "The Rape of the Lock," published in 1712. It is the most brilliant mock-heroic poem ever written. The subject is trifling enough. Lord Petre, a man of fashion at the court of Queen Anne, playfully cut off a lock of hair from the head of Miss Arabella Fermor, a beautiful maid of honor. This freedom was resented by the lady, and the friendly intercourse of the two families was interrupted. To put the two parties into good humor, and thus to effect a reconciliation, Pope devised this humorous epic. Sylphs, gnomes, nymphs, and salamanders form a part of the delicate poetic machinery. Here is a description of the unfortunate lock : —

> "This nymph, to the destruction of mankind,
>   Nourished two locks, which graceful hung behind
>   In equal curls, and well conspired to deck
>   With shining ringlets the smooth iv'ry neck.
>   Love in these labyrinths his slaves detains,
>   And mighty hearts are held in slender chains.
>   With hairy springes we the birds betray;
>   Slight lines of hair surprise the finny prey;
>   Fair tresses man's imperial race ensnare,
>   And beauty draws us with a single hair."

Speaking of the trifling circumstances that gave rise to this poem, Roscoe says : "To Cowley it might have suggested some quaint witticisms or forced allusions ; to Waller or Suckling, a metaphysical song; Dryden would have celebrated it in some strong lines, remarkable for their poetical spirit, and perhaps not less so for their indelicacy; while, by the general tribe of poets, it never could have been extended further than to a sweet epigram or a frigid sonnet. What is it in the hands of Pope? An animated and moving picture of human life and manners; a lively representation of the whims and follies of the times; an important contest, in which we find ourselves deeply engaged: for the interest is so supported, the manner so ludicrously serious, the characters so marked and distinguished, the resentment of the heroine so natural, and the triumph of the conqueror so complete, that we unavoidably partake the emotions of the parties, and alternately sympathize, approve, or condemn."

In 1713 Pope undertook the translation of Homer's "Iliad." The work was published by subscription; and as he had already gained recognition as the first poet of his time, the enterprise met with generous encouragement. Among other influential friends, Swift was active in securing subscriptions.

At first the poet was appalled at the magnitude of his undertaking, and wished, to use his own phrase, that somebody would hang him. But facility increased with practice; and his defective knowledge of Greek was remedied by the use of translations and the aid of scholarly friends.

This translation, in connection with the "Odyssey," was his principal labor for twelve years, and it brought a remuneration that had never before been realized by an English author. He received altogether about eight thousand pounds, which furnished him with a competency the rest of his life.

The translation is wrought out with exceeding care; but in its artificial character, it is far from reproducing the simplicity of the original. It brings Homer before us in a dress-suit. Bentley's criticism was exactly to the point: "It is a pretty poem, Mr. Pope, but you must not call it Homer." Yet it is a wonderful work; and Johnson was not far wrong when he said, "It is certainly the noblest version of poetry which the world has ever seen, and its publication must therefore be considered as one of the great events in the annals of learning."

In the sketch of Addison, reference was made to the ill-feeling existing between the illustrious essayist and Pope. It came to an open rupture in connection with the publication of the "Iliad." Tickell, a friend of Addison's, undertook a rival translation. He had Addison's encouragement, and perhaps also his assistance. It is possible that the essayist felt some jealousy of the rising reputation of the poet, and used his influence, in a civil way, to depreciate the latter's work. At all events, news of this sort came to Pope; and "the next day," he says, "while I was heated with what I had heard, I wrote a letter to Mr. Addison, to let him know that I was not unacquainted with this behavior of his; that if I was to speak severely of him, in return for it, it should not be in such a dirty way; that I should rather tell him, himself, fairly of his faults, and allow his good qualities; and that it should be something in the following manner." He then added what has since become the famous satire on Addison, in which the lack of justice is made up by brilliancy of wit : —

> " Peace to all such; but were there one whose fires
> True genius kindles and fair fame inspires;
> Blest with each talent and each art to please,
> And born to write, converse, and live with ease;
> Should such a man, too fond to rule alone,
> Bear like the Turk no brother near the throne,
> View him with scornful yet with jealous eyes,
> And hate for arts that caused himself to rise,
> Damn with faint praise, assent with civil leer,
> And, without sneering, teach the rest to sneer;
> Willing to wound and yet afraid to strike,
> Just hint a fault and hesitate dislike,
> Alike reserved to blame or to commend,
> A timorous foe and a suspicious friend;
> Dreading e'en fools, by flatterers besieged,
> And so obliging that he ne'er obliged;
> Like Cato give his little Senate laws,
> And sit attentive to his own applause,

> While wits and templars every sentence raise,
> And wonder with a foolish face of praise; —
> Who but must laugh if such a man there be?
> Who would not weep if Atticus were he?"

After becoming independent from the proceeds of his Homeric translations, Pope removed to the villa of Twickenham, where he spent the remainder of his life. Here he received his friends, who were among the most polished men of the time. Gay, Arbuthnot, Bolingbroke, Peterborough, Swift, were all warmly attached to him — "the most brilliant company of friends," says Thackeray, "that the world has ever seen."

We should not forget the filial piety he showed his parents — one of the most beautiful feature's of the poet's life. However spiteful, acrimonious, and exacting toward others, to his mother he was always tender, considerate, patient. In her old age he stayed by her, denying himself the pleasure of long visits and foreign travel. While conventionally courteous and formal in his relations to other women, for whom, after the fashion of the time, he seemed to entertain no high opinion, he was simple and unaffected toward her. And when she died, he spoke of her with peculiar tenderness: "I thank God, her death was as easy as her life was innocent; and as it cost her not a groan, or even a sigh, there is yet upon her countenance such an expression of tranquillity, nay, almost of pleasure, that it is even enviable to behold it. It would afford the finest image of a saint expired that ever painter drew."

As soon as Homer was off his hands, he proceeded to get even with the critics who had attacked his previous writings. The result was the "Dunciad," the most elaborate satirical performance in our language, which was given to the public in 1728.

We cannot think that, as he claims, his object was "doing good" by exposing ignorant and pretentious authors; from what we know of his character, we are justified in supposing that personal pique animated him no less than zeal for the honor of literature. Theobald, whose grievous offence was surpassing Pope in editing Shakespeare, is elevated to the throne of Dulness, though he is afterwards deposed to make place for Cibber.

"On the day the book was first vended," Pope tells us, "a crowd of authors besieged the shop; entreaties, advices, threats of law and battery, nay, cries of treason, were all employed to hinder the coming out of the 'Dunciad;' on the other side, the booksellers and hawkers made as great efforts to procure it. What could a few poor authors do against so great a majority as the public? There was no stopping a torrent with a finger, so out it came."

The satire had the desired effect; it blasted the characters it touched. One of the victims complained that for a time he was in danger of starving, as the publishers had no longer any confidence in his ability. The poem is not interesting as a whole, but contains many splendid flights, as in the concluding lines, which describe the eclipse of learning and morality under the darkening reign of advancing Dulness: —

> "She comes! she comes! the sable throne behold
> Of Night primeval, and of Chaos old!
> Before her Fancy's gilded clouds decay,
> And all its varying rainbows die away.
> Wit shoots in vain its momentary fires,
> The meteor drops, and in a flash expires.
> As one by one, at dread Medea's strain,
> The sickening stars fade off th' ethereal plain;
> As Argus' eyes, by Hermes' wand oppressed,
> Closed one by one to everlasting rest;
> Thus at her felt approach, and secret might,
> Art after art goes out, and all is night;
> See skulking Truth to her old cavern fled,
> Mountains of casuistry heap'd o'er her head!
> Philosophy, that lean'd on Heaven before,
> Shrinks to her second cause, and is no more.
> Physic of Metaphysic begs defence,
> And Metaphysic calls for aid on Sense!
> See Mystery to Mathematics fly!
> In vain, they gaze, turn giddy, rave, and die.

> Religion, blushing, veils her sacred fires,
> And unawares Morality expires.
> Nor public flame, nor private dares to shine;
> Nor human spark is left, nor glimpse divine,
> Lo, thy dread empire, Chaos! is restored;
> Light dies before thy uncreating word:
> Thy hand, great Anarch, lets the curtain fall,
> And universal darkness buries all."

This is, indeed, a fine passage, repaying careful study ; but it hardly deserves the extravagant praise bestowed upon it by Thackeray. "In these astonishing lines," he says, "Pope reaches, I think, to the very greatest height which his sublime art has attained, and shows himself the equal of all poets of all times. It is the brightest ardor, the loftiest assertion of truth, the most generous wisdom, illustrated by the noblest poetic figure, and spoken in words the aptest, grandest, and most harmonious. It is heroic courage speaking ; a splendid declaration of righteous wrath and war. It is the gage flung down, and the silver trumpet ringing defiance to falsehood and tyranny, deceit, dulness, superstition."

The "Essay on Man," his noblest work, appeared in 1733. It consists of four "Epistles :" the first treats of man in relation to the universe ; the second, in relation to himself ; the third, in relation to society ; and the fourth, in relation to happiness.) The "Epistles" are addressed to Bolingbroke, by whom the "Essay" was suggested, and from whom many of its principles proceeded. It is not so much a treatise on man as on the moral government of the world. Its general purpose is to —

> "Vindicate the ways of God to man."

This is done by an application of the principles of natural religion to the origin of evil, the wisdom of the Creator, and the constitution of the world. But, as a whole, the "Essay" does not present a consistent and logical system of teaching. Pope was not master of the deep theme he had undertaken ; and he was content to pick up in various authors whatever he could fit into his general plan.   On the one hand he was attacked for having written against religion.   Certainly moral responsibility disappears if we accept his declaration, —

> " One truth is clear; whatever is, is right."

On the other hand, Warburton came forward to defend his orthodoxy; and his championship was gratefully accepted by the poet.   " You have made my system," Pope wrote to him, " as clear as I ought to have done, and could not. . . .   I know I meant just what you explain, but I did not explain my own meaning as well as you.   You understand me as well as I do myself, but you express me better than I could express myself."

When, however, we turn from the whole to the separate parts, we are astonished at the marvellous expression and inimitable form.   We may call it, with Dugald Stewart, " the noblest specimen of philosophical poetry which our language affords."   Single truths have never had more splendid statement.   Here is his amplification of the truth that all things exist in God : —

> " All are but parts of one stupendous whole,
>   Whose body Nature is, and God the soul;
>   That, changed through all, and yet in all the same,
>   Great in the earth, as in th' ethereal frame,
>   Warms in the sun, refreshes in the breeze,
>   Glows in the stars, and blossoms in the trees;
>   Lives through all life, extends through all extent,
>   Spreads undivided, operates unspent;
>   Breathes in our soul, informs our mortal part,
>   As full, as perfect, in a hair as heart;
>   As full, as perfect, in vile man that mourns,
>   As the rapt seraph that adores and burns:
>   To him no high, no low, no great, no small;
>   He fills, he bounds, connects, and equals all."

The religion of nature, as seen in the savage, has never had better expression than this : —

" Lo, the poor Indian ! whose untutor'd mind
    Sees God in clouds, or hears him in the wind;
    His soul proud science never taught to stray
    Far as the solar walk, or milky way;
    Yet simple nature to his hope has given,
    Behind the cloud-topp'd hill an humbler heaven;
    Some safer world in depth of woods embraced,
    Some happier island in the watery waste,
    Where slaves once more their native land behold,
    No fiends torment, no Christians thirst for gold.
    To be, contents his natural desire,
    He asks no angel's wing, no seraph's fire;
    But thinks, admitted to that equal sky,
    His faithful dog shall bear him company."

Pope died in 1744. A few days before his death he became delirious. On recovering his rationality he referred to his delirium as a sufficient humiliation of the vanity of man. Bolingbroke was told that during his last illness Pope was always saying something kind of his present or absent friends, and that his humanity seemed to have survived his understanding. "It has so," replied the statesman; "and I never in my life knew a man that had so tender a heart for his particular friends, or more general friendship for mankind."

As the end drew near, Pope was asked whether a priest should not be called. He replied, "I do not think it essential, but it will be very right; and I thank you for putting me in mind of it." He had undoubting confidence in a future state. Shortly after receiving the sacrament, he said, "There is nothing that is meritorious but virtue and friendship, and indeed friendship itself is only a part of virtue." He lies buried at Twickenham.

In appearance he was the most insignificant of English writers. He was a dwarf, four feet high, hunch-backed, and so crooked that he was called the "Interrogation Point." His life was one long disease. He required help in dressing and undressing; and to keep erect, he had to encase his body in stays. Extremely sensitive to cold, he wore three or four times the usual amount of clothing. But his face was pleasing, his voice agreeable, and his eyes especially were beautiful and expressive. He was fastidious in dress and elegant in manner. As might naturally be expected, he was punctilious and troublesome, requiring so much attention that he was the dread of servants. Fond of highly seasoned dishes, and unable to control his appetite, he frequently made himself sick by over-eating.

He was singularly lacking in manly frankness, seeking always to attain his ends by artifice. It was said of him that he hardly drank tea without stratagem; and Lady Bolingbroke used to say that " he played the politician about cabbages and turnips." But he carried his artifice to higher matters, and manipulated his correspondence and his writings in the interest of his reputation.

His character was full of contradictions. While professing to disregard fame, he courted it; while affecting superiority to the great, he took pleasure in enumerating the men of high rank among his acquaintances; while appearing indifferent to his own poetry, saying that he wrote when " he just had nothing else to do," he was always revolving some poetical scheme in his head, so that, as Swift complained, he was never at leisure for conversation; and while pretending insensibility to censure, he writhed under the attacks of critics. Yet it is to his credit that he never put up his genius to the highest bidder, and that he never indulged in base flattery for selfish ends. His translation of the " Iliad" he dedicated, not to influential statesmen or titled nobility, but to the second-rate dramatist, Congreve. In his view of life he fixed his attention upon its petty features, forgetting the divine and eternal relations that give it dignity and worth. There is truth in the following lines, but it is only one-sided : —

> " Behold the child, by nature's kindly law,
>   Pleased with a rattle, tickled with a straw:
> Some livelier plaything gives his youth delight,
>   A little louder, but as empty quite;

> Scarfs, garters, gold, amuse his riper age,
> And beads and prayer-books are the toys of age;
> Pleased with this bauble still, as that before,
> Till tired he sleeps, and life's poor play is o'er."

Virtue, love, divine stewardship, and eternal life take away this pettiness, and give our existence here beauty and grandeur.

As a poet, it is too much to claim that his verses attained the highest imaginative flights, such as we find in Shakespeare and Tennyson. He was not swayed by the fine frenzy, the over-mastering convictions, and the tormenting passions that irresistibly force an utterance. He conformed his writings to a conventional form. He sought above all, in imitation of classical models, correctness of style. And, in the words of James Russell Lowell, "in his own province he still stands unapproachably alone. If to be the greatest satirist of individual men, rather than of human nature, if to be the highest expression which the life of the court and the ballroom has ever found in verse, if to have added more phrases to our language than any other but Shakespeare, if to have charmed four generations, make a man a great poet, — then he is one. He was the chief founder of an artificial style of writing, which in his hands was living and powerful, because he used it to express artificial modes of thinking and an artificial state of society. Measured by any high standard of imagination, he will be found wanting ; tried by any test of wit, he is unrivalled."

AN ESSAY ON CRITICISM.

PART I.

'TIS hard to say, if greater want of skill
Appear in writing or in judging ill;
But, of the two, less dangerous is the offence
To tire our patience, than mislead our sense.
Some few in that, but numbers err in this;
Ten censure wrong for one who writes amiss;
A fool might once himself alone expose,
Now one in verse makes many more in prose.
    'Tis with our judgments as our watches, none
Go just alike, yet each believes his own.   10
In poets as true genius is but rare,
True taste as seldom is the critic's share;
Both must alike from Heaven derive their light,
These born to judge, as well as those to write.
Let such teach others who themselves excel,
And censure freely, who have written well.
Authors are partial to their wit, 'tis true,
But are not critics to their judgment, too?
    Yet, if we look more closely, we shall find
Most have the seeds of judgment in their mind: 20
Nature affords at least a glimmering light.
The lines, though touched but faintly, are drawn right;
But, as the slighest sketch, if justly traced,
Is, by ill-coloring, but the more disgraced,
So, by false learning, is good sense defaced:
Some are bewildered in the maze of schools,
And some made coxcombs nature meant but fools.
In search of wit these lose their common sense,
And then turn critics in their own defence:
Each burns alike, who can or cannot write,   30
Or with a rival's or an eunuch's spite.
All fools have still an itching to deride,
And fain would be upon the laughing side.

If Mævius scribble in Apollo's spite,
There are, who judge still worse than he can write.
  Some have at first for wits, then poets, passed,
Turned critics next, and proved plain fools at last.
Some neither can for wits nor critics pass,
As heavy mules are neither horse nor ass.
Those half-learned witlings, numerous in our isle,   40
As half-formed insects on the banks of Nile;
Unfinished things, one knows not what to call,
Their generation's so equivocal:
To tell them would a hundred tongues require,
Or one vain wit's, that might a hundred tire.
  But you, who seek to give and merit fame,
And justly bear a critic's noble name,
Be sure yourself and your own reach to know,
How far your genius, taste, and learning, go;
Launch not beyond your depth, but be discreet,   50
And mark that point where sense and dulness meet.
  Nature to all things fixed the limits fit,
And wisely curbed proud man's pretending wit.
As on the land while here the ocean gains,
In other parts it leaves wide sandy plains;
Thus in the soul while memory prevails,
The solid power of understanding fails.
Where beams of warm imagination play,
The memory's soft figures melt away.
One science only will one genius fit;   60
So vast is art, so narrow human wit:
Not only bounded to peculiar arts,
But oft in those confined to single parts.
Like kings, we lose the conquests gained before,
By vain ambition still to make them more:
Each might his several province well command,
Would all but stoop to what they understand.
  First follow nature, and your judgment frame
By her just standard, which is still the same:
Unerring nature, still divinely bright,   70
One clear, unchanged, and universal light,

Life, force, and beauty, must to all impart,
At once the source, and end, and test of art.
Art from that fund each just supply provides;
Works without show, and without pomp presides:
In some fair body thus the informing soul
With spirits feeds, with vigor fills the whole,
Each motion guides, and every nerve sustains;
Itself unseen, but in the effects remains.
Some, to whom Heaven in wit has been profuse,   80
Want as much more, to turn it to its use;
For wit and judgment often are at strife,
Though meant each other's aid, like man and wife.
'Tis more to guide, than spur the muse's steed;
Restrain his fury, than provoke his speed;
The wingéd courser, like a generous horse,
Shows most true metal when you check his course.

Those rules, of old discovered, not devised,
Are nature still, but nature methodized;
Nature, like liberty, is but restrained   90
By the same laws which first herself ordained.

Hear how learn'd Greece her useful rules indites,
When to repress, and when indulge our flights.
High on Parnassus' top her sons she showed,
And pointed out those arduous paths they trod;
Held from afar, aloft, the immortal prize,
And urged the rest by equal steps to rise.
Just precepts thus from great examples given,
She drew from them what they derived from Heaven.
The generous critic fanned the poet's fire,   100
And taught the world with reason to admire.
Then criticism the muse's handmaid proved,
To dress her charms, and make her more beloved:
But following wits from that intention strayed,
Who could not win the mistress, wooed the maid;
Against the poets their own arms they turned,
Sure to hate most the men from whom they learned.
So modern 'pothecaries, taught the art
By doctors' bills, to play the doctor's part,

Bold in the practice of mistaken rules,   110
Prescribe, apply, and call their masters fools.
Some on the leaves of ancient authors prey,
Nor time nor moths e'er spoil so much as they.
Some dryly plain, without invention's aid,
Write dull receipts how poems may be made.
These leave the sense, their learning to display,
And those explain the meaning quite away.

    You, then, whose judgment the right course would steer,
Know well each ancient's proper character;
His fable, subject, scope in every page;   120
Religion, country, genius of his age:
Without all these at once before your eyes,
Cavil you may, but never criticise.
Be Homer's works your study and delight,
Read them by day, and meditate by night;
Thence form your judgment, thence your maxims bring,
And trace the muses upward to their spring.
Still, with itself compared, his text peruse;
And let your comment be the Mantuan Muse.

    When first young Maro, in his boundless mind,   130
A work to outlast immortal Rome designed,
Perhaps he seemed above the critic's law,
And but from nature's fountain scorned to draw:
But when to examine every part he came,
Nature and Homer were, he found, the same.
Convinced, amazed, he checks the bold design:
And rules as strict his labored work confine,
As if the Stagirite o'erlooked each line.
Learn hence for ancient rules a just esteem;
To copy nature is to copy them.   140

    Some beauties yet no precepts can declare,
For there's a happiness as well as care.
Music resembles poetry : in each
Are nameless graces which no methods teach,
And which a master-hand alone can reach.
If, where the rules not far enough extend
(Since rules were made but to promote their end),

Some lucky license answer to the full
The intent proposed, that license is a rule.
Thus Pegasus, a nearer way to take,   150
May boldly deviate from the common track.
Great wits sometimes may gloriously offend,
And rise to faults true critics dare not mend ;
From vulgar bounds with brave disorder part,
And snatch a grace beyond the reach of art,
Which, without passing through the judgment, gains
The heart, and all its end at once attains.
In prospects, thus, some objects please our eyes,
Which out of nature's common order rise,
The shapeless rock or hanging precipice.   160
But though the ancients thus their rules invade
(As kings dispense with laws themselves have made),
Moderns, beware ! or if you must offend
Against the precept, ne'er transgress its end ;
Let it be seldom, and compelled by need ;
And have, at least, their precedent to plead.
The critic else proceeds without remorse,
Seizes your fame, and puts his laws in force.

    I know there are, to whose presumptuous thoughts
Those freer beauties, even in them, seem faults.   170
Some figures monstrous and misshaped appear,
Considered singly, or beheld too near,
Which, but proportioned to their light, or place,
Due distance reconciles to form and grace.
A prudent chief not always must display
His powers in equal ranks and fair array,
But with the occasion and the place comply,
Conceal his force, nay, seem sometimes to fly.
Those oft are stratagems which errors seem,
Nor is it Homer nods, but we that dream.   180

    Still green with bays each ancient altar stands,
Above the reach of sacrilegious hands ;
Secure from flames, from envy's fiercer rage,
Destructive war, and all-involving age.
See, from each clime the learn'd their incense bring ;

Hear, in all tongues consenting Pæans ring !
In praise so just let every voice be joined,
And fill the general chorus of mankind.
Hail ! bards triumphant ! born in happier days ;
Immortal heirs of universal praise !   190
Whose honors with increase of ages grow,
As streams roll down, enlarging as they flow ;
Nations unborn your mighty names shall sound,
And worlds applaud, that must not yet be found !
Oh may some spark of your celestial fire,
The last, the meanest of your sons inspire,
(That, on weak wings, from far pursues your flights,
Glows while he reads, but trembles as he writes),
To teach vain wits a science little known,
To admire superior sense, and doubt their own !   200

PART II.

Of all the causes which conspire to blind
Man's erring judgment, and misguide the mind,
What the weak head with strongest bias rules,
Is pride, the never-failing vice of fools.
Whatever nature has in worth denied,
She gives in large recruits of needful pride ;
For as in bodies, thus in souls, we find
What wants in blood and spirits, swelled with wind :
Pride, where wit fails, steps in to our defence,
And fills up all the mighty void of sense.   210
If once right reason drives that cloud away,
Truth breaks upon us with resistless day.
Trust not yourself ; but your defects to know,
Make use of every friend — and every foe.

A little learning is a dangerous thing ;
Drink deep, or taste not the Pierian spring :
There, shallow draughts intoxicate the brain,
And drinking largely sobers us again.
Fired at first sight with what the muse imparts,
In fearless youth we tempt the heights of arts,   220

While from the bounded level of our mind,
Short views we take, nor see the lengths behind;
But, more advanced, behold, with strange surprise,
New distant scenes of endless science rise!
So, pleased at first the towering Alps we try,
Mount o'er the vales, and seem to tread the sky,
The eternal snows appear already passed,
And the first clouds and mountains seem the last:
But, those attained, we tremble to survey
The growing labors of the lengthened way,   230
The increasing prospect tires our wandering eyes,
Hills peep o'er hills, and Alps on Alps arise!
    A perfect judge will read each work of wit
With the same spirit that its author writ:
Survey the whole, nor seek slight faults to find
Where nature moves, and rapture warms the mind;
Nor lose, for that malignant dull delight,
The generous pleasure to be charmed with wit.
But, in such lays as neither ebb nor flow,
Correctly cold, and regularly low,   240
That, shunning faults, one quiet tenor keep;
We cannot blame indeed — but we may sleep.
In wit, as nature, what affects our hearts
Is not the exactness of peculiar parts;
'Tis not a lip, or eye, we beauty call,
But the joint force and full result of all.
Thus, when we view some well-proportioned dome
(The world's just wonder, and even thine, O Rome!),
No single parts unequally surprise,
All comes united to the admiring eyes;   250
No monstrous height, or breadth, or length, appear;
The whole at once is bold, and regular.
    Whoever thinks a faultless piece to see,
Thinks what ne'er was, nor is, nor e'er shall be.
In every work regard the writer's end,
Since none can compass more than they intend;
And if the means be just, the conduct true,
Applause, in spite of trivial faults, is due.

As men of breeding, sometimes men of wit,
To avoid great errors, must the less commit :   260
Neglect the rules each verbal critic lays,
For not to know some trifles is a praise.
Most critics, fond of some subservient art,
Still make the whole depend upon a part :
They talk of principles, but notions prize,
And all to one loved folly sacrifice.

    Once on a time, La Mancha's knight, they say,
A certain bard encountering on the way,
Discoursed in terms as just, with looks as sage,
As e'er could Dennis, of the Grecian stage ;   270
Concluding all were desperate sots and fools,
Who durst depart from Aristotle's rules.
Our author, happy in a judge so nice,
Produced his play, and begged the knight's advice ;
Made him observe the subject and the plot,
The manners, passions, unities ; what not ?
All which, exact to rule, were brought about,
Were but a combat in the lists left out.
"What! leave the combat out ? " exclaims the knight.
" Yes, or we must renounce the Stagirite."   280
" Not so, by heaven ! " (he answers in a rage)
" Knights, squires, and steeds must enter on the stage."
" So vast a throng the stage can ne'er contain."
" Then build a new, or act it in a plain."

    Thus critics of less judgment than caprice,
Curious, not knowing, not exact, but nice,
Form short ideas ; and offend in arts
(As most in manners) by a love to parts.

    Some to conceit alone their taste confine,
And glittering thoughts struck out at every line ;   290
Pleased with a work where nothing's just or fit ;
One glaring chaos and wild heap of wit.
Poets, like painters, thus, unskilled to trace
The naked nature and the living grace,
With gold and jewels cover every part,
And hide with ornaments their want of art.

True wit is nature to advantage dressed;
What oft was thought, but ne'er so well expressed;
Something, whose truth convinced at sight we find,
That gives us back the image of our mind.   300
As shades more sweetly recommend the light,
So modest plainness sets off sprightly wit.
For works may have more wit than does them good,
As bodies perish through excess of blood.

    Others for language all their care express,
And value books, as women men, for dress:
Their praise is still — " the style is excellent; "
The sense, they humbly take upon content.
Words are like leaves; and, where they most abound,
Much fruit of sense beneath is rarely found: 310
False eloquence, like the prismatic glass,
Its gaudy colors spreads on every place;
The face of nature we no more survey,
All glares alike, without distinction gay:
But true expression, like the unchanging sun,
Clears and improves whate'er it shines upon;
It gilds all objects, but it alters none.
Expression is the dress of thought, and still
Appears more decent, as more suitable;
A vile conceit, in pompous words expressed,   320
Is like a clown in regal purple dressed:
For different styles with different subjects sort,
As several garbs with country, town, and court.
Some by old words to fame have made pretence,
Ancients in phrase, mere moderns in their sense;
Such labored nothings, in so strange a style,
Amaze the unlearn'd, and make the learned smile.
Unlucky, as Fungoso in the play,
These sparks with awkward vanity display
What the fine gentleman wore yesterday;   330
And but so mimic ancient wits at best,
As apes our grandsires in their doublets dressed.
In words, as fashions, the same rule will hold,
Alike fantastic if too new or old.

Be not the first by whom the new are tried,
Nor yet the last to lay the old aside.
        But most by numbers judge a poet's song,
And smooth or rough, with them, is right or wrong;
In the bright muse though thousand charms conspire,
Her voice is all these tuneful fools admire;   340
Who haunt Parnassus but to please their ear,
Not mend their minds; as some to church repair,
Not for the doctrine, but the music there.
These equal syllables alone require,
Though oft the ear the open vowels tire;
While expletives their feeble aid do join
And ten low words oft creep in one dull line;
While they ring round the same unvaried chimes,
With sure returns of still expected rhymes;
Where'er you find " the cooling western breeze,"   350
In the next line, it " whispers through the trees : "
If crystal streams " with pleasing murmurs creep,"
The reader's threatened (not in vain) with "sleep : "
Then, at the last and only couplet fraught
With some unmeaning thing they call a thought,
A needless Alexandrine ends the song,
That, like a wounded snake, drags its slow length along.
        Leave such to tune their own dull rhymes, and know
What's roundly smooth or languishingly slow;
And praise the easy vigor of a line,   360
Where Denham's strength, and Waller's sweetness join.
True ease in writing comes from art, not chance,
As those move easiest who have learned to dance.
'Tis not enough no harshness gives offence,
The sound must seem an echo to the sense.
Soft is the strain when Zephyr gently blows,
And the smooth stream in smoother numbers flows;
But when loud surges lash the sounding shore,
The hoarse, rough verse should like the torrent roar:
When Ajax strives some rock's vast weight to throw,   370
The line, too, labors, and the words move slow;
Not so, when swift Camilla scours the plain,

Flies o'er the unbending corn, and skims along the main.
Hear how Timotheus' varied lays surprise,
And bid alternate passions fall and rise !
While, at each change, the son of Libyan Jove
Now burns with glory, and then melts with love ;
Now his fierce eyes with sparkling fury glow,
Now sighs steal out, and tears begin to flow :
Persians and Greeks like turns of nature found,   380
And the world's victor stood subdued by sound !
The power of music all our hearts allow,
And what Timotheus was, is Dryden now.

    Avoid extremes ; and shun the fault of such,
Who still are pleased too little or too much.
At every trifle scorn to take offence,
That always shows great pride, or little sense :
Those heads, as stomachs, are not sure the best,
Which nauseate all, and nothing can digest.
Yet let not each gay turn thy rapture move ;   390
For fools admire, but men of sense approve :
As things seem large which we through mist descry,
Dulness is ever apt to magnify.

    Some foreign writers, some our own despise ;
The ancients only, or the moderns prize.
Thus wit, like faith, by each man is applied
To one small sect, and all are damned beside.
Meanly they seek the blessing to confine,
And force that sun but on a part to shine,
Which not alone the southern wit sublimes,   400
But ripens spirits in cold northern climes ;
Which from the first has shone on ages past,
Enlights the present, and shall warm the last ;
Though each may feel increases and decays,
And see now clearer and now darker days.
Regard not then if wit be old or new,
But blame the false, and value still the true.

    Some ne'er advance a judgment of their own,
But catch the spreading notion of the town ;
They reason and conclude by precedent,   410

And own stale nonsense which they ne'er invent.
Some judge of authors' names, not works, and then
Nor praise nor blame the writings, but the men.
Of all this servile herd, the worst is he
That in proud dulness joins with quality.
A constant critic at the great man's board,
To fetch and carry nonsense for my lord.
What woful stuff this madrigal would be,
In some starved hackney sonneteer, or me!
But let a lord once own the happy lines,   420
How the wit brightens! how the style refines!
Before his sacred name flies every fault,
And each exalted stanza teems with thought!

    The vulgar thus through imitation err;
As oft the learn'd by being singular:
So much they scorn the crowd, that if the throng
By chance go right, they purposely go wrong:
So schismatics the plain believers quit,
And are but damned for having too much wit.
Some praise at morning what they blame at night;   430
But always think the last opinion right.
A muse by these is like a mistress used,
This hour she's idolized, the next abused;
While their weak heads, like towns unfortified,
'Twixt sense and nonsense daily change their side.
Ask them the cause; they're wiser still they say;
And still to-morrow's wiser than to-day.
We think our fathers fools, so wise we grow;
Our wiser sons, no doubt, will think us so.
Once school-divines this zealous isle o'erspread, 440
Who knew most sentences was deepest read;
Faith, Gospel, all, seem'd made to be disputed,
And none had sense enough to be confuted:
Scotists and Thomists now in peace remain,
Amidst their kindred cobwebs in Duck Lane.
If faith itself has different dresses worn,
What wonder modes in wit should take their turn?
Oft, leaving what is natural and fit,

The current folly proves the ready wit;
And authors think their reputation safe,   450
Which lives as long as fools are pleased to laugh.
   Some valuing those of their own side or mind,
Still make themselves the measure of mankind :
Fondly we think we honor merit then,
When we but praise ourselves in other men.
Parties in wit attend on those of state,
And public faction doubles private hate.
Pride, malice, folly, against Dryden rose,
In various shapes of parsons, critics, beaux;
But sense survived, when merry jests were past;   460
For rising merit will buoy up at last.
Might he return, and bless once more our eyes,
New Blackmores and new Millbourns must arise:
Nay, should great Homer lift his awful head,
Zoilus again would start up from the dead.
Envy will merit, as its shade, pursue;
But like a shadow, proves the substance true:
For envied wit, like Sol eclipsed, makes known
The opposing body's grossness, not its own.
When first that sun too powerful beams displays,   470
It draws up vapors which obscure its rays;
But even those clouds at last adorn its way,
Reflect new glories, and augment the day.
   Be thou the first true merit to befriend;
His praise is lost who stays till all commend.
Short is the date, alas! of modern rhymes,
And 'tis but just to let them live betimes.
No longer now that golden age appears,
When patriarch-wits survived a thousand years:
Now length of fame (our second life) is lost,   480
And bare threescore is all ev'n that can boast;
Our sons their fathers' failing language see,
And such as Chaucer is, shall Dryden be.
So when the faithful pencil has designed
Some bright idea of the master's mind,
Where a new world leaps out at his command,

And ready nature waits upon his hand ;
When the ripe colors soften and unite,
And sweetly melt into just shade and light ;
When mellowing years their full perfection give,   490
And each bold figure just begins to live,
The treacherous colors the fair art betray,
And all the bright creation fades away !

     Unhappy wit, like most mistaken things,
Atones not for that envy which it brings.
In youth alone its empty praise we boast,
But soon the short-lived vanity is lost :
Like some fair flower the early spring supplies,
That gayly blooms, but ev'n in blooming dies.
What is this wit, which must our cares employ ?   500
The owner's wife, that other men enjoy ;
Then most our trouble still when most admired,
And still the more we give, the more required ;
Whose fame with pains we guard, but lose with ease,
Sure some to vex, but never all to please ;
'Tis what the vicious fear, the virtuous shun,
By fools 'tis hated, and by knaves undone !

     If wit so much from ignorance undergo,
Ah ! let not learning too commence its foe !
Of old, those met rewards who could excel,   510
And such were praised who but endeavored well :
Though triumphs were to generals only due,
Crowns were reserved to grace the soldiers too.
Now they who reach Parnassus' lofty crown,
Employ their pains to spurn some others down ;
And, while self-love each jealous writer rules,
Contending wits become the sport of fools :
But still the worst with most regret commend,
For each ill author is as bad a friend.
To what base ends, and by what abject ways,   520
Are mortals urged, through sacred lust of praise !
Ah, ne'er so dire a thirst of glory boast,
Nor in the critic let the man be lost.

Good-nature and good sense must ever join;
To err is human, to forgive, divine.
　　But if in noble minds some dregs remain,
Not yet purged off, of spleen and sour disdain;
Discharge that rage on more provoking crimes,
Nor fear a dearth in these flagitious times.
No pardon vile obscenity should find,   530
Though wit and art conspire to move your mind;
But dulness with obscenity must prove
As shameful sure as impotence in love.
In the fat age of pleasure, wealth, and ease,
Sprung the rank weed, and thrived with large increase:
When love was all an easy monarch's care;
Seldom at council, never in a war:
Jilts ruled the state, and statesmen farces writ;
Nay, wits had pensions, and young lords had wit:
The fair sat panting at a courtier's play,   540
And not a mask went unimproved away:
The modest fan was lifted up no more,
And virgins smiled at what they blushed before.
The following license of a foreign reign,
Did all the dregs of bold Socinus drain;
Then unbelieving priests reformed the nation,
And taught more pleasant methods of salvation;
Where Heaven's free subjects might their rights dispute,
Lest God himself should seem too absolute:
Pulpits their sacred satire learned to spare,   550
And vice admired to find a flatterer there!
Encouraged thus, wit's Titans braved the skies,
And the press groaned with licensed blasphemies.
　　These monsters, critics! with your darts engage,
Here point your thunder, and exhaust your rage!
Yet shun their fault, who, scandalously nice,
Will needs mistake an author into vice;
All seems infected that the infected spy,
As all looks yellow to the jaundiced eye.

PART III.

LEARN, then, what morals critics ought to show.   560
For 'tis but half a judge's task, to know.
'Tis not enough, taste, judgment, learning, join;
In all you speak, let truth and candor shine:
That not alone what to your sense is due
All may allow; but seek your friendship too.
(Be silent always, when you doubt your sense;)
And speak, though sure, with seeming diffidence:
Some positive, persisting fops we know,
Who, if once wrong, will needs be always so;
But you, with pleasure, own your errors past,   570
And make each day a critique on the last.
    'Tis not enough your counsel still be true;
Blunt truths more mischief than nice falsehoods do;
Men must be taught as if you taught them not,
And things unknown proposed as things forgot.
Without good breeding truth is disapproved;
That only makes superior sense beloved.
    Be niggards of advice on no pretence;
For the worst avarice is that of sense.
With mean complacence, ne'er betray your trust,   580
Nor be so civil as to prove unjust.
Fear not the anger of the wise to raise,
Those best can bear reproof who merit praise.
    'Twere well might critics still this freedom take,
But Appius reddens at each word you speak,
And stares, tremendous, with a threatening eye,
Like some fierce tyrant in old tapestry.
Fear most to tax an honorable fool,
Whose right it is, uncensured, to be dull
Such, without wit, are poets when they please,   590
As, without learning, they can take degrees.
Leave dangerous truths to unsuccessful satires,
And flattery to fulsome dedicators,
Whom, when they praise, the world believes no more,
Than when they promise to give scribbling o'er.

'Tis best sometimes your censure to restrain,
And charitably let the dull be vain:
Your silence there is better than your spite,
For who can rail so long as they can write?
Still humming on, their drowsy course they keep, 600
And, lashed so long, like tops, are lashed asleep.
False steps but help them to renew the race,
As, after stumbling, jades will mend their pace.
What crowds of these, impenitently bold,
In sounds and jingling syllables grown old,
Still run on poets in a raging vein,
Even to the dregs and squeezing of the brain;
Strain out the last dull droppings of their sense,
And rhyme with all the rage of impotence!

Such shameless bards we have; and yet, 'tis true, 610
There are as mad, abandoned critics, too.
The bookful blockhead, ignorantly read,
With loads of learned lumber in his head,
With his own tongue still edifies his ears,
And always listening to himself appears.
All books he reads, and all he reads assails,
From Dryden's Fables down to Durfey's Tales.
With him most authors steal their works, or buy;
Garth did not write his own Dispensary.
Name a new play, and he's the poet's friend, 620
Nay, showed his faults — but when would poets mend?
No place so sacred from such fops is barred,
Nor is Paul's Church more safe than Paul's Churchyard:
Nay, fly to altars; there they'll talk you dead;
For fools rush in where angels fear to tread.
Distrustful sense with modest caution speaks,
It still looks home, and short excursions makes;
But rattling nonsense in full volleys breaks,
And, never shocked, and never turned aside,
Bursts out, resistless, with a thundering tide. 630

But where's the man who counsel can bestow,
Still pleased to teach, and yet not proud to know?
Unbiassed, or by favor, or in spite;

Not dully prepossessed, nor blindly right;
Though learn'd, well-bred; and though well-bred, sincere;
Modestly bold, and humanly severe;
Who to a friend his faults can freely show,
And gladly praise the merit of a foe?
Blessed with a taste exact, yet unconfined;
A knowledge both of books and human kind;   640
Generous converse; a soul exempt from pride;
And love to praise, with reason on his side?
    Such once were critics: such the happy few,
Athens and Rome in better ages knew.
The mighty Stagirite first left the shore,
Spread all his sails, and durst the deeps explore;
He steered securely, and discovered far,
Led by the light of the Mæonian star.
Poets, a race long unconfined and free,
Still fond and proud of savage liberty,   650
Received his laws; and stood convinced 'twas fit,
Who conquered nature, should preside o'er wit.
    Horace still charms with graceful negligence,
And without method talks us into sense;
Will, like a friend, familiarly convey
The truest notions in the easiest way.
He who, supreme in judgment as in wit,
Might boldly censure, as he boldly writ,
Yet judged with coolness, though he sung with fire;
His precepts teach but what his works inspire.   660
Our critics take a contrary extreme.
They judge with fury, but they write with phlegm:
Nor suffers Horace more in wrong translations
By wits, than critics in as wrong quotations.
    See Dionysius Homer's thoughts refine,
And call new beauties forth from every line!
    Fancy and art in gay Petronius please,
The scholar's learning, with the courtier's ease.
    In grave Quintilian's copious work, we find
The justest rules and clearest method joined: 670
Thus useful arms in magazines we place,

All ranged in order, and disposed with grace,
But less to please the eye, than arm the hand,
Still fit for use, and ready at command.
        Thee, bold Longinus! all the Nine inspire,
And bless their critic with a poet's fire.
An ardent judge, who, zealous in his trust,
With warmth gives sentence, yet is always just:
Whose own example strengthens all his laws;
And is himself that great sublime he draws.   680
        Thus long succeeding critics justly reigned,
License repressed, and useful laws ordained.
Learning and Rome alike in empire grew;
And arts still followed where her eagles flew;
From the same foes, at last, both felt their doom,
And the same age saw learning fall, and Rome.
With tyranny then superstition joined.
As that the body, this enslaved the mind;
Much was believed, but little understood,
And to be dull was construed to be good;   690
A second deluge learning thus o'errun,
And the monks finished what the Goths begun.
        At length Erasmus, that great injured name
(The glory of the priesthood, and the shame!)
Stemmed the wild torrent of a barbarous age,
And drove those holy Vandals off the stage.
        But see! each muse, in Leo's golden days,
Starts from her trance, and trims her withered bays;
Rome's ancient genius, o'er its ruins spread,
Shakes off the dust, and rears his reverent head.   700
Then sculpture and her sister arts revive;
Stones leaped to form, and rocks began to live;
With sweeter notes each rising temple rung;
A Raphael painted, and a Vida sung.
Immortal Vida! on whose honored brow
The poet's bays, and critic's ivy grow:
Cremona now shall ever boast thy name,
As next in place to Mantua, next in fame!
        But soon by impious arms from Latium chased,

Their ancient bounds the banished muses passed.   710
Thence arts o'er all the northern world advance,
But critic-learning flourished most in France ;
The rules a nation born to serve, obeys ;
And Boileau still in right of Horace sways.
But we, brave Britons, foreign laws despised,
And kept unconquered and uncivilized ;
Fierce for the liberties of wit, and bold,
We still defied the Romans, as of old.
Yet some there were, among the sounder few
Of those who less presumed and better knew,   720
Who durst assert the juster ancient cause,
And here restored wit's fundamental laws.
Such was the muse, whose rule and practice tell
" Nature's chief masterpiece is writing well."
Such was Roscommon, not more learned than good,
With manners generous as his noble blood ;
To him the wit of Greece and Rome was known,
And every author's merit, but his own.
Such late was Walsh — the muse's judge and friend,
Who justly knew to blame or to commend ;   730
To failings mild, but zealous for desert ;
The clearest head, and the sincerest heart.
This humble praise, lamented shade ! receive,
This praise at least a grateful muse may give :
The muse, whose early voice you taught to sing,
Prescribed her heights, and pruned her tender wing,
(Her guide now lost) no more attempts to rise,
But in low numbers short excursions tries ;
Content, if hence the unlearned their wants may view,
The learned reflect on what before they knew :   740
Careless of censure, nor too fond of fame ;
Still pleased to praise, yet not afraid to blame ;
Averse alike to flatter, or offend ;
Not free from faults, nor yet too vain to mend.

NOTES TO ESSAY ON CRITICISM.

(The numbers refer to lines.)

4. *Sense* = understanding, judgment.

15. *Who* has *such* for its antecedent. The meaning is, Let those who excel teach others.

17. *Wit* = genius. As we shall see, *wit* is used in a variety of meanings in the poem.

20. *Most* qualifies *persons* understood. The full form of expression would be, "We shall find (that) most (persons) have," etc.

26. *Schools* = different systems of philosophy, science, and theology.

34. *Mævius* = an insignificant poet of the Augustan age, who attacked the writings of Virgil and Horace. He owes the preservation of his name to the fact that these two great poets made him a subject of ridicule. — *Apollo* was the president and protector of the Muses.

35. *Who* has *those* understood as its antecedent. "There are (those) who judge," etc.

36. *Wits* = men of learning or genius.

43. *Their generation*, etc. = their formation is so doubtful, uncertain. A reference to the belief that insects were generated by the mud of the Nile.

52. *Fit* = suitable, proper.

53. *Wit* = intellect, mind.

66. *Several* = separate, particular.

72. *Life, force, and beauty* are in the objective case after *must impart.*

73. This line is in apposition with *nature.*

76. *Informing* = imbuing and actuating with vitality.

80. *Wit* = genius; but as implied in the next line, *judgment.*

84. *'Tis more to guide* = it is more important to guide.

86. *Winged courser* = Pegasus, a winged horse of the Muses.

92. *Indites* = composes, produces.

94. *Parnassus* = a mountain in Greece, celebrated in mythology as sacred to Apollo and the Muses.

97. *Equal steps* = like or corresponding steps.

109. *Bills* = prescriptions.

120. *Fable* = plot.

124. *Homer* = the author of the "Iliad," and the greatest epic poet of antiquity. Seven Grecian cities contended for the honor of having given him birth.

129. *Mantuan Muse* = Virgil, who was born near Mantua, 70 B.C. After Homer, the greatest poet of antiquity. His full name was Publius Virgilius Maro, the latter part of which appears in the next line. It is said that before writing the "Æneid," he contemplated a poem on Alban and Roman affairs, but found the subject beyond his powers.

133. *But* = except.

138. *Stagirite* = Aristotle. He was born at Stagira, a town in Macedonia; hence the name Stagirite.

142. *Happiness* = fortuitous elegance or felicity of expression.

158. *Prospects* = landscapes.

183. *Secure from flames*, etc. — "The poet here alludes to the four principal causes of the ravage among ancient writings. The destruction of the Alexandrine and Palatine libraries by *fire*, the fiercer rage of *Zoilus, Mævius*, and their followers, against wit; the irruption of the Barbarians into the empire; and the long reign of ignorance and superstition in the cloisters." — WARTON.

186. *Pæans* = a song of rejoicing, among the ancients, in honor of Apollo.

216. *Pierian* = pertaining to the Muses. From Mount Pierus, in Thessaly, sacred to the Muses.

218. *Drinking largely* is the subject of *sobers*.

237. *That malignant dull delight*, that is, of seeking to find slight faults.

248. *Even thine, O Rome!* = the dome of St. Peter's, designed by Michael Angelo.

265. *Notions* = judgments, opinions.

267. *La Mancha's Knight* = Don Quixote, the hero of a work written by Cervantes, a Spanish author, in 1605.

270. *Dennis* = a mediocre author, born in 1657. For an account of his literary quarrels, see the sketch of Pope.

286. *Curious* = difficult to please. — *Nice* = over-scrupulous, hard to please.

289. *Conceit* = odd, fanciful notion, affected conception.

308. *Content* = acquiescence without examination.

322. *Sort* = suit, fit.

328. *Fungoso* = a character in one of Ben Jonson's plays, who assumed the dress and tried to pass himself off for another.

329. *Sparks* = gay, showy men.

337. *Most* = most persons or critics.

344. *These* = these persons.

356. *Alexandrine* = a verse consisting of twelve syllables; so called from a French poem on the life of Alexander written in that measure. The next line is an Alexandrine.

361. Sir John Denham was born at Dublin in 1615, and died in 1668. His poems contain here and there an expression of considerable force. — Edmund Waller was born in 1606 and died in 1687. See reference to Waller in preceding pages.

366. *Zephyr* = strictly the west wind; but poetically, any soft, gentle breeze.

370. *Ajax* = a hero of the Trojan war, represented by Homer as, next to Achilles, the bravest and handsomest of the Greeks.

372. *Camilla* = Queen of the Volscians, an army of whom she led to battle against Æneas. She was so remarkable for her swiftness that she is described by the poets as flying over the corn without bending the stalks, and skimming over the surface of the water without wetting her feet.

374. *Timotheus* = a celebrated musician of Thebes in Bœotia. Invited to attend the nuptials of Alexander the Great, he is said to have animated that monarch in so powerful a degree that he started up and seized his arms. Dryden made use of the incident in his celebrated ode, "Alexander's Feast."

376. *Son of Libyan Jove* = a title assumed by Alexander.

394. *Some* is the subject of *despise* understood. "Some (despise) foreign writers."

400. *Sublimes* = exalts.

404. *Each* qualifies *age* understood.

415. *Quality* = high rank, superior birth or station.

418. *Madrigal* = a short lyrical poem, adapted to the quaint and terse expression of some pleasant thought, generally on the subject of love.

424. *The vulgar* = the common people.

440. *School-divines* = school-men; that is, philosophers and divines of the Middle Ages, who adopted the principles of Aristotle, and spent much time on points of abstract speculation, sometimes ridiculous in character.

441. *Sentences* = passages from recognized authorities in the church.

444. *Scotists* = followers of Duns Scotus, one of the most famous school-men of the fourteenth century. He taught at Oxford and Paris. He was distinguished for the zeal and ability with which he defended the immaculate conception of the Virgin — a doctrine that was, in 1854, declared by papal authority to be a necessary article of the Roman Catholic faith. At the Renaissance the Scotists opposed the new learning, and added the word *dunce*, that is, a *Dunsman*, to our language. — *Thomists* = followers of Thomas Aquinas, one of the ablest school-men of the thirteenth century. He taught at Paris, Rome, Bologna, and Pisa. He denied the immaculate conception.

The works of these authors abounded, not in useful knowledge, but in fine-spun theories and argumentation.

445. *Duck Lane* = a place in London where old books were sold.

447. " *What wonder* [is it that] modes in wit," etc.

449. *Ready* = keen, prompt. Understand *to be* after *proves*.

459. *Parsons, critics, beaux.* — Referring to Jeremy Collier, and the Duke of Buckingham.

463. *Blackmores* = Sir Richard Blackmore, one of the court physicians in the reigns of William III. and Anne, and characterized " as the most voluminous and heavy poetaster of his own or any other age." — *Millbourn* = Rev. Luke Millbourn, who criticised Dryden with much justice.

465. *Zoilus* = a grammarian and sophist of Amphipolis, who rendered himself known by his severe criticisms on the poems of Homer, for which he received the nickname, " Chastiser of Homer." See note on line 183.

479. *Patriarch-wits* = the antediluvians.

495. *Brings* = causes.

496. *Its* refers to *wit* or genius.

509. *Commence* = begin or appear to be.

536. *Easy monarch* = Charles II.

545. *Socinus.* — Faustus and Lælius Socinus were Italian theologians of the sixteenth century, who denied the Trinity, the deity of Christ, the personality of the devil, the native and total depravity of man, the vicarious atonement, and the eternity of future punishment.

552. *Titans* = fabled giants of ancient mythology, who made war against the gods.

564. *Sense* = judgment. The same also in line 566.

585. *Appius* = Dennis. See sketch of Pope for an account of the literary quarrel of the two poets.

599. *So long* = to such an extent.

606. " *Run on* [as] *poets*," etc.

617. *Durfey* = Thomas D'Urfey, a writer of plays and poems in the reign of Charles II., with whom he was a favorite for his wit, liveliness, and songs. He is best remembered for his collection of songs, entitled " Pills to Purge Melancholy," the tales here referred to by Pope.

619. *Garth* = Sir Samuel Garth, an eminent physician and poet of some reputation, born in 1660. His professional skill was associated with great conversational powers. His best-known work is " The Dispensary," a poetical satire on the apothecaries and those physicians who sided with them in opposing the project of giving medicine gratuitously to the sick poor.

623. *Paul's Churchyard* = headquarters of the London booksellers before the great fire.

645. *Stagirite.* — See note on line 138.

648. *Mæonian star* = Homer, who is supposed by some to have been born in Mæonia, a district in Asia Minor. Aristotle derived many of his elements of criticism from Homer.

652. *Who conquered nature* = Aristotle, the greatest naturalist of his day. He wrote a Natural History, Physics, and Astronomy, in addition to his metaphysical treatises.

665. *Dionysius* was a learned critic and rhetorician, as well as historian. He was born at Halicarnassus, about 50 B.C., but came to Rome in early manhood, where he spent the remainder of his life. Among his critical works the principal are *Censura Veterum Scriptorum, Ars Rhetorica,* and *De Compositione Verborum,* which are said to possess high literary merit.

667. *Petronius* = a Roman voluptuary at the court of Nero, whose profligacy is said to have been of the most elegant description. He had charge of the royal entertainments. He is the author, it is believed, of a work entitled *Petronii Arbitri Satyricon,* which gives a horrible picture of the depravity of the times.

669. *Quintilian* = a celebrated teacher of rhetoric and oratory at Rome. He was born in Spain in 40 A.D. His chief work, entitled *De Institutione Oratoria,* is a complete system of rhetoric. He stood high in the favor of the Emperor Domitian.

675. *Longinus* = a Platonic philosopher and famous rhetorician, who was born, according to some, in Syria, and, according to others, in Athens, about 213 A.D. His knowledge was so extensive that he was called a " living library " and a " walking museum;" hence Pope speaks of him as inspired of all the nine Muses. He was probably the best critic of antiquity. The only work that has come down to us is a treatise " On the Sublime."

692. *Goths* = a powerful Germanic nation that had no small part in the destruction of the Roman Empire.

693. *Erasmus* = a distinguished scholar of the period of the Reformation. He was born at Rotterdam in 1467. He became a monk, but afterwards was absolved from his monastic vows by the pope. He did much to promote the revival of learning. His best-known work is his *Colloquia,* which contains a vigorous denunciation of monastic life, festivals, and pilgrimages. The best scholar, perhaps, of his day.

696. *Vandals* = monks. The *Vandals* were a famous race of European barbarians, probably of Germanic origin. They successively overran Gaul, Spain, and Italy. In 455 A.D. they plundered Rome; and the manner in which they mutilated and destroyed the works of art in the city has originated the term *vandalism.*

697. *Leo* = Leo X., who reigned as pope from 1513 to 1521. He was a patron of learning and art, and his court was the meeting-point of all the

scholars of Italy and the world. During his pontificate the Reformation began, which he at first described as " a squabble among the friars."

704. *Raphael* was born in 1483, and died in 1520. He is ranked almost by universal opinion as the greatest of painters. He was employed by Leo X., who kept his great powers constantly in exercise. The great frescoes of the Vatican are his work. — *Vida* was a learned Latinist and profound scholar, as well as poet. He was born at Cremona, near Mantua, the birth-place of Virgil, in 1485. Among his best-known works is *De Arte Poetica*, to which the poet here refers.

714. *Boileau* = an illustrious French poet, born near Paris in 1636. As a sage critic, he exerted an immense influence upon French literature. Voltaire pronounced him " the legislator of Parnassus." In 1674 he published *L'Art Poétique*, which Pope has imitated in the present poem.

723. *Such was the muse*, etc. A reference to the Duke of Buckingham's " Essay on Poetry."

725. *Roscommon* = the Earl of Roscommon, born in Ireland in 1634. He wrote an " Essay on Translated Verse," and rendered Horace's *Ars Poetica* into English blank verse.

729. *Walsh* = William Walsh, a poet, man of fashion, and member of Parliament. He was a friend of both Dryden and Pope. He published, in 1691, a " Dialogue concerning Women," in prose. See the sketch of Pope for an account of their relationship.

THE AGE OF JOHNSON.

REPRESENTATIVE WRITERS.

BURNS, GOLDSMITH, JOHNSON.

OTHER PROMINENT WRITERS.

Poets. — AKENSIDE, GRAY, COWPER.

Historians. — HUME, ROBERTSON, GIBBON.

Orators. — PITT, BURKE, SHERIDAN.

VI.

AGE OF JOHNSON.

(1750-1800.)

GENERAL SURVEY. — The age of Johnson includes the second half of the eighteenth century. It is here named after the great literary dictator simply as a matter of convenience. While he was the centre of an influential literary group for many years, and is the most prominent and picturesque literary figure of his time, other and mightier influences were giving a new tone to literature.

In great measure Johnson bore the impress of the preceding period. In his poetry he is coldly classical; and in a part at least of his prose, he is an imitator of Addison. (The real characteristic of this second half of the eighteenth century is transition.) By the side of the literary forms and canons of the age of Pope, there arose a new kind of writing distinguished by a return to nature. Artificial poetry had already been carried to its utmost limits; and if literature was to reach a higher excellence, it was obliged to assume a new form. And to this it was urged by the momentous social, political, and religious changes that took place, not only in England, but on the Continent and in America during the latter part of the century.

In their onward course mankind made a marked advance. In social and political relations the rights of men were more clearly recognized, and the brotherhood of mankind began to affect existing customs and institutions. As in all great forward movements of the world, a variety of causes co-operated in bringing about great changes. Unwilling hands often played an important part. The stupidity and obstinacy of George III. and of some of his ministers hastened the formal declaration of those principles of liberty which mark a new era in civil government.

A strong tendency of the age was crystallized in the Declaration of Independence. " We hold these truths to be self-evident," said the wise and courageous representatives of the American colonists, "that all men are created equal ; that they are endowed by their Creator with certain unalienable rights ; that among these are life, liberty, and the pursuit of happiness ; that, to secure these rights, governments are instituted among men, deriving their just powers from the consent of the governed ; that, whenever any form of government becomes destructive of these ends, it is the right of the people to alter or to abolish it, and to institute a new government, laying its foundation on such principles, and organizing its powers in such form as to them shall seem most likely to effect their safety and happiness." This solemn declaration sounded the knell of absolutism in the world. It is a political gospel that is destined to leaven the whole lump.

But how came the American colonists to a recognition of the weighty truths embodied in this declaration ? They simply voiced the growing spirit of the age. The greater diffusion of knowledge had opened the eyes of men to a better perception of truth. The force of custom and prejudice was in a measure broken. The claims of superiority set up by privileged classes were seen to be baseless, and injustice and oppression in the state were discerned and denounced.

In England there was a noteworthy advance in popular intelligence. Remarkable inventions in the mechanic arts placed new power in the hands of the producing classes. The use of coal in smelting iron; the opening of canals throughout England; the invention of the spinning-jenny and power-loom; the perfecting of the steam-engine with its wide application to manufacturing purposes — all this brought people together in large communities, greatly raised the average intelligence, and established the industrial supremacy of England.

Printing-presses were set up in every town; circulating libraries were opened; newspapers were multiplied; and monthly magazines and reviews fostered the general intelligence that called them into being. The proceedings of Parliament were regularly published, and naturally became the subject of discussion in every club-room, and at many a hearthstone.

The principles of political economy, especially after the publication of Adam Smith's "Wealth of Nations," received increased and more intelligent attention.

The result of all this was inevitable; men came to a clearer recognition of their interests and their rights.

The moral and religious state of society showed marked improvement. Grossness gave way to decorum in life. Indecency was almost wholly banished from the stage and from literature. This happy change is illustrated in an incident told us by Sir Walter Scott. His grand-aunt assured him that, when led by curiosity to turn over the pages of a novel in which she had delighted in her youth, she was astonished to find that, sitting alone at the age of eighty, she was unable to read without shame a book which sixty years before she had heard read out for amusement in large circles, consisting of the best society in London.

This improved moral tone was not restricted to sentiment. One of the noble features of this period was the active efforts to improve the condition of the unfortunate and the oppressed. The slave-trade, which Englishmen had long made a source of profitable commerce, was abolished. Hospitals were established. Howard, by his noble enthusiasm and incessant labors, secured a reform in prison discipline. Robert Raikes of Gloucester established the Sunday-school, which for England was the beginning of popular education.

These facts help us to understand one of the noteworthy literary features of the period. It is the relative predominance of prose. Poetry retires somewhat into the background. Fancy gives way to reason. It was a practical age, largely absorbed in material advancement and political and social reform. The task laid on the age was too serious to encourage merely the pleasures of the imagination. It was a time for thought and action.

Historical writing attained an excellence that has scarcely been surpassed. There arose three great historians, who brought to their narratives philosophical insight, and a finished excellence of style. Hume, Robertson, and Gibbon are imperishable names.

It was an age noted for its oratory. The world has never seen a group of greater orators than Chatham, Pitt, Burke, and Sheridan. Great questions of government presented themselves for consideration and action.

Through the activity of the press, eloquence was no longer confined within the walls of Parliament.

The principles of human liberty, of sound political economy, and of manly integrity have never had better utterance. The spirit of true patriotism never found nobler embodiment. " Sir," exclaimed Pitt, after the passage of the Stamp Act had aroused resistance, " I rejoice that America has resisted. Three millions of people so dead to all the feelings of liberty as voluntarily to submit to be slaves would have been fit instruments to make slaves of the rest."

ROBERT BURNS.

THE greatest poet of Scotland and the best song writer of the world — such is but a moderate estimate of Burns. Scarcely any one will be found to claim less, and some to claim more. A careful study of his writings, in connection with the unfavorable circumstances of his life, impresses us with his extraordinary genius. He was the greatest poetic genius produced by Great Britain in the eighteenth century. A peculiar interest attaches to him. His great natural gifts were hampered by poverty and manual toil, and enslaved by evil habits, so that he accomplished only a small part of what was possible for him. That his genius was chained by untoward circumstances awakens our profound pity and regret; and that he weakly yielded to intemperance and immorality arouses our censure and indignation.

His life was a tragedy — a proud and powerful mind overcome at length in the hard struggle of life. The catastrophe was unspeakably sad; yet — let not our admiration of his gifts blind our judgment — Burns himself, and not an unkind destiny, was chiefly to blame. Genius has no exemption from the ordinary rules of morality. If he had abstained from drunken carousals and illicit amours, his life might have been crowned with beauty and honor. No doubt, as is often charitably said, he had strong passions and severe temptations; but these he ought to have resisted; for, as Carlyle says, "Nature fashions no creature without implanting in it the strength needful for its action and duration; least of all does she so neglect her masterpiece and darling, the poetic soul."

Robert Burns was born in a clay-built cottage two miles from the town of Ayr in 1759. His father was a man of strict integrity and deep piety. We have an imperishable portrait of him in "The Cotter's Saturday Night." His early years were spent on a small, unfruitful farm in poverty and toil. His strength was overtaxed, his shoulders became stooped, and his nervous system was weakened. He afterwards spoke of this period as combining "the cheerless gloom of a hermit with the unceasing moil of a galley slave."

Yet this hardship was not without some relief. His humble home was sweetened with kindness and love ; and the future poet was taught, first in school and afterwards by his father, the elements of learning. His mind was enlarged and his taste refined by works of the highest merit. His early reading included "The Spectator," Shakespeare, Pope, and Locke's "Human Understanding."

In his fifteenth year his genius was awakened under the sweet spell of love. "You know," he says, "our country custom of coupling a man and woman together as partners in the labors of harvest. In my fifteenth summer my partner was a bewitching creature, a year younger than myself. My scarcity of English denies me the power of doing her justice in that language ; but you know the Scottish idiom. She was a bonnie, sweet, sonsie lass. In short, she, altogether unwittingly to herself, initiated me into that delicious passion which, in spite of acid disappointment, gin-horse prudence, and bookworm philosophy, I hold to be the first of human joys here below." The first offspring of his muse was entitled "Handsome Nell," which, though he afterwards spoke of it as puerile, still contains a touch of that charming simplicity of thought and expression which characterizes so much of his poetry. Is not this stanza delightful ?

> " She dresses aye sae clean and neat,
>   Baith decent and genteel,
> And then there's something in her gait
>   Gars [1] ony dress look weel."

At the age of nineteen he went to Kirkoswald to study mensuration and surveying. It turned out to be a bad move. The

---

[1] Makes.

town was frequented by smugglers and adventurers; and Burns was introduced into scenes of what he calls "swaggering riot and roaring dissipation." He worked at his mensuration with sufficient diligence till he one day met a pretty lass and fell in love. The current of his thought was turned from mathematics to poetry, and put an end to his studies. Love-making now became a common business with him. He composed a song on every pretty girl he knew. The most beautiful of the songs of this period is his " Mary Morison," which was inspired by a real affection : —

> " Yestreen, when to the trembling string,
>   The dance gaed thro' the lighted ha',
> To thee my fancy took its wing,
>   I sat, but neither heard nor saw :
> Tho' this was fair, and that was braw,
>   And yon the toast of a' the town,
> I sigh'd and said amang them a',
>   Ye are na Mary Morison.
>
> Oh, Mary, canst thou wreck his peace,
>   Wha for thy sake wad gladly die;
> Or canst thou break that heart of his,
>   Whase only faut is loving thee?
> If love for love thou wilt na gie,
>   At least be pity to me shown;
> A thought ungentle canna be
>   The thought o' Mary Morison."

In spite of his sweet love songs his suit was rejected — an incident that long cast a shadow over his inner life. He was a great reader. He possessed a " Collection of English Songs ; " and this he says, " was my vade-mecum. I pored over them driving my cart, or walking to labor, song by song, verse by verse ; carefully noticing the true, tender, or sublime, from affectation or fustian ; and I am convinced I owe to this practice much of my critic craft, such as it is." A consciousness of his strength began to dawn upon him and to fill his mind with a great ambition. Amidst his varied labors on the farm, as a beardless boy, he felt —

> " E'en then a wish, I mind its power,
>   A wish that to my latest hour
>   Shall strongly heave my breast :
>   That I for poor auld Scotland's sake,
>   Some useful plan or book could make,
>   Or sing a sang at least."

In the summer of 1781 he went to Irvine to learn the flax-dressing business in the hope of increasing thereby the profits of farming. It turned out to be a disastrous undertaking. As at Kirkoswald, he fell into the company of smugglers and adventurers, by whom he was encouraged in loose opinions and bad habits. With the unsettling of his religious convictions, he overleaped the restraints that had hitherto kept him in the path of virtue.

His flax-dressing came to an abrupt close. He was robbed by his partner ; and his shop took fire at a New Year's carousal, and was burnt to the ground. Dispirited and tormented with an evil conscience, he returned to his home, which was soon to be overshadowed by the death of his father. " Whoever lives to see it," the old man had said, " something extraordinary will come from that boy." But he went to the grave sorely troubled with apprehensions about the future of his gifted son.

Burns now made an effort to reform. In his own words, " I read farming books, I calculated crops, I attended markets, and, in short, in spite of the devil, the world, and the flesh, I should have been a wise man ; but the first year, from unfortunately buying bad seed, the second, from a late harvest, we lost half our crops. This overset all my wisdom ; and I returned like the dog to his vomit, and the sow that was washed to her wallowing in the mire." He came under ecclesiastical discipline for immorality, and revenged himself by lashing the minister and church officers with keen and merciless satire. His series of religious satires, in spite of all their inimitable brilliancy of wit, reflect little credit either on his judgment or his character. While his harvests were failing, and his business interests were all going against him, he found solace in rhyme. As he says, —

> "Leeze me [1] on rhyme ! it's aye a treasure,
>   My chief, amaist my only pleasure,
>   At hame, a-fiel', at wark, at leisure,
>   The Muse, poor hizzie !
>   Tho' rough and raplock [2] be her measure,
>   She's seldom lazy."

The year (1785) while he was laboring with his brother on a farm at Mossgiel, saw the greatest activity of his muse.   It was at that time that he composed "To a Mouse," "The Cotter's Saturday Night," "Address to the Deil," "Man Was Made to Mourn," and "The Mountain Daisy," which established his fame on a lasting foundation.   They were composed behind the plough, and afterwards written in a little farmhouse garret. "Thither," says Chambers, "when he had returned from his day's work, the poet used to retire, and seat himself at a small deal table, lighted by a narrow skylight in the roof, to transcribe the verses which he had composed in the fields.   His favorite time for composition was at the plough."

His immoral conduct again brought him into serious trouble. The indignant father of Jean Armour put the officers of the law upon his track.   By a subsequent marriage with Jean, he did something in the way of repairing the wrong.   While lurking in concealment, he resolved to emigrate to Jamaica ; and to secure the necessary means for the voyage, he published a volume of his poems in 1786.

The result altered all his plans.   The volume took Scotland by storm.   "Old and young," says a contemporary, "high and low, grave and gay, learned and ignorant, were alike delighted, agitated, transported.   I was at that time resident in Galloway, contiguous to Ayrshire, and I can well remember how even plough-boys and maid-servants would have gladly bestowed the wages they earned most hardly, and which they wanted to purchase necessary clothing, if they might procure the works of Burns."

As a financial venture, the volume brought him only twenty

----

[1] I am happy in rhyme.   [2] Coarse.

pounds ; but what was of more importance, it retained him in his native country, and introduced him to the noble and the learned of Edinburgh. He has left a humorous account of the first time he met a nobleman socially, and " dinner'd wi' a Lord " : —

> " But wi' a Lord ! stand out my shin,
> A Lord — a Peer, an Earl's son !
> Up higher yet my bonnet !
> And sic a Lord ! lang Scotch ells twa,
> Our Peerage he o'erlooks them a',
> As I look o'er a sonnet."

Professor Dugald Stewart has given an interesting account of Burns's bearing on the same occasion : " His manners were then, as they continued ever afterwards, simple, manly, and independent ; strongly expressive of conscious genius and worth, but without anything that indicated forwardness, arrogance, or vanity. He took his share in conversation, but not more than belonged to him ; and listened with apparent attention and deference on subjects where his want of education deprived him of the means of information."

In November, 1786, Burns deemed it wise to visit the Scottish metropolis. His journey thither on horseback was a continued ovation. He occupied very humble quarters, lodging in a small room costing three shillings a week. From this lowly abode he went forth into the best society of Edinburgh, to which his genius gained him ready admission. He was the social lion of the day.

The Scottish capital was noted at this time for the literary talent gathered there. In the most polished drawing-rooms of the city, Burns met Dugald Stewart, William Robertson, Adam Smith, Hugh Blair, and others of scarcely less celebrity. He did not suffer from this contact with the ablest men of his country. Indeed, it has been said by one who knew him well that poetry was not his forte: His brilliant conversation — his vigorous thought, sparkling wit, and trenchant style — sometimes eclipsed his poetry.

His manner was open and manly, a consciousness of native strength preserving him from all servility. He showed, as Lockhart says, "in the strain of his bearing his belief that in the society of the most eminent men of his nation he was where he was entitled to be, hardly deigning to flatter them by exhibiting a symptom of being flattered." He was especially pleasing to ladies, "fairly carrying them off their feet," as one of them said, "by his deference of manner and the mingled humor and pathos of his talk."

He cherished a proud feeling of independence. He emphasized individual worth, and looked with contempt on what may be regarded as the mere accidents of birth or fortune. To this feeling, which finds a response in every noble breast, he gave powerful expression in his song, "A Man's a Man for a' That ": —

> " Is there, for honest poverty,
>   That hangs his head, and a' that?
> The coward slave, we pass him by;
>   We dare be puir for a' that.
> For a' that, and a' that,
>   Our toils obscure and a' that,
> The rank is but the guinea-stamp —
>   The man's the gowd [1] for a' that."

He chafed under the inequalities of fortune he discovered in society, and sometimes showed an inconsiderate bitterness of feeling. "There are few of the sore evils under the sun give me more uneasiness and chagrin," he writes in his diary, "than the comparison how a man of genius, nay, of avowed worth, is received everywhere, with the reception which a mere ordinary character, decorated with the trappings and futile distinctions of fortune meets." "He had not yet learned — he never did learn" — says Principal Shairp, "that lesson, that the genius he had received was his allotted and sufficient portion ; and that his wisdom lay in making the most of this rare inward gift, even on a meagre allowance of this world's external goods."

[1] Gold.

Unfortunately for Burns he did not confine himself to the cultivated circles of Edinburgh. He frequented the social clubs that gathered nightly in the taverns. Here he threw off all restraint, and the mirth frequently became fast and furious. Deep drinking, rough raillery, and coarse songs made up the sum of these revellings, which served at once to deprave the poet's character and to ruin his reputation.

In 1787 the ostensible purpose for which Burns had come to Edinburgh was accomplished, and a second volume of his poems was issued by the leading publisher of the city. He then made two brief tours through the border districts and the highlands of Scotland for the purpose of visiting points celebrated for beauty of scenery or consecrated by heroic deeds. He returned for a few months to Edinburgh; but the coarse revelries of his previous visit had undermined his influence, and he met with only a cold reception.

Before leaving the city he received an appointment in the Excise. He had hoped for something better. But he wrote to a friend: "The question is not at what door of fortune's palace shall we enter in, but what doors does she open for us." He also leased a farm at Ellisland, which he had long set his heart on.

Returning to Ayrshire, he married Jean Armour, whom the poet had a second time betrayed, and whom an angered father had thrust from his door. The poet writes: "I have married my Jean. I had a long-and much-loved fellow-creature's happiness or misery in my determination, and I durst not trifle with so important a deposit, nor have I any cause to repent it. If I have not got polite tittle-tattle, modish manners, and fashionable dress, I am not sickened and disquieted with the multiform curse of boarding-school affectation; and I have got the handsomest figure, the sweetest temper, the soundest constitution, and the kindest heart in the country." The truth of this characterization is established by the patience with which Jean bore the irregularities of her husband's life.

His farm at Ellisland proved a failure. His duties as exciseman, besides leading him into bad company, prevented that strict supervision of farm work which was necessary to success. He suffered much from depression of spirits, to which the recollections of his wayward life contributed no small part. "Alas!" he writes, "who would wish for many years? What is it but to drag existence until our joys gradually expire, and leave us in a night of misery, like the gloom which blots out the stars, one by one from the face of heaven, and leaves us without a ray of comfort in the howling waste?"

He continued to find at intervals solace in poetry. One morning he heard the report of a gun, and shortly after saw a poor wounded hare limping by. The condition of the little animal touched his heart, and called forth the excellent poem "On Seeing a Wounded Hare Limp by Me," written in classic English : —

> " Go live, poor wanderer of the wood and field,
>   The bitter little that of life remains:
>   No more the thickening brakes and verdant plains
> To thee shall home, or food, or pastime yield."

We meet with this tender sympathy with nature, and strong sense of fellowship with lower creatures, in many of his poems. It is one secret of their charm. In the poem "To a Mouse" is the following : —

> " I'm truly sorry man's dominion
>   Has broken Nature's social union,
>   An' justifies that ill opinion
>   Which makes thee startle
>   At me, thy poor earth-born companion
>   An' fellow-mortal ! "

The cold blasts of a winter night remind him of —

> " Ilk happing bird, wee helpless thing,
>   That in the merry months o' spring
>   Delighted me to hear thee sing,
>   What comes o' thee?
>   Where wilt thou cower thy chittering wing,
>   And close thy e'e? "

The choicest products of this sojourn at Ellisland are the immortal "Tale o' Tam o' Shanter," and "To Mary in Heaven." The latter is a song of deep pathos. Years before he had loved his "Highland Mary" with a deep devotion. Their parting by the banks of Ayr — which the untimely death of Mary made the last — was attended with vows of eternal constancy. Her memory never vanished from the poet's mind. On the anniversary of her death, in October, 1786, he grew sad and wandered about his farmyard the whole night in deep agitation of mind. As dawn approached he was persuaded by his wife to enter the house, when he sat down and wrote those pathetic lines, beginning : —

> " Thou lingering star with lessening ray,
> That lov'st to greet the early morn,
> Again thou usherest in the day
> My Mary from my soul was torn.
> O Mary, dear departed shade !
> Where is thy place of blissful rest ?
> See'st thou thy lover lowly laid ?
> Hear'st thou the groans that rend his breast ? "

In 1791 Burns removed to Dumfries, and gave his whole time to the duties of the Excise, for which he received seventy pounds a year. At Ellisland he had written : —

> " To make a happy fireside clime,
> For weans and wife,
> Is the true pathos and sublime
> Of human life."

Unfortunately he did not live as wisely as he sang. His spirit became soured toward those more favored by fortune. His nights were frequently spent at the tavern with drinking cronies. His life is summed up in one of his letters : " Hurry of business, grinding the faces of the publican and the sinner on the merciless wheels of the Excise, making ballads, and then drinking and singing them ; and over and above all, correcting the press of two different publications."

In 1792 his aid was solicited in the preparation of "Melodies of Scotland." He entered into the undertaking with enthusiasm. When the editor, George Thompson of Edinburgh, once sent him some money in return for a number of songs, the poet wrote: "I assure you, my dear sir, that you truly hurt me with your pecuniary parcel. It degrades me in my own eyes. However, to return it would savor of affectation; but, as to any more traffic of that debtor and creditor kind, I swear by that honor which crowns the upright stature of Robert Burns's integrity, on the least motion of it, I will indignantly spurn the by-pact transaction, and from that moment commence entire stranger with you." In view of the financial straits into which he shortly afterwards came, this must be regarded as an unwise sacrifice of prudence to sentiment.

Burns strongly sympathized with the revolutionary movement in France; and to this feeling no less than to his Scottish patriotism, if we may believe his own account, we owe the thrilling lines of "Bruce's Address," which Carlyle says "should be sung with the throat of the whirlwind." The excellence of this poem has been questioned by Wordsworth and others; but let the following lines be read with something of the heroic fervor with which they were composed, and all doubts will be set at rest: —

> "Wha will be a traitor knave?
> Wha can fill a coward's grave?
> Wha so base as be a slave?
> Let him turn and flee."

The end was drawing near. The irregularities of his life had undermined his strong constitution. He was often serious. "I find that a man may live like a fool," he said to his friend, "but he will scarcely die like one." In April, 1796, he wrote: "Alas, my dear Thompson, I fear it will be some time before I tune my lyre again! By Babel streams I have sat and wept, almost ever since I wrote you last; I have known existence only by the pressure of the heavy hand of sickness, and have counted time by the repercussions of pain! Rheumatism, cold, and fever have formed to me a terrible combination. I close my eyes in misery and open them without hope. I look on the vernal day, and say, with poor Ferguson, —

> ' Say wherefore has an all-indulgent heaven
> Light to the comfortless and wretched given?' "

His last days were illumined now and then by flashes of poetic fire. For Jessie Lewars, a young girl that had seen the poet's need, and from sympathy had come into his home to assist in domestic duties, he wrote the following beautiful lines : —

> " Oh! wert thou in the cauld, cauld blast,
>   On yonder lea, on yonder lea,
> My plaidie to the angry airt,[1]
>   I'd shelter thee, I'd shelter thee.
> Or did misfortune's bitter storms
>   Around thee blaw, around thee blaw,
> Thy bield[2] should my bosom be,
>   To share it a', to share it a'.
>
> Or were I in the wildest waste,
>   Sae black and bare, sae black and bare,
> The desert were a paradise,
>   If thou wert there, if thou wert there:
> Or were I monarch o' the globe,
>   Wi' thee to reign, wi' thee to reign,
> The brightest jewel in my crown
>   Wad be my queen, wad be my queen."

The (21st of July, 1796,) with his children around his bed, the great poet of Scotland passed away. Let our final judgment of him as a man be tempered by the gentle spirit he commends in the " Address to the Unco Guid: " —

> " Then gently scan your brother man,
>   Still gentler sister woman;
> Tho' they may gang a kennin[3] wrang,
>   To step aside is human:

---

[1] Point of the compass.   [2] Shelter.   [3] Trifle.

> One point must still be greatly dark
>   The moving *why* they do it;
> And just as lamely can ye mark,
>   How far perhaps they rue it.

> Who made the heart, 'tis He alone
>   Decidedly can try us;
> He knows each chord — its various tone,
>   Each spring — its various bias;
> Then at the balance let's be mute,
>   We never can adjust it;
> What's *done* we partly may compute,
>   But know not what's *resisted*."

As a poet Burns's life was incomplete. His struggle with poverty and his bad habits left him only fragments of his power to be devoted to literature. He was not guided by the controlling influence of a great purpose. His efforts were spasmodic — the result of accidental circumstances. His genius has not the range of Shakespeare's; but within its limits it is unsurpassed. He was the greatest peasant poet that ever lived. Unlike Wordsworth, in whom the reflective element is largely developed, Burns is a painter of nature. He has glorified the landscape of his native land. Beyond all other poets he has caught the beauty, the humor, the pathos, of every-day life. He was thoroughly honest in his best writings. There is no attitudinizing in his poems, no pretence to unreal sentiment. He was a poet —

> "Whose songs gushed from his heart,
>   As drops from the clouds of summer,
>   Or tears from the eyelids start."

He felt deeply, and then poured forth his song because he could not otherwise find peace. He could not endure affectation, rant, hypocrisy. At heart devout before the great Author and Preserver of all things, he yet rebelled against some of the hard features religion had assumed. In his "Epistle to a Young Friend," his real feelings are indicated: —

"The great Creator to revere,
    Must sure become the creature;
But still the preaching cant forbear,
    And ev'n the rigid feature:
Yet ne'er with wits profane to range,
    Be complaisance extended;
An Atheist's laugh's a poor exchange
    For Deity offended.

When ranting round in pleasure's ring,
    Religion may be blinded;
Or, if she gie a random sting,
    It may be little minded:
But when on life we're tempest-driven,
    A conscience but a canker —
A correspondence fixed wi' Heaven,
    Is sure a noble anchor."

More than any other man he saw the beauty of a sincere religious life, to a portrayal of which he devoted the best of his poems. His sensibilities were extraordinarily sensitive and strong. "There is scarcely any earthly object," he says, "gives me more — I do not know if I should call it pleasure — but something which exalts me, something which enraptures me — than to walk in the sheltered side of a wood or high plantation in a cloudy winter day, and hear the stormy wind howling among the trees and raving over the plain. . . . I listened to the birds and frequently turned out of my path, lest I should disturb their little songs or frighten them to another station." With such a sensitive nature it is no wonder that we find contradictions in his poetry. The storm of emotion drives quickly from grave to gay, from high to low. He has written much that ought to be and will be forgotten. But upon the whole, his poetry is elevating in its tone — a treasure for which we ought to be thankful. It is the voice of a man who, with all his weakness and sin, was still, in his best moments, honest, manly, penetrating, and powerful.

THE COTTER'S SATURDAY NIGHT.

INSCRIBED TO R. AIKIN, ESQ.

"Let not ambition mock their useful toil,
    Their homely joys, and destiny obscure;
Nor grandeur hear, with a disdainful smile,
    The short and simple annals of the poor."
                                    GRAY.

I.

My lov'd, my honour'd, much respected friend!
    No mercenary bard his homage pays:
With honest pride I scorn each selfish end;
    My dearest meed, a friend's esteem and praise:
To you I sing, in simple Scottish lays,
    The lowly train in life's sequester'd scene;
The native feelings strong, the guileless ways;
    What Aikin in a cottage would have been:
Ah! tho' his worth unknown, far happier there, I ween.

II.

November chill blaws loud wi' angry sugh:
    The short'ning winter-day is near a close:
The miry beasts retreating frae the pleugh;
    The black'ning trains o' craws to their repose:
The toil-worn cotter frae his labour goes,
    This night his weekly moil is at an end,
Collects his spades, his mattocks, and his hoes,
    Hoping the morn in ease and rest to spend,
And weary, o'er the moor, his course does hameward bend.

III.

At length his lonely cot appears in view,
    Beneath the shelter of an aged tree:
Th' expectant wee-things, toddlin', stacher thro'
    To meet their dad, wi' flichterin' noise an' glee.

His wee bit ingle, blinkin' bonnily,
    His clean hearth-stane, his thriftie wifie's smile,
The lisping infant prattling on his knee,
    Does a' his weary, carking cares beguile,
An' makes him quite forget his labour and his toil.

IV.

Belyve, the elder bairns come drappin' in,
    At service out, amang the farmers roun':
Some ca' the pleugh, some herd, some tentie rin   30
    A cannie errand to a neebor town:
Their eldest hope, their Jenny, woman grown,
    In youthfu' bloom, love sparklin' in her e'e,
Comes hame, perhaps, to show a braw new gown,
    Or deposit her sair-won penny fee,
To help her parents dear, if they in hardship be.

V.

Wi' joy unfeign'd, brothers and sisters meet,
    And each for other's weelfare kindly spiers:
The social hours, swift-wing'd, unnotic'd fleet:
    Each tells the uncos that he sees or hears;   40
The parents, partial, eye their hopeful years;
    Anticipation forward points the view;
The mother, wi' her needle an' her shears,
    Gars auld claes look amaist as weel's the new; —
The father mixes a' wi' admonition due.

VI.

Their master's an' their mistress's command,
    The younkers a' are warnèd to obey;
An' mind their labours wi' an eydent hand,
    An' ne'er, tho' out o' sight, to jauk or play:
" An' O ! be sure to fear the Lord alway !   50
    An' mind your duty, duly, morn an' night !
Lest in temptation's path ye gang astray,
    Implore his counsel and assisting might:
They never sought in vain, that sought the Lord aright !"

VII.

But hark ! a rap comes gently to the door ;
    Jenny, wha kens the meaning o' the same,
Tells how a neebor lad cam' o'er the moor,
    To do some errands, and convoy her hame.
The wily mother sees the conscious flame
    Sparkle in Jenny's e'e, and flush her cheek ;   60
With heart-struck, anxious care, inquires his name,
    While Jenny hafflins is afraid to speak ;
Weel pleas'd the mother hears, it's nae wild, worthless rake.

VIII.

Wi' kindly welcome, Jenny brings him ben :
    A strappin' youth ; he taks the mother's eye ;
Blythe Jenny sees the visit's no ill ta'en ;
    The father cracks of horses, pleughs, and kye.
The youngster's artless heart o'erflows wi' joy,
    But blate and laithfu', scarce can weel behave ;
The mother, wi' a woman's wiles, can spy   70
    What makes the youth sae bashfu' an' sae grave ;
Weel pleas'd to think her bairn's respected like the lave.

IX.

O happy love ! where love like this is found !
    O heart-felt raptures ! — bliss beyond compare !
I've pacèd much this weary, mortal round,
    And sage experience bids me this declare —
" If heaven a draught of heavenly pleasure spare
    One cordial in this melancholy vale,
'Tis when a youthful, loving, modest pair,
    In other's arms, breathe out the tender tale,   80
Beneath the milk-white thorn that scents the ev'ning gale."

X.

Is there, in human form, that bears a heart —
    A wretch ! a villain ! lost to love and truth !
That can, with studied, sly, ensnaring art,
    Betray sweet Jenny's unsuspecting youth ?

Curse on his perjur'd arts! dissembling smooth!
 Are honour, virtue, conscience, all exil'd?
Is there no pity, no relenting ruth,
 Points to the parents fondling o'er their child?
Then paints the ruin'd maid, and their distraction wild?   90

XI.

But now the supper crowns their simple board,
 The halesome parritch, chief o' Scotia's food:
The sowpe their only hawkie does afford,
 That 'yont the hallan snugly chows her cood;
The dame brings forth in complimental mood,
 To grace the lad, her weel-hain'd kebbuck fell —
An' aft he's prest, an' aft he ca's it guid;
 The frugal wifie, garrulous, will tell,
How 'twas a towmond auld, sin' lint was i' the bell.

XII.

The cheerfu' supper done, wi' serious face,   100
 They, round the ingle, form a circle wide;
The sire turns o'er, wi' patriarchal grace,
 The big ha' Bible, ance his father's pride;
His bonnet rev'rently is laid aside,
 His lyart haffets wearing thin an' bare;
Those strains that once did sweet in Zion glide,
 He wales a portion with judicious care;
And " Let us worship God!" he says, with solemn air.

XIII.

They chant their artless notes in simple guise;
 They tune their hearts, by far the noblest aim: 110
Perhaps Dundee's wild warbling measures rise,
 Or plaintive Martyrs, worthy of the name,
Or noble Elgin beets the heav'nward flame,
 The sweetest far of Scotia's holy lays:
Compar'd with these, Italian trills are tame;
 The tickl'd ears no heart-felt raptures raise;
Nae unison hae they with our Creator's praise.

XIV.

The priest-like father reads the sacred page,
   How Abram was the friend of God on high;
Or, Moses bade eternal warfare wage
   With Amalek's ungracious progeny;
Or how the royal bard did groaning lie
   Beneath the stroke of Heav'n's avenging ire;
Or Job's pathetic plaint, and wailing cry;
   Or rapt Isaiah's wild, seraphic fire;
Or other holy seers that tune the sacred lyre.

XV.

Perhaps the Christian volume is the theme,
   How guiltless blood for guilty man was shed;
How He, who bore in heaven the second name,
   Had not on earth whereon to lay his head;   130
How his first followers and servants sped;
   The precepts sage they wrote to many a land:
How he, who lone in Patmos banishèd,
   Saw in the sun a mighty angel stand,
And heard great Bab'lon's doom pronounc'd by Heaven's command.

XVI.

Then kneeling down, to Heaven's Eternal King,
   The saint, the father, and the husband prays:
Hope " springs exulting on triumphant wing,"
   That thus they all shall meet in future days:
There ever bask in uncreated rays,   14c
   No more to sigh, or shed the bitter tear,
Together hymning their Creator's praise,
   In such society, yet still more dear;
While circling time moves round in an eternal sphere.

XVII.

Compar'd with this, how poor Religion's pride,
   In all the pomp of method and of art,
When men display to congregations wide,
   Devotion's ev'ry grace, except the heart!

The Pow'r, incensed, the pageant will desert,
    The pompous strain, the sacerdotal stole;   150
But, haply, in some cottage far apart,
    May hear, well pleased, the language of the soul;
And in the book of life the inmates poor enrol.

XVIII.

Then homeward all take off their sev'ral way;
    The youngling cottagers retire to rest;
The parent-pair their secret homage pay,
    And proffer up to Heaven the warm request,
That He, who stills the raven's clam'rous nest,
    And decks the lily fair in flow'ry pride,
Would, in the way his wisdom sees the best,   160
    For them and for their little ones provide;
But, chiefly, in their hearts with grace divine preside.

XIX.

From scenes like these, old Scotia's grandeur springs,
    That makes her loved at home, rever'd abroad:
Princes and lords are but the breath of kings,
    " An honest man's the noblest work of God : "
And certes, in fair virtue's heavenly road,
    The cottage leaves the palace far behind;
What is a lordling's pomp? — a cumbrous load,
    Disguising oft the wretch of human kind,   170
Studied in arts of hell, in wickedness refin'd!

XX.

O Scotia! my dear, my native soil!
    For whom my warmest wish to Heaven is sent!
Long may thy hardy sons of rustic toil
    Be bless'd with health, and peace, and sweet content!
And, O! may Heaven their simple lives prevent
    From luxury's contagion, weak and vile!
Then, howe'er crowns and coronets be rent,
    A virtuous populace may rise the while,
And stand a wall of fire around their much-lov'd isle.   180

XXI.

O Thou! who poured the patriotic tide
   That stream'd thro' Wallace's undaunted heart,
Who dared to nobly stem tyrannic pride,
   Or nobly die, the second glorious part:
(The patriot's God peculiarly thou art,
   His friend, inspirer, guardian, and reward!)
O never, never, Scotia's realm desert;
   But still the patriot, and the patriot bard,
In bright succession raise, her ornament and guard!

TO A MOUSE.

ON TURNING HER UP IN HER NEST WITH THE PLOUGH, NOVEMBER, 1785.

WEE, sleekit, cow'rin', tim'rous beastie,
O, what a panic's in thy breastie!
Thou need na start awa sae hasty,
        Wi' bickering brattle!
I wad be laith to rin an' chase thee,
        Wi' murdering pattle!

I'm truly sorry man's dominion
Has broken Nature's social union,
An' justifies that ill opinion
        Which makes thee startle
At me, thy poor earth-born companion,
        An' fellow-mortal!

I doubt na, whyles, but thou may thieve;
What then? poor beastie, thou maun live!
A daimen-icker in a thrave
        'S a sma' request:
I'll get a blessin' wi' the lave,
        And never miss't!

10

Thy wee bit housie, too, in ruin!
Its silly wa's the win's are strewin'!   20
An' naething, now, to big a new ane,
    O' foggage green!
An' bleak December's winds ensuin',
    Baith snell and keen!

Thou saw the fields laid bare an' waste,
And weary winter comin' fast,
And cozie, here, beneath the blast,
    Thou thought to dwell,
Till crash! the cruel coulter past
    Out thro' thy cell.   30

That wee bit heap o' leaves an' stibble,
Has cost thee mony a weary nibble!
Now thou's turn'd out, for a' thy trouble,
    But house or hald,
To thole the winter's sleety dribble,
    An' cranreuch cauld!

But, Mousie, thou art no thy lane,
In proving foresight may be vain:
The best laid schemes o' mice an' men,
    Gang aft a-gley,   40
An' lea'e us nought but grief and pain,
    For promis'd joy.

Still thou art blest, compar'd wi' me!
The present only toucheth thee:
But, Och! I backward cast my e'e
    On prospects drear;
An' forward, tho' I canna see,
    I guess an' fear.

TO A MOUNTAIN DAISY.

ON TURNING ONE DOWN WITH THE PLOUGH IN APRIL, 1786.

WEE, modest, crimson-tippèd flow'r,
Thou's met me in an evil hour;
For I maun crush among the stoure
    Thy slender stem;
To spare thee now is past my pow'r,
    Thou bonnie gem!

Alas! it's no thy neebor sweet,
The bonnie lark, companion meet!
Bending thee 'mang the dewy weet,
    Wi' spreckl'd breast,   10
When upward-springing, blithe to greet
    The purpling east.

Cauld blew the bitter-biting north
Upon thy early, humble birth;
Yet cheerfully thou glinted forth
    Amid the storm,
Scarce rear'd above the parent earth
    Thy tender form.

The flaunting flow'rs our gardens yield,
High shelt'ring woods and wa's maun shield; 20
But thou, beneath the random bield
    O' clod or stane,
Adorns the histie stibble-field,
    Unseen, alane.

There, in thy scanty mantle clad,
Thy snawie bosom sun-ward spread,
Thou lifts thy unassuming head
    In humble guise;
But now the share uptears thy bed,
    And low thou lies.   30

Such is the fate of artless maid,
Sweet flow'ret of the rural shade !
By love's simplicity betrayed,
            And guileless trust,
Till she, like thee, all soiled, is laid
              Low i' the dust.

Such is the fate of simple bard,
On life's rough ocean luckless starr'd !
Unskilful he to note the card
            Of prudent lore,   40
Till billows rage, and gales blow hard,
             And whelm him o'er !

Such fate to suffering worth is giv'n,
Who long with wants and woes has striv'n,
By human pride or cunning driv'n
            To mis'ry's brink,
Till wrench'd of ev'ry stay but Heav'n,
             He, ruin'd, sink !

Ev'n thou who mourn'st the Daisy's fate,
That fate is thine — no distant date ;   50
Stern Ruin's plough-share drives, elate,
            Full on thy bloom,
Till crush'd beneath the furrow's weight,
             Shall be thy doom !

NOTES TO THE COTTER'S SATURDAY NIGHT.

(The numbers refer to lines.)

THIS is the best known of Burns's longer poems. As we have already learned from our study of the poet, his father's cottage supplied the principal features. But the poem has a far wider significance. It is a description of the ideal peasant life of Scotland. In its substantial elements, an exemplification might have been found in a thousand homes. Said an old Scotch serving-woman, to whom a copy of "The Cotter's Saturday Night" had been given for perusal, "Gentlemen and ladies may think muckle o' this; but for me it's naething but what I saw i' my faither's house every day, and I dinna see how he could hae tell't it ony ither way."

It would lead us too far to inquire particularly into the causes that have produced this beautiful peasant life. No doubt the basis of it is to be found in the native sturdiness of the Scotch character. But the immediate cause must be sought in religion. The truths and duties of Christianity occupied a large place in the daily thought and life. The sentiment of reverence, which seems to be sadly lacking at the present time, was carefully cultivated. Family worship was general; the Sabbath was strictly observed; the Bible was revered and studied to an unusual degree. "The Cotter's Saturday Night" shows us how a humble, laboring life may be glorified by a simple, earnest, reverent piety.

1. R. Aikin, to whom the poem is inscribed, was an attorney of Ayr, and a man of worth.

2. *Mercenary bard.* — The poem was inspired, not by the hope of pecuniary reward, but simply by the promptings of friendly affection.

5. *Lays* = songs, lyric poems. A favorite word with poets in the last century.

6. *Train* = class, company. Another favorite word, much used by Goldsmith in the "Deserted Village."

9. *Ween* = think, imagine. From A. S. *wenan*, to imagine.

10. *Sugh* = a sighing sound as of wind in the trees. The local features of the poem are in the Ayrshire dialect, the poet's vernacular.

12. *Miry* = covered with mire or wet soil. — *Pleugh* = plough.

14. *Cotter* = cottager; a small farmer.

15. *Moil* = toil, drudgery.

17. *Morn* = morrow.

19. *Cot* = cottage.

21. *Wee-things* = little things, children. — *Stacher* = stagger.

22. *Flichterin'* = fluttering.

23. *Ingle* = fire, fireplace. — *Blinkin' bonnily* = blazing cheerfully.

26. *Carking* = distressing, oppressive.

27. *Toil.* — This word seems to have been pronounced *tile.* In the last century *oi* frequently had the sound of long *i.*

28. *Belyve* = by and by. — *Bairns* = children.

30. *Ca' the pleugh* = drive the plough. Literally, *call.* — *Tentie rin* = heedfully run. *Tentie* is a corruption of *attentive.*

31. *Cannie* = trustworthy, careful. — *Neebor* = neighbor.

34. *Braw* = brave, in the sense of *fine*, handsome.

35. *Deposit* has the accent on the first syllable. — *Sair-won* = hard won. — *Penny fee* = wages paid in money. *Penny* is used vaguely for *money.*

38. *Spiers* = inquires.

40. *Uncos* = news.

44. *Gars auld claes*, etc. = makes old clothes look almost as well as the new.

47. *Younkers* = youngsters.

48. *Eydent* = diligent.

49. *Jauk* = trifle, dally.

51. *Duty* = prayers.

52. *Gang* = go.

56. *Wha kens* = who knows.

58. *Convoy* = accompany.

59. *Conscious* = tell-tale.

62. *Hafflins* = partly, half.

64. *Ben* = in. A. S. *binnan*, within.

67. *Cracks* = talks. — *Kye* = cows.

69. *Blate* = bashful. — *Laithfu'* = hesitating.

72. *Lave* = rest.

88. *Ruth* = pity, tenderness.

92. *Halesome parritch* = wholesome porridge, oatmeal pudding.

93. *Sowpe* = milk. — *Hawkie* = a cow; properly one with a white face.

94. *'Yont* = beyond. — *Hallan* = screen or low partition between the fireplace and the door. — *Chows her cood* = chews her cud.

96. *Weel-hain'd* = well kept. — *Kebbuck* = cheese. — *Fell* = tasty, biting.

99. *How 'twas a towmond*, etc. = how it was a twelvemonth old since flax was in the bloom; that is, the cheese was a year old last flax-blossoming.

103. *Ha'-Bible* = hall Bible; that is, the family Bible kept in the hall or chief room.

104. *Bonnet* = a cap or covering for the head, in common use before the introduction of hats, and still used by the Scotch.

105. *Lyart* = gray, mixed gray. — *Haffets* = temples; literally, *half-heads*.

107. *Wales* = chooses. Cf. Ger. *wählen*, to choose.

111. *Dundee, Martyrs, Elgin* = names of Scottish psalm-tunes.

113. *Beets* = adds fuel to.

121. *Amalek's ungracious progeny* = the Amalekites, a fierce and war-like Canaanitish nation. They were uncompromising in their hostility to the Israelites. See Deut. xxv. 17–19.

122. *Royal bard* = David. See 2 Sam. xii. 16.

133. *He* = the Apostle John. — *Patmos* = an island in the Ægean Sea, to which John was banished in the year 94, and where he wrote *Revelation.*

135. *Babylon* = the figurative Babylon spoken of in Rev. xviii. 2–24. Usually interpreted among Protestants as referring to papal Rome.

138. From Pope's "Windsor Forest."

143. *Society* = social enjoyment.

150. *Sacerdotal stole* = priestly vestments or robes.

156. *Secret homage* = private devotions.

166. From Pope's "Essay on Man."

182. *Wallace* = the national hero of Scotland. He lived in the thirteenth century.

TO A MOUSE.

1. *Sleekit* = sly. — *Cow'rin'* = cowering, crouching through fear.

4. *Bickering brattle* = a short race.

5. *Wad be*, etc. = would be loathe to run.

6. *Pattle* = a paddle for cleaning the soil from the plough.

13. *Whyles* = sometimes.

14. *Maun* = must.

15. *Daimen* = rare, now and then; *daimen-icker* = an ear of corn now and then. — *Thrave* = two shocks or twenty-four sheaves of corn; a considerable quantity.

20. *Silly* = frail, weak. — *Wa's* = walls.

21. *Big* = to build.

22. *Foggage* = coarse grass.

24. *Snell* = bitter, severe.

31. *Stibble* = stubble.

34. *But* = without. A. S. *butan*, without. — *Hald* = home, abiding place.
35. *Thole* = endure. — *Dribble* = drizzling.
36. *Cranreuch* = hoar-frost.
37. *No thy lane* = not alone.
40. *Gang aft a-gley* = go often wrong.

TO A MOUNTAIN DAISY.

3. *Stoure* = dust.
9. *Weet* = wet, rain.
15. *Glinted* = peeped.
21. *Bield* = shelter, protection.
23. *Histie* = dry, barren.

OLIVER GOLDSMITH.

A STRANGE combination of weakness and strength, of genius and folly. ("Inspired idiot") is the terrific phrase with which Horace Walpole once described him. It is a gross caricature indeed, but having truth enough at bottom to be perpetuated. Goldsmith belonged to a literary club, the members of which occasionally dined together. Goldsmith was usually one of the last to arrive. While waiting for him one day, the company playfully composed a number of epitaphs on "the *late* Mr. Goldsmith." The epitaph by Garrick, the celebrated actor, has been preserved as a happy hit : —

> " Here lies poet Goldsmith, for shortness called Noll,
> Who wrote like an angel and talked like poor Poll."

There are other anecdotes illustrating Goldsmith's awkwardness in conversation. He greatly lacked self-confidence, and had a faculty for blundering. His friends sometimes took advantage of his weaknesses, and for amusement tricked him into saying and doing absurd things. He has suffered also from thick-headed critics, who have sometimes misunderstood his delicate humor. Boswell, who was no friendly critic, but who reported facts truthfully, says : " It has been generally circulated and believed that Goldsmith was a mere fool in conversation; but in truth, this has been greatly exaggerated." In spite of his deficiencies, he sometimes got the better of Dr. Johnson, the clearest and strongest talker of his time. Talking of fables once, Goldsmith remarked that the animals introduced seldom talked in character. "For instance," he said, "take the fable of the little fishes who saw birds fly over their heads, and envying them, petitioned Jupiter to be changed into birds.

The skill consists in making them talk like little fishes." Dr. Johnson took exception to the remark. "Ah, Doctor," he replied, "this is not so easy as you may think; for if you were to make little fishes talk, they would talk like whales."

But we turn to his life. Scarcely any other English author has put into his writings so much of his character and experience. Oliver Goldsmith was born at Pallas in the county of Longford, Ireland, in 1728, the son of a Protestant clergyman. About two years later his father moved to the village of Lissoy in the county of Westmeath, where he enjoyed a better living. An unusual interest is connected with that home. The amiable piety, learned simplicity, and guileless wisdom of his father are portrayed in the immortal "Vicar of Wakefield." It was a fireside where a Christian benevolence was inculcated and practised. The memories of this home never left Goldsmith; and years afterwards, in his "Deserted Village," he gave a famous description of "the village preacher's modest mansion:" —

> "A man he was to all the country dear,
> And passing rich with forty pounds a year;
> Remote from towns he ran his godly race,
> Nor e'er had changed, nor wished to change his place."

At the age of six years Goldsmith was sent to the village school taught by Thomas Byrne, an old soldier with a large stock of stories. Of him also we have a portrait in the "Deserted Village:" —

> "A man severe he was, and stern to view,
> I knew him well, and every truant knew:
> Well had the boding tremblers learned to trace
> The day's disasters in his morning face.
> Full well they laughed with counterfeited glee
> At all his jokes, for many a joke had he;
> Full well the busy whisper circling round,
> Conveyed the dismal tidings when he frowned."

As a pupil he was dull — a stupid blockhead he was thought to be; but his amiability and thoughtless generosity, which characterized him all through life, made him popular with his schoolmates. An incident that occurred in his sixteenth year, not only throws light upon his character, but also shows the origin of his most famous comedy. He was returning home from Edgeworthstown, where he had been attending school. He had borrowed a horse for the journey, and received from a friend a guinea. He at once began to put on airs, and to affect the gentleman. Arriving in a village at night-fall, he inquired for the best house in the place, and was directed by a wag to the private house of a gentleman of fortune. Accordingly he rode up to what he supposed to be an inn, ordered his horse to be taken to the stable, walked into the parlor, seated himself by the fire, and demanded what he could have for supper. The gentleman of the house, discovering his mistake, concluded to humor him, and gave him the freedom of the house for the evening. He was highly elated. When supper was served, he insisted that the landlord, his wife, and daughter should eat with him, and ordered a bottle of wine to crown the repast. When next morning he discovered his blunder, his sense of humiliation can easily be imagined. With the literary instinct that turned all his experiences to account, he dramatized this incident many years afterwards in " She Stoops to Conquer ; or, The Mistakes of a Night." Throughout his life, as in this case, the possession of money made a fool of him.

In his seventeenth year Goldsmith entered Trinity College, Dublin, as a sizar. This relation was naturally repugnant to his timid and sensitive nature. His tutor was ill-tempered and harsh ; some studies, especially mathematics and logic, were distasteful to him. His social nature betrayed him into a neglect of his studies, and his love of fun got him into trouble. Having once gained a prize of thirty shillings, he gave a dance at his room to some young men and women of the city. This was a violation of the college rules ; and his tutor, attracted by the sound of the fiddle, rushed to the scene of festivity, gave Goldsmith a thrashing, and turned his guests out of doors.

An anecdote, belonging to this period, illustrates the tender heart and inconsiderate benevolence that characterized his whole life. He had been invited to breakfast by a college friend, and, failing to make his appearance, was visited at his room. There he was found in bed, buried in feathers up to his chin. The evening before, a woman with five children had told him a pitiful tale of her distress and need. It was too much for his sympathetic nature; and bringing the woman to the college gate, he gave her the blankets off his bed, and a part of his clothing to sell and buy bread. Getting cold in the night, he had ripped open his bed and buried himself in the feathers.

In due course he took his bachelor's degree, and returned to his home. It had been sadly changed by the death of his father. The next two or three years were spent in a desultory way; while ostensibly preparing to take orders, he was in reality spending his time in miscellaneous reading and rustic convivialities. He did dot like the clerical profession. "To be obliged to wear a long wig when I liked a short one," he says in explanation of his antipathy, "or a black coat when I generally dressed in brown, I thought such a restraint upon my liberty that I absolutely rejected the proposal."

His fondness for gay dress was a weakness throughout his life, and more than once exposed him to ridicule. When the time for his examination came, he appeared before the Bishop of Elphin arrayed in scarlet breeches. This silly breach of propriety cost him the good opinion of the bishop, and led to his rejection.

Then followed a succession of undertakings and failures without parallel. He became tutor in a good family, and lost his position on account of a quarrel at cards. He then resolved to emigrate to America, and left for Dublin mounted on a good horse and having thirty guineas in his pocket. In six weeks he returned to his mother's door in a condition not unlike that of the prodigal son. Every penny was gone. He explained that the ship on which he had engaged passage had sailed while he was at a party of pleasure. The ship had been waiting for a favorable wind; "and you know, mother," he said, "that I could not command the elements."

His uncle Contarine, who was one of the few that had not lost all confidence in him, gave him fifty pounds with which to go to London for the purpose of studying law. He reached Dublin on his way; but unfortunately he met an old acquaintance, who allured him into a gambling-house. He came out penniless.

He was next advised to try medicine; and a small purse having been made up for him, he set out for Edinburgh. He remained there eighteen months, during which he picked up a little medical science. But most of his time was spent in convivial habits. With gaming, feasting, and reckless generosity, he was often brought into financial difficulties.

Then he went to Leyden, ostensibly for the purpose of completing his medical studies, but really, there is reason to believe, for the purpose of gratifying his roving disposition. He spent a year in that city with his usual improvidence. A friend provided him with money to go to Paris. The mania for tulip culture still prevailed in Holland. One day wandering through a garden, Goldsmith suddenly recollected that his uncle Contarine, his steadfast benefactor, was a tulip fancier. Here, then, was an opportunity to show his appreciation. A number of choice and costly bulbs were purchased; and not till after he had paid for them did he reflect that he had spent all the money designed for his travelling expenses. In this extremity he set out on foot with his flute. "I had some knowledge of music," says the Philosophic Vagabond in the "Vicar of Wakefield," "with a tolerable voice; I now turned what was once my amusement into a present means of subsistence. I passed among the harmless peasants of Flanders, and among such of the French as were poor enough to be merry; for I ever found them sprightly in proportion to their wants. Whenever I approached a peasant's house, I played one of my merriest tunes, and that procured me not only a lodging, but subsistence for the next day." In this way he was able to make the tour of Europe, visiting Flanders, France, Switzerland, Germany, and Italy. At Padua he is said to have taken his medical degree. These travels, as we shall see, were afterwards to be turned to good account.

In 1756 he returned to England. "You may easily imagine," he wrote to a friend afterwards, "what difficulties I had to encounter, left as I was without friends, recommendations, money, or impudence, and that in a country where being born an Irishman was sufficient to keep me unemployed. Many in such circumstances would have had recourse to a friar's cord or the suicide's halter. But, with all my follies, I had principle to resist the one, and resolution to combat the other."

He went to London, where for the next several years he led an existence miserable enough. He became successively an usher in a school, an apothecary's assistant, a practising physician — and failed in them all. At last, after other unlucky ventures, he settled down to the drudgery of a literary hack. From this humiliating station he was lifted by the force of genius alone.

He began by writing for reviews and magazines, and compiling easy histories. His first serious undertaking was "An Inquiry into the State of Learning in Europe," with which his career as an author may be said to begin. His work gradually gained recognition, and brought him better pay. His circle of acquaintance widened, and included the most distinguished literary talent of his time. Burke had discovered his genius; Percy, afterwards Bishop of Dromore, sought him out in his garret; and most important of all, Johnson, the great Cham as he has been humorously styled, sought his acquaintance. He had met Reynolds and Hogarth. In 1763 he became one of the original nine members of the Club, which included among others Johnson, Reynolds, and Burke, and to which were added subsequently Garrick and Boswell. He was thus brought into intimate fellowship with the choicest minds of the English metropolis.

Having attracted their notice by the humor, grace, and picturesqueness of his style in writing, he won their affection by the guilelessness and amiability of his character. There was a charm in his personality that triumphed over his weaknesses, and drew the strongest and best men to him in tender friendship. That same charm exists in his works; and with the possible exception of Addison, he is, what Thackeray claims for him, "the most beloved of English writers."

The lesson of economy he never learned. His growing income had enabled him to take better lodgings. But in 1764 we find him in arrears for his board and in the hands of the sheriff. He sent for Johnson. "I sent him a guinea," says Johnson, "and promised to come to him directly. I accordingly went as soon as I was dressed, and found that his landlady had arrested him for rent, at which he was in a violent passion. I perceived that he had already changed my guinea, and got a bottle of Madeira and a glass before him. I put the cork into the bottle, desired he would be calm, and began to talk to him of the means by which he might be extricated. He then told me that he had a novel ready for the press, which he produced to me. I looked into it, and saw its merit; told the landlady I should return soon; and having gone to a bookseller, sold it for sixty pounds. I brought Goldsmith the money; and he discharged his rent, not without rating his landlady in a high tone for having used him so ill." But speedily relenting, he called her to share in a bowl of punch.

The novel in question was no other than the "Vicar of Wakefield"—"one of the most delicious morsels of fictitious composition," justly observes Sir Walter Scott, "on which the human mind was ever employed." The plot is indeed faulty; but the charm of the characters, the ludicrousness of the situations, the grace of style, and the delicacy of humor, make it a book which we read with delight in youth, and return to with pleasure in maturity and old age. Notwithstanding its high rank as a work of genius, the stupid publisher kept it in hand two years before venturing to give it to the public.

In 1764, while the " Vicar of Wakefield " was being held by the publisher, Goldsmith published a poem called the "Traveller." It was the first work to which he attached his name. The time was favorable for its appearance, inasmuch as the British Muse was doing but little. Johnson kindly lent his assistance in bringing it out, reading over the proof-sheets, and adding here and there a line. The merits of the poem were soon recognized, and the general opinion agreed that nothing better had appeared since the time of Pope. Goldsmith dedicated it to his brother : —

> " Where'er I roam, whatever realms to see,
> My heart untravelled fondly turns to thee;
> Still to my brother turns, with ceaseless pain,
> And drags at each remove a lengthening chain."

It embodies the observations of his tour on the continent; but —

> " Vain, very vain, my weary search to find
> That bliss which only centres in the mind:
> Why have I strayed from pleasure and repose
> To seek a good each government bestows?
> In every government, though tyrants reign,
> Though tyrant kings, or tyrant laws restrain,
> How small, of all that human hearts endure,
> That part which laws or kings can cause or cure?
> Still to ourselves in every place consigned,
> Our own felicity we make or find;
> With secret course which no loud storms annoy,
> Glides the smooth current of domestic joy."

The Earl of Northumberland read the poem and was greatly pleased with it. He sent for Goldsmith ; and after stating that he had been appointed Lord Lieutenant of Ireland, he expressed a willingness to do the poet any kindness in his power. Goldsmith's genius for blundering did not desert him. He said that he had a brother in Ireland that needed help; but as for himself, he did not place much dependence in the promises of the great, and looked to the booksellers for a support.

Goldsmith continued to do hack writing for the booksellers, but did not neglect original composition. In 1768 appeared his comedy of "The Good-Natured Man." It was refused by Garrick, notwithstanding the intercession of Reynolds, and was brought out at Covent Garden. It did not gain the applause it merited, but as a financial venture it was a success. It was acted for nine nights; and including the copyright, it brought the author no less than five hundred pounds. That was a dangerous sum for a man of his improvident habits. He at once rented elegant lodgings at a cost of four hundred pounds, and gave dinners to Johnson, Reynolds, and other friends of note. His chambers were often the scene of gay festivities; and Blackstone, who occupied rooms immediately below, and was engaged on his "Commentaries," used to complain of the racket overhead. At this rate his means were of course soon exhausted.

His labors for the booksellers included his "Animated Nature," "History of Rome," "History of England," and "History of Greece." These compilations were hardly worthy of his genius, but they brought him the means of livelihood. "I cannot afford to court the draggle-tail muses," he once said; "they would let me starve; but by my other labors I can make shift to eat, and drink, and have good clothes." But even his compilations bore the trace of his genius in the clear arrangement of facts and in his felicitous mode of treatment. "Whether indeed, we take him as a poet, as a comic writer, or as an historian," declared Johnson, "he stands in the first class."

In 1770 appeared the "Deserted Village." In this he cast a glory around his native village, to which, as he approached the end of his life, his mind reverted with peculiar tenderness. The political economy presented is indeed false; but the pictures the poem brings before us are as enduring as the language. Every one is acquainted with Paddy Byrne : —

"In arguing, too, the parson owned his skill;
For e'en though vanquished, he could argue still."

And then the village preacher — a portrait of Goldsmith's father and his brother Henry. It is one of the most delightful descriptions in the English language, rivalled alone by Chaucer's parson : —

> "And as a bird each fond endearment tries
> To tempt its new-fledged offspring to the skies,
> He tried each art, reproved each dull delay,
> Allured to brighter worlds, and led the way."

The poem was at once successful, and has since retained, through all changes of taste, its place as a classic.

In 1773 he gave his comedy, " She Stoops to Conquer," to the public. The plot turns on an incident suggested by his blunder as a school-boy. The theatrical manager predicted a complete failure, and Goldsmith was in great distress. But the night of the first presentation the theatre was filled ; and the humorous dialogue and the ridiculous incidents kept the audience in a roar of laughter. It has since retained its place on the stage.

During the last years of his life Goldsmith's income was about four hundred pounds a year. With a little economy this would have enabled him to live in comfort and ease. But his extravagance and heedless benevolence left him in debt.

The end came April 3, 1774. When the news was brought to Burke, he burst into tears. Sir Joshua Reynolds laid aside his pencil. But more significant than all was the lamentation of the old and the infirm on his stairs — helpless creatures to whose supplications he had never turned a deaf ear. Johnson wrote his epitaph, in which it is said that he " left scarcely any style of writing untouched, and touched nothing that he did not adorn." In the words of Thackeray, " Think of him reckless, thriftless, vain if you like — but merciful, gentle, generous, full of love and pity. He passes out of our life, and goes to render his account beyond it. Think of the poor pensioners weeping at his grave ; think of the noble spirits that admired and deplored him ; think of the righteous pen that wrote his epitaph — and the wonderful and unanimous response of affection with which the world has paid back the love he gave it. His humor delighting us still; his song fresh and beautiful as when he first charmed with it; his words in all our mouths; his very weaknesses beloved and familiar — his benevolent spirit seems still to smile upon us; to do gentle kindnesses; to succor with sweet charity; to caress, soothe, and forgive; to plead with the fortunate for the unhappy and the poor."

THE DESERTED VILLAGE.

SWEET AUBURN! loveliest village of the plain;
Where health and plenty cheered the labouring swain,
Where smiling spring its earliest visit paid,
And parting summer's lingering blooms delayed:
Dear lovely bowers of innocence and ease,
Seats of my youth, when every sport could please,
How often have I loitered o'er thy green,
Where humble happiness endeared each scene!
How often have I paused on every charm,
The sheltered cot, the cultivated farm,   10
The never-failing brook, the busy mill,
The decent church that topt the neighbouring hill,
The hawthorn bush, with seats beneath the shade,
For talking age and whispering lovers made!
How often have I blest the coming day,
When toil remitting lent its turn to play,
And all the village train from labour free,
Led up their sports beneath the spreading tree.
While many a pastime circled in the shade,
The young contending as the old surveyed;   20
And many a gambol frolicked o'er the ground,
And sleights of art and feats of strength went round.
And still, as each repeated pleasure tired,
Succeeding sports the mirthful band inspired;
The dancing pair that simply sought renown
By holding out to tire each other down;
The swain mistrustless of his smutted face,
While secret laughter tittered round the place;
The bashful virgin's side-long looks of love,
The matron's glance that would those looks reprove.   30
These were thy charms, sweet village! sports like these,
With sweet succession, taught even toil to please:
These round thy bowers their cheerful influence shed:
These were thy charms — but all these charms are fled.
    Sweet smiling village, loveliest of the lawn,
Thy sports are fled, and all thy charms withdrawn;

Amidst thy bowers the tyrant's hand is seen,
And desolation saddens all thy green:
One only master grasps the whole domain,
And half a tillage stints thy smiling plain.   40
No more thy glassy brook reflects the day,
But, choked with sedges, works its weedy way;
Along thy glades, a solitary guest,
The hollow-sounding bittern guards its nest;
Amidst thy desert walks the lapwing flies,
And tires their echoes with unvaried cries;
Sunk are thy bowers in shapeless ruin all,
And the long grass o'ertops the mouldering wall;
And trembling, shrinking from the spoiler's hand,
Far, far away thy children leave the land.   50

 Ill fares the land, to hastening ills a prey,
Where wealth accumulates, and men decay:
Princes and lords may flourish, or may fade;
A breath can make them, as a breath has made:
But a bold peasantry, their country's pride,
When once destroyed, can never be supplied.

 A time there was, ere England's griefs began,
When every rood of ground maintained its man;
For him light labour spread her wholesome store,
Just gave what life required, but gave no more: 60
His best companions, innocence and health;
And his best riches, ignorance of wealth.

 But times are altered; trade's unfeeling train
Usurp the land and dispossess the swain;
Along the lawn, where scattered hamlets rose,
Unwieldy wealth and cumbrous pomp repose,
And every want to opulence allied,
And every pang that folly pays to pride.
These gentle hours that plenty bade to bloom,
Those calm desires that asked but little room,   70
Those healthful sports that graced the peaceful scene,
Lived in each look, and brightened all the green;
These, far departing, seek a kinder shore,
And rural mirth and manners are no more.

 Sweet Auburn! parent of the blissful hour,
Thy glades forlorn confess the tyrant's power.

Here, as I take my solitary rounds
Amidst thy tangling walks and ruined grounds,
And, many a year elapsed, return to view
Where once the cottage stood, the hawthorn grew,   80
Remembrance wakes with all her busy train,
Swells at my breast, and turns the past to pain.

    In all my wanderings round this world of care,
In all my griefs — and GOD has given my share —
I still had hopes, my latest hours to crown,
Amidst these humble bowers to lay me down;
To husband out life's taper at the close,
And keep the flame from wasting by repose:
I still had hopes, for pride attends us still,
Amidst the swains to show my book-learned skill,   90
Around my fire an evening group to draw,
And tell of all I felt, and all I saw;
And, as an hare whom hounds and horns pursue
Pants to the place from whence at first she flew,
I still had hopes, my long vexations past,
Here to return — and die at home at last.

    O blest retirement, friend to life's decline,
Retreats from care, that never must be mine,
How happy he who crowns in shades like these
A youth of labour with an age of ease;   100
Who quits a world where strong temptations try,
And, since 'tis hard to combat, learns to fly!
For him no wretches, born to work and weep,
Explore the mine, or tempt the dangerous deep;
No surly porter stands in guilty state,
To spurn imploring famine from the gate;
But on he moves to meet his latter end,
Angels around befriending Virtue's friend;
Bends to the grave with unperceived decay,
While resignation gently slopes the way;   110
And, all his prospects brightening to the last,
His heaven commences ere the world be past!

    Sweet was the sound, when oft at evening's close
Up yonder hill the village murmur rose.
There, as I past with careless steps and slow,
The mingling notes came softened from below;

The swain responsive as the milk-maid sung,
The sober herd that lowed to meet their young,
The noisy geese that gabbled o'er the pool,
The playful children just let loose from school,   120
The watch-dog's voice that bayed the whispering wind,
And the loud laugh that spoke the vacant mind; —
These all in sweet confusion sought the shade,
And filled each pause the nightingale had made.
But now the sounds of population fail,
No cheerful murmurs fluctuate in the gale,
No busy steps the grass-grown foot-way tread,
For all the bloomy flush of life is fled.
All but yon widowed, solitary thing,
That feebly bends beside the plashy spring: 130
She, wretched matron, forced in age, for bread,
To strip the brook with mantling cresses spread,
To pick her wintry faggot from the thorn,
To seek her nightly shed, and weep till morn;
She only left of all the harmless train,
The sad historian of the pensive plain.

    Near yonder copse, where once the garden smiled,
And still where many a garden flower grows wild;
There, where a few torn shrubs the place disclose,
The village preacher's modest mansion rose.   140
A man he was to all the country dear,
And passing rich with forty pounds a year;
Remote from towns he ran his godly race,
Nor e'er had changed, nor wished to change his place;
Unpractised he to fawn, or seek for power,
By doctrines fashioned to the varying hour;
Far other aims his heart had learned to prize,
More skilled to raise the wretched than to rise.
His house was known to all the vagrant train;
He chid their wanderings but relieved their pain: 150
The long remembered beggar was his guest,
Whose beard descending swept his aged breast;
The ruined spendthrift, now no longer proud,
Claimed kindred there, and had his claims allowed;
The broken soldier, kindly bade to stay,
Sat by his fire, and talked the night away,

Wept o'er his wounds or tales of sorrow done,
Shouldered his crutch and shewed how fields were won.
Pleased with his guests, the good man learned to glow,
And quite forgot their vices in their woe;   160
Careless their merits or their faults to scan,
His pity gave ere charity began.

　　Thus to relieve the wretched was his pride,
And e'en his failings leaned to Virtue's side;
But in his duty prompt at every call,
He watched and wept, he prayed and felt for all;
And, as a bird each fond endearment tries
To tempt its new-fledged offspring to the skies,
He tried each art, reproved each dull delay,
Allured to brighter worlds, and led the way.   170

　　Beside the bed where parting life was laid,
And sorrow, guilt, and pain by turns dismayed,
The reverend champion stood.　At his control
Despair and anguish fled the struggling soul;
Comfort came down the trembling wretch to raise,
And his last faltering accents whispered praise.

　　At church, with meek and unaffected grace,
His looks adorned the venerable place;
Truth from his lips prevailed with double sway,
And fools, who came to scoff, remained to pray.   180
The service past, around the pious man,
With steady zeal, each honest rustic ran;
E'en children followed with endearing wile,
And plucked his gown to share the good man's smile.
His ready smile a parent's warmth exprest;
Their welfare pleased him, and their cares distrest:
To them his heart, his love, his griefs were given,
But all his serious thoughts had rest in heaven.
As some tall cliff that lifts its awful form,
Swells from the vale, and midway leaves the storm,   190
Tho' round its breast the rolling clouds are spread,
Eternal sunshine settles on its head.

　　Beside yon straggling fence that skirts the way,
With blossom'd furze unprofitably gay,
There, in his noisy mansion, skill'd to rule,
The village master taught his little school.

A man severe he was, and stern to view;
I knew him well, and every truant knew:
Well had the boding tremblers learned to trace
The day's disasters in his morning face;   200
Full well they laughed with counterfeited glee
At all his jokes, for many a joke had he;
Full well the busy whisper circling round
Conveyed the dismal tidings when he frowned.
Yet he was kind, or, if severe in aught,
The love he bore to learning was in fault;
The village all declared how much he knew:
'Twas certain he could write, and cipher too;
Lands he could measure, terms and tides presage,
And even the story ran that he could gauge: 210
In arguing, too, the parson owned his skill,
For, even tho' vanquished, he could argue still;
While words of learnèd length and thundering sound
Amazed the gazing rustics ranged around;
And still they gazed, and still the wonder grew,
That one small head could carry all he knew.
        But past is all his fame. The very spot
Where many a time he triumphed is forgot.
Near yonder thorn, that lifts its head on high,
Where once the sign-post caught the passing eye,   220
Now lies that house where nut-brown draughts inspired,
Where grey-beard mirth and smiling toil retired,
Where village statesmen talked with looks profound,
And news much older than their ale went round.
Imagination fondly stoops to trace
The parlour splendours of that festive place:
The white-washed wall, the nicely sanded floor,
The varnished clock that clicked behind the door;
The chest contrived a double debt to pay,
A bed by night, a chest of drawers by day;   230
The pictures placed for ornament and use,
The twelve good rules, the royal game of goose;
The hearth, except when winter chill'd the day,
With aspen boughs and flowers and fennel gay;
While broken tea-cups, wisely kept for shew,
Ranged o'er the chimney, glistened in a row.

Vain transitory splendours! could not all
Reprieve the tottering mansion from its fall?
Obscure it sinks, nor shall it more impart
An hour's importance to the poor man's heart   240
Thither no more the peasant shall repair
To sweet oblivion of his daily care;
No more the farmer's news, the barber's tale,
No more the woodman's ballad shall prevail;
No more the smith his dusky brow shall clear,
Relax his ponderous strength, and lean to hear;
The host himself no longer shall be found
Careful to see the mantling bliss go round;
Nor the coy maid, half willing to be prest,
Shall kiss the cup to pass it to the rest.   250

Yes! let the rich deride, the proud disdain,
These simple blessings of the lowly train;
To me more dear, congenial to my heart,
One native charm, than all the gloss of art;
Spontaneous joys, where Nature has its play,
The soul adopts, and owns their first born sway;
Lightly they frolic o'er the vacant mind,
Unenvied, unmolested, unconfined.
But the long pomp, the midnight masquerade,
With all the freaks of wanton wealth arrayed —   260
In these, ere triflers half their wish obtain,
The toiling pleasure sickens into pain;
And, e'en while fashion's brightest arts decoy,
The heart distrusting asks if this be joy.

Ye friends to truth, ye statesmen who survey
The rich man's joys increase, the poor's decay,
'Tis yours to judge, how wide the limits stand
Between a splendid and a happy land.
Proud swells the tide with loads of freighted ore,
And shouting Folly hails them from her shore;   270
Hoards e'en beyond the miser's wish abound,
And rich men flock from all the world around.
Yet count our gains. This wealth is but a name
That leaves our useful products still the same.
Not so the loss. The man of wealth and pride
Takes up a space that many poor supplied;

Space for his lake, his park's extended bounds,
Space for his horses, equipage, and hounds:
The robe that wraps his limbs in silken sloth
Has robbed the neighbouring fields of half their growth;　280
His seat, where solitary sports are seen,
Indignant spurns the cottage from the green:
Around the world each needful product flies,
For all the luxuries the world supplies;
While thus the land adorned for pleasure all
In barren splendour feebly waits the fall.

　　As some fair female unadorned and plain,
Secure to please while youth confirms her reign,
Slights every borrowed charm that dress supplies,
Nor shares with art the triumph of her eyes;　290
But when those charms are past, for charms are frail,
When time advances, and when lovers fail,
She then shines forth, solicitous to bless,
In all the glaring impotence of dress.
Thus fares the land by luxury betrayed:
In nature's simplest charms at first arrayed,
But verging to decline, its splendours rise;
Its vistas strike, its palaces surprise:
While, scourged by famine from the smiling land,
The mournful peasant leads his humble band,　300
And while he sinks, without one arm to save,
The country blooms — a garden and a grave.

　　Where then, ah! where, shall poverty reside,
To 'scape the pressure of contiguous pride?
If to some common's fenceless limits strayed
He drives his flock to pick the scanty blade,
Those fenceless fields the sons of wealth divide,
And even the bare-worn common is denied.

　　If to the city sped — what waits him there?
To see profusion that he must not share;　310
To see ten thousand baneful arts combined
To pamper luxury, and thin mankind;
To see those joys the sons of pleasure know
Extorted from his fellow-creature's woe.
Here while the courtier glitters in brocade,
There the pale artist plies the sickly trade;

Here while the proud their long-drawn pomps display,
There the black gibbet glooms beside the way.
The dome where pleasure holds her midnight reign
Here, richly decked, admits the gorgeous train :   320
Tumultuous grandeur crowds the blazing square,
The rattling chariots clash, the torches glare.
Sure scenes like these no troubles e'er annoy !
Sure these denote one universal joy !
Are these thy serious thoughts ? — Ah, turn thine eyes
Where the poor houseless shivering female lies.
She once, perhaps, in village plenty blest,
Has wept at tales of innocence distrest ;
Her modest looks the cottage might adorn,
Sweet as the primrose peeps beneath the thorn :   330
Now lost to all ; her friends, her virtue fled,
Near her betrayer's door she lays her head,
And, pinch'd with cold, and shrinking from the shower,
With heavy heart deplores that luckless hour,
When idly first, ambitious of the town,
She left her wheel and robes of country brown.

    Do thine, sweet Auburn, — thine, the loveliest train, —
Do thy fair tribes participate her pain?
Even now, perhaps, by cold and hunger led,
At proud men's doors they ask a little bread !   340
    Ah, no ! To distant climes, a dreary scene,
Where half the convex world intrudes between,
Through torrid tracts with fainting steps they go,
Where wild Altama murmurs to their woe.
Far different there from all that charm'd before
The various terrors of that horrid shore ;
Those blazing suns that dart a downward ray,
And fiercely shed intolerable day ;
Those matted woods, where birds forget to sing,
But silent bats in drowsy clusters cling ;   350
Those poisonous fields with rank luxuriance crowned,
Where the dark scorpion gathers death around ;
Where at each step the stranger fears to wake
The rattling terrors of the vengeful snake ;
Where crouching tigers wait their hapless prey,
And savage men more murderous still than they ;

While oft in whirls the mad tornado flies,
Mingling the ravaged landscape with the skies.
Far different these from every former scene,
The cooling brook, the grassy vested green, 360
The breezy covert of the warbling grove,
That only sheltered thefts of harmless love.

Good Heaven! what sorrows gloom'd that parting day,
That called them from their native walks away;
When the poor exiles, every pleasure past,
Hung round the bowers, and fondly looked their last,
And took a long farewell, and wished in vain
For seats like these beyond the western main,
And shuddering still to face the distant deep,
Returned and wept, and still returned to weep. 370
The good old sire that first prepared to go
To new found worlds, and wept for others' woe;
But for himself, in conscious virtue brave,
He only wished for worlds beyond the grave
His lovely daughter, lovelier in her tears,
The fond companion of his helpless years,
Silent went next, neglectful of her charms,
And left a lover's for a father's arms.
With louder plaints the mother spoke her woes,
And blest the cot where every pleasure rose, 380
And kissed her thoughtless babes with many a tear,
And clasped them close, in sorrow doubly dear,
Whilst her fond husband strove to lend relief
In all the silent manliness of grief.

O luxury! thou curst by Heaven's decree,
How ill exchanged are things like these for thee!
How do thy potions, with insidious joy,
Diffuse their pleasure only to destroy!
Kingdoms by thee, to sickly greatness grown,
Boast of a florid vigour not their own. 390
At every draught more large and large they grow,
A bloated mass of rank unwieldy woe;
Till sapped their strength, and every part unsound,
Down, down they sink, and spread a ruin round.

Even now the devastation is begun,
And half the business of destruction done;

Even now, methinks, as pondering here I stand,
I see the rural virtues leave the land.
Down where yon anchoring vessel spreads the sail,
That idly waiting flaps with every gale, 400
Downward they move, a melancholy band,
Pass from the shore, and darken all the strand.
Contented toil, and hospitable care,
And kind connubial tenderness, are there ;
And piety with wishes placed above,
And steady loyalty, and faithful love.
And thou, sweet Poetry, thou loveliest maid,
Still first to fly where sensual joys invade ;
Unfit in these degenerate times of shame
To catch the heart, or strike for honest fame ; 410
Dear charming nymph, neglected and decried,
My shame in crowds, my solitary pride ;
Thou source of all my bliss, and all my woe,
That found'st me poor at first, and keep'st me so ;
Thou guide by which the nobler arts excel,
Thou nurse of every virtue, fare thee well !
Farewell, and O ! where'er thy voice be tried,
On Torno's cliffs, or Pambamarca's side,
Whether where equinoctial fervours glow,
Or winter wraps the polar world in snow, 420
Still let thy voice, prevailing over time,
Redress the rigours of the inclement clime ;
Aid slighted truth with thy persuasive strain ;
Teach erring man to spurn the rage of gain ;
Teach him, that states of native strength possessed,
Tho' very poor, may still be very blessed ;
That trade's proud empire hastes to swift decay,
As ocean sweeps the laboured mole away ;
While self-dependent power can time defy,
As rocks resist the billows and the sky. 430

NOTES TO THE DESERTED VILLAGE.

(The numbers refer to lines.)

For general remarks on the poem, see the sketch of Goldsmith.

1. *Auburn* = Lissoy probably, though with the addition of imaginative details.

2. *Swain* = peasant. A favorite word among the poets of the last century, by whom it was used in a somewhat vague sense as "shepherd," "lover," or "young man."

4. *Parting* = departing. For the same use of the word, see the first line of Gray's "Elegy."

5. *Bowers* = dwellings. By poets often used somewhat vaguely.

6. *Seats* = abodes.

10. *Cot* = cottage.

12. *Decent* = neat, becoming.

13. *Hawthorn.* — The hawthorn bushes around Lissoy have been cut to pieces to furnish souvenirs of the locality.

16. *Remitting* = ceasing for a time.

17. *Train.* — See note to line 6 of "The Cotter's Saturday Night."

19. *Circled* = went round. See line 22.

21. *Gambol frolicked* = sportive trick was played in a frolicsome manner.

35. *Lawn* = plain. See line 1.

37. *Tyrant* = Some wealthy land-owner. Goldsmith deplores the accumulation of land in the hands of great land-owners, to be used by them, not for careful tillage, but in great measure for ostentation and pleasure.

39. *One only master* = one sole master.

40. *Stints* = deprives of fruitfulness and beauty.

43. *Glades* = open spaces, usually low and moist or marshy.

45. *Walks* = range, region. — *Lapwing* = a wading bird of the plover family. See Webster.

49. *Shrinking*, etc. — Owing to the absorption of the land by great proprietors, the peasantry were forced to emigrate.

52. *Decay* = decrease in number.

55. Goldsmith is here partly right and partly wrong. "A bold peasantry" is undoubtedly necessary to the highest welfare of a country. But when, in the following lines, he inveighs against commerce and manufacture,

he makes a mistake. These do not injure a country, but increase its wealth, population, and intelligence. When, however, he denounces luxury, which unfortunately he sometimes confounds with trade, he has the approval of all right-thinking men.

63. *Trade's unfeeling train* = those enriched by commerce and manufacture.

81. *Busy train* = thronging reminiscences of the past.

85. These lines express a real wish of Goldsmith's, but one that was destined not to be fulfilled. The reality of the desire renders these lines pathetic.

88. *By repose* modifies *keep*.

100. *Age* = old age.

105. *Guilty state.* — *State* here means *livery;* and it is called *guilty* because regarded by the poet as an evidence of criminal avarice and luxury.

107. *He* = the person spoken of in line 99. — *Latter end* = a Biblical phrase meaning *death*. See Prov. xix. 20.

110. *Slopes* = eases.

115. *Careless* = without care or anxiety.

121. *Bayed* = barked at. O. Fr. *abayer*, to bark.

122. *Spoke* = indicated.

123. *The shade* = the shadows of " evening's close."

126. *Fluctuate in the gale* = float on the breezes.

128. *Bloomy* = blooming.

130. *Plashy* = puddle-like.

132. *Mantling* = covering as with a cloak or mantle.

136. *Pensive* = expressing thoughtfulness with sadness.

137. *Copse* = a thicket of underwood. Cf. *coppice*.

139. *Disclose* = reveal, mark.

140. *Mansion* = house, habitation; usually one of some size or pretensions.

142. *Passing rich* = more than rich, very rich.

144. *Place* = post, position.

149. *Vagrant train* = wandering company; tramps.

155. *Broken* = broken down by age, sickness, or some other cause.

159. *Glow* = kindle with interest or enthusiasm.

171. *Parting.* — See line 4.

189. *As some tall cliff*, etc. — This has been pronounced one of the sublimest similes in the English language.

194. *Furze* = a thorny evergreen shrub. It is called " unprofitably gay " because, in spite of its beautiful yellow flowers, it is of no practical use.

196. *The village master* = Paddy Byrne. See sketch of Goldsmith.

199. *Boding* = foreboding.

209. *Terms and tides* = seasons and times.

210. *Gauge* = measure the capacity of vessels.

221. *Nut-brown draughts* = draughts of nut-brown ale. With his convivial habits, we may be sure that Goldsmith was not a stranger to the scenes he here describes.

229. *Double debt to pay* = to serve a double use.

231. *For ornament and use.* — They were probably used to hide defects in the walls.

232. *Twelve good rules.* — These are worth repeating: 1. Urge no healths. 2. Profane no divine ordinances. 3. Touch no state matters. 4. Reveal no secrets. 5. Pick no quarrels. 6. Make no comparisons. 7. Maintain no ill opinions. 8. Keep no bad company. 9. Encourage no vice. 10. Make no long meals. 11. Repeat no grievances. 12. Lay no wagers. — *Game of goose* = the game of the fox and the geese.

236. *Chimney* = fireplace.

243. *Farmer's news.* — His visits to the neighboring markets would naturally make him the newsman. — *Barber's tale.* — The endless loquacity of barbers is a continual theme for jest or disgust among the writers of the time.

244. *Woodman's ballad* = perhaps some tale of Robin Hood.

248. *Mantling bliss* = foam-covered ale.

257. *Vacant* = unembarrassed with care.

259. *Pomp* = procession.

269. *Freighted* = loaded for shipment.

276. *Poor* is the object of *supplied*.

285. *All* = entirely.

293. *To bless* = to bestow her heart and hand.

300. *Band* = family.

305. *Common* = enclosed tract of land belonging, not to an individual, but to the public.

316. *Artist* = artisan.

319. *Dome* = palace.

321. *Blazing square*, that is, filled with torches, which the rich used before the introduction of street-lights.

344. *Altama* = Altamaha in Georgia. "The various terrors" enumerated are apt to provoke a smile.

355. *Crouching tigers.* — These exist in Georgia only in the poet's imagination.

403. *Shore, strand.* — By *strand* the poet means the line of sand next the sea; by *shore*, the ground above the sand.

418. *Torno's cliffs* = the heights around Lake Tornea in the north of Sweden. — *Pambamarca* = a mountain near Quito in South America.

SAMUEL JOHNSON.

THERE is no other English author with whom we are so intimately acquainted. Through the hero-worship of his biographer Boswell we are permitted to see and hear him as he appeared in the circle of his most intimate friends. We get close to the man as he actually was. We know his prejudices, foibles, and peculiarities; and, strange to say, this minute acquaintance does not lessen, but increase our admiration and love. He was a piece of rugged Alpine manhood. But his towering greatness was softened by a benevolence that never failed to reach out a helping hand to the needy; and his brusqueness of manner was relieved by an integrity of character that scorned every form of hypocrisy. In the midst of so much pettiness and cant it is delightful to contemplate his sturdy uprightness and independence; as Carlyle said of Luther, "a true son of nature and fact, for whom these centuries, and many that are to come yet, will be thankful to Heaven."

His peculiarities of person and manner are well known. He was ponderous in body as in intellect. A scrofulous affection, for which Queen Anne had laid royal hands upon him, had disfigured his face, and also tinged his mind, perhaps, with whim and melancholy. He had a rolling walk, and made it a habit to touch the posts as he passed. His appetite for tea was enormous; and he ate with an absorbing interest that might properly be called ravenous. His sight was defective; but when Reynolds painted him with a pen held close to his eye, he protested that he did not want to descend to posterity as ("blinking Sam.") He was singularly insensible to music; and when a musical performance was praised as being difficult, he simply said that he wished it had been impossible. After he had published his dictionary he was once with a friend at the top of a hill. "I haven't had a roll for a long time," said the great lexicographer; and, emptying his pockets, he stretched himself on the ground, turning over and over, like a barrel, till he reached the bottom.

But in spite of physical defects and eccentric manners, he dominated, by the sheer force of genius, the most brilliant club of London, and became the most imposing literary figure of his age. In conversation he was ready and eloquent, though apt to bear down an opponent by mere vociferation or savage personality. "There is no arguing with Johnson," said Goldsmith; "for if his pistol misses fire, he knocks you down with the but-end of it." He looked upon conversation as an intellectual wrestling, and delighted in it as a skilled and powerful athlete. "That fellow," he once said when sick, "calls forth all my powers. Were I to see Burke now, it would kill me."

He sometimes offended his friends by his rude personalities; but his repentance was so prompt and genuine that he was speedily forgiven. He set a high value on friendship, which, he said, one ought to keep in constant repair. "I look upon a day as lost," he said in his later years, "in which I do not make a new acquaintance." With all his clearness of judgment and honesty of purpose, he was sometimes narrow and prejudiced in his opinions. Not everything he says is to be taken as true, though expressed in the most dogmatic way. "No man but a blockhead," he said, "ever wrote except for money." His principles as a Tory and Churchman sometimes warped his literary criticism. Upon the death of Dr. Bathurst, a friend of his earlier years, he said, "Dear Bathurst was a man to my very heart's content: he hated a fool, and he hated a rogue, and he hated a Whig; he was a very good hater."

Samuel Johnson was born at Lichfield in 1709, the son of a bookseller of considerable ability and reputation. As a boy he was fond of athletic exercises, in which he excelled; and he possessed a constitutional fearlessness that made him a natural

leader. At the grammar school of his native town he acquired
the rudiments of Latin under a stern discipline. Though he
afterwards complained of the severity of his teachers, he remained a believer in the virtues of the rod. "A child that is
flogged," he said, "gets his task, and there's an end on't;
whereas by exciting emulation and comparisons of superiority,
you lay the foundations of lasting mischief; you make brothers
and sisters hate each other."

He left school at sixteen, and spent the next two years
at home, probably learning his father's business. He continued his studies, became a good Latin scholar, and accumulated large stores of general information. He was a vora-
cious reader. In 1728 he entered Pembroke College, Oxford,
with an unusual store of knowledge. He suffered from poverty; and at the end of three years he left the University without taking a degree. Attacks of melancholy sometimes drove
him to the verge of insanity. When reminded in after-years that
he had been "a gay and frolicsome fellow," he replied, "Ah,
sir, I was mad and violent. It was bitterness which they mistook for frolic. I was miserably poor, and I thought to fight
my way by my literature and my wit; so I disregarded all
power and all authority." In his poverty he remained proud;
and when a new pair of shoes was placed at his door by some
benevolent person, he ungraciously flung them away.

In 1731 he left the University to make his way in the world.
For the next thirty years his life was a constant struggle with
poverty and hardship. Though of a deeply religious nature, he
did not turn to the church for a living. He tried teaching, and
failed. At the age of twenty-six he married a fat, gaudy widow
of forty-eight. To Johnson's defective sight she always remained a "pretty creature," while she had discernment enough
to see the worth and ability of her husband. Though his
declaration that "it was a love match on both sides" is apt to
meet with some incredulity, the marriage did not prove an unhappy one, and there is something pathetic in the tenderness
with which he always referred to her.

In 1737 he went to London with three or four guineas and half of the tragedy of "Irene" in his pocket. Literature at this time did not offer an inviting field. It generally meant poorly paid hack-work for publishers. Long afterwards, in recalling the trials of this period, Johnson burst into tears. One of the publishers to whom he applied for work advised him, after surveying his athletic frame, to get a "porter's knot and carry trunks." He was often in want of food, clothes, and lodging. In these days of precarious livelihood he was befriended by Harry Hervey, toward whom he ever afterwards cherished a lively sense of gratitude. "Harry Hervey," he said shortly before his death, "was a vicious man, but very kind to me. If you call a dog Hervey, I shall love him."

Notwithstanding his dependent condition, he did not become obsequious. His feeling of manly independence and self-respect never deserted him. He was employed once by Osborne to make a catalogue of the Harleian Library. Reproved by his employer in an offensive manner for negligence, Johnson knocked him down with a huge Greek folio.

The year after his arrival in London we find him at work on the *Gentleman's Magazine*, a periodical of wide circulation. His most important contributions were his reports of the proceedings of Parliament, which the publisher, as a measure of precaution, sent forth as "Reports of the Debates of the Senate of Lilliput." He was furnished with notes, generally meagre and inaccurate ; and on these as a basis it was his business to write the speeches. He did the work marvellously well. Many years afterwards one of Pitt's speeches was pronounced superior to anything in Demosthenes. Johnson replied, "I wrote that speech in a garret in Exeter Street." When his impartiality was once praised in a friendly company, he answered with charming frankness, "That is not quite true; I saved appearances pretty well, but I took care that the Whig dogs should not have the best of it."

In 1738 appeared a poem entitled "London," an imitation of the third satire of Juvenal. It met with a favorable reception ;

and though it brought the author only ten guineas in money, it served to direct attention to him as a man of genius. It was published anonymously; but Pope declared on reading it that the author could not long remain concealed. Its general theme is found in the following lines, which were written doubtless with all the conviction of bitter experience: —

> " This mournful truth is everywhere confessed,
> Slow rises worth by poverty depressed;
> But here more slow, where all are slaves to gold;
> Where looks are merchandise and smiles are sold;
> Where, won by bribes, by flatteries implored,
> The groom retails the favors of his lord."

Another work appearing in 1744 added much to Johnson's reputation. One of his Grub Street acquaintances was Richard Savage, a man of noble birth but profligate life. In spite of an insolent manner, he was of agreeable companionship and wide experience. He had passed through great vicissitudes of fortune; and on his death, Johnson wrote his life in a masterly manner. "No finer specimen of literary biography," says Macaulay, "existed in any language, living or dead." It had the effect of pretty well establishing Johnson's fame.

In 1747 he was applied to by several eminent booksellers to prepare a "Dictionary of the English Language." The remuneration agreed upon was fifteen hundred guineas. The plan was issued and addressed to Lord Chesterfield, the most polished man of his time. This distinguished lord had at one time given the burly scholar encouragement; but repelled at last by his boorishness of manner, he had politely shaken him off. He characterized Johnson as a "respectable Hottentot, who throws his meat any where but down his throat." "This absurd person," he says again, "was not only uncouth in manners and warm in dispute, but behaved exactly in the same way to superiors, equals, and inferiors; and therefore, by a necessary consequence, absurdly to two of the three." Johnson's opinion of Chesterfield contained just as little flattery. He denounced that nobleman's "Letters" as teaching the morals of a harlot and the manners of a dancing-master. At another time· he said, "I thought this man had been a lord among wits ; but I find he is only a wit among lords."

After seven years of drudgery Johnson brought his work to a close. In hopes of having it dedicated to himself, Chesterfield took occasion to recommend it in two letters published in the *World*, a periodical to which men of rank and fashion frequently contributed. The proud scholar was not to be appeased ; and his reply was terrific — "the far-famed blast of doom proclaiming into the ear of Lord Chesterfield," says Carlyle, "and through him of the listening world, that patronage should be no more." "Is not a patron, my lord," wrote Johnson, "one who looks with unconcern on a man struggling for life in the water, and when he has reached the ground encumbers him with help? The notice which you have been pleased to take of my labors, had it been earlier, had been kind ; but it has been delayed till I am indifferent, and cannot enjoy it ; till I am solitary, and cannot impart it ; till I am known, and do not want it. I hope it is no very cynical asperity not to confess obligations where no benefit has been received, or to be unwilling that the public should consider me as owing that to a patron which Providence has enabled me to do for myself."

Johnson defined a lexicographer as a "harmless drudge." This is fairly descriptive of the nature of his work, which consisted in collecting, defining, and illustrating all the words in the language. Judged by present high standards, the work is defective. Scientific etymology was not yet in existence. But it far surpassed anything before it, and was received with enthusiasm by the English people.

Johnson's energies were not wholly expended on the drudgery of the "Dictionary." In 1749 he published another imitation of Juvenal entitled the "Vanity of Human Wishes." It is written with much vigor, and in passages surpasses the original. The vanity of the warrior's pride is illustrated by Charles XII. of Sweden : —

> "He left a name at which the world grew pale,
> To point a moral, or adorn a tale."

To the ambitious scholar he says : —

> "Deign on the passing world to turn thine eyes,
> And pause awhile from letters to be wise;
> There mark what ills the scholar's life assail,
> Toil, envy, want, the patron, and the jail.
> See nations, slowly wise, and meanly just,
> To buried merit raise the tardy bust.
> If dreams yet flatter, once again attend,
> Hear Lydiat's life and Galileo's end."

The poem brought him little besides a growing reputation. A few days after the publication of the "Vanity of Human Wishes," his tragedy of "Irene" was brought upon the stage by Garrick. It was heard with respectful attention. After running nine nights, it was withdrawn, and has never since been acted. "When Johnson writes tragedy," said Garrick, "declamation roars and passion sleeps; when Shakespeare wrote he dipped his pen in his own heart." Johnson took the failure of his tragedy with philosophical calmness. It brought him all together about three hundred pounds, in which no doubt he found substantial consolation.

In 1750 he began the publication of the *Rambler*, a periodical resembling the *Spectator*. It appeared twice a week for two years. The range of subjects is wide and interesting. The prevailing tone is serious and moral. Though coldly received at the time of first issue, yet afterwards collected into volumes, the papers had an extraordinary circulation. No fewer than ten editions appeared during the author's life.

His style is characterized by an artificial stateliness, and a preponderance of Latin words. "I have labored," he says in the closing paper, "to refine our language to grammatical purity, and to clear it from colloquial barbarisms, licentious idioms, and irregular combinations. Something, perhaps, I have added to the elegance of its construction, and something to the harmony of its cadence." He lacked the delicate touch of Addison. Of his moral aim he says: "The essays professedly serious, if I have been able to execute my own intentions, will be found exactly conformable to the precepts of Christianity, without any accommodation to the licentiousness and levity of the present age. I therefore look back on this part of my work with pleasure, which no praise or blame of man can diminish or augment. I shall never envy the honors which wit and learning obtain in any other cause, if I can be numbered among the writers who have given ardor to virtue, and confidence to truth." The *Rambler* is a delightful book with which to spend an occasional half-hour. It is filled with sober wisdom, and some of the papers are singularly beautiful.

In 1759 Johnson's mother died at Lichfield at the age of ninety. He was still involved in financial troubles. In order to gain money for her funeral expenses, he wrote in a single week the story of "Rasselas." It is his most popular work. Its main theme is announced in the opening sentence: "Ye who listen with credulity to the whispers of fancy, and pursue with eagerness the phantoms of hope; who expect that age will perform the promises of youth, and that the deficiences of the present day will be supplied by the morrow; attend to the history of Rasselas, prince of Abyssinia." The story makes no pretensions to historical accuracy; the Abyssinians brought before us are in reality highly cultivated Europeans. But it is written with Johnson's peculiar eloquence, and exhibits fully his moral and reflective temperament.

The year 1762 saw an important change in Johnson's condition. He received a pension of three hundred pounds a year. In his "Dictionary" he had defined a pension as "generally understood to mean pay given to a state hireling for treason to his country." Being assured that he did not come within the definition, and that the pension was accorded in recognition of past services, he accepted it after some hesitation. It placed him for the first time in circumstances of independence, and allowed him to indulge his constitutional indolence. He talked at night and slept during the day, rising at two in the afternoon. "I cannot now curse the House of Hanover," he said in appreciative reference to his pension ; "but I think that the pleasure of cursing the House of Hanover and drinking King James's health, all amply over-balanced by three hundred pounds a year."

No longer driven by necessity, his pen became less busy. His principal influence was exerted through conversation. His colloquial powers were of the highest order. In the Club, which included, among others, Goldsmith, Burke, Reynolds, and Garrick, he was easily first. The opinion of the Club carried great weight; and for a time his position might be described as literary dictator of England. Meeting the King one day in the royal library, he was asked by his Majesty if he intended to give the world any more of his compositions. " I think I have written enough," said Johnson. " And I should think so too," replied his Majesty, "if you had not written so well " — a compliment of which Johnson was very proud.

In 1773 Johnson made a journey to the Hebrides. He was kindly received on his journey through Scotland. His prejudices against the Scotch were softened to a harmless foible. He made inquiries concerning the poems of Ossian. He denounced Macpherson's work as a forgery. Receiving a furious and threatening letter from the author of " Ossian," Johnson replied : " I hope I shall never be deterred from detecting what I think a cheat by the menaces of a ruffian." In anticipation of personal violence, he provided himself with a heavy stick, of which, had occasion offered, he would doubt-less have made vigorous use.

The results of this trip are given in a pleasant volume entitled "Journey to the Hebrides." The style is, as usual, elaborate and stately. Writing to an intimate friend from the Hebrides, he says with colloquial ease and pith, " When we were taken up-stairs, a dirty fellow bounced out of the bed on which one of us was to lie." In his book this incident is trans-lated into his artificial literary style as follows : " Out of one of the beds on which we were to repose, started up, at our entrance, a man black as a Cyclops from the forge."

In 1777 a number of London booksellers decided to publish a collection of English poetry. Johnson was asked to prepare the introductory biographical and critical sketches. The result was his "Lives of the Poets," the work, perhaps, by which he will be longest known. In the judgment of Macaulay it is more interesting than any novel. In many respects it is an admirable production. Without much patient research after biographical material, it gives the leading facts in the life of each poet, together with a masterly analysis of his character and a critical examination of his works. It is less ponderous in style than his earlier writings. That it is independent in judgment goes without saying. His criticisms, always worth attention, are not always just. He was sometimes influenced by his prejudices, as in the case of Milton and Gray ; and he attached too much importance to the logical and didactic elements of poetry. He had no ear for the music of poetry ; and that subtle, ethereal quality, which raises it above prose, could not be grasped by his clumsy critical principles.

One of the great charms of the "Lives of the Poets" consists in the shrewd observations upon life and character with which the book abounds. Discussing Dryden's financial difficulties, he remarks : "It is well known that he seldom lives frugally who lives by chance. Hope is always liberal, and they that trust her promises make little scruple of revelling to-day on the profits of the morrow." The work contains the materials for a collection of maxims as interesting as those of La Rochefoucauld, and much more truthful. "Very near to admiration," he says, "is the wish to admire." The rich treasures of wisdom which long experience and reflection had stored in his spacious mind are scattered through his pages with lavish hand.

Much of interest in Johnson's life is necessarily omitted : the strange crowd of dependants he maintained at his home ; his relation with the Thrales ; a great store of interesting anecdote preserved to us by his satellite Boswell. Though for a time oppressed with a dread of death, he met it, as the end drew near, with manly courage. In his last sickness he was visited by many of his old friends. " I am afraid," said Burke, " that so many of us must be oppressive to you." — " No, sir, it is not so," replied Johnson ; " and I must be in a wretched state indeed when your company would not be a delight to me." — " You have always been too good to me," said Burke with a breaking voice, as he parted from his old friend for the last time. Now and then there was a flash of the old vigor and humor. Describing a man who sat up with him, he said : " Sir, the fellow's an idiot ; he's as awkward as a turnspit when first put into the wheel, and as sleepy as a dormouse." His last words were a benediction. A young lady begged his blessing. " God bless you, my dear," he said with infinite tenderness. Nothing could have been more characteristic of his great, benevolent heart. He peacefuly died Dec. 13, 1784. He had once playfully said to Goldsmith, when visiting the poets' corner of Westminster Abbey,

" Forsitan et nostrum nomen miscebitur istis." [1]

The prediction and the wish were fulfilled. And among the wise and great who repose there, there is no one whose massive intellect, honest worth, and great heart command our admiration and love in a higher degree than Samuel Johnson.

: Perhaps our names will be mingled with them.

AKENSIDE.

(From Johnson's "Lives of the Poets.")

MARK AKENSIDE [1] was born on the 9th of November, 1721, at Newcastle-upon-Tyne. His father, Mark, was a butcher, of the Presbyterian sect; his mother's name was Mary Lumsden. He received the first part of his education at the grammar school of Newcastle; and was afterwards instructed by Mr. Wilson, who kept a private academy.

At the age of eighteen he was sent to Edinburgh, that he might qualify himself for the office of a dissenting minister,[2] and received some assistance from the fund[3] which the dissenters employ in educating young men of scanty fortune. But a wider view of the world opened other scenes, and prompted other hopes; he determined to study physic,[4] and repaid that contribution, which, being received for a different purpose, he justly thought dishonorable to retain.

Whether, when he resolved not to be a dissenting minister, he ceased to be a dissenter, I know not. He certainly retained an unnecessary and outrageous zeal[5] for what he called liberty; a zeal which sometimes disguises from the world, and not rarely from the mind which it possesses, an envious desire of plundering wealth or degrading greatness; and of which the immediate tendency is innovation and anarchy, an impetuous eagerness to subvert and confound, with very little care what shall be established.

Akenside was one of those poets who have felt very early the motions of genius, and one of those students who have very early stored their memories with sentiments and images. Many of his performances were produced in his youth; and his greatest work, "The Pleasures of Imagination,"[6] appeared in 1744. I have heard Dodsley, by whom it was published, relate, that when the copy was offered him, the price demanded for it, which was a hundred and twenty pounds, being such as he was not inclined to give precipitately, he carried the work to Pope, who, having looked into it, advised him not to make a niggardly offer, for "this was no every-day writer."

In 1741 he went to Leyden in pursuit of medical knowledge; and there three years afterwards (May 16, 1744) became doctor of physic, having, according to the custom of the Dutch universities, published a thesis or dissertation.[7] . . .

Akenside was a young man, warm with every notion that by nature or accident had been connected with the sound of liberty, and, by an eccentricity which such dispositions do not easily avoid, a lover of contradiction, and no friend to anything established.[8] He adopted Shaftesbury's foolish assertion of the efficacy of ridicule for the discovery of truth. For this he was attacked by Warburton, and defended by Dyson;[9] Warburton afterwards reprinted his remarks at the end of his dedication to the Freethinkers.

The result of all the arguments which have been produced in a long and eager discussion of this idle question may easily be collected. If ridicule be applied to any position as the test of truth, it will then become a question whether such ridicule be just; this can only be decided by the application of truth, as the test of ridicule. Two men fearing, one a real, the other a fancied danger, will be for a while equally exposed to the inevitable consequences of cowardice, contemptuous censure, and ludicrous representation; and the true state of both cases must be known, before it can be decided whose terror is rational, and whose is ridiculous; who is to be pitied, and who to be despised. Both are for a while equally exposed to laughter, but both are not therefore equally contemptible.

In the revisal of his poem, though he died before he had finished it, he omitted the lines which had given occasion to Warburton's objections.[10]

He published, soon after his return from Leyden (1745), his first collection of odes, and was impelled, by his rage of patriotism, to write a very acrimonious epistle to Pulteney,[11] whom he stigmatizes, under the name of Curio, as the betrayer of his country.

Being now to live by his profession, he first commenced physician at Northampton, where Dr. Stonehouse then practised with such reputation and success that a stranger was not likely to gain ground upon him. Akenside tried the contest a while; and having deafened the place with clamors for liberty, removed to Hampstead, where he resided more than two years, and then fixed himself in London, the proper place for a man of accomplishments like his.

At London he was known as a poet, but was still to make his way as a physician; and would perhaps have been reduced to great exigencies but that Mr. Dyson, with an ardor of friendship that has not many examples, allowed him three hundred pounds a year. Thus supported, he advanced gradually in medical reputation, but never attained any great extent of practice, or eminence of popularity. A physician in a great city seems to be the mere plaything of fortune; his degree of reputation is, for the most part, totally casual : they that employ him know not his excellence; they that reject him know not his deficience. By any acute observer, who had looked on the transactions of the medical world for half a century, a very curious book might be written on the " Fortune of Physicians."[12]

Akenside appears not to have been wanting to his own success; he placed himself in view by all the common methods; he became a Fellow of the Royal Society; he obtained a degree at Cambridge; and as admitted into the College of Physicians; he wrote little poetry, but published from time to time medical essays and observations; he became physician to St. Thomas's Hospital; he read the Gulstonian Lectures in Anatomy; he began to give, for the Crounian Lecture, a history of the revival of learning, from which he soon desisted; and, in conversation, he very eagerly forced himself into notice by an ambitious ostentation of elegance and literature.

His " Discourse on the Dysentery " (1764) was considered as a very conspicuous specimen of Latinity; which entitled him to the same height of place among the scholars as he possessed before among the wits; and he might, perhaps, have risen to a greater elevation of character, but that his studies were ended with his life, by a putrid fever, June 23, 1770, in the forty-ninth year of his age.

Akenside is to be considered as a didactic and lyric poet. His great work is " The Pleasures of Imagination; "[13] a performance which, published as it was at the age of twenty-three, raised expectations that were not very amply satisfied. It has undoubtedly a just claim to very particular notice, as an example of great felicity of genius, and uncommon amplitude of acquisitions, of a young mind stored with images, and much exercise in combining and comparing them.

With the philosophical or religious tenets of the author I have nothing to do; my business is with his poetry. The subject is well chosen, as it includes all images that can strike or please, and thus comprises every species of poetical delight. The only difficulty is in the choice of examples and illustrations; and it is not easy, in such exuberance of matter, to find the middle point between penury and satiety. The parts seem artistically disposed, with sufficient coherence, so as that they cannot change their places without injury to the general design.

His images are displayed with such luxuriance of expression, that they are hidden, like Butler's moon, by a "veil of light;" they are forms fantastically lost under superfluity of dress. *Pars minima est ipsa puella sui.* The words are multiplied till the sense is hardly perceived; attention deserts the mind, and settles in the ear. The reader wanders through the gay diffusion, sometimes amazed, and sometimes delighted, but, after many turnings in the flowery labyrinth, comes out as he went in. He remarked little and laid hold on nothing.

To his versification justice requires that praise should not be denied. In the general fabrication of his rhymes he is, perhaps, superior to any other writer of blank verse; his flow is smooth, and his pauses are musical; but the concatenation of his verses is commonly too long continued, and the full close does not recur with sufficient frequency. The sense is carried on through a long intertexture of complicated clauses, and, as nothing is distinguished, nothing is remembered.

The exemption which blank verse affords from the necessity of closing the sense with the couplet betrays luxuriant and active minds into such self-indulgence, that they pile image upon image, ornament upon ornament, and are not easily persuaded to close the sense at all. Blank verse will, therefore, I fear, be too often found in description exuberant, in argument loquacious, and in narration tiresome.

His diction is certainly poetical as it is not prosaic, and elegant as it is not vulgar. He is to be commended as having fewer artifices of disgust than most of his brethren of the blank song.[14] He rarely either recalls old phrases, or twists his meter into harsh inversions. The sense of his words, however, is strained, when " he views the Ganges from Alpine heights ; " that is from mountains like the Alps. And the pedant surely intrudes (but when was blank verse without pedantry?) when he tells how " Planets *absolve* the stated round of time." [15]

It is generally known to readers of poetry that he intended to revise and augment this work, but died before he had completed his design. The reformed work as he left it, and the additions which he had made, are very properly retained in the late collection. He seems to have somewhat contracted his diffusion ; but I know not whether he has gained in closeness what he has lost in splendor. In the additional book, " The Tale of Solon " is too long.

One great defect of this poem is very properly censured by Mr. Walker, unless it may be said, in his defence, that what he has omitted was not properly in his plan. His " picture of man is grand and beautiful, but unfinished. The immortality of the soul, which is the natural consequence of the appetites and powers she is invested with, is scarcely once hinted throughout the poem. This deficiency is amply supplied by the masterly pencil of Dr. Young; who, like a good philosopher, has invincibly proved the immortality of man, both from the grandeur of his conceptions, and the meanness and misery of his state; for this reason, a few passages are selected from the 'Night Thoughts,' which, with those of Akenside, seem to form a complete view of the powers, situation, and end of man."

His other poems are now to be considered; but a short considera-tion will despatch them. It is not easy to guess why he addicted himself so diligently to lyric poetry, having neither the ease and airi-ness of the lighter, nor the vehemence and elevation of the grander ode. When he lays his ill-fated hand upon his harp, his former powers seem to desert him; he has no longer his luxuriance of ex-pression, nor variety of images. His thoughts are cold, and his words inelegant. Yet such was his love of lyrics, that, having written with great vigor and poignancy his " Epistle to Curio," he transformed it afterwards into an ode disgraceful only to its author.

Of his odes nothing favorable can be said: the sentiments com-monly want force, nature, or novelty; the diction is sometimes harsh and uncouth, the stanzas ill-constructed and unpleasant, and the rhymes dissonant, or unskilfully disposed; too distant from each other, or arranged with too little regard to established use, and there-fore perplexing to the ear, which in a short composition has not time to grow familiar with an innovation.[16]

To examine such compositions singly cannot be required; they have doubtless darker and brighter parts; but when they are once found to be generally dull, all further labor may be spared; for to what use can the work be criticised that will not be read?

NOTES TO JOHNSON'S AKENSIDE.

1. This sketch of Akenside is from the "Lives of the Poets." It is one of the shortest, but it exhibits very well Johnson's manner of criticism. As is frequently the case in the "Lives," the biographical matter is scanty.

2. Dr. Johnson was a strong Churchman; and his prejudices against the Dissenters kept him from doing Akenside full justice.

3. This was a fund used by the Church of Scotland to educate young men of limited means for the ministry.

4. The reason for the change is a matter of conjecture. It probably sprang from a disinclination to assume the responsibilities of the clerical office, or perhaps from the drawings of worldly ambition.

5. Here the prejudices of the Tory and Churchman are apparent.

6. The title was suggested to Akenside by Addison's papers on the "Pleasures of the Imagination," in the *Spectator*. But the treatment in the poem is quite different.

7. This dissertation was characterized by acute professional research and sound reasoning.

8. Dr. Johnson's prejudices against Presbyterians and Whigs again get the better of his judgment.

9. Jeremiah Dyson — "a name never to be mentioned by any lover of genius or noble deeds without affection and reverence" — was the steadfast friend and benefactor of Akenside. The passage in question occurs in the third book of the "Pleasures of Imagination." The sense of ridicule was implanted "in mortal bosoms,"

> " Wherefore, but to aid
> The tardy steps of reason, and at once
> By this prompt impulse urge us to depress
> The giddy whims of folly ? "

10. This omission would indicate that he recognized the justice of Warburton's strictures.

11. William Pulteney, Earl of Bath. Once the friend, he afterwards became the enemy of Robert Walpole, and the leader of the opposition in Parliament. His weakness in forming a ministry after Walpole's downfall in 1741 gave rise to the charge of betraying his country. Of Akenside's

epistle, Macaulay said that it indicated "powers of elevated satire, which, if diligently cultivated, might have disputed the eminence of Dryden."

12. This may be taken as an illustration of Johnson's interesting side remarks.

13. This is the first of the series known as the " Poems of the Pleasures." The others are " The Pleasures of Memory," by Samuel Rogers; " The Pleasures of Hope," by Thomas Campbell; and " The Pleasures of Friendship," by James McHenry.

14. Johnson had an unreasonable aversion to blank verse. In the sketch of Milton he says: " Poetry may subsist without rhyme, but English poetry will not often please; nor can rhyme ever be safely spared, but where the subject is able to support itself. Blank verse . . . has neither the easiness of repose, nor the melody of numbers, and therefore tires by long continuance."

15. These paragraphs illustrate the points to which Dr. Johnson devotes his criticism. It is chiefly external qualities upon which he dwells — the essential element of poetry is untouched.

16. These observations are a little too severe.

THE NINETEENTH CENTURY.

REPRESENTATIVE AUTHORS.

SCOTT, BYRON, WORDSWORTH, TENNYSON.

OTHER PROMINENT WRITERS.

Poets. — COLERIDGE, SOUTHEY, MOORE, SHELLEY, KEATS, CAMPBELL, BROWNING.

Historians. — GROTE, MACAULAY, HALLAM, CARLYLE.

Essayists. — JEFFREY, HAZLITT, LAMB, DE QUINCEY.

Novelists. — JANE AUSTEN, CHARLOTTE BRONTÉ, MARRYATT, DICKENS, THACKERAY, LYTTON, TROLLOPE, GEORGE ELIOT.

VII.

THE NINETEENTH CENTURY.

GENERAL SURVEY. — Upon the whole there has been no grander age in the history of the world. It may lack the æsthetic culture of the age of Pericles; the great martial spirit of ancient Rome; the lofty ideals of the age of chivalry. But as we compare the conditions of the present day with those of any period of the past, who can doubt the fact of human progress? The world has grown into a liberty, intelligence, happiness, and morality unknown at any previous time. To be sure, the true golden age has not been reached. That lies, and perhaps far distant, in the future. Many evils in society, in the state, and in the church, need to be corrected. But the advancement during the present century has been marvellously rapid. Let us consider for a moment some of the characteristics of this age.

If we think of the wonderful improvements in the mechanic arts, we recognize this century as an age of invention. Within a few decades are comprised more numerous and more important inventions than are found in many preceding centuries taken together. Think of the wonders accomplished by steam! It has supplied a new motive power, accelerated travel, and built up manufacturing inland towns and cities. Electricity is at present accomplishing scarcely less. It carries our messages and lights our cities. The capacity of the printing-press has been vastly increased. While the sewing-machine has taken the place of the needle in the house, the reaper and the mowing-machine have supplanted the sickle and the scythe in the field. The breech-loading and repeating rifle has driven out the muzzle-loading flint-lock. Swift armored battle-ships have taken the place of slow, high-decked wooden vessels.

These are but a few of the inventions belonging to our time. Many a man is now living who has seen the entire system of manufacturing, travel, agriculture, and transmission of intelligence, completely revolutionized, seeing more than if he had lived, in some ages of the world, a thousand years.

The present is an age of scientific inquiry. The Baconian spirit prevails. Tradition has lost much of its power ; men are not guided by mere authority ; the conclusions of empty speculation are little valued. Careful and patient toilers are at work in every department of learning. Nature is being questioned as never before. All the natural sciences — physics, zoölogy, botany, geology, chemistry, physiology, astronomy — have been wonderfully expanded. We are able to penetrate more deeply the mysteries of the world about us. A school-boy now knows more of the constitution and laws of the physical world than the greatest sages of antiquity. The same patient methods of investigation are applied to the study of the mind, the origin of man, the history of the past, the laws of society. The result is seen in a modification or destruction of many old beliefs ; but at the same time it has brought us greater light and a more receptive attitude of mind.

This is pre-eminently a practical age. It aims at visible results. Science and invention have placed vast resources at our command. The Baconian maxim that "knowledge is power" now has abundant exemplification. The material wealth of every country is being developed; and daring explorers, supported by private enterprise or royal bounty, are sent to examine unknown regions. Railroads are built; mines are opened; towns are established; commerce is encouraged. Every effort is put forth to make living less costly and more comfortable. Food and clothing were never so abundant.

Common-sense reigns. Unwilling to be imposed upon in any way, men strive to see things as they are. Utility is the test applied to everything. Whatever in traditional institutions cannot justify itself by this standard, is slowly undermined and abolished. No doubt this practical tendency sometimes goes too far, subjecting æsthetic and spiritual interests to material gains. The ideal is in too great a degree banished from life. Wealth, luxury, power, become in too many cases the object of men's endeavor, instead of a pure and lofty character. But while attended with this drawback, the practical tendency of our age deserves to be considered one of its claims to superiority.

It is an age of educational advancement. Schools of every class are being multiplied. Education is brought within the reach of common people, and in many countries compulsory attendance is enforced. The methods of instruction are more nearly conformed to the nature of the child, and the subjects of study are designed to fit the pupil for the duties of practical life. In higher education the change is no less remarkable. The traditional curriculum, consisting largely of Latin and Greek, has been greatly expanded. Subjects of great practical importance — the modern languages, natural and political science, the mother tongue, and history — receive increased attention.

Education is brought into closer relations with practical life. Intelligence was never so generally diffused. The periodical press exerts an immense influence. Not only the news from all parts of the world, but also the leading political, social, scientific, and religious questions of the time, are daily discussed and read in newspapers and magazines. The horizon of thought is greatly broadened for the masses.

It is a time of political advancement. The democratic principles announced and defended in America and France at the close of the last century have become more widely diffused. It is now commonly recognized that governments exist, not for sovereigns or favored classes, but for the people. The right of suffrage has been greatly extended. The science of government is better understood, and legislative enactments have become more intelligent and equitable. The public administration has become purer. If bribery, self-aggrandizement, and dishonesty still exist, these evils are much less frequent than in former ages. Our public men live in the light, and are held accountable at the bar of public opinion.

Wars are becoming less frequent and less barbaric. Minor international differences are usually settled by diplomacy and arbitration. The treatment of the unfortunate and the criminal classes has become more humane. The insane are no longer chained in loathsome cells, the unfortunate debtor is not thrown into jail, a petty criminal is not hanged. As compared with any other period in the history of the English-speaking race, the present is an age of political freedom, justice, and humanity.

The age is one of social advancement. It is true that much remains yet to be accomplished. The agitation of social questions makes us observant of existing evils. However much may be lacking in comparison with an ideal condition, there is great improvement in comparison with the past. The facilities of modern manufacture and commerce have greatly multiplied and cheapened the necessities and comforts of life. Wages have increased. The poor, as well as the rich, live better than ever before.

With increased intelligence, the popular taste has become more refined. Amusements have become less coarse and brutal. Public libraries and museums give the laboring classes the means of intellectual culture and refined enjoyment. Machinery has decreased the amount of drudgery. The hours of work have been shortened. Children are protected from the cruelty of parents and the inhumanity of employers. A great levelling process is lessening the inequalities of social condition. Serfs and slaves are things of the past.

The religious advancement of the time is specially noteworthy. Christian doctrines have felt the touch of a broadened culture and a scientific spirit. Superstition has become a thing of the past. The emphasis of religious teaching is now centred upon fundamental truths. We understand more clearly the nature and the works of God. A new life, begotten and sustained by Christianity, receives increased emphasis. Piety in the daily life is considered of more importance than the formal acceptance of elaborate creeds. Christ has become more and more the conscious ideal of the world. The ascetic spirit has given place to an active spirit that bravely meets the duties of every-day life.

Religion never had greater power. Its principles pervade every department of life. Christian churches are multiplied ; religious literature is widely extended ; the Bible is more carefully studied. The asperities of religious sects are softening, and the general tendency is to Christian unity. The Evangelical Alliance and the Young Men's Christian Association are the practical manifestation of the general desire for closer union and co-operation among Christian people.

In accordance with the practical tendencies of the age, religion is more benevolent in its activities. The fatherhood of God and the brotherhood of man are appreciated as never before. The church is active in missionary work at home and abroad. It is foremost in every work that seeks to relieve the unfortunate and reclaim the lost. It seeks to bring a pure and benevolent spirit to the settlement of the great social and political problems of the day.

Literature, in sympathy with the intellectual movements of the age, has shown a many-sided activity. It is at once creative and diffusive. Both prose and poetry have been cultivated to an extraordinary degree. Old forms of literature have been expanded, and new forms devised to contain the rich intellectual fruitage of the present century. In style there has been a return to nature ; at the same time there has been an artistic finish unknown in previous eras.

With the establishment of many periodicals, essay writing has attained a new importance and excellence. In the days of Addison and Johnson, the essay was devoted chiefly to brief discussions of light social and moral topics. It is different now. In the form of reviews and magazine articles, the essay deals with every subject of interest or importance. The scholar, the scientist, the philosopher, the historian, — each uses the periodical press to set forth the results of his studies and investigations. The cream of human thought and activity is contained in our leading magazines and reviews. Without an acquaintance with their contents, it is difficult to keep abreast with the times.

A notable advance is discernible in the writing of history. Greater prominence is given to the social condition of the people. The sources of information have been greatly enlarged, and historians are expected to base their statements on trustworthy data. Besides, a philosophy of history has been recognized. Greater attention is given to the moving causes of events, and to the general tendencies in national life. With this greater trustworthiness and more philosophic treatment, history has lost nothing of its excellence of style. If it has given up the uniform stateliness of Robertson and Gibbon, it has become more graphic, more varied, and more interesting.

No other department of literature has shown a richer development during the present century than fiction. It occupies the place filled by the drama during the Elizabethan period. The plot is skilfully conducted ; the characters represent every class of society ; the thoughts are often the deepest of which our nature is capable. Fiction is no longer simply a means of amusement. Without laying aside its artistic character, it has become in great measure didactic. In the form of historical romance, it seeks to reproduce in a vivid manner the thoughts, feelings, and customs of other ages. The novel of contemporary life often holds up to view the foibles and vices of modern society. In many cases fiction is made the means of popularizing various social, religious, and political views.

The many changes in politics, science, and religion have produced a notable change in poetry. The poetic imagery inherited from Greece and Rome has been swept away. Modern science has been too strong for the mythology of the ancients.

Yet the general effect upon poetry of the modern scientific spirit has been salutary. While it has swept away what was unessential and temporary, it has led the way to deeper verities. Poetry now penetrates more deeply into the secrets of human nature and of the physical universe. The revolutionary social and political ideas, with which the century opened, have likewise proved favorable to poetry. For a time, as in Shelley and Byron, it resulted in productions outrageously hostile to existing institutions. But after a time the perturbed current of poetry began to run clear, and it was seen to have gained in volume and power. Throwing aside its anarchical tendencies, it became the advocate of justice, freedom, and truth.

With clearer views of divine truth, poetry has gained in geniality, and in power to reach the profound spiritual part of man. The hardness of Puritanic asceticism has been laid aside. In Christian lyrics of unsurpassed sweetness, poetry breathes the spirit of divine and human love ; and in elegies, it draws strength and comfort from the deepest resources of philosophy and inspiration.

While in large measure realistic, poetry has not cast aside its ideal character. Modern progress in culture has placed it on a high vantage ground — far in advance of all the preceding ages ; and from this new position, its penetrating vision pierces farther into the realms of unexplored and undiscovered truth. With its present expansion in thought and feeling, poetry has naturally assumed new forms. While in dramatic poetry there is a humiliating decay in comparison with the Elizabethan era, yet in lyric, narrative, and didactic poetry we find almost unrivalled excellence. With naturalness of form and expression, there is a careful and conscientious workmanship not found in previous periods.

SIR WALTER SCOTT.

THE greatest literary figure during the first quarter of the present century is undoubtedly Sir Walter Scott. He occupied scarcely less relative prominence for a time than did Samuel Johnson a few decades earlier. It is not uncommon to associate his name with the period in which he was pre-eminent. He distinguished himself in both poetry and prose. He created a species of romantic poetry that was received with great applause until it was eclipsed by the intenser productions of Byron. "Why did you quit poetry?" a friend once inquired of Scott. "Because Byron beat me," was the remarkably frank reply. He then turned to fiction; and in his splendid series of historical romances he stands pre-eminent not only among the writers of England, but of the world.

Sir Walter Scott descended from a line distinguished for sports and arms rather than letters. One of his remote ancestors was once given the choice of being hanged, or marrying a woman who had won the prize for ugliness in four counties. After three days' deliberation he decided in favor of "meikle-mouthed Meg," who, be it said, made him an excellent wife. It was from her that our author possibly inherited his large mouth. His father was a dignified man, orderly in his habits, and fond of ceremony. It is said that he "absolutely loved a funeral;" and from far and near he was sent for to superintend mortuary ceremonies. As a lawyer he frequently lost clients by insisting that they should be just — a sturdy uprightness that was transmitted to his illustrious son.

Sir Walter's mother was a woman of superior native ability and of excellent education. She had a good memory, and a talent for narration. "If I have been able to do anything in the way of painting past times," he once wrote, "it is very much from the studies with which she presented me." He loved his mother tenderly; and the evening after his burial, a number of small objects that had once belonged to her were found arranged in careful order in his desk, where his eye might rest upon them every morning before he began his task. This is an instance of filial piety as touching as it is beautiful.

Walter Scott, the ninth of twelve children, was born in Edinburgh, Aug. 15, 1771. On account of sickness he was sent into the country, where his childhood was spent in the midst of attractive scenery. Left lying out of doors one day, a thunder-storm arose; and when his aunt ran to bring him in, she found him delighted with the raging elements, and shouting, "Bonny, bonny!" at every flash of lightning. One of the old servants spoke of him as "a sweet-tempered bairn, a darling with all about the house." But at the same time he was active, fearless, and passionate. The Laird of Raeburn, a relative, once wrung the neck of a pet starling. " I flew at his throat like a wild cat," said Sir Walter, as he recalled the circumstance fifty years afterwards, "and was torn from him with no little difficulty."

At school he established a reputation for irregular ability. He possessed great energy, vitality, and pride, and was naturally a leader among his fellow-pupils. He had the gift of story-telling in a remarkable degree. He found difficulty in confining himself to the prescribed studies, and persistently declined to learn Greek. In Latin he made fair attainments. He delighted in the past, reverenced existing institutions, sympathized with royalty, and as a boy, as in after life, he was a Tory.

As a student of law at the University of Edinburgh, Scott was noted for his gigantic memory and enormous capacity for work. His literary tastes ran in the direction of mediæval life, and he devoured legend and romance and border song with great avidity. He learned Italian to read Ariosto, and Spanish to read Cervantes, whose novels, he said, " first inspired him with the desire to excel in fiction." ⟩ But his memory retained only what suited his genius. He used to illustrate this characteristic by the story of an old borderer who once said to a Scotch divine: "No, sir, I have no command of my memory. It only retains what hits my fancy; and probably, sir, if you were to preach to me for two hours, I would not be able, when you finished, to remember a word you had been saying."

As a lawyer Scott was not notably successful. He was fond of making excursions over the country to visit localities celebrated for natural beauty or historic events. In view of this habit, his father reproached him as being better fitted for a pedler than for a lawyer. He was rather fond, it must be said, of living, —

> "One crowded hour of glorious life."

"But drunk or sober," such is the testimony of one of his companions at this time, "he was aye the gentleman." Scott practised at the bar fourteen years; but his earnings never amounted to much more than two hundred pounds a year. In 1799 he was made sheriff of Selkirkshire on a salary of three hundred pounds; and a few years later he became Clerk of the Session, — an officer in the Court of Edinburgh, — a position that increased his income to sixteen hundred pounds. He was not eloquent as a pleader; his tastes were averse to legal drudgery; and his proclivities for poetry and for rambling over the country did not enhance his reputation as a lawyer. But whether practising at the bar or wandering over the country, "he was makin' himself a' the time" — storing his mind with the facts, legends, and characters which he was afterwards to embody in his immortal works.

The life of Scott was not without its romance, and, — but for the effect upon his character and works, we might say, — alas, its sorrow. He one day offered his umbrella to a beautiful young lady who was coming out of the Greyfriars church during a shower. It was graciously accepted. The incident led to an acquaintance, and, at least on the part of Scott, to a deep attachment. His large romantic nature was filled with visions of happiness. Then came disappointment. For some reason the fair Margaret rejected his attentions, and married a rival. After the first resentment was past, this attachment remained throughout his life a source of tender recollections. Years afterwards he went to visit Margaret's mother, and noted in his diary: " I fairly softened myself, like an old fool, with recalling old stories till I was fit for nothing but shedding tears and repeating verses for the whole night." Within a twelve-month of his disappointment, urged on it may be by his pride, he married Miss Carpenter, a lady of French birth and parentage. Though it was "a bird of paradise mating with an eagle," she made a good wife, and the union was upon the whole a happy one.

Though Scott's greatest literary work was to be in prose, he began with poetry. His first undertaking was a translation from the German of Bürger's spectral ballad, " Lenore." Though his rendering is spirited, he was far too healthy-minded to be perfectly at home in treating spectral themes. He soon turned to more congenial subjects. From his college days he had been making a collection of old Scottish ballads. In 1802 he published in two volumes " The Minstrelsy of the Scottish Border," which was an immediate success.

The native bent of his mind, and his studies for many years, peculiarly fitted him to restore and illustrate the simplicity and violence of the old border life. The transition to original poems, in which the legends and history of the same region were embodied, was easily made. " The Lay of the Last Minstrel" was published in 1805, and at once became widely popular. More than two thousand copies were sold the first year; and by 1830 the sales reached forty-four thousand copies, bringing the author nearly a thousand pounds.

Three years later " Marmion," his greatest poem, appeared; and this was followed in 1810 by " The Lady of the Lake." They were read with enthusiasm. They were new in subject and treatment. Without any pretension to classical regularity and finish, they were rapid, energetic, and romantic — the style exactly suited to the subject. " I am sensible," the author said, " that if there be anything good about my poetry or prose either, it is a hurried frankness of composition, which pleases soldiers, sailors, and young people of bold and active dispositions." They are so simple in structure and thought as to be easily comprehended ; they abound in wild scenes and daring deeds; they are suffused with a patriotic, martial spirit, and the delirious enjoyment of wild out-door life.

Nearly all of Scott's poetry was written in a beautiful little country house at Ashestiel. The locality is vividly depicted in the first canto of " Marmion " : —

> " November's sky is chill and drear,
> November's leaf is red and sear ;
> Late, gazing down the steepy linn,
> That hems our little garden in,
> Low in its dark and narrow glen,
> You scarce the rivulet might ken,
> So thick the tangled greenwood grew,
> So feeble trilled the streamlet through;
> Now, murmuring hoarse, and frequent seen,
> Through bush and briar no longer green,
> An angry brook, it sweeps the glade,
> Brawls over rock and wild cascade,
> And, foaming brown with double speed,
> Hurries its waters to the Tweed."

He devoted the first part of the day to his literary work. " Arrayed in his shooting-jacket, or whatever dress he meant to use till dinner-time, he was seated at his desk by six o'clock, all his papers arranged before him in the most accurate order, and his books of reference marshalled around him on the floor, while at least one favorite dog lay watching his eye, just beyond the line of circumvallation. Thus, by the time the family assembled for breakfast, between nine and ten, he had done enough, in his own language, ' to break the neck of the day's work.' "

During the seven years of his residence at Ashestiel, his

literary labors included, besides his poetry, a " Life of Dryden," "The Secret History of James I.," and many other works of less importance.

In 1812 Scott moved to Abbotsford, where he spent the rest of his life. He was a man of great personal and family pride. It was his ambition to live in great magnificence, and to dispense hospitality on a large scale. He bought a large area of land at an aggregate expense of twenty-nine thousand pounds, and erected a baronial castle. Here he realized for a time his ideal of life. He was visited by distinguished men and hero-worshippers from all parts of the world. Indeed, his fame became oppressive. His correspondence was enormous, and as many as sixteen parties of sight-seers visited Abbotsford in a single day.

For his friends Scott was the prince of hosts. Devoting only the earlier part of the day to work, he placed his afternoons wholly at the service of his guests. Hunting was his favorite sport, and he led many a brilliant party over the hills and through the valleys to the echoing music of his hounds. His large, benevolent nature drew men to him. To all classes he was thoroughly kind. " Sir Walter speaks to every man as if they were blood relations," was a common description of his demeanor. Even the dumb animals recognized in him a friend.

Apart from his social enjoyments, Scott found most delight in planting trees. He greatly beautified his estate, and imparted a taste for arboriculture to the landholders about him. "Planting and pruning trees," he said, " I could work at from morning to night. There is a sort of self-congratulation, a little self-flattery, in the idea that while you are pleasing and amusing yourself, you are seriously contributing to the future welfare of the country, and that your acorn may send its future ribs of oak to future victories like Trafalgar."

The great mistake in Scott's life lay in his business ventures. Through them came ultimately embarrassment and disaster. In the hope of increasing his income, he established the publishing house of John Ballantyne & Co., in Edinburgh. John Ballantyne was a frivolous, dissipated man, wholly unfit for the management of the enterprise. Scott, though possessing sufficient discernment, was easily led away by his feelings. As a consequence, the warehouses of the new firm were soon filled with a great quantity of unsalable stock. Only the extensive sale of his novels saved the company from early bankruptcy. But ultimately the crash came, and in 1825 Scott found himself personally responsible for the enormous debt of one hundred and thirty thousand pounds.

For years he had been the literary sovereign of Great Britain. He had lived in the midst of great splendor at Abbotsford. To find his means swept away in a single moment was a terrific blow, sufficient to crush an ordinary man. But at no time in his career did Scott exhibit so fully his heroic character. Instead of crushing him, misfortune only called forth his strength. With indomitable will and sturdy integrity, he set to work to meet his immense obligations. There is nothing more heroic in the course of English literature. Work after work came from his pen in rapid succession. He well-nigh accomplished his purpose; but at last, as we shall see, his mind and body gave way under the tremendous strain, and he fell a martyr to high-souled integrity.

In 1814, when the affairs of Ballantyne & Co. were in a perplexing condition, Scott took up a work in prose, which he had begun in 1805, and pushed it rapidly to completion. This was "Waverley," the first of that wonderful series which has placed his name at the head of historical novelists. Though published anonymously, as were all its successors, it met with astonishing success. It decided his future literary career. His poetic vein had been exhausted, and Byron's verse was attracting public attention. Henceforth he devoted himself to historical fiction, for which his native powers and previous training were precisely adapted.

For the remainder of his life he composed, in addition to other literary labors, on an average two romances a year, illustrating every period in Scottish, English, and Continental history from the time of the Crusades to the middle of the eighteenth century. The series is, upon the whole, remarkably even in excellence; but among the most interesting may be mentioned "Old Mortality," which describes the sufferings of the Covenanters; "The Heart of Midlothian," to which many critics assign the highest rank; "Ivanhoe" which is very popular; and "Quentin Durward," which holds a distinguished place.

In the composition of these works, Scott wrote with extraordinary rapidity. "Guy Mannering" is said to have been written in six weeks. Carlyle finds fault with what he calls the "extempore method." But in reality it was not extempore. It had been Scott's delight from childhood to store his capacious memory with the antiquarian and historical information which he embodied in his novels. Instead of laborious special investigations, he had but to draw on this great reservoir of learning. He did not wait for moments of inspiration; but morning after morning, he returned to his task with the same zest, and turned out the same amount of work.

Even acute physical suffering did not overcome his creative power. He dictated "The Bride of Lammermoor," "The Legend of Montrose," and "Ivanhoe" to amanuenses. His suffering sometimes forced from him cries of agony. When his amanuensis once begged him to stop dictating, he only answered, "Nay, Willie, only see that the doors are fast; I would fain keep all the cry as well as all the wool to ourselves." A few other writers have equalled or even surpassed Scott in the number of novels; but, if we consider the quality of work and the many centuries covered by his romances, we must regard him as still without a successful rival.

The Waverley novels are characterized by largeness of thought and style. They turn on public rather than private interests. In place of narrow social circles, we are introduced into the midst of great public movements. Crusaders, Papists, Puritans, Cavaliers, Roundheads, Jacobites, Jews, freebooters, preachers, schoolmasters, gypsies, beggars, move before us with the reality of life. The past is made to live again. The style corresponds to the largeness of the subjects. Scott could not have achieved distinction in domestic novels, with their petty interests and trifling distinctions.

He was an admirer of Miss Austen, in reference to whose manner he said: "The big bow-wow strain I can do myself, like any now going; but the exquisite touch which renders ordinary commonplace things and characters interesting, from the truth of the description and the sentiment, is denied me." "Scott needed," observes Hutton, "a certain largeness of type, a strongly marked class-life, and where it was possible, a free out-of-doors life, for his delineations. No one could paint beggars and gypsies, and wandering fiddlers, and mercenary soldiers, and peasants, and farmers, and lawyers, and magistrates, and preachers, and courtiers, and statesmen, and best of all perhaps queens and kings, with anything like his ability."

In 1825, after the failure of Ballantyne & Co., Scott resolutely set to work to pay his creditors. His only resource was his pen. Although his cherished hopes were all blasted, he toiled on indomitably till nature gave way. Two days after the news of the crash reached him, he was working on "Woodstock." In three years he earned and paid over to his creditors no less than forty thousand pounds. If his health had continued, he would have discharged the enormous debt. But unfavorable symptoms began to manifest themselves in 1829, and the following year he had a stroke of paralysis. Though he recovered from it, his faculties never regained their former clearness and strength. Nevertheless, in spite of the urgent advice of physicians and friends, he continued to toil on. "Count Robert of Paris" and "Castle Dangerous" appeared in 1831. But they showed a decline in mental vigor — his magic wand was broken. An entry in his diary at this time is truly pathetic: "The blow is a stunning one, I suppose, for I scarcely feel it. It is singular, but it comes with as little surprise as if I had a remedy ready; yet God knows I am at sea in the dark, and the vessel leaky, I think, into the bargain." It is the pathos of a strong man's awaking to a consciousness that his strength is gone.

A sea voyage was recommended; and in October, 1831, he sailed in a vessel, put at his disposal by the government, for Malta. He visited various points on the Mediterranean, but without material benefit. With the failing of his strength, he longed for Abbotsford. As he caught sight of the towers once more, he sprang up with a cry of delight. A few days before his death he called his son-in-law Lockhart to his bedside. "Lockhart," he said, "I may have but a minute to speak to you. My dear, be a good man, — be virtuous, — be religious, — be a good man. Nothing else will give you any comfort when you come to lie here." These were almost his last words. Four days afterwards, during which time he showed scarcely any signs of consciousness, he quietly passed away, Sept. 21, 1832 — one of the grandest, but, also — if we think of his disappointed hopes — one of the saddest characters in English literature.

THE TALISMAN.

CHAPTER FIRST.

They, too, retired
To the wilderness, but 'twas with arms.
Paradise Regained.

THE burning sun of Syria had not yet attained its highest point in the horizon, when a knight of the Red-cross,[1] who had left his distant northern home, and joined the host of the Crusaders in Palestine, was pacing slowly along the sandy deserts which lie in the vicinity of the Dead Sea, or, as it is called, the Lake Asphaltites,[2] where the waves of the Jordan pour themselves into an inland sea, from which there is no discharge of waters.

The warlike pilgrim had toiled among cliffs and precipices during the earlier part of the morning ; more lately, issuing from those rocky and dangerous defiles, he had entered upon that great plain, where the accursed cities[3] provoked, in ancient days, the direct and dreadful vengeance of the Omnipotent.

The toil, the thirst, the dangers of the way, were forgotten, as the traveller recalled the fearful catastrophe, which had converted into an arid and dismal wilderness the fair and fertile valley of Siddim,[4] once well watered, even as the Garden of the Lord, now a parched and blighted waste, condemned to eternal sterility.

Crossing himself, as he viewed the dark mass of rolling waters, in color as in quality unlike those of every other lake, the traveller shuddered as he remembered, that beneath these sluggish waves lay the once proud cities of the plain, whose grave was dug by the thunder of the heavens, or the eruption of subterraneous fire, and whose remains were hid, even by that sea which holds no living fish in its bosom, bears no skiff on its surface, and, as if its own dreadful bed were the only fit receptacle for its sullen waters, sends not, like other lakes, a tribute to the ocean.   The whole land around, as in the days of Moses, was "brimstone and salt; it is not sown, nor beareth, nor any grass groweth thereon ; "[5] the land as well as the lake might be termed dead, as producing nothing having resemblance to vegetation, and even the very air was entirely devoid of its ordinary winged inhabitants, deterred probably by the odor of bitumen and sulphur, which the burning sun exhaled from the waters of the lake, in steaming clouds, frequently assuming the appearance of waterspouts.[6] Masses of the slimy and sulphurous substance called naphtha,[7] which floated idly on the sluggish and sullen waves, supplied those rolling clouds with new vapors, and afforded awful testimony to the truth of the Mosaic history.

Upon this scene of desolation the sun shone with almost intolerable splendor, and all living nature seemed to have hidden itself from the rays, excepting the solitary figure which moved through the flitting sand at a foot's pace, and appeared the sole breathing thing on the wide surface of the plain. The dress of the rider and the accoutrements of his horse were peculiarly unfit for the traveller in such a country. A coat of linked mail, with long sleeves, plated gauntlets, and a steel breastplate, had not been esteemed a sufficient weight of armor; there was also his triangular shield suspended round his neck, and his barred helmet[8] of steel, over which he had a hood and collar of mail, which was drawn around the warrior's shoulders and throat, and filled up the vacancy between the hauberk[9] and the head-piece.[10] His lower limbs were sheathed, like his body, in flexible mail, securing the legs and thighs, while the feet rested in plated shoes, which corresponded with the gauntlets. A long, broad, straight-shaped, double-edged falchion, with a handle formed like a cross, corresponded with a stout poniard, on the other side. The knight also bore, secured to his saddle, with one end resting on his stirrup, the long steel-headed lance, his own proper weapon, which, as he rode, projected backward, and displayed its little pennoncelle,[11] to dally with the faint breeze, or drop in the dead calm. To this cumbrous equipment must be added a surcoat[12] of embroidered cloth, much frayed and worn, which was thus far useful, that it excluded the burning rays of the sun from the armor, which they would otherwise have rendered intolerable to the wearer. The surcoat bore, in several places, the arms[13] of the owner, although much defaced. These seemed to be a couchant leopard, with the motto, "I sleep—wake me not." An outline of the same device might be traced on his shield, though many a blow had almost effaced the painting. The flat top of his cumbrous cylindrical helmet was unadorned with any crest.[14] In retaining their own unwieldy defensive armor, the northern Crusaders seemed to set at defiance the nature of the climate and country to which they had come to war.

The accoutrements of the horse were scarcely less massive and unwieldy than those of the rider. The animal had a heavy saddle plated with steel, uniting in front with a species of breastplate, and behind with defensive armor made to cover the loins. Then there was a steel axe, or hammer, called a mace-of-arms, and which hung to the saddlebow ; the reins were secured by chain-work, and the front-stall of the bridle was a steel plate, with apertures for the eyes and nostrils, having in the midst a short sharp pike, projecting from the forehead of the horse like the horn of the fabulous unicorn.

But habit had made the endurance of this load of panoply [15] a second nature, both to the knight and his gallant charger. Numbers, indeed, of the western warriors who hurried to Palestine, died ere they became inured to the burning climate ; but there were others to whom that climate became innocent and even friendly, and among this fortunate number was the solitary horseman who now traversed the border of the Dead Sea.

Nature, which cast his limbs in a mould of uncommon strength, fitted to wear his linked hauberk with as much ease as if the meshes had been formed of cobwebs, had endowed him with a constitution as strong as his limbs, and which bade defiance to almost all changes of climate, as well as to fatigue and privations of every kind. His disposition seemed, in some degree, to partake of the qualities of his bodily frame ; and as the one possessed great strength and endurance, united with the power of violent exertion, the other, under a calm and undisturbed semblance, had much of the fiery and enthusiastic love of glory which constituted the principal attribute of the renowned Norman line, and had rendered them sovereigns in every corner of Europe, where they had drawn their adventurous swords.

It was not, however, to all the race that fortune proposed such tempting rewards ; and those obtained by the solitary knight during two years' campaign in Palestine had been only temporal fame, and, as he was taught to believe, spiritual privileges. Meantime, his slender stock of money had melted away, the rather that he did not pursue any of the ordinary modes by which the followers of the Crusade condescended to recruit their diminished resources, at the expense of the people of Palestine ; he exacted no gifts from the wretched natives for sparing their possessions when engaged in warfare with the Saracens, and he had not availed himself of any opportunity of enriching himself by the ransom of prisoners of consequence. The small train which had followed him from his native country had been gradually diminished, as the means of maintaining them disappeared, and his only remaining squire was at present on a sick-bed, and unable to attend his master, who travelled, as we have seen, singly and alone. This was of little consequence to the Crusader, who was accustomed to consider his good sword as his safest escort, and devout thoughts as his best companion.

Nature had, however, her demands for refreshment and repose, even on the iron frame and patient disposition of the Knight of the Sleeping Leopard; and at noon, when the Dead Sea lay at some distance on his right, he joyfully hailed the sight of two or three palm-trees, which arose beside the well which was assigned for his mid-day station. His good horse, too, which had plodded forward with the steady endurance of his master, now lifted his head, expanded his nostrils, and quickened his pace, as if he snuffed afar off the living waters, which marked the place of repose and refreshment. But labor and danger were doomed to intervene ere the horse or horseman reached the desired spot.

As the Knight of the Couchant Leopard continued to fix his eyes attentively on the yet distant cluster of palm-trees, it seemed to him as if some object was moving among them. The distant form separated itself from the trees, which partly hid its motions, and advanced toward the knight with a speed which soon showed a mounted horseman, whom his turban, long spear, and green caftan [16] floating in the wind, on his nearer approach, showed to be a Saracen cavalier.[17] " In the desert," saith an Eastern proverb, " no man meets a friend." The Crusader was totally indifferent whether the infidel, who now approached on his gallant barb, as if borne on the wings of an eagle, came as friend or foe — perhaps, as a vowed champion of the Cross, he might rather have preferred the latter. He disengaged his lance from his saddle, seized it with the right hand, placed it in rest with its point half elevated, gathered up the reins in the left, waked his horse's mettle with the spur, and prepared to encounter the stranger with the calm self-confidence belonging to the victor in many contests.

The Saracen came on at the speedy gallop of an Arab horseman, managing his steed more by his limbs, and the inflection of his body, than by any use of the reins, which hung loose in his left hand; so that he was enabled to wield the light round buckler of the skin of the rhinoceros, ornamented with silver loops, which he wore on his arm, swinging it as if he meant to oppose its slender circle to the formidable thrust of the western lance. His own long spear was not couched or levelled like that of his antagonist, but grasped by the middle with his right hand, and brandished at arm's length above his head. As the cavalier approached his enemy at full career, he seemed to expect that the Knight of the Leopard should put his horse to the gallop to encounter him. But the Christian knight, well acquainted with the customs of Eastern warriors, did not mean to exhaust his good horse by any unnecessary exertion; and, on the contrary, made a dead halt, confident that if the enemy advanced to the actual shock, his own weight, and that of his powerful charger, would give him sufficient advantage, without the additional momentum of rapid motion. Equally sensible and apprehensive of such a probable result, the Saracen cavalier, when he had approached toward the Christian within twice the length of his lance, wheeled his steed to the left with inimitable dexterity, and rode twice round his antagonist, who, turning without quitting his ground, and presenting his front constantly to his enemy, frustrated his attempts to attack him on an unguarded point; so that the Saracen, wheeling his horse, was fain to retreat to the distance of a hundred yards. A second time, like a hawk attacking a heron, the Heathen renewed the charge, and a second time was fain to retreat without coming to a close struggle. A third time he approached in the same manner, when the Christian knight, desirous to terminate this elusory warfare, in which he might at length have been worn out by the activity of his foeman, suddenly seized the mace which hung at his saddlebow, and, with a strong hand and unerring aim, hurled it against the head of the Emir,[18] for such and not less his enemy appeared. The Saracen was just aware of the formidable missile in time to interpose his light buckler betwixt the mace and his head; but the violence of the blow forced the buckler down on his turban, and though that defence also contributed to deaden its violence, the Saracen was beaten from his horse. Ere the Christian could avail himself of this mishap, his nimble foeman sprung from the ground, and calling on his horse, which instantly returned to his side, he leaped into his seat without touching the stirrup, and regained all the advantage of which the Knight of the Leopard hoped to deprive him. But the latter had in the meanwhile recovered his mace, and the Eastern cavalier, who remembered the strength and dexterity with which his antagonist had aimed it, seemed to keep cautiously out of reach of that weapon, of which he had so lately felt the force, while he showed his purpose of waging a distant warfare with missile weapons of his own. Planting his long spear in the sand at a distance from the scene of combat, he strung, with great address, a short bow which he carried at his back, and putting his horse to the gallop, once more described two or three circles of a wider extent than formerly, in the course of which he discharged six arrows at the Christian with such unerring skill, that the goodness of his harness alone saved him from being wounded in as many places. The seventh shaft apparently found a less perfect part of the armor, and the Christian dropped heavily from his horse. But what was the surprise of the Saracen, when, dismounting to examine the condition of his prostrate enemy, he found himself suddenly within the grasp of the European, who had had recourse to this artifice to bring his enemy within his reach! Even in this deadly grapple, the Saracen was saved by his agility and presence of mind. He unloosed the sword-belt, in which the Knight of the Leopard had fixed his hold, and thus eluding his fatal grasp, mounted his horse, which seemed to watch his motions with the intelligence of a human being, and again rode off. But in the last encounter the Saracen had lost his sword and his quiver of arrows, both of which were attached to the girdle which he was obliged to abandon. He had also lost his turban in the struggle. These disadvantages seemed to incline the Moslem to a truce. He approached the Christian with his right hand extended, but no longer in a menacing attitude.

"There is truce betwixt our nations," he said, in the Lingua Franca [19] commonly used for the purpose of communication with the Crusaders; "wherefore should there be war betwixt thee and me? — Let there be peace betwixt us."

"I am well contented," answered he of the Couchant Leopard; "but what security dost thou offer that thou wilt observe the truce?"

"The word of a follower of the Prophet was never broken," answered the Emir. "It is thou, brave Nazarene, from whom I should demand security, did I not know that treason seldom dwells with courage."

The Crusader felt that the confidence of the Moslem made him ashamed of his own doubts.

"By the cross of my sword," he said, laying his hand on the weapon as he spoke, "I will be true companion to thee, Saracen, while our fortune wills that we remain in company together."

"By Mohammed, Prophet of God, and by Allah, God of the Prophet," replied his late foeman, "there is not treachery in my heart toward thee. And now wend we to yonder fountain, for the hour of rest is at hand, and the stream had hardly touched my lip when I was called to battle by thy approach."

The Knight of the Couchant Leopard yielded a ready and courteous assent; and the late foes, without an angry look, or gesture of doubt, rode side by side to the little cluster of palm-trees.

NOTES TO THE TALISMAN.

THE extract given is the first chapter of "The Talisman." It well illustrates Scott's largeness of style, and his powers of graphic description.

The events narrated in "The Talisman" are supposed to have occurred during the Third Crusade. This was undertaken by Frederick Barbarossa, Emperor of Germany, with the support of Phillip II. of France, and Richard I., surnamed *Cœur de Lion*, of England. It accomplished nothing farther than the establishment of a truce with Saladin, during which the privilege of visiting the holy places of Palestine was accorded to Christians.

"The Talisman" was Scott's first attempt to treat an Eastern theme. In this field he had been preceded by other distinguished English writers. Southey in his "Thalaba," Moore in his "Lalla Rookh," and Byron in several of his romantic tales, had treated Oriental scenes and characters with eminent success. Scott felt a hesitancy, as he tells us, about entering into rivalry with his illustrious contemporaries, especially as he had never had an opportunity to observe the landscape and people that he undertook to describe. The result, however, showed his fears to be groundless, and served only to increase his overshadowing reputation.

1. *Knight of the Red-cross* = Sir Kenneth of Scotland.

2. A name derived from the ancient classical writers. In Lat. *Lacus Asphaltites.*

3. *Accursed cities* = Sodom and Gomorrah. See Gen. xix. 24, 25.

4. This name is taken from Gen. xiv. 10.

5. See Deut. xxix. 23.

6. These features are exaggerated. Birds abound; and no noisome smell nor noxious vapor arises from the lake.

7. *Naptha* contains no sulphur; hence the adjective must be taken as referring only to color.

8. *Barred helmet.* — See Webster.

9. *Hauberk* = a shirt of mail formed of small steel rings interwoven. The "coat of linked mail" referred to above. See Webster.

10. *Head-piece* = helmet.

11. *Pennoncelle* = a small flag or streamer borne at the top of a lance. Called also *pencel.*

12. *Surcoat* = the long and flowing drapery of knights, anterior to the introduction of plate armor.

13. *Arms* = armorial device or coat of arms.

14. *Crest* = the plume of feathers, or other decoration, worn on a helmet.

15. *Panoply* = complete armor. From Gr. *pan*, all, and *hoplon*, implement of war, harness.

16. *Caftan* = a Persian or Turkish vest or garment.

17. *Saracen cavalier* = Sheerkohf, the Lion of the Mountain, from Kurdistan.

18. *Emir* = an Arabian prince. As he informed Sir Kenneth afterwards, ten thousand men were ready to take the field at his word.

19. *Lingua Franca* = a kind of corrupt Italian, with a considerable admixture of French words.

LORD BYRON.

No other poet has so embodied himself in his poetry as Byron. Had he not possessed a powerful individuality, his works would long since have perished. He was utterly lacking in the independent creative power of Shakespeare, who never identified himself with his characters. Throughout Byron's many works, we see but one person — a proud, misanthropic, sceptical, ungovernable man. Whatever exaggerations of feature there may be in the portrait, we recognize the essential outlines of the poet himself.

His poetry is largely biographical, and his utterance intense. Without the careful artistic polish of many minor poets, his manner is rapid, stirring, powerful. He was, perhaps, the most remarkable poetic genius of the century ; yet his powers were not turned to the best account. He lacked the balance of a noble character and a well-regulated life. On reading a collection of Burns's poems, he once exclaimed : " What an antithetical mind ! — tenderness, roughness — delicacy, coarseness — sentiment, sensuality — soaring and grovelling — dirt and deity — all mixed up in that one compound of inspired clay." The same antitheses might be applied with equal truth to himself.

His place in literature is not yet fixed. " In my mind," wrote Carlyle, " Byron has been sinking at an accelerated rate for the last ten years, and has now reached a very low level." On the other hand, Taine declares that " he is so great and so English, that from him alone we shall learn more truths of his country and his age than from all the rest put together."

When the final verdict is made up, the Scotchman will probably be nearer the truth than the Frenchman. The finest strains of poetry are not to be found in his productions; and the moral sense of the world has become too strong to approve his flippant scepticism or condone his shameful immoralities. He once called himself, " The grand Napoleon of the realms of rhyme." The comparison is not unjust; but in both cases alike, the glamour of brilliant achievement has been stripped off, and the forbidding personal character brought to light. Byron was endowed with extraordinary ability; but in large measure he used his powers to vent his misanthropy, to mock at virtue and religion, and to conceal the hideousness of vice.

George Gordon, Lord Byron, was born in London, Jan. 22, 1788. His ancestry runs back in an unbroken line of nobility to the time of William the Conqueror. His father was an unprincipled and heartless profligate, who married an heiress to get her property, and who, as soon as this was squandered, abandoned her. His mother was a proud, passionate, hysterical woman, who alternately caressed and abused her child. At one moment treating him with extravagant fondness, at the next she reproached him as a "lame brat," and flung the poker at his head. " Your mother's a fool," said a school companion to him. " I know it," was the painful and humiliating answer. With such parentage and such rearing, it becomes us to temper somewhat the severity of our judgment of his character.

He was sent to school at Harrow. " I soon found," wrote the head-master soon afterwards, "that a wild mountain colt had been submitted to my management." Byron did not take much interest in the prescribed studies, and never became an accurate scholar. His reading, however, was extensive, and he learned French and Italian. He formed a few warm friendships. During one of his vacations, he fell in love with Mary Ann Chaworth, whose father the poet's grand uncle had slain in a tavern brawl. He was fifteen, and she was two years older. Looking upon him as a boy, she did not take his attachment seriously, and a year later married another. To Byron, who loved her with all the ardor of his nature, it was a grievous disappointment; and years afterwards, when he him-

self stood at the altar, recollections of her disturbed his soul.
The story is told in " The Dream," a poem of much beauty : —

> " The boy had fewer summers, but his heart
> Had far outgrown his years, and to his eye
> There was but one belovèd face on earth."

In 1805 Byron entered Trinity College, Cambridge, with
which he was connected for nearly three years. Like many of
his predecessors of independent genius — Bacon, Milton, Locke,
Gibbon — he cared little for the university training. He was
fond of out-door sports, and excelled in cricket, boxing, riding,
and shooting. Along with a good deal of miscellaneous reading, he wrote verses, and in 1808 published a volume entitled
" Hours of Idleness." The work gave little evidence of poetic
genius, and was the subject of a rasping critique in the *Edinburgh Review.* "The poesy of this young lord," it was said
with some justice, "belongs to the class which neither gods
nor men are said to permit. Indeed, we do not recollect to
have seen a quantity of verse with so few deviations in either
direction from that exact standard."

While affecting contempt for public opinion, Byron was
always acutely sensitive to adverse criticism ; and the exas-
perating attack of the *Edinburgh Review* stung him like a blow,
rousing him to fury. The result was, a little later, the furious
and indiscriminate onslaught known as " English Bards and
Scotch Reviewers." "Prepare," he shouted, —

> " Prepare for rhyme — I'll publish right or wrong;
> Fools are my theme, let satire be my song."

The first edition was exhausted in a month. Though violent, indiscriminate, and often unjust, the satire indicated
something of his latent power.

In 1809, after a few weeks of wild revel at his ancestral seat
of Newstead Abbey, he set out upon his travels, and visited
Portugal, Spain, Greece, and Turkey. His restless spirit found
some degree of satisfaction in roving from place to place.

While continuing to lead an ill-regulated life, he carried with him the eyes of a keen observer, and the sentiments of a great poet. His experience and observation are given in the first two cantos of "Childe Harold's Pilgrimage." Though he affirmed that Childe Harold is a fictitious character, it is impossible not to identify him with the poet himself.

> "Whilome in Albion's isle there dwelt a youth,
> Who ne in virtue's ways did take delight;
> But spent his days in riot most uncouth,
> And vexed with mirth the drowsy ear of night.
>
> .   .   .   .
>
> And now Childe Harold was sore sick at heart,
> And from his fellow bacchanals would flee;
> 'Tis said at times the sullen tear would start,
> But pride congealed the drop within his ee :
> Apart he stalked in joyless reverie,
> And from his native land resolved to go,
> And visit scorching climes beyond the sea;
> With pleasure drugged he almost longed for woe,
> And e'en for change of scene would seek the shades below."

The poem is written in the Spenserian stanza ; and the antiquated style which he affected at first was soon cast aside. It opened a new field ; and its rich descriptions seized the public fancy. It ran through seven editions in four weeks; and to use the author's words, " he woke up one morning and found himself famous." The other results of his Eastern travels are " The Giaour," " The Bride of Abydos," " The Corsair," and " Lara " — poetical romances of passion and violence, which were received with outbursts of applause. They surpassed Scott in his own field — a fact which he had the judgment to recognize and the manliness to confess.

Byron had returned to England in 1812, after an absence of two years ; and while the various works mentioned were appearing, he was leading a fashionable and dissipated life in London. When the right mood was on him, he had the power of making himself highly entertaining.   His presence was striking.   " As for poets," says Scott, " I have seen all the best of my time and country ; and though Burns had the most glorious eye imaginable, I never thought any of them could come up to an artist's notion of the character except Byron.   His countenance is a thing to dream of."

Byron was naturally idolized by women ; but never discerning the nobler elements of their character, he set a low estimate upon them.   " I regard them," he says, " as very pretty but inferior creatures, who are as little in their place at our tables as they would be in our council chambers. . . .   I look upon them as grown-up children."

In 1815 he married Miss Milbanke ; but there was no love on either side, and it proved an ill-assorted match.   Though an excellent woman, his wife was exacting and unsympathetic. Impatient at his late hours, she inquired when he was going to leave off writing verses.   On the other hand, he was fitful, violent, and immoral.

At the end of a year, and after the birth of their daughter Ada, she went to her father's, and informed Byron that she did not intend ever to return to him.   The separation created a sensation ; and the burden of blame, as was no doubt just, fell upon him.   He sank in popular esteem as suddenly as he had risen.   He dared not go to the theatres for fear of being hissed, nor to Parliament for fear of being insulted.   The result is given in his own words : " I felt that, if what was whispered and muttered and murmured was true, I was unfit for England ; if false, England was unfit for me."   Accordingly in 1816, disappointed and burdened at heart, he left his native shore never to return.

> " I depart,
> Whither I know not ; but the hour's gone by,
> When Albion's lessening shores could grieve or glad mine eye.

> Once more upon the waters ! yet once more !
> And the waves bound beneath me as a steed
> That knows his rider.   Welcome to their roar !
> Swift be their guidance, wheresoe'er it lead !

> Though the strained mast should quiver as a reed,
> And the rent canvas fluttering strew the gale,
> Still I must on ; for I am as a weed
> Flung from the rock, on ocean's foam to sail,
> Where'er the surge may sweep, the tempest's breath prevail.''

With this voluntary exile he entered upon a new era of authorship, in which he attained to the full maturity of his powers. At Geneva he wrote the third, and at Venice the fourth canto of "Childe Harold," and at once placed himself among the great masters of English verse. Landscapes of unsurpassed majesty and beauty are portrayed ; history lives again ; our feelings are stirred with deep emotion. Treasures are found on every page. For example : —

> '' The sky is changed ! — and such a change ! O night,
> And storm, and darkness, ye are wondrous strong,
> Yet lovely in your strength, as is the light
> Of a dark eye in woman ! Far along,
> From peak to peak, the rattling crags among,
> Leaps the live thunder ! Not from one lone cloud,
> But every mountain now hath found a tongue,
> And Jura answers through her misty shroud,
> Back to the joyous Alps, who call to her aloud.''

Or again : —

> '' I see before me the gladiator lie :
> He leans upon his hand — his manly brow
> Consents to death, but conquers agony,
> And his drooped head sinks gradually low —
> And through his side the last drops, ebbing slow
> From the red gash, fall heavy, one by one,
> Like the first of a thunder shower; and now
> The arena swims around him — he is gone,
> Ere ceased the inhuman shout that hailed the wretch who won.''

Once more : —

> '' There is a pleasure in the pathless woods,
> There is a rapture on the lonely shore,
> There is society where none intrudes,
> By the deep sea, and music in its roar :

> I love not man the less, but nature more,
> From these our interviews, in which I steal
> From all I may be or have been before,
> To mingle with the universe, and feel
> What I can ne'er express, yet cannot all conceal."

At Geneva he wrote the touching story of Bonnivard, "The Prisoner of Chillon."

From Switzerland, Byron went to Italy, living for a time at Venice, Ravenna, Piza, and Genoa. His Italian life was voluptuous and immoral. In every place of sojourn, however, he continued to write, composing many works of high excellence. "Cain" is a powerful drama. One of the characters is Lucifer, of whom Byron apologetically says, "It was difficult for me to make him talk like a clergyman upon the same subjects." "Manfred" and "Sardanapalus" are other dramas. The "Vision of Judgment," a satire on George the Third and "Bob Southey," is not reverent, but it is the wittiest production of its class in our language. "Don Juan," his longest poem, is a conglomerate of wit, satire, and immorality, relieved at intervals by sage reflection and delicate poetic sentiment. It shows at once the author's genius and degradation.

At length the aimless and voluptuous life he was leading filled him with satiety. He had drained the cup of pleasure to its dregs of bitterness. He began to long for a life of action. "If I live ten years longer," he wrote in 1822, "you will see that it is not all over with me. I don't mean in literature, for that is nothing— and I do not think it was my vocation ; but I shall do something."

Greece was at this time struggling for independence from Turkish tyranny. Byron was a friend of liberty ; the struggling Greeks touched his sympathies. Accordingly he embarked for Greece in 1823 to aid them in their struggle. As he was about to depart, the shadow of coming disaster fell upon him. "I have a sort of boding," he said to some friends, "that we see each other for the last time, as something tells me I shall never return from Greece."

He was received at Mesolonghi with salvoes of musketry and music. He received a military commission, and in his subsequent movements displayed ability and courage. But before he had been of much assistance to the Greeks, he was seized with a virulent fever, and died April 9, 1824. The cities of Greece contended for his body; but it was taken to England, where, sepulture in Westminster Abbey having been refused, it was conveyed to the village church of Hucknall.

Such lives are unutterably sad. Byron possessed what most men spend their lives for in vain — genius, rank, power, fame ; yet he lived a wretched man. His peace of mind was broken and his body prematurely worn by vicious passions. He was himself oppressed with a sense of failure ; and less than three months before his death he wrote : —

> " My days are in the yellow leaf;
>   The flowers and fruits of love are gone;
>   The worm, the canker, and the grief,
>   Are mine alone ! "

Life had lost its charm ; and all he sought was a martial death in that land of ancient heroes.

> " Seek out, less often sought than found,
>   A soldier's grave — for thee the best;
> Then look around, and choose thy ground,
>   And take thy rest."

THE PRISONER OF CHILLON.

I.

My hair is gray, but not with years,
  Nor grew it white
  In a single night,
As men's have grown from sudden fears:
My limbs are bow'd, though not with toil,
  But rusted with a vile repose,
For they have been a dungeon's spoil,
  And mine has been the fate of those
To whom the goodly earth and air
Are bann'd and barr'd — forbidden fare;   10
But this was for my father's faith
I suffer'd chains and courted death;
That father perish'd at the stake
For tenets he would not forsake;
And for the same his lineal race
In darkness found a dwelling-place;
We were seven — who now are one,
  Six in youth, and one in age,
Finish'd as they had begun,
  Proud of persecution's rage;   20
One in fire, and two in field,
Their belief with blood have seal'd;
Dying as their father died,
For the God their foes denied;
Three were in a dungeon cast,
Of whom this wreck is left the last.

II.

There are seven pillars of Gothic mould,
In Chillon's dungeons deep and old,
There are seven columns, massy and gray,
Dim with a dull imprison'd ray,   30
A sunbeam which hath lost its way,

And through the crevice and the cleft
Of the thick wall is fallen and left;
Creeping o'er the floor so damp,
Like a marsh's meteor lamp:
And in each pillar there is a ring,
  And in each ring there is a chain;
That iron is a cankering thing,
  For in these limbs its teeth remain,
With marks that will not wear away,   40
Till I have done with this new day,
Which now is painful to these eyes,
Which have not seen the sun to rise
For years — I cannot count them o'er,
I lost their long and heavy score
When my last brother droop'd and died,
And I lay living by his side.

III.

They chain'd us each to a column stone,
And we were three — yet, each alone:
We could not move a single pace,   50
We could not see each other's face,
But with that pale and livid light
That made us strangers in our sight:
And thus together — yet apart,
Fetter'd in hand, but joined in heart,
'Twas still some solace, in the dearth
Of the pure elements of earth,
To hearken to each other's speech,
And each turn comforter to each
With some new hope, or legend old,   60
Or song heroically bold;
But even these at length grew cold.
Our voices took a dreary tone,
An echo of the dungeon-stone,
  A grating sound — not full and free
  As they of yore were wont to be:
  It might be fancy — but to me
They never sounded like our own.

IV.

I was the eldest of the three,
    And to uphold and cheer the rest   70
    I ought to do — and did — my best,
And each did well in his degree.
    The youngest, whom my father loved,
Because our mother's brow was given
To him — with eyes as blue as heaven,
    For him my soul was sorely moved:
And truly might it be distress'd
To see such bird in such a nest;
For he was beautiful as day —
    (When day was beautiful to me   80
    As to young eagles, being free) —
    A polar day, which will not see
A sunset till its summer's gone,
    Its sleepless summer of long light,
The snow-clad offspring of the sun!
    And thus he was as pure and bright,
And in his natural spirit gay,
With tears for nought but others' ills,
And then they flow'd like mountain rills,
Unless he could assuage the woe   90
Which he abhorr'd to view below.

V.

The other was as pure of mind,
But form'd to combat with his kind;
Strong in his frame, and of a mood
Which 'gainst the world in war had stood,
And perish'd in the foremost rank
    With joy: — but not in chains to pine:
His spirit wither'd with their clank,
    I saw it silently decline —
    And so perchance in sooth did mine: 100
But yet I forced it on to cheer
Those relics of a home so dear.
He was a hunter of the hills,
    Had follow'd there the deer and wolf;

To him this dungeon was a gulf,
And fetter'd feet the worst of ills.

VI.

    Lake Leman lies by Chillon's walls:
A thousand feet in depth below
Its massy waters meet and flow;
Thus much the fathom-line was sent   110
From Chillon's snow-white battlement,
    Which round about the wave enthrals:
A double dungeon wall and wave
Have made — and like a living grave
Below the surface of the lake
The dark vault lies wherein we lay,
We heard it ripple night and day;
    Sounding o'er our heads it knock'd;
And I have felt the winter's spray
Wash through the bars when winds were high   120
And wanton in the happy sky;
    And then the very rock hath rock'd,
    And I have felt it shake, unshock'd,
Because I could have smiled to see
The death that would have set me free.

VII.

I said my nearer brother pined,
I said his mighty heart declined,
He loathed and put away his food;
It was not that 'twas coarse and rude,
For we were used to hunter's fare,   130
And for the like had little care:
The milk drawn from the mountain goat
Was changed for water from the moat,
Our bread was such as captives' tears
Have moisten'd many a thousand years,
Since man first pent his fellow-men
Like brutes within an iron den;
But what were these to us or him?
These wasted not his heart or limb;
My brother's soul was of that mould   140

Which in a palace had grown cold,
Had his free breathing been denied
The range of the steep mountain's side;
But why delay the truth ? — he died.
I saw, and could not hold his head,
Nor reach his dying hand — nor dead —
Though hard I strove, but strove in vain,
To rend and gnash my bonds in twain.
He died — and they unlock'd his chain,
And scoop'd for him a shallow grave   150
Even from the cold earth of our cave.
I begg'd them, as a boon, to lay
His corse in dust whereon the day
Might shine — it was a foolish thought,
But then within my brain it wrought,
That even in death his freeborn breast
In such a dungeon could not rest.
I might have spared my idle prayer —
They coldly laugh'd — and laid him there:
The flat and turfless earth above   160
The being we so much did love;
His empty chain above it leant,
Such murder's fitting monument!

VIII.

But he, the favourite and the flower,
Most cherish'd since his natal hour,
His mother's image in fair face,
The infant love of all his race,
His martyr'd father's dearest thought,
My latest care, for whom I sought
To hoard my life, that his might be   170
Less wretched now, and one day free;
He, too, who yet had held untired
A spirit natural or inspired —
He, too, was struck, and day by day
Was wither'd as the stalk away.
Oh, God! it is a fearful thing
To see the human soul take wing
In any shape, in any mood:

I've seen it rushing forth in blood,
I've seen it on the breaking ocean 180
Strive with a swoln convulsive motion,
I've seen the sick and ghastly bed
Of sin delirious with its dread :
But these were horrors — this was woe
Unmix'd with such — but sure and slow :
He faded, and so calm and meek,
So softly worn, so sweetly weak,
So tearless, yet so tender — kind,
And grieved for those he left behind ;
With all the while a cheek whose bloom 190
Was as a mockery of the tomb,
Whose tints as gently sunk away
As a departing rainbow's ray —
An eye of most transparent light,
That almost made the dungeon bright,
And not a word of murmur — not
A groan o'er his untimely lot, —
A little talk of better days,
A little hope my own to raise,
For I was sunk in silence — lost 200
In this last loss, of all the most ;
And then the sighs he would suppress
Of fainting nature's feebleness,
More slowly drawn, grew less and less,
I listen'd, but I could not hear —
I call'd, for I was wild with fear ;
I knew 'twas hopeless, but my dread
Would not be thus admonished ;
I call'd and thought I heard a sound —
I burst my chain with one strong bound, 210
And rush'd to him : — I found him not,
I only stirred in this black spot,
I only lived — *I* only drew
The accursed breath of dungeon-dew ;
The last — the sole — the dearest link
Between me and the eternal brink,
Which bound me to my failing race,
Was broken in this fatal place.

One on the earth, and one beneath —
My brothers — both had ceased to breathe: 220
I took that hand which lay so still,
Alas! my own was full as chill;
I had not strength to stir, or strive,
But felt that I was still alive —
A frantic feeling, when we know
That what we love shall ne'er be so.
      I know not why
      I could not die,
I had no earthly hope — but faith,
And that forbade a selfish death.   230

IX.

What next befell me then and there
    I know not well — I never knew —
First came the loss of light, and air,
    And then of darkness too:
I had no thought, no feeling — none —
Among the stones I stood a stone,
And was, scarce conscious what I wist,
As shrubless crags within the mist;
For all was blank, and bleak, and gray;
It was not night — it was not day;   240
It was not even the dungeon-light,
So hateful to my heavy sight,
But vacancy absorbing space,
And fixedness — without a place:
There were no stars — no earth — no time —
No check — no change — no good — no crime —
But silence, and a stirless breath
Which neither was of life nor death;
A sea of stagnant idleness,
Blind, boundless, mute, and motionless!   250

X.

A light broke in upon my brain, —
    It was the carol of a bird;
It ceased, and then it came again,
    The sweetest song ear ever heard,

And mine was thankful till my eyes
Ran over with the glad surprise,
And they that moment could not see
I was the mate of misery;
But then by dull degrees came back
My senses to their wonted track; 260
I saw the dungeon walls and floor
Close slowly round me as before,
I saw the glimmer of the sun
Creeping as it before had done,
But through the crevice where it came
That bird was perch'd, as fond and tame,
    And tamer than upon the tree;
A lovely bird with azure wings,
And song that said a thousand things,
    And seem'd to say them all for me! 270
I never saw its like before,
I ne'er shall see its likeness more:
It seem'd like me to want a mate,
But was not half so desolate,
And it was come to love me when
None lived to love me so again,
And cheering from my dungeon's brink,
Had brought me back to feel and think.
I know not if it late were free,
    Or broke its cage to perch on mine, 280
But knowing well captivity,
    Sweet bird! I could not wish for thine!
Or if it were, in wingèd guise,
A visitant from Paradise;
For — Heaven forgive that thought! ...e while
Which made me both to weep and smile;
I sometimes deem'd that it might be
My brother's soul come down to me;
But then at last away it flew,
And then 'twas mortal well I knew, 290
For he would never thus have flown,
And left me twice so doubly lone, —
Lone — as the corse within its shroud,
Lone — as a solitary cloud,

A single cloud on a sunny day,
While all the rest of heaven is clear,
A frown upon the atmosphere,
That hath no business to appear
    When skies are blue, and earth is gay.

XI.

A kind of change came in my fate,   300
My keepers grew compassionate;
I know not what had made them so,
They were inured to sights of woe,
But so it was:— my broken chain
With links unfasten'd did remain,
And it was liberty to stride
Along my cell from side to side,
And up and down, and then athwart,
And tread it over every part;
And round the pillars one by one,   310
Returning where my walk begun,
Avoiding only, as I trod,
My brothers' graves without a sod;
For if I thought with heedless tread,
My step profaned their lowly bed,
My breath came gaspingly and thick,
And my crush'd heart fell blind and sick.

XII.

I made a footing in the wall,
    It was not therefrom to escape,
For I had buried one and all   320
    Who loved me in a human shape;
And the whole earth would henceforth be
A wider prison unto me:
No child — no sire — no kin had I,
No partner in my misery;
I thought of this, and I was glad,
For thought of them had made me mad;
But I was curious to ascend
To my barr'd windows, and to bend
Once more upon the mountains high,   330
The quiet of a loving eye.

XIII.

I saw them — and they were the same,
They were not changed like me in frame;
I saw their thousand years of snow
On high — their wide long lake below,
And the blue Rhone in fullest flow;
I heard the torrents leap and gush
O'er channell'd rock and broken bush;
I saw the white-wall'd distant town,
And whiter sails go skimming down;   340
And then there was a little isle,
Which in my very face did smile,
        The only one in view;
A small green isle, it seem'd no more,
Scarce broader than my dungeon floor,
But in it there were three tall trees,
And o'er it blew the mountain breeze,
And by it there were waters flowing,
And on it there were young flowers growing,
        Of gentle breath and hue.   350
The fish swam by the castle wall,
And they seem'd joyous each and all;
The eagle rode the rising blast,
Methought he never flew so fast
As then to me he seem'd to fly,
And then new tears came in my eye,
And I felt troubled — and would fain
I had not left my recent chain;
And when I did descend again,
The darkness of my dim abode   360
Fell on me as a heavy load;
It was as is a new-dug grave,
Closing o'er one we sought to save, —
And yet my glance, too much oppress'd,
Had almost need of such a rest.

XIV.

It might be months, or years, or days,
        I kept no count — I took no note,
I had no hope my eyes to raise,

And clear them of their dreary mote;
At last men came to set me free, 370
　　I ask'd not why, and reck'd not where,
It was at length the same to me,
Fetter'd or fetterless to be,
　　I learn'd to love despair.
And thus when they appear'd at last,
And all my bonds aside were cast,
These heavy walls to me had grown
A hermitage — and all my own!
And half I felt as they were come
To tear me from a second home: 380
With spiders I had friendship made,
And watch'd them in their sullen trade,
Had seen the mice by moonlight play,
And why should I feel less than they?
We were all inmates of one place,
And I, the monarch of each race,
Had power to kill — yet, strange to tell!
In quiet we had learn'd to dwell —
My very chains and I grew friends,
So much a long communion tends 390
To make us what we are: — even I
Regain'd my freedom with a sigh.

NOTES TO THE PRISONER OF CHILLON.

(The numbers refer to lines.)

THIS poem was written in Switzerland in 1816, after Byron's final departure from his native land. It belongs to the group of poems to which we may give the name of *romantic tales*. There is no resemblance between the hero of the poem and the historic prisoner of Chillon, of whom Byron knew little or nothing at the time he wrote. " When the foregoing poem was composed," he frankly confesses, " I was not sufficiently aware of the history of Bonnivard, or I should have endeavored to dignify the subject by an attempt to celebrate his courage and his virtues." The Bonnivard of history, on whom the poet afterwards wrote a sonnet, was imprisoned for six years — from 1530 to 1536 — for political reasons. He was a man of extensive knowledge, upright aims, and heroic will. No brothers shared his imprisonment. After his liberation he lived in honor in Geneva, for the liberties of which he had suffered. A sight of the dungeon, without an extended acquaintance with the history of the illustrious prisoner of Chillon, was sufficient material for the poet's powerful imagination to work upon. The story of the prisoner of Chillon, as here given, is almost pure fiction.

3. *In a single night*, etc. — Byron has this note: " Ludovico Sforza, and others. The same is asserted of Marie Antoinette's, the wife of Louis XVI., though not in quite so short a period. Grief is said to have the same effect: to such, and not to fear, this change in *hers* was to be attributed."

6. *Rusted* = made weak and sluggish.

10. *Bann'd* = forbidden, interdicted. From A. S. *bannan*, to proclaim. The word appears in its original sense in the phrase *the banns of marriage*.

11. *This* should be *it;* or else line 12 should be omitted. The construction here may be taken as an illustration of Byron's occasional carelessness of style.

13. *That father*, etc. — He is represented as a Protestant.

22. *Seal'd* = confirmed, ratified. O. Fr. *seel*, Lat. *sigillum*, a seal.

28. *Chillon* = a celebrated castle and fortress in Switzerland. It is situated at the east end of Lake Geneva, on an isolated rock, almost entirely surrounded by deep water, and connected with the shore by a wooden bridge. The castle dates from the year 1238.

30. *Dim with a dull*, etc. — The poet has here taken some liberties with

the facts. "The dungeon of Bonnivard," says Murray, in his "Handbook of Switzerland," "is airy and spacious, consisting of two aisles, almost like the crypt of a church. It is lighted by several windows, through which the sun's light passes by reflection from the surface of the lake up to the roof, transmitting partly also the blue color of the waters."

41. *This new day.* — The prisoner, as we learn from stanza 14, had been released after years of imprisonment; and the light of the open sky seemed new to him.

45. *Score* = account or reckoning. From A. S. *sceran,* to cut. Accounts were once kept by *cutting* notches on a stick.

55. *Fettered in hand.* — Fetters were originally shackles for the *feet,* as manacles were shackles for the *hands.*

57. *Pure elements* = air and light.

63. *Our voices,* etc. — Privations and suffering sometimes materially change the voice. On one occasion, when two Arctic exploring parties were reunited after a protracted separation, "the doctor," says Franklin, "particularly remarked the sepulchral tone of our voices, which he requested us to make more cheerful if possible, not aware that his own partook of the same key."

71. *Ought* = was under obligation. Here a past tense, though commonly used in the present.

95. *Had stood* = would have stood.

97. *To pine* depends on *was formed* in line 93.

101. *I forced it on.* — He speaks of his spirit as of a weary, fainting soldier.

102. *Those relics* = his two brothers. Literally, that which is left. Lat. *relinquere,* to leave.

107. *Lake Leman* = Lake of Geneva.

108. *A thousand feet,* etc. — Byron says in a note: "Below the castle, washing its walls, the lake has been fathomed to the depth of eight hundred feet. . . . The château is large, and seen along the lake for a great distance. The walls are white."

112. *Wave* is the subject of *enthralls.* See line 28.

122. *Rock hath rocked.* — We cannot consider this word-play as felicitous. The noun *rock* and the verb *rock* are of different origin.

142. *Had his free,* etc. = if his free breathing had been denied.

148. *Gnash* = break by violent bitings.

152. *Boon* = a favor, deed of grace. From Fr. *bon,* Lat. *bonus,* good.

155. Compare the following lines in Coleridge's "Christabel": —

> "And to be wroth with one we love
> Doth work like madness in the brain."

172. *Yet* = hitherto, thus far.

189. *And grieved for those*, etc. — "There is much delicacy," says Hales, "in this plural. By such a fanciful multiplying of the survivors, the elder brother prevents self-intrusion; himself and his loneliness are, as it were, kept out of sight and forgotten. There is a not unlike sensitiveness in the Scotch phrase, 'them that's awa',' of some single lost one. The grief is softened by vagueness."

230. *Selfish death* = self-inflicted death.

231. *What next befell*, etc. — The following description of the prisoner's deadly stupor is graphic and powerful. It has been much admired.

237. *Wist* = knew; past tense of A. S. *witan*, to know.

252. *It was the carol*, etc. — The sympathies of his nature were awakened again. In a similar manner the spell of the Ancient Mariner was broken by the sight of iris-hued serpents disporting in the water: —

> "A spring of love gushed from my heart,
> And I blessed them unaware."

In Goethe's great work, Faust is recalled from despair by a chime of bells and a choral song. Dashing the cup of poison from his lips, he exclaims: —

> "Sound on, ye hymns of Heaven, so sweet and mild!
> My tears gush forth: the earth takes back her child."

327. *Had made* = would have made.

335. *The blue Rhone.* — This statement is not strictly correct. At its entrance into the lake, the Rhone is of the common color of glacier streams; it does not become blue till it leaves the lake at Geneva.

339. *White-walled, distant town* = Villeneuve.

341. *Little isle.* — In a note to this passage Byron says: "Between the entrances of the Rhone and Villeneuve, not far from Chillon, is a very small island; the only one I could perceive, in my voyage round and over the lake, within its circumference. It contains a few trees (I think not above three), and from its singleness and diminutive size has a peculiar effect upon the view."

WILLIAM WORDSWORTH.

IN striking contrast with the restless, passionate life of Byron stands the peaceful, uneventful life of Wordsworth. Instead of furious, tormenting passions, there is a self-poised, peaceful life of contemplation. Byron imparted to the beautiful or sublime scenes of nature the colorings of his turbulent thoughts and violent emotions; Wordsworth brought to mountain, stream, and flower the docility of a reverent and loving spirit. His soul was open to the lesson of the outward world, which to him was pervaded by an invisible presence. In his pride and misanthropy, Byron felt no sympathy with the sufferings and struggles of humanity. His censorious eye perceived only the foibles and frailties that lie on the surface. With a far nobler spirit and a keener insight, Wordsworth discerned beauty and grandeur in human life, and aspired to be helpful to his fellow-men. "It is indeed a deep satisfaction," he wrote near the close of his life, "to hope and believe that my poetry will be, while it lasts, a help to the cause of virtue and truth, especially among the young." While Byron trampled on the laws of morality, ruined his home, and turned the joys of life to ashes, Wordsworth lived in the midst of quiet domestic happiness — humble indeed, but glorified by fidelity, friendship, and love. Byron died in early manhood enslaved by evil habits and oppressed with the emptiness of life; Wordsworth reached an honored old age, and passed away upheld with precious hopes. The one may be admired for his power and meteoric splendor; the other will be honored and loved for his upright character, his human sympathy, and his helpful teachings.

William Wordsworth was born at Cockermouth in Cumberland County, April 7, 1770, of an ancient family. His violent and moody temper as a child filled his mother with anxiety about his future. He in no way distinguished himself at school, though some of the verses he then composed were well spoken of.

At the age of seventeen he entered Cambridge, where he gave no promise of his future greatness. His genius developed slowly. It was not from books, but from nature, that he derived the greatest inspiration and help. The celebrated Lake District, in which he was born and in which his school days and the greater part of his maturity were spent, is a region of varied and beautiful scenery. With its mountains, forests, and lakes, it is grander than the typical English landscape, yet without the overpowering sublimity of Switzerland. It was a region specially suited to awaken and develop the peculiar powers of Wordsworth. He moved among the natural beauties of the country with an ill-defined but exquisite pleasure. In his own words, —

> " The ever-living universe
> Turn where I might, was opening out its glories;
> And the independent spirit of pure youth
> Called forth at every season new delights
> Spread round my steps like sunshine o'er green fields."

In 1791 Wordsworth took the degree of Bachelor of Arts, and left the university without having decided upon a vocation. " He did not feel himself good enough for the church," he said years afterwards; " he felt that his mind was not properly disciplined for that holy office, and that the struggle between his conscience and his impulses would have made life a torture." He was disinclined to the law; and though he fancied that he had talents for the profession of arms, he feared that he might fall a prey to disease in foreign lands. He passed some time in London without a definite aim and also without much profit. He felt out of place amidst the rush and din of the city. Like the " Farmer of Tilsbury Vale," whom he afterwards described : —

> " In the throng of the town like a stranger is he,
> Like one whose own country's far over the sea;
> And nature, while through the great city he hies,
> Full ten times a day takes his heart by surprise."

After a few months he went to France for the purpose of learning the language. His sympathies, which had been with the revolutionists, were intensified by an acquaintance at Orleans with the republican general Beaupuis. Returning to Paris, Wordsworth contemplated placing himself at the head of the Girondist party — a step that would inevitably have brought him to the guillotine. From this danger he was saved by his friends, who, not in sympathy with his republicanism, stopped his allowance, and thus compelled him to return to England. The excesses into which the Revolution ran were a rude shock to him. He was driven to the verge of scepticism: —

> "Even the visible universe
> Fell under the dominion of a taste
> Less spiritual, with microscopic view
> Was scanned, as I had scanned the moral world."

But his thoughtful nature could not rest in unbelief. A sympathetic study of nature, the beautiful devotion of his sister Dorothy, and a deeper insight into the lives of men, restored his healthfulness and peace of mind. As he advanced in years, he gave up the ardent republican hopes of his youth, and settled down into a staid conservatism.

There are few lives that might better serve to illustrate the doctrine of a special providence. All through his career, the needed help came to him at the right moment. Wordsworth had nursed with tender care a young man attacked by consumption. Upon his death it was found that he had left the poet a legacy of nine hundred pounds. Nothing could have come more opportunely. With this small sum Wordsworth settled with his sister in a little cottage at Racedown in Dorsetshire. Here he began to devote himself to poetry in earnest. In his sister he found a congenial and helpful companion. She filled his home with sunshine. Her poetic sensibilities were keenly alive to the beauties of nature. In grateful recognition of her helpfulness, the poet says : —

> " She gave me eyes, she gave me ears,
> And humble cares, and delicate fears;
> A heart the fountain of sweet tears;
> And love, and thought, and joy."

With a beautiful devotion she found her life-work in aiding her gifted brother to fulfil his mission.

The first volume of Wordsworth is entitled "Lyrical Ballads." It was published in 1798, and contained, besides Coleridge's "Ancient Mariner," and several pieces that were ridiculed for triviality, "We are Seven," "Expostulation and Reply," "The Tables Turned," and above all "Tintern Abbey," all of which contain the essential principles of Wordsworth's poetry. Indeed, the "Tintern Abbey" more than any other single poem contains the revelation that the poet had to make to the world.

Unfortunately the trivial pieces attracted most attention, and the work was received with coldness and ridicule. "The Idiot Boy" — a delightful poem to those who can feel the pathos of childish imbecility and the beauty of maternal love and solicitude — was the subject of one of the cruelest passages in the "English Bards and Scotch Reviewers." Speaking of Wordsworth, whom he denominates "a mild apostate from poetic rule," Byron continues : —

> " Thus when he tells the tale of Betty Foy,
> The idiot mother of an idiot boy,
> A moon-struck silly lad who lost his way,
> And like his bard confounded night with day,
> So close on each pathetic part he dwells,
> And each adventure so sublimely tells,
> That all who view the idiot in his glory,
> Conceive the bard the hero of the story."

Immediately after the publication of the "Lyrical Ballads," Wordsworth and his sister went to Germany in order to improve their imperfect acquaintance with the German language. They passed the winter at Goslar; but as they seem to have made no acquaintances, their means of advancement was confined to reading German books privately.

The winter was severe, and their comforts were few. Wordsworth says: "I slept in a room over a passage that was not ceiled. The people of the house used to say, rather unfeelingly, that they expected that I should be frozen to death some night." Notwithstanding these discomforts, his muse was active, and he produced some of his most charming and characteristic pieces, among which are "Lucy Gray," "Ruth," "Nutting," and the "Poet's Epitaph." It was here, too, that the "Prelude," the poetical autobiography of the author's mental growth, was begun. "The Prelude," says a biographer, "is a book of good augury for human nature. We feel in reading it as if the stock of mankind were sound. The soul seems going on from strength to strength by the mere development of her inborn power."

Wordsworth returned to England in 1799, and settled at Grasmere in the Lake District, in which he spent the rest of his life. The following year he published a new edition of the "Lyrical Ballads," containing many new pieces and the famous preface in which he laid down his poetical canons. These canons may be briefly stated as follows: 1. Subjects are to be taken from rustic or common life, "because in that condition the essential passions of the heart find a better soil, in which they can attain their maturity, are less under restraint, and speak plainer and more emphatic language." 2. The language of common life, purified from its defects, is to be adopted, because men of that station "hourly communicate with the best objects from which the best part of language is originally derived; and because, . . . being less under the action of social vanity, they convey their feelings and notions in simple and unelaborated expressions." 3. "There neither is nor can be any essential difference between the language of prose and metrical composition."

The most, perhaps, that can be said in favor of these principles is that, without being absolutely true, they contain elements of truth. Like Burns, Wordsworth has conferred a blessing on humanity in pointing out the beauty of commonplace objects and incidents. We cannot spare "We are Seven," or "Michael," which ought to be one of our most popular poems. His naturalness of diction is to be commended. Yet it must be said that Wordsworth sometimes carries his principles to a ridiculous extent. When he hits upon phrases like "dear brother Jim," and objects like "skimmed milk," and —

> "A household tub, like one of those
> Which women use to wash their clothes,"

his greatest admirers are forced to grieve.

Wordsworth's life in the Lake District was characterized by great simplicity. There were no stirring events, no great changes. His resources were increased by the payment of an old debt due his father's estate. His marriage, in 1802, to Miss Mary Hutchinson, brought into his home a real helpmate. Though decidedly domestic in her turn, she was not without poetic feeling, and appreciated her husband's genius. The poet paid her this glowing tribute : —

> "A being breathing thoughtful breath,
> A traveller between life and death;
> The reason firm, the temperate will,
> Endurance, foresight, strength, and skill;
> A perfect woman nobly planned,
> To warn, to comfort, and command;
> And yet a spirit still, and bright
> With something of angelic light."

With true feminine tact she presided over the poet's home, and softened as far as possible the unconscious egotism into which his retirement and contemplation had betrayed him. Dorothy Wordsworth shared their home. The life of this happy family was an illustration of "plain living and high thinking." Much time was spent in the open air, and every foot of ground in the neighborhood was traversed by the poet and his sister.   A large part of his verse was composed during these daily rambles.   While extending a cordial welcome to congenial friends, — DeQuincey, Coleridge, Wilson, Southey, and others, — he cared little for neighborhood gossip.   To him it was a fruitless waste of time.   As he tells us in the sonnets entitled " Personal Talk : " —

> " Better than such discourse doth silence long,
>   Long, barren silence, square with my desire;
>   To sit without emotion, hope, or aim,
>   In the loved presence of my cottage fire,
>   And listen to the flapping of the flame,
>   Or kettle whispering its faint undersong."

This quiet, humble, reflective life is beautiful ; yet it has its objectionable features.   It leads to narrow and one-sided views of life.   It is not the way in which to develop a strong or heroic character.   Yet it was adapted to Wordsworth's genius, and produced a rich fruitage.

The first great sorrow that came into the poet's life was the death of his brother John, captain of an East Indiaman.   His vessel was wrecked in 1805, and sank with the captain at his post of duty.   He had several years previously spent a few months at Grasmere, and was looking forward to the time when he might settle there for life.

A strong attachment existed between him and his brother. It was but natural, therefore, that the poet should write : " For myself, I feel that there is something cut out of my life which cannot be restored.   I never thought of him but with hope and delight.   We looked forward to the time, not distant, as we thought, when he would settle near us — when the task of his life would be over, and he would have nothing to do but reap his reward. . . .   I never wrote a line without the thought of giving him pleasure; my writings, printed and manuscript, were his delight, and one of the chief solaces of his long voyages."   The same year saw the death of Nelson at Trafalgar. The death of the hero brought grief to the national heart.

Combining the traits of his brother John and Admiral Nelson, Wordsworth composed "The Happy Warrior," a poem of great dignity and weight — a veritable manual of greatness. Who is the happy warrior? He who owes,—

> "To virtue every triumph that he knows;
> Who, if he rise to station of command,
> Rises by open means; and there will stand
> On honorable terms, or else retire,
> And in himself possess his own desire;
> Who comprehends his trust, and to the same
> Keeps faithful with a singleness of aim;
> And therefore does not stoop nor lie in wait
> For wealth, or honors, or for worldly state;
> Whom they must follow, on whose head must fall,
> Like showers of manna, if they come at all."

Every year increased the number of notable poems. There are two or three that deserve especial mention as embodying peculiar views — to some extent Wordsworth's philosophy of life. In a little poem called "The Rainbow," he says : —

> "My heart leaps up when I behold
> A rainbow in the sky:
> So was it when my life began;
> So is it now I am a man;
> So be it when I shall grow old,
> Or let me die!
> The child is father of the man;
> And I could wish my days to be
> Bound each to each by natural piety."

Far more is here expressed than appears at first reading. "Wordsworth holds," to adopt the excellent interpretation by Myers, "that the instincts and pleasures of a healthy childhood sufficiently indicate the lines on which our maturer character should be formed. The joy which began in the mere sense of existence should be maintained by hopeful faith ; the simplicity which began in inexperience should be recovered by medita-tion ; the love which originated in the family circle should expand itself over the race of men." In the "Ode to Duty," one of Wordworth's noblest productions, we meet with this " genial sense of youth : " —

> "Serene will be our days and bright,
>   And happy will our nature be,
> When love is an unerring light,
>   And joy its own security.''

In the " Ode on Immortality,'' in which we have perhaps the highest attainment of poetry in this century, he makes use of the Platonic doctrine of the pre-existence of the soul to account for the glory that hovers over the visible world in childhood. As the child looks upon the various objects of earth and sky, he unconsciously invests them, the poet says, with the splendor of the spiritual world from which he has come. But as life advances, these recollections of a previous existence become fainter and fainter, and at last the world degenerates into a commonplace reality. Now read these splendid lines : —

> " Our birth is but a sleep and a forgetting:
>   The soul that rises with us, our life's star,
>   Hath had elsewhere its setting,
>   And cometh from afar:
>   Not in entire forgetfulness,
>   And not in utter nakedness,
>   But trailing clouds of glory do we come
>   From God, who is our home:
>   Heaven lies about us in our infancy!
>   Shades of the prison house begin to close
>   Upon the growing boy,
>   But he beholds the light and whence it flows,
>   He sees it in his joy;
>   The youth, who daily further from the east
>   Must travel, still is nature's priest,
>   And by the vision splendid
>   Is on his way attended;
>   At length the man perceives it die away,
>   And fade into the light of common day.''

In 1813 Wordsworth removed to Rydal Mount, where he spent the rest of his life. With increasing family — three sons and two daughters had been born unto him — came increasing wants and expenditures. His good fortune did not desert him. He was appointed distributer of stamps for the county of Westmoreland — an office that brought him little labor, but five hundred pounds a year.

The following year he published " The Excursion," a tedious and prosaic poem relieved here and there with passages of surpassing beauty. It was coldly received, and proved a financial loss. Jeffrey began a famous review with the contemptuous sentence, " This will never do." Up to this time Wordsworth had been the subject of continuously unfavorable criticism. No other writer, perhaps, ever had so protracted a struggle to gain a proper recognition.

But through all this long period of misrepresentation and detraction, Wordsworth did not lose confidence in himself. His genius was its own sufficient witness. He felt a pity for the ignorance of the world, but looked forward to a time when the merits of his poetry would be recognized. Writing to a friend, he says : " Let me confine myself to my object, which is to make you, my dear friend, as easy hearted as myself with respect to these poems. Trouble not yourself upon their present reception. Of what moment is that compared with what I trust is their destiny ? — to console the afflicted ; to add sunshine to daylight, by making the happy happier ; to teach the young and the gracious of every age to see, to think and feel, and therefore to become more actively and securely virtuous ; this is their office, which I trust they will faithfully perform long after we (that is, all that is mortal of us) are mouldered in our graves." What in many a man would savor of egotism comes from the lips of Wordsworth with the calm dignity of conscious strength.

His hopes were not disappointed. The latter years of his life brought him great popularity and honor. In 1839 the University of Oxford conferred upon him the degree of Doctor of Civil Law ; three years later the government granted him a pension of three hundred pounds ; and upon the death of

Southey he became poet laureate.　His pure and peaceful life came to an end April 23, 1850.　And surely of him, if of any one, we may think as of a man who was so in accord with nature, so at one with the very soul of things, that there can be no mansion of the universe which shall not be to him a home, no Governor who will not accept him among his servants, and satisfy him with love and peace."

LINES

COMPOSED A FEW MILES ABOVE TINTERN ABBEY, ON REVISITING THE
BANKS OF THE WYE, DURING A TOUR.

JULY 13, 1798.

FIVE years have past; five summers, with the length
Of five long winters! and again I hear
These waters, rolling from their mountain-springs
With a sweet inland murmur.   Once again
Do I behold these steep and lofty cliffs,
That on a wild secluded scene impress
Thoughts of more deep seclusion, and connect
The landscape with the quiet of the sky.
The day is come when I again repose
Here, under this dark sycamore, and view   10
These plots of cottage-ground, these orchard-tufts,
Which at this season, with their unripe fruits,
Are clad in one green hue, and lose themselves
Among the woods and copses, nor disturb
The wild green landscape.   Once again I see
These hedgerows — hardly hedgerows — little lines
Of sportive wood run wild; these pastoral farms,
Green to the very door; and wreaths of smoke
Sent up, in silence, from among the trees,
With some uncertain notice, as might seem   20
Of vagrant dwellers in the houseless woods,
Or of some hermit's cave, where by his fire
The hermit sits alone.
                         These beauteous forms,
Through a long absence, have not been to me
As is a landscape to a blind man's eye;
But oft, in lonely rooms, and 'mid the din
Of towns and cities, I have owed to them,
In hours of weariness, sensations sweet,
Felt in the blood, and felt along the heart;
And passing even into my purer mind,   30
With tranquil restoration: feelings too

Of unremembered pleasure; such, perhaps,
As have no slight or trivial influence
On that best portion of a good man's life —
His little, nameless, unremembered acts
Of kindness and of love.   Nor less, I trust,
To them I may have owed another gift,
Of aspect more sublime : that blessed mood,
In which the burden of the mystery,
In which the heavy and the weary weight   40
Of all this unintelligible world,
Is lightened; that serene and blessèd mood
In which the affections gently lead us on,
Until, the breath of this corporeal frame
And even the motion of our human blood
Almost suspended, we are laid asleep
In body, and become a living soul ;
While with an eye made quiet by the power
Of harmony, and the deep power of joy,
We see into the life of things.
                              If this   50
Be but a vain belief, yet, oh! how oft,
In darkness, and amid the many shapes
Of joyless daylight, when the fretful stir
Unprofitable, and the fever of the world,
Have hung upon the beatings of my heart —
How oft, in spirit, have I turned to thee,
O sylvan Wye!   Thou wanderer thro' the woods,
How often has my spirit turned to thee !

    And now, with gleams of half-extinguished thought,
With many recognitions dim and faint,   60
And somewhat of a sad perplexity,
The picture of the mind revives again ;
While here I stand, not only with the sense
Of present pleasure, but with pleasing thoughts
That in this moment there is life and food
For future years.   And so I dare to hope,
Though changed, no doubt, from what I was when first
I came among these hills ; when like a roe
I bounded o'er the mountains, by the sides

Of the deep rivers and the lonely streams,   70
Wherever nature led : more like a man
Flying from something that he dreads than one
Who sought the thing he loved.   For Nature then
(The coarser pleasures of my boyish days,
And their glad animal movements all gone by)
To me was all in all.   I cannot paint
What then I was.   The sounding cataract
Haunted me like a passion ; the tall rock,
The mountain, and the deep and gloomy wood,
Their colors and their forms, were then to me   80
An appetite, a feeling and a love,
That had no need of a remoter charm,
By thought supplied, nor any interest
Unborrowed from the eye.   That time is past,
And all its aching joys are now no more,
And all its dizzy raptures.   Not for this
Faint I, nor mourn nor murmur ; other gifts
Have followed, for such loss, I would believe,
Abundant recompense.   For I have learned
To look on Nature, not as in the hour   90
Of thoughtless youth ; but hearing oftentimes
The still, sad music of humanity,
Nor harsh nor grating, though of ample power
To chasten and subdue.   And I have felt
A presence that disturbs me with the joy
Of elevated thoughts : a sense sublime
Of something far more deeply interfused,
Whose dwelling is the light of setting suns,
And the round ocean and the living air
And the blue sky, and in the mind of man :   100
A motion and a spirit, that impels
All thinking things, all objects of all thought,
And rolls through all things.   Therefore am I still
A lover of the meadows and the woods
And mountains, and of all that we behold
From this green earth ; of all the mighty world
Of eye and ear, both what they half create
And what perceive ; well pleased to recognize
In Nature and the language of the sense

The anchor of my purest thoughts; the nurse,   110
The guide, the guardian of my heart, and soul
Of all my moral being.
                  Nor, perchance,
If I were not thus taught, should I the more
Suffer my genial spirits to decay:
For thou art with me here upon the banks
Of this fair river; thou, my dearest friend,
My dear, dear friend, and in thy voice I catch
The language of my former heart, and read
My former pleasures in the shooting lights
Of thy wild eyes. Oh! yet a little while   120
May I behold in thee what I was once,
My dear, dear sister! and this prayer I make,
Knowing that Nature never did betray
The heart that loved her; 'tis her privilege,
Through all the years of this our life, to lead
From joy to joy: for she can so inform
The mind that is within us, so impress
With quietness and beauty, and so feed
With lofty thoughts, that neither evil tongues,
Rash judgments, nor the sneers of selfish men,   130
Nor greetings where no kindness is, nor all
The dreary intercourse of daily life,
Shall e'er prevail against us, or disturb
Our cheerful faith, that all which we behold
Is full of blessings. Therefore let the moon
Shine on thee in thy solitary walk;
And let the misty mountain winds be free
To blow against thee; and in after-years,
When these wild ecstasies shall be matured
Into a sober pleasure, when thy mind   140
Shall be a mansion for all lovely forms,
Thy memory be as a dwelling-place
For all sweet sounds and harmonies; oh! then,
If solitude or fear or pain or grief
Should be thy portion, with what healing thoughts
Of tender joy wilt thou remember me,
And these my exhortations! Nor, perchance
If I should be where I no more can hear

Thy voice, nor catch from thy wild eyes these gleams
Of past existence, wilt thou then forget   150
That on the banks of this delightful stream
We stood together; and that I, so long
A worshipper of Nature, hither came
Unwearied in that service: rather say
With warmer love, oh! with far deeper zeal
Of holier love.   Nor wilt thou then forget,
That after many wanderings, many years
Of absence, these steep woods and lofty cliffs,
And this green pastoral landscape, were to me
More dear, both for themselves and for thy sake.   160

ODE.

INTIMATIONS OF IMMORTALITY FROM RECOLLECTIONS OF EARLY CHILDHOOD.

THERE was a time when meadow, grove, and stream,
    The earth, and every common sight
            To me did seem
            Apparelled in celestial light,
The glory and the freshness of a dream.
It is not now as it hath been of yore; —
            Turn wheresoe'er I may,
            By night or day,
The things which I have seen I now can see no more.

            The rainbow comes and goes,   10
            And lovely is the rose;
            The moon doth with delight
Look round her when the heaven is bare;
            Waters on a starry night
            Are beautiful and fair;
    The sunshine is a glorious birth;
    But yet I know, where'er I go,
That there hath passed away a glory from the earth.

Now, while the birds thus sing a joyous song,
    And while the young lambs bound   20
            As to the tabor's sound,
To me alone there came a thought of grief:
A timely utterance gave that thought relief,
            And I again am strong:
The cataracts blow their trumpets from the steep;
No more shall grief of mine the season wrong;
I hear the echoes through the mountains throng,
The winds come to me from the fields of sleep,
            And all the earth is gay;
            Land and sea   30
    Give themselves up to jollity,

And with the heart of May
Doth every beast keep holiday; —
Thou child of joy,
Shout round me, let me hear thy shouts, thou happy
Shepherd boy!

Ye blessèd creatures, I have heard the call
Ye to each other make; I see
The heavens laugh with you in your jubilee;
My heart is at your festival,
My head hath its coronal,
The fulness of your bliss, I feel — I feel it all.
Oh evil day! if I were sullen
While earth herself is adorning,
This sweet May morning,
And the children are culling
On every side,
In a thousand valleys far and wide,
Fresh flowers; while the sun shines warm,
And the babe leaps up on his mother's arm;
I hear, I hear, with joy I hear!
— But there's a tree, of many, one,
A single field which I have looked upon,
Both of them speak of something that is gone:
The pansy at my feet
Doth the same tale repeat:
Whither is fled the visionary gleam?
Where is it now, the glory and the dream?

Our birth is but a sleep and a forgetting:
The soul that rises with us, our life's star,
Hath had elsewhere its setting,
And cometh from afar:
Not in entire forgetfulness,
And not in utter nakedness,
But trailing clouds of glory do we come
From God, who is our home.
Heaven lies about us in our infancy!
Shades of the prison-house begin to close
Upon the growing boy,

But he beholds the light, and whence it flows ;   70
      He sees it in his joy.
The youth who daily farther from the east
    Must travel, still is nature's priest,
      And by the vision splendid
      Is on his way attended ;
At length the man perceives it die away,
And fade into the light of common day.

Earth fills her lap with pleasures of her own ;
Yearnings she hath in her own natural kind,
And, even with something of a mother's mind,   80
      And no unworthy aim,
    The homely nurse doth all she can
To make her foster-child, her inmate man,
    Forget the glories he hath known,
And that imperial palace whence he came.
Behold the child among his new-born blisses,
A six-years' darling of a pigmy size !
See where, 'mid work of his own hand, he lies,
Fretted by sallies of his mother's kisses,
With light upon him from his father's eyes !   90
See at his feet some little plan or chart,
Some fragment from his dream of human life,
Shaped by himself with newly learnèd art ;
    A wedding or a festival,
    A mourning or a funeral ;
      And this hath now his heart,
    And unto this he frames his song ;
      Then will he fit his tongue
To dialogues of business, love, or strife.
      But it will not be long   100
      Ere this be thrown aside,
      And with new joy and pride
The little actor cons another part,
Filling from time to time his " humorous stage "
With all the persons, down to palsied age,
That life brings with her in her equipage,
      As if his whole vocation
      Were endless imitation.

Thou, whose exterior semblance doth belie
      Thy soul's immensity ;   110
Thou best philosopher, who yet doth keep
Thy heritage ; thou eye among the blind,
That, deaf and silent, read'st the eternal deep,
Haunted for ever by the eternal mind, —
      Mighty prophet, seer blest !
      On whom those truths do rest,
Which we are toiling all our lives to find,
In darkness lost, the darkness of the grave ;
Thou, over whom thine Immortality
Broods like the day, a master o'er a slave,   120
A presence which is not to be put by ;
Thou little child, yet glorious in the might
Of heaven-born freedom on thy being's height,
Why with such earnest pains dost thou provoke
The years to bring the inevitable yoke,
Thus blindly with thy blessedness at strife?
Full soon thy soul shall have her earthly freight,
And custom lie upon thee with a weight
Heavy as frost, and deep almost as life !

      O joy ! that in our embers   130
        Is something that doth live,
        That nature yet remembers
        What was so fugitive !
The thought of our past years in me doth breed
Perpetual benediction ; not indeed
For that which is most worthy to be blest ;
Delight and liberty, the simple creed
Of childhood, whether busy or at rest,
With new-fledged hope still fluttering in his breast :
      Not for these I raise   140
        The song of thanks and praise ;
      But for those obstinate questionings
      Of sense and outward things,
      Fallings from us, vanishings,
      Blank misgivings of a creature
Moving about in worlds not realized,
High instincts before which our mortal nature

Did tremble like a guilty thing surprised;
 But for those first affections,
 Those shadowy recollections   150
  Which, be they what they may,
Are yet the fountain-light of all our day,
Are yet a master-light of all our seeing;
  Uphold us, cherish, and have power to make
Our noisy years seem moments in the being
Of the eternal silence: truths that wake
  To perish never;
Which neither listlessness nor mad endeavor,
  Nor man, nor boy,
Nor all that is at enmity with joy,   160
Can utterly abolish or destroy!
  Hence in a season of calm weather,
   Though inland far we be,
Our souls have sight of that immortal sea,
   Which brought us hither;
   Can in a moment travel thither,
And see the children sport upon the shore,
And hear the mighty waters rolling evermore.

Then sing, ye birds, sing, sing a joyous song!
   And let the young lambs bound   170
   As to the tabor's sound!
 We in thought will join your throng,
   Ye that pipe and ye that play,
   Ye that through your hearts to-day
   Feel the gladness of the May!
What though the radiance which was once so bright
Be now for ever taken from my sight —
Though nothing can bring back the hour
Of splendour in the grass, of glory in the flower;
We will grieve not, rather find   180
Strength in what remains behind;
In the primal sympathy,
Which having been must ever be;
In the soothing thoughts that spring
Out of human suffering;
In the faith that looks through death,

In years that bring the philosophic mind.
And, O ye fountains, meadows, hills, and groves,
Forebode not any severing of our loves !
Yet in my heart of hearts I feel your might;   190
I only have relinquished one delight
To live beneath your more habitual sway.
I love the brooks which down their channels fret,
Even more than when I tripped lightly as they ;
•The innocent brightness of a new-born day
          Is lovely yet ;
The clouds that gather round the setting sun
Do take a sober colouring from an eye
That hath kept watch o'er man's mortality ;
Another race hath been, and other palms are won.   200
Thanks to the human heart by which we live,
Thanks to its tenderness, its joys, and fears ;
To me the meanest flower that blows can give
Thoughts that do often lie too deep for tears.

NOTES TO TINTERN ABBEY.

(The numbers refer to lines.)

TINTERN ABBEY is a famous ecclesiastical ruin on the right bank of the Wye in Monmouthshire. It was founded in 1131. Though the Abbey is mentioned in the title, it is not referred to at all in the poem itself.

The poem was composed in a single day. In the words of Myers, "The lines written above *Tintern Abbey* have become, as it were, the *locus classicus*, or consecrated formulary of the Wordsworthian faith. They say in brief what it is the work of the poet's biographer to say in detail."

1. *Five summers*, etc.— The poet had visited the same spot five years before, during the restless period that followed his graduation at Cambridge.

4. *Once again*, etc.— As we have already learned, Wordsworth's love of nature was intense. Having once seen this beautiful spot, he could not forget it. In the following lines of this paragraph, he dwells with loving tenderness on the various objects of beauty — the lofty cliffs, the secluded landscape, the cottages, orchards, hedgerows, —

> " And wreaths of smoke
> Sent up, in silence, from among the trees."

27. *I have owed to them*, etc.— Wordsworth cared but little for books; nature was his great teacher. Nature filled him with feelings of deep tranquillity and delight, and taught him something of the significance of this "unintelligible world."

65. *There is life and food*, etc.— The beautiful landscape would not fade from his memory. Both its forms and its teachings would continue to abide with him as a blessing.

67. *From what I was*, etc.— On his first visit, he had not yet learned the meaning of nature. Its forms and scenes filled him with a wild delight, as is beautifully described in the following lines, but they brought him no lesson of wisdom.

89. *For I have learned*, etc.— Here we find the soul of Wordsworth's poetry. Nature and humanity are in fundamental harmony. An invisible presence pervades all things, both animate and inanimate. His highest aim is to live in sympathy with that divine presence, and to make it —

> " The nurse,
> The guide, the guardian of my heart, and soul
> Of all my moral being."

115. *For thou art*, etc. — His sister Dorothy. Her sympathy with nature was scarcely less than that of the poet himself. See sketch of Wordsworth.

126. *For she can so inform*, etc. — The poet realized in his own character what he here describes. Calmness of soul, loftiness of thought, and —

> " Our cheerful faith, that all which we behold
> Is full of blessings," —

these are traits that make Wordsworth's life so beautiful.

138. *And in after-years*, etc. — The poet expects that his sister will pass through the same experience as himself; that her wild ecstasies in the presence of nature will be sobered by reflection and intelligent sympathy with the soul of things.

NOTES TO INTIMATIONS OF IMMORTALITY.

(The numbers refer to lines.)

IN addition to what has been said in the sketch of Wordsworth, the following account given by him of the poem will form a valuable introduction. He says: " This was composed during my residence at Town-End, Grasmere. Two year at least passed between the writing of the first four stanzas and the remaining part. To the attentive and competent reader the whole sufficiently explains itself, but there may be no harm in adverting here to particular feelings or experiences of my own mind on which the structure of the poem partly rests. Nothing was more difficult for me in childhood than to admit the notion of death as a state applicable to my own being. I have elsewhere said, —

> " A simple child
> That lightly draws its breath
> And feels its life in every limb,
> What should it know of death ? "

But it was not so much from the source of animal vivacity that my difficulty came, as from a sense of the indomitableness of the spirit within me. I used to brood over the stories of Enoch and Elijah, and almost persuade myself that, whatever might become of others, I should be translated in something of the same way to heaven. With a feeling congenial to this, I was often unable to think of external things as having external existence, and

I communed with all that I saw as something not apart from, but inherent in, my own immaterial nature. Many times, while going to school, have I grasped at a wall or tree to recall myself from this abyss of idealism to the reality. At that time I was afraid of mere processes. In later periods of life I have deplored, as we have all reason to do, a subjugation of an opposite character, and have rejoiced over the remembrances, as is expressed in the lines "Obstinate Questionings," etc. To that dream-like vividness and splendor which invests objects of sight in childhood, every one, I believe, if he would look back, could bear testimony, and I need not dwell upon it here; but having in the poem regarded this as a presumptive evidence of a prior state of existence, I think it right to protest against the conclusion which has given pain to some good and pious persons that I meant to inculcate such a belief. It is far too shadowy a notion to be recommended to faith as more than an element in our instincts of immortality. But let us bear in mind that though the idea is not advanced in Revelation, there is nothing there to contradict it, and the fall of man presents an analogy in its favor. Accordingly, a pre-existent state has entered into the creed of many nations, and among all persons acquainted with classic literature is known as an ingredient in Platonic philosophy. Archimedes said that he could move the world if he had a point whereon to rest his machine. Who has not felt the same aspirations as regards his own mind? Having to wield some of its elements when I was impelled to write this poem on the immortality of the soul, I took hold of the notion of pre-existence as having sufficient foundation in humanity for authorizing me to make for my purpose the best use of it I could as a poet."

6. *Of yore* = the childhood days of the poet. The usual sense is *of old time.*

9. *The things*, etc. — Compare with this Shelley's "A Lament:" —

> "O World! O life! O time!
> On whose last steps I climb,
> Trembling at that where I had stood before, —
> When will return the glory of your prime?
> No more — oh never more!
>
> Out of the day and night
> A joy has taken flight;
> Fresh spring, and summer, and winter hoar,
> Move my faint heart with grief, — but with delight
> No more — oh never more."

21. *Tabor* = a small drum.

25. *The cataracts*, etc. — The poet had in mind the numerous cascades of the beautiful Lake District.

28. *Fields of sleep.* — The time is morning, and the quiet of night has not yet been broken by the noises of the day.

37. *Ye blessed creatures* = the objects of nature, animate and inanimate, mentioned in the preceding stanza.

39. *Jubilee* = joyfulness, exultation. From the Hebrew *yobel*, a blast of a trumpet, a shout of joy, through the Lat. and Fr.

41. *Coronal* = wreath or garland as worn at Roman and Grecian banquets.

55. *Pansy* = a species of violet. From Fr. *pensée*, a thought; " thus, it is the flower of thought or remembrance.''

57. *Visionary* = vision-like.

59. *Our birth*, etc. — In this stanza the poet explains the source of that glory which invests objects in childhood. He adopts for the time the Platonic doctrine of the pre-existence of the soul, and makes the glory of nature as seen in childhood a reflection of the splendor of our previous state of existence. As we grow older objects are apt to become commonplace. Compare the lines of Hood : —

> " I remember, I remember,
>   The fir-trees dark and high ;
> I used to think their slender tops
>   Were close against the sky.
> It was a childish ignorance ;
>   But now it's little joy
> To know I'm farther off from heaven
>   Than when I was a boy."

An interval of more than two years came between the writing of the fourth and the fifth stanza. The transition seems a little abrupt.

73. *Nature's priest* = one living in close fellowship with nature, discerning its beauty and understanding its secrets.

82. *Homely nurse* = this world; called *homely* in comparison with " that imperial palace," whence her foster-child has come. Compare the following lines from Pope's " Essay on Man : " —

> " Behold the child, by Nature's kindly law,
>   Pleased with a rattle, tickled with a straw ;
> Some livelier plaything gives his youth delight,
>   A little louder, but as empty quite :
> Scarfs, garters, gold, amuse his riper stage,
>   And beads and prayer-books are the toys of age :
> Pleased with this bauble still, as that before,
>   Till tired he sleeps, and life's poor play is o'er."

86. *Behold the child*, etc. — Wordsworth had in mind a particular child, Hartley Coleridge, but the language is applicable to childhood in general.

87. *Pigmy* = a very diminutive person. From Gr. *pugme*, the distance from the elbow to the knuckles, through the Lat. and Fr. Originally applied to a fabulous race of dwarfs.

89. *Fretted* = vexed, annoyed.

103. *Cons* = to study over, examine into. From A. S., *cunnian*, to test, examine.

104. *Humorous stage* = the stage on which the whims, follies, and caprices of mankind are exhibited.

105. *Persons* = *dramatis personæ*, characters.

111. *Bèst philosopher*, because of his spontaneous love, joy, trust. See sketch of Wordsworth.

128. *Custom* = the ordinary usage and requirements of practical life.

144. *Fallings from us, vanishings*, etc. — Refer to the shadowy remembrances of a previous life — remembrances that startle us at times with a consciousness of our immortality, and lead our thoughts to higher things than the material world about us. See Wordsworth's note above.

ALFRED TENNYSON.

For half a century Alfred Tennyson stood at the head of English poetry. It is hardly too much to claim that he was the best representative of the culture of the Victorian age. His extraordinary poetic genius was supported by broad scholarship. He absorbed the deepest and best thought of his age; and instead of mere passing fancies, his poetry embodies a depth of thought and feeling that gives it inexhaustible richness. Viewed from an artistic standpoint, his work is exquisite. He surpassed Pope in perfection of form; he equalled Wordsworth in natural expression; he excelled both Scott and Byron in romantic narrative; and he wrote the only great epic poem since the days of Milton.

Few poets have been more fortunate than Tennyson. His life was one of easy competence. In the retirement of a cultivated home, and in a narrow circle of congenial friends, he steadily pursued his vocation. Never did a poet consecrate himself more entirely to his art. He wrote no prose. He did not entangle himself in business, which has fettered many a brilliant genius. He encumbered himself with no public office, by which his poetic labors might have been broken. His career, like an English river, quietly flowed on among fertile hills and blooming meadows. Perhaps it might have been better had he lived a little less in retirement. Contact with the rude world might have given a more rugged strength to his verse, relieving in some measure the excessive refinement that is possibly its greatest fault.

The principal events in the life of Tennyson are the publication of his successive volumes. He was born at Somersby in Lincolnshire in 1809, the son of a clergyman, and the third of twelve children. It was a gifted family, which Leigh Hunt called "a nest of nightingales." After a careful training in the parsonage under his father, Alfred was sent, with two brothers, to Trinity College, Cambridge. The bent of his mind early showed itself; and in 1827, in connection with his brother Charles, he sent forth, as yet an undergraduate, a volume entitled "Poems, by Two Brothers." As in the case of Byron, this first volume gave no token of genius. The poetry was correct, but unreadably dull.

In 1829, in competition with Arthur Hallam, Tennyson won a medal for his prize poem on the subject of "Timbuctoo." This work contained some faint intimations of his latent powers. His literary career really opened in 1830 with a volume of "Poems, Chiefly Lyrical." With much that was faulty and immature — suppressed by the author in subsequent editions of his works — this volume announced the presence of a genuine poet. He did not, however, receive the recognition he deserved. Christopher North, in *Blackwood's Magazine*, mingled censure and praise — his censure being of the positive kind then in vogue. The poet resented the criticism; and in a volume published a little later, we find the following reply :—

> "You did late review my lays,
>   Crusty Christopher;
> You did mingle blame and praise,
>   Rusty Christopher;
> When I learnt from whom it came,
> I forgave you all the blame,
>   Musty Christopher;
> I could *not* forgive the praise,
>   Fusty Christopher."

Among the pleasing lyrics in this volume are "Lilian," "Recollections of the Arabian Nights," and especially "Mariana."

> "The sparrow's chirrup on the roof,
>   The clock slow ticking, and the sound
> Which to the wooing wind aloof
>   The poplar made, did all confound

> Her sense; but most she loathed the hour
>   When the thick-moted sunbeam lay
>   Athwart the chambers, and the day
> Was sloping toward his western bower.
>   Then said she, " I am very dreary,
>   He will not come," she said;
>   She wept, " I am aweary, aweary,
>   O God, that I were dead ! "

At this period the poet's muse was very active. In 1832 appeared another volume, which exhibited more fully his poetic gifts, and made a notable contribution to English verse. He easily took his place at the head of the younger race of singers. His lyrical power, his mastery of musical rhythm, his charm of felicitous expression, and his exquisite handling of form and color, are everywhere apparent. His breadth of sympathy is shown by his successful treatment of ancient, mediæval, and modern themes. The " May Queen," with its tender pathos, at once touched the popular heart. In " Lady Clara Vere de Vere," the nobility of character is presented in proud contrast with the nobility of birth : —

> " Howe'er it be, it seems to me,
>   'Tis only noble to be good.
> Kind hearts are more than coronets,
>   And simple faith than Norman blood."

In " The Lotus-Eaters," how exquisitely the sound is wedded to the sense : —

> " In the afternoon they came unto a land,
>   In which it always seemèd afternoon.
> All round the coast the languid air did swoon,
>   Breathing like one that hath a weary dream.
> Full-faced above the valley stood the moon;
>   And like a downward smoke, the slender stream
> Along the cliff to fall and pause and fall did seem."

Among the other pieces deserving mention in this volume are " The Lady of Shalott," " Œnone," " The Miller's Daughter," " The Palace of Art," and " A Dream of Fair Women."

For ten years Tennyson published nothing except a few pieces in periodicals. Perhaps he had been discouraged by the want of appreciation on the part of professional critics. But he was by no means driven from his art. This intervening period was devoted to serious study. He enlarged his intellectual range, and perfected himself in artistic expression. He ripened into maturity.

In 1842 appeared a new volume, in which are found many of his choicest pieces. He was no longer simply a master of lyrical harmony; he had become also a thinker and teacher. Here appears his first work in connection with the legend of Arthur and the Round Table. Milton and Dryden had both thought of the Arthurian cycle as the subject of an epic poem. It was reserved for Tennyson to realize the idea; and so well has he done his work, that we may congratulate ourselves that the older poets left the field unoccupied. Listen to the forceful beginning of the " Morte d'Arthur : " —

> " So all day long the noise of battle rolled
> Among the mountains by the winter sea."

Where can we find a more graphic touch than the description of the flinging of Arthur's sword ? —

> " *The great brand*
> *Made lightnings in the splendor of the moon,*
> And flashing round and round, and whirl'd in an arch,
> Shot like a streamer of the northern morn,
> Seen where the moving isles of winter shock
> By night, with noises of the northern sea."

Here is a picture from "The Gardener's Daughter : " —

> " For up the porch there grew an Eastern rose,
> That flowering high, the last night's gale had caught,
> And blown across the walk. One arm aloft —
> Gown'd in pure white that fitted to the shape —
> Holding the bush, to fix it back, she stood.
> A single stream of all her soft, brown hair
> Pour'd on one side : the shadow of the flowers

Stole all the golden gloss, and, wavering
Lovingly lower, trembled on her waist —
Ah, happy shade — and still went wavering down,
But, ere it touched a foot that might have danced
The greensward into greener circles, dipt,
And mixed with shadows of the common ground!
But the full day dwelt on her brows, and sunn'd
Her violet eyes, and all her Hebe bloom,
And doubled his warmth against her lips,
And on the bounteous wave of such a breast
As never pencil drew.   Half light, half shade,
She stood, a sight to make an old man young.''

"Dora" has the charm of a Hebrew idyl — a poem that can hardly be read without tears.   "Locksley Hall," a story of disappointed love, is known to all, and many of its lines have passed into daily use : —

"In the spring a livelier iris changes on the burnish'd dove;
In the spring a young man's fancy lightly turns to thoughts of love.

. . . .

Yet I doubt not through the ages one increasing purpose runs,
And the thoughts of men are widened with the process of the suns.''

"Godiva" is a story of heroic self-sacrifice with many an exquisite passage.   As the heroine returned to the palace, —

" All at once,
With twelve great shocks of sound, the shameless noon
Was clash'd and hammer'd from a hundred towers.''

Almost every poem deserves particular mention.   "Edward Gray" and "Lady Clare" are delightful ballads in the old style.   "Ulysses" is a strong treatment of a classic theme.   In "The Two Voices," "St. Simeon Stylites," and "The Vision of Sin," the poet enters the domain of theology.   The little song called "Farewell" gives expression to a feeling of sadness that has arisen in every sensitive bosom.

" Flow down, cold rivulet, to the sea,
Thy tribute wave deliver;
No more by thee my steps shall be,
Forever and forever.''

The burdening sense of loss on the death of a loved one never had stronger expression than in the little poem beginning, " Break, break, break : " —

> " And the stately ships go on
> To their haven under the hill ;
> But oh, for the touch of a vanish'd hand,
> And the sound of a voice that is still."

In 1847 appeared " The Princess." The author called it " A Medley ; " and such it is, composed of mediæval and modern elements. Half jest, and half earnest, it yet reaches a serious solution of the vexed problem of woman's education : —

> " For woman is not undeveloped man,
> But diverse ; could we make her as the man,
> Sweet love were slain : his dearest bond is this,
> Not like to like, but like in difference.
> Yet in the long years must they liker grow ;
> The man be more of woman, she of man ;
> He gain in sweetness and in moral height,
> Nor lose the wrestling thews that throw the world ;
> She mental breadth, nor fail in childward care,
> Nor lose the childlike in the larger mind ;
> Till at the last she set herself to man,
> Like perfect music unto noble words."

The romantic story is delightfully told ; and the songs interspersed among the several parts are, perhaps, the finest in our language. Where can we match the " Bugle Song ? "

> " The splendor falls on castle walls
> And snowy summits old in story :
> The long light shakes across the lakes,
> And the wild cataract leaps in glory.
> Blow, bugle, blow, set the wild echoes flying,
> Blow, bugle ; answer, echoes, dying, dying, dying."

In 1850 appeared " In Memoriam," the best elegiac poem ever written, and one that will perhaps never have a rival. It is written in memory of Arthur Hallam, a bosom friend of

Tennyson's, and a young man of rich gifts of mind and heart. A bright career seemed open to him ; but while travelling in Germany for his health, he suddenly died at Vienna, in 1833. The poet's heart was wrung with grief ; and under the weight of bereavement, he set himself resolutely to a consideration of the great mysteries of life, death, God, providence, eternal life. He does not deal with these subjects like a theologian or philosopher ; but rising above the plane of the understanding, he finds his answers in the cravings of the heart and the intuitions of the spirit.

No other poem is so filled with the thought and feeling peculiar to our age. It rejects the seductive materialism of recent scientific thought ; it is larger and less dogmatic than our creeds. With reverent heart the poet finds comfort at last in the "strong Son of God : " —

> " Thou wilt not leave us in the dust:
>   Thou madest man, he knows not why;
>   He thinks he was not made to die;
> And thou hast made him: thou art just.
>
> Thou seemest human and divine,
>   The highest, holiest manhood, thou:
>   Our wills are ours, we know not how;
> Our wills are ours, to make them thine.
>
> Our little systems have their day;
>   They have their day and cease to be:
>   They are but broken lights of thee,
> And thou, O Lord, art more than they.
>
> We have but faith: we cannot know;
>   For knowledge is of things we see;
>   And yet we trust it comes from thee,
> A beam in darkness: let it grow."

But no single quotation is sufficient to illustrate the depth and richness and beauty of this wonderful production.

The year in which " In Memoriam " appeared, Tennyson succeeded Wordsworth as poet laureate. The greater part of his busy life he spent in retirement on the Isle of Wight, and more recently at Petersfield in Hampshire. He was greatly beloved by the circle of friends he admitted into his intimacy; but the greater portion of his time was spent among his books and flowers. In 1855 appeared "Maud, and Other Poems." The principal poem in this volume has much divided critical opinion, but it is safe to say that it falls below his usual high achievement. The meaning of the poem, as explained by the poet himself, is the reclaiming power of love: "It is the story of a man who has a morbid nature, with a touch of inherited insanity, and very selfish. The poem is to show what love does for him. The war is only an episode. You must remember that it is not I myself speaking. It is this man with the strain of madness in his blood, and the memory of a great trouble and wrong that has put him out with the world." [1]

"The Brook" is a charming idyl, containing a delicious, rippling inter-lyric:

> "I come from haunts of coot and hern,
>   I make a sudden sally,
> And sparkle out among the fern,
>   To bicker down a valley."

Whatever doubts touching the poet's genius may have been started by "Maud," they were forever cleared away in 1859 by the appearance of the "Idyls of the King." These poems were received with enthusiasm. Consisting at first of only four — Enid, Vivien, Elaine, and Guinevere — the poet afterwards wrought in the same field, until his ten idyls constitute a great epic poem. "Nave and transept, aisle after aisle," to use the language of Stedman, "the Gothic minster has extended, until, with the addition of a cloister here and a chapel yonder, the structure stands complete." These "Idyls" embody the highest poetic achievement of Tennyson's genius, and belong to the mountain summits of song. Brave knights, lovely women, mediæval splendor, undying devotion, and heart-breaking tragedies, are all portrayed with the richest poetic art

[1] Century Magazine, February, 1893.

and feeling. Unlike the "Iliad" or "Paradise Lost," which appeal to us largely through their grandeur, the "Idyls of the King" possess a deep human interest. They arouse our sympathies. We weep for Elaine, "the lily maid of Astolat," the victim of a hopeless love for Lancelot. How worthy of his praise!

> " Fair she was, my King,
> Pure, as you ever wish your knights to be.
> To doubt her fairness were to want an eye,
> To doubt her pureness were to want a heart —
> Yea, to be loved, if what is worthy love
> Could bind him, but free love will not be bound."

The agonies of Arthur and Guinevere at Almesbury go to the heart : —

> " Lo! I forgive thee, as Eternal God
> Forgives; do thou for thine own soul the rest.
> But how to take last leave of all I loved?
> O golden hair, with which I used to play,
> Not knowing! O imperial-moulded form,
> And beauty such as never woman wore,
> Until it came a kingdom's curse with thee.
> I can not touch thy lips, they are not mine,
> But Lancelot's: nay, they never were the King's.
>
> . . . .
>
> My love thro' flesh hath wrought into my life
> So far, that my doom is, I love thee still.
> Let no man dream but that I love thee still.
> Perchance, and so thou purify thy soul,
> And so thou lean on our fair father Christ,
> Hereafter in that world where all are pure,
> We two may meet before high God, and thou
> Wilt spring to me, and claim me thine, and know
> I am thine husband — not a smaller soul,
> Nor Lancelot, nor another. Leave me that,
> I charge thee, my last hope."

How beautiful the words of Arthur, as he seeks in his last moments to comfort the lonely and grief-stricken Sir Bedivere : —

> "The old order changeth, yielding place to new,
> And God fulfils himself in many ways,
> Lest one good custom should corrupt the world.
> Comfort thyself: what comfort is in me?
> I have lived my life, and that which I have done
> May he within himself make pure! but thou,
> If thou shouldst never see my face again,
> Pray for my soul.   More things are wrought by prayer
> Than this world dreams of.   .   .   .
>   I am going a long way
> With these thou seest — if indeed I go
> (For all my mind is clouded with a doubt) —
> To the island valley of Avilion;
> Where falls not hail, or rain, or any snow,
> Nor ever wind blows loudly; but it lies
> Deep-meadow'd, happy, fair with orchard lawns
> And bowery hollows crown'd with summer sea."

In 1864 appeared "Enoch Arden," a work of great beauty. It depicts with deep pathos the heroism to be found in humble life. Beauty, pathos, heroism — these are qualities that give it high rank, and have made it perhaps the most popular of all Tennyson's writings.   Human nature is portrayed at its best; and like all our author's poetry, "Enoch Arden" unconsciously begets faith in man, and makes us hopeful of the future of our race.

Of Tennyson's other works we cannot speak.   It is enough to say that they add nothing to his fame.

The quiet beauty of his death formed a fitting close to his long and uneventful career.   On the evening of the 6th of October, 1892, the soul of the great poet passed away.   The prayer he had breathed two years before in the little poem "Crossing the Bar," was answered:

> " Sunset and evening star,
>   And one clear call for me!
> And may there be no moaning of the bar
>   When I put out to sea.
>
> But such a tide as moving seems asleep,
>   Too full for sound and foam,
> When that which drew from out the boundless deep
>   Turns again home.

Twilight and evening bell,
  And after that the dark!
And may there be no sadness of farewell
  When I embark.

For tho' from out our bourn of Time and Place
  The flood may bear me far,
I hope to see my Pilot face to face
  When I have crossed the bar."

He was entombed by the side of Chaucer in Westminster Abbey, while two continents were lamenting his death.

Whatever changes of taste or fashion may hereafter come in poetry, surely we are justified in believing that Tennyson will continue to hold a high rank. There is nothing in his character to detract from his reputation as a poet. Though we know comparatively little of his life, we clearly read his character in his works. He commands our confidence and reverent regard. Without exhibiting heroic traits, for which there was no special occasion, he appears to us as a man of exquisite and healthful culture. While tenderly sensitive to all that is beautiful in nature and humanity, he possessed profound ethical feeling and spiritual insight. Keenly sympathetic with the eager and restless search after truth characteristic of our time, he avoided its dangers, and continued a strong and trustworthy teacher, inspiring confidence in man, hope in the future, and faith in God.

ELAINE.

ELAINE the fair, Elaine the lovable,
Elaine, the lily maid of Astolat,
High in her chamber up a tower to the east
Guarded the sacred shield of Lancelot;
Which first she placed where morning's earliest ray
Might strike it, and awake her with the gleam;
Then, fearing rust or soilure, fashion'd for it
A case of silk, and braided thereupon
All the devices blazon'd on the shield
In their own tint, and added, of her wit,   10
A border fantasy of branch and flower,
And yellow-throated nestling in the nest.
Nor rested thus content, but day by day,
Leaving her household and good father, climb'd
That eastern tower, and, entering, barr'd her door,
Stript off the case, and read the naked shield,
Now guess'd a hidden meaning in his arms,
Now made a pretty history to herself
Of every dint a sword had beaten in it,
And every scratch a lance had made upon it,   20
Conjecturing when and where: this cut is fresh;
That ten years back; this dealt him at Cærlyle;
That at Cærleon; this at Camelot:
And ah, God's mercy, what a stroke was there!
And here a thrust that might have kill'd, but God
Broke the strong lance, and roll'd his enemy down,
And saved him: so she lived in fantasy.

How came the lily maid by that good shield
Of Lancelot, she that knew not ev'n his name?
He left it with her when he rode to tilt   30
For the great diamond in the diamond jousts
Which Arthur had ordain'd, and by that name
Had named them, since a diamond was the prize.

For Arthur, long before they crown'd him king,
Roving the trackless realms of Lyonnesse,

Had found a glen, gray boulder, and black tarn.
A horror lived about the tarn, and clave
Like its own mists to all the mountain side:
For here two brothers, one a king, had met,
And fought together; but their names were lost.   40
And each had slain his brother at a blow,
And down they fell and made the glen abhorr'd:
And there they lay till all their bones were bleach'd,
And lichen'd into color with the crags:
And he that once was king had on a crown
Of diamonds, one in front, and four aside.
And Arthur came, and laboring up the pass
All in a misty moonshine, unawares
Had trodden that crown'd skeleton, and the skull
Brake from the nape, and from the skull the crown   50
Roll'd into light, and, turning on its rims,
Fled like a glittering rivulet to the tarn:
And down the shingly scaur he plunged, and caught,
And set it on his head, and in his heart
Heard murmurs, " Lo, thou likewise shalt be king."

Thereafter, when a king, he had the gems
Pluck'd from the crown, and show'd them to his knights,
Saying, " These jewels, whereupon I chanced
Divinely, are the kingdom's, not the king's —
For public use: henceforward let there be,   60
Once every year, a joust for one of these:
For so by nine years' proof we needs must learn
Which is our mightiest, and ourselves shall grow
In use of arms and manhood, till we drive
The heathen, who, some say, shall rule the land
Hereafter, which God hinder."   Thus he spoke:
And eight years past, eight jousts had been, and still
Had Lancelot won the diamond of the year,
With purpose to present them to the Queen
When all were won; but, meaning all at once   70
To snare her royal fancy with a boon
Worth half her realm, had never spoken word.

Now for the central diamond and the last
And largest, Arthur, holding then his court

Hard on the river nigh the place which now
Is this world's hugest, let proclaim a joust
At Camelot, and when the time drew nigh
Spake (for she had been sick) to Guinevere,
" Are you so sick, my Queen, you cannot move
To these fair jousts? " " Yea, lord," she said, " ye know it."   80
" Then will ye miss," he answer'd, " the great deeds
Of Lancelot, and his prowess in the lists,
A sight ye love to look on."   And the Queen
Lifted her eyes, and they dwelt languidly
On Lancelot, where he stood beside the King.
He, thinking that he read her meaning there,
" Stay with me, I am sick; my love is more
Than many diamonds," yielded; and a heart,
Love-loyal to the least wish of the Queen
(However much he yearn'd to make complete   90
The tale of diamonds for his destined boon),
Urged him to speak against the truth, and say,
" Sir King, mine ancient wound is hardly whole,
And lets me from the saddle;" and the King
Glanced first at him, then her, and went his way.
No sooner gone than suddenly she began:

       " To blame, my lord Sir Lancelot, much to blame!
Why go ye not to these fair jousts? the knights
Are half of them our enemies, and the crowd
Will murmur, ' Lo, the shameless ones, who take   100
Their pastime now the trustful king is gone!'"
Then Lancelot, vexed at having lied in vain:
" Are ye so wise? ye were not once so wise,
My Queen, that summer, when ye loved me first.
Then of the crowd ye took no more account
Than of the myriad cricket of the mead,
When its own voice clings to each blade of grass,
And every voice is nothing.   As to knights,
Them surely can I silence with all ease.
But now my loyal worship is allow'd   110
Of all men: many a bard, without offence,
Has link'd our names together in his lay,
Lancelot, the flower of bravery, Guinevere,

The pearl of beauty: and our knights at feast
Have pledged us in this union, while the king
Would listen smiling.   How then? is there more?
Has Arthur spoken aught? or would yourself,
Now weary of my service and devoir,
Henceforth be truer to your faultless lord?"

She broke into a little scornful laugh.   120
"Arthur, my lord, Arthur, the faultless King,
That passionate perfection, my good lord—
But who can gaze upon the sun in heaven?
He never spake word of reproach to me,
He never had a glimpse of mine untruth,
He cares not for me: only here to-day
There gleam'd a vague suspicion in his eyes:
Some meddling rogue has tamper'd with him—else
Rapt in this fancy of his Table Round,
And swearing men to vows impossible,   130
To make them like himself: but, friend, to me
He is all fault who hath no fault at all:
For who loves me must have a touch of earth;
The low sun makes the color: I am yours,
Not Arthur's, as ye know, save by the bond.
And therefore hear my words: go to the jousts:
The tiny-trumpeting gnat can break our dream
When sweetest; and the vermin voices here
May buzz so loud—we scorn them, but they sting."

Then answer'd Lancelot, the chief of knights: 140
"And with what face, after my pretext made,
Shall I appear, O Queen, at Camelot, I
Before a King who honors his own word,
As if it were his God's?"

                        "Yea," said the Queen,
"A moral child without the craft to rule,
Else had he not lost me: but listen to me,
If I must find you wit: we hear it said
That men go down before your spear at a touch
But knowing you are Lancelot; your great name,
This conquers: hide it, therefore; go unknown: 150

Win! by this kiss you will: and our true King
Will then allow your pretext, O my knight,
As all for glory; for, to speak him true,
Ye know right well, how meek soe'er he seem,
No keener hunter after glory breathes.
He loves it in his knights more than himself:
They prove to him his work: win and return."

Then got Sir Lancelot suddenly to horse,
Wroth at himself: not willing to be known,
He left the barren-beaten thoroughfare,   160
Chose the green path that show'd the rarer foot,
And there among the solitary downs,
Full often lost in fancy, lost his way;
Till, as he traced a faintly-shadow'd track,
That all in loops and links among the dales
Ran to the Castle of Astolat, he saw
Fired from the west, far on a hill, the towers.
Thither he made, and wound the gateway horn.
Then came an old, dumb, myriad-wrinkled man,
Who let him into lodging, and disarm'd.   170
And Lancelot marvell'd at the wordless man;
And, issuing, found the Lord of Astolat
With two strong sons, Sir Torre and Sir Lavaine,
Moving to meet him in the castle court;
And close behind them stept the lily maid,
Elaine, his daughter: mother of the house
There was not: some light jest among them rose
With laughter dying down as the great knight
Approach'd them: then the lord of Astolat:
"Whence comest thou, my guest, and by what name   180
Livest between the lips? for, by thy state
And presence, I might guess thee chief of those,
After the King, who eat in Arthur's halls.
Him have I seen: the rest, his Table Round,
Known as they are, to me they are unknown."

Then answered Lancelot, the chief of knights:
"Known am I, and of Arthur's hall, and known
What I by mere mischance have brought, my shield.
But, since I go to joust, as one unknown,

At Camelot for the diamond, ask me not.   190
Hereafter you shall know me — and the shield —
I pray you lend me one, if such you have,
Blank, or at least with some device not mine."

    Then said the Lord of Astolat, " Here is Torre's :
Hurt in his first tilt was my son, Sir Torre,
And so, God wot, his shield is blank enough.
His ye can have."   Then added plain Sir Torre,
" Yea, since I cannot use it, ye may have it."
Here laugh'd the father saying, " Fie, Sir Churl,
Is that an answer for a noble knight?   200
Allow him : but Lavaine, my younger here,
He is so full of lustihood, he will ride,
Joust for it, and win, and bring it in an hour,
And set it in this damsel's golden hair,
To make her thrice as wilful as before."

    " Nay, father, nay, good father, shame me not
Before this noble knight," said young Lavaine,
" For nothing.   Surely I but play'd on Torre :
He seem'd so sullen, vext he could not go :
A jest, no more : for, knight, the maiden dreamt   210
That some one put this diamond in her hand,
And that it was too slippery to be held,
And slipt, and fell into some pool or stream,
The castle-well, belike ; and then I said
That *if* I went, and *if* I fought and won it
(But all was jest and joke among ourselves),
Then must she keep it safelier.   All was jest.
But, father, give me leave, an if he will,
To ride to Camelot with this noble knight :
Win shall I not, but do my best to win :   220
Young as I am, yet would I do my best."

    " So ye will grace me," answer'd Lancelot,
Smiling a moment, " with a fellowship
O'er these waste downs whereon I lost myself,
Then were I glad of you as guide and friend ;
And you shall win this diamond — as I hear,
It is a fair large diamond — if ye may ;

And yield it to this maiden, if ye will."
" A fair, large diamond," added plain Sir Torre,
" Such be for queens and not for simple maids." 230
Then she, who held her eyes upon the ground,
Elaine, and heard her name so tost about,
Flush'd slightly at the slight disparagement
Before the stranger knight, who, looking at her
Full courtly, yet not falsely, thus return'd :
" If what is fair be but for what is fair,
And only queens are to be counted so,
Rash were my judgment, then, who deem this maid
Might wear as fair a jewel as is on earth,
Not violating the bond of like to like." 240

He spoke and ceased : the lily maid Elaine,
Won by the mellow voice before she look'd,
Lifted her eyes, and read his lineaments.
The great and guilty love he bare the Queen,
In battle with the love he bare his lord,
Had marr'd his face, and mark'd it ere his time.
Another sinning on such heights with one,
The flower of all the west and all the world,
Had been the sleeker for it : but in him
His mood was often like a fiend, and rose 250
And drove him into wastes and solitudes
For agony, who was yet a living soul.
Marr'd as he was, he seem'd the goodliest man
That ever among ladies ate in hall,
And noblest, when she lifted up her eyes.
However marr'd, of more than twice her years,
Seam'd with an ancient swordcut on the cheek,
And bruised and bronzed, she lifted up her eyes
And loved him, with that love which was her doom.

Then the great knight, the darling of the court, 260
Loved of the loveliest, into that rude hall
Stept with all grace, and not with half-disdain
Hid under grace, as in a smaller time,
But kindly man moving among his kind :
Whom they with meats and vintage of their best,
And talk and minstrel melody entertain'd.

And much they ask'd of court and Table Round,
And ever well and readily answer'd he:
But Lancelot, when they glanced at Guinevere,
Suddenly speaking of the wordless man   270
Heard from the baron that, ten years before,
The heathen caught, and reft him of his tongue.
" He learnt and warn'd me of their fierce design
Against my house, and him they caught and maim'd;
But I, my sons, and little daughter fled
From bonds or death, and dwelt among the woods
By the great river in a boatman's hut.
Dull days were those, till our good Arthur broke
The Pagan yet once more on Badon hill."

    " Oh, there, great Lord, doubtless," Lavaine said, rapt   280
By all the sweet and sudden passion of youth
Toward greatness in its elder, " you have fought.
Oh, tell us — for we live apart — you know
Of Arthur's glorious wars."   And Lancelot spoke
And answer'd him at full, as having been
With Arthur in the fight which all day long
Rang by the white mouth of the violent Glem;
And in the four wild battles by the shore
Of Duglas; that on Bassa; then the war
That thunder'd in and out the gloomy skirts   290
Of Celidon the forest; and again
By castle Gurnion, where the glorious King
Had on his cuirass worn our Lady's Head,
Carved on one emerald, centr'd in a sun
Of silver rays, that lighten'd as he breathed;
And at Cærleon had he help'd his lord,
When the strong neighings of the wild White Horse
Set every gilded parapet shuddering;
And up in Agned-Cathregonion too,
And down the waste sand-shores of Trath Treroit,   300
Where many a heathen fell; " And on the mount
Of Badon I myself beheld the King
Charge at the head of all his Table Round,
And all his legions crying Christ and him,
And break them; and I saw him, after, stand

High on a heap of slain, from spur to plume
Red as the rising sun with heathen blood.
And, seeing me, with a great voice he cried,
' They are broken, they are broken,' for the King,
However mild he seems at home, nor cares   310
For triumph in our mimic wars, the jousts —
For, if his own knight cast him down, he laughs,
Saying his knights are better men than he —
Yet in this heathen war the fire of God
Fills him : I never saw his like : there lives
No greater leader."

     While he utter'd this,
Low to her own heart said the lily maid,
" Save your great self, fair lord ; " and, when he fell
From talk of war to traits of pleasantry, —
Being mirthful he but in a stately kind, —   320
She still took note that when the living smile
Died from his lips, across him came a cloud
Of melancholy severe, from which again,
Whenever, in her hovering to and fro,
The lily maid had striven to make him cheer,
There brake a sudden-beaming tenderness
Of manners and of nature : and she thought
That all was nature, all, perchance, for her.
And all that night long his face before her lived.
As when a painter, poring on a face,   330
Divinely thro' all hindrance finds the man
Behind it, and so paints him that his face,
The shape and color of a mind and life,
Lives for his children, ever at its best
And fullest ; so the face before her lived,
Dark-splendid, speaking in the silence, full
Of noble things, and held her from her sleep.
Till rathe she rose, half-cheated in the thought
She needs must bid farewell to sweet Lavaine.
First as in fear, step after step, she stole   340
Down the long tower-stairs, hesitating :
Anon, she heard Sir Lancelot cry in the court,
" This shield, my friend, where is it ? " and Lavaine

Past inward, as she came from out the tower.
There to his proud horse Lancelot turn'd, and smooth'd
The glossy shoulder, humming to himself.
Half-envious of the flattering hand, she drew
Nearer and stood.   He look'd, and more amazed
Than if seven men had set upon him, saw
The maiden standing in the dewy light.   350
He had not dreamed she was so beautiful.
Then came on him a sort of sacred fear,
For silent, tho' he greeted her, she stood
Rapt on his face as if it were a God's.
Suddenly flashed on her a wild desire
That he should wear her favor at the tilt.
She braved a riotous heart in asking for it.
"Fair lord, whose name I know not — noble it is,
I well believe, the noblest — will you wear
My favor at this tourney?"   "Nay," said he,   360
"Fair lady, since I never yet have worn
Favor of any lady in the lists.
Such is my wont, as those who know me know."
"Yea, so," she answer'd; "then in wearing mine
Needs must be lesser likelihood, noble lord,
That those who know should know you."   And he turn'd
Her counsel up and down within his mind,
And found it true, and answer'd, "True, my child.
Well, I will wear it: fetch it out to me:
What is it?" and she told him, "A red sleeve   370
Broider'd with pearls," and brought it: then he bound
Her token on his helmet, with a smile
Saying, "I never yet have done so much
For any maiden living," and the blood
Sprang to her face and fill'd her with delight;
But left her all the paler, when Lavaine,
Returning, brought the yet-unblazon'd shield,
His brother's; which he gave to Lancelot,
Who parted with his own to fair Elaine;
"Do me this grace, my child, to have my shield   380
In keeping till I come."   "A grace to me,"
She answer'd, "twice to-day.   I am your Squire."
Whereat Lavaine said, laughing, "Lily maid,

For fear our people call you lily maid
In earnest, let me bring your color back ;
Once, twice, and thrice : now get you hence to bed : "
So kiss'd her, and Sir Lancelot his hand,
And thus they moved away ; she stay'd a minute,
Then made a sudden step to the gate, and there —
Her bright hair blown about the serious face   390
Yet rosy-kindled with her brother's kiss —
Paused in the gateway, standing by the shield
In silence, while she watch'd their arms far-off
Sparkle, until they dipt below the downs.
Then to her tower she climb'd, and took the shield
There kept it, and so lived in fantasy.

Meanwhile the two companions past away
Far o'er the long backs of the bushless downs,
To where Sir Lancelot knew there lived a knight
Not far from Camelot, now for forty years   400
A hermit, who had pray'd, labor'd, and pray'd,
And, ever laboring, had scoop'd himself,
In the white rock, a chapel and a hall
On massive columns, like a shorecliff cave,
And cells and chambers : all were fair and dry ;
The green light from the meadows underneath
Struck up and lived along the milky roofs ;
And in the meadows tremulous aspen-trees
And poplars made a noise of falling showers.
And, thither wending, there that night they bode.   410

But when the next day broke from underground,
And shot red fire and shadows thro' the cave,
They rose, heard mass, broke fast, and rode away :
Then Lancelot, saying, " Hear, but hold my name
Hidden, you ride with Lancelot of the Lake."
Abash'd Lavaine, whose instant reverence,
Dearer to true young hearts than their own praise,
But left him leave to stammer, " Is it indeed ? "
And after muttering, " The great Lancelot,"
At last he got his breath and answer'd, " One,   420
One have I seen — that other, our liege lord,
The dread Pendragon, Britain's King of kings,

Of whom the people talk mysteriously,
He will be there — then, were I stricken blind
That minute, I might say that I had seen."

So spake Lavaine, and, when they reach'd the lists
By Camelot in the meadow, let his eyes
Run thro' the peopled gallery, which half round
Lay like a rainbow fall'n upon the grass,
Until they found the clear-faced King, who sat   430
Robed in red samite, easily to be known,
Since to his crown the golden dragon clung.
And down his robe the dragon writhed in gold,
And from the carven-work behind him crept
Two dragons gilded, sloping down to make
Arms for his chair, while all the rest of them
Thro' knots and loops and folds innumerable
Fled ever thro' the woodwork, till they found
The new design wherein they lost themselves,
Yet with all ease, so tender was the work: 440
And, in the costly canopy o'er him set,
Blazed the last diamond of the nameless king.
Then Lancelot answer'd young Lavaine and said,
"Me you call great: mine is the firmer seat,
The truer lance: but there is many a youth,
Now crescent, who will come to all I am
And overcome it; and in me there dwells
No greatness, save it be some far-off touch
Of greatness to know well I am not great:
There is the man."   And Lavaine gaped upon him   450
As on a thing miraculous, and anon
The trumpets blew; and then did either side,
They that assail'd, and they that held the lists,
Set lance in rest, strike spur, suddenly move,
Meet in the midst, and there so furiously
Shock, that a man far-off might well perceive,
If any man that day were left afield,
The hard earth shake, and a low thunder of arms.
And Lancelot bode a little, till he saw
Which were the weaker; then he hurl'd into it   460
Against the stronger: little need to speak

Of Lancelot in his glory!   King, duke, earl,
Count, baron — whom he smote he overthrew.

But in the field were Lancelot's kith and kin,
Ranged with the Table Round that held the lists,
Strong men, and wrathful that a stranger knight
Should do and almost overdo the deeds
Of Lancelot; and one said to the other, " Lo !
What is he?   I do not mean the force alone —
The grace and versatility of the man.   470
Is it not Lancelot?"   " When has Lancelot worn
Favor of any lady in the lists ?
Not such his wont, as we, who know him, know."
" How then? who then? " a fury seized them all,
A fiery family passion for the name
Of Lancelot, and a glory one with theirs.
They couch'd their spears and prick'd their steeds and
        thus,
Their plumes driv'n backward by the wind they made
In moving, all together down upon him
Bare, as a wild wave in the wide North-sea,   480
Green-glimmering toward the summit, bears, with all
Its stormy crests that smoke against the skies,
Down on a bark, and overbears the bark,
And him that helms it, so they overbore
Sir Lancelot and his charger, and a spear,
Down-glancing, lamed the charger, and a spear,
Prick'd sharply his own cuirass, and the head
Pierced thro' his side and there snapt and remain'd.

Then Sir Lavaine did well and worshipfully ;
He bore a knight of old repute to the earth,   490
And brought his horse to Lancelot where he lay.
He up the side, sweating with agony, got,
But thought to do while he might yet endure,
And, being lustily holpen by the rest,
His party, — tho' it seemed half-miracle
To those he fought with — drave his kith and kin,
And all the Table Round that held the lists,
Back to the barrier; then the trumpets blew
Proclaiming his the prize who wore the sleeve

Of scarlet, and the pearls ; and all the knights,   500
His party, cried, " Advance, and take thy prize,
The diamond ; " but he answer'd, " Diamond me
No diamonds ! for God's love, a little air !
Prize me no prizes, for my prize is death !
Hence will I, and, I charge you, follow me not."

He spoke, and vanish'd suddenly from the field
With young Lavaine into the poplar grove.
There from his charger down he slid, and sat
Gasping to Sir Lavaine, " Draw the lance-head : "
" Ah, my sweet lord Sir Lancelot," said Lavaine,   510
" I dread me, if I draw it, ye shall die."
But he, " I die already with it : draw —
Draw," — and Lavaine drew, and that other gave
A marvellous great shriek and ghastly groan,
And half his blood burst forth, and down he sank
For the pure pain, and wholly swoon'd away.
Then came the hermit out and bare him in,
There stanch'd his wound ; and there, in daily doubt
Whether to live or die, for many a week,
Hid from the wide world's rumor by the grove   520
Of poplars, with their noise of falling showers,
And ever-tremulous aspen-trees, he lay.

But on that day when Lancelot fled the lists,
His party, knights of utmost North and West,
Lords of waste marches, kings of desolate isles,
Came round their great Pendragon, saying to him,
" Lo, Sire, our knight thro' whom we won the day
Hath gone sore wounded, and hath left his prize
Untaken, crying that his prize is death."
" Heaven hinder," said the King, " that such an one,   530
So great a knight as we have seen to-day —
He seemed to me another Lancelot,
Yea, twenty times I thought him Lancelot —
He must not pass uncared for.   Wherefore, rise,
O Gawain, and ride forth and find the knight.
Wounded and wearied, needs must he be near.
I charge you that you get at once to horse.
And, knights and kings, there breathes not one of you

Will deem this prize of ours is rashly given:
His prowess was too wondrous.   We will do him   540
No customary honor: since the knight
Came not to us, of us to claim the prize,
Ourselves will send it after.   Rise and take
This diamond and deliver it and return
And bring us where he is and how he fares,
And cease not from your quest until you find."

So saying, from the carven flower above,
To which it made a restless heart, he took,
And gave, the diamond: then, from where he sat,
At Arthur's right, with smiling face arose,   550
With smiling face and frowning heart, a Prince
In the mid might and flourish of his May,
Gawain, surnamed The Courteous, fair and strong,
And after Lancelot, Tristram, and Geraint,
And Gareth, a good knight, but therewithal
Sir Modred's brother, of a crafty house,
Nor often loyal to his word, and now
Wroth that the king's command to sally forth
In quest of whom he knew not made him leave
The banquet, and concourse of knights and kings.   560

So all in wrath he got to horse and went;
While Arthur to the banquet, dark in mood,
Past, thinking, " Is it Lancelot who has come,
Despite the wound he spake of, all for gain
Of glory, and has added wound to wound,
And ridd'n away to die?"   So fear'd the King,
And, after two days' tarriance there, return'd.
Then, when he saw the Queen, embracing, ask'd,
" Love, are you yet so sick?"   " Nay, lord," she said.
" And where is Lancelot?"   Then the Queen, amazed,   570
" Was he not with you? won he not your prize?"
" Nay, but one like him."   " Why that like was he."
And when the King demanded how she knew,
Said, " Lord, no sooner had ye parted from us,
Than Lancelot told me of a common talk
That men went down before his spear at a touch
But knowing he was Lancelot; his great name

Conquer'd : and therefore would he hide his name
From all men, ev'n the King, and to this end
Had made the pretext of a hindering wound   580
That he might joust unknown of all, and learn
If his old prowess were in aught decay'd :
And added, ' Our true Arthur, when he learns,
Will well allow my pretext, as for gain of purer glory.' "

            Then replied the King,
" Far lovelier in our Lancelot had it been,
In lieu of idly dallying with the truth,
To have trusted me as he hath trusted you.
Surely his King and most familiar friend
Might well have kept his secret.   True, indeed,   590
Albeit I know my knights fantastical,
So fine a fear in our large Lancelot
Must needs have moved my laughter : now remains
But little cause for laughter : his own kin —
Ill news, my Queen, for all who love him, this ! —
His kith and kin, not knowing, set upon him ;
So that he went sore wounded from the field :
Yet good news too : for goodly hopes are mine
That Lancelot is no more a lonely heart.
He wore, against his wont, upon his helm   600
A sleeve of scarlet, broider'd with great pearls,
Some gentle maiden's gift."

                    " Yea, lord," she said,
" Your hopes are mine," and, saying that, she choked,
And sharply turn'd about to hide her face,
Past to her chamber, and there flung herself
Down on the great King's couch, and writhed upon it,
And clench'd her fingers till they bit the palm,
And shriek'd out " Traitor " to the unhearing wall,
Then flash'd into wild tears, and rose again,
And moved about her palace, proud and pale.   610

    Gawain the while thro' all the region round
Rode with his diamond, wearied of the quest,
Touch'd at all points, except the poplar grove,
And came at last, tho' late, to Astolat.

Whom, glittering in enamel'd arms, the maid
Glanced at, and cried, " What news from Camelot, lord?
What of the knight with the red sleeve?"   " He won."
"I knew it," she said.   " But parted from the jousts
Hurt in the side," whereat she caught her breath ;
Thro' her own side she felt the sharp lance go ;   620
Thereon she smote her hand : well-nigh she swoon'd ;
And, while he gazed wonderingly at her, came
The lord of Astolat out, to whom the Prince
Reported who he was, and on what quest
Sent, that he bore the prize and could not find
The victor, but had ridden wildly round
To seek him, and was wearied of the search.
To whom the lord of Astolat, " Bide with us,
And ride no longer wildly, noble Prince !
Here was the knight, and here he left a shield ;   630
This will he send or come for: furthermore
Our son is with him : we shall hear anon,
Needs must we hear."   To this the courteous Prince
Accorded with his wonted courtesy, —
Courtesy with a touch of traitor in it.
And stay'd ; and cast his eyes on fair Elaine :
Where could be found face daintier? then her shape —
From forehead down to foot, perfect — again
From foot to forehead exquisitely turn'd :
" Well — if I bide, lo ! this wild flower for me !"   640
And oft they met among the garden yews,
And there he set himself to play upon her
With sallying wit, free flashes from a height
Above her, graces of the court, and songs,
Sighs, and slow smiles, and golden eloquence,
And amorous adulation, till the maid
Rebell'd against it, saying to him, " Prince,
O loyal nephew of our noble King,
Why ask you not to see the shield he left,
Whence you might learn his name?   Why slight your King, 650
And lose the quest he sent you on, and prove
No surer than our falcon yesterday,
Who lost the hern we slipt him at, and went
To all the winds?"   " Nay, by mine head," said he,

" I lose it, as we lose the lark in heaven,
O damsel, in the light of your blue eyes:
But, an ye will it, let me see the shield."
And when the shield was brought, and Gawain saw
Sir Lancelot's azure lions, crown'd with gold,
Ramp in the field, he smote his thigh, and mock'd; 660
" Right was the King! our Lancelot! that true man!"
" And right was I," she answer'd merrily, " I,
Who dream'd my knight the greatest knight of all."
" And if *I* dream'd," said Gawain, " that you love
This greatest knight, your pardon! lo, you know it!
Speak therefore: shall I waste myself in vain?"
Full simple was her answer, " What know I?
My brethren have been all my fellowship,
And I, when often they have talk'd of love,
Wish'd it had been my mother, for they talk'd, 670
Meseem'd, of what they knew not; so myself —
I know not if I know what true love is,
But, if I know, then, if I love not him,
Methinks there is none other I can love."
" Yea, by God's death," said he, " ye love him well,
But would not, knew ye what all others know,
And whom he loves." " So be it," cried Elaine,
And lifted her fair face and moved away:
But he pursued her, calling, " Stay a little!
One golden minute's grace: he wore your sleeve: 680
Would he break faith with one I may not name?
Must our true man change like a leaf at last?
Nay — like enough: why then, far be it from me
To cross our mighty Lancelot in his loves!
And, damsel, for I deem you know full well
Where your great knight is hidden, let me leave
My quest with you; the diamond also: here!
For, if you love, it will be sweet to give it;
And, if he loves, it will be sweet to have it
From your own hand; and, whether he love or not, 690
A diamond is a diamond.   Fare you well
A thousand times! — a thousand times farewell!
Yet, if he love, and his love hold, we two
May meet at court hereafter: there, I think,

So you will learn the courtesies of the court,
We two shall know each other."

                         Then he gave,
And slightly kissed the hand to which he gave,
The diamond, and, all wearied of the quest,
Leapt on his horse, and, carolling, as he went,
A true-love ballad, lightly rode away.   700

       Thence to the court he past; there told the King
What the King knew, " Sir Lancelot is the knight."
And added, " Sire, my liege, so much I learnt;
But failed to find him tho' I rode all round
The region : but I lighted on the maid
Whose sleeve he wore; she loves him; and to her,
Deeming our courtesy is the truest law,
I gave the diamond : she will render it;
For, by mine head, she knows his hiding-place."

       The seldom-frowning King frown'd, and replied,   710
" Too courteous truly ! ye shall go no more
On quest of mine, seeing that ye forget
Obedience is the courtesy due to kings."

       He spake and parted.   Wroth, but all in awe,
For twenty strokes of the blood, without a word,
Linger'd that other, staring after him ;
Then shook his hair, strode off, and buzz'd abroad
About the maid of Astolat and her love.
All ears were prick'd at once, all tongues were loosed :
" The maid of Astolat loves Sir Lancelot,   720
Sir Lancelot loves the maid of Astolat."
Some read the King's face, some the Queen's, and all
Had marvel what the maid might be ; but most
Predoom'd her as unworthy.   One old dame
Came suddenly on the Queen with the sharp news.
She, that had heard the noise of it before,
But sorrowing Lancelot should have stoop'd so low,
Marr'd her friend's point with pale tranquillity.
So ran the tale, like fire about the court,
Fire in dry stubble a nine days' wonder flared :   730
Till ev'n the knights at banquet twice or thrice

Forgot to drink to Lancelot and the Queen;
And, pledging Lancelot and the lily maid,
Smiled at each other, while the Queen, who sat
With lips severely placid, felt the knot
Climb in her throat, and with her feet unseen
Crush'd the wild passion out against the floor
Beneath the banquet, where the meats became
As wormwood, and she hated all who pledged.

    But far away the maid in Astolat, 740
Her guiltless rival, she that ever kept
The one-day-seen Sir Lancelot in her heart,
Crept to her father, while he mused alone,
Sat on his knee, stroked his gray face and said,
"Father, you call me wilful, and the fault
Is yours who let me have my will, and now,
Sweet father, will you let me lose my wits?"
"Nay," said he, "surely!" "Wherefore, let me hence,"
She answer'd, "and find out our dear Lavaine."
"Ye will not lose your wits for dear Lavaine; 750
Bide," answer'd he: "we needs must hear anon
Of him and of that other." "Ay," she said,
"And of that other, for I needs must hence
And find that other, wheresoe'er he be,
And with mine own hand give his diamond to him,
Lest I be found as faithless in the quest
As yon proud Prince who left the quest to me.
Sweet father, I behold him in my dreams
Gaunt as it were the skeleton of himself,
Death-pale, for lack of gentle maiden's aid. 760
The gentler-born the maiden, the more bound,
My father, to be sweet and serviceable
To noble knights in sickness, as ye know,
When these have worn their tokens; let me hence
I pray you." Then her father, nodding, said,
"Ay, ay, the diamond: wit you well, my child,
Right fain were I to learn this knight were whole,
Being our greatest; yea, and you must give it —
And sure I think this fruit is hung too high
For any mouth to gape for save a Queen's — 770

Nay, I mean nothing : so then, get you gone,
Being so very wilful you must go."

    Lightly, her suit allow'd, she slipt away ;
And, while she made her ready for her ride,
Her father's latest word humm'd in her ear,
" Being so very wilful you must go,"
And changed itself, and echoed in her heart,
" Being so very wilful you must die."
But she was happy enough, and shook it off
As we shake off the bee that buzzes at us ;   780
And in her heart she answer'd it and said,
" What matter, so I help him back to life ? "
Then far away, with good Sir Torre for guide,
Rode o'er the long backs of the bushless downs
To Camelot, and, before the city-gates,
Came on her brother with a happy face
Making a roan horse caper and curvet
For pleasure all about a field of flowers :
Whom when she saw, " Lavaine," she cried, " Lavaine,
How fares my lord Sir Lancelot ? " He, amazed,   790
" Torre and Elaine ! why here ? Sir Lancelot !
How know ye my lord's name is Lancelot ? "
But when the maid had told him all her tale,
Then turn'd Sir Torre, and, being in his moods,
Left them, and under the strange-statued gate,
Where Arthur's wars were render'd mystically,
Past up the still, rich city to his kin,
His own far blood, which dwelt at Camelot ;
And her, Lavaine across the poplar grove
Led to the caves : there first she saw the casque   800
Of Lancelot on the wall : her scarlet sleeve,
Tho' carved and cut, and half the pearls away,
Stream'd from it still ; and in her heart she laugh'd,
Because he had not loosed it from his helm,
But meant once more, perchance, to tourney in it.
And, when they gain'd the cell in which he slept,
His battle-writhen arms and mighty hands
Lay naked on the wolfskin, and a dream
Of dragging down his enemy made them move.

Then she that saw him lying unsleek, unshorn,   810
Gaunt as it were the skeleton of himself,
Uttered a little, tender, dolorous cry.
The sound, not wonted in a place so still,
Woke the sick knight; and, while he roll'd his eyes
Yet blank from sleep, she started to him, saying,
" Your prize, the diamond sent you by the King : "
His eyes glisten'd : she fancied, " Is it for me?"
And, when the maid had told him all the tale
Of King and Prince, the diamond sent, the quest
Assign'd to her not worthy of it, she knelt   820
Full lowly by the corners of his bed,
And laid the diamond in his open hand.
Her face was near, and, as we kiss the child
That does the task assign'd, he kiss'd her face.
At once she slipt like water to the floor.
" Alas," he said, " your ride has wearied you.
Rest must you have." " No rest for me," she said ;
" Nay, for near you, fair lord, I am at rest."
What might she mean by that? his large, black eyes,
Yet larger thro' his leanness, dwelt upon her,   830
Till all her heart's sad secret blazed itself
In the heart's colors on her simple face ;
And Lancelot look'd, and was perplext in mind,
And, being weak in body, said no more ;
But did not love the color ; woman's love,
Save one, he not regarded, and so turn'd,
Sighing, and feign'd a sleep until he slept.

    Then rose Elaine and glided thro' the fields,
And past beneath the weirdly-sculptured gates
Far up the dim, rich city to her kin ;   840
There bode the night : but woke with dawn, and pas
Down thro' the dim, rich city to the fields,
Thence to the cave : so day by day she past
In either twilight, ghost-like to and fro
Gliding, and every day she tended him,
And likewise many a night : and Lancelot
Would, tho' he call'd his wound a little hurt
Whereof he should be quickly whole, at times

Brain-feverous in his heat and agony, seem
Uncourteous, even he : but the meek maid   850
Sweetly forebore him ever, being to him
Meeker than any child to a rough nurse,
Milder than any mother to a sick child,
And never woman yet, since man's first fall,
Did kindlier unto man, but her deep love
Upbore her ; till the hermit, skill'd in all
The simples and the science of that time,
Told him that her fine care had saved his life.
And the sick man forgot her simple blush,
Would call her friend and sister, sweet Elaine,   860
Would listen for her coming, and regret
Her parting step, and held her tenderly,
And loved her with all love except the love
Of man and woman when they love their best,
Closest, and sweetest, and had died the death
In any knightly fashion for her sake.
And, peradventure, had he seen her first,
She might have made this and that other world
Another world for the sick man ; but now
The shackles of an old love straiten'd him,   870
His honor rooted in dishonor stood,
And faith unfaithful kept him falsely true.

   Yet the great knight in his mid-sickness made
Full many a holy vow and pure resolve.
These, as but born of sickness, could not live :
For, when the blood ran lustier in him again,
Full often the sweet image of one face,
Making a treacherous quiet in his heart,
Dispersed his resolution like a cloud.
Then, if the maiden, while that ghostly grace   880
Beam'd on his fancy, spoke, he answer'd not,
Or short and coldly, and she knew right well
What the rough sickness meant, but what this meant
She knew not, and the sorrow dimm'd her sight,
And drave her ere her time across the fields
Far into the rich city, where alone
She murmur'd, "Vain, in vain : it cannot be,

He will not love me : how then ? must I die ? "
Then as a little, helpless, innocent bird,
That has but one plain passage of few notes,   890
Will sing the simple passage o'er and o'er
For all an April morning, till the ear
Wearies to hear it, so the simple maid
Went half the night, repeating, " Must I die ? "
And now to right she turn'd, and now to left,
And found no ease in turning or in rest ;
And " Him or death " she mutter'd, " Death or him,"
Again and like a burthen, " Him or death."

    But when Sir Lancelot's deadly hurt was whole,
To Astolat returning rode the three.   900
There, morn by morn, arraying her sweet self
In that wherein she deem'd she look'd her best,
She came before Sir Lancelot, for she thought,
" If I be loved, these are my festal robes ;
If not, the victim's flowers before he fall."
And Lancelot ever prest upon the maid
That she should ask some goodly gift of him
For her own self or hers ; " And do not shun
To speak the wish most dear to your true heart ;
Such service have ye done me that I make   910
My will of yours, and Prince and Lord am I
In mine own land, and what I will I can."
Then like a ghost she lifted up her face,
But like a ghost without the power to speak.
And Lancelot saw that she withheld her wish,
And bode among them yet a little space
Till he should learn it ; and one morn it chanced
He found her in among the garden yews,
And said, " Delay no longer, speak your wish,
Seeing I must go to-day : " then out she brake,   920
" Going ? and we shall never see you more.
And I must die for want of one bold word."
" Speak : that I live to hear," he said, " is yours."
Then suddenly and passionately she spoke :
" I have gone mad.   I love you : let me die."
" Ah, sister," answer'd Lancelot, " what is this ? "

And, innocently extending her white arms,
" Your love," she said, " your love — to be your wife."
And Lancelot answer'd, " Had I chos'n to wed,
I had been wedded earlier, sweet Elaine :   930
But now there never will be wife of mine."
" No, no," she cried, " I care not to be wife,
But to be with you still, to see your face,
To serve you, and to follow you thro' the world."
And Lancelot answer'd, " Nay, the world, the world,
All ear and eye, with such a stupid heart
To interpret ear and eye, and such a tongue
To blare its own interpretation — nay,
Full ill then should I quit your brother's love,
And your good father's kindness."   And she said,   940
" Not to be with you, not to see your face —
Alas for me, then, my good days are done."
" Nay, noble maid," he answer'd, " ten times nay !
This is not love : but love's first flash in youth,
Most common : yea I know it of mine own self :
And you yourself will smile at your own self
Hereafter, when you yield your flower of life
To one more fitly yours, not thrice your age :
And then will I, for true you are and sweet
Beyond mine old belief in womanhood,   950
More specially, should your good knight be poor,
Endow you with broad land and territory,
Even to the half my realm beyond the seas,
So that would make you happy ; furthermore,
Ev'n to the death, as tho' ye were my blood,
In all your quarrels will I be your knight.
This will I do, dear damsel, for your sake,
And more than this I cannot."

                While he spoke
She neither blush'd nor shook, but deathly-pale
Stood grasping what was nearest, then replied,   960
" Of all this will I nothing ; " and so fell,
And thus they bore her swooning to her tower.

    Then spake, to whom thro' those black walls of yew
Their talk had pierced, her father.   " Ay, a flash,

I fear me, that will strike my blossom dead.
Too courteous are you, fair Lord Lancelot.
I pray you, use some rough discourtesy
To blunt or break her passion."

                        Lancelot said,
" That were against me : what I can I will ; "
And there that day remain'd, and toward even   970
Sent for his shield : full meekly rose the maid,
Stript off the case, and gave the naked shield ;
Then, when she heard his horse upon the stones,
Unclasping, flung the casement back, and look'd
Down on his helm, from which her sleeve had gone.
And Lancelot knew the little clinking sound ;
And she by tact of love was well aware
That Lancelot knew that she was looking at him.
And yet he glanced not up, nor waved his hand,
Nor bade farewell, but sadly rode away.   980
This was the one discourtesy that he used.

   So in her tower alone the maiden sat :
His very shield was gone ; only the case,
Her own poor work, her empty labor, left.
But still she heard him, still his picture form'd
And grew between her and the pictured wall.
Then came her father, saying in low tones,
" Have comfort," whom she greeted quietly.
Then came her brethren, saying, " Peace to thee,
Sweet sister," whom she answered with all calm.   990
But, when they left her to herself again,
Death, like a friend's voice from a distant field
Approaching thro' the darkness, call'd ; the owls'
Wailing had power upon her, and she mixt
Her fancies with the sallow-rifted glooms
Of evening, and the moanings of the wind.

   And in those days she made a little song,
And call'd her song " The song of Love and Death."
And sang it : sweetly could she make and sing.

    " Sweet is true love tho' given in vain, in vain ;   1000
And sweet is death, who puts an end to pain ;
I know not which is sweeter, no, not I.

" Love, art thou sweet? then bitter death must be:
Love, thou art bitter; sweet is death to me.
O Love, if death be sweeter, let me die.

" Sweet love, that seems not made to fade away,
Sweet death, that seems to make us loveless clay,
I know not which is sweeter, no, not I.

" I fain would follow love, if that could be;
I needs must follow death, who calls for me;   1010
Call and I follow, I follow! let me die."

High with the last line scaled her voice; and this,
All in a fiery dawning wild with wind,
That shook her tower, the brothers heard, and thought
With shuddering, " Hark the Phantom of the house
That ever shrieks before a death," and call'd
The father, and all three in hurry and fear
Ran to her, and lo! the blood-red light of dawn
Flared on her face, she shrilling, " Let me die!"

As when we dwell upon a word we know,   1020
Repeating, till the word we know so well
Becomes a wonder and we know not why,
So dwelt the father on her face and thought,
" Is this Elaine? " till back the maiden fell,
Then gave a languid hand to each, and lay,
Speaking a still good-morrow with her eyes.
At last she said, " Sweet brothers, yester night
I seem'd a curious, little maid again,
As happy as when we dwelt among the woods,
And when ye used to take me with the flood   1030
Up the great river in the boatman's boat.
Only, ye would not pass beyond the cape
That has the poplar on it: there ye fixt
Your limit, oft returning with the tide.
And yet I cried because ye would not pass
Beyond it, and far up the shining flood
Until we found the palace of the king.
And yet ye would not; but this night I dream'd
That I was all alone upon the flood,

And then I said, ' Now shall I have my will : '　　　　1040
And there I woke, but still the wish remain'd.
So let me hence that I may pass at last
Beyond the poplar and far up the flood,
Until I find the palace of the king.
There will I enter in among them all,
And no man there will dare to mock at me ;
But there the fine Gawain will wonder at me,
And there the great Sir Lancelot muse at me ;
Gawain, who bade a thousand farewells to me,
Lancelot, who coldly went nor bade me one :　　　　1050
And there the King will know me and my love,
And there the Queen herself will pity me,
And all the gentle court will welcome me,
And after my long voyage I shall rest ! "

　　" Peace," said her father, " O my child, ye seem
Light-headed, for what force is yours to go
So far, being sick? and wherefore would ye look
On this proud fellow again, who scorns us all?"

　　Then the rough Torre began to heave and move,
And bluster into stormy sobs, and say,　　　　1060
" I never loved him : an I meet with him,
I care not howsoever great he be,
Then will I strike at him and strike him down.
Give me good fortune, I will strike him dead,
For this discomfort he hath done the house."

　　To which the gentle sister made reply,
" Fret not yourself, dear brother, nor be wroth.
Seeing it is no more Sir Lancelot's fault
Not to love me, than it is mine to love
Him of all men who seems to me the highest."　　　　1070
" Highest?" the father answer'd, echoing " highest?"
(He meant to break the passion in her) " nay,
Daughter, I know not what you call the highest ;
But this I know, for all the people know it,
He loves the Queen, and in an open shame :
And she returns his love in open shame.
If this be high, what is it to be low?"

Then spake the lily maid of Astolat,
" Sweet father, all too faint and sick am I
For anger : these are slanders : never yet   1080
Was noble man but made ignoble talk.
He makes no friend who never made a foe.
But now it is my glory to have loved
One peerless, without stain : so let me pass,
My father, howsoe'er I seem to you,
Not all unhappy, having loved God's best
And greatest, tho' my love had no return :
Yet, seeing ye desire your child to live,
Thanks, but ye work against your own desire ;
For, if I could believe the things ye say,   1090
I should but die the sooner ; wherefore cease,
Sweet father, and bid call the ghostly man
Hither, and let me shrive me clean, and die."

So when the ghostly man had come and gone,
She, with a face bright as for sin forgiven,
Besought Lavaine to write, as she devised,
A letter, word for word ; and, when he ask'd,
" Is it for Lancelot, is it for my dear lord?
Then will I bear it gladly ; " she replied,
" For Lancelot and the Queen and all the world,   1100
But I myself must bear it."   Then he wrote
The letter she devised ; which, being writ
And folded, " O sweet father, tender and true,
Deny me not," she said — " ye never yet
Denied my fancies — this, however strange,
My latest : lay the letter in my hand
A little ere I die, and close the hand
Upon it ; I shall guard it even in death.
And when the heat is gone from out my heart,
Then take the little bed on which I died   1110
For Lancelot's love, and deck it like the Queen's
For richness, and me also like the Queen
In all I have of rich, and lay me on it.
And let there be prepared a chariot-bier
To take me to the river, and a barge
Be ready on the river, clothed in black.

I go in state to court to meet the Queen.
There surely I shall speak for mine own self,
And none of you can speak for me so well.
And therefore let our dumb, old man alone   1120
Go with me ; he can steer and row, and he
Will guide me to that palace, to the doors."

She ceased : her father promised ; whereupon
She grew so cheerful that they deem'd her death
Was rather in the fantasy than the blood.
But ten slow mornings past, and on the eleventh
Her father laid the letter in her hand,
And closed her hand upon it, and she died.
So that day there was dole in Astolat.

But when the next sun brake from underground,   1130
Then, those two brethren slowly, with bent brows,
Accompanying the sad chariot-bier,
Past like a shadow through the field, that shone
Full-summer, to that stream whereon the barge,
Pall'd all its length in blackest samite, lay.
There sat the lifelong creature of the house,
Loyal, the dumb old servitor, on deck,
Winking his eyes, and twisted all his face.
So those two brethren from the chariot took
And on the black decks laid her in her bed,   1140
Set in her hand a lily, o'er her hung
The silken case with braided blazonings,
And kiss'd her quiet brows, and saying to her,
" Sister, farewell for ever," and again,
" Farewell, sweet sister," parted all in tears.
Then rose the dumb old servitor, and the dead,
Steer'd by the dumb, went upward with the flood —
In her right hand the lily, in her left
The letter — all her bright hair streaming down —
And all the coverlid was cloth of gold   1150
Drawn to her waist, and she herself in white
All but her face, and that clear-featured face
Was lovely, for she did not seem as dead
But fast asleep, and lay as though she smiled.

That day Sir Lancelot at the palace craved
Audience of Guinevere, to give at last
The price of half a realm, his costly gift,
Hard-won and hardly won with bruise and blow,
With death of others, and almost his own, —
The nine-years-fought-for diamonds : for he saw   1160
One of her house, and sent him to the Queen
Bearing his wish, whereto the Queen agreed
With such and so unmoved a majesty
She might have seem'd her statue, but that he,
Low-drooping till he well-nigh kiss'd her feet
For loyal awe, saw with a sidelong eye
The shadow of a piece of pointed lace,
In the Queen's shadow, vibrate on the walls,
And parted, laughing in his courtly heart. —

All in an oriel on the summer side,   1170
Vine-clad, of Arthur's palace toward the stream,
They met, and Lancelot, kneeling, utter'd, " Queen,
Lady, my liege, in whom I have my joy,
Take, what I had not won except for you,
These jewels, and make me happy, making them
An armlet for the roundest arm on earth,
Or necklace for a neck to which the swan's
Is tawnier than her cygnet's : these are words :
Your beauty is your beauty, and I sin
In speaking, yet O grant my worship of it   1180
Words, as we grant grief tears.   Such sin in words
Perchance we both can pardon : but, my Queen,
I hear of rumors flying through your court.
Our bond, as not the bond of man and wife,
Should have in it an absoluter trust
To make up that defect : let rumors be :
When did not rumors fly ? these, as I trust
That you trust me in your own nobleness,
I may not well believe that you believe."

While thus he spoke, half turn'd away, the Queen   1190
Brake from the vast oriel-embowering vine
Leaf after leaf, and tore, and cast them off,
Till all the place whereon she stood was green ;

Then, when he ceased, in one cold passive hand
Received at once and laid aside the gems
There on a table near her, and replied:

    " It may be I am quicker of belief
Than you believe me. Lancelot of the Lake,
Our bond is not the bond of man and wife.
This good is in it, whatsoe'er of ill,   1200
It can be broken easier. I for you
This many a year have done despite and wrong
To one whom ever in my heart of hearts
I did acknowledge nobler. What are these?
Diamonds for me? they had been thrice their worth
Being your gift, had you not lost your own.
To loyal hearts the value of all gifts
Must vary as the giver's. Not for me!
For her! for your new fancy. Only this
Grant me, I pray you: have your joys apart.   1210
I doubt not that, however changed, you keep
So much of what is graceful: and myself
Would shun to break those bounds of courtesy
In which, as Arthur's queen, I move and rule:
So cannot speak my mind. An end to this!
A strange one! yet I take it with Amen.
So pray you, add my diamonds to her pearls;
Deck her with these; tell her she shines me down:
An armlet for an arm to which the Queen's
Is haggard, or a necklace for a neck   1220
O as much fairer as a faith once fair
Was richer than these diamonds! hers, not mine —
Nay, by the mother of our Lord himself,
Or hers or mine, mine now to work my will —
She shall not have them."

                  Saying which she seized,
And, through the casement, standing wide for heat,
Flung them, and down they flash'd, and smote the stream.
Then from the smitten surface flash'd, as it were,
Diamonds to meet them, and they past away.
Then, while Sir Lancelot leant, in half disgust   1230
At love, life, all things, on the window ledge,

Close underneath his eyes, and right across
Where these had fallen, slowly past the barge
Whereon the lily maid of Astolat
Lay smiling, like a star in blackest night.

But the wild Queen, who saw not, burst away
To weep and wail in secret ; and the barge,
On to the palace-doorway sliding, paused.
There two stood arm'd, and kept the door ; to whom,
All up the marble stair, tier over tier,   1240
Were added mouths that gaped, and eyes that ask'd,
" What is it? "   But that oarsman's haggard face,
As hard and still as is the face that men
Shape to their fancy's eye from broken rocks
On some cliff-side, appall'd them, and they said,
" He is enchanted, cannot speak — and she,
Look how she sleeps — the Fairy Queen, so fair !
Yea, but how pale ! what are they? flesh and blood?
Or come to take the King to fairy land?
For some do hold our Arthur cannot die,   1250
But that he passes into fairy land."

While thus they babbled of the King, the King
Came girt with knights : then turn'd the tongueless man
From the half-face to the full eye, and rose
And pointed to the damsel, and the doors.
So Arthur bade the meek Sir Percivale
And pure Sir Galahad to uplift the maid ;
And reverently they bore her into hall.
Then came the fine Gawain and wonder'd at her,
And Lancelot later came and mused at her,   1260
And last the Queen herself and pitied her :
But Arthur spied the letter in her hand,
Stoopt, took, brake seal, and read it ; this was all :

" Most noble lord, Sir Lancelot of the Lake,
I, sometime call'd the maid of Astolat,
Come, for you left me taking no farewell,
Hither to take my last farewell of you.
I loved you, and my love had no return,
And therefore my true love has been my death.

And therefore to our lady Guinevere,   1270
And to all other ladies, I make moan.
Pray for my soul, and yield me burial.
Pray for my soul, thou too, Sir Lancelot,
As thou art a knight peerless."

     Thus he read,
And, ever in the reading, lords and dames
Wept, looking often from his face who read
To hers which lay so silent, and at times
So touch'd were they, half-thinking that her lips
Who had devised the letter moved again.

   Then freely spoke Sir Lancelot to them all;   1280
" My lord, liege Arthur, and all ye that hear,
Know that for this most gentle maiden's death,
Right heavy am I; for good she was and true,
But loved me with a love beyond all love
In women, whomsoever I have known.
Yet to be loved makes not to love again;
Not at my years, however it hold in youth.
I swear by truth and knighthood that I gave
No cause, not willingly, for such a love:
To this I call my friends in testimony,   1290
Her brethren, and her father, who himself
Besought me to be plain and blunt, and use,
To break her passion, some discourtesy
Against my nature: what I could, I did.
I left her, and I bade her no farewell.
Though, had I dreamt the damsel would have died,
I might have put my wits to some rough use,
And help'd her from herself."

     Then said the Queen,
(Sea was her wrath, yet working after storm)
" Ye might at least have done her so much grace,   1300
Fair lord, as would have help'd her from her death."
He raised his head, their eyes met and hers fell,
He adding, " Queen, she would not be content
Save that I wedded her, which could not be.
Then might she follow me through the world, she ask'd;

It could not be.   I told her that her love
Was but the flash of youth, would darken down
To rise hereafter in a stiller flame
Toward one more worthy of her.   Then would I,
More specially were he she wedded poor,   1310
Estate them with large land and territory
In mine own realm beyond the narrow seas,
To keep them in all joyance ; more than this
I could not ; this she would not, and she died."

He pausing, Arthur answer'd, " O my knight,
It will be to thy worship, as my knight,
And mine, as head of all our Table Round,
To see that she be buried worshipfully."

So toward that shrine which then in all the realm
Was richest, Arthur leading, slowly went   1320
The marshal'd order of their Table Round,.
And Lancelot sad beyond his wont to see
The maiden buried, not as one unknown,
Nor meanly, but with gorgeous obsequies,
And mass, and rolling music, like a queen.
And, when the knights had laid her comely head
Low in the dust of half-forgotten kings,
Then Arthur spake among them, " Let her tomb
Be costly ; and her image thereupon.
And let the shield of Lancelot at her feet   1330
Be carven, and her lily in her hand.
And let the story of her dolorous voyage
For all true hearts be blazon'd on her tomb
In letters gold and azure ! " which was wrought
Thereafter ; but, when now the lords and dames
And people, from the high door streaming, brake
Disorderly, as homeward each, the Queen,
Who mark'd Sir Lancelot where he moved apart,
Drew near, and sigh'd, in passing, " Lancelot,
Forgive me ; mine was jealousy in love."   1340
He answer'd with his eyes upon the ground,
" That is love's curse ; pass on, my Queen, forgiven."
But Arthur, who beheld his cloudy brows,

Approach'd him, and with full affection flung
One arm about his neck, and spake and said:

" Lancelot, my Lancelot, thou in whom I have
Most love and most affiance, for I know
What thou hast been in battle by my side,
And many a time have watched thee at the tilt
Strike down the lusty and long-practised knight,   1350
And let the younger and unskill'd go by
To win his honor and to make his name,
And loved thy courtesies and thee, a man
Made to be loved ; but now I would to God,
For the wild people say wild things of thee,
Thou couldst have loved this maiden, shaped, it seems,
By God for thee alone, and from her face,
If one may judge the living by the dead,
Delicately pure and marvellously fair,
Who might have brought thee, now a lonely man,   1360
Wifeless and heirless, noble issue, sons
Born to the glory of thy name and fame,
My knight, the great Sir Lancelot of the Lake."

    Then answer'd Lancelot, " Fair she was, my King,
Pure, as you ever wish your knights to be.
To doubt her fairness were to want an eye,
To doubt her pureness were to want a heart —
Yea, to be loved, if what is worthy love
Could bind him, but free love will not be bound."

    " Free love, so bound, were freest," said the King.   1370
" Let love be free ; free love is for the best :
And, after heaven, on our dull side of death,
What should be best, if not so pure a love
Clothed in so pure a loveliness ? yet thee
She fail'd to bind, though being, as I think,
Unbound as yet, and gentle, as I know."

    And Lancelot answer'd nothing, but he went,
And, at the inrunning of a little brook,
Sat by the river in a cove, and watch'd
The high reed wave, and lifted up his eyes   1380
And saw the barge that brought her, moving down,

Far-off, a blot upon the stream, and said
Low in himself, " Ah ! simple heart and sweet,
Ye loved me, damsel, surely with a love
Far tenderer than my Queen's.   Pray for thy soul?
Ay, that will I.   Farewell too — now at last —
Farewell, fair lily.   ' Jealousy in love?'
Not rather dead love's harsh heir, jealous pride?
Queen, if I grant the jealousy as of love,
May not your crescent fear for name and fame   1390
Speak, as it waxes, of a love that wanes?
Why did the King dwell on my name to me?
Mine own name shames me, seeming a reproach,
Lancelot, whom the Lady of the Lake
Stole from his mother — as the story runs.
She chanted snatches of mysterious song
Heard on the winding waters ; eve and morn
She kiss'd me saying, ' Thou art fair, my child,
As a king's son,' and often in her arms
She bare me, pacing on the dusky mere.   1400
Would she had drown'd me in it, where'er it be !
For what am I ? what profits me my name
Of greatest knight ? I fought for it, and have it :
Pleasure to have it, none ; to lose it, pain ;
Now grown a part of me : but what use in it?
To make men worse by making my sin known?
Or sin seem less, the sinner seeming great?
Alas for Arthur's greatest knight, a man
Not after Arthur's heart ! I needs must break
These bonds that so defame me : not without   1410
She wills it : would I, if she will'd it? nay,
Who knows? but, if I would not, then may God,
I pray Him, send a sudden angel down
To seize me by the hair and bear me far,
And fling me deep into that forgotten mere,
Among the tumbled fragments of the hills."

    So groan'd Sir Lancelot in remorseful pain,
Not knowing he should die a holy man.

NOTES TO ELAINE.

(The numbers refer to lines.)

KING ARTHUR was a Celtic hero, who fought against the early Saxon invaders. What his real character was, it is now impossible to discover. A cycle of legends has gathered about him, and hidden the actual facts. The Arthurian legends are widely extended. From England they crossed the Channel to France, and from that country passed into the literature of the leading nations of Europe. These legends were a favorite topic with the poets and storytellers of the Middle Ages. The scenes of Arthur's exploits are laid chiefly in the south-western part of England. Cærleon on the Usk is given as his principal place of residence. He established a magnificent court, gathered about him the bravest knights and fairest ladies of his realm, and sought to regenerate the world. Twelve of the noblest knights, who enjoyed the special confidence of the king, and sat with him at meat, constituted the famous " order of the Table Round." In " Guinevere " Arthur is represented as saying:—

> " But I was first of all the kings who drew
> The knighthood errant of this realm, and all
> The realms, together under me, their head,
> In that fair order of my Table Round,
> A glorious company, the flower of men,
> To serve as model for the mighty world,
> And be the fair beginning of a time.
> I made them lay their hands in mine and swear
> To reverence the King, as if he were
> Their conscience, and their conscience as their King,
> To break the heathen and uphold the Christ,
> To ride abroad redressing human wrongs,
> To speak no slander, no, nor listen to it,
> To lead sweet lives in purest chastity,
> To love one maiden only, cleave to her,
> And worship her by years of noble deeds
> Until they won her ; for, indeed, I knew
> Of no more subtle master under heaven
> Than is the maiden passion for a maid,
> Not only to keep down the base in man,
> But teach high thoughts and amiable words
> And courtliness and the desire of fame
> And love of truth and all that makes a man."

But alas for Arthur's beautiful hopes! Passion and sin invaded his court; and finally the unfaithfulness and treachery of his friends brought devastation and death.

Among the knights of the Round Table, Lancelot was pre-eminent for deeds of prowess. He stood highest in the favor of the king. His birthplace and possessions were in Brittany. In his infancy he was carried away and fostered by Vivien, the Lady of the Lake; and from this circumstance he is called sometimes "Lancelot du Lac." Unfortunately, he cherished a secret passion for the queen. This unholy attachment, which is referred to in " Elaine," and still more fully in " Guinevere," brought unspeakable sorrow, not only to the guilty lovers, but also to the noble and unsuspecting king. It was this love for the queen that steeled his heart against the touching devotion of Elaine.

" Elaine " is justly regarded as one of the most beautiful " Idyls of the King." The story is as follows : " On his way to Camelot to joust, *incognito*, for the last and greatest of the nine diamonds offered as prizes by King Arthur, Lancelot spends the night at Astolat, the castle of Elaine's father. Here unwittingly he wins Elaine's love. At the joust, whither he is accompanied by Lavaine, Lancelot, wearing her sleeve of pearls on his helmet, is sorely wounded. Elaine learns of this, and, with her father's consent, goes to him and nurses him through his serious illness. Recovering, he returns with her and her brother to Astolat for his shield, left with her that he might not be recognized by it. Here she confesses to him her love. Unable to give his own in return, he tenderly, yet without farewell, departs. Elaine sickens and dies ; but not till her father has promised her that, with the letter she has written to Lancelot and the queen in her dead hand, she shall be dressed in her richest white, placed on the deck of the barge, and rowed up the river to the palace. This is done ; and the majestic poem concludes with the appearance of her body at court and the burial, with a painful interview between the king and Lancelot, and with Lancelot's sad reflections."

2. *Lily maid*, in reference to her complexion.

4. *Sacred*, that is, in the eyes of Elaine.

9. *Blazoned* = to portray armorial bearings. From O. Fr. *blazon*, a coat of arms.

10. *Tinct* = color, tinge. Lat. *tingere*, to stain.

17. *Arms* = coat of arms.

22. *Cærlyle*, etc. — See introductiõn.

26. *Him* = Lancelot.

35. *Lyonnesse* = a district in Cornwall.

44. *Lichen'd* = covered with lichen — flowerless, parasitic plants.

46. *Aside* = on each side.

53. *Shingly scaur* = steep rocky bank.

62. *Proof* = trial, test.

65. *Heathen* = Saxons. Arthur is represented as a Christian king. See introduction.

67. *Still* = always.

69. *The Queen* = Guinevere, between whom and himself there existed a guilty attachment.

71. *Boon* = gift, present. From Fr. *bon*, Lat. *bonus*, good.

76. *World's hugest* = London, on the Thames.

91. *Tale* = number.

94. *Lets* = hinders. There are two *lets* in English; the one from A. S. *lætan*, to allow; and the other from A. S. *lettan*, to hinder.

104. *That summer*, etc. — Lancelot had been sent to conduct Guinevere to the court to become the wife of King Arthur. It was on this journey, when all their talk was on " love and sport and tilts and pleasure," that their attachment sprang up.

106. *Cricket*, here used as a collective noun. Cf. *creak*.

108. *Nothing*, that is, cannot be located.

110. *Allow'd* = approved, sanctioned.

118. *Devoir* = duty.

129. *Table Round*. — See introduction.

135. *Bond*, that is, of marriage.

137. *Gnat* = mosquito.

146. *Craft* = skill.

148. *Wit* = understanding, reason.

149. *But knowing* = only knowing or simply knowing.

162. *Downs* = hills. From A. S. *dun*, a hill.

167. *Fired* = lighted up by the setting sun.

168. *Gateway horn* = the horn used by visitors to announce their presence.

181. *Livest between the lips* = art known or called by.

193. *Blank* = without coat of arms or other device.

196. *Wot* = knows.

202. *Lustihood* = vigor of body.

214. *Belike* = perhaps.

218. *An if* = if.

222. *So* = if.

259. *Doom* = destruction.

263. *Smaller time* = time of less noble thought and feeling.

269. *Glanced* = referred or alluded to.

287. *Glem*, etc. — See introduction.

293. *Lady's Head* = image of the Virgin Mary.

294. *Centred*, etc. — The emerald was set in the centre of a pictured sun.

297. *White Horse* = standard of the northern invaders.

338. *Rathe* = early. It is the positive form, now little used, of *rather*.

356. *Favor* = something worn as a sign of regard.

382. *Squire* = shield-bearer.

411. *Broke from underground* = rose above the horizon.

416. *Lancelot of the Lake.* — See introduction.

422. *Pendragon* = dragon's head, a title descending to Arthur from his reputed father, Uther.

431. *Samite* = a rich silk stuff, usually adorned with gold.

442. *Nameless king.* — See line 40.

456. *Shock* = strike together, collide.

482. *Smoke* = are blown into mist by the wind.

489. *Worshipfully* = honorably, worthily. From A. S. stem *weorth*, worthy, honorable.

502. *Diamond me*, etc. = do not speak to me of diamonds.

529. *Marches* = borders, frontiers. From A. S. *mearc*, border.

545. *Bring us* = bring us word.

552. *Mid might* = the might of vigorous manhood.

556. *Sir Modred* was Arthur's nephew, and finally became a traitor. See "Guinevere" and "The Passing of Arthur."

654. *To all the winds* = in all directions.

660. *Ramp* = stand rampant; that is, upright on their hind legs.

681. *One I may not name* = Queen Guinevere.

703. *Liege* = sovereign. In the older sense, a *liege* lord was a *free* lord. Common meaning, faithful, loyal.

715. *Twenty strokes*, etc. = twenty beats of the pulse.

739. *Wormwood* = a plant of bitter, nauseous taste. From A. S. *wermod*, ware-wood, mind-preserver. So called, says Skeat, from its curative properties in diseases of the mind. Thus it has no connection with either *worm* or *wood*.

798. *Far blood* = distant relations.

844. *Either twilight* = morning and evening.

857. *Simples* = medicinal plants. "So called," says Webster, "because each vegetable is supposed to possess its particular virtue, and therefore to constitute a simple remedy."

870. *Straitened* = confined, bound.

880. *Ghostly grace* = the image of the Queen seen vaguely in fancy.

898. *Burthen* = chorus or refrain of a song.

939. *Quit* = repay, requite.

953. *Realm beyond the seas.* — See introduction.

995. *Sallow-rifted* = streaked or seamed with pale yellow.

1012. *Scaled* = ascended, rose in pitch.

1084. *Pass* = die.

1092. *Ghostly man* = priest. From A. S. *gast*, spirit; the *h* has been inserted.

1114. *Chariot-bier* = hearse; a vehicle on which dead bodies are *borne*.

1129. *Dole* = grief, sorrow.

1131. *With bent brows* = with heads bowed in sorrow.

1134. *Full-summer* = with light and beauty of mid-summer.

1176. *Armlet* = an ornament for the arm.

1254. *From the half face*, etc. = from a side view to look the king full in the face.

1300. *Sea was her wrath*, etc. = her wrath was like the sea raging after a storm.

1316. *Worship* = honor.   See line 489.

INDEX.

Addison, referred to, **349;** sketch of, **352;** character of writings, **352;** early life, **353;** politics, **353;** travels, **354;** "The Campaign," **355;** in Parliament, **356;** *Tatler* and *Spectator*, **356, 357;** "Cato," **358;** attacked by Dennis, **358;** marriage, **360;** secretary of state, **360;** death, **360;** Thackeray's estimate, **360;** quarrel with Pope, **384.**

Age of Johnson, 421; poetry of, **421;** predominance of prose, **424.**

Akenside, Johnson's sketch of, **490;** notes to, **495.**

Alcuin on study, **7.**

Alfred the Great, 12.

Angles, Saxons, and Jutes, **3.**

Augustan Age in France, **312;** in England, **347.**

Augustine in England, **5.**

Augustus, 347.

Austen, Miss, referred to, **516.**

Bacon, referred to, **2;** sketch of, **137;** philosophy, **137;** purpose of knowledge, **137;** early life, **138;** as lawyer, **140;** political career, **141;** as orator, **141;** befriended by Essex, **141;** "Essays," **142, 150;** mode of living, **143;** trial, **144;** "Instauratio Magna," **144;** estimate of, **148;** notes to "Essays," **164.**

Beaumont, quoted, **175.**

Bede, father of English prose, **10;** quoted, **5, 9.**

Bentley, quoted, **383.**

Beowulf, 8.

Bertha, wife of Ethelbert, **5.**

Bible, influence on literature, **79.**

Blackstone, referred to, **462.**

Boccaccio, 23.

Boileau, 312, 353.

Bolingbroke, Lord, referred to, **315, 387;** quoted, **389.**

Book of Common Prayer, 80.

Boswell, quoted, **454.**

Boyle, referred to, **313.**

Buckingham, Duke of, 274, 313; satirized, **320.**

Buffon, referred to, **348.**

Butler, Joseph, referred to, **315.**

Burke, referred to, **424;** anecdote of, **489.**

Burns, sketch of, **426;** rank, **426;** early life, **427;** "Mary Morison," **428;** effort to reform, **429;** "Cotter's Saturday Night," **430;** first volume of poems, **430;** in Edinburgh, **431;** marriage, **431;** sympathy with nature, **434;** "Tam o' Shanter," **435;** as exciseman, **435;** "Bruce's Address," **436;** death, **437;** glorifies the commonplace, **438;** religious feeling, **438.**

Byron, sketch of, **526;** characterized, **526;** place in literature, **526;** ancestry, **527;** early life, **527;** "Hours of Idleness," **528;** "English Bards and Scotch Reviewers," **528;** "Childe Harold's Pilgrimage," **529;** life in London, **529;** marriage, **530:** voluntary exile, **531;** "Prisoner of Chillon," **532, 534;** "Don Juan," **532;** in Greece, **532;** death, **533;** quoted, **551.**

Caedmon, 9; extract from, **10.**

Canterbury Tales, plan of, **30.**

Carew, quoted, **278.**

Carlyle, quoted, **426, 436, 526.**

Cato, Addison's, **358.**

Cavaliers, 276; Cavalier poets, **277, 278.**

Caxton, 76.

Celt and Teuton contrasted, **1.**

Celts in British Isles, **3.**

Charles I., 273.

Charles II., 312.

Chatham, referred to, **424.**

Chesterfield and Johnson, **483.**

Chaucer, sketch of, **24;** pre-eminence of, **24;** biographical facts, **25;** personal appearance, **25;** character and culture, **26, 27;** love of nature, **27;** keen observer, **27;** treatment of woman, **28;** courage in misfortune, **29;** literary career, **29;** "Canterbury Tales," **30;** language and versification, **55.**

Christianity, effects on Anglo-Saxon character, **6.**

Church and education, **7.**

Civil War Period, 273.

Clubs of London, **351.**

Collier, Jeremy, referred to, **318.**

Compass, Mariner's, 77.

Congreve, quoted, **325.**

Corneille, referred to, **312;** imitated by Dryden, **318.**

Cotter's Saturday Night, 430, 440; notes to, **450.**

Creative Period, 75.

Cromwell, 276.

Crusades, 22.

Cudworth, Ralph, referred to, **314, 315.**

Danes, incursions of, **13.**

Dante, 23, 30.

Decameron, 30.

Declaration of Independence, 422.

Deism, 314.

Dennis, referred to, **358, 381.**

Deserted Village, 463, 465; notes to, **476.**

Drama, discussion of, **252;** in France, **312.**

Dryden, quoted, **280, 289, 312;** referred to, **313, 349, 383;** sketch of, **316;** his rank and aims, **316, 324;** biographical details, **317;** "Heroic Stanzas," **317;** as dramatist, **318;** as satirist, **319;** "Religio Laici," **320, 327;** turns Cath-

olic, **322;** "Hind and Panther," **322;** "Mac Flecknoe," **323;** as translator, **323;** "Alexander's Feast," **324;** as prose writer, **324;** Congreve's estimate, **325.**

Education in nineteenth century, **501.**

Edwin, King of Northumbria, **5.**

Elaine, Tennyson's, **582, 586;** notes to, **623.**

Elizabeth, reign of, **75, 80, 84;** learning, **77;** character, **80.**

England, in fourteenth century, **21, 22;** under Elizabeth, **81, 82;** at time of Civil War, **273;** at Restoration, **311;** under Queen Anne, **347;** Age of Johnson, **421;** in nineteenth century, **499.**

English language formed, **19.**

English literature defined, **2;** extent of, **3.**

Enoch Arden, 584.

Environment, influence of, **1.**

Epoch, influence of, **1.**

Erasmus, referred to, **77.**

Essay on Criticism, Pope's, **379, 392;** notes to, **412.**

Essay on Man, Pope's, **387.**

Essex, Lord, 141.

Ethelbert, speech of, **5.**

Excursion, Wordsworth's, **557.**

Faery Queene, 83; plan of, **91;** defects of, **92;** criticised, **95;** First Booke of, **96;** notes to, **125.**

Feudalism in England, **21.**

Fiction in nineteenth century, **505.**

Formative Period, 19.

Garrick, quoted, **454, 485.**

George III., referred to, **422.**

Goldsmith, sketch of, **454;** awkwardness in conversation, **454;** early life, **455;** effect of money, **456;** anecdote, **457;** fondness for dress, **457;** failures, **457;** studies medicine, **458;** in London, **459;** literary work, **459;** extravagance, **460;** "Vicar of Wakefield," **460;** "Traveller," **461;** anecdote, **461;** "Good-Natured Man," **462;** compilations, **462;** "Deserted Village," **462;** "She Stoops to Conquer," **463;** death, **463;** quoted, **480.**

Greene, quoted, **174.**

Hallam, quoted, **148.**
Halley, referred to, **313.**
Harvey, Gabriel, 85.
Henry VIII. and the Reformation, **79.**
Herbert, Lord, of Cherbury, **314.**
Herrick, quoted, **279.**
Hilda, abbess at Whitby, **9.**
Hind and Panther, 322.
History, 1 ; advance in style, **505.**
Hobbes, referred to, **315.**
Hooker, " Ecclesiastical Polity," **83.**
Hutton, quoted, **516.**

Idyls of the King, 582.
Independents, 275.
Instauratio Magna, 144.
Inventions, modern, **499.**

Jarrow, monastery of, **11.**
Jeffrey, quoted, **557.**
Johnson, Samuel, quoted, **278, 322,
353, 360, 378, 383 ;** age of Johnson,
421 ; sketch of, **479 ;** character, **479 ;**
peculiarities, **479 ;** in conversation, **480 ;**
early life, **480 ;** anecdote, **481 ;** marriage, **481 ;** in London, **482 ;** as reporter,
482 ; " Life of Savage," **483 ;** dictionary, **483 ;** relations with Chesterfield,
483 ; "Vanity of Human Wishes,"
484 ; as dramatist, **485 ;** *Rambler*, **485 ;**
style, **485 ;** "Rasselas," **486 ;** journey
to the Hebrides, **487 ;** "Lives of the
Poets," **488 ;** death, **489 ;** sketch of
Akenside, **490.**
Jonson, Ben, quoted, **175.**

Lady of the Lake, 511.
L'Allegro, 291 ; notes to, **300.**
Latimer, referred to, **79.**
Laud, Archbishop, 274.
Lay of the Last Minstrel, 511.
Literature, defined, **1 ;** three leading fac-
tors, **1 ;** in relation to causes, **2 ;** Eng-
lish literature defined, **2 ;** substantial
element, **22 ;** influence of French, **22 ;**
in nineteenth century, **504.**
Lives of the Poets, Johnson's, **488.**
Locke, John, referred to, **315, 348, 356.**
Lockhart, quoted, **433.**
Louis XIV., 312, 348.
Lowell, James Russell, quoted, **29,
325, 391.**
Luther, referred to, **2, 78.**

Macaulay, quoted, **483.**
Macpherson, referred to, **487.**
Magna Charta, 21.
Marlborough, referred to, **355.**
Marmion, Scott's, **511.**
Mary, misrule of, **80.**
Mary, Queen of Scots, 80.
Maud, Tennyson's, **582.**
Merchant of Venice, 177, 183 ; notes
to, **252.**
Methodism, rise of, **350.**
Milton, John, referred to, **277 ;** sketch
of, **280 ;** early life, **280 ;** educational
reformer, **281 ;** at Horton, **282 ;** "L'Al-
legro " and " Penseroso," **282 ;** Continen-
tal tour, **283 ;** return to England, **283 ;**
as teacher, **284 ;** prose writings, **284,
285, 287 ;** marriage, **285 ;** definition of
education, **286 ;** course of study, **287 ;**
Latin secretary, **287 ;** blindness, **288 ;**
" Paradise Lost," **289 ;** " Samson Agonistes," **290 ;** character, **290.**
Molière, referred to, **312.**
Montague, Earl of Halifax, **353, 354.**
Montesquieu, referred to, **348 ;** quoted,
350.
More, Henry, referred to, **314.**
More, Sir Thomas, 76.
Myers, quoted, **555.**

Newton, Sir Isaac, referred to, **313.**
Nineteenth Century, some features of,
499.
Norman Conquest, 19, 20.
Normans, 20.

Ode on Immortality, Wordsworth's,
556, 564 ; notes to, **571.**
Ossian, referred to, **487.**

Penseroso, 295 ; notes to, **304.**
Pepys, quoted, **317.**
Petrarch, referred to, **23.**
Pitt, quoted, **425.**
Poetry, the first literature, **8 ;** Anglo-Saxon, **8 ;** in nineteenth century, **506.**
Pope, referred to, **347 ;** quoted, **349 ;**
sketch of, **377 ;** rank, **377 ;** early life,
377 ; precocity, **378 ;** influence of Trumbull, **378 ;** advice of Walsh, **379 ;** relations with Wycherly, **379 ;** " Essay on
Criticism," **379, 392 ;** attack on Dennis,
381 ; sensitive to criticism, **382 ;** " Rape

Pope, (*Continued.*)
of the Lock," **382** ; translation of Iliad, **383** ; quarrel with Addison, **384** ; filial piety, **385** ; "Dunciad," **385** ; "Essay on Man," **387** ; death, **389** ; appearance, **389** ; character, **390** ; estimate of, **391.**

Princess, The, 580.

Printing, introduced into England, **76.**

Prisoner of Chillon, 532, 534 ; notes to, **545.**

Prologue, Chaucer's, **32** ; versification of, **55** ; notes to, **57.**

Puritans, 275, 276, 311.

Quarles, Francis, quoted, **279.**

Queen Anne, 347.

Queen Anne Period, 347.

Race, influence of, **1.**

Racine, referred to, **312.**

Raleigh, Sir Walter, 86.

Rambler, The, 485.

Rape of the Lock, quoted, **349** ; publication of, **382.**

Rasselas, 486.

Raumer, quoted, **148.**

Reformation, influence of, **78, 79.**

Religio Laici, 320, 327 ; notes to, **339.**

Restoration, The, **311** ; relation to natural science, **313.**

Revival of learning, **76, 84.**

Roscoe, quoted, **382.**

Rousseau, referred to, **348.**

Royal Society founded, **313.**

Schools, monastic, **7.**

Sciences, present interest in, **500.**

Scotland and England united, **348.**

Scott, Sir Walter, referred to, **423** ; quoted, **460** ; sketch of, **508** ; rank, **508** ; ancestry, **508** ; early life, **509** ; as a lawyer, **510** ; marriage, **511** ; "Lay of the Last Minstrel," **511** ; "Marmion," **511** ; "Lady of the Lake," **511** ; method of work, **512** ; at Abbotsford, **513** ; as host, **513** ; as publisher, **514** ; "Waverley," **514** ; extempore method, **515** ; anecdote of, **515** ; style, **515** ; failing health, **516** ; death, **517.**

Shadwell, satirized, **323.**

Shaftesbury, Earl of, satirized, **320.**

Shakespeare, referred to, **83** ; sketch of, **172** ; parentage and education, **172** ; marriage, **173** ; goes to London, **173** ; "Venus and Adonis," **174** ; as business man, **174** ; Beaumont and Jonson on, **175** ; retires to Stratford, **175** ; death, **176** ; estimate of, **176** ; development of genius, **177** ; personality concealed, **178** ; knowledge of dramatic art, **178** ; acquaintance with human nature, **179** ; style, **179** ; influence, **181.**

Sheridan, referred to, **424.**

Sidney, Sir Philip, referred to, **86.**

Sir Roger de Coverley, 349, 350, 362 ; notes to, **372.**

Spectator, The, established, **357.**

Spenser, "Faery Queene," **83** ; sketch of, **84** ; biographical facts, **85** ; "The Shepherd's Calendar," **85** ; secretary to Lord Grey, **86** ; visited by Raleigh, **86** ; "Colin Clout's Come Home Again," **87** ; "Mother Hubbard's Tale," **87** ; "Faery Queene," published, **88** ; marriage, **88** ; "View of the State of Ireland," **89** ; Kilcolman Castle burned, **90** ; character, **90** ; death, **90** ; literary gifts, **95** ; reference to Shakespeare, **174.**

Stedman, quoted, **582.**

Steele, Sir Richard, quoted, **357.**

Stephen, Leslie, quoted, **380.**

Stewart, Dugald, quoted, **143, 388, 431.**

Strafford, Earl of, referred to, **274.**

Taine, quoted, **277, 526.**

Talisman, The, 518 ; notes to, **524.**

Tennyson, quoted, **24** ; sketch of, **575** ; rank, **575** ; favorable surroundings, **575** ; early life, **575** ; "Poems, Chiefly Lyrical," **576** ; second volume, **577** ; volume of 1842, **578** ; "The Princess," **580** ; "In Memoriam," **580** ; "Maud," **582** ; "Idyls of the King," **582** ; "Enoch Arden," **584** ; death, **584** ; estimate of, **585.**

Teuton and Celt compared, **1.**

Teutonic character, **3.**

Thackeray, quoted, **360, 385, 387, 463.**

Tillotson, John, referred to, **315.**

Tintern Abbey, 551, 559 ; notes to, **570.**

Tories, 348.

Trumbull, Sir William, referred to, 378.
Turner, quoted, 7.
Tyndale, version of Bible, 79.

Universities founded, 23.

Vanity of Human Wishes, 484.
Vicar of Wakefield, 460.
Voltaire, quoted, 325.

Walpole, referred to, 348; quoted, 454.
Walsh, William, referred to, 379.
Warburton, referred to, 388.
Waverley, 514.
Wesley, John, referred to, 350.
Whately, Archbishop, quoted, 142.
Whigs, 348.

Whitefield, referred to, 350.
William of Normandy, 20.
William of Orange, 314.
Wordsworth, quoted, 290; sketch of, 548; parallel with Byron, 548; early life, 549; in France, 550; favored by fortune, 550; devotion of his sister, 550; "Lyrical Ballads," 551; "Tintern Abbey," 551, 559; satirized by Byron, 551; in Germany, 552; at Grasmere, 552; poetic canons, 552; "Michael," 553; marriage, 553; domestic life, 554; "Happy Warrior," 555; "Ode on Immortality," 556, 564; "Excursion," 557; self-confidence, 557; death, 558.
Wycherly, referred to, 379.

PRICES LARGELY REDUCED.

The Students' Series of English Classics.

Coleridge's Ancient Mariner . . . . 25 cts.

A Ballad Book . . . . 50 "

The Merchant of Venice . . . . 35 "

A Midsummer Night's Dream . . . . 35 "
  Edited by KATHARINE LEE BATES, Wellesley College.

Matthew Arnold's Sohrab and Rustum . . . . . . 25 "

Webster's First Bunker Hill Oration . . . . . . 25 "

Milton's L'Allegro, Il Penseroso, Comus, and Lycidas . 25 "
  Edited by LOUISE MANNING HODGKINS.

Introduction to the Writings of John Ruskin . . . 50 "

Macaulay's Essay on Lord Clive . . . . 35 "
  Edited by VIDA D. SCUDDER, Wellesley College.

George Eliot's Silas Marner . . . . 35 "

Scott's Marmion . . . . 35 "
  Edited by MARY HARRIOTT NORRIS, Instructor, New
  York.

Sir Roger de Coverley Papers from The Spectator . . 35 "
  Edited by A. S. ROE, Worcester, Mass.

Macaulay's Second Essay on the Earl of Chatham . . 35 "
  Edited by W. W. CURTIS, High School, Pawtucket, R.I.

Johnson's History of Rasselas . . . . 35 "
  Edited by FRED N. SCOTT, University of Michigan.

Joan of Arc and Other Selections from De Quincey . . 35 "
  Edited by HENRY H. BELFIELD, Chicago Manual Training School.

Carlyle's The Diamond Necklace . . . . 35 "
  Edited by W. F. MOZIER, High School, Ottawa, Ill.

Macaulay's Essays on Milton and Addison . . . . . 35 cts.
    Edited by JAMES CHALMERS, Ohio State University.

Selections from Washington Irving . . . . 50 "
    Edited by ISAAC THOMAS, Principal of High School,
        New Haven, Conn.

Goldsmith's Traveller and Deserted Village . . . . 25 "
    Edited by W. F. GREGORY, High School, Hartford, Conn.

Burke's Speech on Conciliation with America . . . . 35 "
    Edited by L. DU PONT SYLE, University of California.

Macaulay's Life of Samuel Johnson . . . . 25 "
    Edited by GAMALIEL BRADFORD, JR., Instructor in Lit-
        erature, Wellesley and Boston.

Tennyson's Elaine . . . . 25 "
    Edited by FANNIE MORE MCCAULEY, Instructor in Eng-
        lish Literature, Winchester School, Baltimore.

Pope's Iliad, Books I, VI, XXII, XXIV . . . . . . 35 "
    Edited by W. J. PRICE, St. Paul's School, Concord, N.H.

Milton's Paradise Lost, Books I and II . . . . . . 35 "
    Edited by ALBERT S. COOK, Yale University.

Scott's Lady of the Lake . . . . 35 "
    Edited by JAMES ARTHUR TUFTS, Phillips Exeter Academy.

Tennyson's The Princess . . . . 35 "
    Edited by HENRY W. BOYNTON, Phillips Academy,
        Andover, Mass.

Goldsmith's Vicar of Wakefield . . . . 50 "
    Edited by J. G. RIGGS, School Superintendent, Platts-
        burg, N.Y.

De Quincey's Revolt of the Tartars . . . . 35 "
    Edited by FRANK T. BAKER, Teachers' College, New
        York City.

Carlyle's Essay on Burns . . . . 35 "
    Edited by WILLIAM K. WICKES, High School, Syracuse,
        N.Y.

Macaulay's Lays of Ancient Rome . . . .
    Edited by D. D. PRATT, High School, Portsmouth, Ohio.

Dryden's Palamon and Arcite . . . .
    Edited by W. F. GREGORY, High School, Hartford, Conn.

All are substantially bound in cloth.   The usual discount will be made for these books in quantities.

LEACH, SHEWELL, & SANBORN, Publishers.
BOSTON.   NEW YORK.   CHICAGO.

Annie E. Hood

Annie Hood
"Longwood"

Annie E. Hood

"'Tis only noble to be good."

Tennyson